David
Niven

David Niven

The Moon's
a Balloon

Bring on the
Empty Horses

OCTOPUS BOOKS LIMITED

The Moon's a Balloon first published in the United States
of America in 1972 by G. P. Putnam's Sons
Bring on the Empty Horses first published in the United States
of America in 1975 by G. P. Putnam's Sons

This volume first published in 1984 by
arrangement with G. P. Putnam's Sons

by

Octopus Books Limited
59 Grosvenor Street
London W1

This edition published 1985

ISBN 0 7064 2196 3

Printed in Great Britain by
Richard Clay (The Chaucer Press) Ltd,
Bungay, Suffolk

David Niven

Contents

The Moon's a Balloon

Bring on the Empty Horses

David
Niven

The Moon's
a Balloon

FOR

Kira Triandpyllapopulous

Introduction

Evelyn Waugh penned these words: 'Only when one has lost all curiosity about the future has one reached the age to write an autobiography.'

It is daunting to consider the sudden wave of disillusionment that must have swept over such a brilliant man and caused him to write such balls.

Nearer the mark, it seems to me, is Professor John Kenneth Galbraith of Harvard University who wrote: 'Books can be broken broadly into two classes: those written to please the reader and those written for the greater pleasure of the writer. Subject to numerous and distinguished exceptions, the second class is rightly suspect and especially if the writer himself appears in the story. Doubtless, it is best to have one's vanity served by others; but when all else fails, it is something men do for themselves. Political memoirs, biographies of great business tycoons *and the annals of aging actors* sufficiently illustrate the point.'

The italics are mine.

I apologize for the ensuing name dropping. It was hard to avoid it.

People in my profession, who, like myself, have the good fortune to parlay a minimal talent into a long career, find all sorts of doors opened that would otherwise have remained closed. Once behind those doors it makes little sense to write about the butler if Chairman Mao is sitting down to dinner.

DAVID NIVEN
Cap Ferrat AM

who knows if the moon's
a balloon, coming out of a keen city
in the sky – filled with pretty people?
(and if you and i should

get into it, if they
should take me and take you into their balloon,
why then
we'd go up higher with all the pretty people

than houses and steeples and clouds:
go sailing
away and away sailing into a keen
city which nobody's ever visited, where

always
     it's
         Spring) and everyone's
in love and flowers pick themselves

                     E.E. Cummings

Nessie, when I first saw her, was seventeen years old, honey-blonde, pretty rather than beautiful, the owner of a voluptuous but somehow innocent body and a pair of legs that went on for ever. She was a Piccadilly whore. I was a fourteen-year-old heterosexual schoolboy and I met her thanks to my stepfather. (If you would like to skip on and meet Nessie more fully, she reappears on page 403.)

I had a stepfather because my father, along with 90 per cent of his comrades in the Berkshire Yeomanry, had landed with immense panache at Suvla Bay. Unfortunately, the Turks were given ample time to prepare to receive them. For days, sweltering in their troopships, the Berkshire Yeomanry had ridden at anchor off shore while the High Command in London argued as to the best way to get them on the beach. Finally, they arrived at their brilliant decision and the troops dutifully embarked in the ship's whalers. On arrival they held their rifles above their heads, cheered, and gallantly leaped into the dark waist-high water. A combination of barbed wire beneath the surface and machine guns to cover the barbed wire, provided a devastating welcome.

Woodpigeons were calling on a warm summer evening and my sister, Grizel, and I were swapping cigarette cards on an old tree trunk in the paddock when a red-eyed maid came and told us our mother wanted to see us and that we were not to stay too long.

After a rather incoherent interview with our mother, who was French, and had trouble explaining what 'missing' meant, we returned to the swapping of cigarette cards and resumed our perusal of endless trains lumbering along a distant embankment loaded with guns and waving young men ... 1915.

I am afraid my father's death meant little or nothing to me at the time; later it meant a great deal. I was just five years old and had not seen him much except when I was brought down to be shown off before arriving dinner guests or departing fox-hunting companions. I could always tell which were which because the former smelled of soap and perfume and the latter of sweat and spirits.

I lived with Grizel in a nursery presided over by a warm enveloping creature, Whitty.

Rainy days were spent being taught Highland reels by a wounded piper of the Argyll and Sutherland Highlanders, and listening to a gramophone equipped with an immense horn. Our favourite record had 'The Ride of the Valkyrie' on one side and, on the other, a jolly little number for those days, called 'The Wreck of the Troopship'. We were specially fascinated by the whinnying of the horses as the sharks moved in (the troops were on the way to the South African War).

Occasionally, I was taken to the hospital in Cirencester to 'do my bit'. This entailed trying not to fidget or jump while young VADs practised bandaging any part of me they fancied.

The war days sped by and the house in Gloucestershire was sold. So, too, was one we had in Argyllshire. Everyone, my mother included, was under the misapprehension that my father was very rich. He had cheerfully gone off to war like a knight of old, taking with him as troopers his valet, his under-gardener and two grooms. He also took his hunters, but these were exchanged for rifles in Egypt en route and my father, his valet and one groom were duly slaughtered.

It transpired that he was hugely in debt at the time.

We soon moved to London to a large, damp house in Cadogan Place. Straw had been laid in the street when we arrived to make things quieter for someone dying next door. The sweaty, hearty, red-faced, country squires were replaced by pale, gay, young men who recited poetry and sang to my mother. She was very beautiful, very musical, very sad and lived on cloud nine.

A character called 'Uncle Tommy'* soon made his appearance and became a permanent member of her entourage. Gradually the pale, gay young men gave way to pale, sad, older men.

'Uncle Tommy' was a second line politician who did not fight in the war. A tall, ramrod straight creature with immensely high, white collars, a bluish nose and a very noisy cuff-link combination which he rattled at me when I made an eating error at mealtime.

I don't believe he was very healthy really. Anyway he got knighted for something to do with the Conservative Party and the Nineteen Hundred Club, and Cadogan Place became a rendezvous for people like Lord Willoughby de Broke, Sir Edward Carson, KC, and Sir Edward Marshall Hall, KC. I suppose it bubbled with the sort of brilliant conversation into which children these days would be encouraged to join, but, as soon as it started, Grizel and I were sent up to a nursery which had a linoleum floor and a string bag

* Sir Thomas Comyn-Platt. Liked to be known as 'the mystery man of the Conservative Party'. Contested Portsmouth Central in the Election of 1926.

full of apples hanging outside the window during the winter. Grizel, who was two years older than me, became very interested during this period in the shape and form of my private parts; but when after a particularly painful inspection, I claimed my right to see hers too, she covered up sharply and dodged the issue by saying, 'Well, it's a sort of flat arrangement.'

The Germans raided London. High in the night sky, I saw a Zeppelin in flames.

One day my mother took me to buy a pair of warm gloves. Some Fokkers came over and everyone rushed into the street to point them out to each other. Then as the possibility of what might be about to drop out of the Fokkers dawned on them they rushed back indoors again.

My mother didn't leave the glove shop. She was busy giving a discourse on the superior quality of French gloves when the manager said, 'This place will come down like a pack of cards.' By this time the Fokkers must have been fifty miles away but I was nevertheless lugged across the street and we joined an undignified Gadarene swine movement down the steps of the Knightsbridge Tube station. One woman had a parrot. Another had hysterics and between screams, ate handfuls of marmalade out of a stone jar, a spectacle I found highly enjoyable.

Uncle Tommy's marriage to my mother coincided with my sixth birthday. The wedding took place at All Saints, Sloane Street. Purple with embarrassment, I was press-ganged into being a page and pressure-fed into a primrose coloured suit with mother-of-pearl buttons, a white lace collar, shorts and socks.

I did everything I could do to wreck the show and fidgeted and picked my nose till an aquiline creature, later identified as the famous Margot Asquith, came and knelt in the aisle to comfort me. I decided she was a witch and again and again informed the congregation of this discovery in a shrill treble.

I was removed and Uncle Tommy, forever politically sensitive, treated me from that moment on with frosty distaste.

My eldest brother, Henri (known as Max), was a naval cadet at Dartmouth, longing to get into the war. My eldest sister, Joyce, was at home helping my mother and Grizel had gone away to boarding school in Norfolk. I was the youngest. And, overcoming my mother's apprehensions, 'Tommy' soon saw to it that I was packed off to a boarding school near Worthing.

Apart from the Chinese, the only people in the world who pack their sons off to the tender care of unknown and often homosexual schoolmasters at the exact moment when they are most in need of parental love and influence, are the British so-called upper and middle classes.

I had not been long at boarding school before I discovered that life could be hell. There was a great deal of bullying and for a six-year-old, the spectacle of a gang of twelve-year-olds bearing down, cracking wet towels like whips, can be terrifying.

For the most part, the masters were even more frightening. It would be charitable to think that they were shell-shocked heroes returned from the hell of Mons and Vimy, but it seems more probably that they were sadistic perverts who had been dredged up from the bottom of the educational barrel at a time of acute manpower shortage.

One, a Mr Croome, when he tired of pulling ears half way out of our heads (I still have one that sticks out almost at right angles thanks to this son of a bitch), and delivering, for the smallest mistake in declension, back-handed slaps that knocked one off one's bench, delighted in saying, 'Show me the hand that wrote this', and then bringing down the sharp edge of a heavy ruler across the offending wrist.

He took the last class on Friday evening and I remember praying every week that he would die before then so that I could somehow reach the haven of Saturday and Sunday and the comparative safety of the weekend.

I don't think I have ever been so frightened of a human being in my life. Once he made me lean out of a fourth floor window – a stupefying height for a little boy – then he shut the window across the small of my back, ordered two other equally terrified boys to hold my feet and laid into me mightily with a cane. All this for some mistake in – 'common are sacerdos dux vates parens et conjux . . .'

Years later, when I was at Sandhurst and playing in the Rugby football fifteen, big enough and ugly enough to take care of myself, I had an overpowering urge to see the bastard again, face to face.

I went down to the school, filled with vindictiveness. I don't know what I intended to do really, but when I got there I found the school deserted; its prison-like exercise yard full of rubbish and old newspapers. The fourth floor window, out of which I had dangled, was broken and open to the rain – it didn't even look very high.

My mother, at the time, however, would not believe my tales of woe or rather Uncle Tommy persuaded her that they were nonsense, telling her that all boys exaggerated and that anyway she could not be expected to know anything about English schools.

After two years of this purgatory, I got a large and painful boil as a result of the bad food. 'Oh!' said the matron, 'that's nothing, don't make such a fuss!', and lopped off the top of it with a pair of scissors. The ensuing infection was pretty horrible and put me in hospital.

The next term, I was removed and sent to Heatherdown at Ascot.

At this point, I don't believe my mother was actually taking in washing, but, as sure as hell, she was sending very little out, and it must have been a fearful drain on her resources. Heatherdown was far more expensive than Worthing; certainly only a token subscription to the family coffers was being made by Uncle Tommy and she still had her thumb in the dyke of my father's debts, but I was blissfully unconscious of all this and wallowed in my good fortune.

Heatherdown was a very different cup of tea, very carriage-trade, very protected and, compared to Worthing, very soft, very snobbish. Everybody went from there to Eton. Gone were the sadistic masters and the school bullies tying small boys to hot radiators; no more scissor-wielding matrons; no more ex-naval cooks with finger nails like toe nails doling out their nauseous confections; and, receding like a bad dream, were the flinty playground and the evil-smelling doorless lavatories, open to the elements and to the helpful advice of schoolmates.

Instead, I found a world of cleanliness and kindly masters; motherly matrons; green playing fields; a lake; delicious food and a swimming pool. In short . . . schoolboy heaven.

The only grown-ups who hit me were the headmaster who, under great provocation, occasionally uncorked a dose of the cane; and a dear old gentleman who taught divinity, called Mr Hodgson, who sometimes brandished a clothes brush known as 'Dixon and Parker' because if, as rarely happened, he hit someone with it, the name of the maker was left imprinted on the bum.

After the appalling apprenticeship of Worthing, I could not believe that life could be so perfect. Released from fear and oppression, the whole thing went to my head.

Almost nine, I became something of a clown. This was hastened on when, for some strange reason, my balls dropped three years earlier than they should have done.

I was in the choir at the time, the possessor of a voice of guileless purity. Sometimes I was entrusted with solo passages and it was on such an occasion, and in front of a full house, that disaster struck.

17

Ascot Sunday – parents staying for the race meeting in smart country houses nearby had filled the chapel to capacity. Alone, I was piping my way through 'There is a green hill far away, without a city wall'. . . . Suddenly, on the word 'wall' a fearful braying sound issued from the angelic face of the soloist. I tried for the note again: this time it sounded like a Rolls-Royce klaxon of the period. The paper-thin discipline of the choir quickly disintegrated . . . repressed laughter became contagious and finally, general.

Immediately after chapel, I was caned by the headmaster – Sammy Day. He had once played cricket for England and still had one of the best late cuts in the business. It hurt a lot and, considering the medical evidence that was from then on permanently with me, was rather unfair.

Boys are terrible snobs and I was annually unnerved when the school list came out, to see some of my contemporaries sniggering because in between the young marquesses and dukes with their splendid addresses, was –

Niven, D. Rose Cottage, Bembridge, I.W.

It had become necessary for the house in London to be sold and our permanent address was now as advertised – a converted fisherman's cottage which had a reputation for unreliability. When the East wind blew, the front door got stuck and when the West wind blew, the back door could not be opened – only the combined weight of the family seemed to keep it anchored to the ground. I adored it and was happier there than I had ever been, especially because, with a rare flash of genius, my mother decided that during the holidays she would be alone with her children.

Uncle Tommy was barred – I don't know where he went – to the Carlton Club, I suppose.

After the sudden descent of my testicles, I was removed from the choir as a bad risk and became the 'bellows man' and the musical success of each service (we suffered through two a day) depended entirely on my prowess behind the organ. This was a position of great trust, but the newly found clown in me could not resist the opportunities it offered. For a small price – two chocolate whirls, one Cadbury's Milk Flake or a brace of Turkish delights – I could be bribed to let the air out of the bellows on important occasions. The whole school, on the selected day, would be in the know and would sit through an endless sermon hugging itself with delicious anticipation.

It took careful preparation but I could generally arrange matters so that a rude noise could be subtly injected into the proceedings, usually just after an Amen. I could redress the situation rapidly by quick pumping and only the connoisseurs could detect that it was not a mistake . . . the boys were all connoisseurs.

Once I tried it when the Bishop of Ripon was in the middle of a special address. This was my masterpiece and also my downfall but the bribes were mountainous.

It was a highly technical job and involved surreptitiously and noiselessly keeping the bellows half-filled for several minutes after the end of the preceding hymn. I had intended to let this air out in a series of well-spaced small squeaks and trills thus keeping the boys happy during what promised to be a long, trying period, but something went wrong and it all came out at once and on a most unfortunate cue . . . a quotation from Proverbs 7, 'I have perfumed my bed with myrrh, aloes and cinnamon. . . .'

It was as if the bellows could not contain themselves any longer – a tremendous fart rent the air. All was confusion.

The school was infiltrated with informers and I was soon dealt with once more by the long-suffering Sammy Day.

I loved Heatherdown and tried hard to uphold the agricultural standards of the landed gentry with whom I was rubbing shoulders.

Every summer on the First Sunday after the Derby (it is not thus described in the Book of Common Prayer but so many boys of noble birth had racehorse owner fathers that at Heatherdown, it far outranked Rogation Sunday, the Sunday after Advent, and the Twenty-first Sunday after Trinity) a prize was given to the boy with the most beautiful garden. Each boy had one about the size of a lavatory mat in a small commercial hotel, but immense ingenuity and forethought was displayed by the owners. Actually, these allotments were status symbols of the worst kind, and boys whose family estates employed an army of gardeners proudly displayed the most exotic flowers and shrubs, delivered for planting hot from the family greenhouses while the more modest smallholders nurtured colourful annuals and arranged them in intricate patterns.

I could only manage a bi-annual crop of mustard and cress.

The year that Humorist won the Derby saw that rare phenomenon, a drought in England, and my crop, carefully timed for the Flower Show, failed, burned to a crisp.

By now the self-appointed jester to the upper classes, I decided to fill the gap, and creeping out of the dormitory after dark, I made my way downstairs and flitting from tree to tree in the moonlight, arrived at a well-known gap in the wall which separated Heatherdown from Heathfield – the girls' school next door.

From preliminary reconnaisance, I knew that this gap opened on to the kitchen garden. I selected a huge vegetable marrow plant, pulled it up by the roots and once safely back on the male side of the wall, hid it behind a piece of corrugated iron.

It took some while and several near heart attacks but I finally made it back to bed. The next morning I retrieved the marrow and in the hubbub caused by the arrival of other boys' parents in Daimlers and Rolls-Royces, managed to plant my prize on my poor piece of desert.

It didn't go down very well. The Countess of Jersey – one of the parents – presented the prizes.

She didn't give one to me and later, I was caned again by a no longer affable Sammy Day: not for making a nonsense of the Flower Show which could have been justified – but for *stealing* which put a totally different connotation on the thing.

After this, I went rapidly downhill from popular school clown to unpopular school nuisance. Striving to maintain my waning reputation, I fell in the lake and nearly drowned, purposely split the seat of my trousers on the school walk through Ascot and was caught trying to get into the Racecourse – a hideous crime. Poor Brian Franks, a Bembridge friend, near death's door with pneumonia at Wixenford, a school nearby, received from me on the day of his 'crisis', a large chocolate box inside which was a smaller box, then a smaller box and so on down the scale to a match box with a piece of dog's mess in it.

Not a funny joke, especially for the Matron who opened it, but then I didn't know Brian was ill.

Brian* overcame his illness and my gift and has remained a life-long friend but the Matron took a dim view, the smoke signals went up between Wixenford and Heatherdown and Sammy Day decided that this school could get along without me.

I was ten and a half when I was expelled.

---

* Later as a Lieut-Col in the Special Air Services in World War II, Brian, for great gallantry after being dropped behind the German lines, was decorated with the DSO and MC. It is rather depressing to think that his mother complained to mine because I told him the facts of life when we were both ten years old. He, not believing this phenomenal piece of news, had asked her for up-to-date information.

There is a Chinese proverb to the effect that when everything in the garden is at its most beautiful, an ill wind blows the seeds of weeds and suddenly, when least expected, all is ugliness.

The decision to remove me from Heatherdown, I am sure, was not taken lightly because in those days expulsion from school was tantamount to ruin for a boy of my age. Public schools with bulging waiting lists could pick and choose among far more desirable applicants and any boy without a public school education started life at an incalculable disadvantage. Sure enough my mother soon received a polite letter from Mr Tuppy Headlam for whose house at Eton I had hopefully been entered, saying that unfortunately, he had decided that he was going to have to 'shorten his entry list etc. etc.'

But of this I knew nothing. It was the end of term anyway, and in the excitement I noticed no chill on the part of Sammy Day, nor any of the other masters, as I said goodbye and went off whooping and hollering with the rest of the boys to board the school train for the trip to London.

On arrival at Waterloo Station, the shouting, laughing hysterically happy boys were clutched to parental bosoms while eyes were averted from filthy nails, grease spots and ink stains.

I braced myself for my usual encounter with 'Tommy'. He was enlisted on these occasions to meet the school train at one platform, collect my trunk and see me safely ensconced in a third-class compartment on the train for Portsmouth Harbour where my mother would be waiting to take me on the ferry across the Solent to Ryde and thence to my beloved Rose Cottage, Bembridge, I.W. Once this had been accomplished, Tommy's contribution to the proceedings ended.

'Tommy' was easily identifiable. Above his beetling eyebrows and Duke of Wellington nose, he wore a top hat, the wont of his ilk whenever the King was in London. He bore down upon me, uttered no word of greeting and with an imperious gesture of his umbrella commanded me to follow. Everything so far had been perfectly normal. He hardly ever wasted conversation on me, so the silent march through the station following a porter with my trunk gave me no sense of foreboding.

Soon I was alone in a sooty compartment that smelled of stale smoke and orange peel, watching the retreating figure of my stepfather stalking towards the exit. Hanging out of the window I saw him pause and speak to the guard and point in my direction. The guard nodded his understanding. Soon we were off.

I sat back and savoured the delicious aroma of my compartment, then, after examining the framed, faded pictures of Freshwater Bay and Shanklin, I snuggled into my corner seat, gazed out of the window and gave myself up to delicious anticipation of the four weeks' holiday ahead.

My mother had beautiful teeth and a beautiful smile. I imagined her standing by the barrier, the harbour behind her, waiting for me. Would I run to meet her as I longed to do? No, I thought, the little kids at Waterloo had looked pretty soppy doing that; I would play the whole thing cool – saunter, that's what I'd do, saunter, and then suddenly, shove out my hand and give her the wooden bracket I had made for her in the carpentry class. I had clutched this bracket in my hand wrapped in brown paper ever since I left Heatherdown.

Two hours later, the green Hampshire countryside gave way to the drab outskirts of Portsmouth and as the train slowed down for its first stop, Portsmouth Town, I looked down into the busy heart of the city – another five minutes, then at the most and I would see my mother and the holidays really would start. I wondered if the tyres of my bicycle were flat and if Grizel and Joyce were there and above all if Brian Franks was back from Wixenford yet. Max I knew was away on a six months' training cruise as a cadet on HMS *Thunderer* but I squirmed with excitement, little knowing that the Chinese wind had blown a whole cart load of weeds into my garden and I was, at that very moment, waist deep in nettles.

The train stopped. The guard opened the door, jerked his thumb in my direction and addressed someone behind him. 'That's the little bastard.'

A gigantic man in a trench coat with a magenta coloured face and tufts of hair sprouting on his cheek bones, filled the doorway.

'Get your things,' he commanded, 'you are coming with me.'

'No, sir,' I quavered, 'my mother is waiting for me at the next stop.'

'Don't argue, get your bloody things.'

Stupefied with fear, I cowered into my corner.

'Oh, Christ!' said the man to the guard, 'get his bloody things down, will you? I'll lug him out.'

With that, while the guard lowered my suitcase and mackintosh, this huge creature picked me up bodily. I grabbed wildly at the luggage rack as I was carried out and dropped my mother's bracket. I don't think I fought much or even cried. I was paralysed with terror.

I was dragged along the platform, outside into the station yard and shoved into an ancient car.

'What are you doing with that little boy?' asked a woman with a baby.

'Mind your own — business,' was the answer. I noticed a heavy smell of spirits.

Through Portsmouth we lurched and out to the genteel suburbs of Southsea. I now sobbed uncontrollably. My brain refused to consider what could be happening to me. I cried for my mother.

'Stop that bloody noise and when you do, I'll tell you where you're going.'

My sobs dried up into a snivelling kind of hiccups.

'First of all, you have been expelled from Heatherdown because you are a dirty little — . You are not going home for the holidays, you are staying here with me and if you don't behave yourself, I'll tan the arse off you – Any questions?'

I shall always remember Southsea Common: flat, greasy, wet and windswept, with a dejected flock of dirty sheep morosely munching its balding surface.

Half way across he stopped the car and slapped me hard several times across the face.

'Stop it, for Christ's sake . . . You're not a bloody girl.'

I was still whimpering with fear when we arrived at a dreary house in a shoddy row. Grimy net curtains and an aspidistra filled half of a bleak downstairs window which looked on to a brick path and a muddy garden: the other half was filled by the curious faces of half a dozen boys.

Commander Bollard ran a school for 'difficult' boys.

I don't know how my stepfather found him. He was an unlovable man who fulminated constantly against the terrible injustice he had suffered by being 'axed' from the Navy when a promising Lieuten-ant-Commander. Now he and his thin-lipped, blue-veined, tweedy, terribly 'refained' wife added to his meagre pension and indulged their mutual passion for pink gin by taking in a dozen or so boarders.

The boarders were without exception pretty hard cases. Nearly all had been expelled from one or more schools and despairing parents had committed them to the tender care of Commander and Mrs Bollard, hoping that stern discipline would work where kindness or indifference had so far failed.

A few eventually pulled themselves together and clawed their way back to acceptance by lesser public schools. Others ran away and joined the merchant navy. Several ended up in Borstal.

The gallant Commander laid about him with a will on the smallest excuse, and there was hardly a bottom in the house that did not bear witness to his Dickensian brutality.

We were treated like young criminals and soon began to feel that we might as well behave like them. Pocket money was not allowed as part of our 'cure', but extra food was essential because the gin-sodden labours of Mrs Bollard only half-filled our bellies.

The house was a three-storeyed rabbit warren and terribly over-populated, but oh! it was clean. We scrubbed and re-scrubbed every inch of it daily. It must have been the only building in existence where the wooden floors were holy-stoned twice a day. Oil lamps had to be spotless too – there was no electric light – and an ill-trimmed wick was evil-smelling evidence of highly punishable inefficiency.

The ghastly dining room was called the 'Gun Room', the kitchen 'the Galley', the cellar 'the Brig' and so forth. We did not sleep in hammocks but on wooden shelves, four to a room. The Commander and his wife prowled about at night in stockinged feet hoping to catch us talking.

A couple of grey-faced ex-schoolmasters came every day to give us almost continuous lessons and there were no games. Saturday afternoons were free and we made full use of them.

One of the few useful things I learned there was the Morse Code which the Commander taught himself. I suspect it was all he knew but it made it unnecessary to speak when talking after lights out. It did, however, make flashlights and batteries an essential part of our survival kit. These were procured in the same way as food – by stealing.

On Saturday afternoon, 'the ship's company', as the Commander liked to refer to his charges, split up into highly organized gangs of four or six and went shop-lifting for chocolate, condensed milk, cakes, batteries, flashlights, and other essentials.

Every day was torture for me. I received no word from my mother and when once I borrowed enough money, sevenpence I believe, to put through a telephone call to wish her a happy Easter, somebody at Rose Cottage hung up as soon as they heard my voice. Feeling a complete outcast and worst of all, within sight of Bembridge seven miles away across the water, I gradually became the best and most dedicated 'front man' in the establishment.

'Curly' and 'Dusty' were the two unchallenged gang leaders. I worked mostly in Curly's group. A large foxy-faced boy with a mop of sandy hair, protruding teeth and freckles, he called the shots on Saturdays. He was a brilliant organizer.

On Saturday mornings he decided exactly what was to be lifted during the afternoon and it was never an excessive amount – food for consumption during the coming week or saleable goods to provide purchasing power. Curly knew a 'fence' in Southampton who worked with smugglers in the merchant navy and with the exception of our most ambitious effort, a 'hot' motorcycle, which had to be dumped in a chalk quarry on the Downs, this man took everything we had to offer.

One Saturday I was paid the supreme compliment of being chosen to travel with Curly on the bus to Southampton to visit the 'fence'.

Curly had decided that as summer was coming on, thin cotton shirts and singlets would be most acceptable to the 'fence's' regular customers – sailors heading for the Indian Ocean, Dakar or Panama. We lifted that day about two dozen saleable articles. As front man for candy, cigarettes and buns, my job was simple: to open big blue eyes wide and engage the owner of a tobacconist's or cake shop in long conversation about the price of various items which I hoped to be able to buy for my crippled uncle in hospital. While this was going on, one or two of the rest of the gang pocketed necessities from the far end of the counter. It was easy, in the small shops but the big stores, with the possibility of store detectives, called for a more advanced technique – the marbles.

Once I saw that 'the lifters' were exactly in position for their grab, I burst a large paper bag full of glass marbles. The crash of falling glass turned all heads – many willing souls stooped to aid the poor little boy who even on occasions could summon up a few tears of embarrassment.

We never 'worked' the same store twice.

Three weeks passed and as a relief from the Commander's crude and vicious discipline – I once spent a whole day in 'the brig': alone in the darkness of the cellar listening to the rats scrabbling about among piles of old newspapers around me – Saturday afternoons became oases in the desert of my loneliness.

Thrashed by the Commander for the smallest offence, ill-fed, apparently deserted by the family, expelled from a well-known school and facing my future through a bead curtain of question marks, I was, after ten years of life, already at a very low ebb.

But if, Dear Reader, you should think that I was a victim of circumstances, a magnet for bad luck, or just plain 'hardly done by', I beg you also to consider the possibility that I was a thoroughly poisonous little boy.

After a month under the command of Commander Bollard, his wife one day came to find me. A cigarette permanently waggled from her tight mouth. Her upper lip was yellow.

'May husbind wants yew,' she announced.

I followed her to the 'Captain's Cabin' – a dreadful little study full of leather furniture and old navy lists. Around the place plenty of bottles were in evidence – none held sailing ships.

The Commander lounged behind his desk.

'All right, you little bugger, you have been sprung. Get packed, don't steal anybody else's stuff because you go through Customs here before you leave – you're catching the three o'clock ferry to the Island.'

My heart nearly stopped beating. I could hardly believe it. I rushed upstairs and started packing furiously, terrified that he would change his mind.

No mother met the ferry on which I was dumped unceremoniously by the gallant Commander. With a strange last-minute change of character, he thrust a stick of Southsea Rock into my hand along with my ticket.

On the short train trip to Bembridge I reflected on what sort of welcome would be awaiting me.

It was my ally, Grizel, very distressed, bless her, who met me and as we walked up the hill to the cottage, she filled me in as to my immediate fate.

I was to be sent into the Navy, if they would have me and if I could pass the exam, about two years hence.

'How is Mum? Is she very angry with me?'

'I think she is terribly unhappy about Heatherdown. They wouldn't have you at Eton after being expelled, you know.'

I had a poor welcome at Rose Cottage, but it was no worse than I had expected. My mother was in her room. I went upstairs with leaden feet and watery knees.

Coldly she went over my miserable performance at Heatherdown – the damage was done, she said, but it was far more serious than I realized – I wouldn't be able to get into anything now. The Navy might take me but everything depended on getting very high marks in the exam: if I got those they might overlook my being expelled from school.

My mother explained that I had been brought over from Portsmouth, not for a holiday but to repack my trunk and to leave the very next morning for Penn Street, in Buckinghamshire, where 'Uncle Tommy' had arranged for me to go to a crammer's who would try to get me past the entrance examination for Dartmouth.

Another of 'Uncle Tommy's' selections? I quailed at the thought but I couldn't see that things could get very much worse than they had been lately so after a silent family supper, I borrowed Grizel's bicycle and pedalled up to the Mill House where Brian Franks lived, knowing I would find a sympathetic ear.

Still shaky from his illness, Brian gave me an eye-witness account of the opening of my gift. It seemed that the Matron had unwrapped the box with quite a flourish and the contents had flown into a medicine cabinet whence it had been extracted with forceps.

Brian said he had begun to feel better from that moment.

I have noticed again and again that when things are really black and one feels that they can't possibly get any worse – they often do. This time, however, things improved.

The crammer at Penn Street was the Vicar – the Reverend Arthur Browning, a magnificent looking grandson of Robert Browning – clear, blue eyes and white, wavy hair.

Chorus: 'It's the roast beef of old England,
            That makes us what we are today!'
Verse: 'What makes the Vicar's hair so nice and wavy?
            It's simply becos he was brought up on the gravy,
            Of the Roast Beef of old Engerlund
            That makes us wot we are today.'

                               etc. etc.

So we dutifully and sycophantically warbled at the village fête, a week after I arrived.

Sycophantically because beneath his benign and exotic exterior, he was an evil-tempered, vain old tyrant. The parents uniformly adored him: the boys without exception loathed him.

The Victorian vicarage nestled next to the Victorian church in a damp dell, enfolded by dripping beechwoods, part of the well-known pheasant shoot of Lord Howe's Penn House estate, three miles away.

Mrs Browning was a plump partridge of a woman who wore

pince-nez which were attached to a little chain. These in turn were controlled by a spring concealed inside a round enamel receptacle pinned to her generous left bosom.

There was a nice sporting master called Mr Keeble who took us for long walks to Amersham and bicycle rides to Beaconsfield, and a nice scholarly old gentleman called Mr Woodcock whose ill-fitting false teeth had a distressing habit of flying out on to the carpet or into the soup. At the village fête they became embedded in a macaroon.

Ma Browning was immensely greedy and the high fees paid by our parents enabled her to provide a very good 'board' indeed. She had a brace of pretty daughters aged eighteen and twenty whose woollen bloomers hung in steaming festoons in the bathroom and an elder son who enlivened Sunday luncheons by arriving flushed and late with garrulous business friends from London.

All in all, with the exception of 'Pa' Browning's rages, which were the twittering of little birds compared to the exhibitions of Mr Croome and Commander Bollard, Penn Street vicarage was a very pleasant interlude.

I worked hard but many of Pa Browning's tantrums were certainly brought on when it became apparent to him that mathematics of all sorts would for ever be beyond me.

It began to look probable that the Royal Navy would not entrust the navigation of several million pounds' worth of battleship and several hundred lives to an officer who could not work out his position; but there was still some hope as the most important part of the naval entrance exam was said to be the interview by the Board of Admirals, and many encouraging stories were in circulation to prove that he who impressed the Admirals personally was well on his way to conquering the written papers.

There were about a dozen boys at the vicarage, some of my age trying to pass the common entrance exam to public schools and an older group who had finished with school and were trying to pass examinations for universities. Some of these had been removed under a cloud from public schools.

Having been expelled myself from Heatherdown, I had a certain amount in common with these, but not nearly so much as one large ex-Etonian thought. At first I was flattered by his attentions and was naive enough to think he liked me for myself. He took me for bicycle rides and stood me ice-cream cornets by the gross. Then one day he took me for a walk in the beech-woods.

It was a very dreary experience and the laws on homosexuality being what they still are, I am certainly not going into it in any great detail here. Suffice to say that I came out of the wood with a ten and sixpenny second-hand accordion which I had admired in a junk shop in Loudwater.

I think I had visions of owning a whole orchestra. In any event, I could not wait to tell everyone how easy it was to obtain musical instruments.

I was interrogated by Pa Browning and a large, black taxi came and took the large ex-Etonian away.

The day of the naval entrance exam finally dawned. I was scrubbed from head to toe and, shining like a new sixpence, was dumped with several hundred other applicants in a forbidding morgue of a building, next to Burlington Arcade.

My French, English, history and geography were all pretty reliable and I had been primed with a few questions in arithmetic, algebra and geometry that Pa Browning was sure would come up. I had those answers down pat, but above all I was rehearsed in how to behave in front of the Admirals.

'Be quick and intelligent without being smug or cheeky,' said Pa Browning.

'If you don't know the answer to a question – make one up quickly – don't just dither. Remember above all the boy who was asked to give the names of the three most famous Admirals in British Naval history – "Admiral Nelson, sir; Admiral Drake, sir; and I didn't quite catch your name, sir".'

The first exam was the medical one.

Half a dozen at a time, we were stripped naked and to test our hearts, made to climb ropes without using our legs; then the usual tapping of knees and peering into ears, mouths and eyes took place.

Finally, 'get on your marks as though you are going to run a hundred yards'. Once in position, a large hand grabbed our testicles from the rear. 'Cough!' came the order. One poor little brute thought the man said 'Off!' and leaped eagerly forward. He was still being rubbed with ice when I was fully dressed and waiting to be summoned by the Admirals.

A bemedalled Master-at-Arms approached me in the ante-room.

'All right you, you're next, now go and sit at that desk. You'll find a pencil and paper there. You have five minutes to write a funny story – got it?'

I repressed my urge to indulge in lavatory humour and I don't remember what I wrote but it was certainly plagiarism in its finest form as I had read it the day before in an old *Punch*.

Clasping my funny story, I followed the Master-at-Arms into a long panelled room. Seated round a table was a drift of Admirals. One or two wore beards; all were bound to the elbows with gold braid and clanking with medals.

They seemed rather bored. One took my funny story and read it then passed it to his neighbour. Out of the corner of my eye I watched it progress as questions were fired at me.

'Have you had any relations in the Navy?'

I dug up a distant cousin who fought at Jutland.

'How does a petrol engine work?'

I knew.

'What was the number of the taxi you came in, this morning?'

'I walked, sir.'

'There is a blank map on the wall over there, go and point out Singapore.'

I jabbed a desperate finger in the region of Bangkok.

'Why do you want to go into the Navy?'

'I want to be an Admiral, sir.'

(I think I overdid it a bit there.)

After a few more fairly inane questions to which I gave answers of equal non-distinction, the most heavily bearded of the Admirals spoke up.

'One last question – why were you expelled from Heatherdown?'

That really rocked me but I should have realized they would have done their homework.

There was no point in trying to work round that one so I put on what I hoped was 'the boy stood on the burning deck' expression –

'I put some dog's mess in a box, sir, and sent it to a sick friend.'

It sounded quite awful the way I said it and a long silence followed my announcement.

'You thought that was funny?'

'Yes, sir.'

'But your headmaster did not – correct?'

'Yes, sir.'

'I see. Well, fortunately, we don't have dogs aboard ship.'

Hearty laughter greeted this sally, and I was so grateful to the old man. I quite oddly said,

'Thank you, sir.'

I believe I passed the interview and I was bullish after most of the written papers. The last one to confront me was mathematics.

Not one of the carefully learned problems so confidently predicted by Pa Browning came up and my total score in the subject was 28 out of a possible 300.

Not unnaturally, the Royal Navy decided that it could rub along without me. So, aged twelve and a half, it was 'back to the old drawing board'.

The English public schools have been operating for a long time: some for a very long time indeed. Eton was founded in 1440, and Winchester even earlier, in 1378. Rugby, where that horrible little boy picked up a soccer ball and charged off with it, started in 1567 and Oundle, ten years before that. Cheltenham and Marlborough, having opened their doors for the first time in the early eighteen forties, were probably the youngest additions to the well-known list, until in 1923, Stowe came along.

Stowe School was established not, as were the others, by Kings, Archbishops or Lord Mayors but by a consortium of educators and hard-headed businessmen who saw the possibilities for a new public school and hoped to make a good thing out of it.

Stowe House, the vast Georgian home of the extinct Dukes of Buckingham, had become the debt-ridden property of a kinsman – the Master of Kinloss.

He, like my father, was slaughtered during the war to end all wars, and his mother, like mine, was forced to liquidate.

The consortium obtained this magnificent house and several hundred acres of grounds. Clough Williams-Ellis, the architect of Portmeirion in North Wales, was enlisted to transform it. A prospectus was issued and Stowe was on its way – heralded as 'the New Great Public School'.

In these early post-war years, a whole stratum of suddenly well-to-do industrialists found the established public schools, to which they longed to send their sons, already bulging at the seams, so the consortium had no problem whatever in finding clients. Discovering a young aggressive headmaster with new ideas was far more difficult. They made a most fortunate choice – a young housemaster from Lancing College – J.F. Roxburgh.

In May of 1923, the school opened with less than a hundred boys. Somewhere in the depths of the Carlton Club, 'Tommy' heard rumblings; they could have been fulminations because a leading article in *The Times* and the Headmaster of Eton, Edward Lyttelton, in that year both opined that instead of starting a new public school it would be far more sensible to enlarge the facilities of the old ones. Whatever they were, the rumblings sank in. Pa

Browning was instructed to investigate this last resort and in July, I was sent over to Stowe, 30 miles in the dilapidated village taxi, to be interviewed by 'J.F.' Roxburgh.

Stowe must be the most beautiful school in England. Golden stone colonnades, porticos by Vanbrugh, sweeping lawns, huge lakes, long green valleys, glorious avenues, a Corinthian arch, a Palladian bridge and scores of assorted grottoes and 'temples d'amour' from each of which, through spectacular beech woods, rides open up to show other more fascinating 'follies'. Robert Adam, Grinling Gibbons, Kent, Valdré and Borra combined to produce glowing, beautifully proportioned interiors. Roxburgh, in his first public speech as Headmaster, said, 'Every boy who goes out from Stowe will know beauty when he sees it for the rest of his life.'

How true, but the apprehensive, small boy who waited in the Headmaster's flower-filled garden on that warm summer evening, saw nothing of the architectural and landscaped beauties around him. All he knew was that he had never in all his life wanted anything so much as to be accepted for that school – it just felt right and he longed passionately to be part of it.

Roxburgh finally appeared. Very elegant, he seemed, with a spotted bow tie, very tall, curly hair parted in the middle.

He came out through the french windows of his study and crooked his finger at me. Then he smiled, put an arm round my shoulders and led me to a stone bench.

'Now, my dear man,' he said, 'you seem to have had a lot of ups and downs – tell me all about it.'

I don't pretend to have total recall but I do remember those words – I will never forget them.

He listened sympathetically as I told him my version of my life so far. When I had finished, he remained silent for what seemed like an eternity. Then he stood up and said, 'I'll walk with you to the car.' On the way through the school, he showed me the Assembly Hall and the Library and pointed out the fabulous view from the top of the South Front steps across sloping, green pastures to a lake, then up to the towering Corinthian arch. Several times he spoke to boys who passed us, each time addressing them by their Christian names.

When he reached the ancient taxi, he looked down at me and smiled again, then he said, 'There will be two hundred new boys coming next term and you will be in Chandos House. Your housemaster will be Major Haworth.'

I mumbled something then climbed into the taxi and wept.

In September I arrived at Stowe along with the other new boys.

As we outnumbered the old boys by two to one, everybody, masters included, for the first couple of weeks, sported pieces of white cardboard pinned to their coats showing their name in bold print, rather like a dentists' convention in Chicago.

One of Roxburgh's better new ideas was to break with the traditional prison garb of the older establishments; no top hats, stiff collars or straw boaters for us . . . the boys wore grey flannel suits on weekdays and blue suits on Sunday.

Rules were sensible and good manners were encouraged: for instance hands had to be removed from pockets when passing masters or visiting parents. There were no 'bounds' and boys were allowed to have bicycles. As, however, one had to pedal three miles to get out of the school grounds, this was a little more strenuous than it sounded.

I could not believe my good fortune. The boys seemed nice and friendly albeit as bemused for the first few days as I was and Major Haworth, lately a company commander at Sandhurst, was one of the kindest and gentlest of men.

People are sharply divided about their schooldays and contrary to what one tells one's children about their being the best days of one's life, most people remember them with distaste.

Stowe, in those early days, was different from any other school. At the start, we were all the same age – around thirteen. Within four years, as the number of boys swelled from three hundred to five hundred, there was an annual intake of younger ones but somehow it seemed as though we all grew up together and I for one enjoyed the whole thing immensely. Inevitably, my inherent weakness of not being able to stand prosperity got me into trouble, but for the first couple of years, I was a fairly reliable citizen.

Roxburgh dominated the scene and I worshipped the man.

The first to notice some special interest being shown by a boy, Roxburgh nurtured it, fostered it and made the boy feel a litle bit special because of it. How he did this, I shall never know, but he made every single boy at the school feel that they, and what they did, were of real importance to the Headmaster. Boys were always addressed by their first names and encouraged to build radio sets, to fence and play golf and tennis besides the usual school games, to paint, play the piano or the bagpipes and to keep pets, though this last got a little out of control as the boys grew older and instead of rabbits and ferrets being the status symbols, monkeys, bears, hyenas and skunks filled the cages. Finally, the school zoo was shut down for reasons of noise and smell.

I played the trombone and the drum in the school band and started a house magazine, to which 'J.F.' subscribed, called *The Chandosian*. I also by the age of fourteen fell in love once more with milk chocolate and became almost entirely conical in shape. My nickname was Podger or Binge and I went bright pink after Rugger. Another boy, named Smallman, was even fatter than I was; his nickname was unoriginal – 'Tiny'. 'Tiny' Smallman was very large indeed and we both became selfconscious about our physical defects. Tiny found an ad in a boys' paper and we spent our pocket money on strange tubes containing a foul-smelling green paste which, when rubbed on the stomach or bottom, was guaranteed to reduce it in size. After football, we waited till the others had left the changing room rather than take a shower in public.

Because of my shape, I was enlisted in the school plays, usually playing a mushroom or something fairly unobtrusive.... I got the call of the greasepaint, however, and before I left, I was running the school concerts and giving myself all the best parts.

I studied fairly hard, though permanently stymied by mathematics, and my immediate goal was the School Certificate, a public exam for which one sat between 15 and 16 and which, provided one obtained enough 'credits', was comparable with 'O' and 'A' levels today. One of the 'credits' which one had to obtain in order to get the School Certificate was mathematics, so from a very early date 'J.F.' saw to it that I took special tuition to try and defeat the monster.

My long-term goal, thanks to some pretty nifty salesmanship by Major Haworth, became the Royal Military College, Sandhurst, followed by a commission in the Argyll and Sutherland Highlanders.

School, between thirteen and fifteen, therefore, presented no great problems and the holidays, too, went along very nicely during this period of formation. Tommy being persona non grata at Rose Cottage, the summers were bliss: for Christmas Grizel and I were packed off to spend the holiday at Nanpanton, in Leicestershire, with the Paget family – where the children, Peter and Joan, were of identical vintage.

Their father, Edmund, was, with a splendid figure named Algy Burnaby, joint-Master of the Quorn Hunt; Barbara, their mother, was a garrulous, gossipy, enchanting, shop-talking, fox huntress who rode side-saddle under a top hat bigger than Tommy's, swore like a trooper and, along with the rest of her family, never could grasp the fact that Grizel and I were not actually afraid of horses – we were just too impecunious to hunt. We loved the Pagets.

Easter holidays in English schools being short – three weeks –

Tommy would arrange to be away while my mother found a variety of places in which to house us. Sometimes, it was Bembridge, but Rose Cotage was barely habitable at that time of year. Once we were sent to a sister of Tommy's who lived in a noisome little flat in Portsmouth – far too near the Bollards and the scenes of my crimes for comfort – but the worst was when Tommy decided to be a real estate tycoon.

He bought a poky little house in a back street behind Windsor Castle. It was a dark panelled purgatory, whose sole charm lay in the fact that it had once belonged to Nell Gwyn and much Royal thrashing around was said to have gone on in the four-poster upstairs. It poured with rain for the entire holiday and Grizel and I, wearing overcoats, played Mah-Jongg in semi-darkness for three weeks. I hope I never again have to set eyes on the Bamboos, the Flowers, the Winds, the Seasons and all those miserable Dragons. I couldn't wait to get back to Stowe.

The memorable Easter holiday of this period came just after my fourteenth birthday.

Tommy's real estate operations found us, for a while, the inhabitants of 110 Sloane Street, a small house of many floors which shook as the buses went past the door: petrol-driven red Metropolitan buses, numbers 19 and 22 and – far more fascinating to me because they were driven by steam – the white Nationals, No. 30.

My brother, who had left the Navy because of chronic sea sickness and sensibly switched to the Army, was abroad with his regiment in India. Joyce and Grizel both had tiny bedrooms but there was no room for me so I slept in a minute cubicle in a boarding-house in St James's Place, some distance away.

Every night after dinner, I walked to Sloane Square, boarded a 19 or a 22 headed for Piccadilly, got off at the Ritz Hotel and proceeded down St James's Street to my iron bed, wooden floor, stained jug and basin and po under the bed.

The next morning, I had to be back for breakfast at eight o'clock and I was given fourpence a day for the round trip. Even my rudimentary mathematics could work out that by walking four miles a day, I could save almost half a crown a week.

I enjoyed my nocturnal travels very much and soon gave up going straight from Sloane Street to St James's Place and took to going all the way down Piccadilly to Piccadilly Circus to watch the electric signs.

Every night, I became more adventurous and after a week or so, I knew the area bounded by Park Lane, Oxford Street, Regent Street and Pall Mall like the back of my hand. This was a pretty safe area for a fourteen-year-old, indeed, it never crossed my mind that it could be otherwise, and apart from being spoken to a few times by strange men who asked me if I would like to go home with them to meet their dogs or see their paintings, I tramped around unhindered.

It seemed to me perfectly normal for a boy to be walking around the West End of London at night so I saw nothing out of the ordinary in the number of girls who were doing the same thing; cloche hats, flesh-coloured stockings and the forerunner of the mini-skirt being the vogue, I saw a vast amount of female legs and ankles twinkling their way up and down the same streets that I frequented.

Bond Street was a great favourite of mine because many of the shops were lit up all night, and I made it a point, after watching BOVRIL, IRON JELLOIDS and OWBRIDGE'S LUNG TONIC change colours in Piccadilly Circus, to check on how things looked in the windows of Garrards, Aspreys and Ciro Pearls.

Some of the girls, I noticed, were walking every night on the same streets and I was soon on nodding terms with them though I didn't understand at all the remarks made as I passed, nor the giggles that followed me.

One night, in Bond Street, I noticed a really superior pair of legs in front of me and I became so fascinated by them that I followed them for quite a distance. The girl seemed to have many friends and stopped and spoke to them from time to time.

The next night, I skipped going to watch the electric signs and went looking for those legs instead. I searched up and down Bond Street and cased the side streets too, Clifford Street, Savile Row and even Burlington Street, the scene of my naval defeat.

Just as I was about to give up, the girl came out of a house right in front of me and walked rapidly off towards Piccadilly. I followed and when she stopped on a corner to talk to a couple of lady friends, I crossed the street and pretended to look into a shop window. I managed to get a fairly good view of her face. She was laughing and talking . . . very lively, very gay, and her face looked beautiful in an open, fresh, English rose kind of way – blonde, blue eyes, high colour – you know the sort of thing.

She stayed there talking to her friends and as I didn't want to be conspicuous, I moved off towards my boarding-house.

When I woke up in the morning I knew I must be in love. At least, I suspected that I was because I could think of nothing else but this girl. The day dragged on interminably, a shopping morning with my mother and in the afternoon, playing among the stunted, grimy bushes of the gardens opposite our house with some stunted, grimy, Spanish children.

That night, after dinner, I didn't walk, I was in a hurry. I took the bus and was lucky. After cruising up and down for what seemed an age, my patience was rewarded and my heart gave a lurch as I saw her lovely, long legs approaching from the Piccadilly direction. She was with a distinguished-looking, grey-haired man in a dinner jacket. He wore an opera hat and was smoking a cigar – obviously her father. Together they went into the house in Cork Street and, deliriously happy that I had found out where my dream lived, I took myself off to bed.

It took three days or rather nights of patient toil and careful sleuthing before I finally met Nessie.

I was following her at what I imagined to be a discreet distance, my eyes glued to her wondrous underpinnings, when she stopped and turned so suddenly and so unexpectedly, that I nearly bumped into her.

'Wot the 'ell are you followin' me for?' she demanded.

I went purple.

'I wasn't following you', I lied. 'I was just on my way to bed.'

'Well, for Gawd's sake go on 'ome, mate. For the last four nights you've been stuck to me like my bleedin' shadow. Wot d'yer want anyway?'

I stammered and looked wildly to right and left. Suddenly she softened and smiled.

'All right, it's still early and you're a bit young but come on home and I'll give yer a good time.'

Soon she turned into her doorway and in a daze I followed, unable to believe my good fortune.

'A good time' she had said – it had to be at least a ginger beer and listening to the gramophone ... Eileen Stanley singing 'When it's moonlight in Kaluha' perhaps. In a high state of expectancy, I mounted to the second floor behind my glorious new friend.

The flat, above a tailor's shop, was small and smelled of cabbage. In the living room there was a large divan with a lot of satin cushions and some dolls on it and nearby a small lamp with a red shade. A small kitchen stove was behind a screen. The other room was a bedroom, also rather poorly lit: a tiny bathroom was just discernible in the gloom beyond the huge bed that seemed to sag quite a lot in the middle.

'Three quid,' she said, as she took off her coat.

I didn't quite get the message so she came very close to me and peered into my eyes.

'Three quid,' she repeated, 'that too much?'

I gulped and floundered –

'For what?'

'For the best yer've ever 'ad, mate, but then you 'aven't 'ad a lot 'av yer? 'Ow old are yer anyway?'

I was still unsure as to exactly what ground I was on and I kept wondering if her father lived downstairs but I managed to mumble the truth.

'*Fourteen*!!' she practically shrieked. 'Wot the 'ell d'yer think I am – a bleedin' nannie?'

Then she started giggling, 'Oh my Gawd, wot a larf. 'Ow old d'yer think I am anyway?'

'Twenty,' I suggested tentatively.

'Three years yet before that 'appens', she said, 'Well, come on, let's get on wiv it, *fourteen* . . . Gawd, you are a one aren't yer?'

I watched half in fascination, half in apprehension as she walked about the living room, taking of her little hat and blouse and unhooking her skirt.

''ere, take a look at these in case you need any 'elp.' With that she sat me down on the divan and left me to look at a large album of photographs.

'I'll be ready in a jiffy, dear.' She disappeared into the bedroom.

I had not so far been exposed to any pornography so the contents of that album very nearly finished off my sex life before it got under way. Hideous over-weight ladies, clad only in shoes and stockings, being mounted from every angle by skinny little men with enormous 'prongs': combinations of every shot in threes and twos, all with expressions of the greatest sincerity – and all apparently in advanced middle age.

The awful truth began to filter through my brain.

When Nessie appeared in the bedroom door dressed in the same uniform as the buxom ladies in the album – naked except for black stockings, held up above the knees by pink garters with blue roses on them and pink high-heeled shoes – she had a small towel in her hand.

'Come along, ducks, let's see 'ow good you are . . . you can wash in 'ere . . . I've put in permanganate,' she added. In a daze, I followed her into the dark little bedroom . . . another red shaded lamp was beside the bed . . . 'over there, dear,' she said, indicating a kidney shaped enamel bowl on a collapsible knee-high stand. She threw me the towel, lay down on the bed and put a record on a portable gramophone. The tune has, rather naturally, haunted me ever since. 'Yes . . . we have no bananas'. As I was to discover later, Nessie had a wonderful native wit but I still believe her selection at that particular moment was a random one.

'Get a move on, ducks, you don't get all night for three quid, yer know. Get your shirt off for a start.'

I took off my coat and my shirt and started to wash my hands in the bowl.

'Christ!' she yelled, sitting bolt upright, 'not your bleedin' 'ands yer dickie bird! Just a minute,' she went on more gently, 'come 'ere, come and sit on me bed. I want to talk to you. . . . Now look me in the eye, straight . . . is this the first . . . 'ave yer ever done it before? . . . ever done any — ?'

Miserably, I shook my head.

'And you 'aven't got three quid either I'll bet?'

Again I shook my head and mumbled some inane explanation.

'Aw you poor little bastard,' she said, 'you must be scared out of yer — wits.' She looked at me reflectively. 'Ever seen a naked woman before?'

'No,' I confessed.

'Well, this is wot it looks like – 'ow d'yer like it?' I smiled weakly and tried not to lower my eyes. Nessie snuggled down and started to giggle again, a deliciously infectious sound.

'Well, you've got this far – why don't you take the rest of your clobber off and pop into bed?'

'What about the . . .' I began.

'Oh, you owe me three quid,' she interrupted. 'Christ, I never thought I'd be seducing children . . . FOURTEEN . . . come on, jump in then.'

'Yes . . . we have no bananas' was substituted for something a little more encouraging – the bedside lamp with the red shade was left on and Nessie with her wondrous skin became a most understanding teacher. 'There we are, dear, that's it now – take a little weight on your elbows like a gentleman. Slowly, dear, more slowly – whoa! yer not a — woodpecker yer know . . . slowly . . . *that's* it, enjoy yerself ,. . . there, that's nice isn't it, dear . . . are yer 'appy? . . . 'appy now?'

By the time the Easter holidays ended, Nessie had become the most important thing in my life: my education at her hands, and in a way at her expense, had continued. She 'worked' at night and slept late but on many afternoons we met, usually at the entrance to a small movie house – she loved W.S. Hart – or we went to the music halls, the Coliseum, the Alhambra or the Palladium, to see Herbert

Mundin, Lily Morris, Rebla, the juggler, or a marvellous pair of young acrobats – Nervo and Knox. The seats cost one shilling and threepence and after the shows we had a cup of tea and a bun in a little tea shop, or we skipped the tea and the bun and went directly back to her flat. Afterwards, I would walk down to Sloane Street for a dreary family dinner during which Tommy would rattle those damn cuff-links in his starched shirt to draw attention to the fact that I had my elbows on the table.

Quite early in my relationship with Nessie, I made the elementary mistake of asking her why she did it. . . . 'a sweet girl like you'. She rounded on me like a tigress: 'Now don't *you* start trying to reform me. About three times a week some silly bugger asks the same friggin' question.

'Look, I'm three years older than you and I'm doing it because I want to do it . . . why I want to do it is none of your — bizness so if you don't like it – piss off back to school.'

Back at school for the summer term, I found that my life had changed fundamentally. Nessie or the thoughts of Nessie became the focal point of my existence. What I saw in her was fairly obvious but there were other things too; quite apart from the normal and very special physical attachment to 'the first', she gave me something that so far had been in rather short supply – call it love, understanding, warmth, female companionship or just 'ingredient X' – whatever it was, it was all over me like a tent.

I can't believe that I contributed very much to Nessie's well-being or peace of mind during this period – a fat fourteen and a half with no money and less experience – but apart from the 'hurly burly of the chaise longue', as Mrs Patrick Campbell once described a splendid activity, there also grew up between us a brother-sister relationship that was to last for many years.

Thanks to Nessie's insistence, I lost weight, a lot of extra padding turned to muscle and I became quite a proficient athlete of the second rank . . . house colours for practically everything and a frequent performer before I left Stowe in the 1st XI cricket, the 1st XV Rugby Football and in the fencing and boxing teams.

Nessie came down to Stowe to see me in summer and brought a picnic basket and a tartan rug. Together we took full advantage of the beauties of the school grounds. She had never been out of London before and these trips to the country, she told me later, gave her a peace she never knew existed. She took a great interest in my progress at the school and became so intrigued by my hero worship of Roxburgh, that she insisted on meeting him. Basely, I tried to avoid this confrontation but Nessie was not easily put off.

'Look, dear, 'e'll never know I'm an 'ore. 'e'll think I'm yer bleedin' aunt or somefing... Do I look like an 'ore?'

I told her she looked beautiful and like a duchess – not that looking like a duchess was much of a compliment but she was as easily flattered as she was hard to dissuade.

'That's 'im, innit?' she cried one Saturday afternoon, looking across towards the cricket pavillion. Roxburgh was approaching our tartan rug, resplendent in a pale grey suit topped by the inevitable spotted bow tie.

Nessie stood up, bathed in sunlight. She was wearing a short white silk summer dress that clung lovingly to her beautiful body; her honey coloured hair was cut in the fashion of the time – the shingle; she had a small upturned nose; she looked wonderfully young and fresh.

Roxburgh came over smiling his famous smile, 'May I join you?'

I introduced him.

''e's just like you told me,' said Nessie in a stage whisper.

''e's beautiful,' and then to Roxburgh. 'Don't look a bit like a schoolmaster dew yew, dear?'

J.F. setting himself on the rug missed a tiny beat but thereafter never gave any indication that he was not talking to a beautiful duchess.

He stayed about ten minutes, extolling the glories of Stowe House and its history, and Nessie bathed in the full glow of his charm. Never once did he ask any loaded questions and when he got up to leave he said, 'David is very lucky to have such a charming visitor.' The charming visitor nearly got me expelled a year later but it was certainly not her fault.

In the summer of 1926, by now a robust sixteen-year-old and appreciably ahead of my time in worldly experience, Roxburgh must have sensed a change in me. He sent for me and told me that I was one of four boys he had selected to become 'monitors' in a new house – Grafton, which was to open the following term.

The housemaster was coming from Fettes, Mr Freeman, and the boy chosen as prefect or head of the house was Bernard Gadney.* It was a huge compliment for any boy, but for me to feel that J.F. had this faith in me was an enormous boost. However, before I could bask in the glories of my new responsibilities, I had to overcome a slight hazard – the School Certificate. I was to sit for the exam in two weeks' time. It was a sort of long shot really ... if I failed this first

* B.C. Gadney was later to captain the English XV in many Rugby Internationals.

time, I would still have three more chances but I had to obtain the certificate soon in order to qualify to sit for the entrance exam to the Royal Military College, Sandhurst, eighteen months hence.

Apart from the dreaded mathematics, I was quite confident that I could pull it off this first time. My prospects in the new house were very exciting, my fat had disappeared, I had many friends at school and at Bembridge, I had Nessie in the background and I was at last beginning to get to know and to love my mother. In fact, everything was 'roses' for me. Then that damn wind started puffing those weeds in my direction once more.

I sat for the exam in the big school gymnasium and made mincemeat of the first two papers, French and history, and after the science, geography and English papers, I remained supremely confident. The last two tests were mathematics and Latin translation. In mathematics, as already explained, a 'credit' (about 80 per cent) was obligatory; without it, I would fail in the whole exam. When the questions were put on my desk, and all over the country at that particular moment identical papers were being put in front of thousands of nervous boys, I took a deep breath and started to read.

One glance was enough. It was hopeless. I knew that I just couldn't cope and there is no more suffocating feeling when sitting for a public examination.

I made a few vague stabs at the geometry questions and a token effort at the algebra but there was no point in my even trying to tackle the arithmetic.

I was the first boy to hand in his answers and leave the gymnasium. I went out to the cricket nets and faced the fact that the School Certificate was certainly not going to be mine this time.

Nessie was coming to see me the next day – a Saturday – and her train was due at Buckingham Station at midday. The Latin exam was scheduled from ten o'clock till eleven-thirty, so I decided to get through this now useless and unprofitable period as quickly as possible, pedal down to the station and surprise her there instead of meeting her as planned near the Corinthian arch at twelve-thirty.

It so happened that my Latin teacher was the supervisor of the candidates on that Saturday morning, which meant that it was he who would hand out the questions at the start, collect the answers at the end and in between, wander about the rows of desks making sure that there was no talking, or, perish the thought, any use of notes.

He knew that I could easily pass the Latin exam but only I knew that it was now useless to try.

The trick then was to complete the whole paper in half the time

43

and be on my way to Buckingham Station. Archie Montgomery-Campbell was a good and outstanding friend who occupied the desk on my right during the whole week of exams. He was also an excellent Latin scholar, so I enlisted his help.

The Latin paper was in two parts, prose and verse. It was agreed that I would quickly dispose of the prose while Archie coped first with the verse. Then, after making his fair copy, he would crumple up his first draft and drop it on the floor between the two desks. It was clearly understood between us that if anything went wrong, Archie would merely say that he had thrown away his first translation after he had made his fair copy and if somebody picked it up it was none of his business. The dirty work was to be done by me alone; he was to be blameless.

It all went beautifully according to plan. I copied out Archie's verse translation beneath my own effort at the prose, handed in my paper, and bicycled happily off in plenty of time to surprise Nessie.

We spent a blissful day together, eating shrimp paste sandwiches and sausage rolls, drinking shandy-gaff* and rolling around on the tartan rug. Nessie had begun to tell me a little more about herself and I listened adoringly that afternoon to her descriptions of her childhood in a Hoxton slum; six children in a tiny room, the three youngest in the bed, the others sleeping on the floor and all cowering away from the drunken Friday night battles between the parents.

At fifteen she and her sister of a year older had run away. For a while, they found work as waitresses in dingy tea shops and restaurants in Battersea and Pimlico. A few months later they were engaged as hostesses in a sleazy 'club' in Wardour Street. Then the sister started taking drugs and one night told Nessie she was going North with a boy friend to avoid the police. Nessie didn't miss her much and soon was employed by Mrs Kate Meyrick at the 43 Club. She had to be on hand in evening dress as a 'dancing partner', making a fuss of 'Ma' Meyrick's rather high class clientele and persuading them to buy champagne at exorbitant prices.

She was not allowed to solicit on the premises – a rule that was strictly enforced because 'Ma' Meyrick's establishment was often infiltrated by police officers in evening clothes, posing as the tipsy aftermath of regimental dinners or bachelor parties, but. in fact, contacts were easily enough made and Nessie soon built up the basis of an enthusiastic clientele.

'I'm not an 'ore wiv an 'eart of bleedin' gold, you know, dear, I'm out for everything I can get out of this game for another couple of

* A mixture of beer and ginger beer.

years – then I'm going to marry some nice Yank or Canadian and —
off abroad and 'ave kids.

'The only reasons I work the streets is that I'm on me own. I don't
'ave to sit in a Club all bleedin' night talkin' to a lot of drunks. When
I git tired, I can go 'ome and lock me — door . . . I make much more
money too, and the best bit, it's not like bein' one of those wotsits
on the end of a phone. I can see wot I'm gettin'. If I don't like the
look of a bloke, I don't ask 'im up, see.'

Watching Nessie while she talked, it seemed incredible that she
could be leading this sort of existence – her very youth and yes, her
very freshness were in complete contradiction to everything she was
describing – 'A lot of blokes want to 'ave me all to themselves . . .
you know, set me up in a bleedin' flat in Maida Vale with a maid
an' a — puppy but when the time comes – I'll set meself up. I've got
to move out of Cork Street tho', it's gettin' so — noisy, dear, with
that big ginger who's moved in above. An army officer by all
accounts. 'E goes round the coffee stalls at Hyde Park Corner and
picks up them corporals in their red tunics an' all, then he brings
'em 'ome and dresses himself up as a — bride, make-up, white
satin, 'igh 'eels, a bleedin' veil, orange blossom – the lot. Then 'e
chooses one of these blokes – 'e always 'as about 'arf a dozen of
'em up there at the same time – and 'e — *marries* him! Goes
through a sort of service, then, arm in arm wiv 'is 'usband, 'e walks
under a — archway of swords 'eld up by the other blokes. I've
talked to a coupla the soldiers – they're not gingers, mark you, far
from it, but they pick up a coupla quid apiece for the job and a fiver
for the 'usband.

''E doesn't lay an 'and on any of them, just plays the Weddin'
March on 'Is Master's Voice an' shoots 'is wad walking under them
— swords. But the noise, dear – Christ! I can't stand it! Everythink
is very military, 'im being an ex-officer an' all, and when it's all over
'e gets back into 'is nice blue suit, sits down be'ind a table with a —
army blanket on it and they all form up like a bleedin' Pay Parade.
"Guardsman So-and-So." "Sir!" one pace forward march . . . crash!
Forty shillings . . . SIR! about turn . . . crash! NEXT MAN . . .
CRASH! SIR!! . . . CRASH! CHRIST! . . . those — army boots,
dear. I'm going to 'ave to move.' . . . She shook with delicious
laughter.

'Of course, I don't get mixed up with no funny business myself . . .
it's just me and a bloke that's all . . . No exhibitions, none of that
stuff. Of course, I'm not saying I don't occasionally pick up a little
fancy money – watchin' 'em sit in cakes sometimes an' there's this

Aussie millionaire, dear, about fifty, who gets about eight of us up to 'is 'otel, then we all strip down to the stockin's and 'igh 'eels and 'e takes off everything! Then he gives us each an 'en pheasant's tail feather to stuff up the arse – 'ell of a job keepin' it in there it is because we 'ave to walk round in a circle – then, would you believe it, dear, 'e stands there in the middle with a cock pheasant's feather up 'is own arse and sprinkles corn on the — carpet. Of course we 'ave a terrible time not larfin' but if we do larf, we don't get paid and it's a tenner each too ... Well, there he stands, kind of crowin' or whatever the 'ell cock pheasants do, and we all 'ave to kinda peck at the — corn ... it's amazin' really, he shoots off right there all by 'isself in the middle of the circle. We never 'ave to touch 'im ... pathetic really when you think.'

When Nessie went back to London after these outings, I always felt terribly lonely. I loved walking about the fields and woods with her. I've never seen anyone get such real pleasure out of trees and flowers and birds and it gave me a feeling of importance to be able to point out different animals and to tell her about life in the country.

Sadly, I waved her away at Buckingham station and pedalled up the long avenue in time for evening chapel.

The whole school attended chapel twice a day and, after the evening service, announcements of special importance were made by the Headmaster.

In chapel about three weeks after Nessie's visit, J.F. motioned the boys to remain in their places. An expectant murmur arose.

'All over the country,' J.F. began, 'overworked examiners have been correcting several thousand papers sent in for this year's School Certificate examinations.

'Stowe is a new school and these same examiners have been looking at the papers sent in by us with special interest.

'Boys who sit for a public examination are representing their schools in public and they, therefore, have a very great responsibility. Schools are judged by the boys who represent them.

'It is, therefore, with grief and great disappointment that I have to tell you that two boys representing Stowe in the School Certificate have been caught cheating. I shall question the two concerned this evening and I shall deal with them as I see fit.'

Only when I saw Archie Montgomery-Campbell's ashen face did the horrible truth sink in. As the school rose to leave the chapel, my legs turned to water.

Ratings of the Royal Navy have always prided themselves on the fact that without any official signals being made, news and gossip passes between ships at anchor with a rapidity that makes African tribesmen blush over their tom-toms. The ratings themselves would have blushed that day: ten minutes after chapel, the whole school knew who were the two culprits. Perhaps like being attacked by dogs or run away with on horses, Archie and I smelled of fear.

Poor Archie was the first to be summoned to the Headmaster's study – he went off like Sydney Carton at the end of *A Tale of Two Cities*. A quarter of an hour later, I was located near the lavatories where I had been spending the interim.

No smile on J.F.'s face this time, just a single terse question, 'Have you anything to say for yourself?'

For the lack of any flash of genius that might have saved me, I told him the truth – that I had failed the exam anyway and wanted to get out early. I also added that Archie was completely guiltless and stood to gain nothing by helping me.

J.F. stared at me in silence for a long time, then he crossed the quiet, beautifully furnished room and stood looking out of the open french windows into the flower garden where he had first interviewed me. Cheating in a public examination is a heinous crime and it seemed inevitably that I would be expelled. I braced myself for the news as he turned towards me.

'Montgomery-Campbell made a stupid mistake in helping you with your Latin translation and I have given him six strokes of the cane. Until you stood there and told me the truth, I had every intention of expelling you from the school. However, in spite of your very gross misbehaviour, I still have faith in you and I shall keep you at Stowe. Now, I propose to give you twelve strokes with the cane.'

My joy at not being thrown out was quickly erased by the thought of my short-term prospect . . . Twelve! that was terrifying! J.F. was a powerfully built man and his beatings, though rare, were legendary.

'Go next door into the Gothic Library. Lift your coat, bend over and hold on to the bookcase by the door. It will hurt you very much indeed. When it is over, and I expect you to make no noise, go through the door as quickly as you wish. When you feel like it, go back to your house.'

The first three or four strokes hurt so much that the shock somehow cushioned the next three or four, but the last strokes of my punishment were unforgettable. I don't believe I did make any noise, not because I was told to avoid doing so, or because I was brave or anything like that – it hurt so much, I just couldn't get my breath.

When the bombardment finally stopped, I flung open the door and shot out into the passage. Holding my behind and trumpeting like a rogue elephant, down the stone passage, past the boiler rooms I went, out into the summer evening and headed for the woods.

After the pain subsided, the mortification set it. How was I going to face the other boys – a cheat? Obviously, my promised promotion to monitor would be cancelled and my remaining time at Stowe would be spent as an outcast.

Eventually, about bedtime, I crept up to my dormitory. It was a large room that accommodated twenty-five boys. The usual pillow fights and shouting and larking about were in full swing. They died away to an embarrassed silence as I came in. I took off my clothes, watched by the entire room. My underpants stuck to me and reminded me of my physical pain. Carrying my pyjamas I slunk off to the bathroom next door. An ominous murmur followed my exit.

In the bathroom mirror, I inspected the damage. It was heavy to say the least. Suddenly, Major Haworth's cheery voice made me turn, 'Pretty good shooting I'd call that . . . looks like a two-inch group'. He was his usual smiling, kindly self. 'When you've finished in here, get into bed. I'm going to read out a message the Headmaster has sent round the School . . . nothing to worry about.'

When everyone was in bed and quiet, the Major stood by the dormitory door and read from a piece of paper.

'I have interviewed the two boys connected with the School Certificate irregularities. Their explanations have been accepted by me and the boys have been punished. The incident is now closed and will not be referred to again by anyone.'

'Goodnight, everybody,' said the Major, and then with a wink at me – 'When that sort of thing happened to me I used to sleep on my stomach and have my breakfast off the mantelshelf.'

In the darkness, the whispers started – 'How many did you get?' . . . 'Did you blub' . . . 'What sort of cane is it?' . . . 'Promise to show us in the morning.' All friendly whispers. In the darkness, I buried my face in my pillow.

I determined there and then that, somehow, I would repay J.F. I never could, of course, but I became, I think, a good and responsible monitor the next term and, in due course, after squeaking past a mathematical barrier, I passed into the Royal Military College, Sandhurst, and became one of the first three Stowe boys to gain commissions in the Regular Army.

Summer holiday at Bembridge followed immediately after ten days of Officers' Training Corps camp on Salisbury Plain. It was at one such camp that I first smelled success in front of an audience. Several hundred boys from many different schools were attending the camp concert in a huge circus tent. Someone had told Major Haworth that as Stowe was a new school, it would be a good thing if we were part of the programme and he had asked me to do something about it.

There was at that time in England a monologuist named Milton Hayes. I had one of his records at school and had memorized some of his stuff for the benefit of my friends. I must now belatedly apologize to Milton Hayes for stealing from his material, which is what in part I did, adding topical touches of my own to fit the situation at the camp.

His monologue was a take-off of a half-witted politician electioneering. I made mine a half-witted General inspecting the camp. On the night of the concert, I sat outside the tent, waiting for my turn to go on. The boys were a rowdy audience and the noise from inside was deafening. There were a lot of boos. I experienced, for the first time, that delicious terror that has never left me – stage fright, and with rubbery knees, dry lips and sweating palms, I fought against the urge to dash madly away, grow a beard and emigrate to the Seychelles. At last I was called and I heard the Master of Ceremonies announce – 'Niven of Stowe'.

Miserably, I mounted the steps on to the stage, wearing the baggy General's uniform which Major Haworth had concocted for me. In my eye was a monocle and on my upper lip, a huge grey moustache.

Scattered applause and some laughter greeted my appearance.

The MC put up his hand – 'Major General Sir Useless Eunuch!' More laughter.

I gulped and prayed that the stage would open and swallow me up. Hundreds of boys in khaki filled the benches. The first three rows were occupied by officers in red Mess kit. I screwed my monocle into my eye and gazed at the officers. . . .

'Sergeant-Major, why is it that these members of the band have no instruments?' I asked. A roar of delighted laughter filled the tent and suddenly, it was easy. Then lapsing into pilfered Milton Hayes –

'What we must do with this camp, Sergeant-Major, is find out where we stand, then get behind ourselves and push ourselves forward. We must get right down to the very roots, right down to rock bottom, then bring the whole thing up into one common pool ... and looking around here at Salisbury Plain – and how very plain it looks – we should keep the ships at sea ... the harbours will be much cleaner for one thing ...' and so on for about ten minutes.

Milton Hayes and I were a riotous success that night and the harpoon of craving success as a performer was planted deep inside me.

Sailing entered my life about this time. My mother bought Grizel and me a twenty-five-year-old 14 ft sailing dinghy for £12. She was called *Merlin* and is still being sailed by children at Bembridge.

I became a good 'hand' and the pinnacle of my sailing career came later while I was still at Sandhurst and was chosen as a member of Great Britain's International Crew in the Cumberland Cup, a race for 8-metre yachts, during Ryde Week. With Sir Ralph Gore, the famous helmsman, in command, we in *Severn* easily defeated the French challenger *L'Etoile* in a best of three final.

First, however, Brian Franks and I formed the Bembridge Sailing Dinghy Club for children between twelve and eighteen. I was the first Secretary, Brian the first Captain. At the end of the first year, the Club showed a profit of £2 12s. 6d. which Brian and I transferred into liqueur brandy. We were both found next morning, face down in some nettles.

When you are a senior boy in an English Public School, you perhaps reach the pinnacle of your self-importance. Given hitherto un-dreamed of responsibilities and privileges, often receiving the acclaim, even the adulation, of your juniors and sometimes served by 'fags',* it is very easy to get carried away.

The Royal Military College, Sandhurst, soon took care of that ... it is never pleasant to be treated like mud but Sandhurst, at least, did it with style and no malice aforethought: it just came naturally.

We were called 'Gentlemen Cadets'. The officers and non-commissioned officer instructors were the pick of the whole British Army and the drill instructors were exclusively, the pick of the Brigade of Guards. Knowing you were due to become an officer in eighteen months' time, the NCOs could call you anything they

* American friends are often appalled by this description of younger boys who clean the rooms and run messages for their seniors ... they need not be ... it is not an abbreviation of faggot.

liked provided they prefaced it with a 'Mr So-and-So, Sir.'

There were about one thousand cadets at Sandhurst divided into Seniors, Intermediates and Juniors. The course was eighteen months so one spent six months in each category.

The Commandant was Major-General Sir Eric Girdwood, DSO, etc., etc.; the Adjutant was the famous Major 'Boy' Browning, Grenadier Guards, DSO etc., later to command all British Airborne troops in World War II.

In No. I Company my Company Commander was Major Godwin Austen, South Wales Borderers, MC; my Chief Instructor was Major 'Babe' Alexander,* Irish Guards, DSO, and the Company Sergeant Major was 'Robbo' Robinson, Grenadier Guards.

All these were completely splendid soldiers, with impeccable and gallant records, and however tough they may sometimes have been, they always had a deep understanding and sympathy for the cadets under their command.

The Cadet under-officer† in charge of the Junior platoon to which I was assigned, was a shifty-looking customer with a broken nose named Wright – a singularly unattractive piece of work. It was small wonder to any of us who knew him at Sandhurst that later, after changing his name to Baillie-Stewart and joining the Seaforth Highlanders he was caught selling military secrets to the Germans, court-martialled and imprisoned in the Tower of London.

The 'mud treatment' started on the first day of our ten weeks of concentrated drill 'on the square'. We were paraded in the civilian clothes in which we had arrived the day before. A strange assortment wearing suits, tweed jackets, plus-fours, hats, caps, boots, shoes and some with umbrellas, we smiled nervously at each other as we awaited the ministrations of 'Robbo'.

Rapidly and with the minimum of trimmings, Robbo explained that although it looked unlikely at the moment, we were supposed to be officer material and it had fallen to his unfortunate lot to try, within eighteen months, to transform this ''orrible shower' into being worthy of the King's commission.

'I shall address you as "Sir" because that's orders but when you speak to me you'll stand at attention, look me right in the eye and call me Staff . . . got it?'

Scattered murmurs of 'yes', 'right-ho' and 'jolly good' were silenced by one of the mightiest roars in the British Army.

* Brother of the famous wartime 'Alex'.
† In each Company, the five top cadets from Senior term became 'under officers'. They were the élite and wore Sam Browne belts.

'GOT IT !!!! ??? Now let me hear the answer, Gentlemen ...
ONE, TWO, THREE' ... 'GOT IT STAFF,' we roared back.

Quickly and efficiently we were stripped of umbrellas and walking
sticks and shown how to come to attention, how to march and how
to halt. Then, at a hair-raising speed we were marched one and a
half miles to be issued with boots and canvas uniforms. Round and
round the College we whizzed, sweating and apprehensive beneath
the patronizing glances of beautifully turned out older cadets to the
barbers to be shorn like sheep, to the gym to be fitted with physical
training outfits, to the stables for breeches, brown boots and
leggings, to the laundry 'because I don't want to see a speck of dirt
for the next year an' 'arf mind' and finally to the Chapel 'because
'ere, gentlemen, you can thank Almighty Gawd at the end of each
week if you are still breathin'. Got it?' 'GOT IT STAFF!'

It was very hard and very exhausting – for the ten weeks on the
square, we never stopped running, saluting, marching, drilling,
climbing ropes, riding unmanageable charges and polishing and
burnishing everything in sight ... boots, belts, chinstraps, buttons,
bayonets and above all our rifles ... 'the soldier's best friend, mind.'

Normally, there were about fifteen minutes between being
dismissed from one parade and being inspected for the next in a
totally different and spotless outfit. The slightest lapse, a finger
mark on a brass button, a cap at the wrong angle or hair not mown
like a convict was rewarded with 'Defaulters' – a particularly
gruelling extra drill in full battle order at the end of the day when
everyone else was resting.

A rifle barrel imperfectly cleaned invariably meant 'Pack Drill' at
the hands of the dreaded Wright – full battle order but with a
difference: the Pack was filled with sand and in place of normal drill
movements, it was a case of being forced after supper to run up and
down several flights of stairs with the offending rifle at arm's length
above the head, shouting at the top of our lungs 'Parade, Parade.'

The cadets incarcerated in their rooms, cleaning their equipment,
made bets on how long each individual could stand the punishment.
Many defaulters found it a matter of honour to prolong their agony
in order to impress their listening friends. I was a firm supporter of
the doctrine of another group which sought kudos by pretending to
pass out long before they would normally have collapsed.

In the riding school, the rough riding Sergeant Majors were
particularly heartless. We had a beauty, an Irishman from the
Inniskilling Dragoons called McMyn. At 6.30 on a Monday morning, winter and summer, he would be waiting for us with the same

grisly joke ... 'Now then, gentlemen, I'm supposed to make mounted officers of all of you so let's see how many dismounted showers we can have here on this lovely morning ... Knot your reins. Cross your stirrups. Fold your bleedin' arms and split ass over the jumps ... go!' Carnage, of course, but in those strange days all officers, even in infantry regiments, had to know how to ride, and ride well.

The great thing abut those first ten weeks was that although one was being treated like mud, it was at least grown-up mud. We were treated like men for the first time in our lives and as men we were expected to react.

Those weeks 'on the square' were sheer, undiluted hell. At weekends we were allowed no dining-out passes but by Saturday night we were so exhausted anyway that all we wanted to do was to fall into bed, underneath which was a dreadful receptacle described in Military Stores as 'one pot, chamber, china with handle, Gentlemen Cadets for the use of.'

At the end of the purgatory, we 'passed off the square' and settled down to learning other things in addition to physical training, drill, riding, bayonet fighting and more drill. Instruction was given us in organization and administration, in the manual of military law and of course in tactics and man management.

Of the two hundred and fifty 'Juniors' who passed off the square and still remained in one piece, four in each Company were promoted to Lance-Corporal. I was one of the lucky four in No. 1 Company and as there was now a little more time for leisure, I managed also to get a Rugger 'Blue' and played regularly for two seasons with the 1st XV.

I furthermore performed in a couple of College concerts, writing my own sketches, and played the lead opposite Mrs Barcus, the wife of one of our Company officers, in *It Pays to Advertise*.

Nessie came down one Saturday to see the show which opened after a particularly gruelling afternoon's rugger battle against the RAF College, Cranwell.

'Yew looked ever so nice up there on that stage, dear, but the sport's better for yew isn't it? – more balls, if yew know what I mean.'

My liaison with Nessie continued more or less full time all through my year and a half at Sandhurst. She still insisted that 'pretty soon I'm goin' to find that nice feller and — off to the Fiji Islands'. In the summer term, she came down for the June Ball, the big social event of the year. For the occasion she borrowed a magenta-coloured taffeta ball gown from a friend who danced in competitions on the outer London circuit. Her very great beauty and again, I say, her freshness overcame this extraordinary garment and I basked in her success as we waltzed and fox-trotted round the dusty gymnasium to the fluctuating rhythms of the Royal Military College Band.

Nessie was very specific about my seeing other girls – 'We're just together for the larfs and the — , dear, so don't go gettin' serious wiv me or yew'll spoil it.'

In her wisdom she encouraged my friendships and listened apparently with enthusiasm when I told her I had met a beautiful young actress playing in a naval comedy in London by Ian Hay and Stephen King-Hall – *The Middle Watch* – Ann Todd.

Ann had a tiny part and was infinitely glamorous. I had never been backstage in my life before and she was single-handedly responsible for my becoming incurably stage-struck. I had an allowance of five pounds a month so I was not exactly a well-heeled 'stage door Johnny' but Ann was often sent free tickets for the opening of restaurants or night clubs which helped enormously.

Cadets in their Intermediate and Senior terms were allowed cars. Obviously, I did not own one but the wheels of friends were always available and Saturday night in London on a late pass became the focal point of the week.

In the Intermediate Term, I was promoted to full Corporal and received the ultimate accolade for that rank. Along with one other Corporal, Dick Hobson of No. 3 Company, I was appointed Commandant's Orderly for six months. This post was highly coveted and besides announcing to all and sundry that the holder of it was practically bound to become an Under Officer in his senior term, it also carried various 'perks'. One was excused Saturday morning Drill Parade, which meant early to London, and on Sunday, came the big moment . . . breakfast with the General, Sir Eric Girdwood.

Those breakfasts must have been pure hell for this splendid officer but week after week, he toyed with toast and coffee while Dick and I ploughed through acres of scrambled eggs and miles of sausages. Afterwards, while the General was being dressed in highly polished riding boots, Sam Browne belt and sword, Dick and I waited in the garden proudly holding silver sticks, on which were engraved the names of a hundred years of Commandants' Orderlies. Across our chests were white pipe-clayed belts to which, between our shoulder blades, very beautiful and heavily embossed silver Victorian message boxes were attached. Upon the appearance of the General, we formed up on either side of him and escorted him on to the parade, slow marching together ahead of him up the front rank and down the rear as he inspected his battalion of one thousand spotless cadets: then into chapel, trying not to skate with our hobnailed boots on the black marble of the nave and, afterwards, leading his Sunday morning inspection of the College buildings, gymnasium, hospital, stables and so on.

The General was a most imposing and awe-inspiring figure with his chest full of medals and his bristling white moustache. He was also God. A creature so far above the lowly cadet as to make his every word and gesture seem, to us, divine. Of the thousand at that moment under his command, perhaps one would ultimately attain his exalted position.

The silver message box nearly proved to be my undoing. So many cadets asked me what was in it that I decided to give them a little food for thought, and I filled it with various commodities. There-after upon being asked the usual question I would reply, 'Comman-dant's personal supplies – take a look.' Inside they were delighted to find a packet of Woodbines, a box of Swan Vestas matches, a roll of toilet paper and a dozen French letters. I believe my purchases went a long way towards relieving the tedium of those Sunday mornings, and cadets, kept standing to attention far too long in all weathers, were deeply appreciative of the fact that visiting dignitaries, Kings, Presidents, Prime Ministers and Archbishops were invariably pre-ceded in their inspection of the ranks by the pompous passing of this curious cargo.

One cloudless Sunday morning after breakfast, Dick Hobson and I were waiting for the General amidst the rhododendrons of his garden when he suddenly changed his routine. Normally, he would issue from the house, booted, spurred, shining like a new pin and we would fall into step on either side of him, listening to his extremely engaging and relaxed small talk as he headed towards the barrack square where the battalion would be drawn up ready for inspection by him and on occasion by his VIP guests.

Some five hundred yards from his house and just out of sight of the parade it was taken for granted that all informality would melt away and Dick and I would put our silver-headed orderly sticks under our left armpits and start our slow march for the tour of the ranks.

This beautiful June morning, however, he came out of the garden door and stopped in front of us.

'I think I'd better inspect you two fellers today,' he said.

We immediately sprang to attention secure and relaxed in the knowledge that we, too, were faultlessly turned out. I was on Dick's right, so the General looked first at my cap, chin, my buttons, my belt, my creases and my boots. Then, with a pace to the side and in the usual army fashion, he started on Dick from his boots up to his cap. Round the back he went, inspecting Dick from the rear when Christ! I heard a little click as he opened Dick's Message Box.

The joke of what mine contained had long since been over, hardly anybody bothered to ask me any more what was in it – everyone knew – in fact I had forgotten all about it myself. The few seconds that it took the Commander to inspect Dick's rear view seemed to me to take until autumn. Finally, I heard his breathing directly behind me. I prayed he would move round to the front again without looking into my Box. I promised God all sorts of rash things if he would arrange this for me, but he failed me. I felt rather than heard the General open my Box and sensed him rustling about among its horrible contents – Woodbines, matches, lavatory paper and French letters! My military career was obviously over before it had even started and I toyed with the idea of falling on my bayonet among the rhododendron petals. Dick too had realized the full possibilities of the situation and started to vibrate like a harp string on my left, a condition brought about my a mixture of concern for his partner, suppressed laughter and keen anticipation of impending doom.

After an eternity, Major-General Sir Eric Girdwood stood before me. He looked for a long time at my sea-green face without saying a word. Staring blankly ahead, I waited for the axe to fall.

'Niven', he said, 'I had heard about that . . . thank you very much . . . you are very considerate. . . .'

It was never referred to again, but immediately after Church Parade that day I cleared out my Message Box.

Life at Sandhurst was tough but it was exhilarating and the cadets were a dedicated corps d'élite. Some went on to command Divisions and even armies. Several among the dignified Sikhs and Pathans became leaders in their countries but a heartbreakingly high percentage were destined in little more than ten years' time to meet death on the beaches, deserts and hillsides of World War II, for this was the vintage of professional soldiers that suffered most heavily when the holocaust came.

Led by Major Godwin Austen and goaded almost beyond endurance by the much loved Robbo Robinson, No. 1 Company became champion Company and for the eighteen months I was at Sandhurst, I was one of the privileged, proudly wearing the red lanyard of the Champions.

If the work was hard, so was the play. Cadets in their senior term were allowed motor cars and a few well-heeled young men could be seen whizzing up the Great West Road, London-bound for weekends in an assortment of jalopies. Jimmy Gresham in my platoon owned a Hillman Huskie and was most generous about giving his friends lifts. A very bright fellow destined for the Welsh Guards, he was highly resilient when it came to contretemps. For some misdemeanour he was not allowed to use his car for several weeks but he solved this temporary inconvenience by keeping a chauffeur's uniform and a false moustache at White's Garage in Camberley and our weekly forays to the capital continued without missing a beat.

Reggie Hodgkinson, an old Bembridge friend, also headed for the Welsh Guards, was a member of No. 3 Company housed across the Barrack Square in the new buildings. One night, having persuaded some kind friend to sign in for him before midnight, he was almost caught by the watchful Robbo crossing our Parade ground at 3 a.m. wearing a dinner jacket. Reggie arrived beating at my door, breathless – 'Give me a pair of pyjamas for Christ's sake, that bloody Robbo nearly nabbed me.' He quickly donned the pyjamas over his dinner jacket and dashed out again.

From the window, I watched, fascinated, as Reggie, with closed eyes, gave it the full 'I come from haunts of coot and hern' treatment; arms stretched out before him, he ambled in the bright moonlight, straight across the Barrack Square towards No. 3 Company.

He soon realized that Robbo was walking beside him.

'Wot d'you think you're doin', Mr 'Odgkinson, Sir?'

'Sleep walking, Staff.'

'Then sleep walk into the bleedin' Guard Room. Lef rite, lef rite ... smartly now, swing the arms, Sir,' and my pyjamas disappeared at high speed in the direction of 'the cooler'.

It had long been decided that no stone would be left unturned for me to be commissioned in the Argyll and Sutherland Highlanders once I had successfully passed out of Sandhurst. When I say it had been decided, I really mean that my mother had gone to a great deal of trouble to raise old influential friends of my father's from the days when we had lived in Argyllshire. For my part I was delighted at the prospect of joining such a glamorous regiment and revelled in the meetings that were arranged by one of my mother's advisers, the Colonel of the Regiment, The McClean of Loch Buie.

The McLean, three times during my days at Sandhurst, took me, all spruced up, to visit Princess Louise, sister of King George V, who was the honorary Colonel of the Regiment and who took a great interest in all things pertaining to that famous outfit.

The first time I was taken to visit her, I was instructed to meet the McClean at his London club so that he could check me over and among other things, teach me how to bow properly to Royalty – never, but never, any arching of the back or movement from the waist – that he informed me was strictly for headwaiters.

'Stand upright, my boy, look 'em right in the eye, then, with a completely stiff back, a sharp, very definite inclination of the head, bringing the chin almost to the chest.'

I tried this rather painful manœuvre several times and each time a peculiar squeaking sound issued from my undergarments. A minute inspection disclosed the fact that the new braces which I had purchased for the occasion, complete with a very complicated gadget – a sort of pulley effect ... little wheels over which passed elastic straps – had been delivered with a faulty wheel and this was complaining bitterly at the unusual strain that was being placed upon it. The McClean solved the problem by oiling the offending part with a dab of hair lotion.

The elderly Princess became a great ally and it was at her suggestion that I was invited to spend the day with the officers of the Regiment just before they embarked for service in the West Indies where I hoped to be joining them later. They were a gay and friendly group and Colonel and subalterns alike all made me feel confident of a warm welcome in about one year's time. All I had to do, they assured me, was to pass the final Sandhurst exams and I would be with them for sure.

Before I returned to Sandhurst for my last term and final exams, I spent what was to be my last holiday at Bembridge. The whole family, minus Tommy, was there. My mother, whom I had finally grown to love and to appreciate, presided over the gathering. 'Max' was back from India, having become disenchanted with soldiering. He had resigned his commission and gone to work as the Starter on the Bombay Race Course. This, too, had palled and his adventurous spirit had taken him to Australia, where for the past five years he had been working as a jackaroo (cowboy) on a cattle station near Yarra Weir. Now he was having a last long look at England before sailing away to take a job as manager of a banana plantation on Norfolk Island in the South Pacific.

Looking back on that period, I now realize that at eighteen I must, by today's standards, have been a very square member of a very square group. There seems to have been the minimum of rebellion against the Establishment. There was mass unemployment; conditions in the mines and shipyards were appalling. There were hunger marches and general strikes but my generation of students remained shamefully aloof. We did little or nothing in protest. Perhaps we were still very much in shock from realizing that the cream of the generation immediately before ours had been wiped out. Perhaps there was no one left worth rebelling against and in my case, discipline was being pumped and bashed into me to such an extent that any sort of organized student revolt against authority, such as has now become the norm, was unthinkable. We drank a great deal, it is true, but we were immensely physically fit. Pot, speed, hashish and LSD were as yet unheard of so instead of sitting around looking inwards, we rushed about noisily and happily extroverted.

My final term at Sandhurst was a breeze. I had never had it so good. By now promoted to Under-Officer, I was also for the second season running a rugger blue and even found time to produce a couple of concerts and to play the juvenile lead in *The Speckled Band*. I had also discovered girls in a big way and although Nessie might with certain justification have been called 'the head mistress', I had a heart like a hotel with every room booked.

Nessie, as always describing herself as 'an 'ore wiv an 'eart of — gold', was staying with a gentleman friend on a yacht for Cowes week but managed a few clandestine meetings with me in Seaview. She was still the same, as funny and forthright and as beautiful as ever and, as always, most solicitous as to my sexual wellbeing. 'Gettin' plenty, dear?'

When I sat for the final exams I discovered with pleasure mixed with surprise that they came quite easily to me and as I had also accumulated a very nice bonus of marks for being an Under-Officer, my entry into the Argylls seemed purely a formality. Everything in the garden was beautiful – a fatal situation for me.

Just before the end of term, all cadets who were graduating were given a War Office form to fill in:

'Name in order of preference three regiments into which you

desire to be commissioned.'

I wrote as follows:

1. The Argyll and Sutherland Highlanders
2. The Black Watch

and then for some reason which I never fully understood, possibly because it was the only one of the six Highland Regiments that wore trews instead of the kilt, I wrote

3. Anything but the Highland Light Infantry.

Somebody at the War Office was funnier than I was and I was promptly commissioned into the Highland Light Infantry.

I cushioned my mother from the blow of my not being commissioned into the Argylls by a lot of military double-talk about vacancies and people with short service commissions coming from the universities and I told her, with truth, that anyway the HLI was a much older Highland regiment than the Argylls and persuaded her with a big, black lie that, also, I much preferred being sent to Malta instead of to Bermuda.

I had, however, a sizeable problem explaining to her, when I displayed my uniform, why I was wearing 'those funny striped trousers instead of a kilt'. After reading up the regimental history of the Argylls for eighteen months I was woefully short of material about the HLI, but I did remember hearing that this, the second oldest Highland regiment, had so distinguished itself at some point in its history that the men of the regiment were paid the supreme compliment of being allowed to dress like the officers in the other Highland regiments – in trews – the kilt being, they were told, the symbol of serfdom. An unlikely story, I always felt, particularly since the HLI insisted on wearing white spats with their trews to make quite sure that nobody confused them with the Lowland regiments, and a campaign to be allowed to wear the kilt was always simmering on the regimental hob. It finally came to the boil soon after I joined and the kilt was restored to us.

Nessie accompanied me to various pompous tailors and bootmakers in London while I was being outfitted and eyebrows flew up and down like lifts at some of her observations.

'Don't like that — black bonnet at all, dear. Makes you look like a bleedin' judge 'andin' out the death sentence.

'Better not sit down in them tight trousers, dear, or you'll be singin' alto in the — choir.'

When one considers that the most expensive tailors in London at that time charged only fourteen guineas for a suit, it must have come as a body-blow to my mother to receive bills for £250 for tropical clothes all 'suggested' in a list provided by the Adjutant. Salt was doubtless rubbed into my poor mother's financial wound when I handed over my 'clothing grant' from a grateful Government – £50.

Nessie took me in uniform to a photographer in Piccadilly called 'Cannons of Hollywood' and had me preserved for posterity. She also insisted on coming to see me off at Tilbury Docks on a bleak, January morning when I embarked in the *Kaisar-i-Hind* for Malta, two months before my nineteenth birthday. At the last moment, my mother, who had been suffering one of her increasingly frequent bouts of what the family called 'Mum's pain', decided to get out of bed and come too.

'Don't worry about me, dear,' said Nessie when I told her, 'I won't embarrass your mum, I'll hide behind a — packin' case or somefink, I just want to wave goodbye, that's all.'

In the event it was my spats that brought them together. I put on my outfit, Glengarry, cut-away short khaki jacket with one 'pip' on the shoulders, McKenzie tartan trews and my mother took me, with a mound of tin mothproof uniform cases, in a taxi to the docks. Far from hiding behind a packing case, Nessie was very much in evidence standing by the barrier wearing a little beret over her fair hair and a very short white tightly belted raincoat that took nothing away from her fabulous figure and long slim legs. She was doing a very poor job of pretending not to look in my direction; she looked ravishing and I realized with a lurch of the heart just how much I was going to miss her. As my mother and I walked towards the barrier, a noise like castanets came from the region of my shoes. A few heards turned in our direction and suddenly Nessie doubled up with laughter. 'Christ, yer — spats are on the wrong feet.' My mother caught Nessie's laughter and I caught hers and in the ensuing hysteria, I introduced one to the other. My mother's famous disdain for punctuality had already brought our arrival at the docks perilously close to sailing time so with Nessie in tow we barely had time to inspect the cabin which the aforesaid grateful Government had arranged that I share with three others before the booming gong and a cry of 'all visitors ashore please' sent them both scurrying back down the gangplank. I have always been embarrassed by long drawn out farewells: once I have got to the point of departure – like an operation – I want to get the damn thing over. We had all agreed that there would be none of that business of smiling bravely and waving while swearing dock-hands wrestled with gangplanks so the last I saw of them was walking away through the damp, dreary Customs Shed. Nessie was holding my mother's arm.

The ship was filled mostly with Service families heading for Egypt, India and the Far East.

'Posh' – I soon learned the origin of the word: Port Out Starboard

Home, and it summed up the suburban snobbery of my shipmates whose supreme status symbol was a cabin on the shady side of the ship. Although civilian clothes were worn aboard, rank was still strictly observed, and if the Navy tended to feel superior to the Army both turned up their noses at the Air Force and all combined to ignore the few civilians. The wives were the worst and in the prevailing atmosphere I clung like a drowning man to a very attractive Jewish couple who nobody spoke to and who had misguidedly booked passage to Alexandria.

One wonders what sort of welcome they would receive there today but at that time Mr and Mrs Marks were a boon and a blessing. On the voyage they invited me to sit at their table and took me with them when we went ashore at Marseilles. We spent the day at Arles where I was initiated into the glories of the art galleries and the Roman amphitheatre.

There was one other officer on board from my own regiment. I had spotted him from his uniform on the dock and I knew that he had also identified me for the same reason, but he chose not to speak to me until the day we arrived at Malta. It was a pretty ridiculous situation because between us we represented fifteen per cent of the total complement of officers in the 1st Battalion, the Highland Light Infantry, and would presumably be living cheek by jowl for the foreseeable future – but for ten days on a smallish ship he preferred to avoid me. This behaviour later turned out to be typical of a large percentage of my brother officers but I was in no position to argue about it and I had a nasty cold feeling that the comedian at the War Office might have passed on the happy news of my three choices of regiment.

The *Kaisar-i-Hind* dropped anchor in the deep blue Grand Harbour of Valletta just as the sun was setting and it was an unforgettable sight, tier upon tier of honey-coloured houses rising on one side and Fort Ricasoli, built in 1400 by the Knights of Malta, brooding benevolently on the other. In between lay the leviathans of the greatest navy in the world. 'Retreat' was being sounded by the massed bands of the Royal Marines on the Flight Deck of the giant carrier *Eagle* whilst astern of her lay three more – *Furious*, *Argus* and *Ark Royal*.

Ahead there was a line of huge battleships and beyond them again, the tall rather old-fashioned looking country class cruisers. The harbour was filled with these giants and their escorts, the light cruise squadrons, the destroyer and submarine flotillas, with their mother ships and oilers and the battered old target ship *Centurion*.

Pinnaces, Admirals' barges and shore boats slashed the blue water with white as they fussily dashed about on their errands leaving hordes of gaily coloured local dghajjes with their lowly civilian passengers humbly bobbing about in their wake.

As the final plaintive notes of the Retreat floated out from *Eagle*, the sinking sun kissed the topmost houses and churches of Valletta with gold and all over the Grand Harbour as the signal lights winked from a hundred mastheads, the White Ensign and Union Jacks of the Royal Navy were lowered, rolled up and put reverently away for the night. If my vintage at Sandhurst was to be decimated in the war that the Germans were to unleash only ten years later, it is even more horrifying to speculate on the fate of those magnificent ships and their ships' companies that I glimpsed for the first time on that balmy evening.

Captain Henry Hawkins had been a trooper in the Life Guards but through a combination of bravery and efficiency, he had been commissioned from the ranks and was now Adjutant of my regiment. Tall, almost Phoenician-looking with his swarthy features and black moustache, resplendent in Glengarry, blue patrols and strapped evening tartan trews, he came aboard the liner to meet me. Flashing white teeth and a hearty hand-shake did much to de-congeal me from the chilling apprehension that had descended upon me when I had put on my new uniform for the first time since I had left Tilbury Docks.

'Of course you have been with Jimmy for the whole voyage so at least you know somebody in the Battalion.'

'Jimmy, sir?'

'Don't call me "Sir" except on Parade. Colonel and Majors you address as "Sir", always; everybody else by their Christian names once you get to know them. Jimmy McDonald – he's on board isn't he? Ah! here he is now.'

Henry Hawkins then gave a rather restrained welcome to my shipmate and snorted when he learned that we had so far not met.

'How bloody silly', he said and introduced us.

Jimmy McDonald was a fairly senior subaltern with rather shifty eyes, the complexion of a hotel night porter and a blonde straggly moustache. I was relieved to learn from Hawkins that I was to be in 'C' Company while McDonald was to join the Headquarters wing.

Hawkins brought McDonald up to date on various regimental news while we were gathering our hand baggage together and being ferried ashore by Carlo, the regimental boatman. The Markses pressed an antique Hebrew silver amulet into my hand for good luck and waved from the upper deck till I could no longer see them.

On the deck were several tough-looking 'Jocks' from the regiment working under the supervision of a sergeant. They were busy loading our heavy baggage and a mound of regimental stores on to mule-drawn drays. Only a few years before the German blitzkrieg would shatter the British Army, mechanization had still not come to our infantry regiments.

'Just room for two comfortably in the gharry', said Henry Hawkins, 'so you and I'll go ahead to the Mess. Jimmy knows the way so he can follow.' Actually there was room for four in the rickety horse carriage that now transported us up from the landing-stage down the main street of Valletta and out across the vast underground granaries to Floriana Barracks.

'Watch the driver,' said Henry Hawkins, 'they are so superstitious here that, now the sun has gone down, he'll keep changing his position so that the devil can't come and sit beside him.'

We clip-clopped along at a good pace but I had a chance to notice the ornate sandstone buildings on either side and the Sunday evening promenade in the streets, the men walking up and down on one side, the women on the other. All the men in dark suits and clean white shirts; the women in black and a large percentage wearing the *faldetta* – a large black crescent-shaped hood.

'Yells, bells and smells – that's how the Jocks describe Malta,' chuckled Hawkins. 'Just listen to their bloody bells now, Sunday evening is the worst. They all have a go but you'll get used to them. You may get used to the yelling too. Most of that is the poor sods trying to sell goat's milk, hot from the udder, but I don't think you'll ever get over the smells – I haven't.

'Now let me tell you a few things and ask me any questions you like. When we get to the Mess, you'll meet Jackie Coulson – he's orderly officer today. He's about a year senior to you and he's going to look after you and give you a shove in the right direction. Being Sunday evening, there probably won't be anybody else about. Incidentally, people in this regiment make it a point to take a long time to get to know newly joined officers. They reckon that they don't have to rush things because joining a regiment is for a lifetime. So don't worry if some of them, specially the more senior ones, are not very forthcoming for a little while. I had a hell of a time.'

He smiled to himself and tickled the back of his neck with his swagger cane.

Mine was a rather daunting prospect; being abroad for the first time in my life; joining a regiment in which I did not know one single soul; taking command of a platoon of hardened professionals, many of whom had been soldiering abroad for a dozen years or more, all under the watchful eyes of brother officers who, I gathered, were not going to be very helpful – and my nineteenth birthday still some way off.

To say that I was relaxed during our half-hour to Floriana would be a slight exaggeration. I was damp with apprehension which was not eased when H.H. told me that we would probably go on an Active Service 'Stand to' the following week.

'The whole Mediterranean Fleet is pulling out for two months for their Spring exercises and we are expecting serious trouble – riots and sabotage at the Dockyard – that sort of thing. The Italians have been stirring up the Maltese for a long time and getting them all excited about kicking out the British and becoming part of Italy. When the Navy leaves we'll be on our own – just one miserable battalion to control this whole bloody island.'

The officers' mess of Floriana Barracks was glued to the side of a huge church which housed the biggest and busiest and noisiest bells in Malta. They were banging away as we arrived.

Jackie Coulson met us at the door and Hawkins effected our introductions with sign language then, roaring above the din, explained that his wife and his dinner were waiting for him; he was driven off in the evil-smelling gharry.

Coulson signed to me to drop my two pieces of hand luggage inside the courtyard and to follow him. We passed through a door in a far corner and I found myself in a monstrosity, typical of the living quarters of British Army officers at home and abroad ... brown leather sofas and chairs, a few functional writing desks, a large round table in the middle of the room covered with elderly copies of English daily and weekly papers; a large fireplace and mantelshelf with, above it, two signed sepia reproductions of pictures of King George V and Queen Mary and below it a large bum-warmer. Two morose and to my eyes middle-aged officers in mufti were seated on this piece of furniture with drinks in their hands. The bells were a little fainter in here but the room had a gloom all its own and was covered entirely with a thin layer of dust.

'This is Niven,' said Coulson, jerking a thumb in my direction. Like the guns of a battleship, two pairs of cold eyes swivelled towards me. There was a long silence. The elder and more mauve coloured of the two finally spoke. 'Oh,' he said.

They both continued to stare at me.

Coulson pressed a bell on the right hand side of the fireplace and a

Corporal appeared in a white mess jacket with two gold stripes on his arm. 'Sir?'

'Double whisky,' said Coulson.

'Same,' said the most mauve man finishing his glass.

'Same,' reiterated the less mauve man draining his.

'If you want something,' said Coulson to me, 'order it yourself. We don't stand drinks in the Mess.'

'Same, please,' I said faintly.

Nothing much happened till the drinks arrived, the two mauve men returning to their interrupted conversation about Maltese priests.

'Not a bad job, really,' said the most mauve man, 'if some woman can't have a baby, she sends for the priest and he has a go to help things along in the name of the Church.'

'Always remembering to hang his umbrella on the doorknob to warn the husband to stay away till he's finished' said the least mauve man. Knowing winks and chuckles followed this exchange.

Coulson led me to a far corner of the anteroom and in subdued whispers, or at least in subdued shouts against the clamour of the Sunday evening bells, proceeded to bring me up to date. No one could have described Coulson as a warm and friendly man but he was better at first sight than the two highly coloured gentlemen on the bum-warmer. He was thin, sandy and weedy. He exuded an aura of defeat.

'Malta is a sod of a place,' he said, 'you'll hate it. Nobody knows how long we'll be here. The second battalion is in India and we were supposed to be on home service for the next ten years but they suddenly winkled us out of Aldershot and shipped us out here a couple of years ago. It's a bloody mess being a home battalion on service abroad, they don't even give us tropical kit. Just wait till you have to wear full mess kit with a stiff shirt and waistcoat in August when the sirocco is blowing. . . . Christ, you'll melt!'

'Who are those officers?' I asked, nodding at the other occupants of the room.

'McDougall and Galt,' said Coulson. 'Subalterns both in D Company.'

'Subalterns' – I was amazed.

'Both subalterns,' said Coulson, divining my thoughts, 'about halfway up the list. Nobody ever gets promoted in the regiment. It takes at least ten or twelve years to become a captain.'

'Twelve years!' I gasped – my dream of becoming a general fading rapidly.

'At least,' said Coulson, 'and then it will be another seven or eight till you have a chance of commanding a company and if you ever get that and become a major, it will be four to one against you ever commanding a battalion. So the chances are that at the age of forty-five you'll be out on your arse with a pension of a hundred and eighty pounds a year, after twenty-five years' service!'

I must have looked fairly shaken because he added almost kindly, 'Well, we're all in the same boat, aren't we? They never told us about this at Sandhurst did they? Anyway if some silly bugger starts another war, we'll get plenty of promotion tho' it seems pretty quiet at the moment. In the meanwhile, you get two months' leave a year; after you've completed a year's service, you get about ten shillings a day pay and messing allowance but whisky we get in bond so that's only six shillings a bottle.'

Coulson morosely painted thumb-nail portraits of some of the senior officers and ended by giving the following advice – 'The only people you have to look out for are the Colonel, the Adjutant, your Company Commander and, of course, Trubshawe.'

'Trubshawe?'

'Trubshawe, look out for him – he's nothing but trouble. If it hadn't been for Henry Hawkins covering up for him, he would have been flung out months ago ... he's a disaster!'

'Which company is Trubshawe in?'

'"B" Company, thank God, and they're over there on the other side of Grand Harbour in Fort Ricasoli. He's confined to barracks anyway at the moment so he's practically locked up and a good job, too!'

Just as I was about to ask a few pertinent questions about this intriguing character my erstwhile shipmate, Jimmy McDonald, stormed in.

'These — Malts!' he said, addressing the bum-warmer, 'they think they own the bloody island – said I had to go through Customs. Told 'em where to get off, of course, but the head grease ball got quite offensive till I threatened to put him under close arrest.' He jabbed the bell with his finger and ordered a double whisky.

'Have a good leave, Jimmy?' asked one of the mauve men.

'Not bad, spent most of it at home. Nearly got married but managed to talk my way out of it. Any supper left?' The three of them disappeared into the dining room carrying their glasses.

'Cold food on Sunday nights', said Coulson, 'go on in if you want anything ... I've eaten.'

I was very hungry but the thought of sitting alone with the three who had just gone in there filled me with alarm.

'So have I', I said. 'I think I'll go and unpack.'

Coulson showed me my room. 'Your batman is McEwan. He looks like a decent sort of Jock. I'll tell the Mess Corporal to send him over.' He turned to go then paused at the door.

'Oh, you'll need a mosquito net, did you bring one?'

'No, nobody told me.'

'Well, I have a spare one you can have. It's never been used so you can have it for what I paid for it.'

'Very good of you thanks!'

I've forgotten what I paid Coulson for his net but it was about double, I subsequently discovered, the going rate in Valletta.

I looked around the room. It was on the ground floor, large, stone-floored and almost bare. The smell of horse, donkey, mule and goat dung which came through the window was very strong indeed. I was very depressed.

'Private Ewan, sorr,' said a voice behind me.

I turned to find a stocky, fresh complexioned soldier of about my own age.

'Corporal Deans sent me over tae help ye unpack.'

My boxes and bags were in a corner and in silence we bent to the task.

'I've no done this sort o' work before, sorr – ye'll have tae tell me what ye want me tae do.'

'What are you supposed to do, McEwan?'

The square bandy-legged figure stood up very straight. 'Sorr, in time o' war I'm yer runner. I carry yer messages tae the Platoon and see that ye have food and a place tae sleep . . . in time o' peace, sorr, I look after ye as best I can.' He paused and then added, 'That's what the Company Sarnt Major told me this morning.'

When the recitation ended, we continued the unpacking and I learnt a little more about Private McEwan.

Like many others he had joined the Army because he was sick of being unemployed. A day labourer from the Glasgow slums, he had grown weary of standing in line in drizzling rain, week after week, waiting to collect the dole. A man of fierce pride and stainless steel integrity, as I was to learn during the four years he remained with me, for him it must have been a degrading experience. So one day, he and five cronies sauntered in to Maryhill Barracks and announced that they were joining the Highland Light Infantry.

As was the custom, they were deloused, given a bath, a hot meal and a bed for the night. Next day four of the cronies disappeared before breakfast but McEwan signed on for five years with the Colours and two with the Reserve. His remaining chum opted for seven and five because he was wanted by the Glasgow police for housebreaking, assault and battery. Like many others in that tough town he had decided that the best way to avoid civil justice was to change his name, join the Army and disappear abroad.

'Have ye no had yet supper, sorr?' McEwan asked when we had got everything stowed away as best we could.

Before I had time to answer he went on,

'Corporal Deans said that maybe as this is yer first night in the Mess, yer'd like tae eat in yer room and he said tae tell ye that he has some cold grub and a bottle o' beer for ye . . . I'll go an' get it the noo.'

When McEwan came back with this most welcome repast he also brought me the news that I was to report to my Company Commander at the Company Office at 0800 hours the following morning.

'I'll wake ye at seven o'clock, soor, wi a cup o' gunfire and then I can show ye the way to t'Office.'

I slept fitfully and during the long periods I was awake, I became increasingly excited at the prospect of taking over my Platoon. In the morning I avoided the Mess as I was extremely apprehensive of meeting brother officers on an empty stomach and fortified by 'gunfire',* I was escorted across the granaries by McEwan, past the guardroom, across the Barrack Square and deposited outside the door marked 'C' Company Office.

Company Sergeant Major 'Sixty' Smith was the sole occupant, arranging papers on a trestle table covered with a grey Army blanket. He sprang to attention as I came in and I caught a glimpse of the medal ribbons of the DCM and MM on his chest. A rather portly figure with a friendly and revealing smile – revealing the absence of four front teeth. He had spent his whole life in the regiment, having joined as a band boy aged fourteen.

'You'll be Mister Niven, sorr? The Company Commander will be here in a wee while. Welcome to "C" Company, sorr.'

'Sixty' Smith was a regimental character recommended for the Victoria Cross in 1917. He was renowned for his toughness and the fact that his Company Commander was hardly ever called upon to deal with small 'offences' was not so much a measure of the high standard of discipline in 'C' Company, as a tribute to the strong right arm of 'Sixty' meting out his own brand of punishment behind

* The very strong, very sweet tea the Jocks made.

the latrines with a big leather belt.

'Company Commander crossing the Barrack Square, sorr.'

I looked out of the window with interest well mixed with apprehension. For the foreseeable future the officer approaching would be both my boss and my judge; answerable only to the Commanding Officer, it would be in his hands alone to make my life pleasant or very unpleasant, interesting or deadly dull. I saw a long sleek Lagonda swing up to a stop outside the Company office. The morning sun was beginning to beat down and the glare from the parade ground hurt my eyes. Dust from the sudden stop billowed up around the car. From the driver's seat a tall and powerfully built figure emerged. Major Harry Ross-Skinner was a man of about forty-five – on his chest his bravery, DSO and MC, in hand, a battered briefcase, on his head, nothing.

He unhurriedly addressed a well-turned out soldier who was sliding over behind the controls – 'Wash the car, then pick up my wife at 11 o'clock, and take her shopping. At noon be back here for me and don't forget to tell them at the stables that I'll be playing six chukkas this afternoon.' He picked up Glengarry, Sam Browne belt and swagger cane from the back seat, and ambled towards the door. As he entered, silhouetted against the fierce glare from outside, he was even larger than I had first thought. His complexion was florid; his eyes, bright blue; his hair and rather large moustache sand and salt. He gazed at me with vague alarm as I snapped off my best Sandhurst salute.

'Oh, hullo,' he said amicably, 'what can we do for you?'

Niven, sir . . . posted to "C" Company!'

'Well, that's nice,' he said, 'who told you so?'

'The orderly officer, sir, Coulson.'

'I wonder why nobody told me.' He raised his voice very slightly, 'Sixty!'

The Company Sergeant Major could only have been out of sight by a couple of feet. He shot round the door and stood to attention. 'SORR?'

'Do we know anything about this?'

'Yessir, it was in Battalion Orders last week and the Adjutant sent you a personal memo two days ago.'

'Oh, I see . . . well splendid . . . do you play polo?'

'I'm afraid not, sir.'

'Why not?'

'I don't think I could afford it, sir.'

It seemed to take an appreciable time for this to sink in.

'Which platoon have we given him?'

'Yer said No. 3, sorr,' said 'Sixty' Smith gently.

'Ah, yes . . . well he can have that or No. 2 or No. 4 whichever he likes. . . .'

He brushed up his moustache between the forefinger and thumb of his left hand and looked down on me. . . . 'Any preference?'

'Er . . . no, sir . . . er, anything will do.'

'All right then, No. 3 ∴. let's see, "Sixty", who's the Platoon Sergeant of No. 3?'

'Sarnt Innes, sorr.'

'Oh yes, of course.' Ross-Skinner was putting on his belt and cap during this conversation.

'Anybody for Company Office?' he asked.

'No charges today, sorr, but the storeman has reported the loss of seven blankets and a pickaxe. He thinks he can make them up before the next Quartermaster's Inspection.'

'How's he going to do that d'you suppose?'

Sixty chuckled. 'Best not ask, sorr.'

Ross-Skinner took off his belt and bonnet again and sat down behind the table with a sigh. Then he opened his briefcase and spread out on the grey blanket some saddlery catalogues. A solidly built old soldier appeared in the doorway with a great stamping of feet.

'Adjutant's compliments, sorr', he bellowed towards the ceiling. 'Commanding Officer wants to see Mister Newton.' He made this statement with such tremendous authority that it was a moment before I realized that he was referring to me.

'You'd better cut along there,' said Ross-Skinner. 'Pity about the polo,' he added.

Across the barrack square, the old soldier set a rapid pace and between keeping up with him, and proudly answering meticulously the first salutes ever thrown in my direction, I was bathed in perspiration by the time I arrived at Battalion HQ. I was shown in to the Adjutant's Office.

Henry Hawkins smiled up from behind his desk – 'Shaking down all right? It's very strange at first I know. Just let me finish signing all this bumph and I'll take you in to meet the CO.' For a few minutes the scratching of his pen was the only sound in the warm office, then he spoke again.

'Incidentally, when you were posted to us, some joker at the War Office sent us a memo about you, something about your preference for Regiment.'

My sweating increased a hundredfold. Hawkins never looked up, he continued signing documents.

'It came directly to me and it is now locked up in the Adjutant's confidential file. Nobody else can see it.'

He looked up, put down his pen and smiled again.

'Now˙... let's go and see the Colonel.'

This was an awesome moment. The Commanding Officer was seated behind his desk, that is to say like Ross-Skinner, Henry Hawkins and everyone else in Floriana Barracks who was seated behind anything, he was seated behind a trestle table on which was spread a grey army blanket.

'Mr Niven, Colonel,' announced Henry Hawkins, loosing off a salute. I did the same.

It took weeks for my Commanding Officer to address a word to me directly. I never discovered whether he thought it was impressive or whether he was shy or whether he just didn't know what the hell to say, but for whatever reason, he preferred to address the junior officers of his battalion through an intermediary. Nobody had warned me of this and it came as something of a shock when he turned to the Adjutant and said,

'Did he have a good trip?'

'Yes, sir, very good,' said Hawkins firmly.

'I hate those bloody P and Os. They always smell of sick,' said the Colonel.... 'What sports does he play?'

Henry consulted with a file he had in his hand, 'School Rugby XV and Cricket XI, School teams for Boxing and Swimming. Rugby Blue at Sandhurst, good horseman and passed for Hunting.'

'Is he going to play polo?'

Hawkins made a question-mark face in my direction.

'I may not be able to, sir,' I said now addressing Hawkins, 'It might be a bit ... er ... too much for me.'

'Well, tell him about the fifteen bobbers, Henry,' said the Colonel, 'and explain that people in the Navy always have ponies they want exercised ... I think we can expect him down at the Marsa.'

To show that the interview was now concluded, the Colonel rose from behind his desk. Unfortunately, he was so short that his head remained almost exactly the same distance from the floor. Sitting down in the darkened office he had seemed quite impressive – large brown eyes set in a deeply tanned face, dark hair, grey at the temples and at least three rows of medal ribbons – but when he walked to the window and displayed tartan trews that somehow managed to look both skimpy and baggy at the same time, he looked like a little bird, a similarity that to any astonished eyes became even more pronounced when, with his back to the room, he raised both arms high above his head with the palms flat and fingers extended. . . . he reminded me instantly of a cormorant drying its wings.

'Wait behind, will you, Henry,' said the Commanding Officer over his shoulder. I saluted his strange back view and went out into the hot sunlight.

Back at the Company Office, Sergeant Innes was waiting for me and a splendidly reassuring sight he was too. Strong as an ox, he was also comparatively tall, about five feet ten. Most of the men in the Regiment were much more stocky. He had bright red hair, very close cropped and a deep scar under his cheek bone which raised one corner of his mouth in a permanent grin. It was probably a razor slash. The Jocks had a great partiality for the razor as an offensive weapon and invariably had a couple of safety blades sewn just inside the peak of their Glengarrys. In a brawl, an adversary was well advised to stay out of range because with one quick movement, the bonnet was off and swinging in a wide arc held by the ribbons at the back.

'Ginger' Innes saluted. 'I'll take ye tae the Barrick Room, sorr, so ye can see yer platoon.'

So this was it – the moment of truth! At last I was about to come face to face with the forty-odd professionals who would be under my command. This was the crunch. In a strange mood of exaltation, I marched confidently alongside Sergeant Innes. Outside a Barrack Room door, excitingly marked 'No. 3 Platoon', Sergeant Innes stopped – then flung it open. A stentorian bellow rent the sultry air.

'STAND TAE YER BEDS! !'

A sound of scuffling feet came from within. After that, silence.

'No. 3 Platoon ready fer yer inspection, sorr.'

Proudly, I passed him to confront, for the first time, my long-awaited charges.

Seven rather crestfallen soldiers in various stages of undress stood waiting for me beside their beds.

Only seven stood by their beds but there seemed to be many other beds displaying kits laid out for inspection.

'Why only seven, Sergeant Innes?' I asked.

'Four on Regimental Guard, sorr, six on Palace Guard, three on cookhouse fatigues, three on Regimental fatigues, two on Officers' Mess fatigues, four awa' sick wi' sandfly fever and two doing sixty-eight days detention in Military Prison for attempted desertion, sorr.'

Even my faulty mathematics could work out that my platoon was woefully under strength, but I swallowed my disappointment and inspected my meagre flock.

They were a hard-faced lot and although they stared unblinkingly at some fixed point about two feet above my head, I was pretty sure that within thirty seconds of my having walked through the door they had all thoroughly inspected me.

Foot regiments in the Regular Army consisted of two battalions; one of which was permanently on service abroad in different parts of the Empire, while the other, based in the British Isles, acted as a holding and training battalion for the one overseas which, perforce, had to be kept up to full strength.

Back at 'C' Company office 'Sixty' Smith gently explained that for a young officer still in his teens, trained to the hilt, and pumped full of ambition and enthusiasm to find himself in a Home Service battalion of very diminished strength, trying to fulfil overseas garrison duties while completing its own training programme and at the same time being constantly drained of its best men, the result was almost inevitable – deadening frustration. It didn't descend on me like a cloud that very first day, but slowly like the damp of a disused house it bored its way into me during the next few months. Meanwhile so much was new, so much was exciting and everything was different.

Nothing much else happened that morning. My company commander disappeared in his Lagonda at about eleven-thirty, two other subalterns of the company appeared briefly, peered at me and went about their business. The other subaltern and the second in command were away on leave so I hung about the company office till lunch time, not knowing what to do.

Luncheon in the mess was a hazard. About twenty officers were present including the birdlike Colonel but nobody spoke to me except Mr Gifford, the civilian steward employed by the officers' mess. A charming Jeeves-like character, Mr Gifford was responsible for the catering and for keeping the officers' mess bills. At dinner time, in white tie and tails, he acted as a glorified butler and at all times he was the supreme boss of Corporal Deans and two permanent mess orderlies. On guest nights or other highly charged occasions, a roster of officers' batmen was also pressed into service and those too he ruled with a rod of iron.

Mr Gifford seated me at a long mahogany table, gleaming with hideous pieces of Victorian silver donated by retiring officers, horses and pheasants mostly, but also a profusion of cigar and cigarette boxes, lighters, ash-trays and menu holders.

The menu displayed in the holders was extensive but my nerves were not quite up to it so I settled for something cold off a groaning sideboard, washed it down quickly with some beer, and fled to my room.

Soon Private McEwan appeared. 'Adjutant's compliments, sorr, ye'll be playing cricket fer the Battalion at fifteen hundred hours this afternoon.'

I must have looked a little dazed because he added, 'We've a verra poor team just noo, but the lads all say, ye'll be a big help, an we're playing against the Gunners an' they're good.'

'Christ,' I said, 'I haven't played cricket since I left school – I can't possibly play for the Battalion.' McEwan smiled encouragingly, 'Ye'll be one o' the best if ye've played at all, sorr.' He was tactfully explaining that in a regiment recruited from Highland villages and the slums of Glasgow, cricket was almost unknown.

At three o'clock that afternoon, I presented myself at the Marsa cricket ground. The heat was like a blast furnace. A jovial deaf major, the shape of an avocado, called with heavy humour 'Roundy' by his contemporaries, greeted me and introduced me to the team, mostly elderly sergeants and young officers. They seemed a friendly and cheerful lot and I began to relax.

Suddenly, an ear-splitting belch rent the air. I spun round and perceived a truly amazing sight. Trubshawe was approaching. Six feet six, with legs that seemed to start at the naval, encased in drain-pipe tight white flannels. He sported a blue blazer with so many brass buttons on it that he shone like a gypsy caravan on Derby Day; on his head a panama hat with MCC ribbon; on his face the biggest moustache I had ever seen: a really huge growth which one could see from the back on a clear day. Part of it was trained to branch off and join the hair above his ears. It was in fact not so much a moustache as an almost total hirsute immersion.

'My dear fellow,' boomed this splendid apparition. 'Welcome! I'm delighted to meet you.' A row of very white teeth blazed out of the foliage as Trubshawe shook my hand. The sergeants, I noticed, were nudging each other and smiling with great affection in his direction but the officers tended to drift away and busy themselves with their cricket gear.

'This, old man,' said Trubshawe, tapping a brief case he was carrying, 'is an invention of mine. It's called "the dipsomaniac's delight".' He flicked the lock and inside, set in green baize slots, I perceived a bottle of whisky, a soda water syphon and two glasses.

'Come, let us drink to your most timely arrival with a glass of Scottish wine.' In the heat of that blazing afternoon I downed what was to be the forerunner of many thousands of toasts in the company of this amazing and wondrous creature.

Never in the history of human conflict has there been a more unlikely officer in a Highland regiment. Just for a start he was English – a felony which he compounded by not being Sandhurst-trained but by arriving via Cambridge University and the sup-plementary reserve of a smart cavalry regiment. He was also highly eccentric with a wild and woolly sense of the ridiculous, an unabashed romantic who had a grand piano in his room on which for hours he played sixteenth-century folk music and Peter Warlock's haunting melodies. His reading matter was influenced by an old Cambridge chum, T.H. White. He was, in short, an Elizabethan with a hunting horn.

I don't remember too much about that afternoon's cricket but I believe I acquitted myself adequately. With the shortage of bowlers I was made to trundle down my slow off breaks for hours on end. The Royal Artillery gleefully dispatched these to various boundaries but I managed to take a few wickets – one a glorious catch on the boundary by Trubshawe who was not supposed to be there at all; he was easing his way back to be close to the 'dipsomaniac's delight.'

I made a few runs and for a brief spell was joined at the wicket by Trubshawe. He was a fascinating sight, full of confidence, taking guard before each ball, patting non-existent divots on the matting wicket and inspecting the positions of the fielders with an imperious and disdainful gaze. But something was very wrong with his timing for although each individual stroke was immaculate in style and execution, it was played so late that the ball was well on its way back to the bowler by the time he had completed his shot.

The match was drawn but not because our team was of the same standard as the Gunners. Cook Sergeant Winters, who was extremely portly as befitted his station, had considerable difficulty in bending down while fielding, a shortcoming he gallantly overcame by stopping ground shots with his shins. A hard drive to mid-off had just connected with a horrible 'crack' just below his knee when a dispatch rider roared on to the field and gave 'Roundy' Cavendish a message. 'Roundy' gathered both teams together and sombrely told us to return to our barracks at once. The situation caused by the Italian-inspired troublemakers, which Henry Hawkins had outlined on the day of my arrival, had deteriorated rapidly and we were to stand by for riot duty and for the guarding of important points against a possible 'coup'.

Back at Floriana Barracks, everything was hustle and bustle but I managed to locate Jackie Coulson and ask him what I should do. 'Battle order, I should think, and report to your company office,' he said curtly over his shoulder, hurrying away. Private McEwan, already himself caparisoned like someone during the retreat from Mons, buttoned me into webbing equipment, water bottle, revolver, map case and steel helmet and with, admittedly, a certain number of Cabbage Whites in my stomach, I made my way across the Granaries. At the company office, the other subalterns were already waiting. 'Sixty' Smith was issuing them with revolver ammunition and maps. We all came to attention when Major Ross-Skinner strode in. Gone was the vague and bumbling sportsman and in his place was the fully efficient, calm, professional commander. As we stood in front of him, he quickly and lucidly issued his orders.

I scribbled frantically as he laid down the duties of No. 3. Platoon, the positions to be occupied, the organization of rations and ammunition, the arrangements for communications, evacuation of wounded and numerous other pieces of vitally important information. He even included a brief résumé of the political situation that had just come to a head: according to Ross-Skinner, the Maltese had been British subjects for a hundred and twenty years but somehow during that time, while English had become the official language of the Administration, Italian had remained the legal language used in all disputes. The local Strickland Government had lately fallen out with the island's Church leaders. The Vatican had consequently become involved with the British Foreign Office and now it had mushroomed into a full showdown between Italy and Great Britain.

It sounded complicated to me but when I recited it to my amazed platoon a few minutes later, it resembled one of the more unlikely plots by Gilbert and Sullivan.

The platoon as presented to me that afternoon by Sergeant Innes had grown to more respectable proportions and I was relieved to note that our fighting strength was now about thirty. They were a tough-looking bunch – mostly Glaswegians, and when I first entered the barrack room, they were clustered round a highly nervous middle-aged Maltese in a sweat-soaked singlet. Like a man possessed, he was turning the heavy stone wheel of a giant knife sharpener. One of the Corporals stepped forward proudly. 'He hoppened tae be passin', sorr, so I persuaded him tae come in wi' his wee contraption and touch up the laddies' bayonets.'

We soon embarked in two local buses that had been commandeered for the occasion and were driven to the Customs sheds on the St Elmo side of the Grand Harbour – our responsibility till relieved. I made a quick reconnaisance with 'Ginger' Innes and issued my orders for the disposition of my troops. Later, Ross-Skinner arrived in his Lagonda and had a look round. To my great relief, he altered nothing, just made a few suggestions about drinking water and a better place to be used as a latrine.

For hours nothing happened. Then some confused shouting around midnight heralded a half-hearted attack by a few hooligans, armed with stones and iron bars. A Jock standing next to me was hit on the steel helmet with a loud clang: ' — THAT!' he roared and charged out with his bayonet flashing in the moonlight. That was the last appearance of any opposition and incidentally, the one and only piece of active service I was to take part in during four years with the Highland Light Infantry.

The next morning, the platoon was withdrawn and the general order to 'stand down' was given. The crisis was over. The British Empire was intact.

Trubshawe, always a mine of information on questions political, told me later that it had all been very simply arranged. The British Government had promptly suspended the Maltese Constitution, forbidden Italian as the official legal language and put His Majesty's Governor in sole charge of everything, 'thereby, old man, putting the whole place back at least a hundred and twenty years.'

Once this little flurry of excitement was over, the battalion settled back into its dreary, soporific routine of garrison duties. Training programmes were issued but there were few men available to train.

With the advent of the hot weather, the leave season moved into high gear and many officers headed for England.

Aided by Trubshawe, whose period of incarceration in Fort Ricasoli was now ended and who had, much to my delight, appointed himself my guide and sponsor, my shaking-down period proceeded apace. First I had to make official calls on all the married officers. The routine was simple. First Private McEwan would find out from the batman at the quarters in question just when the people would be out and I would then slip a couple of calling cards on to the silver tray just inside the door. The wives had a nasty habit of testing the surface of these cards with their thumbs to make sure they were engraved: no 'gentleman', of course, would ever have printed cards. I had also to make the rounds and sign my name in various visitors' books, including the Governor's at Government House and certain Admirals' establishments.

After a few weeks, one or two officers in addition to Trubshawe occasionally spoke to me. But it was a great joy when Trubshawe's Company 'B' (Machine Gun) arrived at Floriana Barracks; things perked up a lot. The Major was 'Tank' Ross, a famous Army and Scotland Rugby footballer, the second in command a young Captain, R.E. 'Wallard' Urquhart. A serious soldier of great charm and warmth, he was unfailingly kind and helpful to me and his splendid qualities, from all accounts, were never seen to greater advantage than in 1944 when, as a Major-General, he led the daring air-drop on Arnhem.

The first regimental guest night which I attended was, quite simply, a nightmare. As the newly joined subaltern, in a sort of travesty of welcome, I was ordered to sit at the Colonel's right hand.

About forty officers were present, including a few guests – Greville Stevens, ADC to the Governor, an amusing pink-faced, sandy-haired Captain in the 60th Rifles, known locally as 'the amorous prawn'; a brace of Admirals; an Air-Marshal, some assorted soldiers and two naval guests of Trubshawe's, a Lieutenant Anthony Pleydell-Bouverie and a midshipman David Kelburn* – two, incidentally, of the gayest and brightest men ever to put on naval uniform.

Round after round of drinks in the anteroom and finally just as I was headed for a most necessary trip to the lavatory, Mr Gifford announced dinner. Like a lamb to the slaughter, I was led with bursting bladder to my chair next by my Commanding Officer. As he had still not spoken to me directly during my service, I was in no

* Now Admiral the Earl of Glasgow.

position to ask him if I might be excused, an unthinkable request as officers and gentlemen never left the table under any circumstances until the end of the meal when the King's health had been drunk. Sweat broke out all over me as I contemplated the hours of agony ahead.

I've long since forgotten who sat on my right. Whoever he was, he too never directed a word in my direction.

So I sat in miserable silence with crossed legs, perspiration trickling down inside my stiff shirt front, my stand-up wing collar wilting with pain.

Cold soup (more strain on the bladder) was followed by other courses, each washed down by a different wine. I drank everything that was placed in front of me in the vague hope that something might act as an anaesthetic and reduce the torture.

By the time we arrived at the cheese, I was desperate, past caring. As far as I was concerned my career could end in a pool right there under the polished mahogany and the regimental silver, but succour was at hand. Mr Gifford bent over and whispered in my ear, 'With Mr Trubshawe's compliments, sir, I have just placed an empty magnum underneath your chair.' Relief, when I heard his words, did not flow over me – it spurted out of me. In an apparently endless stream, but thanks to a firm grip on the bottle with my knees, I was able to aim with one hand and leave the other available to crumble, nonchalantly, a water biscuit. This proved just as well because suddenly the Colonel zeroed in on me and spoke to me for the first time. I was so unnerved by this sudden reversal of form that I nearly released my grip on the warm and by now heavy receptacle below the table.

His words were few and his point was made with admirable clarity. 'I have', he said, ' — women of every nationality and most animals, but the one thing I cannot abide is a girl with a Glasgow accent. Pass the port.' He never spoke to me again.

After the port completed its circle, a toast was given to 'The King'. Many glasses I noticed were ostentatiously passed over the top of a glass of water on their way to the lips in a rather juvenile gesture to show that Highlanders were still drinking to the exiled Stuarts – 'the King over the water'.

After the toast, the Mess pipers filed in, eight in number. From the top drone of each instrument fluttered a heavily embroidered silken banner – the coats of arms of the senior regimental officers present. The eardrums of the diners, particularly those of the Sassenach guests, were subjected in the confined space of the dining room to a veritable barrage of sound. Round and round the table marched the pipers, and round and round the table went the port, brandy, Kummel and Drambuie.

Finally, after the pipe major had played his solo pibroch, the hauntingly lovely 'Desperate Battle of the Birds', the Colonel tottered from the room followed by the survivors who then indulged in a monstrous barging match, punctuated by wild cries, which passed for Highland reels. These in turn further deteriorated into a competition to see who, by using the furniture, could make the fastest circuit of the ante room without touching the floor. Trubshawe, Pleydell-Bouverie, Kelburn and I left in some alarm when a visiting air commodore ate a champagne glass whole, stem and all, and the majors decided to have a competition to see which one could pick up a box of matches off the floor with his teeth while balancing a bottle of champagne on his head.

Anthony and David borrowed some civilian clothes and the four of us, now more suitably attired, Trubshawe in a strange green almost knee-length hacking jacket, made a memorable tour of the late bars of the Strada Stretta known to the Jocks as 'the Gut'.

At five in the morning after hoovering down 'prairie oysters', raw egg yolks mixed with equal portions of port and Worcestershire sauce in 'Aunties' – a red plush establishment run by an enchanting elderly ex-whore from Leeds – I was sick at the top of the Marsamacetta Cliffs.

In the months that followed, my military ambitions suffered a certain seepage as, slowly, but surely, it dawned on me that there was very little point in being a keen young officer. The Army list was kept in the Mess and the pages devoted to the Highland Light Infantry were grubby from the probing fingers that had endlessly traced the inevitable promotions that would come in the long, long years ahead.

However, there was so much new, so much to enjoy that it was almost two years before the deadening horror of the whole thing finally descended upon me and enveloped me like a black Bedouin tent. In the meanwhile Trubshawe's guidance continued apace. He explained to me that I could hire polo ponies for fifteen shillings a month and that apart from buying some mallets, I had nothing to worry about financially, the grooms being soldiers and the ponies all belong on the regimental strength as officers' chargers. In addition, as I got better at the game, he assured me that many naval officers would be delighted to lend me their ponies just to keep them exercised during the long periods they would be away at sea.

All this was indeed true and I found myself quite soon with as many mounts as I could play and quite a respectable handicap.

The Marsa Polo Club was the smart place to be – smart in the most colonial sense of the word; it was mounted suburbia. It was parasols and fraightfully refained voices. It was 'Boy, bring me a stingar', and naval wives who announced with a smirk – 'We're going in to have our bottom scrubbed next week,' but it was still heady stuff compared with what I had been exposed to before and I thrived on it. Girls there were in plenty. Apart from the resident ones, daughters of senior officers and officials, there were also for several months a year hundreds of young and lonely naval officers' wives. There was in addition the 'Fishing Fleet', a motley collection of passed-over debs and pink-cheeked country cousins who annually timed their arrival to coincide with the return, after many months at sea, of several thousand sex-starved mariners. Finally, there were the whores, and Valletta was full of professionals busily catering to the needs of all ranks of the biggest fleet in the world. Many were mid-Europeans or Russians, refugees of impeccable lineage with sisters plying the same desperate trade in Singapore and fathers driving taxis in Paris.

There was a professionally languid Captain in the Headquarters wing who wore a monocle. His wife was very pretty in a sort of chocolate boxy way and could have been described in polite society as a flirt; anywhere else she would have been called a cock teaser.

I had, it is true, nibbled her ear and snapped her garter a couple of times while watching the polo from her car, but nothing more, so I was all unsuspecting when a runner informed me that the Captain wished to see me immediately in his company office. I entered and saluted. He was busy looking over some ammunition returns with the Quartermaster Sergeant. I fidgeted around for a while but he still did not look up. Finally, head still down, he spoke.

'Niven, are you very much in love with my wife?'

My toes tried to grip the floor through my brogues to stop me from keeling over.

'No, sir . . . not at all, sir,' I murmured and then, for no apparent reason, I added,

'Thank you very much, sir.'

'Well, if you're not,' said the Captain, putting some papers in a folder, 'be a good chap, don't go on telling her you are . . . upsets her you know. Now, Quartermaster Sergeant, about the Range Allotment of 303. . . .'

I saluted the top of his head and withdrew.

After that I decided to be a good deal more selective in my nibbling and snapping.

The Fleet was sailing for several weeks of exercises off the Greek islands, leaving behind literally hundreds of ladies in different stages of availability. I discussed the situation with the wife of the Signals Officer of a destroyer who had made it very obvious that she had no intention of sitting around twiddling her thumbs during his absence.

It was a nasty little intrigue really but quite exciting especially when the husband gave a party in his cabin before he sailed and said to me, 'Look after Eunice for me till I get back.'

'I certainly will,' I said, avoiding her eye.

When sailing time came, Eunice and I climbed to the top of the cliffs and watched the splendid spectacle of the entire Mediterranean Fleet steaming out of the harbour, Royal Marine bands playing and bunting fluttering.

We used my field glasses and paid particular attention to her husband's destroyer. He was on the bridge. We had told him where we would be watching and with his binoculars he found us. Lots of waving went on and we even staged a big amorous embrace to make him laugh. I wish I could report that I felt a twinge of shame at that moment but I didn't. I had other feelings of a more animal nature to contend with.

The Fleet sailed away into the sunset and disappeared over the horizon bearing the poor cuckold-to-be towards Corfu; never has a safer stage been set for infidelity but Eunice was in no rush and decided to savour the moment. After all, we had at least six weeks ahead of us in which to indulge ourselves so she insisted that I take her to the Sliema Club to a party with some others, escort her home to her house and then. . . .

So we danced close and drank champagne and toasted each other over the rim of our glasses, all very high powered romantic stuff; finally I found myself in her bed.

Some far from routine thrashing around was going on because Eunice was an expert at prolonging everything when suddenly she went rigid.

'Christ!' she hissed, 'he's back!'

He was too and downstairs in the sitting room.

'Get in that cupboard,' ordered Eunice.

It was pretty ridiculous because my clothes were all over the floor but I did as I was told and stood quaking in a black hole that smelled of mothballs.

I didn't have time to reflect on the old French farce situation that I was in. All I could think of was the certain death that would soon come up those stairs.

Eunice was made of different stuff. She went down naked to meet him.

'Darling, how did you get back?'

'Stripped a bloody turbine thirty miles out . . . towed back.'

Somehow she persuaded him to get in the car and go and get a bottle of champagne so they could celebrate.

I dressed in about eleven seconds and with my shoes on the wrong feet shot downstairs and out of the house. I was impotent for days.

So long as the ex-ranker, Henry Hawkins, was Adjutant, my interest in things military remained at least dormant. Somehow, he could revive it after telling me the frustrating news that, after months of training, the twenty best men in my platoon had been posted to the Second Battalion in India. Somehow, he encouraged me when a great favourite of mine, a gigantic piper from the Western Isles, was listed as a deserter and caught trying to stow away on a tanker bound for Cardiff.

'Johnstone will be court-martialled,' said Hawkins, 'he is in cells now and wants you to defend him.' Any man had the right to nominate any officer he wished to defend him before a court-martial. Flattered by this demonstration of respect but alarmed by his poorly developed sense of self-preservation, I hurried off to the military prison where Johnstone was incarcerated.

'Hoo mony days d'ye think I'll git, sorr?' demanded the prisoner before I was half way in his cell.

'Well,' I said, 'I'll do everything I can to prove you intended to come back so they might make it "absent without leave" instead of "desertion" but I'm afraid you'll get between sixty days and six months whichever way it goes.'

'Naebody's goin' tae put me awa' in the glass hoos for six months,' said Johnstone slowly and with that he put his left hand round the edge of the great iron door of the cell and with his right hand, slammed it shut. All four fingers of his left hand were smashed and dangling like those of a rag doll.

A few weeks later, when he was back in a cell once more awaiting his court-martial, he asked to see me again. It is incredible that I fell into the trap.

'Hoo mony days will they put me awa' for noo, sorr?' he asked but before I could answer, the door clanged shut and he was grinning triumphantly at the same mangled hand.

He never did go to prison. He was dismissed from the service as an undesirable character. He came to say goodbye before he left and was very depressed that he would never be able to play the pipes again.

One sad day, Henry Hawkins, the subalterns' friend, was promoted to Major, and his place was temporarily taken by 'The Weasel'.

'The Weasel' was a most unsavoury piece of work. Yellow teeth protruded from beneath a small nicotine-stained moustache and a receding chin did nothing much to help a pair of shifty eyes that were pinned together like cuff-links above a beaky nose. On his thin chest there were no medals for valour. He made a bad move early. He called Trubshawe in and informed him that he drank too much. Questioned as to how he could have arrived at such an outlandish conclusion, the Weasel announced that he had carefully checked Trubshawe's mess bill and would check all subalterns' mess bills each month in the future. Trubshawe quickly made arrangements with Mr Gifford for a sizeable proportion of his future alcoholic intake to be charged as 'COD packages', but the Weasel's spy system was born that day and from then on none of us felt secure, least of all myself when he said to me, 'I've been looking through your file, Niven – I wouldn't say that the Argylls have missed very much, would you?'

He was never openly hostile to me till one day when platoon training was at its height. I was given the task of attacking a small hill across a mile and a half of completely barren land. The Colonel, accompanied by the second in command and several other officers, was on top of the hill. He listened uninterestedly while the Weasel gave his orders.

'No. 3 Platoon will attack demonstrating the fullest possible use of cover: road and sea are your boundaries, both inclusive.'

As we marched down the dusty road to our start point out of sight in a dip, 'Ginger' Innes and I held a council of war. At all costs we must try to avoid cutting ourselves to pieces crawling in full view across a mile and a half of razor-sharp volcanic outcrop, but nobody in the platoon could swim unnoticed a mile and a half naked, let alone wearing full equipment. The road, too, was in full view and so dusty that the approach of a goat sent a cloud of telltale white puffs billowing into the sky. Salvation, however, in the shape of a half-empty bus stood waiting in the hollow as we descended below the line of vision of the group on the hill. Country women, wearing voluminous black *faldetta* headdresses, were already seated in the bus clasping on their knees baskets of chickens, fish and other goodies which they were taking to market.

'Road inclusive' had been the Weasel's orders so, blessing my good fortune, I judiciously scattered the platoon about the bus. Some lay on the floor with the goats and shielded from view by the black tent-like confections on the good ladies' heads, the whole platoon motored peacefully past the unsuspecting brass. Half a mile behind them was another dip in the road. There we debussed and with their backs towards us, our quarry were easy to stalk. Thirty yards from the group, while our two Lewis guns happily opened up with their football rattles, the rest of us charged with fixed bayonets and blood-curdling yells. Perhaps I overdid it a little on arrival by saying to a stunned Weasel, 'Bang bang, you're dead!'

Not only did he give me a monumental bollocking in front of my own men, calling me among other things a 'bloody boy scout', but he sent us, at the double, a mile and a half to our original starting point and then made us crawl back across the volcanic razors. Far from holding this purgatory against me, the Jocks said they had enjoyed the whole day hugely and the episode was ever after referred to as 'The Desperate Battle of the Bus'.

Trubshawe was not the Weasel's type of man at all and his wonderful eccentricities were like a red rag to a bull. Trubshawe's steel helmet caused a certain strain on an important parade.

'Can't possibly wear the bloody thing, old man, it's too heavy and red hot to boot so I've had this little number run up for the occasion.'

He then placed on his head a papier-mâché replica that was as light as a feather and from three feet away was indistinguishable from the original.

'Can't go wrong, old man, I'll get one for you next time.'

Throughout that increasingly sulphurous morning, I watched Trubshawe jealously as he strode about at the head of his platoon as fresh as a daisy with his helmet at rather a rakish angle like a yachting cap.

Just before the end of the parade, the threatening storm broke and in the torrential downpour, Trubshawe's hat melted and closed over his eyes. An uncertain tittering came from the ranks behind him as the soldiers beheld their splendid officer transformed into something resembling a very lanky hirsute pantomine gnome with a bluebell on his head.

The Weasel confined Trubshawe to barracks for that but Trubshawe hired a string quartet to play for him in the evening in his room. As his quarters happened to be immediately above the Weasel's lair, he was soon released.

I don't believe that Trubshawe was ever a very serious soldier though he was full of compassion for those who were. He was able to indulge this rather aloof, though never patronizing attitude towards the military because, like many officers in the regiment, he had a private income which handsomely papered over the bare patches between a subaltern's pay and the financial facts of garrison life. I had no such cushion but Trubshawe's generosity, which was boundless, made it possible for me to be constantly in his company without feeling a sponger.

I was two years on the island before the Weasel gave me an affirmative answer to my many requests for two months' leave and permission to spend them in the United Kingdom.

One night on a dilapidated ferry boat, *The Knight of Malta*, and I was in Tunis whence a freighter took me to Marseilles, followed by a long train journey to Calais, Dover, Portsmouth and Bembridge.

Two years had wrought awful havoc with the beauty of my mother but when Grizel told me that 'Mum's pains' were more and more frequent, so selfishly occupied was I with my immediate pleasures that I only dimly realized how serious her illness had become. She herself was gay and vague and wonderful and pushed it all aside as something boring she had to live with.

Tommy was nowhere to be seen and my brother, who was now busy growing bananas on Norfolk Island, was back from the South Pacific. Bembridge was in full swing and I had an unforgettable home-coming.

Nessie had never been a great correspondent and her last letter had filled me with unease. It had ended ominously ... 'I've a bit put by now, dear, and I've found a bloke who might suit very nicely, so I might say thanks ever so and piss off to America. He knows all about me and says it makes no difference. If I do decide, I hope you get back before I go so I can see you. I'll close now – love – Nessie.'

I never did see her again. When I arrived in London, I gathered from her friends and co-workers that she had left a month before to get married in Seattle. Most unreasonably, I felt jealous and jilted. She never wrote to me again.

After my leave, I pondered deeply about my military and, with increasing pressure, my financial future.

Brian Franks had been at Bembridge and was learning the hotel business. At the moment, he was working his way up through the kitchens of the Dorchester but was filled with enthusiasm and painted a glowing picture of his prospects.

Most of my other friends had, by now, left University, and were launched on glamorous and seemingly profitable careers in business. I felt rather left out of the scheme of things, a feeling that was not helped by meeting two young officers on leave from the Argylls in Bermuda. Their regiment was not only heading soon for China but in every way it sounded a far happier and more human situation than the one in which I found myself on my return to Malta.

For a start, Trubshawe had fallen in love and much of his time was taken up by a beautiful blonde called Margie Macdougall who was spending a few weeks with Celia Tower, the equally beautiful wife of a lieutenant commander in destroyers. Trubshawe in love was something to behold. He went about looking pale and interesting. I charged him with being off his feed but he refuted this in a dazed way and mumbled that Margie was a Christian Scientist and that although he did not wholeheartedly agree with much of her indoctrination, he was prepared, under certain conditions, to forgo a sizeable percentage of his daily ration of bottled goods. Sinister cracks were appearing in the Trubshavian façade. 'We should give up blood sports, old man. No more the chase, be it fox, stag or field mouse. Amateur theatricals – that's something for us.'

In a day or two my bemused friend and I presented ourselves to Captain Hoskins of the Rifle Brigade who was Military Secretary to the Governor and the undisputed leading light of the Malta Amateur Dramatic Society. After reading a few lines from Frederick Londsdale's *The Last of Mrs Cheyney*, we would-be amateurs were dusted aside with the classic, professional brush-off – 'Nothing for you at the moment but don't call us – we'll call you!'

We drowned our disappointments in a sea of 'gimlets' in the 'snake-pit' – the ladies' annex of the Union Club in Valletta, while

Margie looked on with an apprehensive eye and Celia with a twinkle.

'It's a plot, old man. We'd better get our own show together and break the monopoly.'

So, we resuscitated an old regimental concert part called 'The Hornets' and presented an abysmal confection for three consecutive nights at the Coronado Canteen above the Dockyards.

As in all 'amateur dramatics', the performers had a wonderful time and went on far too long in front of a stoic and partisan audience. We regaled ourselves, and spasmodically our friends, with scenes stolen from the Co-Optimists, and the Hulberts, interlarded with Highland dancing and Sauchiehall Street wit.

Trubshawe had designed the posters which announced the forthcoming event in these terms – 'OFF LIKE A FLASH!!! (AS THE NIGHTLIGHT SAID TO THE NIGHTDRESS)'

These posters were sent round to all the wardrooms and gunrooms of the Mediterranean Fleet so the Weasel, in an ugly scene in which he invoked regimental honour, ordered us to visit every ship in turn, to apologize to the Mess President of each one and to retrieve the offending advertisements. Anthony Pleydell-Bouverie and David Kelburn came with us and it was a miracle that we didn't all drown in pink gin during our futile efforts to obtain the surrender of documents which the Royal Navy had no intention of giving up. At least it had the beneficial result of getting Trubshawe further off the wagon – 'Weasel's orders, old man'. Trubshawe and I had by now become the focal point of the Weasel's distaste. Hardly a week went by when we were not saluted by his orderly – 'Report immediately to Battalion Orderly Room, gentlemen, please,' and off we'd trot to collect another raspberry. So many did we collect at one point, that when the whole shooting match marched out of barracks and went under canvas for summer manœuvres, we decided not to be outdone when it came to the decoration of our tents. The Colonel had a little marker stuck in the ground at the entrance to his marked 'CO', and there were others denoting the denizens of all the important tepees – '2nd 1/C', 'Adj.' 'QM' 'RSM' etcetera so Trubshawe and I persuaded the Armourers' painter to install a couple for us 'Chief Raspberry Picker' and 'Asst Raspberry Picker'. The Jocks were delighted but the Weasel hammered another nail in our coffin.

The summer manœuvres were something that Lady Baden-Powell would have been ashamed of if conducted by a group of Brownies and I was still close enough to Sandhurst to be staggered by the fact that a long halt in the proceedings was always called at midday. While the Jocks sat in searing heat among the crickets and lizards devouring their 'stew and duff' and swigging down their 'gunfire', the officers repaired to a huge marquee where Mr Gifford, in a white tropical suit and white shoes aided by three mess waiters, presided over an Ascot-type meal of gargantuan proportion.

About this time, the Raspberry Pickers received a reinforcement – John Royal, a vast young man of phenomenal physical strength and an anarchist at heart. He appeared one day straight from Sandhurst and I want to introduce him clearly because he will turn up again much later in this dull story and, as he may enliven it, I don't want him, on his reappearance, to pass unnoticed.

His opening line was memorable. Trubshawe and I were sipping something cool on the balcony of the Sliema Club when a voice behind us said 'I've been looking all over Valletta for you two: that twerp in the Orderly Room told me that I should avoid you at all costs!'

John was almost as tall as Trubshawe but built like a heavyweight fighter in his prime. A broken nose did nothing to dispel this impression. He was extremely handsome in a dark, Celtic way and extremely hostile when drunk. Also, as Trubshawe succinctly put it, 'the man puts in some very plucky work with the elbow.' Very soon after his arrival in Malta, John was posted to the Second Battalion and departed for India but during the few weeks he was with us, he made an indelible impression.

He was devoted to animals and could not bear to see the Maltese drivers ill-treating their horses. When he saw one poor emaciated beast, straining uphill with a huge load of sandstone blocks, being belaboured with a heavy stick, he pulled the man off the shafts, put him across his knee and gave him six of the best with his swagger cane.

John also introduced us to green beer.

Trubshawe and I had been ordered by the Weasel to make all the arrangements for the annual Regimental Party at the Marsa Polo Club. Knowing we were given this assignment in the hopes that a normally deadly supper dance might be infused with something perhaps a little unusual, we went to great lengths planning to decorate the place differently and while Trubshawe spent days bashing some sort of rhythm into the regimental band, I busied myself with the catering aided by Mr Gifford.

Three weeks before the part, John told us about the green beer. It appeared that a brewer in Edinburgh had come up with this novelty and he quickly talked us into ordering it for the occasion. Cables were exchanged and to obtain a decent price per crate, we ordered an enormous amount of the stuff. The shipment arrived at the Docks just in time and the mule teams in the transport lines were hastily pressed into service to cart it to the Polo Club where Trubshawe and John and I were waiting to try it.

It tasted all right but the colour, far from being the joyous sparkling crème de menthe we had anticipated, was that of some loathsome opaque and polluted pond.

On the night of the party, acres of green bottles stood hopefully on the tables while the guests avoided them like the plague and drank everything else in sight.

The next day, the Weasel sent for the Raspberry Pickers and said that it was our responsibility to get rid of the green beer. We thought we might be able to 'con' the sergeants' mess into buying some. So together with John Royal we organized, one Sunday, a sergeants' mess picnic, the idea being that if we gave the sergeants enough of it free and slipped them a lot of whisky to help it down, they might overlook its horrendous colour and relieve the officers' mess of a sizeable portion of the stock.

It didn't work, of course. We took several carloads of sergeants, sandwiches, whisky and crates and crates of beer to a remote bay and for hours a glorious time was had by all – swimming, singing, telling exaggerated regimental anecdotes, boasting and drinking. In an effort to get them hooked on the stuff, the three of us, while carefully leaving the whisky out of our own mugs, dreamed up toast after toast, but as evening approached, wild Highland cries became fewer, and the sound of snores and throwing up became the norm.

When finally we delivered our subdued charges back to the sergeants' mess, it was all too plain that we had overplayed our hand: to a man they swore they would never touch the stuff again.

I remember the end of that picnic very clearly because the pipe major was so drunk that 'Sixty' Smith and I had to put him to bed and valiantly trying to get his kilt off while he was thrashing around and muttering obscenities in Gaelic, we unveiled an elderly pair of green regimental boxing shorts. There is always speculation about what a true Scot wears under the kilt: here was additional evidence that it is a very personal decision.

John Royal departed for India the same day that Trubshawe became engaged to Margie Macdougall. Neither event ended well but John's problem came to a head first.

Soon after his arrival, the officers of the Second Battalion were invited to a ball given by the local maharajah and John became sleepy, so after dinner he lay down behind some potted palms and stole forty winks. He was awakened by a captain of a cavalry regiment who stirred him, none too gently, with his foot.

'Stand up', said the Captain. John stood.

'You are drunk,' said the Captain.

'You are right,' said John and flattened him with a left hook. He then composed himself once more behind the potted palms. Pretty soon he was awakened again, this time by a full colonel of Artillery.

'Stand up', said the Colonel. John stood.

'You are drunk,' said the Colonel and collected a right cross.

John was court-martialled and insisted on conducting his own defence. He had been dropped on his head as a baby, he said, and this had the unfortunate effect of making him lash out at the first person he saw when he was woken from a deep sleep.

The prosecuting officer smiled faintly. 'Perhaps you would tell the court what happens to your batman when he wakes you up in the morning?'

'Nothing,' said John, unmoved. 'I have issued him with a fencing mask.'

John left India and the Army and I did not see him again for ten years.

Margie Macdougall left Malta and Trubshawe was saddened. He was comforted by the beautiful Mrs Tower and rallied strongly. Trubshawe had decided that perhaps the Weasel had a point when he hinted that there were other things that Trubshawe might do better than soldiering.

'When Margie and I marry, old man, we'll live in the depths of the country in some beautiful village. I'll run the cricket club and Margie can hand out pheasants to the tenants ... of course a lot depends on the local brewer.'

My twenty-first birthday came and went and I was still on that island. Every day it seemed to get smaller. Rumours were constantly flying that the battalion was to be reinforced and sent to Egypt, to China, or to Singapore but nothing ever happened and after each flurry of excitement, the battalion settled further back into its torpor. Trubshawe was now determined to resign his commission within a year so I asked officially to be seconded for service with the West African Frontier Force, a ploy that would have given me an exciting change of scenery and considerably more pay. The Weasel refused to recommend it.

My last year in Malta was enlivened by two things. First, I was made transport officer and as such, spent my days in the stables with several dozen chargers, draft-horses and mules. The mules were a belligerent lot; probably they had an inferiority complex because they did nothing except pull the company cookers. It was a splendid sight to see a company on the march. At the back and always falling further and further behind, were a couple of mules hauling an immense black cauldron on wheels. Inside this, depending on the time of day, was either boiling tea or boiling stew. Both tasted much the same but, at all times, behind the cauldron, was the company cook enveloped in a cloud of steam and stirring the contents as he marched.

Sergeant Fensham was the transport sergeant, a gay bandy-legged little man with the broken-veined complexion that goes with the proximity of horses. He was ready for every four-legged emergency. If the Colonel's horse was too fresh, before an important ceremonial parade, he would calm it down with a jab of tranquilliser. Once he gave it too much and we both watched apprehensively as, with rolling eyes, it tottered about with its precious cargo in front of several thousand onlookers.

Someone with a distinguished military background died in Sliema and a military funeral was arranged so I was ordered to produce a team and gun-carriage to bear the coffin. Sergeant Fensham paraded the six blackest draft horses we had and towing the black gun carriage, we set off to pick up our cargo.

In the middle of Valletta, one of the horses fell down and grazed its knee. Somehow it knocked off a divot of black hair and exposed a few square inches of hard chalky-white skin. This ruined our carefully arranged black ensemble but Fensham reached into his saddle bag, produced a box of black Cherry Blossom boot polish, and we went on our way without missing a beat.

The other boredom reliever of those last twelve months was the fancy dress ball in the Opera House. It was a predictable show – admirals dressed as pierrots, their wives as columbines. Bo-peeps were plentiful and there was a sprinkling of Old Bills and Felix the Cats among the military. Parties took boxes in the lovely tiered building and everyone tried hard to pretend that it was every bit as gay and abandoned as the Chelsea Arts Ball.

Trubshawe and I went as goats.

First we put noisome rugs on our backs. Then horns on bands were fixed to our heads and finally, between our legs, for the goat fittings, footballs swung with rubber gloves sewn on to them by the

94

regimental cobbler. Half a pint of dry martinis apiece and we were ready for the fray.

We arrived just in time for the Grand March for the prizegiving. The judges for the best costumes were on the stage and round and round in front of them, two by two, like the animals going into the Ark, were the clowns with their red hot pokers, the ballet dancers and the Mickey Mice. Rumblings of disapproval rose from the boxes as the two drunken goats joined in at the back of the parade.

'Trubshawe ... Niven ... goats! Bad show! Damn bad show!' Military moustaches and naval eyebrows bristled from every floor.

'I'm getting dizzy, old man,' said the goat behind me after we had completed several circuits.

'Left wheel!'

Obediently, I turned out of the parade towards the empty centre of the floor.

'Now squat!' commanded Trubshawe.

'What?' I asked, apprehensively.

'Squat, you bloody fool.'

So there at the very hub of the wheel with a kaleidoscope of colour circling round us and the focus of hundreds of disapproving eyes, I squatted. Trubshawe produced a brown paper bag from the folds of his smelly rug and sprinkled black olives on the floor directly behind me.

Except in the box that held David Kelburn and Anthony Pleydell-Bouverie, this flourish was coldly received by the ticket holders, particularly by a party of Maltese students who had a very short fuse when they thought that someone was mocking the local institutions. They jostled and shoved us as we left the floor and made threatening noises.

'Better take off, old man,' said my leader as he headed for the exit and the last I saw of Trubshawe that night he was pounding down the main street of Valletta towards the sanctuary of the Union Club pursued by the hornet students and tripping over his 'udders'.

We were confined to barracks for that little adventure but the boredom of our incarceration was soon relieved by the arrival of a whole new spate of rumours. This time they had a ring of truth to them. The Quarter-Master was seen checking the winter stores and, in the Transport Lines, Sergeant Fensham hinted darkly that he had heard that we might have to find buyers for some of our animals. The Weasel was seen strutting around, obviously having tucked into a sizeable canary.

In fact the battalion had been ordered home to the British Isles –

to the Citadel Barracks, Dover. It was like some gloriously prolonged 'end of term' and when the evacuation order was finally given, the whole battalion set about their allotted tasks with a willingness I had not hitherto seen.

'Sixty' Smith, who had become my friend and adviser, was ill in hospital. It started with sandfly fever, then complications and now he was much more sick than anybody realized. Pleurisy had set in and there was no question of him sailing home with the rest of us. I went to see him the day before we embarked on the troopship and was shocked by his appearance.

'Would you ask the Colonel a favour for me, sorr? Would ye ask if the battalion could march a wee bit oot the road on their way tae the Docks so I can hear the pipes for the last time – it's nae far ... aboot five minutes.'

I suddenly felt chilly in the warm little room.

'What the hell are you talking about, Sixty? ... hearing the pipes for the last time?'

'Becos I'm gonna dee,' Sixty replied quietly and I found it impossible to look into his clouded eyes.

The Weasel was oddly sympathetic to the request and when he gave me the answer he told me the Colonel had added that he would like me to be with the old man when the troops passed the hospital the following day.

It was late afternoon when they passed and the sun was golden on the church spires that Sixty could see from his bed. In the distance he could hear the swinging march: 'Wi' a Hundred Pipers ...' and he asked me to prop him up in his bed. Nearer and nearer came the battalion and as he lifted his head to listen, he must have been thinking of a whole lifetime in the regiment he had joined as a boy. Just before the column reached the hospital, the tune changed: changed to the regimental march – 'Scotland the Brave' – and tears of pride slid down his granite cheeks. He sat bolt upright till the last stirring notes faded away into the distance, then he slid down into his bed and turned his face to the wall.

That night Sixty died.

The troopship was a hell-ship of about 11,000 tons and bursting at the seams with men from every regiment on their way home from various parts of the Empire. For four days she was hove-to in the Bay of Biscay in a storm of Wagnerian proportions. Life in the troop decks in the bowels of the ship was unbelievably awful but the Jocks rose above the overcrowding and the smell of vomit by keeping their minds on the fact that at last they were off the island of Malta and headed in the right direction.

We arrived in the Citadel Barracks, Dover, a few days before Christmas. It was a place of undiluted gloom. A grass-covered fortress, high in the mist above the slate-roof Victorian horror of the town below, but as we marched into the barracks, on that drizzly December evening, there was not a man among us who did not rejoice.

The Weasel sent practically everyone in the battalion home on leave. A skeleton party of caretakers stayed behind and as we were still under the cloud caused by the goat episode, the two officer skeletons were Trubshawe and myself. It was really quite enjoyable and a great relief to be de-Weaseled for a while.

Hogmanay at the turn of the year was as boisterous an affair as usual and over at the canteen Cook Sergeant Winters gave the fifty members of the caretaker party a sizeable spread of haggis with all the trimmings and, following regimental tradition, the officers waited on the men. Trubshawe was at his very best belting out on endless stream of songs on the tinny canteen piano while toasts were offered and accepted.

The following day was a day of shock for the Raspberry Pickers. We rose late with appalling hangovers and were gloomily gazing out of the window of the officers' mess whence far below it was sometimes possible to see the English Channel through the murk. After the sauna-bath climate of Malta, the penetrating damp of the Dover heights could only be combated by a concoction of Trubshawe's called 'The Heart Starter' – port and brandy mixed. We were doing our best to get warm when the door behind us opened and the solitary mess waiter stood there making spastic movements of the head and shoulders, rolling his eyes and jerking his thumb over his shoulder. When he stepped aside, the reason for his alarm became clear. Behind him was a real live Major General. A lean and very formidable figure, he walked briskly into the room. The red band on his hat and red tabs on his collar sowed instant alarm in our breasts and this was not diluted by the sight of General Staff armbands on the Major and Captain immediately behind him.

'Where is your Commanding Officer?'

'On leave, sir,' said Trubshawe.

'Adjutant?'

'On leave, sir,' said I.

'Who is the senior officer present?'

'I am, sir,' said Trubshawe.

'I don't mean in this room,' snapped the General, 'in the barracks.'

'Still me, sir,' said Trubshawe and tried a misguided smile of welcome. 'Can we offer you a little something to keep out the cold?'

There was an ominous silence while the man treated us to a long, penetrating stare. Then he turned and held some sort of low-keyed, high-level military discussion with his staff. The Major and the Captain changed colour noticeably and we got the distinct impression that someone had blundered.

'All right . . . then you show me round,' said the General.

'Well,' began Trubshawe like some obsequious house agent with a prospective client, 'this is the anteroom and the dining room is up these steps to the right, the kitchen is below and the bedrooms, such as they are . . .', he trailed off as the General looked at him speculatively for a long time, tapping his highly polished riding boot with his leather cosh.

'Show me round the barracks', said the General in a controlled voice, 'that is, if it's not too much trouble.'

'Pray follow me, sir,' said Trubshawe (greasy head waiter routine now leading way to a bad table). 'Come, Mr Niven,' he added over his shoulder as an afterthought.

The grisly little procession wound across the almost deserted barrack square; a few bedraggled and hung-over Jocks looked up apprehensively from whitewashing some stones around the guard room.

'Fatigue party "shun",' yelled a corporal rising from behind a sporting paper. Unfortunately, his snappy salute was ruined by the fact that he omitted to take a cigarette out of his mouth.

'Mr Niven! take that corporal's name,' roared Trubshawe, all military efficiency now and pulling the big switch.

'Sir!' I yelled back and rushed over to the offending man. 'For Christ's sake,' I hissed at him, 'it's a General doing a surprise inspection – get the word round quick – get everybody looking busy.'

I rejoined the group just in time to see the General pointing towards a squat building.

'What's that?' he demanded.

Trubshawe and I had a somewhat sketchy idea of the layout of the Citadel but it still came as a rude shock when I realized that the Chief Raspberry Picker was shamelessly passing the buck to his trusted lieutenant.

'Mr Niven,' he said sweetly, 'what's that?'

'Er . . . the library, sir,' I faltered hazarding a guess. Trubshawe must have misheard me, 'The lavatory, sir,' he said. We went inside what was quite evidently the band practice room. In the far corner was the pipe major, who hated going on leave, frantically beating life into the bag of his pipes while his trembling fingers groped for the first plaintive notes of 'The Flowers of the Forest'. The General looked grim.

The inspection of the barracks proceeded on its nightmare course. Trubshawe heard my whispered cue of 'latrines', headed in the indicated direction, took one look at several pairs of protruding white spats belonging to Jocks who had decided to seek sanctuary there, lost his head and made the sort of noises reserved for orderly officers in the dining hall at mealtimes.

'Any complaints?' he asked.

Bewildered and aggrieved Scotsmen rose from their individual thrones.

'No complaints, sorr,' they mumbled.

We correctly identified the cookhouse only because Cook Sergeant Winters, in a white apron, was standing outside it beckoning with heavy-handed helpfulness with a ladle, but we received some timely reinforcements in the shape of Ginger Innes wearing the red sash of orderly sergeant and a smart-looking corporal from Trubshawe's platoon. Our morale rose as, with their whispered help, we successfully fielded searching questions in the quartermaster's stores, the miniature range and the domain of the Pioneer Sergeant.

By now the full complement of fifty caretakers had been mobilized by brush telegraph and whenever we went there were groups of men frantically cleaning, polishing, leaf sweeping and wheelbarrowing.

Trubshawe, as we headed for the General's car, felt that victory was within his grasp. He relaxed and was in an expansive mood when the General fired his last enquiry.

'What's in there?' he asked, indicating a large building with red double doors and FIRE HOUSE written above them. Almost smugly Trubshawe said,

'Why, the fire engine, sir,'

'Get it out,' ordered the General.

'Yes, sir,' Trubshawe looked as though he had been hit with a halibut. Then he turned, almost apologetically to me.

'Mr Niven, get the engine out, please.'

'Very good, sir,' I said, giving him a real killer look.

'Sergeant Innes – get the engine out.'

'Sir! – Corporal MacQuire, th' engin' – git it oot.'

The buck was now passing with great rapidity.

'Lance-Corporal Bruce, git th' engine oot...'

'Private Dool, git th' engin' oot.'

The cry echoed round the Citadel.

The General had started once more on that ominous metronome bit with the leather cosh and the riding boots.

'What sort of engine is it?' he asked with ominous calm.

'Oh – a beauty,' said Trubshawe.

'Merryweather,' I piped up from the back.

'Yes,' said Trubshawe, 'made by Merryweather & Company and it has a lot of brasswork and coils and coils of hose.'

'Get it *OUT!*' said the General much louder now.

Trubshawe seemed almost on the point of surrender – then, like a lookout at Mafeking seeing relief approaching, he let out a long sigh. A soldier bearing a huge key was approaching at the double from the direction of the Guard Room but I could hardly believe my ears when I heard Trubshawe pressing his luck.

'Many's the night, sir, when this trusty engine has been called out to help the honest burghers of Dover.'

'*Get it out!!*'

At last the key was inserted in the lock and with the flourish of a guide at Hampton Court opening the door of Henry VIII's bedchamber, Trubshawe pushed open the double doors.

Inside, against the far wall stood two women's bicycles: a dead Christmas tree from another era lay in the centre of the floor and in the foreground was a bucket of hard and cracked whitewash from a bygone cricket season.

The General turned and stalked to his car without a word. The staff officers gave us pitying glances before they followed him. In silence they all drove away and in silence Trubshawe and I returned to the officers' mess.

In the next few months a tremendous upheaval took place in the battalion. We received a new Commanding Officer; and there was a change of Adjutant. The new Colonel – Alec Telfer-Smollett, DSO, MC – was nothing short of a miracle. In no time at all he shook the battalion out of its warm climate garrison complex. The whole atmosphere became charged with a sense of purpose. It became possible to perform the dullest chores and at the same time to feel one was doing so for a good reason.

Telfer-Smollett was patience itself with me, in fact he took special pains with all the junior officers to make them feel at home, and I use that word advisedly because he was a firm believer in an ancient concept of a regiment – that it should be a family.

I found myself often dining alone with the Colonel and his wife and, unbelievably, at least twice a week I was invited to play golf with him. He laughed at my tales of Malta, nurtured my flagging military ambitions, sympathized with my permanent financial straits and cheated blatantly in the scoring.

He was a wonderfully warm and understanding human being and came within an ace of persuading me to become once more a serious soldier but this was quite unwittingly sabotaged by a petite snub-nosed blonde, a very pretty American girl with the smallest feet I had ever seen – Barbara Hutton.

In the spring of that fateful year, my grandmother died. For years she had lived in rooms in Bournemouth and as children, my sister Grizel and I had paid her annual visits, travelling from the Isle of Wight on a paddle steamer as day trippers. I remember her as a very beautiful old lady with a cloud of carefully coiffed white hair and a little lace choker at her throat kept high under the chin with bones. She had very pale and strangely lifeless skin on her cheeks which I always tried to avoid kissing. She left me £200 in her will.

I immediately invested about half of this windfall in a secondhand Morris Cowley and gleefully entered the London social scene.

Soon I found myself on the Mayfair hostesses' lists – as usual they were desperately short of available young men – and every post brought its quota of invitations to debutantes' parties or weekends in smart country houses. Dover being near to London and weekend leave plentiful, I indulged myself to the hilt with the minimum of outlay and became a crashing title snob in the process. For a short while I really believed that dukes and baronets were automatically important.

One evening at a dance I met Barbara. She was spending a few weeks in London with her uncle Frank and at the time she was engaged to Alex Mdivani, a Georgian prince who was to be her first husband. A gay and sparkling creature, full of life and laughter, she became a great ally at some of the more pompous functions. When she left London she made me promise to come to New York for Christmas, an invitation as lightly made as it was lightly taken.

In November I was sent on a physical training course for several weeks at Aldershot. One night I was called to the telephone and found myself talking to 'Tommy' whom I had not seen for over three years.

'Your mother is very ill,' he said, 'she is in a nursing home in

London and you should come and see her immediately.' He gave me very little further information except the address.

I quickly obtained leave and rushed to Queen's Gate. Although I had seen her only a few weeks before, she was so ravaged by cancer that I was utterly and completely horrified by what I saw. She did not recognize me before she died.

I went back to Aldershot and completed my course in a sort of daze. I simply could not comprehend what had happened. I had never had to cope with a loss of this magnitude and I endlessly chastised myself for always taking her presence for granted, for not doing much, much more to make her happy and for not spending more time with her when I could so easily have done so.

Alec Telfer-Smollett was a father figure and when I got back to Dover he helped me with great wisdom and infinite patience to get over the worst part. With Christmas approaching and with four weeks' leave coming to me, he suggested that I should go far away somewhere and be with people who could not remind me of what he knew well was a gnawing feeling of guilt.

It was then that I remembered Barbara Hutton's invitation. In reply to my cable asking if she had really meant it, I received one which said – 'Come at once love Barbara.'

I flogged the Morris Cowley, borrowed a little money from the bank and a little more from Grizel who had become a very clever sculptress and was now installed in a tiny house in Chelsea, and ten days before Christmas, I embarked on the one-class liner S.S. *Georgic* and throbbed my way to New York. Throbbed was the word; I had the cheapest berth in the ship – directly above the propellers.

The trip from Southampton to New York should have taken eight days but we met a gale head on, so it took ten.

My little throbbing box of a cabin I shared with an enchanting middle-aged American who had been making his first ever visit to Europe on the strength of having sold his clothing store in Milwaukee. He was much exercised by the thought of going home to face, once more, the rigours of Prohibition and during the trip he proceeded to make up for the lean times ahead. He was none too fussy either about mixing his intake.

'Dave', he said, one evening, 'I've gotta great idea . . . tonight you and me are gonna drink by colours.'

We settled ourselves at the bar and he decided to drink the colours of the national flags of all the countries he had visited on his trip – Stars and Stripes first of course. Red was easy – port. White was simple – gin, but blue was a real hazard till the barman unveiled a vicious Swiss liqueur called gentiane. The French and British flags fell easily into place but a horribly snag was placed in our path by the Belgians. Black, yellow and red. Black beer was used to lay a foundation for yellow chartreuse and burgundy, but it was the green crème de menthe of the Italian flag that caused me to retire leaving my new-found friend the undisputed champion.

The crossing was my first confrontation with Americans en masse and I found it a delightful experience. Their open-handed generosity and genuine curiosity about others came as something of a shock at first. What a change, though, to be asked the most searching personal questions in the first few minutes of contact, or to be treated to a point-by-point replay of the private life of a total stranger. What a difference as an unknown foreigner to be invited to sit at a table of friends or to join a family. I suppose it is the fact that we have fifty-odd million people crammed on to an island the size of Idaho, and unable ever to get more than eighty miles from the sea, that makes us so defensive. Who else but the British would spread hats, handbags, umbrellas and paper bags on the seats of railway carriages and then glower furiously through the windows at anyone who shows signs of entering and ruining our privacy?

I had my first brush with the American language in that ship. For a partner in the ping-pong doubles championship, I had snagged a delicious lady from Sioux City. 'Now we have a practice tomorrow,' I warned her, 'if you're not on deck by eleven o'clock, I'll come down to your cabin and knock you up.' She put me straight.

I do not, with my poor pen, have the impertinence to try and describe a first impression of the New York skyline because no one I have ever read has done it justice so far, but that forest of gleaming white set against an ice blue sky is something I will never forget.

Barbara had cabled that she would meet me at the dock so as the Moran tug company's fussy little work-horses pushed and tooted us into our berth, I went below and gathered together my hand baggage.

My Milwaukee friend was there having fitted himself into a strange forerunner of today's space suits. Inside and beneath the armpits were cavernous pockets which concealed large aluminium tanks, each capable of holding about two and a half gallons of Scotch whisky. He was in the process of being topped by the steward.

He pressed speakeasy cards on me, telephone numbers of friends in New York and issued a permanent invitation to visit with him at his home and meet some lovely people.

'Goddam Prohibition,' he muttered as I left, 'take a man's balls off.'

I walked down the gangplank and looked back at the good ship, *Georgic*. A few years later she was sunk by the Germans. Barbara was waiting for me at the dock and had brought two or three carloads of friends to welcome this strange young man, with the funny voice. I was a bit of a freak in the United States in those days as the vast majority of people had still never met a Briton nor heard an 'English accent'. Nobody went to see English movies because they couldn't understand them.

They gave me a rousing reception and I am happy to think that several of those I met on that Christmas Eve are still my friends today.

Barbara's family lived on Long Island but for a town house they utilized several suites in the Pierre Hotel. I was to be installed there and on the way – it was now growing dark – I beheld a breathtaking sight. The limousine swept round the corner of the Grand Central building and stopped. In the frosty evening, there stretched before me as far as the eye could see, a straight line of enormous illuminated Christmas trees. Also, as far as the eye could see, was a necklace of red lights. Suddenly, these lights changed to green and we shot forward. At that time, traffic lights were only being experimented with in London so I could be forgiven if I was unduly impressed by New York's Christmas decorations.

I was given a very nice room at the Hotel Pierre and Barbara, the pefect hostess, made it clear that she hoped I would spend as long as I liked there but feel perfectly free to come and go as I wished and not to feel bound to her or her family.

That night, she gave a party at the Central Park Casino. The incomparable Eddie Duchin was at the piano leading his orchestra and a very attractive couple of young ballroom dancers were the stars of the Cabaret – George and Julie Murphy. (George later became Senator from California.)

It may have been Prohibition but so far I had not noticed it. A vague pretence was certainly made to keep bottles out of sight and many people made extra trips to the lavatory or to their cars to uncork a flask there, but otherwise it was business as usual.

Christmas Day with Barbara's family and presents for the unknown young man of Homeric generosity. Next a visit to Princeton to watch the annual football battle with Yale. The trip to Princeton was organized by a cousin of Barbara's – Woolworth Donahue – and for the occasion, for our comfort and refreshment, he thoughtfully provided a special coach on the train.

The long ride passed in a flash. The men were all about my own age and the girls were the result of their very competitive selection for this high point of the College year. The result was spectacular. I had never seen such beautiful girls in my life and there were more to come. Jack and Marshall Hemmingway were our hosts at Princeton and there the train group joined about forty more for a colossal spread before the game. Finally, we set off for the Stadium with our Princeton pennants, our rosettes, our bottles of Bourbon and our wonderful, wonderful girls. Coonskin and camel-hair coats were very much in evidence.

I didn't see very much of the game. Once the college bands had left the pitch to the players, excitement was at such boiling point that the moment anything important happened, everyone leaped to his feet thereby obscuring my view. I did not have the same built-in springs in my knees as the others and trained, as I was, in the Twickenham school of indulging in a little polite hand clapping while seated, the most exciting moments were blanketed by vast expanses of coonskin and camel-hair ... but no matter, I had a wonderful day and have since become an aficionado of American football.

The days in New York passed in a blaze of parties, speakeasies and nightclubs with daytime forays to visit people on Long Island, sometimes in specially chartered and bar-equipped motor buses. There were also boxing matches and ice hockey games to see at Madison Square Garden, big Broadway musicals to visit, great bands and singers to listen to.

The headquarters of the group I was adopted by was Jack & Charlie's '21' Club – the best speakeasy in New York run by goodlooking Jack Kreindler and the amiable rotund and folksy Charlie Berns. The doorman was named 'Red' and 'Jim' was the watchdog peering through the big bullet-proof door. If an alarm was given of an impending raid by the law, the first thought was to protect the customers – no one would be caught drinking – so waiters were trained to seize all bottles and glasses from the tables and put them on the bar where 'Gus' the barman was in position to throw a switch, the whole bar then tilted up and the offending evidence slid down a chute to the cellar.

No evening was complete without ending up in some dive in Harlem. I don't think I'll try that today.

Prices in New York were bloodcurdling but such was the generosity of my new-found friends, that it was just taken for granted that I was never to be allowed to pay for anything. It was made clear that if I attempted to do so, I would no longer be invited. I didn't feel too bad about this arrangement because there were one or two members of the group who were also financially embarrassed at the time and they too were carried by those in funds. One was a struggling reporter on the *Sun*, a huge teddy bear of a man, named John McClain, destined to become my friend for life. McClain used to point to a slightly older man on the periphery of the group, always with the prettiest girl, a tall, shy, silent, slightly deaf, and compared to the rest of us, very serious minded citizen. 'Let that son of a bitch pay for once', McClain would rumble. The tall man's name was Howard Hughes.

Phil Ammidown had a Pierce Arrow convertible and was leaving for Florida. 'Come with me, Dave,' he said, 'I have a home in St Augustine, we can spend a couple of days there, take in a party at the girls' college in Tallahassee, then go on down to Palm Beach.'

The night before we set off, A. C. Blumenthal, the diminutive financial genius – once described by Dorothy Parker as 'a pony's ass' – gave a party, just six of us. Blumenthal's wife, Peggy Fears, and two other glamorous members of the Hollywood scene – Mary Duncan and Bubbles Haynes, Ammidown and myself. Blumenthal arrived bearing a suitcase almost as big as himself, a glorified model of Trubshawe's dipsomaniac's delight of beloved memory and the farewell party went on at various places all over town till Phil and I were waved away in the Pierce Arrow en route for Florida.

First stop, Richmond, Virginia, and my eyes now gummed together with tiredness, snapped open with amazement when, just as I was signing the hotel register, I noticed a full sized alligator in a small pool about six feet from the reception desk.

Phil was a demon driver and the Pierce Arrow was a very fast car – a combination that provoked a movie-style chase by a speed cop from the State Highway Patrol who was gaining on us with siren blaring when we shot across the State line into Florida and safety.

St Augustine is the oldest town in the United States, indeed the oldest house in the country is still standing there. Phil's house nestled peacefully in lush woods just outside and for two or three days, I was able to charge up my batteries after the hectic days of New York. I revelled in the peace and charm of the place and after the frenetic pace of the big city, I sniffed the warm magnolia-scented air, stared at the hibiscus, listened to the cicadas and the lazy drawling voices of the inhabitants and found it hard to believe I was in the same country. The Citadel Barracks, Dover, were every minute receding further and further into their grey clammy and depressing mists.

The party at Tallahassee took place just before the end of the year. The girls of the college had a tradition that during Leap Year they had the right to ask the men to dance and also to cut in on them. I had witnessed this rather barbaric tribal ritual of cutting in at parties in New York and had many times been highly frustrated having cut in on a beauty only to feel, as she melted into my arms, an ominous pat on the back from the next customer from the stag line, watching and choosing his moment from the middle of the floor. I had also suffered, once or twice, by getting stuck with a comparatively unattractive girl and not receiving that now welcome and relieving tap on the shoulder but I had never sunk so low as to dance round with some poor unprepossessing creature in my arms holding a ten-dollar bill behind her back as bribery to a rescuer. However, having sweated out my first invitation to dance, I kept my ears pricked for the rustling of currency behind my head.

Through forest and swamp, the arrow-straight US Highway No. 1 connects Jacksonville with St Augustine and half way between the two, Phil and I nearly died. Five o'clock in the morning, and travelling fast, we could see the lights of a car coming towards us at least ten miles away. As we shot past the other headlights and into the dark beyond, there was an almighty crash. We were both knocked unconscious. When we came to we were in the swamp on the left hand side of the road, incredibly, the car was the right side up and we were sitting in it pinned against the high back of the seat by the bronze frame of the now glassless windshield bent hard against our chests. The front of the car had been completely demolished. Water and mud were up to the floor boards and we knew we were covered in warm blood. From the swamp beside us came a terrible grunting and splashing –

'Alligators', whispered Phil, 'don't make a sound.'

As we sat, cowering and waiting for the foul slavering jaws to come snapping at us through the non-existent front of the car, we felt ourselves all over: the blood could not have come from us, we were unscratched.

'We didn't hit the other car,' I whispered. 'We were past it when it happened.'

The awesome noises continued for a long time then just as the first grey light of dawn was beginning to silhouette the moss-festooned trees, they stopped. The light grew stronger and we saw what had happened.

In that split second when we were blinded by the too-quickly turned up headlights of the other car, two large black mules had emerged from the swamp and we had hit them broadside. Poor brutes, one must have been flung up in the air and over our heads. Its body had bashed us against the high soft seat-back knocking us out, but, by a miracle, not breaking our necks. The noises had come from the wretched animals dying in the swamp. The Sun Life Insurance Company used a photograph of what was left of the car as a warning and a reminder.

Phil Ammidown, if not a man of great means was certainly a man of style – he bought a new car that same day, and in the afternoon, we continued south to Palm Beach.

Phil found us rooms in a small hotel and got busy on the telephone. Soon the days were flying by, girls everywhere, glorious golden ones, and golf, tennis, fishing in the blue Gulf Stream for marlin, dancing in roofless restaurants – 'How deep is the ocean? How high is the sky?' Parties, love-making, kindness and over-whelming generosity on all sides. Lili Damita, a gorgeous French actress, paraded about with a leopard on a leash and Winston Guest put a shark in his mother's swimming pool. I hoped it would never end but, suddenly, it was Pumpkin Time.

One of the glorious golden girls sidetracked me and I missed the last plane that would carry me north to catch my ship for home. I despatched a cable to Colonel Telfer-Smollett: DEAR COLONEL MAGNIFICENT OPPORTUNITY BIG GAME HUNTING WHALE FISHING FLORIDA REQUEST ONE WEEK EXTENDED LEAVE. This would give me ample time to catch the German ship *Europa* but if permission was not granted I would be in deep trouble overstaying my leave.

The answer came back – NO WHALES OR BIG GAME WITHIN A THOUSAND MILES STOP TAKE TWO SMOLLETT.

The parties and the hospitality reached a crescendo till finally, deafened and petrified by flying for fourteen hours in a non-sound proofed Tri-Motor Ford through the most hideous weather, I crawled on board the *Europa* and made for another rabbit hutch of a cabin in the bowels of the ship. As I unpacked I realized with a tinge of guilt that I had hardly thought about my mother . . . oh! the callousness of youth!

The Great American Kindness went on all the way across the Atlantic. The little cabin was full of goodbye telegrams and Barbara had arranged for a most welcome delivery of champagne. McClain had alerted a friend of his that I was on board and one night I was invited to a dinner in the First Class given by 'Jock' Whitney, a wonderfully intelligent and witty man who can light up a room and who quite lately was one of the most popular and successful US Ambassadors to the Court of St James.

On another occasion I was asked to dine in the First Class and my host insisted, after dinner, in cutting me in on his syndicate that was bidding for a number in the ship's sweep. My contribution was minimal, a fiver, I think, all I could afford anyway. I don't know how my host arrived at the result but when his number won, he told me my share was £160.

Thanks to this wonderful and, I am ashamed to say, now nameless man, I arrived back at the Citadel Barracks with more money than when I had left. I had tasted the fleshpots, in fact I had stuck all my trotters in the trough and had gorged myself: it had all been too rich for my blood, and in a welter of false values, I knew that one day, somehow, I would go back to America.

Trubshawe was on his last legs militarily. 'Can't go on much longer, old man. It's all getting too much like the Army . . . it's hunting four days a week and checking on the young pheasants for me.'

I soon noticed the change myself. Telfer-Smollett was determined to shake the battalion out of its Maltese malaise and bring it to a peak of efficiency and this meant first of all a great sharpening up of the officers.

The Colonel was wonderful to me and the off-duty golf games were as frequent as ever. There was nothing I could not discuss with him. His good advice was boundless. He understood perfectly the itchy feet I had contracted during my flying visit to the United States. He also saw the limited possibilities in the Army for an impatient young man of very slender means. We discussed the possibility of my following Trubshawe's example and resigning my commission and he counselled caution. 'Give it a few more months', he said, 'don't rush it.' I could become a good soldier but I had seen that grass on the other side of the fence and oh! Brother! was it green!

Trubshawe helped me find an old car. 'A man must have wheels.' We settled for a 1927 3-litre sports Bentley. It had done over a hundred and twenty thousand miles, had a strap over the bonnet, a handbrake outside, a compass, an altimeter, and a pressure pump on the dashboard, a cut-out that made the exhaust roar like an aeroplane and a three-tone horn. With a car like that one could only wear a chequered cap. It was the complete cad's car. It was cheap, because it was about to fall apart and the terms of payment were long. When I had handed over the down payment, I didn't have enough to pay for the licence – £25. Luckily the colour of the licence for 1932 was a light fawn so it was a simple matter to put a Guinness label in the licence holder. Guinness labels at that time were numbered, so from five yards my home-made licence was indistinguishable from the real McCoy.

Although I kept my promise to Telfer-Smollett and worked hard, I also used my wheels to good effect and London saw almost as much of me as Dover.

Ann Todd's career was booming and because of my friendship with her, I began to get a little stage-struck. She introduced me to a strikingly good-looking young actor who was even then electric on the stage. Since then, he has two major claims to fame – he is godfather to one of my children and has become the first in his profession to be made a Baron .... Laurence Olivier.

One day in the spring, I received a letter from Tommy. I had not seen him since my mother died. He suggested a Sunday luncheon at the Carlton Club and thinking that perhaps we were about to find some kind of rapprochement after years of hostility, I went.

I gave my name to the porter and was led through several gloomy rooms. My stepfather rose from a chair, ignored my out-stretched hand and said, 'The solicitors tell me that, so far, you have paid nothing towards the grave.' I did not stay for luncheon and I never saw him again.

Trubshawe decided to leave the Army and get married. Although I had been given plenty of warning of this impending, as it turned out, disaster, I was shattered by the news.

'I'll wait for the Levée and the Caledonian Ball, old man, but I've come to the end of the Tartan Trail.'

The prospect of soldiering on without my friend was horrendous and my thoughts turned even more towards taking the plunge into the unknown of civilian life.

The Levée took place at St James's Palace in June. Officers of all arms holding the King's Commission were supposed to present themselves to their Sovereign once or twice during their careers. Many people in the battalion were due for this ceremony and Telfer-Smollett entered wholeheartedly into the arrangements. The biggest problem was where to find regimental full dress. Some of the older officers had their own, but the rest of us, with few exceptions, had no wish to go £250 into the hole for one morning of peacock glory, so we hired from costumiers.

About ten of us attended the Levée and everyone seemed to have everything on and everything on right. The smell of mothballs made our eyes water but we were, I thought, quite an imposing sight as we strode down St James's Street in the June sunshine, shakos on our heads, McKenzie tartan plaids over our silver-buttoned scarlet doublets, claymores flashing and dirks at our sides. Sir Arthur Balfour was the Colonel of the Regiment and as we followed in his wake, for he was technically there to present us to the King, Trubshawe remarked that we looked like 'a gaggle of Highland Postmen.'

Inside St James's Palace was most impressive; two large ante-rooms were filled with several hundred officers from all branches of the three services. It was a blaze of colour – Highlanders, Hussars, Greenjackets, Gentlemen at Arms, Indian cavalry officers in turbans, Gurkhas and Maharajas. There was a suppressed bonhomie in the first ante-room and many old friends were recognized, some from Sandhurst days. The second ante-room into which we were later directed was quiet and one sensed a certain nervousness. In all it took about two hours to percolate through the two anterooms and into the Throne Room where we were to pay our respects to King George V.

Finally, my turn came. I was ushered through the door and remembering my minute instructions from Colonel Balfour, I handed my calling card to the Gentleman-at-Arms. Ahead of me was a slowly moving single line of officers, inching forward towards the dais at the end of the long beautiful room. About twelve men were in front of me and as I, in turn, began to move forward, I had plenty of time to take in the scene.

On the dais and standing at the back were about forty very impressive gentlemen – the most senior in the Royal Household and Services. They stared out impassively from beneath beetling brows. At the centre, on a gold throne, sat the King in Field Marshal's uniform, and standing immediately behind him to right and left, his four sons – the Prince of Wales in the uniform of the Welsh Guards, the Duke of York in naval uniform, the Duke of Gloucester in his Hussar uniform and the Duke of Kent in the sky blue of the Royal Air Force.

I found myself filled with great emotion. When I reached the end of the line, my calling card had miraculously arrived at the same instant and was being handed to a senior official who glanced at it and announced ... 'Mr David Niven – The Highland Light Infantry'. I turned to the right, my shako under my arm, praying I would not trip over my claymore and marched the regulation number of steps that would bring me opposite the King, then a smart left turn and I was face to face with my monarch. I bowed. He acknowledged me with a sight inclination of the head. A smart right turn and I marched out into another ante-room. It had been an unexpectedly moving experience for me and for the others too. We gathered in silence till Sir Arthur Balfour joined us and told us that the Colonel-in-Chief of our Regiment, the elderly uncle of the King, the Duke of Connaught, wished to receive us in his apartments behind the Palace.

During the short walk I was brought down to earth by Trubshawe who said, 'I hope the poor old sod doesn't get gassed by all this camphor.' Standing in a line in his dining room, we were presented to the Duke. He seemed a very old man and his German accent was most pronounced.

'It's good to see the old uniform again,' he intoned, peering at us over a white moustache and a huge beak of a nose.

'Jesus!' whispered Trubshawe, standing next to me. 'Somebody's got one of his old ones on.'

The next night was the Caledonian Ball held at Grosvenor House, a most colourful spectacle awaited us. Scots from all over the world were present in full regalia and the pièce de résistance was always the set reels. The huge ballroom was cleared and in the middle the Duke of Atholl's private sixteensome took up position, then around it were placed the eightsomes of the six Highland Regiments, the Black Watch, ourselves, the Gordons, the Camerons, the Seaforths and Argylls.

Trubshawe and I with, luckily, two very special friends, Keith Swettenham and Michael Bell, were the four subalterns selected by Telfer-Smollett to represent the Highland Light Infantry. The four girls we were to partner wore the sashes of their clans and had been carefully selected by the Ball Committee for their territorial connections with the Regiment and not, we noticed, with some alarm, for their good looks. However, we had just arrived from a riotous dinner in a private room at the Mayfair Hotel which Brian Franks had arranged, so we were not too unnerved when introduced to our horse-faced partners from far-away glens. Also, the dinner party was there to cheer us on, headed by Margie Macdougall, Celia Tower, David Kelburn, Anthony Pleydell-Bouverie and Brian Franks.

The Pipe Major had been polishing up our dancing for days before the big night and we were quietly confident of holding up the good name of the regiment in front of hundreds of pairs of critical eyes.

Now, in an eightsome reel, it doesn't matter how well the individuals dance the steps if the whole eightsome fails to stay in its allotted position. The unknown girls were expert dancers and it was the dawning look of horror on their faces that alerted me to a very nasty situation ... somehow our entire eightsome, performing perhaps with too much verve and abandon, had started to creep slowly down the ballroom floor towards the Gordons. A crash was imminent. The 'Gay' Gordons turned rather nasty, and hissed oaths came our way. We recoiled and began travelling inexorably in the direction of the Camerons who tried to avoid us and got into a really horrible mix-up with the Seaforths. Having started the rot and cleared a large portion of the floor for our own use, our eightsome settled down beautifully and never moved again. The other eightsomes were left cannoning into each other and generally behaving like goods trains at Clapham Junction often ricocheting off the Duke of Atholl's sixteensome in the centre. Trubshawe observed the Argylls trying to ignore a couple from the Black Watch who were now dancing dazedly in their midst and summed up things – 'Bit of a ——-up at the other end of the room, old man.'

Trubshawe adhered to his timetable and by midsummer, he had left the regiment and married Margie Macdougall.

The junior officers, non-commissioned officers and men of the battalion were sad to see him go. The senior officers had mixed feelings. For me it was disaster, compounded when, almost immediately, over half of my platoon were drafted to India and I was sent on a course to the Machine Gun School at Netheravon. Gloom descended on me like a blanket.

I was befriended around this time by the Weigall family who lived in a large white Georgian house in Ascot. Sir Archibald was tall, charming, good-looking, pink-faced and vague. Lady Weigall, permanently in a wheel chair, wearing a blonde wig with a blue bow in it, was plump, vivacious, a tremendous gourmet who loved laughing and being shocked. She was attended by two resident doctors, a youngish male social secretary and a mysterious old gentleman called 'C.J.' who read *Horse & Hound* all day long, and who was rumoured to have been Lady Weigall's boy friend before Sir Archibald showed up. Priscilla, the only child, was a flashing brunette with a delicious sense of humour who was quite correctly considered 'Deb of the Year'.

I spent many happy weekends at Ascot and the Weigalls took a great interest in my future. Sir Archie and Lady Weigall thought it fitting that I should go to Australia as ADC to the Governor General. Priscilla had other ideas.

'You should be a movie actor,' she declared flatly and promptly went to work to promote the idea. First, she introduced me to my boyhood hero, the great Douglas Fairbanks. A chronic anglophile, Fairbanks was enjoying a period of playing the country squire and had rented Mimms, a lovely Queen Anne house in Hertfordshire.

Fairbanks invited me to play golf with him at Sunningdale which I did and basked happily for eighteen holes in his reflected glory. I was so impressed by the gaiety and simplicity of the great man, I never dared mention Priscilla's project.

Undeterred by my cowardice, she next presented me to Bunty Watts, a producer at Sound City, a minute studio nearby, and one Sunday, I appeared in front of the cameras as an extra in a racing film – *All the Winners* with Allan Jeayes as its star. Greatly to Priscilla's disappointment, I was not immediately signed to a million-pound contract and returned to Netheravon in time for parade on Monday morning.

My loathing of the Machine Gun School was only equalled by my pathological hatred of the Vickers Mark IV machine gun, a foul piece of machinery of such abysmal design that it was subject to countless stoppages, all of which we were supposed to be able to diagnose and rectify at a moment's notice. There were about a hundred officers on the course drawn from every conceivable regiment. Henry Clowes of the Scots Guards was my constant companion and although I nearly killed him one day, when the vintage Bentley skidded and somersaulted on Salisbury Plain, pinning us underneath it, he forgave me and did all he could to help me through the hot mornings when I arrived, sleepless, from London.

One such morning was the harbinger of military doom. I had escorted Priscilla to a dance and a night club and I screeched up in the Bentley only just in time to take off my tail coat, jump into my brown canvas overalls, cram my Glengarry on my head and relieve Henry of a hideously heavy tripod before my name was called on the early parade.

'Present, sir,' I puffed.

All morning we laboured, putting that damn gun together then taking it to pieces again.

'All right, gentlemen,' said the chief instructor, a full colonel, 'it's a very warm day, you may remove your overall jackets and work stripped to the waist.'

Sighs of relief all round as the officers peeled

'Mr Niven, you may remove your overalls,' said the chief instructor.

'No thank you, sir, I have a sniffle.'

'Remove your overalls, Mr Niven,' ordered the colonel.

'Yes, sir.'

I stood in the middle of Salisbury Plain unveiled in white tie, stiff collar, shirt and white waistcoat ... Glengarry still on my head.

After that I was a marked man.

The end, militarily speaking, came for me on another stiflingly hot day during the last week of the course. I was much looking forward to a particularly exciting rendezvous in London and my timetable was in grave danger of being ruined by a long-winded address being delivered by a visiting major-general. In the hot tin-roofed lecture hut he was droning on about fields of fire, close support and trajectories. Bluebottles were buzzing about and my head was nodding. Finally he closed his notes.

'Any questions, gentlemen?'

My hand went up. I will never know what prompted me to do it, four years of frustration, I suppose, but I opened my mouth and heard myself say,

'Could you tell me the time, please, I have to catch a train.'

'Stand up that officer'.

I stood – 'Your name?' I told him.

'Go to your quarters and remain there.' I departed.

Soon an officer of the Seaforths of the same rank as myself joined me in my room, ominously he was wearing a sword. He was very embarrassed. 'I'm afraid I have been told to ... er ... stay with you,' he said.

'Close arrest?' I asked.

'Looks like it,' he said.

The embarrassment deepened as we sat staring at each other in the hot little room, he in the leather chair, me on the bed. After about an hour, with an exasperated flourish, he took off his sword.

'This is bloody ridiculous,' he said, 'let's have a drink.'

I agreed eagerly and summoned the room orderly who was lurking suspiciously close determined not to miss a moment of this juicy situation. A bottle of whisky arrived from the mess and almost in silence the Seaforth Highlander and I drank it, and when I say 'it' – we drank the whole bottle.

'I've a suggestion,' said the Seaforth as the last dram was drained, and he said it slowly and with great deliberation.

'I'll go to the lavatory, which I badly need to do, and you escape.'

The beauty and simplicity of this plan would have shamed Field Marshal Montgomery's famous 'Left Hook' at El Alamein.

The Seaforth, with brimming eyes, then clasped both my hands in his, shook his head mournfully, and tottered off in the general direction of the latrines. I climbed hurriedly out of the window, closed my eyes and leapt into space. Luckily my room was on the ground floor so I found myself in no time up to my chin in rhododendron bushes.

I ran to the Bentley and drove rapidly, and luckily without incident, to London.

The girl with whom I had a date I never saw again. I arrived comparatively sober and utterly appalled by what I had done. I rounded up two friends, old friends whom I admired ... Victor Gordon-Lennox, an ex-Major of the Grenadier Guards, then the diplomatic correspondent of the *Daily Telegraph*, and Philip Astley who, as Adjutant of the Life Guards, had been asked to resign his commission for committing a henious crime – he had married an actress – the gorgeous Madeleine Carroll.

The three of us dined at White's; outside, Guinness label gleaming, stood the Bentley. The two ex-Guards officers listened attentively while I told them what had happened. With the port came the inquest.

'How much do you like the Army?' asked Victor.

'I hate it,' I answered.

'You're bound to be court-martialled, why don't you pack up before you're thrown out?'

'Because I'm broke,' I said.

'Do you have any money at all?' asked Victor.

'A few pounds and about half that old Bentley outside.'

They left me nursing a large glass of Cockburn's while they murmured together in a bay window overlooking St James's Street. I tried to avoid the eyes of an ex-member of White's who stared down on me disapprovingly from a large gilt frame – the Duke of Wellington.

Finally the jury returned to their seats.

'There is no question that you are through in the Army,' said Philip, 'but Victor has a possible solution.'

Victor, lately married to a Canadian girl, then spoke, 'I am sailing on the *Empress of Britain* tomorrow to pick up Diana from her parents' island in the Rideau Lakes, then I'm off to Washington. Give me the Bentley or the part you have paid for and I'll give you a return trip ticket to Quebec – come and stay on the island for a week or two and you can decide what to do next.'

I was stunned by my good fortune.

'Now, we'll go downstairs,' said Philip, 'and you can write your colonel your resignation – I'll help you – I've done it.'

Below, by the porter's desk – the only place in White's where guests can use the Club stationery – I wrote out a cable to Alec Telfer-Smollet at the Citadel Barracks, Dover:

'DEAR COLONEL REQUEST PERMISSION RESIGN COM-MISSION. LOVE NIVEN.'

I sailed for Canada in the morning.

The *Empress of Britain*, like my earlier transatlantic carrier the *Georgic*, was sunk a few years later by the Germans. She was a beautiful ship and the September crossing was perfect. We ran into fog only once about one day out of the Gulf of St Lawrence; suddenly, it got much colder and we reduced speed. I remarked on this to a steward.

'Icebergs about,' he said.

'How do you know?' I asked.

'We smell 'em,' he replied.

As yet there was no radar in passenger ships and the steward gave it as his considered opinion that the Captain wetted his pants every time they entered these particular waters.

The fog lifted and everyone was pointing. A mile or so away was a gigantic fortress sailing majestically along. Pale pink in the setting sun on one side and blue-green on the other. It towered out of the water and with nine-tenths out of sight below the surface, imagination boggled at the size of the whole.

Diana Kingsmill Gordon-Lennox was a rarity – a genuine Canadian eccentric. Dark, with beautiful teeth and a lovely smile, she was highly intelligent, smoked small cigars and wore a monocle. She met us in Quebec and we drove and drove to Portland, Ontario. Diana seemed not at all put out that Victor had arrived with an unknown friend, she intimated that her father and mother were looking forward to having me on the island and was delighted when I told her I loved fishing. 'Then Daddy will have a playmate,' she said.

When we approached the island a loon was calling plaintively across the lake. The maples were turning and I had never seen such blazing beauty, great splashes of red, brown, yellow and gold were reflected in the still water and behind rose the foothills of the Gatineau Mountains all clothed in the same breath-taking colours.

The island was of about five acres. The main house was surrounded by perhaps four guest cabins, all of wood. Admiral Kingsmill and his wife were walking down to the boathouse as we arrived. The Admiral was a famous old Canadian sea-dog and with his forthright manner, pointed white beard and ramrod carriage, he certainly looked the part. Diana had heard my story on the long drive from Quebec and has said it would be better to forget my true exit from the British Army. 'Just settle for a straight resigning of the commission when talking to the old man,' she said firmly.

Lady Kingsmill was a gentle motherly creature and I was immediately made welcome.

The days slid by. People came from other islands to visit. The Admiral and I endlessly went fishing for the big green bass, the fighting, jumping, black bass; the giant pike and the ferocious muskellon.

Victor and Diana took me on excursions into the back country and we discussed my future endlessly. Return to England? Hardly. Because of my lack of training in any useful profession the chances of employment seemed brighter in the US than in Canada, so when the time came to move on I made up my mind to cash in my return trip ticket to England and cast my lot in New York.

On the day of my departure I had an agonizingly sore throat. I didn't say anything about it because the Kingsmills might have felt they were getting stuck with a permanent guest so when Victor and Diana headed for Washington, I accompanied them as far as Ottawa, where I said goodbye to my saviour and his wife and visited a doctor who said I had chronically infected tonsils which should come out immediately. I imagine he must have done something about the infection first, but anyway he stuffed me into Ottawa General Hospital. Sodium pentathol not having yet come on the market, the operation was carried out after I had first been rendered unconscious by a mixture of gas and ether being pumped into a rubber mask over my face. After the operation, I lay for days with a throat of greatly increased soreness and to take my mind off my misery, I am afraid I indulged in a little gentle plagiarism.

I hope that the statute of limitations applies in this case and that the Mounties will not be sent to pull me in, and if it will help at all, I offer my belated apologies to the author, Tyrwhitt-Drake, who long before had written a book called *Fox Hunting in Canada*. I found it in the hospital library, copied some of it assiduously and sold four articles to the local newspaper under the title 'Hunting of the Canadian Fox'. It paid the doctor's bill.

I had met some friends of the Kingsmills, Pete and Ginny Bate, and one day they appeared at my bedside.

'We've talked to the doctor,' they said, 'and he has agreed that we can take you home with us. There's a room at the top of the house you can have while you are convalescing and it'll be much more comfy for you. Besides, we would love to have you.'

I was overwhelmed by such a wonderfully warm-hearted gesture by the slightest of acquaintances, though it is typical of Canadians as a whole.

I had at least a week more to spend in bed – apparently it has been an operation with 'complications' so I jumped at the idea and, swathed in blankets, was installed, as promised, in a bright chintzy room at the top of their house.

On a Sunday night Ginny and Pete came up to see me.

'Were going over to Pete's mother's for supper but we'll be back before eleven. Do you mind being left alone?'

Of course I didn't. I was feeling better and due to get up in a day or so. They left me with a radio and departed.

I went to sleep about ten and woke up some time later literally drowning in my own blood. I had had a terrible haemorrhage in the throat and when I turned on my side, it poured out like a tap onto the floor. The bright chintzy room looked like an abattoir. I had not the faintest idea where the telephone was or what was the doctor's number but I had a vague idea that the operator could somehow help me.

I collapsed at the top of the stairs where the poor Bates found me, mercifully a short while later.

Back to hospital and blood transfusions but finally I made it by train to New York. It was now mid-October and becoming exceedingly cold. I found a room in a cheap hotel on Lexington Avenue – the Montclair – and for a week I lay in bed without the energy to pick up the telephone to try to find some of last year's companions.

Finally, I began to make contact with the old group and although they went through the motions of being pleased to see me, I soon realized that there was a big difference between an irresponsible young man over for a short holiday, and an anxious young man badly in need of a job. The background was none too welcoming for a foreigner either, the United States was still in the grip of the Depression and there were millions of United States citizens unemployed. I could not have chosen a worse time for my arrival.

However, good health can overcome the gloomiest thoughts and as my strength returned, my morale improved. I registered with an employment agency and picked up a few dollars here and there working at night for catering companies who handled cocktail parties. It was not a very technical job. The host produced the booze via his bootlegger and the caterers provided the hors d'oeuvres, the barman, the glasses and the waiters. I invested in a white jacket and took great care to check the addresses I was sent to, only accepting jobs where it was very unlikely I would be seen by any of my erstwhile acquaintances.

John McClain, the reporter, was doing better. He had just been given a daily column to write for the *Sun* – 'Up the Gangplank', interviews with interesting arrivals on the ocean liners. One day McClain had a brainwave. . . .

'Look,' he said, 'prohibition was repealed in April and is due to be ratified in a few days and all booze becomes legal. Jack and Charlie are going to become wine merchants – maybe they'll give you a job. I'll have a word with them.'

The next day I had a meeting with Jack Kriendler and found myself employed on a forty dollars a week retainer against ten per cent of what I brought in in the way of orders. Jack explained that Frank Hunter of the world champion doubles team of Tilden and Hunter would be president of the company and my immediate boss.

Frank Hunter, a man of great charm and humour, introduced me to my co-worker, a tough professional salesman named Harry Rantzman.

During the months I held my job, I hardly ever topped four hundred dollars a week in sales which would have 'augmented' my 'retainer'. Harry Rantzman ended up owning several apartment buildings in the Bronx, a real professional.

The first day at work Kriendler sent me to FBI Headquarters to have my fingerprints taken and to be photographed with a number round my neck and to this day at '21' is that picture of me: underneath is written – *Our First and Worst Salesman*.

The products we had to sell were Justerini and Brooks' whole line, Ballantyne's Scotch, George Goulet champagne and a peculiar brandy called Jules Robin.

'Go out now and get the orders,' said Charlie Burns airily. They gave me a price list and told me my beat.

'East of Lexington over to the river and between 42nd St and 90th St, that's for the restaurants and bars – the private customers you pick up anywhere you can.'

I made my first sale the day before drinking became legal – a case of champagne to 'Woolly' Donahue – he needed it at once, Gus the barman gave me the case out of stock and 'Red' the doorman and I delivered it in a Yellow Cab just before midnight on December 4 – '21 Brands Inc' was in business.

In the days that followed, three things became apparent. The first was that with all the ex-bootleggers and gangsters leaping into the

legitimate wine and spirits trade, I was in for a rough time in the
very rough sector of the city that had been allotted to me.

Secondly, most private customers, in a sudden wave of self-
righteousness, preferred to deal with old-time wine merchants and
looked down their noses at the upstarts who had erupted from the
gangster-ridden world of speakeasies, though this was an excuse I
preferred not to make to Jack and Charlie when my shortcomings as
a salesman came up for periodic review.

And thirdly, I found it impossible to try and sell to friends and
acquaintances. I just could not bring myself to say 'Thank you so
much for having me to dinner – now, how about buying a case of
Scotch?'

The Montclair Hotel was pretty awful and the steam heat in my
tiny room was suffocating but it was cheap and right on the edge of
my 'territory'. The front door of the Montclair was on Madison
Avenue, exactly opposite the back door of the Waldorf-Astoria so
during that miserable cold winter, I made it a point to come out each
morning from the Montclair, carrying my bag of samples, cross
Madison, climb the long stairs at the rear entrance to the Waldorf,
wend my way through the vast gilded lobbies of the most luxurious
hotel in New York, descend the steps to the front entrance, pass
through the revolving doors and issue on to Park Avenue to start my
day....

'Good morning, Mr Niven,' said the doorman, saluting deferentially.

'Morning, Charles.'

Very good for the morale. Then I turned right at the first corner
heading for the sleazy restaurants and bars of my domain and
making the most of the warmth from the exhausts of the heating
plants coming through grills in the sidewalks, I started my dreary
rounds.

'Stand over there and wait your turn – okay, Jerk, let's see your
list – what's this — ? Never heard of it. Git yer ass outta here.'

Fourteen degrees below zero outside and stamping into stifling
sandwich counters for lunch then off again to try and corner
restaurant owners sitting hunched over their own meals while
'waiters' in filthy aprons wiped off tables and removed the debris of
departed customers.

'Wait till I finish eating for Chrissake. Okay, let's look at the
list.... Who expects to get these goddam prices anyway? "21
Brands", never heard of 'em.... Take off twenty per cent and
maybe I'll talk to you: now beat it.'

Back at the end of the day with little success.

'Good evening, Mr Niven.'

''Evening, Charles.'

Up the front stairs – through the warm rich-people-fragrant lobbies of the Waldorf, down the back stairs, across Lexington, avoiding skidding taxis and clanging street cars and then going to ground like a bedraggled fox in my lair in the Montclair.

Big cities can be the loneliest places in the world, especially when cash is in short supply, but on New Year's Eve I decided to splurge so I took in the show at the Radio City Music Hall and stood myself a decent supper in a bar-grill off Broadway. There I met, or rather picked up, a show-girl who said she had been stood up by her date. We had a few drinks and she asked me to take her to see the marathon dancers. The Depression had produced some desperate people but none could have sunk to greater depths of degradation than those poor creatures, shuffling round twenty-four hours a day for days on end sleeping occasionally in each other's arms. Zombies with exhausted pinched faces competing for a few hundred dollars in purse money and for the sadistic pleasure of jaded onlookers like my pick-up. She lived in a gaudy apartment on the West Side. A large number of vacuous satin-clad dolls were propped upon her bed. She was attractive in a brassy but curiously vulnerable way. She too seemed lonely.

The next day, I got a call from Jack Kriendler, he must have got the news with his breakfast, he was very highly strung, 'Jesus, kid, you gotta watch your step ... you outta your mind or something? You wanna get rubbed out? ... Lay off that dame you had last night for Chrissake ... she's dynamite!'

He told me the name of the man who had stood her up. It didn't mean anything to me, but McClain whistled when he heard it.

'Jack's right,' he said, 'forget it unless you want to wind up at the bottom of the East River in a barrel of cement.'

An awful lot happened in 1934 and I had a funny feeling that things might be going to get better when one evening in early January, passing homeward through the Waldorf, I ran into Tommy Phipps, an old friend from England. There were three famous Langhorne sisters from Virginia – all very beautiful. One married Dana Gibson, the artist, and became the prototype of the Gibson Girls, another, Nancy, married Lord Astor and became Britain's famous female Member of Parliament representing Plymouth from 1919 to 1945 and was presiding at the very time I met Tommy over the much publicized Cliveden Set. The third, Norah the youngest, and gayest, married an English army officer, Paul Phipps. Tommy, the result of this union, had been sent to Eton and now, a few years later, had come to America to live with his mother and a newly acquired stepfather.

Tommy insisted that I leave with him that moment to spend the weekend with his family in Greenwich, Connecticut. While I was flinging a few things into a bag, Tommy filled me in on the details.

'Lefty' Flynn had been one of the most famous of all Yale athletes. Full-back and all-American, he had also created impossible records in track, winning everything except the high jump and he only failed to win that, according to Tommy, because he was busy winning the mile which took place at the same time.

He became a leading light in the Yale Glee Club and toured with it all over the country. When they were performing in Los Angeles, his monumental physique and good looks caught the eye of William Wellman, the director, and almost overnight Lefty was starring in cowboy pictures.

His instantaneous success had made him, for a while, unreliable, and during his third and last film, he had asked one day to be excused in the middle of shooting to go to the lavatory. Eight days later he had been located by distraught studio executives, in an hotel in Oklahoma City, sitting up in bed playing a guitar and painted bright blue from head to foot. In the room with him was a six-piece Haiwaiian orchestra which he had picked up en route in San Francisco.

Somewhere during his travels he had met Tommy's mother and the resulting *coup de foudre* had only lately resolved itself and resulted in a new home life for Tommy.

I fell in love with the whole family immediately and I am forever grateful to them for the home they gave me from that weekend on. Not a frame house home ... though that was available to me at any time ... something much more important ... a home inside myself from which I felt to venture forth and do battle.

Norah and Lefty did not go to parties in New York, preferring the simple life, in Greenwich, but they had a very soft spot for that inveterate international party giver, Elsa Maxwell. One evening they waited for me at the end of my day's work and took me to tea with this legendary figure in her apartment in the Waldorf Towers.

Rumours abounded as to how Elsa managed to pay for all the extravaganzas she presided over. Some said she was backed by the nouveaux riches who picked up the tab in exchange for being launched surrounded by Elsa's formidable list of the socially desired: others, less generous, hinted that she made a good living out of the by-products of these parties and having talked someone into paying for one, she then collected a handsome percentage from the caterers, orchestras and decorators involved. The truth was that she was personally enormously generous and died leaving very little money. I liked her the moment I saw her.

A small, dumpy figure of sixty-odd in a sacklike garment relieved by not a single bauble, she dispensed tea and dropped names with great expertise. She reminded me somewhat of Lady Weigall so it didn't surprise me when she said, 'Selling liquor . . . that's no good, no good at all . . . get you nowhere . . . you should go to Hollywood . . . nobody out there knows how to speak English except Ronald Colman.'

Norah and Lefty made encouraging noises so she went on, 'Next week I'm giving a party for Ernst Lubitsch, just a small dinner up here for about forty . . . plenty of people are dropping in after the theatre so you be here about twelve and I'll introduce you to Ernst and tell him to do something about it.'

The following week, I showed up at the appointed hour to find about a hundred and fifty people milling around all with the indelible stamp of self-assurance and wealth. 'If I could only sell each one of them a bottle of Scotch . . .' I thought. Instead of trying, I grabbed a glass for myself and looked around for Elsa Maxwell. She was sitting on a sofa at the far end of the room, surrounded by admirers, and didn't seem to show too much enthusiasm when she caught my eye, just lifted a hand in greeting, so I decided to get on with the job myself.

Beside me stood a little dark man with a pale face, slicked down black hair and a huge cigar. He was regarding the social scene with evident distaste.

'Which is Lubitsch?' I asked.

'I am,' he said and moved away.

A few days later, Elsa called me at the Montclair and said, 'I talked to Ernst about you but he says this is not a good moment to start in pictures so I've thought of something else for you – you should marry a rich wife.'

'How do I do that?'

'Become the most popular man in New York, of course.'

'On forty dollars a week?' I said but Elsa started issuing instructions like a demented Field Marshal.

'I'm giving the party of the year for the Milk Fund. It will be at the Casino de Paris. I shall have all the most eligible bachelors in New

York as professional dancing partners at a hundred dollars a dance for the Fund, and afterwards there will be a big auction and people will vote with dollars for the most popular man in New York. I want you to be one of the contestants. You will all wear green carnations . . . goodbye', and she hung up.

The Casino de Paris was filled with the brightest, the most beautiful and the richest in New York. I had dusted off my ageing dinner jacket and reported for duty as ordered. Elsa gave me my badge of office – the green carnation and stood me in line with about twenty other fellows. I was probably the youngest. I was certainly the worst dancer.

A number of people bought dances from me and I was able to hand over a considerable sum to the Lady Treasurer but I was ill prepared for the shame of the auction.

After a midnight show featuring that classic mime, Jimmy Savo, a huge imitation section of the Big Board on the New York Stock Exchange was wheeled on to the stage.

There were twenty names on it. I remember only five of them, Jock Whitney, Sonny Whitney, Lytel Hull, William Rhinelander Stewart and Clifton Webb, the current rage of Broadway. My name, spelled David Nevins, was at the bottom of the list. As I watched the auction progressing a cold sweat of embarrassment broke out all over me. Blocks of shares worth thousands of dollars were bought and the amount registered in lights beside the name after each sale. For a while I had hopes that people would think I was the maker of the machine or something and in fact NEVINS might have gone unnoticed if Fifi and Dorothy Fell had not felt sorry for me and bought a hundred dollars' worth of stock between them. My value and my shame remained at that level for all to see. The winner Jock Whitney, notched up a colossal sum for the Fund. Everyone, with one exception, was highly delighted with the evening.

I couldn't take the Montclair any longer – as a matter of fact it was mutual because on the coldest night of the year I managed to loosen enough layers of cracked and grimy paint round the window to open it about four inches at the bottom. When I woke up my radiator was frozen solid and the heating system for an entire floor had ceased to function.

I found a basement room on Second Avenue. My view was of feet hurrying by and up beyond them, silhouetted against the yellow sky, the rattling, banging Elevated Railway.

The freezing winter seemed endless. Lefty took me skating, something I had never tried before. On a pond near Greenwich I got out of control and charged a girl who was figure skating round an orange. I cut the orange in half and knocked the girl over. Not the best way to start a romance but this was no ordinary girl as I noticed while she was helping me to my feet. She was small, almost tiny, with a wonderfully alive and pretty face, huge brown eyes, and a cloud of auburn hair pushed out from beneath a woolly skating bonnet. We had hot chocolate together and I asked where she lived.

'May I call you when I come back to New York?'

'Sure, if you want to, my name is Hudson and you can find it in the book. My father's a doctor and we live at 750 Park ... Donald Hudson.'

A few days later I called her, 'May I speak to Miss Hudson, please?'

'This is she.'

'Oh, well, this is David Niven – you said I might call you.'

'Who is this?'

'David Niven.'

'I'm sorry ... I don't know the name.'

'Don't you remember me ... cutting your orange in half?'

'I *beg* your pardon.'

'Last weekend ... skating at Greenwich ... don't you remember? I knocked you over?'

'You must be mistaken ... I've never been to Greenwich in my life and I never go skating.'

'You are Miss Hudson?'

'*MRS* Hudson.'

'Oh, I'm terribly sorry. You see the 'Miss Hudson I thought I was calling said that her father was a doctor – Donald Hudson – living at 750 Park ... I looked him up and. . . .'

She interrupted, 'Well, you found my husband's number and he's a lawyer, Dennis Hudson, and his address is 250 Park.' She had a most attractive voice; and safe at the end of the telephone I decided to press on.

'How is he anyway?'

'Who?'

'Your husband, Dennis.'

'Very well, thank you.'

'Is he a *good* lawyer?'

There was a tiny intake of breath but I sensed that she had missed the logical moment to put down the receiver.

'Very good, thank you.'

'Where does he work?'

'Downtown.'

'Well, then, how about meeting me for lunch somewhere uptown?'

She still didn't cut me off.

'Certainly not, I don't have lunch with total strangers.'

'That's the trouble with all you middle-aged American women – no sense of adventure. . . .'

'I'm not middle-aged. I'm twenty-two.'

I settled smugly on my dungeon bed.

'Then that's really awful. I suppose you go off to one of those terrible hen parties, nibbling on a salad and gossiping?'

'Would you please not bother me any more. I'm not going to have lunch with you.'

I said nothing . . . just waited.

'I mean . . . how do I know that you're not a murderer or a kidnapper or something?'

'I tell you what I'll do,' I said. 'I'll wear a blue and white spotted scarf and a red carnation and I'll stand on any street corner you name at one o'clock. Then you can walk or drive by and you'll know me but I won't know you. You can take a good look and if what you see seems all right and not like a murderer or a kidnapper then we'll have lunch uptown . . . how about that?'

A long, long pause. Finally she said,

'Madison and 61st street, one o'clock,' and hung up.

I was well pleased with myself so I bought a dozen roses for Mrs Hudson and a few minutes before 1 o'clock took up my position, round my neck my blue and white scarf, in my buttonhole, my red carnation.

Keep moving in sub-zero weather whatever happens. Don't stand on windy street corners. By one-thirty, I was shivering and blue. By a quarter to two, I couldn't feel the end of my nose and the roses were turning black I was beginning to feel pretty stupid.

Just before two o'clock, a girl walked by and smiled sweetly, 'Good afternoon, Mr Niven,' she said. I took off my hat but she kept walking. Then a girl approached from the opposite direction, 'Good afternoon, Mr Niven.' Off came the hat . . . she kept going. Next three came by, arm in arm. 'Good afternoon, Mr Niven', they chorused.

Two went by on bicycles and four more in a taxi – she must have been awfully busy rounding up her friends but her masterstroke was the singing group from Western Union.

'Mr Niven?'

'Yes.'

'We have a message for you, sir. One! two! three! Happy lunchtime to you ... happy lunchtime to you ... happy lunchtime, dear David ... happy lunchtime to you.' I wish I could report a romantic aftermath to that episode but there was none.

In March I dropped in at a bar on 58th Street hoping to pull off a big sale. I didn't and was soon sipping a consoling drink and staring at the back-view of the first cowboy I had ever seen. He sported a black ten-gallon hat, black shirt with white buttons, a white kerchief at his throat and black levis tucked inside heavily worked high-heeled boots. He also wore a large pair of spurs. From the back he didn't look much like the traditional tall, lean, leathery man of the saddle. There was a white pudginess about his neck and a very definite bulge at his waistline. He stood no more than five feet four inches.

He finally got his drink and turned away from the bar, a bad move because his spurs became locked together, his drink went flying and he fell into my arms.

Doug Hertz, for as such he introduced himself, had a round, white face, small black eyes and a little black pencil moustache. It seemed doubtful that he could ever have been west of Brooklyn. The stories he told later of his childhood were conflicting, but I am sure I detected in his accent a mixture of the Mersey and Whitechapel somewhere under the other layers.

'Sorry, pardner,' he said, 'some dude gave me the elbow.'

Doug Hertz was a promoter of extravaganzas and sporting events. As the evening wore on it appeared that he had gone down with the *Lusitania*, bobbed up again and had the top of his head blown off in the Argonne.

'Under this,' he said, rapping two knuckles on a thick black thatch of curly hair, 'you'll find a steel plate ... hair grows like moss ... pull it out tonight and it's back in the morning.'

He had also it seemed worked as ranch hand, circus roustabout, oil rigger, bouncer and strike breaker. Looking at his small soft hands, I was doubtful.

'You got any dough, son?'

'None, I earn forty bucks a week.'

'That's tough, find me forty grand and I'll make you a million.'

The scheme he uncorked was wondrous.

'You've seen a rodeo, son, and you've seen a horse race. I'm gonna combine the two. Races that will last fifteen minutes.' He leaned forward, conspiratorially – 'INDOORS,' he hissed.

'Tell me more', I said.

'You kidding? I'm on to a goddam goldmine and I'm not giving it away to some jerk in a bar. . . . You come up with some heavy dough and I'll make you a partner. I'm gonna make me a fortune so if you want "in" . . . scratch around and come up with some rich pals. Here's my card – I'm at the Astor Hotel.'

I called Hertz early the next morning and invited him to meet me at '21' for lunch.

'You outta your skull?' he said, 'eating in joints like that? Boy, have you gotta lot to learn.'

He suggested I meet him in the lobby of the Astor and he would then show me the way to eat less expensively. I found him and we started walking. I told him about Lefty Flynn and Hertz immediately sparked to the idea that Lefty with his connections was the ideal man to enlist in the project. Then he initiated me into his cheap eating plan. It was beautiful in its simplicity. He chose a big busy restaurant around 48th Street. I entered alone and sat at a table for two. Then I ordered a cup of coffee and a doughnut and opened my daily paper. After a suitable interval, Hertz came in and joined me. Not a flicker of recognition passed between us. Hertz then commanded a huge meal of soup, steak, potatoes, pie and coffee. I continued reading my paper, drank a second cup of coffee and nibbled at my doughnut.

When Hertz had finished eating, he summoned the waitress and called for his check. This was my cue.

'Would you give me mine too, please?'

The waitress slapped the two checks on the table. When she had moved away and was busy elsewhere, Hertz picked up my check for the doughnut and two cups of coffee, marched briskly over to the cashier, paid and went out into the street.

I took my time, finished my reading, then picked up Hertz's very sizeable account.

'Oh waitress . . . look, there's a mistake here! I haven't had all this steak and pie and stuff . . . I've just had a doughnut and a couple of cups of coffee.'

Consternation and consultations followed but there was nothing for them to do but write out a second bill for two cups of coffee and a doughnut. I paid and joined Hertz at a prearranged street corner far away. A second busy restaurant was selected and there, following the same routine, Hertz got the doughnuts and coffee and I tucked in to a sizeable repast.

Lefty Flynn was always becoming involved in schemes to make his fortune overnight, so it was only natural that when I told him about Doug Hertz, he insisted on meeting him the very next day.

They made an extraordinary couple walking side by side down Fifth Avenue. Lefty towered over Doug by a good twelve inches in spite of Doug's high-heeled boots and high crowned hat.

Doug was obviously impressed by Lefty and I could see that he agreed with me that this great ex-athlete with his mass of friends could be more than useful in finding backing for his dream. Horse races lasting fifteen minutes! Over coffee he explained it to us in detail.

'Simple,' said Doug, 'you have four jockeys in each race and each jockey rides fifteen horses for one minute.'

Lefty's arithmetic was no stronger than mine and his fingers were working like a Turkish bazaar dealer's on an abacus.

'Why, that's sixty horses for each race,' he said finally.

'You said it . . . so we'll need about 150 horses all told for a card of six races – each horse running several times. Mind you this is the time to buy . . . polo ponies! That's what we want for this set-up. Who needs polo ponies in the winter? Nobody wants to feed the sons of bitches. . . . Polo ponies: that's what we have to get.'

'That' right,' echoed Lefty, slapping the lunch counter. 'We need polo ponies!'

I looked at him out of the corner of my eye . . . there was no question . . . he was hooked.

'It's just like a relay!' said Lefty, eyes gleaming.

'Just like a relay,' repeated Hertz, 'except the jockeys will have to ride a different way, for each minute, one bareback, another facing the pony's ass, another changing saddle, another changing mounts without touching the ground and so on.'

'Gee whiz,' said Lefty.

'And get this,' said Hertz, 'we'll be having better concessions, peanut concessions, liquor, hot-dogs, – kids, we're gonna clean up.' said Hertz.

Later that day we formed our company – *The American Pony Express Racing Association* – and pencilled in its officers. President, Maurice B. Flynn, Secretary and Treasurer, D. Niven. The experienced D. Hertz prudently kept his name off the books.

'We'll open in Atlantic City,' said Hertz.

'Where do we get the ponies?' I asked.

'Sales. Pick 'em up for peanuts. So long as they're sound, doesn't matter how mean they are.'

'Who's going to ride them?'

131

'Cowboys – I'll find them, a few ads in Montana and Oklahoma and we'll have all we want . . . thirty'll be enough.'

Lefty and I sat goggle-eyed as Hertz expanded.

'Atlantic City, Municipal Auditorium, then the Boston Garden, then the big one – Madison Square . . . we need working capital right now for offices and my living expenses so you fellas can get going and raise that dough. Forty people putting up a thousand bucks each'll do it.'

Lefty and I were mesmerized by Hertz. We became like two schoolboys who had wandered into a power station and pulled a switch. Everything suddenly started to happen.

The first person Lefty decided to approach was Damon Runyon.

Runyon loved the idea, promptly bought a thousand dollars' worth of stock and gave us a word of warning.

'Skip Atlantic City.'

'Why?'

'Unless you can make a deal with the guy who runs it.'

'Who's that?'

'"Pinkie", he runs the numbers, the protection and the whores. He even gets a piece of every slot machine on the Steel Pier . . . nobody gets into Atlantic City without Pinkie . . . don't try it.'

When we reported this conversation to Hertz, he pooh-poohed it. 'Oh, Pinkie won't bother us'.

Armed with our first thousand dollars, and with Damon Runyon's name as an investor, we soon found that it was not all that difficult to raise some more. Jack and Charlie bought a few shares and stifled sighs of relief when I told them I was leaving. Elsa Maxwell campaigned for us and the sudden arrival of two old friends from England, Dennis Smith-Bingham and Ian Galloway who both became shareholders and officers of the Board, helped to lay a fairly solid financial foundation.

Many people however were sceptical of our chances and at 1, William Street, the headquarters of Lehman Brothers, we had to throw in our reserves. I went downstairs and retrieved Hertz. We had left him sitting in full regalia in a waiting room.

Hertz was subjected to a barrage of technical questions about cash flow, contracts and projected earnings. He fielded them admirably but the day was not won till I remembered the steel plate on the top of his head.

'Oh, Doug . . . tell Mr Lehman about the Argonne.'

Hertz went into his routine about the hair growing like moss but still Lehman wavered.

'Pull a little out for Mr Lehman,' suggested Lefty.

Hertz was a brave as a lion. Without a murmur he seized a great hank of his forelock and pulled it out by the roots. Victory was ours. The hair never grew in again, of course. We didn't use this impressive 'ploy' too often but even so, by the time we had raised twenty-five thousand dollars, Doug Hertz's head looked like a diseased moorhen.

Hertz made a deal with a decaying Polo Club at Poughkeepsie, eighty miles away up the Hudson River. There was a ramshackle hotel on the property and Hertz persuaded the proprietors that they should give us free stabling for our ponies. In return we would provide a rodeo every Sunday for which they could sell tickets. The advance guard of ponies went to Poughkeepsie followed by a bus load of cowhands from Marland, Oklahoma, and six Indians whom 'Colonel' Zack Miller had persuaded to leave their reservation. I went up to take care of this group while Lefty and Hertz went to Atlantic City. A week later they returned, flushed with success, having landed a contract with the Municipal Auditorium for a Grand Opening in May.

Smith-Bingham and Galloway, both expert horsemen, moved up and training started with a vengeance ... it was needed. The cowboys, mostly old rodeo and circus hands, operated in a haze of bourbon and rye whisky, and the ponies, bought at an average price of around a hundred and twenty dollars, though sound in wind and limb were mostly quite mad.

'Excellent,' said Hertz, 'We'll have 'em running through the orchestra and jumping into the ringside seats.'

Our spartan life at Poughkeepsie was enlivened by the appearance of Hertz's blonde, statuesque wife who took an instant shine to Ian Galloway. One night there was an ugly scene when Hertz accused Ian of trying to seduce her in the stables. It ended with everyone getting drunk in the hotel and swearing eternal friendship but in the middle of the celebrations, Dennis Smith-Bingham rushed in. 'Come on, quick! somebody's left the door open and about forty ponies have got out ... they're all over the bloody country.' We dashed out.

It was a pitch black night so it took hours to round them up. The only casualty was Hertz who ran very fast straight into a large carthorse which was standing perfectly still in the middle of a field. The impact knocked him cold.

Training progressed and in a few weeks, we could see that we had a very exciting spectacle on our hands: the only problem was money. We were approaching our Grand Opening in Atlantic City and the cost of moving the whole cavalcade from Poughkeepsie was going to be astronomical. Hertz called an emergency meeting.

'We're in trouble, boys, we've gotta have another ten grand to get us to the opening. From there on in the show'll pay for itself but I've gotta have ten big ones this week or we fold.'

We were silent.

'Get on down to New York fellas and beat the bushes – I mean it – or we fold.'

Somehow we raised the money, and set off for Atlantic City on the appointed day.

The advance man had done his job with enthusiasm. Hoardings and walls were plastered with announcements of our coming and promises of what we were going to deliver. 'CHILLS, SPILLS AND THRILLS' – screamed the posters. Doug Hertz organized a parade from the railway station and tied up traffic all over town as a result. He rode at its head himself, an oval pouter-pigeon figure rolling slightly in the saddle as his round thighs tried to grip: he didn't really ride, he 'conned' horses into letting him sit on them.

The American Pony Express Racing Association was in Atlantic City for a week before the Grand Opening and Lefty and I often broached the subject of Damon Runyon's warning about the mysterious Pinkie which still nagged us.

'Nothing to worry about at all,' said Hertz confidently, 'I've seen the police, nobody's going to interfere with us.'

'How do we get any betting? It's illegal in the State of New Jersey.'

Hertz winked broadly. 'Everything is just Jim Dandy'.

On the night of the Grand Opening, it was pouring with rain but the lines were at the box office and by the time the parade started, the auditorium was packed—fifteen thousand people. Dorothy Fell and McClain came down with a big party from New York to cheer us on but we were so short of cash that we couldn't afford an orchestra for our opening night. The best we could provide was an organist. The organ blared out stirring music as the parade trotted round the arena.

A Master of Ceremonies, wearing full fox hunting regalia, explained over the loud speaker the finer points of the races. The teams of ponies were guaranteed to be evenly matched, he said, so it was a question of picking the jockey with the most prowess.

I had a feeling of cement in my stomach when the teams came out for the first race, but Hertz waddled about exuding confidence.

'Good luck, kids,' he said, to the riders, 'you're gonna be great.'
The ponies sensed the tension and acted up like thoroughbreds.
One or two which had been tubed whistled loudly through holes in
their necks. Suddenly the auditorium went dark except for the
bright floodlit track. Crack went the opening gun and away went the
first race. The entire audience rose to its feet. Terrible chances were
taken at the sharp turns. The cowboys excelled themselves, the
courageous Indians staged some hair-raising falls and at the end of
the evening we listened almost unbelievingly to loud and prolonged
applause.

'We're in business, kids,' said Hertz, clapping Lefty and me on
our backs. 'Next stop, Boston, then the Garden!'

The morning after, I was sitting in our little office in the
Auditorium smugly reading the reviews of our show in the local
press when four extremely hostile characters barged in. They wore
fedoras and tight double-breasted suits.

'Where's Hertz?' they demanded.

Almost before I could answer the avocado shape of our leader
appeared in the doorway behind them. When Hertz saw his visitors,
he went the colour of cat-sick.

'Okay,' said one of the hostile men to me, 'we don't need you –
beat it.' I left with what dignity I could summon.

For about twenty minutes, I watched the approach to our office
from a discreet distance and when I saw the men depart, I hurried
back in. Hertz was sitting slumped behind the desk. He looked
stricken.

'What did they want?' I asked.

Hertz smiled wanly.

'It was a shakedown,' he said, 'but nothing's gonna happen. Like
I said, I'm right in there with the cops.' He didn't sound too
confident and in the event, a number of things did happen. That
second night, we had a 'house' only slightly less well filled than the
previous one. Everything was going according to plan and the
audience was enjoying itself hugely. Suddenly, in the middle of the
second race, all the lights in the Auditorium went out. For a while
chaos reigned, ponies were crashing into each other, cowboys were
swearing and women were screaming. The lights stayed out for
fifteen minutes and the slow handclaps started. Finally, the lights
came on again and we restarted the show. During the fourth race,
the same thing occurred—Only this time, when the lights went on
again the people were streaming towards the exits and many went to
the box office and demanded their money back.

On the third night, it was discovered that at least half the cowboys had packed up and left during the day.

The next day, the forage for the animals never arrived and during the night a large number of saddles mysteriously disappeared.

On the fifth night, the lights went out again. More cowboys defected the next day and on the Saturday night, our show was pitiful. It didn't matter any more, the audiences had eroded to a point where only a handful had turned up.

Hertz, who had certainly never lacked courage, was stoic in defeat, but all chance of selling the show to other Auditoriums in the country had evaporated. We were living on a shoestring. Everything had depended on making a big profit during that first week.

It was decided to liquidate our assets immediately and salvage what we could from the wreck.

Lefty could take all the disappointments except the desertion of the cowboys. He had loved them dearly and he couldn't believe that they had allowed themselves to be induced to sink us. Sadly, he left for Greenwich and I stayed on to help Hertz arrange a sale of the livestock and remaining saddlery – all the assets we had. They didn't fetch much and by the time we had tied everything up in Atlantic City, I am afraid our gallant band of backers did not see very much of their original investment.

When I came to think of it, I too, was in far worse financial shape than when I had first become involved with the American Pony Express Racing Association and in addition, I had given up my job with Jack and Charlie but please don't feel that, at the end of this chapter, you are leaving me, like Pearl White, strapped to the financial railroad tracks, because, thank God, succour was already puffing towards me aboard the American Express.

10

Back in New York, I found a letter from Grizel. My mother, it appeared, had left everything to 'Tommy' in trust for the four of us, but she had stipulated something very important. Max had once borrowed £300 from her to bail himself out of debt, so if either Joyce or Grizel or I were in desperate need, the small estate must try to provide the same amount for us.

Within a week, I had collected my share. It came to a little over eight hundred dollars – I was rich.

Lefty and Norah had gone to Bermuda where they had rented a small cottage at Devonshire Bay. Lefty met me in Hamilton and I spent several blissful weeks on that spectacular island at a time that must have been its golden era. No cars, no motor cycles – just bicycles or horse-drawn carriages, no muttering groups at street corners, no sullen looks from under pork-pie hats, no cut-off conversations, just smiling happy faces and music everywhere.

Joe Benevides was our carriage driver, a mixture of negro and Portuguese blood. He had bright blue eyes and the broadest smile I had ever seen.

As we clip-clopped along the dazzling white coral road, we passed through orchid farms and dense plantations of palm trees. Bright hued little birds darted in and out of the oleander and giant hibiscus bushes and when we arrived at the cottage, the bay in front of it was aquamarine and the seagulls flying lazily in the blue above had long graceful forked tails.

'Norah's got a big surprise for you, Davey,' said Lefty, 'somebody very special is coming to supper tonight.'

In a day spent swimming on pink sand beach, reminiscing about our ill-fated venture and laughing – oh! how much we laughed – I forgot about my big surprise until Anthony Pleydell-Bouverie walked into the cottage, accompanied by a diminutive Finnish wife called Peanut.

Anthony was now flag lieutenant to Admiral Sir Ernle Erle Drax, commander-in-chief of a large fleet based on Bermuda. It was a classic reunion.

A week later, Tommy Phipps arrived. He had lately come back from California and was full of stories of Hollywood. He had also sold his first piece of writing, a short story, to *Harper's Bazaar*. The days flew by. We bicycled off in the mornings to various beaches or explored the Islands. We were never out of the water and became burned the colour of mahogany. I fell slightly in love with a dark haired beauty of eighteen from Richmond, Virginia. She wore a camellia in her hair on the night I took her for a romantic drive in the full moon. Joe Benevides, though himself the soul of tact on these occasions, sitting bolt upright on his box and staring straight ahead oblivious to what was going on behind him, had unknowingly sabotaged my very delicate preliminary moves by feeding his horse some wet grass. It is quite impossible to impress a beautiful girl with your sincerity if your carefully worded murmurings into a shell pink ear have to compete with a barrage of farts.

A lot of the time we spent planning our lives. Lefty and Norah had made up their minds to leave the suburbia of Greenwich for the real country. They had masses of places to choose from and plans and prospectuses went with us everywhere. Their hearts were more or less set on the little village of Tryon, North Carolina, nestling at the foot of the Smoky Mountains. There they had their eyes on a delicious low white frame farmhouse called Little Orchard.

Tommy had more or less decided to follow a literary career and looked like installing himself in New York.

I was the problem and much of the planning time was allotted to my future moves. A letter from Dennis Smith-Bingham decided them.

Lefty's stories of his time in Hollywood had fired my imagination. Then Tommy had stoked the fires. Now Dennis's letter clinched it.

Immediately after Atlantic City, he had left for California: 'This is a great spot. Come out and see for yourself,' he wrote. 'I'll find you a place to live.'

Deep down I had a sneaking feeling that I might be able to make a go of it in the movies. Norah and Lefty urged me on when I broached the idea but Tommy was more forthright – 'Your legs are too big,' he said.

Big legs or not, at the end of July, I packed my worldly belongings in my suitcase and the Flynns, Tommy, Anthony and the Peanut came to see me off. I sailed on a dirty old freighter for Cuba.

I had a week to wait in Cuba before the *President Pierce* sailed for the Panama Canal and California.

Havana enthralled me and I loved the gay jostling mobs but there was a strange undercurrent of uneasiness and much that I did not understand. A lot of heavily armed soldiers were about and almost as soon as I arrived I witnessed a very brutal arrest.

One night in Sloppy Joe's Bar, I met an Irishman. He explained what was going on. The power behind President Mendieta was his Chief of Staff, Batista – 'a ruthless bastard' according to my informant. 'He won't even let them have an election.' The Irishman was fascinating and, I think, a little mad. I met him every evening. He tried to sell me the idea of becoming a soldier of fortune with him and joining some strange group who were forming 'to fight for the rights of the people'.

One night, on my way to Sloppy Joe's, an English voice spoke to me from a doorway near the entrance to my cheap hotel.

'May I have a word with you?' The man was about 35 and wore a white linen suit.

'Of course.'

'You hold a British passport do you not?'

'Yes.'

'I'm from the British Embassy – how long are you planning to stay here?'

'I'm sailing on the *President Pierce*, the day after tomorrow.'

'Good. I hope you'll do just that. You've been seen with a man whom the local authorities don't view too highly. We got the word from them this morning. I suspect you have been followed, because they told me where to find you. Take my tip, don't miss that ship.'

He refused to join me for a drink and hurried away. I avoided Sloppy Joe's that night and was the first in the line when the gangway of the *President Pierce* was lowered.

When travelling I have always lived in the hope that I will find myself seated on planes next to the most beautiful girl. It never happens. Usually it is a mid-European business man who spreads himself over my seat and smokes a foul cigar.

I knew I would be sharing my cabin on the *President Pierce* with someone and I prayed that the agents might have slipped up and that I would find myself with one of the several attractive ladies I noticed going through the Immigration. My room mate turned out to be an Indian male – a Red Indian male but this was no lean copper-coloured warrior, mine was about two hundred and fifty pounds of pure blubber and he smelled like a badger. According to the purser, he had just become a millionaire because oil had been found on a small plot of land he owned in Oklahoma.

The *President Pierce* had started her cruise in New York so by the time I joined her everyone was more or less acquainted and I was the new boy in the school. Most of the passengers were elderly but there were a few families headed for Panama and California. It came as a rude shock when I realized the ship was 'dry'. I was fascinated by the passage through the Canal and at Panama, where we spent a day, I went ashore and played golf in a thunderstorm.

The smell of hot Indian was so overpowering in my cabin that I regularly slept in a deck chair behind a funnel.

I spent a great deal of time and energy avoiding the cruise director, a man who looked and behaved like a games-mistress.

'Come, come,' he would say, clapping his hands. 'Who's for shuffle board ... we don't want to get "pepless" do we? You look like a perfect ping-pong type', he said to me, just as I was settling down to a good book. 'This is Miss Weyhauser from Toledo, Ohio. She'll give you a good game ... come ... come....'

Miss Weyhauser had a small brother of nine and he became the bane of my existence – a really horrid little boy who wore white plus-fours, a white shirt and a red bow tie and a white peaked cap with a pom-pom on the top of it. His name was Cyrus – Cy for short – he never left my side. He was intrigued by my 'English accent' and followed me round all day saying, 'Pip-pip, old chappie. Jolly good show – what! any teabags anyone ... ?'

His father, not surprisingly, was a Hollywood scriptwriter.

Finally, after several warnings, I hit him. I was playing ping-pong with his sister and when Cyrus was not picking up the ball and throwing it overboard, he was pinching my bottom and crying out 'The Redcoats are coming,' so I let him have one really hard with the flat of my hand. It made a noise like a pistol shot. Everyone looked up from their chairs to find Cyrus lying on the deck holding the side of his face, pointing and howling, 'The Limey hit me! the Limey hit me!'

Miss Weyhauser took a backhander at me with her ping-pong racquet and said, 'Oh! how dare you strike a child!' The cruise director materialized as if by magic.

'Well, we all thought you were a gentleman!' he swished off and picked up the blubbering little brute and cradled him in his arms.

That night the cruise director said he thought it might be a nice gesture if I apologized publicly to Cyrus and his mother after dinner. I had nothing to lose; no one was speaking to me anyway, so in the lounge, I stood up and asked for attention. I said that I was really sorry that it had happened and begged them all not to think it was typical of my race. 'I am an orphan,' I said. 'I was abandoned in a cemetery by my mother when I was a few weeks old. I never knew who my father was. I was brought up by the parson but he drank the

Communion wine and beat me every Sunday night.' I went on along those lines. I was good – there was no question, and as I warmed to my work, I saw several good ladies sniffling and taking out their handkerchiefs. I began to wonder if my trip to Hollywood might perhaps not be in vain.

I sat down to rapturous applause. My apology was accepted with smug bad grace by Cyrus and his mother and for the remaining days of the voyage, he redoubled his efforts to annoy me. I got even with the little sonofabitch on the day we docked at San Pedro.

'I'm really sorry, Cy, about what happened,' I said.

'Oh, that's okay, Limey, forget it.'

'No, really, Cy, to show there's no hard feelings, come and have an ice cream soda with me.'

'Okay.'

We sat on two stools at the only bar in the ship.

'Banana split with cream?'

'Okay.'

Then a little later,

'How about a chocolate sundae with pistaccio nuts?'

'Okay.'

'A nice prune whip and caramel sauce?'

'Okay.'

I must say it was an expensive revenge. He was a veritable human disposal, but finally, after about seven mountainous concoctions his colour began to change.

His mother's last-minute packing must have been interesting.

Dennis had cabled that he would meet the ship and there he was with a beautiful golden-haired girl. I recognized her at once as Sally Blane, a fast-rising young star of the movies.

The usual shipboard reporters were sniffing around for stories. They spotted Sally and I found myself improvising about the pony racing and my plans. The next day, there was a picture of me in the Los Angeles *Examiner* with the caption – 'BRITISH SPORTSMAN ARRIVES, PLANS TO BUY OVER A HUNDRED HEAD OF POLO PONIES.'

Sally was marvellous, endowed with a lovely open face. 'It's all arranged,' she said. 'Mom's got a room for you. You are going to come and visit with us till you find somewhere to live.'

Mrs Belzer was Sally's mother and with her three other daughters she lived in a charming colonial style house on Sunset Boulevard between Holmby Hills and Westwood.

On the drive up from San Pedro, we passed first through oil fields and citrus groves, then we stayed on the Coastal Highway with the endless sandy beaches and pounding Pacific surf on the left. In the distance, were the high hills behind Los Angeles and far away to our right, the snowy top of Mount Baldy.

Mrs Belzer was a beautiful woman, wonderfully sweet and seemingly vague with an impeccable taste in antique furniture. The girls all worshipped her.

When I met the others I gaped. They were all spectacular beauties. Blonde Georgiana was the youngest, only about eleven. Polly Ann Young, an excellent and successful actress, was the oldest, probably twenty-two, a glowing brunette. Then there was Gretchen, Gretchen was already a big movie star and her working name of Loretta Young was known all over the world.

There has never been in my experience such a beautiful family to look at, and the beauty came from within because each and every one of them was filled with concern for others, and kindness, and generosity.

They have never changed.

It was impossible to lie to people like these so when Dennis, a few days later, left suddenly for England, I confessed one night to Mrs Belzer and the girls that I was hoping to break into movies. I felt an idiot doing it in front of three already established professionals but they took it in their stride and took great care not to put me off by telling me too many facts that I was soon to discover for myself.

The next day I got my first taste of a major studio. Loretta was making a picture at Fox, something about hospital nurses and it was arranged that when the family car came to fetch her in the evening, I would be smuggled past the eagle-eyed police at the gate lying on the floor under a rug.

Once inside the gate it was a dream world. The car slipped through Indian villages, jungles, sections of Venice, complete Western streets, New York streets and past a French château and a lake with a large schooner and native canoes on it.

The studio buildings, the executive offices, cutting rooms, fire department, casting office and the huge towering sound stages seemed like a miniature city and everywhere the streets teemed with cowboys, Indians, Southern gentlemen, soldiers, policemen, troupes of dancers and tall willowy show girls. I just gaped and gaped and wondered if I could ever be part of it.

Loretta's driver took me inside stage 19 and I watched fascinated from a dark corner while she was powdered and primped and prepared for a close-up. What a strange, wonderful secret world! It pulled me like a magnet.

I really cannot remember what I was using for money at that time. I know I didn't borrow any and I don't remember stealing but I do know that within a few days of arrival, I realized the vastness of the distances and the urgent necessity for some wheels and for an augmentation of my funds.

The girls took me to a used car lot in Culver City and I bought a very old Auburn for ninety dollars. It went quite well on the flat but hated hills and the small incline of the Bel Air driveway could only be negotiated in reverse.

They also helped me in my search for a place to live. They never gave any sign of it but they must have prayed that I would soon be successful. It is with great embarrassment that I have to record that nothing suitable was found for a considerable time.

The Central Casting Office was down on Western Avenue. It handled only the 'extras'. Anybody who spoke lines was a 'bit player' or a 'small part actor' – these the studios employed through agents. In the Auburn I drove to Central Casting thinking that all I had to do was enrol myself and go to work. It was a forbidding moment. Outside the building was a large sign:

'DON'T TRY TO BECOME AN ACTOR. FOR EVERYONE WE EMPLOY, WE TURN AWAY A THOUSAND.'

I stood in a long line and finally was interviewed by a brisk elderly woman with protruding teeth and glasses so dark that I could not see her eyes.

'Yes?'

'I'd like to be a movie actor.'

'So would millions of others. What professional experience have you?'

'None, I'm afraid.'

'Nationality?'

'British.'

'Do you realize how many Americans there are looking for work these days?' Before I could answer, she went on, 'Well, the studios are making a lot of British stories right now so we might find something for you ... fill in this form and mail it to us ... you got a work permit okay?'

'Work permit?'

'You can't work without one – it's against the law. You got one?'

'No.'

'Give me back that form ... the way out's over there.'

There is an antidote to everything, even, we are told, hopefully, to the Intercontinental Ballistic Missile, and usually, when those old Chinese weeds we wrote about earlier start clogging up the garden and things look pretty hopeless, out of the blue comes a weed-killer.

The weed-killer at this point was Alvin Weingand, later a highly respected Congressman from California, but then a junior reception clerk at the Roosevelt Hotel on Hollywood Boulevard. My search for cheap accommodation had not been going well and Al gave me a room between a service elevator and a huge machine that shrieked and thumped all night as it inhaled warm air, cooled it and belched it downstairs for the benefit of the guests. When I say 'gave' me the room, he charged me so little that it amounted almost to a gift. I had a bed, a shower and a telephone. I needed no more.

Unpacking, I came across a telephone number – a girl I had met in New York, Lydia Macy, who lived in Montecito, eighty miles away. I called her and was invited for the weekend.

Not feeling I could trust the Auburn to undertake such a long trip, I packed my bag, including my frayed and frightful dinner jacket, and thumbed a ride up the US Highway 101 arriving in Montecito in a fruit truck, in plenty of time for dinner. Montecito has more resident millionaires per acre than any other community in the United States. The houses are beautiful; the mountains behind them are purple in the evening light and between them and the white sandy beaches lies a palm-covered plateau, inhabited by charming lotus-eaters.

On the Saturday morning, I looked out of my bedroom window and, riding at anchor in the bay, off Santa Barbara, I beheld an old friend, HMS *Norfolk*, a county class cruiser. She had been in Malta when I was there and more lately, I had found her again in Bermuda. Now, she was on a goodwill tour of the West Coast of Mexico, the United States and Canada.

I told Lydia that I would love to go and visit her as I knew several people on board – 'Well, you're going tonight,' said Lydia. 'The officers are giving a party and all of Montecito is going.'

That night, in a dinner jacket that had been rejuvenated by Lydia's maid, I escorted her on board *Norfolk*.

A huge awning covered the after-deck and she was dressed with garlands of lights and bunting. The Royal Marine Band was grinding out a foxtrot . . . I looked around for a familiar face and nearly fell over the side – there stood Anthony Pleydell-Bouverie. Apparently, Admiral Sir Ernle Erle Drax had decided to join the cruise and his flag lieutenant had come too.

Poor Lydia! I didn't behave very well. The reunions were continuous and strenuous and I spent far too long in the wardroom. She left without me. All guests were asked to be off the ship by three a.m. At about that time, I mumbled to Anthony that it was time I left.

'Nonsense,' he said, 'don't go ashore ... we'll look after you ... there's a bunk you can have ... go to bed and have a nice rest.'

It sounded fine and I was past being analytical anyway, so I removed my clothes and fell immediately into a deep black sleep.

Next morning, about ten-thirty, I woke with a mouth like the inside of a chauffeur's glove – nobody was around. It was Sunday and the ship's company was at Divine Service. I looked out of the port-hole and couldn't see much except sea and the sea was passing the window at a great rate.

I lay there wondering what to do next. Whatever Anthony had said, it made no sense to be at sea, in the middle of the Pacific, in one of His Majesty's county class cruisers ... in broad daylight ... in a dinner jacket.

I continued to lie there. About noon a sailor poked his head round the door.

'Compliments of the Ward Room, sir, the officers would like to see you.'

I doused my head with cold water, donned my crumpled suit and followed him through the humming interior maze of the ship. Sailors gave me surprised glances as I passed.

Several of last night's drinking companions were already at the bar.

'Morning, Niven – pink gin?'

'Yes, thanks.'

'Enjoy yourself, last night? Pretty girl you had with you,' – small talk, chatter, more pink gin, no sign of Anthony and nobody bringing up the question of why I was still with them.

I thought to myself, 'Well, I'd better just play this by ear ... if they're not going to mention it – I'm not' – so I relaxed, joined in the small talk, accepted the pink gins and closed my mind to the future.

At last, Anthony appeared. 'Sorry,' he said. 'I've been with the Admiral. He wants to see you!'

'Like this?' I said, looking down.

'You look fine,' said Anthony, 'let's go – he's waiting for you.'

By now I was sure I was going to be made to walk the plank.

In the Captain's dining-room, the Admiral was waiting, a spare, ruddy, typical sailor.

'Morning, Niven.'
'Morning, sir.'
'Enjoy yourself last night?'
'Very much, thank you, sir.'
'Care for a pink gin?'
'Thank you, sir.'

There I stood in my dinner jacket, wondering, and there half an hour later, I sat having luncheon, still wondering. Small talk, shop talk, Malta talk, Bermuda talk but the subject of my presence never broached.

Towards the end of the meal, a signalman knocked and entered. He handed the Admiral a message using the flat white top of his headgear as a tray.

'H'm,' said the Admiral, 'HMS *Bounty* off the starboard bow . . . Niven, look out there and see if you can see her, will you?'

I moved to the indicated port-hole wondering if delirium tremens was always so fascinating. I had just finished reading Nordhoff and Hall's brilliant historical novel which Lefty had taken to Bermuda.

Sure enough, I beheld the *Bounty* with all sails set, moving gently on the Pacific swells. Suddenly, little white puffs of smoke like cotton wool erupted from her side, followed by the champagne cork pops of her cannon. HMS *Norfolk* slowed to a dead stop. The *Bounty* came close and I could see her crew wearing pig-tails and striped stockings, then victory cheers floated across the water. I turned towards the Admiral and Anthony and they both burst out laughing.

'This is where you get off, young man,' said the Admiral.

As he led me on deck, Anthony explained that the great Metro Goldwyn Mayer producer, Irving Thalberg, was about to make a film of *Mutiny on the Bounty*. A complete replica of the original eighteenth-century warship had been built and now, as a publicity stunt for the promotion of the picture, a meeting with its modern counterpart had been arranged in the Catalina Channel.

A rope ladder was dropped over the side and, an incongruous figure in my dinner jacket and cheered on by Anthony and a large number of the ship's company, I clambered nervously down on to the deck of the press tender which had materialized alongside.

Several of today's Hollywood Press Corps, including Jimmy Starr of the Los Angeles *Herald Express* and Bill Mooring of *Tidings*, witnessed my arrival and I got the reputation of being the first man to crash Hollywood in a battleship.

Also on the tender were Frank Lloyd, the director of the picture, and Robert Montgomery, one of the reigning Hollywood stars. Clark Gable and Charles Laughton who were to make the film as Fletcher Christian and Captain Bligh were not present. Bob Montgomery had come along for the ride. The camera crews, the press, Frank Lloyd and Montgomery were most hospitable to their unexpected charge and as *Norfolk* gathered speed and resumed her course south, I was carried unprotesting for the second time in about three weeks to the port of San Pedro.

Montgomery had a new sports Bentley – very impressive for me to see this beautiful machine so far from home and very helpful to me when he offered me a lift to MGM studios, which lay some hundred miles north.

We arrived at about seven o'clock just as the day's work was coming to an end. The departing crowds of extras stood, respectfully, aside as Montgomery was saluted through the main gate by the studios' police.

Frank Lloyd offered me a drink in his office and there I met another great director of the day, Edmund Goulding.

Goulding had lately completed the epic *Grand Hotel* with Garbo, John Barrymore, Joan Crawford, Wallace Beery and a host of other great names as his stars. He was about to start a film with Ruth Chatterton.

Goulding was about five feet ten of square stocky build, sandy hair and a broken nose spread half way across his face. About forty, a man of enduring charm, I owe more to him than to anyone else in the business.

Goulding was wearing the Goulding uniform – sweat shirt, silk handkerchief round his neck, a blue blazer and white slacks turned up at the bottoms displaying highly polished loafers. He laughed with a deep rumble when he heard from Frank Lloyd about my arrival on *Norfolk*.

'Ever done any acting?' he asked.

'None to speak of.'

'Good. I'm looking for a new face to play the drunken, dissolute, younger brother of Chatterton. Will you make a test for me tomorrow?'

I thought it better with this wonderful opportunity being dangled before me to leave nothing unsaid that ought to be said so I told him about my abortive trip to Central Casting a few days before.

'No problem,' said Goulding, 'you don't need any permit to make a test ... if it works out, the studio will arrange things.'

147

'What do I have to do?'

'Just be yourself . . . Harry Bouquet, the test director, will make it – he'll give you something easy to do.' Goulding then invited me to his home for dinner. He was married to the famous dancer, Marjorie Moss. Even then she was dying. Goulding knew, she didn't.

After dinner when I made a move to go home, Goulding and Marjorie would have none of it.

'Why?' they asked.

'To sleep, shave and change.'

'You can sleep and shave here,' said Goulding, 'but I want that test made exactly as you are now – in that dinner jacket.'

The next morning at 8.30 a.m. I presented myself to Harry Bouquet on stage 29. I had been painted a strange yellow ochre by Bill Tuttle in the make-up department and my eyes and lips were made up like a Piccadilly tart – I felt ridiculous.

Harry Bouquet, a frustrated man, was in a hurry. 'Christ,' he said, 'I've got six of these goddamned things to get through by lunch time; whaddaya gonna do?'

'Mr Goulding said you'd give me something easy,' I said.

'Jesus! nothing's easy in this business! Okay, stand over there by that table while they light you.'

The set was decorated as a New York apartment. Under the bright lights I could vaguely make out the outlines of the camera and about forty people. A man with evil-smelling fingers stuck a light meter immediately beneath my nose.

'Light 'em all,' came a voice from the camera – 'Okay, Harry, let's go.'

Bouquet loomed out of the shadows.

'Okay now, start off facing the camera, then turn slowly when I tell you – wait a beat at each profile. Then wind up facing the camera again, got it?'

'Yes, sir.'

'Turn 'em over.'

I stood blinded by the lights and stared in the direction of the camera like a dog watching a snake.

'Turn slowly,' said Bouquet, 'hold the profile, goddammit . . . Okay, now hold the full face . . . try to come alive for Chrissake . . . tell us a funny story.'

Out of my panic and my subconscious came a very old school boy limerick. I recited it.

There once was an old man of Leeds
Who swallowed a packet of seeds,
Great tufts of grass
Shot out of his arse
And his cock was covered in weeds

'Cut ! ! !'

Bouquet loomed up again. 'Whattayou trying to do for Chrissake! Get me fired? Everyone sees these things ... L.M. Mayer ... Mannix, the whole bunch.'

He softened and smiled, 'Okay, kid, now relax, we'll pick it up from there ... think of some little story. When you're ready tell me and we'll shoot it ... clean it up though willya.'

Finally, I recounted a story that had happened to Tommy Phipps when he first went into an automat. Not knowing how it worked, he put five cents in the slot machine for a cup of coffee and collected a jet of hot fluid in the fly buttons. Later somebody ate his sandwich and somebody else dunked their doughnut in the coffee he had finally managed to collect in a cup.

I had laughed when Tommy told it and there was, I thought, quite a gratifying reaction when I had finished this homely little tale.

The next day, Goulding called me and told me to meet him at his office.

'That test was really pretty bad – apart from the natural bit when you told the limerick. Except for that you were all frozen up. You won't get the part this time. L.B. wants Louis Hayward anyway ... but I think you can make it and I'm going to help you. I'll be through with my picture in about twelve weeks, till that's over I can do nothing – call me in three months and we'll see what can be done.'

Al Hall was Mae West's director and she was about to start a picture at Paramount – *Going to Town*. Goulding told Hall about me. Hall got hold of my test and a week later I got a call from the Paramount Casting Office. Mae West would like to interview me as her possible leading man.

I was welcomed at Paramount almost with eagerness. Anybody Mae West might want, they might want too, so before I was even seen by Miss West, I found myself being asked if I would be interested in a seven-year contract with options. Did I have a work permit? – 'No.' – 'Never mind, we can fix that.'

I was ushered into a huge office and seated behind a Mussolini-type desk was a small round platinum blonde woman flanked on one

149

side by a large American-Irish manager, and on the other by the diminutive Al Hall.

She never spoke. The men asked various questions. Then, after a whispered conversation Al Hall said, 'Would you mind taking off your coat? And your shirt?'

'Now turn around, please.'

More whispers, then the manager spoke.

'Who is your agent?'

'I don't have one.'

Incredulous looks were passed.

'We'd like to see you again. Please be sure that Casting knows where you are.'

The men rose and shook hands cordially, Mae West said nothing.

The next day, I had an urgent call from the Paramount Casting Office. I also had a visitor. A pale-faced man in a dark suit was waiting for me in the hotel lobby.

'I'm from United States Immigration Service, Mr Niven. Now let me see . . .' he had some documents, 'you arrived in San Pedro four week ago. You asked for and were granted a ten days' visitors' visa. You are, therefore, now in this country illegally. We also understand you are contemplating signing an employment contract with a US firm, so you are about to break the law on a second count.'

'What do I do?' I asked.

He was a kind man but a tired one. He must have been through this a thousand times. His voice was weary.

'You have twenty-four hours to be off United States territory – you understand that don't you?'

'Yes.'

'Then sign this.'

I glanced at a mimeographed slip, it was a statement admitting that I had been told to leave and that I understood the dire penalties involved if I did not comply.

'Where the hell do I go?'

'That's your problem, son. If you want to work in this country, you must get a Resident Alien Visa. So long now.'

Al Weingand advised me and that afternoon I boarded a train that clanked and bumped for hours through a sandstorm to the border post of Calexico. There I left the United States and walked on foot into Mexico.

Mexicali may be a thriving metropolis by now. I hope it is, for its own sake. In late 1934, it was the most awful dump I had ever seen. A single dirt road ran through the centre of a small township and petered out at each end into dry brown hills. In the centre of the town there was one dilapidated hotel, a few broken-down lodging houses, a grocery store that must have been the official breeding ground for all the flies in Northern Mexico and one small clean-looking house, the American Consulate.

The American Consul was a busy man, mostly because he had to cope with the problems and grievances of the sad daily flow of underpaid Mexicans who crossed the border to be driven in stinking buses to work crippling hours picking fruit, cotton and vegetables in the Imperial Valley.

He advised me kindly that he would be able to arrange a visa for me as a Resident Alien in the US but first I must produce my birth certificate and a copy of my police record from Scotland Yard.

I took a room for a dollar a night in a loathsome lodging house and sent my sister Grizel a cable – 'SEND BIRTH CERTIFICATE IMMEDIATELY'. She got the cable two weeks later when she returned from a trip to Spain. She did not distinguish herself by her reply – WHOSE BIRTH CERTIFICATE? I really had to sweat it out – there was little transatlantic air mail in those days. The mail service to Mexicali via Mexico City must have gone by donkey. My little pile of money was dwindling alarmingly but many Americans came to Mexicali to hunt quail and other game in the surrounding brown hills. I became the 'gun man' in the only moderately clean bar in the town and in exchange for chili or tortillas, I cleaned and polished the guns while their owners drank and boasted. Sometimes I was given a tip. I never refused.

It was just after New Year's Day 1935 when I triumphantly presented myself at the US Border at Calexico, in my hand was my Resident Alien Visa – my permit to work.

I jumped trucks back to Los Angeles. Al Weingand let me have my old room back and manfully swallowed the difficulties of payment.

I telephoned Goulding, but he had finished his picture and gone to New York. Mae West, I learned, was halfway through her picture with an unknown English actor called Paul Cavanagh playing opposite her.

I visited Central Casting and after an agonizing wait of several days, was finally accepted and enrolled as 'Anglo-Saxon Type No. 2008'.

Such was the efficiency of Central Casting that the first call I got to work as a professional actor, was as a Mexican.

Los Angeles is one of the largest cities in area in the world. The film studios are mostly strategically placed in far away suburbs miles from its centre. Universal Studios is in the San Fernando Valley. I was told to be there at 5 a.m. The Auburn broke down the night before so I started a zig-zag journey across the city by street car at 3 o'clock.

Once at the studios, I was handed a chit through a small window and instructed to report to wardrobe. There, I waited in line, showed my chit which was stamped, and was issued with a baggy white suit, a large sombrero, some sandals and a blanket.

I changed in a huge barn-like dressing room. Other 'Mexicans' were putting on their outfits. 'Indians' were also preparing themselves and honest townsfolk were getting in to tail-coats, top hats and bowlers. The women 'extras' were dressing in an adjacent barn.

I followed my fellow 'Mexicans' to the make-up department and once more stood in line. While those, including myself, who had fair skins were sprayed with a brown mixture from a spray gun, on some of us they glued moustaches. The 'Indians' lined up opposite were being similarly treated all over their bodies with a reddish colour. Somewhere the Chinese were getting it in yellow.

There was not much happy chatter, I noticed.

At six-thirty, we were all marshalled by an assistant director and loaded into buses for a one hour drive to a remote movie ranch where the permanent Western town had been erected. There we were positioned by other assistants and told when to move slowly, when to scatter in alarm, etc., etc. The cowboy star, whoever he was, appeared and at eight o'clock sharp shooting started. The director's name was Aubrey Scotto. He did not bother with us, we were pushed around all day by a harrassed assistant.

At one o'clock we were given a cardboard box and told we had half an hour to eat. The contents consisted of a piece of chicken fried in batter, some cookies, an orange and a small carton of milk. After lunch we resumed shooting till the sun became too low and its light too feeble to continue.

There had been a lot of pushing and pulling by the extras during the filming of the last scene, it being essential to be 'established' so that you would automatically be called back the following day.

Back at the studios, I waited my turn to wash the make-up off in a basin. When I handed in my moustache and clothing, my chit was stamped again – then a last long wait at the cashier's office to present my chit and be paid.

I was lucky enough to get a lift back to Hollywood from a group who had lived there but even so it was ten o'clock before I sat down on a stool in the drugstore for the '50 cents Blue Plate Special.' My salary for my first day as a professional actor amounted to two dollars and fifty cents.

My fellow extras, I discovered during the next few weeks, fell into two distinct categories. There were the professional 'crowd artistes' and the actors who were 'would-be stars'.

The professionals were content to remain extras. They had no acting ambitions. They worked all the angles and were not above slipping a percentage of their daily salaries to unscrupulous assistant directors to guarantee being 'called' next day. Among these 'professionals' could be counted the specialists such as the mounted extras, who worked almost exclusively in Westerns, and the Dress Extras. This last named group were much more highly paid, getting as much as twenty dollars a day because they provided their own modern wardrobe for every occasion, including evening dress for the women, white tie and tails for the men, beach outfits, city outfits, and the correct clothes for race meetings, football games, fox hunting and graduation days.

The acknowledged leaders of the professional Dress Extras were two elderly English people, Mrs Wicks and a white-moustached ex-Indian Army man known as 'the Major'.

This couple were in great demand, lending dignity and refinement to the drabbest pictures. They had their own little coterie of friends and, sitting in full evening dress, they all played bridge together from morning to night.

There were a few younger professional Dress Extras also totally devoid of acting ambition and perfectly content to put on their smart clothes and work two or three days a week. Stuart Hall was one of these. Born in Cyprus, he had been brought to California as a child and had drifted into the movies. Stuart was a striking looking man of my age. He was constantly being offered small speaking parts: he always refused them.

I did not have the finances to set myself up as a Dress Exra but Stuart became a good friend and if we were called to the same studio, he always gave me a lift.

The 'would-be stars' did everything decently or indecently possible to get themselves placed in foregrounds with a chance of being noticed, and people in this group were occasionally singled out to say a line or play a small 'bit'. At night they went to acting schools or formed small theatre groups. The studios sent talent scouts to cover these showcases. Unless you were a big star brought out specially from Broadway, the only door into Hollywood was within Hollywood itself.

These were the golden days. The movie business was booming. Hundreds of films were being made each year and there was little competition in the entertainment world. Television had not been heard of. Night football and night baseball were in the future. Nobody played bingo or went bowling.

This was the era of the Great Stars. The studios had not yet been emasculated by the Supreme Court in anti-trust suits and the newspapers still had several pages each day devoted to nothing but Hollywood news and gossip.

The studios looked ahead and carefully built up their stables of favourites. When I worked in crowds at Metro Goldwyn Mayer I used to stare in awe at the names on the dressing room doors ... Garbo, Gable, Norma Shearer, Jean Harlow, Joan Crawford, W.C. Fields, Wallace Beery, Spencer Tracy, Hedy Lamarr, William Powell, Myrna Loy, Louise Rainer, Robert Montgomery, Lionel Barrymore, John Barrymore, Charles Laughton and the Marx Brothers.

The supporting actors were a powerful lot too. Frank Morgan, Louis Calhern, Robert Young, Franchot Tone, Reginald Owen, Lewis Stone, H.B. Warner. And the 'babies', some of them doing their school work in little canvas cubicles on the sound stages – so many hours each day by Californian law ... Elizabeth Taylor, Mickey Rooney, Lana Turner, Judy Garland and Ava Gardner. All those under contract to one studio at the same time.

Other studios had their stables too. James Cagney, Pat O'Brien, Edward G. Robinson and Bette Davis were at Warners, Gary Cooper, Charles Boyer, Claudette Colbert and Marlene Dietrich at Paramount, while Fred Astaire, Ginger Rogers and Cary Grant reigned at RKO.

Small wonder that young people with stars in their eyes flocked to Hollywood from all parts of the world. There was hardly a beauty contest winner anywhere who didn't hopefully book a one way ticket.

Small wonder ... outside Central Casting ... 'DON'T TRY AND BECOME AN ACTOR. FOR EVERYONE WE EMPLOY WE TURN AWAY A THOUSAND'. And small wonder that behind cosmetic counters, serving as car hops and waitresses, selling theatre tickets, swim suits, ice creams, or their bodies, were the most beautiful girls in the world.

I soon got the feel of it and was able to take short cuts. Friends among the extras tipped me off about jobs that might be coming up, and riding very much with the Sandhurst 'forward seat', I worked in a number of Westerns.

I got to know a few assistant directors and they put me on their personal lists. I also made the rounds of all the studio casting offices when the Auburn was in the mood.

Once or twice a week, I worked as deck-hand on a swordfish boat operating out of Balboa.

Chet Leibert had a forty-five foot charter boat rigged up for marlin fishing with rod and line from the stern and a ten-foot spear platform forward for tackling the giant broadbill. He was a dour, rather unpleasant man, but a wonderful fisherman, and generous. He gave me six dollars a day, more if we had fish to sell, and allowed me to keep my tips. I enjoyed the fishing more than the filming.

I don't believe this is one of the thoughts of Chairman Mao but breaks, good or bad, do come when you least expect them.

I had been doing a fruitless round of the studio casting offices and my last port of call was the United Artists studio on Santa Monica Boulevard... 'Nothing just now, call next week'.... So that the sanctity of the studio could be preserved, the entrance to the Casting Office was separated from the main gate by a twelve foot high wall of wire netting. I was walking out again when I was hailed from a large limousine on the other side of the cage. 'Hi! how's the golf?' It was the great Douglas Fairbanks himself. He never forgot a face but he had the greatest difficulty in coming up with a name to match it.

Soon I was on his side of the barricade and setting him right that I was not Bobby Sweeny. He asked what I was doing in Hollywood and I told him. He thought for a moment and said kindly,

'Gee, I hope you make it ... I'm here with Sylvia at the Beach House and we'd love to see you any time you like. I'd like to take you to play at Bel Air – it's a great course. Come around, I mean it, any time but please don't ask me to help you with your career.'

This was the completely honest expression of a completely honest man and a breath of fresh air in a place where the empty promise was the easy way out.

'Now,' he said, 'I'm going to take a steam – come on in and join me.'

Actually, I would have preferred the offer of a good hot meal but I gratefully tagged along. He greeted everyone he passed with a wide smile and 'Hi! how are you'. It was obvious that he was greatly loved but he was never quite sure who was loving him.

Inside the steam room, I was introduced to various mist-shrouded figures and I found myself sitting stark naked on a marble slab between Darryl Zanuck, the head of Twentieth Century, a new thrusting company which he was just forming, and Joe Schenck, his partner. Opposite sat Charlie Chaplin and Sid Grauman, a famous theatre owner. Present too were Bill Goetz, another associate of Zanuck's, Lew Schreiber, his casting director, Bill Dover, Sam the Barber and Aiden Roark.

The sight and proximity of these great men, combined with the intense heat was almost too much for me but I decided to sit there if it took all night. It might lead to something. They were used to these steam baths. I wasn't. After ten minutes, my lungs felt scalded and my head was spinning.

Fairbanks, above all, loved jokes of any sort, funny jokes, practical jokes, any jokes. He had, of course, caught on that I was practically broke so he couldn't resist saying,

'Oh, Niven, what are you planning this winter? Playing polo or bringing the yacht round?'

'Polo . . . polo,' I croaked and made for the exit. Sam the Barber grabbed me before I fell to the marble floor and put me forcibly into the ice-cold plunge. I was reviving when the others came out of the steam room.

'Doug says you played for the British Army,' said Zanuck.

'Well, I played a bit in Malta,' I mumbled.

'Come and play a few chukkas on Sunday. We'll have a good game.'

'Er . . . my clothes haven't arrived yet, I'm afraid.'

'Aiden here will fix you up.'

Aiden Roark was a ten goal international. He and his brother Pat both played for Great Britain. Now he was employed by Zanuck in some capacity and organized Zanuck's polo team. A quiet, dark haired, olive-skinned Irishman, he looked more like a South American. I decided to tell him the truth and in a corner, I explained my limitations.

'Don't worry about it – I'll lend you all the stuff you need. Just play a couple of chukkas – you'll have fun.'

So it was arranged. I was to play polo at the Uplifters Club the following Sunday afternoon with Darryl Zanuck! How many two dollars and fifty cents 'extras' were getting that break?

On the fateful day, Aiden Roark lent me some jodhpurs that were much too tight and drove me to the ground. The first thing that worried me was when I noticed that the stands were full of people.

Douglas Fairbanks and the gorgeous Sylvia Ashley were in a box. The second thing which unnerved me was the sight of the other players. Among them were 'Big Boy' Williams, a formidable performer, Elmer Boseke and Cecil Smith, both ten-goal internationals. The final thing, and this nearly completed my disintegration, was the sight of 'Saint George'.

'Saint George' was a white Arab stallion. He bit savagely at everything in sight and at that moment, a groom was struggling to put him into a muzzle.

'You can play Saint George,' said Aiden. 'Play him in the first and fourth chukkas. It's only a pick up game. You play at number one and I'll hit the ball up to you ... Mark Darryl, he's playing back on the other team ... wear the red vest.'

The bell went. It was a nightmare. I didn't know who was playing in which position on what team. Those great experts were hitting the ball like a rocket from every direction but during that first chukka, I was far too busy stopping Saint George from leaving the ground altogether to care. When Aiden passed the ball up to me, I made vague flourishes at it with my stick but quickly needed both hands again to control the brute. It was during one of these mad dashes that Saint George kicked a goal.

Zanuck I tried to cover but generally passed him at high speed without making contact.

At the end of the first chukka, Aiden was laughing so much he could hardly change ponies.

'Come back in for the fourth one ... you'll find him easier now he's worked some of it off.'

I toyed with the idea of slinking from the ground but I still hoped that I might impress Zanuck and further my movie career so I waited apprehensively for my next appearance. My riding muscles, suddenly forced into violent action, were now reacting and causing me to shake like a leaf. This did not go unnoticed by Saint George when I mounted him once more for the fourth chukka.

I was determined to make my mark on Zanuck and I stayed as close to him as Saint George would let me. I even hit the ball a couple of times which encouraged me enormously. The experts continued to charge about playing a spectacular game shouting oaths and instructions at each other but Aiden, I suspected, had deliberately stopped sending the ball up to me. It all seemed more peaceful.

Suddenly, 'Big Boy' Williams, renowned as one of the longest hitters in the game, connected from the far end of the ground and the ball sailed over Zanuck's head towards the goal. Zanuck turned fast and galloped off to backhand it away. I chased after him to try and ride him off the line, and if miracles could happen, to score. The two of us were now the focal point of all eyes. People were shouting and clods of earth were flying up into my face from Zanuck's pony's hooves.

Saint George was the faster and we gained inexorably.

As we drew almost level and I was getting into position to bump Zanuck off the line of the ball, Saint George leaned forward and through his muzzle sank his teeth into the seat of Zanuck's breeches. Zanuck roared with alarm and pain and in the ensuing shambles, his pony trod on the ball. It became embedded in the turf. I caught a momentary glimpse of the white mushroom top passing below us and, trying to ignore the embarrassing action at the front end of my steed, I made a vague swipe at it as it fell astern. I missed and my stick passed beneath Zanuck's pony's tail. His mount being extremely sensitive in that area, with a maidenly reaction, clamped its tail to its behind. The head of my stick was thus imprisoned. I was attached by a leather thong around my wrist to the other end of the stick. Saint George had a firm grip on Zanuck's buttocks and our horrible triangle galloped past the stands.

Zanuck was good about it. I was not invited to play polo with him again but he mentions it to this day when I see him.

Goulding came back from New York and kept his word . . . he really tried to help me.

'You must stop being an "extra" and have a good agent,' he said.

He talked to Bill Hawks, an important man in that line and I found myself with a representative. It was vitally important to 'have something on film' so I was delighted when I was given 'tests' for various roles. I did tests with Mady Christians, with Elizabeth Allen and with Claudette Colbert but I never landed the parts I was being tested for.

Three men did the same test on the same day with Claudette Colbert for *The Gilded Lily* – a scene on a park bench complete with popcorn and pigeons. The other two both got contracts at Paramount but nothing happened to me . . . their names were Fred MacMurray and Ray Milland. I was a new face and the life blood of movies is 'New Faces'. I also had a good agent and a powerful director pushing me; furthermore, I was meeting 'the people who mattered'. I was interviewed and tested for dozens of roles at all the major studios. I had the contacts and the chances, none could have had more, but I was a hopeless amateur and in front of the camera, I congealed with nerves.

As the weeks went by, I changed from being 'a new face' to being 'a face that's been around and hasn't made it'. Invitations to the houses of the great became fewer. Tests no longer came my way and it began horribly to dawn on me that after all, it might be beyond my reach.

Irving Thalberg had been the boy genius of Hollywood. Now just in his mid-thirties, he was the undisputed master producer of Metro Goldwyn Mayer. Married to the beautiful Norma Shearer, they were the golden couple of Hollywood.

Production of his epic *Mutiny on the Bounty* was getting under way and having being told by Goulding of my bizarre connection with his ship, Thalberg decided that, as an additional drop in the publicity bucket, it might be worth while to sign me up as one of the non-speaking mutineers.

He happened to phrase it more glamorously at some Friday night gathering:

'I'm thinking of signing David Niven to a contract on Monday.'

That did it. The word went around. If the great Irving Thalberg was going to put me under contract, then I must be worth having. Three studios sent people looking for me but I was out chasing marlin. When I got back on Sunday night, Al Weingand gave me a sheaf of messages. I called Goulding and told him of the sudden activity. He and Bill Hawks came over to the hotel and held a council of war. Then Goulding fetched my original and only relaxed test from the MGM studios vault, put it in his car and went directly to the house of Samuel Goldwyn, Hollywood's legendary and most successful independent producer.

Goldwyn ran the test there and then while Frances, his wife, listened sympathetically to Goulding's sales talk.

On Monday morning, Goldwyn sent for me. He sat behind a huge desk in a tastefully furnished office. He was almost entirely bald, very well dressed, with small intense eyes set in a brown face. He was about fifty and looked extremely fit. He spoke without smiling in a strangely high-pitched voice.

'I'm giving you a seven year contract,' he said. 'I'll pay you very little, and I won't put you in a Goldwyn picture till you've learnt your job: now you have a base. Go out and tell the studios you're under contract to Goldwyn, do anything they offer you, get experience, work hard, and in a year or so, if you're any good – I'll give you a role.'

I was ushered out in a daze and taken to see the head of publicity

– Jock Lawrence, a dynamo.

'Jesus,' said Jock, 'you realize what a break you've got? Mr Goldwyn never signs unknowns. He only has three people under contract – Eddie Cantor, Anna Sten and Ronald Colman. Colman's leaving next month and he's taking on Gary Cooper and Joel McCrea.'

He looked at me quizzically, 'What do you think of Mr Goldwyn?'

'He didn't give me time,' I said. 'I was in and out of there in about two minutes.'

'He's the greatest,' said Lawrence. 'All his pictures are hits and he is the only producer in Hollywood who uses his own money – Mr Goldwyn never goes to the banks – he's the greatest all right but boy! can he be rough sometimes. Now, he's told me to build you up so let's hear all about you.'

I gave Jock Lawrence a brief résumé of my life so far while he made notes.

'Mother?'

'French.'

'Good, we can use that.'

'Father?'

'Killed in the war.'

'*Great*! What rank?'

'Lieutenant.'

'Jesus, that's terrible, we'd better make him a General.'

I was taken to see Reeves Espy, Goldwyn's assistant, a gentle, intelligent man who explained that my contract started at a hundred dollars a week for the first two years, with twelve weeks' lay-off each year. During the first two years, Goldwyn had an option every three months to terminate the contract. In the third year, a little more money and fewer options and so on for seven years. I hardly listened ... it was all to unbelievable. I was taken to see Bob McIntyre the Production Manager and Lola Unger his assistant. Lola said, 'We have a nice dressing room for you' and gave me a key. 'We'll put your name on the door tomorrow.'

I found my little cubby hole and sat there in a wicker chair for a long time. Then I wandered about the studio, the same United Artists Studio where Fairbanks had invited me to take a steam.

Near the Main Gate was a familiar high wire fence. On the other side was a shuffling line of extras enquiring for work at the Casting Office.

The Auburn had finally collapsed altogether so I walked to the hotel and told Al Weingand the good news. He was genuinely overjoyed but he also said, 'Thank Christ, now you can pay your goddam bill!'

Together we crossed Hollywood Boulevard to the showroom of the Ford Motor Company. The new models were in the window and priced at just under five hundred dollars. I told the snooty salesman I had just signed a seven year contract with Samuel Goldwyn and at the magic name, he became, immediately, deferential.

'I'll take that one,' I said, pointing. He gave me some forms to sign to do with monthly payments. Then he pulled a chain – the whole window moved aside and I drove out into my Brave New World – and took Goulding and Al Weingand to lunch.

GOLDWYN SIGNS UNKNOWN! – that was the headline of super-powerful columnist, Louella Parsons, the next morning. The *Hollywood Reporter* and *Daily Variety*, the twin bibles of the industry, similarly alerted their readers to this earth-shaking occurrence.

In my new Ford, I drove out to bask in the congratulations of the Belzer-Young family.

Within a week I had evacuated from Al Weingand's haven and found myself a tiny, brown cuckoo-clock of a chalet at the top of North Vista Street, with a view looking over the whole of the Los Angeles Basin. I shared the chalet with several scorpions and black-widow spiders and a garage with the Madam of a well-known whore house situated immediately below me.

I joined the Hollywood Cricket Club.

There were twenty-two cricket clubs in California at that time. The Hollywood Cricket Club was deservedly the most famous and crashes were frequent on Sunset Boulevard on Sunday afternoons when amazed local drivers became distracted by the sight of white flannel trousers and blazers on the football ground of UCLA.

Hollywood was going through a 'British period' and the studios were indulging themselves with such epics as *Mutiny on the Bounty, David Copperfield, National Velvet, Bengal Lancers, Edwin Drood, Disraeli, Lloyds of London* and *Sherlock Holmes* ... it was a bonanza for the British character actors. The captain of the Hollywood Cricket Club was the redoubtable, craggy C. Aubrey Smith. A famous county cricketer, he had a penchant for suddenly nipping out from behind the umpire and firing down his fast ball. ... He had been nicknamed 'Round the Corner Smith'. His house on Mulholland Drive was called 'The Round Corner'; on his roof were three cricket stumps and a bat and ball serving as a weather vane.

Ernest Torrance and his wife Elsie were other leaders of the British colony. Henry Stephenson, E.E. Clive, Eric Blore and H.B. Warner were members. Later arrivals, Basil Rathbone and Nigel Bruce, were fiercely independent of the label 'British colony' and Herbert Marshall spent all his time with Gloria Swanson and Reggie Gardiner with Hedy Lamarr while, aloof from it all, living the life of a hermit in his house at the end of Mound Street, was Ronnie Colman. There he entertained only his intimate circle – William Powell, Richard Bartlemess and Noll Gurney. He had just overcome an unhappy marriage and was trying not to fall in love with Benita Hume.

The hard core British colony took tea on Sundays at the Torrances or the Aubrey Smiths ... the atmosphere was very like the Marsa Polo Club in Malta.

Nigel and Bunnie Bruce became, for me, the Norah and Lefty of the West Coast.

'Willie' Bruce, immortal as Doctor Watson in *Sherlock Holmes*, was fat and jovial and generous. Bunnie was thin and gay and generous. They both adored their two little girls, Pauline and Jennifer. They kept open house in an old Spanish-style mansion on Alpine Drive and happily spent every penny that Willie earned.

It was Willie who made me join the Hollywood Cricket Club. He was keen and had played first class cricket before he collected eleven machine-gun bullets in his left leg at Cambrai. After the war he went on the stage and appeared often with Gerald du Maurier and Gladys Cooper. Once he was invited for the weekend to play country house cricket at some ducal monstrosity.

He arrived the night before the match and was shown his room by the butler with that subtle mixture of alarm and condescension reserved exclusively for actors. Out of his window, Willie saw the house party gathered round the Duke, sitting under a giant yew tree, tea cups and cucumber sandwiches were in evidence and Willie shuddered.

Finally, he plucked up courage to go down and meet his host and fellow guests but to put off the evil moment as long as possible he made a detour through the orchards and greenhouses. There he came across a small peach tree bearing one solitary peach. He ate it and continued on his way to the giant yew. Nobody, including the Duke, took the slightest notice of him so he huddled miserably at the back of the group and toyed with a piece of fruit cake. The butler appeared and announced, 'The Gentlemen of the Press are here, your Grace'. This caused considerable excitement and an anticipatory buzz arose. Willie tapped his nearest neighbour.

'What's all the excitement?'

'Oh, haven't you heard? The Duke is the first man in the world to succeed in growing a full-sized peach on a miniature tree.'

Willie tiptoed away, packed and left before dinner.

Having a highly publicized contract with Goldwyn made it

obvious that I was not about to parlay an invitation to dinner or tennis into an embarrassing hint for work. New doors were ajar. I played tennis with Constance Bennett and Gilbert Roland, with Dolores del Rio and Cedric Gibbons, golf with Jean Harlow and William Powell. When Garbo was not nursing him, I spent sad afternoons with John Gilbert who was fighting a losing battle with the bottle in his hilltop hideaway. The Thalbergs, Douglas Fairbanks and Sylvia became close friends; so did Merle Oberon of unbeatable beauty. Ronald Colman slowly made me persona grata at Mound Street and a lasting bond was formed with Phyllis and Fred Astaire.

John McClain suddenly arrived from the East with a contract to write scripts for RKO and my cup overflowed.

My social life was picking up nicely but my professional career was not in top gear. My first speaking part was at Paramount in *Without Regret*. Elissa Landi was the star and I said 'Goodbye, my dear,' to her on a station platform.

Howard Hawks produced *The Barbary Coast* with Miriam Hopkins – I got the part of a cockney sailor, with drooping moustache.

'Orl rite – I'll go,' I said, and was thrown out of the window of a brothel in San Francisco and into the mud. Miriam Hopkins, Joel McCrea, Walter Brennan, thirty vigilantes and some donkeys walked over the top of me.

I was employed by Woody Van Dyke to play a whole scene with Jeanette MacDonald in *Rose Marie* at MGM. She and Nelson Eddy were the stars and a lanky young actor from New York was making his debut in the same picture. James Stewart was his name.

This looked better – a whole scene in a big important musical!

It was a short piece so I was not given a complete script, just a couple of sides with my stuff on it. It took place in a theatre in Toronto. Jeanette MacDonald had just come off the stage from singing some aria to a packed house and was rushing to the arms of Nelson Eddy, her lover in the Mounties, who was supposed to be waiting in the dressing room.

She flung open the door expectantly and all she found was a top hat protruding above a screen. Underneath the hat was a drunken stage-door Johnnie (me) who, after a short altercation, was forcibly removed.

Van Dyke seemed happy enough with my efforts and by eleven o'clock I was out of the studio.

He was a very fast worker. MGM sent me two tickets to the

preview and I took a girl friend along.

'What's the story?' she asked.

'I've no idea, but when they get to Toronto – that's me after the song – a top hat behind a screen. I'll tell you when it's coming.' We settled back expectantly.

The picture trailed on and finally it was clear that the song in Toronto was over and Jeanette MacDonald was heading for her dressing room.

'Here I come,' I whispered. The girl held my hand.

'There! . . . there's the hat – this is me!!'

The hat moved and a perfectly strange man stepped out from behind the screen and played my scene.

Apparently, I had been so bad that they had got rid of me early and sent for another actor to come and do it correctly.

Van Dyke was a very fast worker.

Al Santell was a director at Columbia and I have blessed him forever. He was directing *A Feather in Her Hat* with Ruth Chatterton. I was employed to play a long and difficult scene in a big party sequence. Leo, the poet, was my character.

The party had been in full swing for some time with much build up towards the arrival of Leo, the poet.

'I *wish* Leo would come, he'll liven it up' etc. etc.

Finally, all gaiety and light, I had to burst in through a door and for at least three minutes, I was supposed, single-handed, to raise the whole tempo of the party, with a wise-crack here and kiss there. The scene was in a continuous shot with the camera on a rail moving with me from group to group.

The 'extras' on the set, some hundred or so, were Dress Extras. Stuart Hall was there full of encouragement but most of the others were of the highly critical 'would-be-star' category. It was an appallingly difficult scene and I hadn't slept all night from anxiety.

I didn't own the tail coat I needed for the occasion so Herbert Marshall lent me his. 'Bart' Marshall had lost a leg on the Somme so for some technical reason, his fly buttons did up the wrong way, like a woman's coat. I was shaking so badly in the wardrobe department that a seamstress had to do my flies up for me with a button hook.

I waited around in an agony of apprehension till finally, I was sent for to do the scene. Santell was kindness and patience itself and walked me gently through many rehearsals but I still couldn't relax.

This was my big chance but I was rigid with terror.

'Okay, Dave, let's take a crack at it – do it just like that last rehearsal – that was just fine.'

Miserable and sweating, I stood outside the door and listened to the happy sounds of the party inside. After an eternity, a red light glowed – my signal to burst in.

I did. My toe caught in the track and I nearly fell over. I bumped a dowager in a chair; I spilled somebody else's drink and said all the wrong lines to the wrong people but somehow, I staggered through to the end.

Everyone on the set applauded.

I couldn't believe my ears. Santell rushed up.

'Hey, that's great, Dave! Just what I wanted . . . perfect! Now we have that one in the can we'll just take another for safety. . . Oh! this time don't hit the track, and watch out for the old dame's chair . . . one or two little changes . . . just clean it up a little . . . but it's great and we have it already – this one's a luxury.'

I stood outside the door looking at the red light . . . I couldn't wait for it to go on. 'This is easy,' I thought, 'this is fun!'

I sailed through the second take, loving every minute of it, completely relaxed.

At the end of the day, Stuart Hall and I were celebrating in a bar: he told me the secret. Santell had addressed the whole 'set' while I had been shivering and shaking in my dressing room.

'The boy who's playing Leo – this is his first big scene in a picture and we've all got to help him loosen up. After the first take, however bad he is, I want you all to applaud then I'll put some film in the camera.'

Santell is in my private Hall of Fame.

'Go get yourself experience,' Goldwyn had said. . . . so I went to the Pasadena Playhouse. This was by far the most highly regarded of all the 'showcases' and almost impossible to break in to. The magic name of Goldwyn opened the door.

I was welcomed by Gilmour Brown, the Playhouse director, and given a minute part in *Wedding*.

It was all very 'arty'. The curtain was up when the audience arrived. It never came down between acts and it remained up when they left.

I was one of the guests. There were sixty others and most of them were queer. One with whom I shared a cubicle dressing room was different. He was an ex-footballer from Notre Dame with a forgettable Polish name. He was a devotee of Scotch whisky and had a large stock of a brand called 'Mist o' the Moors'.

It tasted like rubbing alcohol. I think it was made in Japan.

My part was as follows: Early in Act I I sauntered on carrying a large bowl of punch. This was a very important prop as there was an urgent message for someone underneath it. I arranged the bowl carefully on a table and sauntered off again.

Act II. I had to enter left looking distracted, suddenly see off stage someone I was looking for, smile with relief and exit hurriedly, right.

Act III. Was my big moment. I had a snatch of conversation with my Footballer Friend.

Niven: 'I tell you the King of Siam *does*.'

F.F.: 'Well, I *know* the King of Siam . . . and I tell you he *doesn't*.'

Niven: 'I see.' EXIT

During the two weeks' rehearsal, I went to many parties in Hollywood and without actually lying I propagated the idea that I was starring in a play at the Pasadena Playhouse – good propaganda... 'Yes, I am opening with a very interesting girl at the Playhouse next week . . . I think she'll go a long way . . .' That sort of thing, not lies really.

On opening night, thanks to the ever present Mist o' the Moors, I was completely relaxed. When my moment came, I picked up my bowl of punch and wandered on stage.

I received a thunderous ovation.

In alarm I shielded my eyes from the footlights, an unforgivable thing to do, and saw that 'Bart' Marshall had brought a surprise party of about thirty people to witness my great star debut. I caught a glimpse of Gloria Swanson and Charles Laughton among other famous people filling the first three rows and tottered off the stage with the bowl of punch, thereby ripping irreparable holes in the plot.

Downstairs in our cubicle, the F.F. tried to calm me.

'Have a little Mist, Dave, don't worry about 'em ... screw 'em...'

He gave me a great umbrella stand full of the stuff.

Act II. I thought 'they mustn't see me' – so I shot across the stage from left to right like a meteor.

Act III. And after several more calming draughts of Mist, I had changed considerably – 'Many of these people', I said to the F.F. 'have come from as far as Malibu to see me . . . let's go.' He blinked and shook his head in a dazed way, then followed me meekly on stage for our snatch of conversation.

We swayed on and I led him by the arm right down to the footlights.

'Now look,' I said giving him an intimidating stare, 'I don't want to impose my rather strong personality on your very dull brain . . . but I have it . . . on the very finest authority . . . straight from the horse's mouth . . . that the KING OF SIAM *DOES*.'

The F.F. looked utterly stunned, then in an awed voice he said, 'Jesus Christ!'

Gilmour Brown was waiting for us in the wings – 'Get out of my theatre – both of you.'

Reactions to my performance were mixed. 'Bart' Marshall said he wouldn't have missed it for the world; Charles Laughton gave me an angry lecture about 'bastardizing my profession'. Goldwyn treated me to a mild dressing down. He had been pacified in advance by the news that the great Ernst Lubitsch had just seen my 'relaxed' performance as Leo, the poet, and wanted me to start immediately at Paramount in a very good part in *Bluebeard's Eighth Wife* with Gary Cooper and Claudette Colbert.

Working with Lubitsch in the company of such professional experts and such privately wonderful human beings as Gary Cooper and Claudette Colbert was a joy that lasted for about three months.

The screen play was by another expert – Billy Wilder.

Lubitsch sat, like a little gnome, beside the camera, perched on a small step ladder, giggling and hugging himself at all his own wonderful inventiveness. A vast cigar was always in his mouth. He was patient, understanding and encouraging: what more could any actor ask?

I learned major lessons about playing comedy during that time and will forever remember a statement of his: 'nobody should try to play comedy unless they have a circus going on inside'.

Thank You, Jeeves was the next. I was borrowed from Goldwyn by RKO to play Bertie Wooster and the indelible Arthur Treacher played Jeeves. But it was a 'B' picture, a curtain raiser on the programme for the main feature. It was my first leading role, however. Virginia Field was the leading lady.

Then I was sent for by Warner Brothers, where Michael Curtiz was testing actors for *The Charge of the Light Brigade*. Errol Flynn was the star – his second picture. His first had been a smash hit – *Captain Blood*. Now he was the big white hope of the studio.

Curtiz had a reputation for eating actors for breakfast. An ex-cavalry officer and very Prussian in his approach to subordinates, he was a daunting sight when I reported for work, outfitted in riding boots and breeches and carrying a fly whisk.

I was testing for the part of Flynn's friend: destined for a sticky end in the Charge. The whole scenario was a loose adaptation of the true story and the Charge itself took place on the North West Frontier of India but, no matter, those were the days when Hollywood was reshaping British history to conform to budgets and available locations. I was to play the test scene with Olivia de Havilland so, I realized with dismay, were a dozen other hopeful young actors all dressed in exactly the same uniform as myself ... all standing around and, a refinement of sadism, allowed to watch each other perform.

By the time the scene had been played half a dozen times, and six actors curtly dismissed by Curtiz, everything I had hoped to do had already been done. My mind was a blank when Curtiz, with heavy accent, called out, 'Next man.'

I was led out of the shadows by an assistant and introduced to Miss de Havilland and Curtiz. She smiled a tired resigned smile and shook hands. Curtiz said,

'Where's your script?'

I said, 'You mean the four pages I was given for the scene, Mr Curtiz?'

'Yes ... where is it?'

'Well,' I said, hoping it was true, 'I've learnt it, Mr Curtiz. I don't have it with me.'

'I asked you *where* it is!'

'Well, it's in my dressing room at the other end of the studio.'

'Run and get it,' he shouted.

My uniform was thick and tight. It was 100° in the shade and the sound stage was not air-conditioned ... also, after witnessing the efforts of the others, I reckoned I had no chance of getting the part anyway.

'You — well run and get it,' I said.

His reaction was instantaneous.

'Dismiss the others – this man gets the part.'

We got along famously all through the picture ... 'that goddammed Sandhurst man' Mike called me and built up my part.

My friendship with Flynn dated from that picture. I had met him once or twice at Lili Damita's bungalow in the Garden of Allah and we had reacted to each other with wary distaste. Now he was married to Lili and we made a new appraisal of each other.

Flynn was a magnificent specimen of the rampant male. Outrageously good looking, he was also a great natural athlete who played tennis with Donald Budge and boxed with 'Mushy' Calahan. The extras, among whom I had many old friends, disliked him intensely.

They were a rough lot too, the toughest of the riders from

Westerns, plus the stunt men who specialized in galloping falls. Flynn, they decided, had a swollen head, having made too big a success too soon. They were the 27th Lancers. Flynn was their commander; I was the second in command.

One day they were lined up on the parade ground of our fort, somewhere in the San Fernando valley. Flynn and I were slightly in front of our men when one of them leaned forward with his lance, rubber-tipped to cut down accidents, and wriggled it in Flynn's charger's dock.

The animal reared up and Flynn completed the perfect parabola and landed on his back.

Six hundred very muscular gentlemen roared with laughter.

Flynn picked himself up, 'Which of you sons of bitches did that?'

'I did, sonny,' said a huge gorilla of a man, 'want to make anything of it?'

'Yes, I do,' said Flynn. 'Get off your horse.'

Nobody could stop it and the fight lasted a long time. At the end of it the 'gorilla' lay flat on his back. After that everyone liked Errol much more.

Goldwyn decided that I was ripe to appear in one of his own super-pictures and cast me as Captain Lockert in *Dodsworth* with Walter Huston and Ruth Chatterton. Walter had created the role on Broadway and had now moved to California. His son, John, then a script writer, also worked on the picture. He and his father were wonderful to me, so was Ruth Chatterton. William Wyler, the director, was not.

As his record plainly shows, Willie Wyler is one of the world's all-time great directors. Practically without exception, his films have been hugely successful, both critically and financially. He may have mellowed by now but in 1936 he was a Jekyll and Hyde character.

Kind, fun and cosy at all other times, the moment his bottom touched down in his director's chair, he became a fiend.

Some directors, especially those touched by the Max Reinhardt School, believed in breaking actors down completely so that they became putty in their hands. As practised by Willie, he even managed to reduce the experienced Ruth Chatterton to such a state that she slapped his face and locked herself in her dressing room.

I became a gibbering wreck.

Whenever I was working it was perfectly normal for Willie to sit beneath the camera reading the *Hollywood Reporter* and not even look up till I had ploughed through the scene a couple of dozen times – 'just do it again' he'd say, turning a page.

The picture was a big hit in spite of my wooden performance. I have only kept one 'review' during my life. It is of *Dodsworth* and appeared in the *Detroit Free Press*.

> In this picture we were privileged to see the great Samuel Goldwyn's latest discovery – all we can say about this actor (?) is that he is tall, dark and not the slightest bit handsome.

It has the place of honour in my lavatory.

Irving and Norma, like all the top movie people, had a private projection room in their home. One night Lubitsch brought down a print of *Bluebeard's Eighth Wife* and they ran it after dinner for their friends.

I sat squirming with embarrassment throughout the showing but after it was over, everyone, with one exception, was overly flattering and enthusiastic. Fairbanks and Sylvia, Merle, the Astaires, Paulette Goddard and Frederick Lonsdale, all puffed me up most pleasantly. One guest sat silent in his chair. Finally, I could stand it no longer.

'What did *you* think, Mr Chaplin?'

His answer constituted the greatest advice to any beginner in my profession.

'Don't be like the great majority of actors ... don't just stand around waiting your turn to speak – *learn to listen*.'

By the autumn of 1936, I was very much involved with a GBS (Great Big Star).

The GBS was doing a week of publicity in New York for her latest vehicle and we had a rendezvous to meet there.

I made a side trip to see Lefty and Norah, by now blissfully happy in 'Little Orchard' at Tryon, North Carolina.

Tommy Phipps was there and his highly talented sister, Joyce Grenfell, was over from England. Lefty took me to see the local high school football games and among the glorious colours of the Fall, I rode with him along the foothill trails of the Smoky Mountains. It was a wonderful few days and a most salutary contrast to the life I had been leading in Tinsel City, but I fear the lesson passed almost unnoticed and I hurried off to keep my tryst with the 'GBS' in the St Regis Hotel.

The 'GBS' was gorgeous and quite adventurous.

'Let's not fly back to California – let's take the sleeper to Detroit – buy a Ford and drive it out.'

She bought the car – I drove and the first night we spent together in Chicago.

She disguised her well-known face with a black wig and dark glasses and called herself Mrs Thompson. In the lobby nobody recognized her. Though it was highly unlikely that anyone would recognize me, I went along with the game and called myself Mr Thompson.

The desk clerk handed GBS a telegram,

'For you, Mrs Thompson.' I was mystified.

'How could that happen?' I said.

'I promised Jock Lawrence I'd tell him exactly where we'll be all the way across in case the studio needs me urgently, then I can hop a plane.'

She opened the envelope – 'TELL NIVEN CALL GOLDWYN IMMEDIATELY JOCK.'

'Forget it,' said the GBS, 'call him tomorrow – it's too late now.' We went to bed.

The next night we spent in Cedar Rapids, Iowa.

'Telegram for you, Mrs Thompson', said the desk clerk.

'TELL NIVEN CALL ME TONIGHT WITHOUT FAIL GOLDWYN.

We didn't want the idyll spoiled even though the new signature gave me an eerie feeling of impending doom.

In North Platte, Nebraska, the wording was crisper –

ASK NIVEN WHAT HE THINKS HE'S DOING HAVE HIM CALL TONIGHT OR ELSE   GOLDWYN

Still we pressed happily on across the country, and the telegrams became more alarming at each stop. The one at the Grand Canyon was very unattractive indeed –

TELL NIVEN HE'S FIRED   GOLDWYN.

The GBS was made of stern stuff –

'He can't do that,' she said, 'and anyway he wants me for two more pictures. We'll call him when we get to California – not before.'

I was so besotted by the GBS that I even managed to enjoy the rest of the trip except when we turned off the main road in the middle of New Mexico and got stuck in the desert at sunset.

Finally, the ten-day trip ended and we crossed the State Line into California. From a motel in Needles, with great apprehension, I called Goldwyn.

'Do you know what you're doing, you stupid son of a bitch?' he yelled. 'You're doing about a hundred and thirty-five years in jail. Ever heard of the Mann Act and taking women across State Lines for immoral purposes? Think what Winchell would do to that girl, too, if he got the story – you're through I tell you ... you're ...'

His voice was pitched even higher than usual. The GBS leaned across the bedside table and grabbed the phone out of my hand.

'Sam, darling,' she purred, 'I've had a simply gorgeous time so don't be angry with David ... I'll explain it all to you when we get back tomorrow...' She motioned me to go out of the room and finished her conversation alone. When she found me later, she said,

'Sam's sweet really, everything's okay again, you've been re-instated.'

The 'actor's nightmare' is the role of Edgar in *Wuthering Heights*. Soon after I came back from my trip with the GBS, Goldwyn called me in and told me he had cast me to play it. 'Laurence Olivier will play Heathcliffe and Merle Oberon, Cathy,' he said.

'But it's the most awful part ever written,' I said, 'and one of the most difficult; please don't make me do it.'

'You'll have the best director in the business,' said Goldwyn. 'He'll make it easy for you.'

'Who?'

'Willie Wyler.'

I could not afford it, but I immediately asked to be put on 'suspension' – the combination of 'Edgar' and Wyler was too daunting.

On paper, if a contract actor refused to work, he could not, of course, complain if his weekly salary was suspended, but what happened in practice was that the actor was suspended not only for the duration of the picture (four months for a big one), but the producer had the right to suspend him for half that amount of time again as a punishment, then the whole six months was added on to the end of the original contract. In studios with unscrupulous managements who purposely gave actors assignments which they knew would be refused, players were sometimes trapped for twelve or fifteen years working off a seven-year contract. Years later, Olivia de Havilland fought this and took it all the way to the Supreme Court. She won, and thereafter, if someone refused to work, he didn't get paid but it became illegal for the length of his contract to be altered without his consent.

Olivia struck a great blow for freedom and everyone in the industry should bless her but she hardly ever worked in Hollywood again.

Goldwyn did not offer people roles in order to prolong their contracts, and he found it hard to understand my intransigence.

One day after I had been on suspension for two or three weeks, Willie Wyler called me.

'Come and have dinner at Dave Chasen's,' he said.

Over drinks he asked,

'Tell me truly, why you don't want to play Edgar?'

'Because it is such an awful part,' I said.

'It's not, you know,' said Willie, 'and you are one of the few people in the business who can make it better than it is.'

Now that was pretty heady stuff coming from one of the great directors to someone with my minimal experience.

'There's something else, isn't there?' Willie said.

'Honestly, Willie, I love you, I love being here with you but I was so bloody miserable working for you on *Dodsworth* – I just couldn't go through it again. You're a sonofabitch to work with.' Willie laughed.

'I've changed,' he said, 'come and play the part – it's a wonderful cast . . . it'll be a great picture and I'll make you great in it.'

I weakened at once, of course.

'Okay, under one condition – that the night before I start work, you come and have dinner with me here, and I'll remind you that you've changed – that you're no longer a sonofabitch.'

It was arranged.

I reported to the studio next day and did all the costume fittings and renewed my acquaintanceship with Laurence Olivier who had arrived that morning from England.

Larry appeared with a fantastically beautiful kitten-like creature on his arm – Vivien Leigh.

Viv had come out to be with Larry during the shooting of our picture and within a week of that day, she met David O. Selznick, was tested and over the furious heads of all the big established female stars was handed the role of Scarlett O'Hara in *Gone with the Wind*.

The night before I was to start filming, Willie Wyler kept his word. We had a good dinner at Chasens and played ping-pong on the back patio.

As we bade each other good-night, Willie laughed.

'Don't worry – you'll have fun . . . I'm not a sonofabitch any more.'

The shooting next day was on location in the San Fernando Valley. Goldwyn had reconstructed Wuthering Heights in rolling hills, and except for the fact that the heather of the moors was about four feet high, it looked wonderfully like Yorkshire. In the first scene, I had to drive up in a two horse buggy with Merle looking very demure as Cathy at my side. Once I had stopped at exactly the right mark, the dialogue commenced. Wyler was up on a rostrum about fifty feet in the air, with the camera.

A few rehearsals to practise that tricky stop and we made the first 'take'.

The horses halted just right.
Cathy.   'Come in, Edgar, and have some tea.'
Edgar.   'As soon as I've put the horses away.'
Wyler.   'CUT! Just play it perfectly straight, David – this is not a comedy, you know.'

After a long drive, breasting through the heather, we arrived back for the second 'take'.

'Come in, Edgar, and have some tea.'
'As soon as I've put the horses away.'
'CUT!' What's so funny, David? This is not a Marx Brothers Picture. Do it again! !' Off we drove.

Forty something times I drove those damn horses round the San Fernando Valley. Finally, Wyler said,

'Well, if that's the best you can do, we'd better print the first one I suppose.'

'Willie,' I said, 'remember last night at Chasen's?'

'Yea, I remember – what about it?'

'You really are a sonofabitch, aren't you?'

'Yes – and I'm going to be one for fourteen weeks!'

No one was spared by Willie. The girls were reduced to tears on several occasions and even Olivier was brought up all standing.

The most talented and most reasonable of performers, after being told twenty or thirty times to play some long scene once again, without any specific instructions as to how to alter it, he finally confronted Wyler.

'Willie, look – I've done it thirty times – I've done it differently thirty times – just *tell* me, that's all. *What do you want me to do?*'

Wyler considered this for a long moment –

'Just . . . just be *better*.'

When Cathy was lying dead in her big bed with her family all around her, and a lot of great performers they were too – Flora Robson, Geraldine FitzGerald, Hugh Williams, all weeping silently and Larry circling purposefully round the fireplace. I glanced

175

nervously at the instructions in my script.

(Edgar breaks down at foot of bed and sobs)

'Willie,' I whispered, 'I can't do that.'

'Do what?'

'Sob. I don't know how to.'

'Speak up.'

'I don't know how to sob, Willie.'

'Speak up . . . louder.'

'I DON'T KNOW HOW TO SOB,' I yelled.

Wyler addressed the whole set –

'Well, you've all heard it – here's an actor who says he doesn't know how to act . . . now . . . SOB.'

I tried and it was pretty grisly. 'Tam' Williams got hiccoughs bottling his laughter and Larry looked up the chimney.

I tried again.

'Jesus,' said Wyler, 'can you make a crying face?'

I made some sort of squashed-up grimace.

'Oh, God,' he groaned, *'Irving!'*

Irving Sindler, the prop man, was instantly at his side.

'Give him the blower,' said Wyler.

Greg Toland, the cameraman, gave his signals and the film started passing through the sprockets.

'The blower, Irving!' said Wyler.

Through a handkerchief, Sindler puffed menthol into my open eyes.

'Bend over the corpse,' said Wyler. 'Now make your crying face . . . Blink your eyes . . . Squeeze a little . . . Bend over the corpse . . . Heave your shoulders.'

A terrible thing happened. Instead of tears coming out of my eyes, green slime came out of my nose.

'Ooh! How *horrid!'* shrieked the corpse, shot out of bed and disappeared at high speed into her dressing room.

Thanks to Wyler, the picture was a big hit and has remained one of the all-time classics. And incidentally any time Wyler wants me to work for him – I'll be there.

There was an excitement and generosity of spirit in Hollywood – a minimum of jealousy and pettiness, everyone felt they were still pioneering in a wonderful entertainment medium.

The premières of the big pictures were black tie events and all the big names turned out to cheer on their friends. Outside, 'bleachers' were erected to enable the screaming fans to catch a glimpse of their favourites and searchlights waved weaved patterns across the sky.

After the show, a loudspeaker alerted the fans to the departing of the great –

Mr Clark Gable's car!

Miss Marlene Dietrich's car!

Miss Constance Bennett's car!

Miss Shirley Temple's mother's car! and on one glorious occasion –

Mr Alfred Hitchcar's cock!

Some of the conveyances were a trifle exotic. Connie Bennett sat inside the wicker-box body of a Rolls Phaeton with a spotlight on her . . . outside in all weathers sat her chauffeur.

Tom Mix drove himself in a white open Packard wearing a white ten-gallon hat.

Marlene Dietrich had a black Cadillac driven by a chauffeur named Briggs who carried two revolvers and in winter wore a uniform with a mink collar.

Marlene, the most glamorous of all, was also one of the kindest. Once, I was ill with flu in my chalet shack on North Vista Street. She hardly knew me but Briggs was a friend and he told her I was sick. Marlene arrived with soup and medicine. She then went to work and herself cleaned the whole place from top to bottom, changed my bedclothes and departed. She came back every day till I was well.

Goldwyn continued my build-up and gave me a good part in *The Real Glory* with Gary Cooper. Then I was loaned to Darryl Zanuck to play two important roles at Twentieth Century Fox, both with Loretta Young, still as sweet and as generous as ever. The whole Young family turned up for the first day's shooting. John Ford directed one of these, an experience actors prayed for. So incredibly sure was his touch that he cut the film with his camera as he went along. All the editor could do was join the pieces together in the correct order and there was the picture.

Ford, like many movie greats, had a soft spot for the practical joke. I had a birthday during the picture and Loretta presented me with a cake which the whole crew devoured.

'David,' said Ford, 'tomorrow you have very little to do – you'll just be background so tonight go on out and enjoy yourself – really tie one on.'

I hate getting drunk but I felt that I had more or less been ordered to do so and I did my best to oblige. I started slowly, after work, in Tyrone Power's dressing room, then home where Flynn joined me enthusiastically, continued at the Trocadero with Mike Romanoff, then I visited two German lesbians in Encino and after making the rounds of Chasen's, the Brown Derby and various bars in Hollywood, I finished up in Doc Law's All Night Café in Santa Monica. From there, I went directly to the studio at eight o'clock in the morning, very drunk indeed and thinking how pleased John Ford would be.

We were rehearsing the first scene. All I had to do was bind up George Sanders' arm who had been shot. Suddenly, I heard Ford say,

'Hold it – what's the matter with you, Niven? Why don't you stand still?'

'Sorry, Mr Ford.'

'Just a minute – are you drunk or something?'

'Well, I did have a few, Mr Ford ... I thought you said..'

'Cut the lights,' said Ford.

'Send for Mr Zanuck. Tell him I have a drunken actor on my set – ask him to come down right away.'

I was sobering up rapidly but still not registering too clearly. All I knew was that people were backing away from me, not wanting to be part of the impending showdown.

Zanuck marched on to the set, looking ferocious, followed by his henchmen.

'What's the problem, Jack?'

'Goddam Limeys', said Ford, 'they're all alike.... give 'em an inch ... this actor reported for work drunk.'

'Let me see a "take",' said Zanuck.

'Put a white coat on him,' said Ford, 'and give him the first aid box ... all right, now try to pull yourself together for Christ's sake ... on your cue pull the stethoscope out of your pocket, then open the box and take out a dressing – okay, let's go.' White coat? Stethoscope? dressing? – these were new instructions.

The camera turned and George Sanders and Richard Greene played a lengthy scene. Out of the corner of my eye, I could see Zanuck watching intently. I tried to concentrate on my cue and when it came, I put my hand in the pocket for the stethoscope and pulled out a large snake. Trying manfully to continue the scene. I dropped it on the floor and opened the first aid box when I saw it was full of little green turtles. I let out a yell and flung it in the air.

'Print it,' yelled Ford, amidst the ensuing guffaws. The scene which Zanuck had been a party to was run constantly in private projection rooms thereafter.

By now Flynn had separated from Lili Damita and I was looking for new quarters so together we rented Rosalind Russell's house,

601 North Linden Drive and settled in to a fairly ostentatious bachelor existence.

'601' became a hotbed of fun and bad behaviour, the booze flowed freely, the girls formed an ever changing pattern and after Flynn came back from a trip to North Africa, we went through a long period when we smoked or chewed kif.

Kif had strange effects on me, sometimes everything seemed hilariously funny, sometimes I became quiet and introspective, sometimes I experienced pleasant imaginings or hallucinations. I got bored with it one day and just stopped taking it. Nowadays it is known as marijuana.

Flynn had a more lucrative contract at Warners than I had with Goldwyn so he paid the most rent and consequently had the big double bedroom. I was allowed to borrow it for 'special occasions'.

Fairbanks had a small ranch down near San Diego where he used to take the Astaires and me, duck shooting and coyote hunting. A rather bigger spread lay north, near San Luis Obispo, where the super newspaper tycoon, William Randolph Hearst, had built himself a hilltop castle dominating some two hundred thousand acres.

His sons, George, Bill, Jack, Randy and David, invited me up there constantly. They were all about the same age as myself and all were either just married, about to become engaged or sliding down the other side into divorce. The girls were beautiful, the boys were great fun and I spent some of the happiest times of my life at San Simeon.

W.R. Hearst lived there openly for years with the blue-eyed beauty, Marion Davies. The sons loved their mother who lived on Long Island. They also loved their father and they liked Marion enormously. It was impossible not to ... a warm-hearted scatter-brain who worshipped 'W.R.'

Mr Hearst fascinated me. He was an avid collector of antiques on a massive scale. An entire Greek temple had been dismantled, shipped over and reassembled by the swimming pool. Glorious frescoes, paintings and tapestries were everywhere. Often I slept in Richelieu's bed. Hearst had repositories of treasure still not unpacked and a large private zoo. He enjoyed going for rambles with the young and discoursing on every subject under the sun. One heard rumbles that he was utterly ruthless in business but, rather naturally, I saw no sign of that.

In the huge panelled dining hall, flanked by monks' stalls, and decorated up high by sixty or seventy ducal banners from Venice, Siena and Florence, it always intrigued me that down the centre of the largest refectory table in the world stood clusters of HP sauce, Heinz tomato ketchup and paper napkins.

At the end of 1936, Irving Thalberg died. He was thirty-seven years old. He had caught a chill playing cards out of doors, pneumonia followed and very quickly he was gone. Hollywood was stunned. It was a staggering loss.

Fairbanks organized the ushers at the funeral service at the synagogue, B'nai Brith. He told me to help at the entrance and said that he would seat the family personally in the front as he knew them all by sight. Knowing his penchant for putting the wrong name to the wrong face, this made me rather nervous, a condition that increased when I walked down the aisle to ask him advice about something and he showed me into a pew.

By Hollywood standards, the funeral was conducted with great decorum: the fans were kept at bay so nobody had a chance to repeat an earlier disaster when the widow had her veils ripped off – 'Let's see your face, dearie.'

The only sour note was when some moron in the MGM publicity department saw to it that the child actor, Freddie Bartholomew, who had just completed the name part in the film showed up in his black velvet Little Lord Fauntleroy suit.

It was probably the same source of good taste which, when Jean Harlow died, took out full page 'ads' in the trade papers showing the Metro Lion dressed in white tie and tails with tears pouring down its face, placing a wreath on a tombstone: JEAN HARLOW IN MEMORIAM – and below on a scroll, the full list of her screen credits.

Norma was inconsolable and disappeared from view for months.

David O. Selznick was as big an independent producer as Goldwyn so when he borrowed me to play Fritz von Tarlenheim in *The Prisoner of Zenda*, I was very excited. Not only was it to be one of the biggest pictures of the year, it also had a spectacular cast – Ronald Colman, Madeleine Carroll, Raymond Massey, Douglas Fairbanks Jr, Mary Astor and C. Aubrey Smith.

Colman was now very close to me and I did not doubt that on my behalf, he had put in his two cents' worth with Selznick. Doug. Jr I was meeting for the first time and we immediately struck up a friendship which is just as warm today. An added bonus was that Madeleine's husband, Philip Astley, was coming out to spend three months with her in Malibu.

My part was excellent. Seemingly the only comedy relief, I had never had it so good.

John Cromwell, the director, was rather solemn and steadfastly refused to let me play my part for comedy. I ploughed on, playing it straight as ordered, but was pretty sure the result was dim. Colman found it hard to be encouraging.

After about a week, I decided to make a stand and upon completion of a scene, I said, 'Mr Cromwell, would you let me do it again – my way?'

This was unheard-of insubordination and the entire crew shuffled about looking embarrassed.

'All right,' said Cromwell. 'Do it once more – your way.'

By now, whatever it was I had dreamed up felt profoundly unfunny but I did it anyway.

'Next scene,' said Cromwell with no change of expression.

That night David Selznick called me.

'I'm sorry, David, but somehow you're not giving the part what I thought you would . . . I'm afraid I have to replace you.'

My legs turned to water. I went up to my room and sat on my bed in the dark. So I really couldn't do it after all – Lubitsch and Wyler might have pulled me through but the first big chance had found me out . . . What was I going to tell everyone?

My next option with Goldwyn was just coming up . . . he would surely drop me. I felt panic rising. I heard Flynn come back about two o'clock and still I sat there.

At nine in the morning, Selznick called me.

'I want to see you at once . . . come on down.'

I was taken straight to his office. With him was John Cromwell.

'Look, David,' said Selznick, 'we have just seen yesterday's stuff . . . the last thing you did was exactly what I want from you and John here agrees.

'I certainly do,' said Cromwell. 'It's my fault entirely and David and I are going to build up the part so that we can get much more fun out of it . . . you'll be great . . . go and get dressed.'

How many big directors are really that big, I wonder? Cromwell is another for my private Hall of Fame.

It was a long picture – over four months – and every day was fascinating. We all felt we were making a success and the enthusiasm ran high.

I was given my own 'stand-in' for the first time. I asked Stuart Hall if he would like the job and for years thereafter he stood patiently being lit by cameramen so that I would be fresh when the moment came to play a scene.

I had problems with my old chums among the extras. At 6.30 at night, they automatically went on a quarter extra salary. If I was playing a scene around that magic hour, they would make it clear they expected me to 'blow' my lines and put them safely into overtime. My loyalty to David Selznick, who would have to pay them, also came into question . . . it was very tricky.

In the coronation procession, Colman and Madeleine were in the royal coach, C. Aubrey Smith and I rode alongside and the two heavies, Doug. Jr and Ray Massey, rode behind us.

Knowing the fixation that studios have that leading actors should be seen riding highly strung prancing steeds, I had a little chat with the Head Wrangler and exchanged mine for a quiet old mare. Unfortunately, she was in heat and the stallion that Ray Massey was riding decided to mount her, and me, in the middle of a 'take'. I heard snapping teeth behind my head and just caught a glimpse of Ray's appalled expression far above me as I flung myself to the ground.

Towards the end of the picture, King George VI and Queen Elizabeth visited President Roosevelt.

Someone had the bright idea that the British colony should do a special radio show on the Sunday which would coincide with a hot dog picnic which the president was giving for his royal guests at Hyde Park up the Hudson River.

We rehearsed for days and bashed our brains out being loyal and talented.

Olivier gave the 'Into the breach . . .' speech from *Henry V*, Brian Aherne recited Rupert Brooke's 'The Soldier', Aubrey Smith, Nigel Bruce and Roland Young sang 'Three Little Fishes', Reggie Gardiner imitated a train: Ray Noble's band played and the rest of us – Vivien Leigh, Flynn, Colman, Madeleine, Cary Grant and myself, all did something.

I had an unexpected moment alone with Her Majesty a few years later and asked her how they had all enjoyed our efforts.

'Oh, wasn't it awful,' she said, 'the President's battery ran down just before it came on.'

At the end of *Zenda*, Goulding called in a high state of excitement from his house in Palm Springs.

'Come at once – I have good news, I think.'

I drove down to the desert to find Goulding hopping up and down in the driveway.

He led me down to his pool. There was a naked figure in it.

'Oh, I forgot,' said Goulding. 'Garbo was coming over for a swim . . . we'd better go back up to the house.'

Up there he told me the news.

'You've got it!' he said. 'They just called from Warners and confirmed it.'

'Got what?'

'Scotty in *Dawn Patrol* – it's the best part ever written for an actor.'

Warners borrowed me from Goldwyn and Goulding was right. It was a marvellous part . . . a World War I story of the Royal Flying Corps. Flynn and I were pilots. At one point I was hungover and late and went up in my Sopwith Camel in red and white spotted pyjamas. I was shot down and fell in a lake. The officer's mess was plunged in gloom at the loss when I suddenly walked in, still in pyjamas with an armful of champagne bottles. This was a true incident that had happened near Arras to a certain Flying Officer Pope.

Basil Rathbone played the CO and Donald Crisp was the Adjutant.

Goulding was a most sensitive and inventive director. The picture really hit the jackpot and he achieved what he had always promised – he launched me in a great part in a great picture.

After that, things moved rapidly, I was given star billing and borrowed by Twentieth Century Fox to do a picture in England with the beautiful French actress, Annabella.

Trubshawe came to Southampton to meet the ship. He was now the Squire of Barton Hall in Norfolk and Margie had presented him with two daughters. For old time's sake, he carried the dipsomaniacs' delight. He also displayed a placard:

BARTON HALL VILLAGE FETE
CRICKET MATCH
SIDE SHOWS
RAFFLE
BOWLING FOR THE PIG
CAWSTON SILVER BAND
TO BE OPENED BY FAMOUS HOLLYWOOD STAR
DAVID NIVEN

'Better come, old man,' he said. 'It's tomorrow and I've stuck these bloody things up all over the country.'

It was marvellous to be home again.

The picture was shot at Denham. Angie and Ken Thornton let me be a 'paying guest' in their lovely old house at Ascot, near the

Weigalls, and a hundred old threads were picked up. I had time to go to Bembridge. Everyone made a great fuss of me and I wallowed in it.

On the return journey in the *Ile de France*, I met an Austrian named Felix Schaffcotsh. He was on his way to Sun Valley, Idaho, where, at the request of Averell Harriman, he had designed and built a new ski resort.

A handsome and affable 'Graf', he was also a dyed-in-the-wool Nazi. He spent hours extolling the virtues of Hitler, sympathizing with his problems and enthusing over his plans. I listened politely but took none of it seriously. I was far more interested in the script of my next film.

Shortly before sailing, I had been advised that Goldwyn had loaned me to Walter Wanger to co-star with Loretta in *Eternally Yours*.

Felix said that he was bringing over a dozen good ski instructors from near his home in Austria – 'all Nazis too'. I promised to go to Sun Valley after I finished the picture.

I arrived back in Hollywood to find that Flynn and Lili Damita had signed a truce and I had to find somewhere else to live.

John McClain was at the Garden of Allah so I rented a bungalow there, and although I missed F. Scott Fitzgerald, who had moved to Malibu with Sheilah Graham, I had the great joy of meeting Robert Benchley and Dorothy Parker.

Benchley was one of the wittiest men alive but unlike most people full of funny things to say, he was rather retiring. Long the theatre critic for the *New Yorker*, he was now bravely putting on the other hat and embarking on a highly successful career as an actor. He loved to drink . . . . 'I must step out of these wet things and into a dry martini. . . .'

There had lately been a big influx of 'Easterners' and with McClain and Benchley, I spent fascinating evenings at Cole Porter's house where it was quite usual to listen to Cole or Irving Berlin or George Gershwin playing numbers from the half-written scores of their future smash hit musicals.

When McClain moved back to New York, I moved down to Santa Monica and rented a small guest beach house from Marion Davies. I shared this with Robert Coote, an excellent English actor, and a mysterious Australian named Walter Kerry Davis.

Bob was quickly making a big name for himself as a character actor and Walter was hovering hopefully on the fringe of Los Angeles and Pasadena society where, rumour had it, he was trying to snag a rich wife. He so often failed to pay his share of the rent that he must have been finding the going very uphill.

It was a very happy combination, however, and we entertained twenty-four hours a day . . . so much so that Carole Lombard, Alice Faye, Ida Lupino and Cary Grant christened the house 'Cirrhosis by the Sea'. We had this painted on a board outside the front door where it remained for over a year till we received instructions from W.R. Hearst to take it down.

Fred Astaire and Ginger Rogers decided to make no more musicals together and the whole world mourned.

Fred went on from strength to strength with a series of different dancing partners and Ginger decided to return to straight acting. They were the king and queen of RKO so it was immensely flattering for me when Goldwyn told me that he had loaned me out to co-star with Ginger in her first solo for a long time, *Bachelor Mother* to be directed by the immensely talented writer-director, Garson Kanin.

'Everyone's going to expect you to dance,' said Goldwyn, 'show them that you can act instead.'

The script, by Norman Krasna, was a dream and Goldwyn decided that this picture was so important that he would not put me into anything else before it. It was then February 1938.

I kept my promise and went skiing at Sun Valley. The resort was just open, new and small. Only two hotels were built, 'The Lodge', very good and very expensive and 'The Challenger Inn' where I went, very gay and much cheaper.

Averell Harriman had his own charming chalet and others were building. The skiing was perfect and I had a wonderful six weeks. Felix had made a huge success of the place. Given half a chance he was still liable to lay down the law about 'Lebensraum' but he was a most agreeable companion. Towards the end of my stay, I was surprised to get a phone call from Norma Shearer who had been virtually incommunicado since Irving Thalberg's death.

She sounded desperately lonely so I persuaded her to come on up and booked her a suite in the Lodge. When she arrived Averell Harriman went out of his way to make life pleasant for her. She fell in love with the place, with skiing, and a few years later with a great skier and happily remarried.

Bachelor Mother took most of the summer to shoot and was a most happy assignment. Thanks to Garson's sure hand and novel ideas the result surpassed the highest hopes and it was widely acclaimed as the best comedy of the year. It went straight to my head, of course, and I bought a Leica and went all over Los Angeles taking pictures of my name and likeness on the billboards.

During the filming, Garson said something that gave me pause for thought.

'Do you realize,' he said, 'that I am the director of this picture and you are the co-star but between us we are being paid less than half what the cameraman is getting?'

There was no doubt that every time Goldwyn loaned me out he demanded huge sums for my services but I was still basically amazed that I was being paid at all and Goldwyn, after all, had given me a chance when nobody else would touch me. Nevertheless, the flea was in my ear so I had a talk with Leland Hayward, the top agent in Hollywood.

'Leave Goldwyn to me,' he said, 'you're making a fortune for him – I'm going in there to ask for a lot of money and a contract for five years straight with no lay-off and no options, a limited number of pictures and six weeks' guaranteed vacation each year.'

On the day of Leland's meeting with Goldwyn, he went in to the office brimming with confidence. I waited in the ante-room.

Two minutes later he was back.

'Did you get it?' I asked.

'Not exactly,' said Leland. 'Goldwyn has barred me from the lot – now I can't even talk to him.'

A really ridiculous war of nerves then started with Goldwyn. He didn't speak to me when I met him and when I turned down what I thought was a really awful script, I was promptly put on suspension.

One day I saw a headline in Louella Parsons' daily gossip column read avidly by the whole industry – 'NIVEN IMPOSSIBLE SAY FELLOW WORKERS'. It went on to charge that because of recent successes I had got such a swollen head I refused to speak to old friends in the studio.

I was appalled and when I discovered through a secretary in the publicity department that the story had emanated from there, I confronted Jock Lawrence.

As usual he was urbane.

'Remember that first day you came in here? I told you then Mr Goldwyn is the greatest but he's rough sometimes.'

Being suspended, I started earning a nice amount by working on radio in the Lux Radio Theatre and other programmes – very serious they were, too, with a week's rehearsal and the performance given before a live audience of several hundred to an unseen one of fifty million.

Reeves Espy spoke to me: poor man, he hated to deliver bad news.

'Dave, Mr Goldwyn says that you have been working on radio without his permission. Under the terms of the contract he has the right to everything you earn. However, he'll let you keep half.'

The next radio show I did was with Bing Crosby; the sponsor was Kraft. At the end of the show, as was often the custom, I was presented with a large hamper filled with all the Kraft products, cheeses, spreads, and sardines.

When I got home, Coote helped me, and we meticulously removed half the spread from the jars, cut every cheese in half, every sardine in half, then with an envelope containing a cheque for half my salary from the show, I sent the lot to Goldwyn inside half the basket.

It was ridiculous and childish and I was behaving like a small boy attacking a heavy tank with a water pistol but rather enjoying it.

Fred and Phyllis Astaire arranged a ceasefire and Goldwyn sent for me. All smiles, he received me in his office – he had immense charm. He told me that he wanted to give me a new seven-year contract, mentioned the figures which seemed colossal to me and added that the first picture I would do would be *Raffles*.

I had always wanted to tackle the part of the famous gentleman crook; now it was being dangled before me like a carrot. It all seemed perfect.

'I'll call Leland and have him come over and we'll make a deal,' said Goldwyn. I left in a high state of excitement.

I remember that September evening very vividly because in the car park, outside Leland's office, I listened to the hysterical voice of Hitler, addressing the Nuremberg Rally. The doom-filled tones of the commentator, Gabriel Heatter, left one in no doubt as to the intentions of the man and the rolling Sieg Heils of his massed Storm Troopers underlined them in an ominous and frightening way.

I thought about Felix and his dire prognostications.

Leland blithely turned down Goldwyn's offer.

'You've got to have some guts,' he said, when I remonstrated. 'Sit him out – play it uninterested – your contract is running out. He doesn't want to lose you – he's just playing games – I know Sam – we'll get the deal we want.'

I just hoped that Leland knew what he was doing, and went sailing with Flynn on one of our weekend jaunts to Catalina Island in his ketch *Sirocco*. Normally, the arrangement was that we provided the booze, and the girls, whoever they were, brought the food. There was one lady who had made a habit of showing up with nothing but a loaf of bread and a douche bag.

We were on our way back to the mainland on the Sunday evening. The sea had kicked up quite considerably.

About fifteen miles out of Balboa, we sighted a large cabin cruiser. She was stopped and wallowing about and signalling to us frantically.

When we came near enough, we could see her name *Jobella* and sitting in the stern with a cigar clamped between his teeth, was the owner, Harry Cohn, the head of Columbia Studios.

'Give us a tow for Christ's sake,' yelled Cohn. 'Goddam engines broke down.'

Jobella was a heavy boat and we didn't bring her in to Balboa till well after midnight.

Cohn in his rough, tough, East Side way was only moderately grateful so the next day I thought I'd have a little fun with him. I persuaded a lawyer friend to send him an official letter quoting maritime law on the question of asking for help at sea and, mentioning the Salvage Act of 1912, I claimed one half of the *Jobella*.

No answer came and I forgot all about it. One day Leland called me. 'What the hell have you done at Columbia – you've been barred from the lot for life!!'

'I haven't set foot in the place for three years,' I said.

'Well, you must have done *something*,' said Leland.

Then I remembered and told him about the lawyer's letter.

'But it couldn't be that,' I said.

'Knowing Cohn, that's exactly what it is,' said Leland, 'you'd better call him up and explain.'

I called Cohn and couldn't get him on the phone. I left messages – he never called back.

I became nervous. There were only six major studios. Goldwyn was highly displeased with me at the moment and he had an option coming up in a few days. Suppose Goldwyn dropped me? Out for life at Columbia!! And the 'black list' really did exist. Too many actors who had quarrelled with their studios had sunk without trace. I might never work again anywhere. I panicked.

Leland tried to calm me down but it was obvious that he, too, was concerned.

Finally, Cohn consented to see me and I was granted an interview at 9 a.m.

He kept me waiting in the outer office all morning. At lunch time, he walked out, right past me and never said a word. But I was frightened. I was chicken. I didn't have the guts to leave too.

After lunch, Cohn came back. He never looked at me. All afternoon I sat under the pitying eye of a secretary. Finally at 6.30 –

'Mr Cohn will see you now.'

In his big office he growled at me,

'Waddaya want?'

I said, 'About that night Errol and I towed you home. . . .'

'Yeah . . . well whattabout it?'

'. . . did you get a lawyer's letter about the salvage?'

'Yeah, I got it. D'you want apologize?'

'Look, the idea was to make you laugh – if it made you unhappy, of course, I apologize.'

'Okay, I accept the apology – now get your ass outta here.'

I didn't work at Columbia till after Cohn died twenty years later.

The ridiculous war of nerves with Goldwyn continued, though I suspect that the nerves were strictly on my side.

I was called to the studio to make some costume tests for a picture with Gary Cooper. I began to notice a man hovering about in white tie and tails. He was posing for stills with Bob Coburn, the Goldwyn photographer – posing, I saw, half way up a ladder with a revolver in one hand and a pearl necklace in the other – obviously he was meant to look like 'Raffles', the gentleman crook.

During the afternoon, I approached the man and asked him what he was doing. He was a little mystified himself.

'Well, I've been told to put on these clothes and follow you around having these pictures taken.'

The 'ploy' was pretty juvenile – to get me to rush off and sign the Goldwyn offer for fear of losing *Raffles*. After work, I sent Goldwyn a Boy Scout's outfit.

The name of the man was Dana Andrews.

Finally, in the spring, Goldwyn and Leland made a deal. Goldwyn, who had a great capacity for letting bygones be bygones, welcomed me to his office with open arms and Jock Lawrence had pictures taken of the two of us signing the contract. . . .

Goldwyn, himself, escorted me to one of the huge star suites and ordered it to be redecorated to my taste. Olivia de Havilland was signed to play opposite me and Sam Wood to direct.

I was pampered and spoiled and my every whim was catered to. When I asked for some of my old 'extra' chums to be employed in the English country house sequences, they were immediately and when I walked on the set, I thought it was the Crystal Palace. To a man they were sporting monocles. When Sam Wood fell ill, the picture was completed by a gentle and helpful Willie Wyler.

We finished shooting on September 1st. The picture looked good and Goldwyn was delighted. My contract was munificent. Goldwyn's plans for me were most exciting ... and all this had happened in less than four years ... but at that very moment when I was preening myself, something bigger than a weed was blowing into many people's gardens.

Hitler, without a declaration of war, was invading Poland.

Doug Junior with his attractive new Virginia-born wife, Mary Lee, had chartered a yacht for a weekend trip to Catalina. On board were Larry Olivier and Vivien Leigh. Ronnie Colman and Benita Hume were anchored nearby in Colman's ketch, *Dragoon*. Coote and I were supposedly sailing across to join them in a small sloop, the *Huralu*. Coote and I drank an immense amount of rum at a party in the Balboa Yacht Club and did not quite 'make the tide'.

We were woken up at 6 a.m. by a man in a dinghy banging on the side of our boat.

'You guys English?'

We peered blearily over the side. 'Yes.'

'Well, lotsa luck – you've just declared war on Germany.'

We never spoke a word ... just went below and filled two tea cups with warm gin.

When we finally arrived at Catalina and joined the others, we found a sombre group. Nobody knew quite what to do; like millions all over the world, it was beginning to dawn on us that we were pawns in a game that had got out of control.

After a gloomy couple of days, Coote and I sailed back. I got a call from Felix Schaffcotsh from New York.

'Hello, enemy,' he said gaily, 'what are you going to do?'

'I'll go back to England, I suppose,' I said, very gloomily.

Felix sounded very bright. 'I'm leaving for Germany the day after tomorrow, let's go together.'

The next day, I told Goldwyn that I had been called up and had to leave immediately. Goldwyn, as usual, was far smarter than I gave him credit for. Within half an hour he had checked with the British Embassy in Washington and had been told that nobody outside the British Isles had yet been called up: and furthermore, that all British subjects should continue a normal life until such time as they received a summons. Luckily, nobody told Goldwyn that, having resigned my commission, I was no longer on the Reserve and in all probability would never be called up at all.

I cabled my brother Max with certain instructions and was able to show Goldwyn a cable which read –

REPORT REGIMENTAL DEPOT IMMEDIATELY ADJU-TANT.

Doug Jr gave me a splendid send-off – a bachelor party complete with pipers. The guests included Colman, Nigel Bruce, Olivier, Brian Aherne, George Sanders, Cary Grant, Roland Young, Kerry Davis and Coote, and the next day, I took off from the Burbank airport for New York.

As the plane circled over the San Fernando Valley, gaining sufficient height to cross the mountains, the whole of Los Angeles stretched out below me in the early morning light. Warner Brothers and Universal Studios were easy to pick out. I had a nasty feeling that I might be seeing them for the last time. I also wondered what the hell I was doing up there.

Felix had gone on ahead and made a rendezvous with me in Rome.

Dreading the idea of being back again in the British Army, I decided to save time and money by offering myself to the Canadian Army instead so from New York, I went to Washington to ask the advice of the Military Attaché at the Embassy.

The Military Attaché was sympathetic, but explained that the few divisions at present being raised in Canada were already over-subscribed nine times down to cooks. 'Anyway,' he added, 'the Ambassador would like to see you.'

Lord Lothian was flattering, but gave me a very peculiar directive: 'It is, of course, admirable that you want to join up, but if you really would like my advice, the best thing you can possibly do, is to go back to Hollywood and represent your country on the screen.'

I thanked him and sailed in the Italian liner *Rex* for Naples.

The ship was fairly empty except for a group of extremely hostile young Germans who made it obvious that the war had already started. I was delighted when a British destroyer stopped *Rex* outside Gibraltar. Officers boarded her, interrogated all the passengers and over the vehement protestations of the Italian captain, removed several of the young Germans.

Felix met me at Naples and we embarked on a week of liquid farewells in Rome.

He seemed very well connected and twice I found myself at the Golf Club di Roma, playing with Count Ciano, the Foreign Minister and son-in-law of Mussolini.

Ciano was a highly attractive man, and both times we played, beautiful Roman ladies walked round with us twittering like birds. When he heard that I was on my way to England to join up, he wished me luck very solemnly and said that he was sure it would all be settled very soon.

Felix and I decided that we would both leave Rome on the same day. The night before, he arranged a glorious finale. It started with drinks in somebody's Palazzo and continued through a series of visits to the houses and apartments of Felix's smart Roman friends.

In the early hours, we took two carefully selected girls to a night club – a Spanish one for Felix – a Norwegian for me, and all the time we drank, and drank without getting drunkards' drunk or noisy drunk – an evident danger on this occasion. Towards dawn Felix said: 'Let's go to the Vatican and all kiss a Swiss Guard.'

When we arrived, the sky above St Peter's was changing from black to palest blue and the iridescent beauty of the place was almost unearthly. The Spanish girl surreptitiously crossed herself, the Norwegian whispered irreverently in my ear, 'Every time I've been in the place, I've been groped.'

Soon they were both asking to be taken home.

Ungallantly, we did not accompany them but this was our night and they sensed it.

Alone in a little 'bistro' in Trastevere, we drank Fontana di Candida as though they were never going to make any more – still we didn't get drunk. Felix talked about the new ski lifts he was planning for Sun Valley and I talked of the pictures I was going to make. A long silence enveloped us. We watched the newly awakened swifts wheeling and darting and miraculously missing each other in the darker blue sky. Suddenly, Felix slammed his glass down on the table and jumped to his feet,

'Let's say goodbye now,' he said almost angrily.

I stood up. I think we both wept, anyway, drunk at last, we embraced and parted quickly. A few hours later, Felix headed northeast for the Brenner Pass to join the SS and I headed north-west for the French border at Modane to join God knew what.

Felix was killed in Russia.

12

Duce! Duce! on every station in letters ten feet high and the train services in Italy were running perfectly. By way of Genoa and Turin, I was quickly transported to the French border and crossed into Savoie at Modane.

Not a bomb had yet fallen on the French railway system but chaos was reigning supreme.

I had the greatest difficulty convincing a pompous little official that I was not a spy.

'Why does an Englishman come from Italy, monsieur?'

At last I persuaded him I was trying to be on his side if only he would let me and with a shrug of resignation, he stamped my passport and wrote a special pass.

'*Se rend en Angleterre pour faire la guerre.*'

The distance between Mondale and Paris is a little over five hundred miles. The train took three full days. It was packed with drunken reservists and if I ever found a seat, I vacated it only 'in extremis'. The corridor was jammed with eagle-eyed opportunists. At night, train and stations were blacked out and we stumbled about bitterly cold platforms looking for bread and cheese and wine being sold by ill-tempered ladies with flashlights and no change.

Most of the time, the train stood in sidings. Nothing seemed to go past and rumours of bombings farther up the line ran up and down the coaches.

I was constantly told by thick garlic-laden voices that the whole thing was the fault of England, and now, having forced France to join them against the Germans, the English would never show up to fight – 'just like the last time.'

I thought of the three million British Empire casualties including my own father, and finally, through pure exhaustion, I placated the accusing red faces by explaining that I was half French anyway.

On arrival in Paris, I managed to find a room in an hotel on the Left Bank and slept for twenty-four hours.

Refreshed, I decided to give myself a week in Paris, and then join the RAF. I wondered if, perhaps, I could do this in France so I called at the British Embassy but it was a seething mass of expatriate

British looking for permits, visas and transportation so I gave up and contacted Claude.

Claude had appeared in Hollywood for a very short period and had twice made the hazardous crossing to Catalina aboard *Sirocco*.

She had been a model in a famous Paris fashion house and had graduated to become the mistress of a rich industrialist. He had, rather sneakily, sabotaged her movie ambitions by sending her to Hollywood with a return ticket and just enough money for three months. She was now once more under his roof . . . actually, if not technically. He had built an apartment building in Neuilly and lived on the top floor with his plump wife and two children. Directly beneath, he had installed the beautiful Claude. She was given a certain amount of freedom but he was adamant that she must never receive gentlemen friends alone in her flat.

Although 'Monsieur' paid the concierge on the ground floor, he paid her so poorly that instead of being a built-in spy system for him, she had become the *gardienne* of Claude's freedom.

Once 'Monsieur' was home for the evening, 'en famille', he never made surprise visits below, explaining to Claude, with Gallic logic, that he would never insult his wife. Claude's only enemy then was the extreme cheapness of the materials which 'Monsieur' had used in the construction of his building: he could hear everything, even the squeaking of bed springs, and once had questioned her closely as to why she had got out of bed and used her bidet at four in the morning.

Bumping about for long periods in motor cars, trains or planes always had a strangely exuberant effect on my sexual ambitions: the problem now was how to gratify them without making a sound.

If 'Monsieur' had had the foresight to install a pane of glass in his floor, he could have gazed down on the ridiculous spectacle of two people thrashing around below with handkerchiefs stuffed in their mouths. As it was, it was a miracle he didn't come down to investigate because Claude, towards the end of the evening, decided to freshen me up with an alcohol rub. She intimated this in sign language and fetched a large bottle of eau de Cologne. Unfortunately, as I turned over to have my back done, I knocked the bottle out of her hand with my elbow and most of its contents went straight up my behind. Shrieking agony in whispers is a difficult thing to accomplish.

Noël Coward had come to visit my beach neighbour, Cary Grant, about six months previously and, like hundreds before and since, I had fallen under his spell within a few minutes of meeting him. Quite apart from the searing talent and biting wit, there is a largely unknown gentleness and a kindliness backed by lots and lots of guts. He also has a tremendous sense of loyalty and is a tiger in defence of friends or causes.

When I had last seen him, we had lunched together at 'The Cock 'n Bull' on Sunset Boulevard and he had been quite definite in his prognostications that Neville Chamberlain and his government were leading us all unerringly into war.

Now he was appointed to a job in Naval Intelligence in Paris, though he later had a misunderstanding with Winston Churchill who was never on his wavelength. He was for the moment installed in a beautiful apartment in the Place Vendome.

I went to see him one evening. The apartment was filled with a mixture of French and British diplomats and a sprinkling of officers in uniform. One of them, a very tall RAF Group Captain, cornered me and introduced himself by the name of Pope. 'It might amuse you,' he said, 'but that character you played in *Dawn Patrol* was me! – and I still have the pyjamas.'

Pope told me that I was probably too old to be taken on and trained as a fighter pilot but thought I might get fitted in elsewhere in the Service. I was only twenty-nine so this came as a rude shock. However, he recommended that I go to see John Acheson, the Air Attaché, at the Embassy and I presented myself promptly, the next morning.

'No way to join up here in France,' said Acheson, 'you'll have to get to England . . . keep your mouth shut and I'll get you on the mail plane – it goes every evening.'

He signalled me later in the day and I found myself clasping my suitcase, sitting on a pile of mail bags and gazing down on, of all things, the white cliffs of Dover topped by those ghastly Citadel Barracks.

It was a gloomy, grey, drizzly evening in late October and as the pilot circled over Hendon aerodrome, I caught my first glimpse of the barrage balloons flying like monstrous grey toys over the city. I had not let anybody know I was coming and by the time I found Grizel's studio flat in Chelsea, it was black-out time.

We sat for hours and she brought me up to date. Max had joined my father's old regiment, the Berkshire Yeomanry and was billeted underneath the grandstand of Newbury Racecourse.

Joyce was making camouflage nets and driving for the Women's Volunteer Service and, pointing down at her own coarse blue trousers, Grizel said, 'I've joined the Chelsea Fire Service.'

Max lent me his little flat in Queen Street and, after contacting a few friends and being given a great deal of conflicting advice, I set about the business of getting into uniform myself. There seemed to be a certain amount of difficulty over this because it was the time of the 'phoney war'. The Navy, indeed, was fully involved but the RAF was confined to dropping leaflets on the Germans suggesting politely that it would be much wiser for them to quit before they got hurt and the Army was stagnant on the Belgian border. All reservists had been called, plus sufficient classes of conscripts.

An added snag was that my face was all over London. *Dawn Patrol* and *Bachelor Mother* were enormously successful and the publicity department were excelling themselves. Everywhere, I was grinning out of newspapers or leering down from billboards. It was impossible to go unnoticed and the press quickly caught up with me.

To save myself from endless harrying, it seemed wiser to get the whole thing done at once so I telephoned Goldwyn's representative and, still being Hollywood-minded, I allowed him to arrange a press conference with one or two newspapers. He set it up in the Odeon Cinema, in Leicester Square, and over a hundred reporters and photographers showed up.

I explained that I had come to join up and added that I hoped to get into the RAF.

The next morning Grizel called in a state of shock. When I read the front pages, I wanted to cut my throat.

'HOLLYWOOD'S FIRST RECRUIT!' 'RELAX! THE DAWN PATROL IS HERE!' 'NIVEN SPURNS ARMY!' ... 'IT'S THE RAF FOR ME!'

I stayed hidden with friends in the country for a week to give things time to settle down and then visited the Air Ministry to make enquiries.... On the way, I noticed with rising panic that the 'ads' for *Bachelor Mother* had been altered ... above my name, red stickers had been added –

THE STAR WHO CAME HOME TO JOIN THE RAF.

I was directed to the office of a certain Group Captain. Unfortunately, I was swept into it on the crest of a giggling wave of secretaries, clutching pieces of paper and pencils.

The man restored order and eyed me with distaste. He knew who I was. Unless he had been blind he couldn't have avoided it. Nevertheless, he went through the motions of asking my name and occupation and what I wanted to do.

When I told him, he pursued in some breath with a whistling noise and shook his head.

'Ever heard of Wilfrid Lawson?'

'Yes . . . he's a wonderful actor.'

'Maybe . . . we took him on and we've had trouble, nothing but trouble ever since . . . Drink.'

I said, 'Look – all sorts of people drink, but I've come seven thousand miles at my own expense and I'd like to join the RAF.'

'So I've read,' he said nastily, 'but we don't encourage actors to join *this* service.'

For a moment I sat there stunned, then I felt anger rising from the soles of my feet.

'Then — *you!*' I said.

'Get out of my office,' he shouted. 'Get out!'

We were standing toe to toe when an inner door opened and an Air Commodore appeared,

'What the devil's going on in here?'

'And — *you too!*' I shouted unreasonably and made for the door and the giggling crowd outside it.

A week passed. I heard that Henry Clowes, who had nearly been killed five years before when the Guinness label Bentley overturned on Salisbury Plain, was now Adjutant of the Scots Guards.

Philip Astley was separated from Madeleine Carroll and he offered me a room as a paying guest in his flat at the top of Hay Hill.

'It won't work', he said, 'they have blinkers on about the theatrical profession in the Brigade – look at me – I was Adjutant of the Life Guards when I got engaged to Madeleine, but I was out of the regiment before I married her – don't try it – it's a waste of time.'

I did try it and I asked Henry Clowes if he could get me into the Scots Guards.

'No problem at all,' said Henry when I warned him about the footlight barrier – 'that was in peace time. I'll talk to the Colonel tomorrow – and phone you at once.'

Another week passed so I called Henry at Wellington Barracks.

'It didn't work, did it?' I asked.

'I'm terribly embarrassed,' said Henry. 'No it didn't.'

Goldwyn's representative called me daily.

'Look, Dave, I've got about thirty offers for you on my desk – shall I forward them to Mr Goldwyn?'

I was in no mood to be tampered with by the end of November when David Kelburn, now a full lieutenant just back from a North Atlantic convoy, told me the naval facts of life.

'Of course you can get into the Navy tomorrow if you want to – as a stoker – but you want to be an officer, don't you? ... Well, that means standing in line with thousands of people who know about the sea ... little things like navigation. Go back to your old regiment.'

'No,' I said firmly. 'I'm going to change my butcher. I don't want a lot of childish black marks hanging over me today.'

We were having a late supper on the balcony of the Café de Paris ... I stared gloomily down on the dancers. Most of the young men were in uniform, the regular army men very smart and self-assured in blue patrols, the cavalry men with colourful stripes on their pants and chain-mail on their shoulders and the exotic Rifle Brigade and 60th who wore green patrols with black patent leather cross belts and silver buckles, the newly commissioned, proud but selfconscious in drab khaki. Many RAF and naval officers were also present.

Suddenly, the orchestra leader stopped the music and Poulsen, the owner, stepped forward ... 'Ladies and gentlemen, in case anyone is interested, the air raid warning just sounded.' Such was the effect of the 'phoney war' that this announcement was greeted with cheers, hunting cries and cat-calls ... in ten seconds it was forgotten.

Less than a year later, at the height of the blitz, a bomb shrieked through the roof and exploded on the dance floor, killing Poulsen, nearly all the orchestra and a tragic percentage of the dancers.

David got up to speak to some friends and I was left looking jealously at a table of RAF pilots and their girls immediately below me. Although I was sitting unobtrusively in the balcony, they noticed me and raised their glasses, perhaps mockingly, perhaps not, but I was so selfconscious about the blaring publicity of my arrival in the country that I preferred not to speculate. One girl had her back to me. She, too, was in the powder-blue uniform of the RAF. She turned and looked up. Long blonde hair fell away and I found myself gazing into a face of such beauty and such sweetness that I just stared blankly back.

Her complexion was so perfect that the inevitable description, 'English Rose', would have been an insult. Her eyes were the merriest and the bluest I had ever seen. She looked at me for a long moment and when she got up to dance, I saw that she was tall with a divinely willowy figure.

I had a funny feeling that I would never forget her and in my mind, she became marked down as 'the WAAF'.*

* Women's Auxiliary Air Force.

I was shaken out of my musing by a rude voice behind my chair I turned to see a beefy young man in army uniform. He was swaying slightly.

'When are you going to win the war single-handed?' he asked.

A girl was plucking ineffectually at his sleeve. To avoid him, I looked again down on the scene below. A hefty shove in the back nearly embedded my front teeth in the table top.

'I'm talking to *you*, Niven,' said the young man.

'Please, Sidney,' said the girl. 'You promised not to.'

'Piss off, Janet,' said Sidney, loudly.

Heads were turning and I could see even more unpleasant publicity looming ahead. Luckily, David arrived with some naval reinforcements and Janet led a glowering Sidney back to his table.

'I don't know why you rush it,' said David, 'the bloody war will probably last a hundred years anyway ... everybody's waiting to get into uniform – you're not the only one.'

'My name's Jimmy Bosvile.' I looked up and saw, in the darkness of the night club, what I took to be a small wiry, elderly subaltern, wearing khaki with black buttons.

'I was with an air commodore this morning who was talking about your visit to his office the other day ... how splendid! I wish I'd been there.'

Bosvile sat down and I filled his glass.

'Having trouble finding a home, are you?' he said. 'Why don't you come to the Rifle Brigade?'

'You couldn't get me into the ladies' lavatory in Leicester Square,' I said, sourly.

He laughed. 'I happen to command the Second Battalion.'

Only then did I notice that one of the pips on his shoulder was a crown ... a lieutenant colonel.

So it was arranged. I told him very briefly of my previous military history and he said, 'You'll be commissioned as a second lieutenant, but put your two pips up anyway. Mark Kerr is my adjutant, he'll write and tell you what you'll need in the way of kit.... When you've got it together, come down to Tidworth. I'll expect you in about three weeks.' He smiled and we shook hands.

The Rifle Brigade! Probably the most famous of all the elite light infantry regiments in the British Army.... Army again ... oh! well ... the die was now cast. I had achieved what I had set out to do several weeks before in California ... I had a strange feeling of anti-climax.

Philip Astley was himself waiting to be called up in some capacity.

Some ten years older than me, he was doubtful what jobs could be found for him. 'Ever been to a war cemetery?' he asked, 'it doesn't matter what war or which army . . . the average age on those crosses is about twenty – it'll be the same this time.'

When instructions arrived, I visited a recommended tailor. While he was measuring me for my uniform, I asked him, 'How's business in these days of drastic clothing rationing?'

'Very slow, sir, very slow indeed . . . of course, it'll pick up nicely once we start having heavy casualties.'

I decided to visit my club. My brother and Brian Franks and others had insisted that I join during my last visit to England. My name had been put down and some months later, I had been duly elected to Boodle's.

Mr White, Mr Boodle and Mr Brooks all kept coffee houses in St James's Street in the days of the Prince Regent. The horse racing, gambling 'bloods' had frequented White's, the politicians – Brooks's, and Boodle's had been the haunt of the landed gentry. Upon the demise of the owners, these coffee shops became clubs.

It is arguable which, today, has the most attractive interior but Boodle's, with its cream-coloured columns and bow windows certainly has the most beautiful face.

Davy, the hall porter, showed me round the premises at eleven o'clock one morning. The perfect club servant, he had spent his whole life in Boodle's since he had started there as a page.

'Of course, some of my older members are a little awkward nowadays, sir . . . they don't take to the rationing at all, sir . . . luckily Chef can still put on a good table because so many of my members bring game from home. . . .'

He prattled on as he showed me the beautifully proportioned rooms. 'Of course, the Scarlet Pimpernel, he was a member, sir, and all his gang too . . . very exciting times those must have been, sir.'

He showed me a secluded corner of the main room. Large, leather chairs, discreetly separated one from the other, were placed beneath portraits of former members, Prime Ministers, Dukes and Masters of Foxhounds. 'In this corner, some say Beau Brummel used to sit looking out into the street though personally I fancy he belonged to Whites . . . this is the silence corner, sir . . . in here my members speak only to the waiters, never to each other.

'Welcome to the club, sir, we're never had a movie star in Boodle's before.' He withdrew.

No other members were about at that hour so I settled myself in the silence corner with a weekly magazine and rang the bell. The waiter brought me my glass and tidied up an ash-tray: without looking up he whispered,

'I took my wife to see *Bachelor Mother* last night, sir . . . you're her favourite fan. Lovely pictures of you and Miss Rogers in all the papers today, sir.'

I had seen them. The film had just gone on general release and once more, I was staring out of the movie pages from enormous advertisements.

From the silence corner, I had an interesting view of the passers-by in St James's Street. Always fascinated by the expressions of people who do not know they are being observed, I was too occupied to realize that I was myself being examined, with some distaste, by an elderly gentleman with a white walrus moustache. He stood right over me and flapped at me with a newspaper, a sort of fly-removing underhand flick.

'Hhhrrrump!' he said. I looked up at him.

'Hhhrrrump!' he went again and flicked once more.

I wondered if he wanted me to throw him a fish.

He 'hhhrrrumped' and flicked at me for quite a while and finally subsided angrily into a leather chair directly facing mine. There he breathed heavily, and furious, intolerant, upper-class eyes stared out at me malevolently from beneath cotton wool eyebrows.

I tried to concentrate on my magazine but the tension between us was oppressive. At last, he appeared to relax somewhat. He sat back and opened his newspaper.

Suddenly, he sat bolt upright as though he had sat on a nail. He stared appalled at the paper in front of him, then very slowly, like eighteen inch guns in a warship, his horrified gaze zeroed in on me. His eyes never left my face as he rang the bell beside his chair.

'Bring me a list of members,' he commanded with the voice of doom.

'Very good, m'lord.'

Those terrible orbs bored into me till the members' list was brought to him on a silver tray. Before he opened it he took one last look at his paper, then his finger travelled up and down the pages. The waiter hovered, nervously. Finally, the old man closed the list with a snap, looked at me for fully a minute, then let out a long moaning sound of deep despair—treachery! treachery! it said.

He turned to the waiter and trying to keep his voice steady, said bravely, 'Double brandy – quick!'

'I enjoyed that very much,' said a naval lieutenant-commander, with a pleasant ruddy face and a broad smile. 'That's our oldest member. He hates people sitting in his chair.'

I had moved out of silence corner in a hurry and a few members were now filtering in. Over drinks and luncheon he told me he was in Naval Intelligence 'probably stuck in the Admiralty for the duration'. Ian Fleming was his name and we laughed together at the same things for years to come.

While I was gathering my necessaries together for a second military career, I found Trubshawe.

He was still living at Barton, waiting, like so many others, to be called up, but his marriage to Margie was foundering and he was being comforted increasingly by the solicitous Mrs Tower.

Ditchley Park, in Oxfordshire, was the beautiful home of Nancy and Ronnie Tree.

Nancy was a cousin of Norah Flynn and Ronnie had lately distinguished himself by being one of the small band of rebel Conservative MPs who had voted with Winston Churchill against Chamberlain at the time of Munich. They invited me for the weekend and in the lovely house, decorated with sublime taste by Nancy, I was to spend some of my happiest times.

For some reason I returned on Sunday afternoon instead of Monday morning. Philip had also gone away so I was surprised when I let myself into the flat to find myself greeted by a minute Yorkshire terrier. Further shocks awaited me when I heard strange cries coming from my bedroom. I tiptoed down the passage and peered round the open door.

There, stark naked and strapped to the foot of my bed was a pillar of High Society. Thrashing him with great concentration with a birch, was a large, red-haired lady wearing a black bra, black gauntlets and black thigh boots. . . .

'Mercy, mistress.'

'Mercy, mistress,' he squealed as the birch rose and fell. The little dog sniffed at his heels. Nobody saw me so I left quietly and went to a movie. When I came back later, there was no trace of the activity except for a small puddle in the drawing room. Philip promised to reduce my rent if he lent my room to anyone in the future.

Being the owner of a well-known movie face has opened all sorts of doors. It has also closed a few, but I have had the chance to meet people whom I would only have read about if I had been a successful bank clerk or a well-to-do butcher.

The last weekend before I went to Tidworth, I was invited to the home in Kent of Sir Adrian and Lady Baillie, Leeds Castle. Here, I was to see some of the big wheels of Government at play. David

Margesson was Chief Whip of the Conservative party and later, Secretary of State for War. Geoffrey Lloyd was Minister of Transport and 'Crinks' Johnston was Head of the Liberal party.

Individually charming and for all I knew, performing their tasks with the greatest ability, as a group they depressed me.

I had a feeling that they had no right to eat and drink and dress for dinner, to make small talk and gossip like ordinary people. I was quite unreasonably shocked that they were not locked in their offices for the weekend, working tirelessly to find ways to finish the war before it got properly started.

For £190 I bought a Hillman Minx. With the petrol ration of a few gallons a month, its tiny consumption would at least allow me some freedom.

I spent my last night in London at the Café de Paris, hoping to see the WAAF again, but she did not show up. The next afternoon, I put on my new uniform, threw my baggage on to the back seat of the Hillman and headed out on the Great West Road.

It was a cold, wet, windy and altogether miserable winter's evening when I stopped the car on a hilltop on Salisbury Plain. Woodpigeons were homing into the dark isolated clumps of firs, the sodden turf on either side of the road had been chewed up by tanks. Below me lay Tidworth ... acres and acres of Victorian barrack squares in all their red-brick horror. Grey slate roofs glistened in the drizzle. A band of blue smoke hung above the place and the sound of bugles rose.

With every mile that Tidworth had come nearer, my depression had increased. 'What have you done?' I asked myself. 'Nobody asked you to come – they even told you not to ... you hate the Army ... you certainly are not very brave and you don't want to get hurt ... you've thrown away a wonderful life and career in Hollywood ... you're going to miss all that, you know ... why did you do it? ... are you sure it was not just to show off?'

I put my head on the steering wheel and warm tears of self-pity pricked my eyeballs. After a while, I drove downhill.

The Second Battalion was a motor training battalion. I was, by at least eight years, the oldest of the subalterns under training and being an ex-regular but knowing less than the others, a bit of a freak. It didn't take long to catch up. All too soon, I realized that in the intervening years, there had been pitifully few innovations. We now formed threes instead of fours; the Lewis light automatic had been replaced by the Bren; a few small Bren-carriers with tracks had been added, and instead of marching into battle, we were now driven there in trucks. Once there, we were required to perform in much the same way as before.

Jimmy Bosvile was an excellent Commanding Officer. Dick Southby, my Company Commander, was first class as was Mark Kerr, the Adjutant.

The officers came from all corners of the British Isles, the men recruited almost exclusively from London with a preponderance from the East End.

Conscripts, particularly cockney ones, were I soon discovered, very different from the professional peacetime Jocks of the Highland Light Infantry and it took me a while to get used to the grumbling of bored soldiers who resented being pulled out of good jobs and warm homes to train in acute discomfort for a war they didn't believe would ever come to anything.

Jimmy Bosvile made it clear that I was earmarked for the First Battalion which was already on the Belgian border, and in the meanwhile, I settled down to a deadening routine of teaching men to drive trucks and to march and march and march. . . .

A tall flaxen-haired Danish model, a nymphomaniac of heroic proportions, came down from London most weekends and I installed her in a cottage in a nearby village. The Great Dane did not pack a prodigious intellectual punch but her bed, though every bit as tiring, was a welcome change from spending cold frustrating nights chasing non-existent German parachutists all over Salisbury Plain. I introduced her to a rather dubious Jimmy Bosvile . . . he was convinced she was a spy.

A few days' leave came my way in February and I spent them at Ditchley.

Winston Churchill was there with Mrs Churchill. Also, Brendan Braken, his trusted lieutenant, and Anthony Eden.

I arrived in uniform just in time for dinner – the meal had, in fact, already been announced and a move was being made in the direction of the dining room. Nancy Tree took me by the hand. 'Come and sit next to me,' she said, 'it's too late for introductions.'

We were twenty in number and just as we were about to sit down, Churchill spotted me from the far end of the table. I had heard before that he was an ardent movie-goer but I was unprepared for what was to come. He marched the whole length of the dining room and shook me by the hand.

'Young man,' he growled, 'you did a very fine thing to give up a most promising career to fight for your country.'

I was conscious that the great and the near-great in the room had remained standing and were listening with interest.

I stammered some inane reply and Churchill continued with a twinkle, 'Mark you, had you not done so – it would have been despicable!' He marched back to his seat.

After dinner Churchill talked and expounded on every subject under the sun. Eden took issue with him on several occasions but Bracken, always so opinionated on his own, was very subdued in the presence of the Champion.

After church on Sunday, Churchill requisitioned me for a walk round the walled garden.

He talked at great length about vegetables and the joy of growing one's own. He made it clear that before long, rationing would become so severe that 'every square inch of our island will be pressed into service.' He questioned me about the problems of a junior officer in the Army and listened most attentively to my answers. It saddens me greatly that I had the enormous good fortune to have several of these 'garden tours' with this unique human being and that I remember so little of what he actually said.

That first weekend he extolled the virtues of Deanna Durbin, 'a formidable talent', and whenever he spoke of Hitler, he referred to him either as 'Corporal Hitler' or as 'Herr Schickelgruber'.

Ronnie Tree asked me if I could arrange an occasional private showing of a movie for Churchill. 'He loves films but he doesn't want to go out in public to see them for obvious reasons.'

The next morning I got busy and on the last evening of my leave, I booked a projection room in Soho and obtained a copy of the latest Deanna Durbin musical. I installed a bar in the projection room and gave a small dinner in the private room of a nearby restaurant before the showing.

The Trees and Eden came to dinner. Churchill was detained at the Admiralty but he joined us for the show. When he arrived, he accepted a large liqueur brandy, lit a cigar and settled happily down in his seat. Half way through the film, whispering started at the back and I saw that Churchill was leaving. I followed him out and he thanked me kindly for my efforts but said that 'something important' had come up and he must return to the Admiralty.

The next day the headlines were ecstatic. Churchill had given the order for HMS *Cossack* to enter the Josling Fjord 'to board with cutlasses' the German naval auxiliary *Altmark* and free three hundred British prisoners – seamen of merchant ships sunk by the *Graf Spee*.

The phoney war continued and the deadening boredom of the

training battalion melted into that which I had found so intolerable in the Citadel Barracks, Dover . . . I felt I had never been away.

New battalions were being formed but I still waited for my posting to the First Battalion in France. Suddenly at the beginning of May, all hell broke loose. Norway fell, Holland and Belgium were invaded and Churchill became Prime Minister.

By the end of the month, our First Battalion were fighting desperately in Calais with their backs to the Channel, as a rearguard, protecting the evacuation from Dunkirk. I was ordered to standby to move there with two hundred replacements. Events moved too quickly. By June 4th the last troops had left Dunkirk, and our entire gallant First Battalion was wiped out – all killed or taken prisoner.

My brother decided that this was the moment to get married to a beautiful South African from Durban, Doreen Platt.

After their three-day honeymoon ended, he was sent out to the Eighth Army in the desert and did not see his wife again till he came back in one piece six years later. Miraculously, the marriage also survived.

I was shown an interesting document by Mark Kerr, calling for volunteers for a new 'elite force' of a highly secret nature. There followed qualifications about age and questions about liability to air- and sea-sickness.

'I think it must be parachuting,' said Mark. 'I heard rumours that they are forming something like that.'

'Jesus!' I said. 'I don't want any part of *that*.' But the Tidworth boredom prevailed and 'anything to make a change', I put my name down.

It turned out to be something equally alarming . . . the beginning of the Commandos.

I was accepted and found myself being interviewed by Colonel Dudley Clarke at the War Office.

He told me the whole conception of the quick cut and thrust of raids on the enemy coastline. He had some special ideas, he said, which he might disclose later. In the meanwhile, I was to report to a prohibited area in Scotland – Lochailort Castle in the Western Highlands for special training with the other volunteers.

Before leaving, I made a quick but fruitless reconnaisance of the Café de Paris in the hopes of seeing 'the WAAF' who I could not get out of my mind, and then fulfilled a noisy, bruising late-night rendezvous with the Great Dane.

Volunteers usually fall into two groups. There are the genuinely courageous who are itching to get at the throat of the enemy, and the restless who will volunteer for anything in order to escape from the boredom of what they are presently doing.

There were a few in my category but most of the people I was thrown together with were made of sterner stuff.

Bill Sterling, Brian Mayfield and the Everest climber, Jim Gavin, were the founder members of the group. They were lately recovered from being depth-charged almost to death while returning in a submarine from some secret operation on the coast of Norway. Other instructors were David Sterling,* who later collected a record three DSOs for desert raids deep behind the enemy lines; 'Mad Mike' Calvert, the demolition expert; Lord Lovat, who became the great Commando leader of the Dieppe Raid and the Normandy landings, where he also lost half his stomach; Colonel Newman who collected a Victoria Cross when he raided St Nazaire and blew up the dock gates; the highly decorated Freddie Chapman who spent three and a half years behind the Japanese lines in the Malayan jungle; and two very formidable Shanghai police, Mr Sykes and Mr Fairbairn, who concentrated on teaching us a dozen different ways of killing people without making any noise.

Volunteers of all ranks came from every conceivable outfit and were a tough adventurous group prepared for any hardship. Mixed with us, for a while, were the semi-mutinous remains of the independent companies, defeated in Norway and now awaiting either absorption into the Commandos or disbandment. The Regimental Sergeant Major of this rugged conglomeration was a huge man, brought by Brian Mayfield and Bill Sterling from their parent regiment, the Scots Guards. The first morning I was at Lochailort, this splendid creature passed me, ramrod straight and moustache bristling. He let fly a tremendous salute which I acknowledged. He replied to this with an unmistakable and very loud Bronx cheer or common raspberry.

I spun round as if shot and shouted after him,

'Sergeant Major!'

'SAH!'

'Come back here!'

'SAH!'

He came back, halted and snapped off another salute.

'Did you make that rude noise?'

'YESSIR!'

* The younger brother of Bill.

'Why, may I ask?'

'Because you look such a — in a Rifle Brigade hat – SAH!'

Only then did I catch on – it was John Royal of Green Beer fame! While I gaped at him he said,

'I heard you were coming . . . I have a room in a crofter's cottage, name of Lachlan, just behind the kirk in the village – see you there this evening . . . SAH!'

Another Scots Guards salute and he was gone.

John's cottage was a godsend. Every evening, I repaired there and tried to forget my aching, bruised body and my 'flea-bag bed' on the hard wooden floor of a loft, shared with forty or fifty others.

John, after his problems in India, had found it impossible to obtain a commission so he had joined the Scots Guards as a guardsman and within a few months had risen to his present dizzy height. Later he became a parachutist and at last got back his commission as a gilder pilot. He was killed at Arnhem.

After two months running up and down the mountains of the Western Highlands, crawling up streams at night, and swimming in the loch with full equipment, I was unbearably fit. I spoke to Bill Sterling about my problem and he, most understandingly, allowed me forty-eight hours' leave in London to rectify the situation.

I visited the little village shop which doubled as post office and sent a telegram to the Great Dane.

ARRIVING WEDNESDAY MORNING WILL COME STRAIGHT TO FLAT WITH SECRET WEAPON.

The Great Dane lived in Swan Court and I went there as soon as the night train from Glasgow had deposited me in London.

I was about to ring the bell when I was tapped on the shoulder. A major and two sergeants of the Military Police had materialized from nowhere.

'Come with us, please,' said the major.

'Why? What's the matter?'

'I couldn't say – my superior wants to see you.'

I was taken in a military car to a building in St James's Street almost opposite Boodle's and shown into an office where sat a man in a blue suit. He didn't look very friendly.

'MI5 would like to ask you one little question,' he said grimly. 'You are a member of the most secret outfit in the British Army: you are in training in a Prohibited Area; you have sent a message in code to an enemy alien: WHY?'

I said, 'Sir . . . that's not code – that's — .'

I explained the circumstances and finally persuaded him that all was well. He melted a little but said that he would investigate the whole matter further. The upshot of it was that although I spent my holiday as planned with his daughter, the Great Dane's father was discovered to be working in the Ministry of Supply in a department closely connected with the organization of convoys at sea. He was removed.

By September, I was sent back to Colonel Dudley Clarke who told me that I had been promoted to Captain and was now the liaison officer between MO9 – the War Office department which was responsible for the Commandos and their operations – and the units themselves. When at the War Office, I shared a desk with a portly amiable captain who coped tirelessly and uncomplaining with the mountainous paper work – Quintin Hogg – now Lord Chancellor of Great Britain. The rest of the time, I was on the move.

A weekend leave at Ditchley provided me with a second tour of the walled garden with Winston Churchill, now Prime Minister.

He asked me what I was doing at the moment so, as we walked, I filled him in on the exciting prospects with the Commandos.

He stopped by the greenhouse and said, 'Your security is very lax ... you shouldn't be telling me this.' He was always a superb actor but to this day I don't know whether or not he was joking.

The first big raid was on Guernsey. We trained in the Isle of Wight. RAF crash boats were used because landing craft had not yet been built.

It was a success and a few bemused prisoners were taken out of their beds. One party made a landing by mistake on Sark which had no Germans on it at all. They were invited to the nearest pub by the locals.

The Battle of Britain was now in full swing as Goering tried to break the back of the RAF as a prelude to invasion.

As the battles over London and the south and east coasts raged, friends suddenly disappeared. Billy Fiske, the first American killed in World War II, died flying a Spitfire with 601 Squadron. The phoney war was over with a vengeance.

Dudley Clarke switched the role of Commandos from offence to defence and we trained to be overrun by the invaders and then to form the nucleus of an underground movement.

London was being heavily bombed and moves were made to take the minds of the civilians off their increasing discomfort. At the National Gallery, for instance, as an inducement to relax and forget what was happening over one's head, eminent musicians gave free lunch-time concerts.

I took advantage of this and one day, I walked there from the War Office and wandered round a couple of galleries. From a third, I heard a cello being played by an expert. I watched her complete concentration and bathed myself in the haunting sounds for several minutes before I realized that a few feet away, and totally engrossed, stood – 'the WAAF.'

Almost guiltily, I stared at her. At close quarters and under the overhead lighting of the gallery she was even more beautiful than I had remembered and so sweet looking and gentle.

When the music ended she did not move: she stood quite still, lost in the beauty of what she had heard. People applauded and the cellist picked up her things and left. Still the WAAF did not move. When there was only two of us left in the gallery, she looked up and noticed me.

'Hello,' she said 'wasn't that wonderful?'

I persuaded her to have a sandwich with me at a nearby coffee shop . . . we were both on the point of being late back to work.

I discovered her name, the fact that she was the cypher clerk at the RAF Reconnaissance Squadron at Heston just outside London and that she was billeted on a family friend who lived in the middle of Regent's Park.

There was never a shadow of doubt in my mind that this was the one, but with the whole world flying apart at the seams, there was no time for the niceties of a prolonged courtship. That night I called at the house in Regent's Park and passed in a note saying that I was outside the door, was considering buying the Park from the King and would like advice on the dredging of the lake.

She appeared giggling deliciously and invited me in.

Two days later I was invited to luncheon to meet her mother and by the end of the week, I found myself shaking and sweating and being introduced to her father who lived apart. My mission was to persuade him to allow his daughter to become my wife.

Bill Rollo was an angel. Nobody has ever been able to say a word against him and this despite the fact that he was a famous divorce lawyer.

When I met him he was, though over fifty, also in the uniform of the RAF . . . on his chest an impressive row of ribbons from World War I.

He worked all day at his law office and did night duty in a special war room where on a wall map, the Prime Minister could see at a glance the latest disposition of flotillas, brigades and squadrons.

He protested mightily: 'But, Primmie darling, you *can't* put me in this position because I don't know how to behave!'

'Don't be nervous, papa,' said she, 'leave everything to us.'

He handed me an enormous drink and helped himself liberally. 'Oh, God!' he said, 'this is agony, isn't it? I ought to ask you all sorts of questions . . . do you have any prospects? . . . well, that's bloody silly for a start because the air raid warning has just gone.'

It was the night of a particularly heavy 'blitz' and bombs were soon raining down. It had been arranged that we would go out to dinner but there was so much shrapnel flying about that we decided against it.

'I can't think why you want to marry her,' said Bill, 'she can't cook and she can't sew.'

'You're a big help,' said his daughter.

We opened some wine, some cans of beans and some cheese and as a particularly heavy bombardment made the high old building shudder and sway, with the three of us huddling under the kitchen table, Bill Rollo gave his consent.

War is a great accelerator of events so ten days later, we were married in the tiny Norman church of Huish village at the foot of the Wiltshire Downs. Trubshawe, now in the uniform of the Royal Sussex Regiment, was best man, and friends from far and near came by train, by bicycle or by blowing their petrol rations for a month – some came on horseback.

Primmie looked like a porcelain figure in a simple pale blue dress. The Battle of Britain on that cloudless September day, was raging in the skies above – it was no time for veil and orange blossom. She carried a bouquet of pink flowers picked from her parents' garden a hundred yards away. Half way through the service, as we were singing her favourite anthem, 'Sheep may safely graze', a small flock, as though divinely summoned, wandered in from the Downs and stood chewing benignly round the font.

Our first days of honeymoon were spent finding a place for Primmie to set up a home.

We had no money apart from my army pay so we were lucky to find a fourteenth-century, unheated, thatched cottage between Dorney and Slough. Primmie had left the RAF in order to get married but she was determined to contribute to the war effort so she bicycled to Slough every morning at seven o'clock and worked at Hawker's factory, building Hurricane fighters. She took in an elderly refugee from the London bombing who had just lost her husband and her home near the docks. Mrs Wisden was a little birdlike cockney who wore pince-nez. She kept 'Halfway Cottage' tidy and cooked – after a fashion – but behaved rather strangely during air raid alerts. Hawker's being an obvious target for the Luftwaffe, these were frequent. Thanks to a permanent smoke screen from smudge pots, the factory itself remained untouched but the whole neighbourhood became pitted with bomb craters to Mrs Wisden's apparent satisfaction. The moment the banshee wailings of the sirens started, she would rip down the blackout curtains, turn on all the lights and rush out into the garden, tearing at her blouse.

'Let me 'ave it, 'Itler!' she would scream, 'rite through me bleedin' chest ... I want to join my 'Arry ... Roll on death!'

The Commandos were being prepared for offensive operations but these were held up while landing craft were designed and built. In the meanwhile, the danger of our own invasion by the German Army, poised across the Channel, was very real. A new and highly secret outfit within the Special Services was formed to help deal with this possibility and I was ordered to join it in Richmond Park. Before I went, I did something for which, in my opinion, the military has never adequately rewarded me. I suggested to my new uncle by marriage, Robert Laycock, that he should join the Commandos.

He was then a captain in the Royal Horse Guards and had just received a posting to India to become gas officer of a division and was due to embark in a few days' time. He came to the War Office and I introduced him to Dudley Clarke who immediately decided that this was just the man he wanted.

Bob and I paced the stone corridors of that dreary building while Clarke dashed about, pulling strings as a result of which somebody else went to India and Bob formed No. 8 Commando, embarking on a career of legendary gallantry which included his famous effort to blow up Field Marshal Rommel in the desert some 200 miles behind the German lines in Libya. It culminated, five years later, in his becoming Chief of Combined Operations with the rank of major-general.

Richmond Park was the headquarters of 'Phantom' – the brain-child of 'Hoppy'.

Colonel Hopkinson had realized painfully during the retreat to Dunkirk that if a general fighting a battle is not receiving a steady flow of reliable information from the front, he cannot contribute very much towards the outcome. In the heat of contact, normal communications frequently break down, radio transmitters get destroyed and dispatch riders get killed.

'Phantom' was composed of a number of highly mobile squadrons of 'officer patrols'. These were deployed among the forward units, equipped with radios, endowed with expert dispatch riders and as a last resort, a basket of carrier pigeons. The commanding officer of 'Phantom' stayed at the army commander's right hand and when the situation at a certain point on the map needed clarifying, a message went direct to the nearest 'Phantom' Squadron to find out exactly what was going on. In practice the answer usually came back explaining that the situation was unclear because the place was full of Germans.

After a brief period of intensive training, I was promoted to Major and for over three years I had the great honour to command 'A' Squadron.

'Hoppy' was a short, square officer with a fertile imagination and a great gift for extracting the maximum of loyalty and hard work from all ranks. Before he was killed in action in Italy, he built up a unit that again and again proved its worth in the reconquest of the Continent.

Hugh Kindersley, a handsome giant from the Scots Guards, was second-in-command and the officers and men came from every unit in the British Army.

During the threat of sea-borne invasion, the 'Phantom' squadrons were distributed along the southern and eastern coasts where, apart from our primary function, we also made ourselves ready to go underground and a large stock of disguises was earmarked for distribution if the invasion was successful. I, personally, was ready to re-emerge dressed as a parson.

For a start 'A' Squadron was attached to 5 Corps in the danger area behind Poole Harbour. The Corps Commander was a dynamic little man who demanded a fearsome standard of mental alertness and physical fitness. Just inside his headquarters was a large notice board. . . .

ARE YOU 100% FIT?
ARE YOU 100% EFFICIENT?
DO YOU HAVE 100% BINGE?

We never discovered what he meant by 'BINGE' because nobody dared to ask him. His name was General Bernard Montgomery.

'A' Squadron was my pride and joy. The second-in-command was a sardonic Irish newspaper man and the patrol officers included a Cameron Highlander, a Frenchman, a Lancastrian, a weight lifter, the assistant Bursar at Eton College, an amateur steeplechase jockey and an interior decorator who frequently called me 'dear' instead of 'sir'.

The Squadron Sergeant-Major was a Scots guardsman and the seventy other ranks were made up of bank clerks, burglars, shop assistants, milkmen, garage mechanics, school masters, painters, bookmakers, stockbrokers and labourers.

A rugged corporal told me he was 'a lion tamer in usual life' and of the two men who cooked for and catered to the officers, one came from the Royal Household at Buckingham Palace while the other, a Norfolk man, said he 'liked a bit of poaching better than anything.' In action, of course, these two were 'runners' at Squadron Head-quarters and once when General Montgomery visited us unexpec-tedly, I was waiting under his eagle eye for an important message to be delivered when I was appalled to see my 'runner' approaching with the message in one hand and a pheasant in the other.

In the autumn of '41, the Trees invited Primmie and me to spend my week's leave in the comfort of Ditchley. Walter Monckton, Director General of the Ministry of Information, was there, also a charming American, David Bruce. As the Germans had radio beams from Norway and France pinpointing Chequers, the Prime Minister's country retreat was considered a bad risk so Ronnie and Nancy made a large part of Ditchley available to Winston Churchill and his staff. It was fascinating to rub shoulders with the greats, with Sir Charles Portal, the Commander in Chief of the RAF, and Sholto Douglas, Chief of Fighter Command.

Churchill bade me take another walk in the walled garden. Things were looking grim – the war in the desert was at its lowest ebb with Rommel snapping at the gates of Alexandria and after their spectacular success in Crete, the possibility of an enemy airborne invasion of the UK had now superseded the threat of a conventional one. Food was getting more and more scarce and a glance at the map sent cold shivers down one's back.

The whole of Europe was under German domination and in Russia, Von Rundstedt had just captured 600,000 prisoners at Kiev and Von Bock another 600,000 at Vyazma ... Leningrad was besieged and the road to Moscow appeared wide open.

'Do you think, sir,' I asked, 'that the Americans will ever come into the war?'

He fixed me with that rather intimidating gaze and unloosed the famous jaw-jutting bulldog growl.

'Mark my words – something cataclysmic will occur!'

Four weeks later the Japanese attacked Pearl Harbor.

Months after, when we were once more enjoying the delights of a short leave at Ditchley, I asked in the walled garden if the Prime

Minister remembered what he had said so long ago. His reply gave me goose pimples.

'Certainly I remember.'

'What made you say it, sir?'

'Because, young man, I study history.'

When Primmie became pregnant in the spring of 1942, she stopped building fighter planes, left Mrs Wisden baring her bosoms in the garden at the first sign of a German bomber and followed 'A' Squadron wherever it went, living in a succession of farms, stables and vicarages. We were wonderfully in love and spent a lot of time praying that Phantom would not be sent to the African desert, or the Malayan jungle.

In mid-August, the ambitious raid on Dieppe was carried out. About 8,000 men, mainly Canadians, were employed. Commandos under Lord Lovat were also involved and a specially trained force from Phantom.

Though the raid taught many invaluable lessons that saved devastating loss of life later on the Normandy beaches, the cost was appalling with almost two-thirds of the attacking force wiped out.

Writing and re-writing the letters I had to send to the wives and girl friends of the men lost from 'A' Squadron, I kept thinking of a scene from *Dawn Patrol* when the Commanding Officer was going through the same agonizing ritual. The adjutant watched him for a while and then said, gently, 'It doesn't matter how you word it, sir, it'll break her heart just the same.'

By autumn, Primmie was less mobile so she moved to London during the height of the blitz and calmly waited for the arrival of her baby.

I thought perhaps Philip Astley might let her stay in his comfortable flat and went to see him. The building had been demolished by a direct hit. Fortunately, Philip had been out at the time.

By a great piece of good luck, 'Hoppy' had recalled 'A' Squadron to Richmond to refit with new equipment so I was well within reach when Primmie was whisked off in the middle of a December night and admitted to the Royal Northern Hospital in Camden Town in North London. 'Hoppy' gave me permission to spend the nights in the hospital so, every evening, after work, I borrowed a dispatch rider's motor cycle and rode through the black-out across the whole of London to be with Primmie and her little boy. They were unattractive trips. Hitler's full fury was raining down on the city and shrapnel from the anti-aircraft batteries was also falling like lethal confetti. I wore a steel helmet and, too often aided by the light of the fires, chugged my way past bomb craters and debris, peering ahead at the glow-worm reflection from my dimmed-out headlight. Happily the motor cycle made so much noise that I could not hear the express train whistle of falling bombs.

I slept on the floor beside Primmie's bed and marvelled at her serenity – she was totally unafraid. Camden Town, a working class district, for some reason had become a prime target for the German bombers ... the devastation around the hospital was awful. The bombing started nightly, as soon as darkness fell, and continued till dawn. More than once, on hearing a bomb screaming down in his direction, the brave major on the floor had to steel himself against taking over under his wife's bed.

A few days after Primmie and the baby left for Dorney, the inevitable happened – the hospital received a direct hit.

During 1943, the soldier's oldest enemy – boredom – attacked Phantom. It was quite evident to us that we were being prepared for the final assault on the continent of Europe, but like footballers, we were becoming overtrained, so 'Hoppy' sent his squadrons whizzing all over England.

At one moment, 'A' Squadron found itself isolated outside the walls of Dartmoor Prison.

'Keep the men interested,' ordered 'Hoppy' by radio. 'Think of novel employment for them – turn night into day – make front-line conditions.'

Obediently, I arranged three days on the moors of intensive manœuvres and, at the last minute, to simulate what might easily lie ahead of us, I cancelled the ration trucks.

Naturally, at the end of seventy-two hours on a windswept escarpment, covered with nothing but heather, ferns and wild pony sh it, 'A' Squadron, forced to 'live off the land', were in a sorry condition. All, that is, except their gallant commander who had taken certain precautions and Squadron Sergeant Major Lonsdale of the Scots Guards.

'How is it possible?' I asked him. 'I am the only one who knew that the squadron would have no food or water for three days.'

'Sorr,' he replied, 'I happened to have aboot my person one large fruit cake.'

The naval commander of a flotilla of motor torpedo boats in Dartmouth contacted me.

'We are made of three-ply,' he said, 'and are fitted with last-war 2-pounders. The German E boats have twin Oerlikens operated electrically from armour-plated bridges and we are supposed to protect the convoys from the bastards – do you have any anti-tank weapons? If so, please come and help us.'

'A' Squadron spent many miserable seasick hours as a result of my quixotic acceptance of this dangerous invitation.

'Hoppy' finally gathered all the squadrons into Richmond Park and told me to arrange a concert. I went to beg the help of the Crazy Gang at the Victoria Palace.

Bud Flanagan's response was typical. 'Leave it to us,' he said, 'just provide the transport and we'll provide the show but you be Master of Ceremonies and give us some grub after.'

The concert took place at midnight, in the big movie house on Richmond Hill. It was a classic show business answer to an SOS Flanagan and Allen showed up, also Nervo and Knox, Naughton and Gold, Debroy Somers and his Band, Teddy Brown and his xylophone, Sid Field, Zoe Gail, Frances Day, Naunton Wayne, Arthur Riscoe and Leslie Henson.

The show lasted for four hours and was wildly appreciated. Civilian morale on a small beleaguered island was also in constant need of bolstering and during the time I spent in the Home Forces, I was used for all sorts of capers. I was given four weeks 'special duty' and with a radio transmitter in my dressing room from which I controlled 'A' Squadron, I played a part in a film about the Spitfire, backed by the RAF – *The First of the Few* with Leslie Howard.

Two years later, I collected a few more weeks of 'special duty' and played in an Army-backed film, directed by Carol Reed, written by Eric Ambler and Peter Ustinov – *The Way Ahead* – which was not only a huge public success but for ten years after the war was used as a training film at Sandhurst.

These short bursts of escapism were a bonanza and I was only too happy to sample the first marvellous fruits of a happy married life.

With my Major's pay, Primmie had now left the numbing damp of 'Halfway Cottage' for the roaring draughts of a phoney Tudor villa nearer the centre of the village of Dorney.

It was always full of friends, bringing their own food and drink of course. Larry Olivier did the carving, having been brought up in a low budget parsonage he could make a chicken do for ten people. He and Vivien lived nearby as did Johnny and Mary Mills, Rex Harrison and Lili Palmer. Noël Coward was a frequent and greatly cherished visitor and all of them looked after Primmie while I was away and gave her a wonderful introduction into the strange, half-mad world of show business.

Del Giudice, the Italian dynamo who produced the pictures that took Arthur Rank out of his flour bags and put him at the top of the film world, was another neighbour. A popular guest at Del Giudice's house was the then Minister of Labour and later, one of the greatest Foreign Secretaries that Britain has ever known – Ernest Bevin.

I discussed with him the problem of my soldiers' boredom.

'Make 'em use their noggins,' he said, 'they're all intelligent fellers ... get a few debates going – but don't take side yourself or you'll be in a bloody mess.'

The discussion periods I organized as a result of Bevin's advice were a huge success. The liveliest one was sparked off by a leading article which had appeared in the *Daily Mirror*, '... the accepted tip for Army leadership would, in plain truth, be this: All who aspire to mislead others in war should be brass-buttoned boneheads, socially prejudiced, arrogant and fussy. A tendency to heart disease, apoplexy, diabetes and high blood pressure is desirable in the highest posts. ...'

One thing stuck out a mile during these debates – the vast majority of men who had been called up to fight for their country held the Conservative party entirely responsible for the disruption of their lives and in no circumstances would they vote for it next time there was an election – Churchill or no Churchill.

Weekends at Ditchley afforded close-ups of other members of the Cabinet: Anthony Eden was unfailingly kind and charming but, somehow, left me with the impression that he was floating in the air far above me. Duff Cooper, a much tougher, much more down-to-earth character, was given to bursts of ungovernable fury during which his face would congest and turn an alarming magenta colour. The smallest thing could set him off and the Trees' two sons would come rushing to find me ... 'Come quick ... Duff's doing a turkey cock in the library!'

I got on famously with him once he realized we had one big thing in common – we both loved America and Americans. His wife, the legendary Lady Diana, was, of course, sublime.

My fast-becoming-forgotten movie face was occasionally pressed into service and I was sent to make impassioned speeches in factories in the Midlands during 'Tanks for Russia Week'. I was also sent to Glasgow to head a drive to get more volunteers for the Women's Army – the ATS. There, for a week, I appeared in fog-filled movie houses all over the city and harangued the paying customers whom I could barely see in the gloom.

By the beginning of 1944, the Americans were pouring into Britain and many old Hollywood friends appeared at Dorney. Bob Coote materialized in the Royal Canadian Air Force. Clark Gable, whose adored wife, Carole Lombard, had been killed in an air disaster, appeared as a major in a bombing squadron and Jimmy Stewart showed up – a colonel in the same line of business. John Ford and Douglas Fairbanks Jr were in the US Navy. Willie Wyler and John Huston were with Combat Photographic Units. Garson Kanin was doing something very mysterious in the Army and joy of joys, John McClain arrived, a lieutenant in the US Navy attached to the OSS.

Dorney features so often in this account that I feel I should explain that I was in other places too. At the end of a war one forgets, thank God, the numbing patches of boredom and frustration and remembers only the fright and the fun. I am chiefly concerned with the fun and Dorney, with Primmie, was where my fun lay.

The Free French frequently cooked their rations in our kitchen, among them Claude Dauphin and Jean Pierre Aumont. These two gave a party for us in London and Joseph Kessel ate a champagne glass, stem and all.

Guy Gibson, the master bomber, spent a weekend with us just after he had been awarded the Victoria Cross for blowing up the Eder and Mohne dams. He was in a rare state of excitement because Winston Churchill had invited him to dinner at 10 Downing Street on the Monday. Guy made a date with us for luncheon at one o'clock on the following day so he could report everything the great man said.

Primmie and I were at the Berkeley sharp at one – no Gibson. Two o'clock – no Gibson. We were just finishing our ersatz coffee around three o'clock when he came tottering in looking ghastly, eyes like dog's balls.

'How was it?' we asked.

'Marvellous – fabulous!' he croaked. 'God! I'm tired – that was the best yet!'

'What did he say?'

'Who?' said Gibson.

'Churchill,' I said with a touch of asperity.

Gibson looked stricken – then he clutched his head.

'Jesus Christ! – I *forgot!*'

A month later on his one hundred and twentieth bombing mission, he was shot down.

By the early spring of 1944, it was obvious that the Second Front would soon be opened on the Continent. Training increased in tempo and there were so many American troops in Britain that only the barrage balloons kept the island from sinking beneath the waves under their weight.

Out of the blue, I was ordered to report to General Sir Frederick Morgan at a highly camouflaged headquarters in a wood near Sunningdale. Morgan, although I did not know it, had four months been drawing up the invasion plans that would soon be put to effect in Normandy. He came straight to the point.

'You've lived in America for some years?'

'Yes, sir.'

'Do you like Americans?'

'Very much, sir.'

'Good, because you're going to be seeing a great deal of them . . . I'm taking you out of Phantom and promoting you to Lieutenant Colonel . . . from now on you will be under the direct order of General Barker – an American.'

He told me where to go and I found General Ray Barker in a Nissen hut under the trees. He, it transpired, had been working with Morgan on the overall invasion plan.

'One thing we dread is a repetition of what happened between the British and the French in the last war,' he said. 'Sir John French and General Lanrezac were commanding adjoining armies. They didn't speak each other's language; they detested each other and tried to win private feuds to impress Field Marshal Joffre.

'Their feeling percolated down to the troops. The Germans repeatedly attacked this weak link in the chain and very nearly won the war as a result.'

General Barker was the finest type of contemporary American . . . quiet, courteous and full of humour but underneath his evident compassion and gentleness, one could detect the steel . . . I listened attentively as he went on . . .

'When we land on the Continent, there will be American, British and Canadians to start with. Later there will be Poles and French. I am charged by General Eisenhower with seeing that this time, there are no weak links in the chain. Misunderstandings and rumours are bound to arise but they will have to be dealt with promptly at all levels from friction between army commanders, right down to arguments about what programmes should be beamed to the troops by the BBC and the American Forces Network. After we invade you will be in the field doing odd jobs for me and from now on you take orders only from me.'

'A' Squadron gave me a silver tankard and I handed over to John Hannay, my second-in-command for the past two years. It was a big wrench but my love of change soon dispelled my disappointment and under the highly efficient John the squadron prospered.

A celebration luncheon with Ian Fleming at Boodle's revealed that the place was much changed. A direct hit had demolished the back of the building but the beautiful façade and famous ceilings were still intact. Most of the windows were boarded over. Food had become very scarce.

'My members don't take to whale steaks at all,' said Davy mournfully.

We were peering at the daily menu displayed in the darkened hall when the oldest member growned in my ear.

'Can't see the damn thing in this gloom – what's on the card today?'

'Moules marinières, sir,' I said.

'Good God!' he trumpeted, 'the bloody fellers have got us eatin' moles now!'

We held a belated christening party for little David and with the exception of Bob Laycock, all the godparents came to Dorney.

Larry and Vivien produced a Jacobean drinking mug with 'D.W.' engraved on it. I complained about this to Godmother Vivien who said, 'I'm not going to change it so from now on you'll just have to be called "Wiven", that's all.'

Godfather Noël Coward donated a silver cocktail shaker on which was inscribed –

> 'Because, my Godson dear, I rather
> Think you'll turn out like your father.'

The day, however, was made by a retired Nannie – Miss Maple – who at seventy had decided that she could still 'do her bit' so she struggled with little David to enable Primmie to return to work at Hawker's. Some of my methods, however, had upset this redoubtable old lady and she suddenly appeared and announced to the assembled guests.

'It's bad enough when the Colonel takes Master David's olive oil for the salad dressing – but when he steals his concentrated California orange juice for the cocktails – it's going *too far!*'

I was so proud of Primmie, of her flower-like beauty of course, but everyone loved her and the reason was obvious ... She never thought an unkind thought about anyone. She was incapable of saying an unkind word. On the June night before I left for Normandy we clung together miserably. The parting was not made easier by the news that her uncle, Michael Laycock, had just been killed on the beaches and that her brother, Andrew, had been blown up when his destroyer hit a mine. His captain reported that 'blown up' was the correct description because Andrew was on the foredeck when it happened and the next moment the captain, high on the bridge, saw Andrew above his head. Miraculously, he fell in the sea and survived.

I lied to Primmie about leaving after breakfast and at dawn when she had finally fallen asleep, I slipped out of bed, dressed, looked down at her with the little boy asleep in his cot beside her, and tiptoed out of the house.

The *Empire Battleaxe* was a Liberty ship with elements of an American Division. I boarded her at Southampton.

'That's one helluvan encouraging send-off,' observed a GI as, over the side, we watched hundreds of wounded being helped or carried ashore from a tank landing craft – boys with shocked faces and staring eyes, in their bandages and hastily applied field dressings, grown old in a few short hours.

Once opposite the Normandy beach, we were ordered into the landing craft and, to the continuous roll of gunfire, ferried ashore. Beach Masters pointed to the white taped paths through the minefields and we went our separate ways.

There is no place in these pages for harrowing blood-soaked descriptions of man's inhumanity to man – all that has been raked over a thousand times by a thousand more competent writers since that June of 1944 so let me say at once that lying in a ditch that first night in Normandy, my most vivid recollection was the sound of the nightingales.

Before the war, eminent lady cellists were employed by the BBC to sit in remote black woods to try and coax these timid little birds into song. The nightingales of Normandy were made of sterner stuff – they all but drowned out the gunfire with their racket.

Between British Second Army and American First there was a small bridge at Carentan. It was in fact the one vital link between our very meagre bridgeheads and, consequently, was shelled by the Germans at close range many times a day.

Several spare Bailey bridges were kept handy so that replacement was speedy and the lifeline kept open, but it was a hazardous crossing and I had to make it frequently. Foxholes were dug on either side of the bridge and once, trapped by the shelling, I was cowering in the bottom of one of them when, after what seemed an eternity, the lethal rain seemed to have let up. I peeked timidly out and couldn't believe my eyes. Like a cock-pheasant in the bracken, a familiar head was sticking out of a foxhole a few yards away – John McClain.

After the barrage, my transport was no longer functioning so my old friend gave me a ride in his command car driven by a very disapproving American sergeant. Mcclain also pinned on my chest the Iron Cross.

Cherbourg was still in enemy hands and McClain, with a psychological warfare unit, had been bombarding the defenders with a verbal barrage via a sound truck. General von Schlieben, in an attempt to shore up the morale of the defenders, had for some days been handing out decorations like Lady Bountiful at a village fête. He had radioed for more Iron Crosses to be delivered by parachute and they had been dropped in error on McClain and his outfit.

My work completed at First Army, McClain suggested a light luncheon at a little inn he had heard about from Captain Bob Low, an ex-*Time* reporter, now working in First Army Intelligence.

'Low says it's in a backwater,' he said, 'no krauts there – nobody – untouched by the war – let's go.'

Quetthou, on the coast about five miles south of Barfleur, was all that Bob Low had predicted and the inn, 'Aux Trois Cents Hommes', was unforgettable. The disapproving sergeant refused to join us and sat outside morosely chewing his 'C' rations, while McClain and I, the first Allied combatants they had seen, were treated like royalty by the three bosomy ladies who ran the place. We were given a sumptuous meal of omelettes, delicious little flat fish and Camembert cheese, washed down by bottles of Bordeaux which they dug up from the cabbage patch where they had been hidden from the Germans.

On the way back, we grew strangely silent as we approached Carentan because it became obvious from the noise that we were going to have to run the gauntlet of the bridge once again.

'Er . . . lookit, Sarge,' said McClain. 'Isn't there some way round by the beach so we can cut out that goddam bridge?'

The disapproving one was unbending.

'The way I see it, Lieutenant – it's either got your name on it, or it hasn't.'

McClain's reply was really brave.

'Well – it may have your — name on it – but it doesn't have mine.'

The Normandy battles raged around Caen and St Lô longer than had been expected and this frustration of their plans sparked the first differences of opinion between the Allied commanders. Finally, at the end of July, with the British and Canadians containing the bulk of the German armour, the Americans were able to break out on the Western flank and the charge on Paris and Brussels began.

I found 'B' Squadron of Phantom hidden in a wood behind the Orne. Dennis Russell was still in command. Hugh (Tam) Williams, that fine actor, was still in the squadron. They told me that Hugh Kindersley had been badly wounded and 'Tam' and I agreed that if we had known about the German Nebelwerfer – a six-barrelled mortar – we would never have joined the Army in the first place. (After the war, like many others, 'Tam' found his place had been filled while he had been away and that he had been largely forgotten as an actor. He went bankrupt and then emerged triumphant as one of the most successful playwrights that London has seen.)

In a tent far to the rear lived a group of war correspondents typing out pages of self-glorification ... 'as the bullets sang past my head' etc. There were some heroic and exemplary war correspondents, of course – Ernie Pyle, Bob Capa, and Chester Wilmot, to name a few – but anyone who says a bullet sings past, hums past, flies, pings or whines past, has never heard one – they go *crack*.

Just before the breakout at Falaise, General Barker recalled me for a few hours to England.

The DC3 lumbered off the makeshift runway on a cliff top above the landing beaches. After an alarming dip, it gained height and headed home. Below much of the damage wrought by the disastrous three-day storm at the end of June was still apparent. The 'Mulberry' harbour opposite St Laurent was completely wrecked and of the 800 landing craft originally smashed ashore, at least half still lay there like beached whales.

An American intelligence colonel sitting on the bucket seat beside me, told me that the storm had reduced the unloading of vital stores and reinforcements to a trickle and for two weeks it had been touch and go whether we could hang on in Normandy.

We landed at Croydon at eight o'clock in the morning. Flying bombs were now being directed into London all day long and driving through the City, the damage was much greater than I expected.

General Barker concluded his business with me with great

dispatch, then with his customary thoughtfulness, he said, 'Your plane goes back at seven this evening so go on home and give your wife a surprise.'

I caught the fast train to Reading, got off at Taplow and borrowed the station master's bicycle. I could be in Dorney by one and the five o'clock train back seemed days away.

Land-girls were cutting lettuce and digging potatoes in the fields on either side of the road. They looked up and waved as I pedalled past. My heart was bubbling with excitement. In my mind I rehearsed all sorts of stiff-upper-lip-returning-warrior platitudes. I wished I had a toy for the little boy.

Quietly, I leaned the bicycle against a tree and pushed the back door – it was locked. The front door was locked too. I walked round and round the house . . . nobody was home. I opened a back window by breaking a pane and crawled through . . . The family was gone and judging by the state of the kitchen, had been gone for some days.

Disconsolate and also alarmed, I mounted the bicycle and made enquiries in the village shops.

'Mrs Niven picked up her ration books a week ago but nobody knows where she went.'

Back at the house, I called Bill Rollo in London at his office but he was out.

I had beer, bread and cheese and pickled onions in the village pub then went home again and waited for Bill to call back. While I was waiting, I mowed the lawn and weeded Primmie's little vegetable garden. At three o'clock Bill called and told me she had decided to evacuate the London area and take little David up to the peace and quiet of Quenby in Leicestershire.

I put through a call to Quenby but there was a three-hour delay. I pleaded with the operator but she was granite.

'We all 'ave our little problems these days don't we, luv?'

I drank the remainder of a bottle of gin in the kitchen and weaved off on the stationmaster's bicycle in time to catch the five o'clock for London and Normandy.

13

By mid-August the Canadians had entered Falaise. The Poles were above Chambois and with the British and Americans in full spate, the bulk of the German Seventh Army was wiped out in the Mortain Pocket. Sixteen of the twenty German generals involved, however, managed to escape to fight another day and this touched off more asperity between the Allied commanders with everyone accusing everyone else of being too slow, too quick or too cautious.

The Americans and Free French entered Paris on the twenty-fifth and the British, Canadians and Poles rushed headlong for the Channel ports and Belgium.

With the Germans in full retreat, conflicting plans were put forward for bringing the war to a speedy conclusion and even louder squabbles now broke out between those super primadonnas, Montgomery, Bradley and Patton. Distorted versions of their differences filtered down to the fighting troops and General Barker's department had a lot of fence-mending to do.

I was ordered to Paris to deliver some important documents to an American colonel. 'Meet him in the bar of the Hotel Crillon', was my highly sophisticated directive and I hastened south, most anxious to see my favourite city in the full orgiastic ecstasy of her liberation.

An American corporal was driving my jeep. We got lost in Neuilly till I realized I was only a stone's throw from Claude's apartment. I bade the corporal wait, and leaving him festooned with flowers in the centre of a singing, kissing, bottle-waving throng, I pushed my way into the building.

My welcome was rapturous but the set-up had changed. 'Monsieur' having been deported to a forced labour camp near Essen, Madame and Claude, in their misery, had buried their hatchets, pooled their resources and Claude had moved in upstairs with the family. They nourished me from their sparse supplies of food and drink, heated water in pails so I could have a hot bath and clucked over me like two hens.

Luckily, I had kept the documents with me because when I descended to keep my rendezvous at the Crillon the jeep and corporal had disappeared, borne off, he assured me later, on the crest of a wave of hysterical grateful citizenry ... Claude saved the day.

'It's nothing – you take Madame's bicycle ... I come with you!'

From some long-forgotten celebration, Madame produced two small Union Jacks and with Claude at my side, bells ringing, and flags fluttering bravely from the handle-bars, we free-wheeled down the whole length of the Champs Elysées to the admiring plaudits of the crowd. Mounted on a woman's bicycle, I was probably the first British soldier the French of Paris had seen for five years.

The Guards Armoured Division entered Brussels on September 3rd. Antwerp was freed the next day. The reaction of the French of Paris to their liberation was that of an undertakers' convention compared to the behaviour of the Belgians. The tired faces of the soldiers glowed – it made everything seem worthwhile.

That autumn has been described by the war historians as a 'lull' – the soldiers didn't notice it – particularly the British airborne troops who had to fight for their lives at Arnhem, the Canadians struggling on the Leopold Canal or the Americans at Aachen.

'A' Squadron Phantom, with John Hannay at the helm, was living in great discomfort in flat, water-logged fields near Geldrop. I spent some days when them en route to a chore in Nijmegen near the Meuse where I ran across Tony Bushell, Olivier's production manager in usual life, and now a company commander with the Welsh Guards. We were reminiscing in the tank park when the earth shook under an appalling explosion. Instinctively, I dived for cover. I looked out to see Bushell roaring with laughter.

'What the hell was that?' I asked.

'Oh, that's an old friend,' said Bushell. 'They've got a bloody great gun in a railway tunnel across the river. About once an hour they wheel it out and let off a big one – then they pop back in again. We're used to it.'

In early December in Brussels, I found Bobby Sweeny who had been distinguishing himself with the RAF. He was on leave.

'They tell me,' said Bobby, 'that the wild duck are really flighting in to the flooded farmland on the Scheldt Estuary, let's go and knock some off.'

A great organizer of comfort, Sweeney conjured up a jeep, guns and ammunition and we set off, accompanied by a carload of Bobbie's Belgian friends. The shooting at dusk was spectacular. On the other side of the river it must have been equally good because we could hear the Germans taking full advantage of it.

The Belgian group returned to Brussels after dark but 'the

Comfort King' had a better idea.

'Nothing in the world like wild duck cooked absolutely fresh . . . much better than after they've been hung,' he said. 'One of the best restaurants in Europe is the "Panier d'Or" in Bruges. The Canadians have probably taken the place by now – let's go in there and if the "Panier d'Or" is still standing, we'll get 'em to cook for us.'

At the outskirts of the beautiful little seventh-century Flemish town, the Military Police told us that the Germans had indeed been pushed out several hours before. In the centre of the town there was very little damage and we found the 'Panier d'Or' intact.

Bobbie was right about the duck – they were sensational but we both underestimated the hospitality of the owner and his family.

They plied us for hours with every known kind of drink and before we staggered out, they produced their 'Livre d'Or' for our signatures. A special page was prepared and after five years of German names, the two first Allied ones were scrawled with a flourish. Outside, a full moon was riding in the cold winter sky. The town, with not a chink of light showing, was unnaturally quiet – not a cat was stirring – it was eerie.

We started up the jeep and clattered through the deserted streets and back over the bridge to the main road. A Canadian patrol stopped us and told us the facts of life. During our long meal, the enemy had started a vicious counter-attack and the Canadians had pulled back through the town. Half an hour after we left the 'Panier d'Or', the centre of Bruges was once more swarming with Germans.

In the middle of December, I was passing through Spa, American First Army Headquarters in the Ardennes. I spent the day with Bob Low and he showed me the map room of the Intelligence Section.

'What happens here?' I asked.

'You mean here in Spa?'

'Yes.'

After all these years I can quote what he said, word for word – it was impossible to forget. He pointed out of the window.

'You see the trees on the top of those hills?'

'Yes.'

'Well, the other side of those hills, there is a forest and in that forest they are now forming the Sixth Panzer Army and any day now the Sixth Panzer Army is going to come right through this room and out the other side, cross the Meuse, then swing right and go north to Antwerp.'

'Have you told anyone?' I laughed.

'We've been telling them for days,' said Low. 'Every day we have to give three appreciations of what we *think* may happen – that has been our number one appreciation.'

The next day I went down through the fog-shrouded Forest of the Ardennes to Marche. Within hours the last great German offensive of the war erupted. Ahead of it, Skorzeny's Trojan Horse Brigade, American-speaking and wearing American uniforms, infiltrated everywhere with captured American tanks and half-tracks. Sabotaging as they went, they rushed for the Meuse. The rumours of Skorzeny's men flew wildly. In my British uniform and jeep with 21st Army Group markings, I had some anxious moments at the hands of understandably trigger-happy GIs. Identification papers meant nothing – 'Hands above your head, Buddy – all right – so who won the World Series in 1940?'

'I haven't the faintest idea but I do know I made a picture with Ginger Rogers in 1938.'

'OK beat it, Dave, but watch your step for Chrissake.'

Time and again I was stopped, and, thanks entirely to Sam Goldwyn, survived.

At the end of February, the British Army was fighting bloody battles in the Reichwald where a sudden thaw had turned the frozen forest floor into a quagmire. Great battles were in progress for the Roehr and the Maas. During the first week of March, US First Army reached the Rhine at Cologne and two days later US Third Army did likewise at the junction of the Moselle. 9th US Armoured Division that week made their miraculous discovery that the Ludendorff Railway Bridge at Remagen had not been blown, and secured the first small bridgehead across the Rhine, bridgehead that cried out for exploitation. Montgomery was all set to cross in strength further down and surge across the Ruhr plain, but first a big build-up, he felt, was necessary. This stoked up all the old friction between Montgomery's dedication to 'tidy battles' and the American genius for improvisation. The super primadonnas were at it in earnest this time and the heights, or rather the depths of idiocy were surely reached when, according to military historians, Patton telephoned Bradley and said,

'I want the world to know Third Army made it before Monty starts across.'

I crossed the Rhine at Wesel and I had never seen such destruction – the smoking town had ceased to exist. At Munster nothing was left standing except a bronze statue of a horse. In the open country between Hanover and Osnabrück, both of which were totally ruined, was a huge hastily erected prisoner-of-war cage.

There must have been a hundred thousand men already inside when the American Unit I was then with passed them. The first warming rays of the sun were just touching the prisoners. It had rained heavily during the night and now a cloud of steam was rising from this dejected field-grey mass of humanity.

The Burgomaster of Hanover said that at least 60,000 corpses were still under the rubble of his city. Bremen was no better.

Hitler had started the whole horrible shambles but looking at the places where his chickens had come home to roost, I watched the miserable survivors picking around in the ruins of their towns and was unable to raise a glimmer of a gloat.

In a siding near Liebenau, I came across a freight train, its flat cars loaded with V2 rockets destined for London. In the woods nearby, was a slave labour camp where they had been made. The notices in the camp were in Italian, French, Czech, Polish, Dutch, Yugoslav, Russian and Ukrainian. The liberated workers were wandering dazedly all over the place, asking how to get home, mingling with the dead-eyed prisoners from the concentration camps, gaunt and shuffling, conspicuous in their black and white stripes.

By May 8th, the war in Europe was officially over, but people were still being killed and Hitler's werewolves were still hopefully stretching piano wire at head height from trees on either side of the roads. To avoid decapitation, the wiser jeeps now carried sharpened iron stanchions welded to their radiators. The routes west out of Germany were becoming clogged with an estimated eight million homeward-bound displaced persons pushing their pathetic belonging on bicycles or dragging them in little home-made carts. One became hardened to the sight of people lying under trees or in ditches too exhausted or too hungry to take another step.

On a country road near Brunswick, I drove through an attractive red-roofed village on the outskirts of which was a large manor house. Two tow-headed little boys were playing in the garden. A mile or so away, I passed a farm wagon headed for the village. I glanced casually at the two men sitting up behind the horse. Both wore typical farmer headgear and sacks were thrown over their shoulders protecting them from a light drizzle. We were just past them when something made me slam on the brakes and back up. I was right, the man who was not driving was wearing field boots. I slipped out from behind the wheel, pulled my revolver from its holster and told the corporal to cover me with his Tommy gun.

I gestured to the men to put their hands over their heads and told them in fumbling German to produce their papers.

'I speak English,' said the one with the field boots, 'this man has papers – I have none.'

'Who are you?' I asked.

He told me his name and rank – 'General.'

'We are not armed,' he added, as I hesitated.

Sandhurst did it – I saluted, then motioned to them to lower their hands.

'Where are you coming from sir?'

He looked down at me. I had never seen such utter weariness, such blank despair on a human face before. He passed a hand over the stubble of his chin.

'Berlin,' he said quietly.

'Where are you going, sir?'

He looked ahead down the road towards the village and closed his eyes.

'Home,' he said almost to himself, 'it's not far now ... only ... one more kilometre.'

I didn't say anything. He opened his eyes again and we stared at each other. We were quite still for a long time. Then I said,

'Go ahead, sir,' and added ridiculously ... 'please cover up your bloody boots.'

Almost as though in pain, he closed his eyes and raised his head, then with sobbing intake of breath, covered his face with both hands and they drove on.

On 13th May, Churchill spoke from London and the whole world listened – or did it?

'... we have yet to make sure that the simple and honourable purposes for which we entered the war are not brushed aside or overlooked in the months following our success, and that the words "freedom", "democracy" and "liberation" are not distorted from their true meaning as we have understood them. There would be little use in punishing the Hitlerites for their crimes if law and justice did not rule, and if totalitarian or police governments were to take the place of the German invaders ...'

I cannot claim to have exerted much pressure on the squabbling field marshals and generals but way down the scale, attached to various units, I must have done what General Barker wanted. At any rate, in September, he pinned the American Legion of Merit on me and the British Army gave me –

1 suit, worsted grey
1 hat, Homburg, brown

2 shirts, poplin, with collars
1 tie, striped
1 pair shoes, walking black –
and above all my FREEDOM.

Such was the stringency of the clothing rationing that Major General Robert Laycock, DSO, Chief of Combined Operations, asked me if I could spare him my discarded khaki shirts.

It was an unbelievable feeling to be free again. Primmie was due to have the second baby in November so we took little David and treated ourselves to a holiday of luxury at the Ferryboat Inn on the Helford River. Then I cabled Goldwyn to the effect that I was 'available'.

Goldwyn generously replied that he was giving me a new five-year contract at a mouth-watering figure and that in the meanwhile, he was loaning me out to Michael Powell and Emeric Pressburger to star in *A Matter of Life and Death* (*Stairway to Heaven* in the US).

This was a huge relief because although I had been disguising it from Primmie, I was extremely nervous about my future. Six months is too long for an actor to be out of business – six years is almost certain disaster.

A whole new breed of stars had taken over the movie audiences and at thirty-five I had good reason to be worried. I was also highly apprehensive lest I had forgotten how to do it.

Powell and Pressburger wrote a brilliant screenplay. Kim Hunter played the girl and my old friend, Raymond Massey, the 'heavy'. Jack Cardiff's fantastic colour photography helped enormously to make the picture a big success on both sides of the Atlantic and in Britain it was chosen as the first Royal Command Film.

After Primmie produced Jamie, we set about planning our new life. Although she had never seen California, I had described it all to her so carefully that she knew exactly what she wanted – 'an old house, falling down, that we can do over, a big rambling garden for the children and dogs, and a view of the mountains or the ocean.'

She was wildly excited at the prospect of going, but nervous about the people she would meet.

'I'm not nearly beautiful enough,' she would say. 'I'll be lost in all that glamour.'

She started buying old furniture, Regency mostly, for the house she could visualize. Vivien Leigh, a great expert, spent hours with her foraging around in the antique shops of Windsor, Amersham and Beaconsfield.

The problem of obtaining transportation to the US appeared insurmountable; with over two million American servicemen champing at the bit to get home, there was obviously no room for a family of foreigners. General Barker came to the rescue and told me that he had secured a berth for me, alone, with the 101 Airborne Division leaving in a week's time in the *Queen Mary* but Primmie and the children would have to wait at least three months. We decided that I should go on ahead to take up my contract and find, if possible, our dream house.

I gave myself a farewell party for two hundred at Claridge's. So that nobody could be wrongly dressed, Primmie borrowed a tiara and a ball gown and I wore an open-necked shirt and my trousers, worsted, grey.

All the guests had one thing in common; at some time in our lives they had been specially nice to us. It was a funny mixture – duchesses, policemen, actors, generals, privates, hospital nurses, taxi drivers, country squires and Mrs Wisden.

I took a sadistic delight in standing at the door and personally winkling out the gatecrashers.

'Please go away . . . you've never been nice to me in your life.'

The evening cost a fortune but no matter – great days were ahead – we could save money later.

Next morning, I went to collect my sailing permit.

'Sorry, old man,' said the official, 'can't give you that till you show us your income tax clearance from the Inland Revenue.'

Off I went to another dreary government office. Thick white tea cups with GR on them littered the untidy desks.

The man who interviewed me was a thin, self-important civil servant with a particularly active Adam's apple. He produced a file.

'Now, let's see, you want to leave the Old Country do you – emigrating are you?'

'No, I'm going back where I came from . . . to the United States. I have a contract to work there.'

He turned the pages of a file.

'Now let me see . . . in 1939 you left the United States and came back to this country. Why was that?'

'To join up . . . for the war.'

'Yes, we all know that, we read the papers at the time but nobody *asked* you to come, did they? It's not as if you were called up, is it? You paid your own way, didn't you?'

'Yes.'

'Well, then, obviously you came here intending to reside again in

233

Great Britain, so that confirmed you a resident of Great Britain for tax purposes and we are back-taxing you on your world earnings from the time you left here in 1934.'

The *Queen Mary* was sailing in two days' time and I had to have that sailing permit.

He was very generous. On condition that I did not come back during that time, he allowed me to pay over the next three years but it still cost me several thousand pounds for the privilege of spending six years in the British Army.

The *Queen Mary* carried fifteen thousand troops. We were packed like sardines. It didn't matter. We ate in shifts, slept in shifts and lay about in shifts. The teak rails of the upper decks bore the carved initials of countless GIs who had made the journey to Europe – how many, I wondered, were left behind for ever.

On the night I landed in New York, my old employers at '21' gave a large cocktail party for me in the upstairs room of their establishment and I spent the evening with John Huston.

Next day I shopped for some badly needed clothes and took a sleeper on the transcontinental train for California. I was feeling very tired and rather odd so the trip would rest me up, I thought. David Selznick was on the train and he brought me up to date on who was who now in Hollywood and what was going on. David was a friend who never minced words, however ominous.

'It's going to be tough for you,' he said. 'It's a whole new ball game now – a lot of new stars and new directors have come up while you've been away – you're lucky to have Goldwyn behind you.'

At Chicago, a telegram was delivered from Eddie Goulding saying that he was giving me a welcome home bachelor party of a hundred at Romanoff's on the night of my arrival. Another came from Goldwyn saying there was to be a big press luncheon the same day. I looked forward to it all but I also dreaded it . . . I really was very tired and coughed a lot.

WELCOME HOME DAVID!!

A big banner was strung across the main gate of the studio. Stage 8 had been transformed into a restaurant and several hundred studio employees and members of the press listened to speeches of welcome by Goldwyn, Hedda Hopper, the head prop man, Dave Chasen and others. The room was spinning, I was sweating and I had a terrible headache. I wondered how I was going to get through it. I might have been Hollywood's first recruit but I was being treated as if I had won the war single-handed.

After luncheon, 'Willie' Bruce said, 'I'm taking you home,

putting you to bed and getting you a doctor – you look awful.'

'I can't let Goulding down,' I said. 'He's asked a hundred people tonight.'

'Nonsense,' said Willie, 'if the doctor says you can go – all right – otherwise, bed.'

The doctor took my temperature – it was 104° – and told me I had bronchial pneumonia. Goulding was marvellous when he was told. He came to see me and insisted on going through with the party without me.

'I'll have a direct line to your room and an amplifier. You'll be able to hear what's going on and you can talk to old pals on the phone.'

Among the hundred bachelors, Goulding rounded up most of my actor friends including Clark Gable, Doug Jr, Flynn, Gary Cooper and 'Ty' Power. Also, I noticed from the book of photographs he sent me later of the proceedings, an impressive body of the Hollywood super-brass had also dusted off their dinner jackets including Goldwyn, Selznick, Pandro Berman, Eddie Mannix, Billy Wilder, Howard Hawks, Mervyn Le Roy, Hal Wallis and even Harry Cohn.

There was a pipe band. My name was carved in a huge block of ice and the whole place was festooned with American and British flags.

It was extremely generous of Goulding, highly flattering and completely unwarranted.

I convalesced in the desert at Palm Springs and, as soon as I was well enough, Goldwyn put me to work. He loaned me to Paramount to do a picture with, of all people, Loretta Young.

Primmie cabled that she hoped to get passage soon and I went, frantically, house hunting.

The Fairbanks's found it for me, right next door to theirs, exactly what she had always said she wanted – old and rambling with a big garden and a view of both the Santa Monica Mountains and the ocean. The basement had about three feet of water in it when the agent showed it so I was able to buy it very cheaply. Vicki Baum, author of *Grand Hotel*, had built it forty years before.

'The Pink House', as it was known for obvious reasons, became of tremendous importance to me. It was the first home I had ever owned, and with my adored family, I longed to settle down at last. I seemed to have been running and running all my life.

I decided to give the place to Primmie as a surprise when she arrived, then let her do it over and, with her wonderful taste, decorate it in her own good time – in the meanwhile, I rented a big Spanish-style monstrosity in Beverly Hills.

The picture at Paramount finished just in time for me to fly East to meet my family. They had taken eighteen days in terrible gales to cross the Atlantic in an old Liberty ship. They finally docked in Portland, Maine.

Primmie looked radiant as she came running down the gangplank. Little David was full of chat and questions. As a typical war baby, he noticed the skeleton of a house being built,

'Look, Daddy,' he said, 'a bomb.'

Jamie, now five months old, slept all the time in a carrying cot. The handle broke in New York and I dumped him on his head in the middle of Penn Station, which may account for the fact that he became an extremely efficient merchant banker.

Primmie fell in love with California on sight and was over the moon when she saw the 'Pink House'.

'The furniture will be perfect in it,' she cried, her eyes shining like a little girl's. 'I'm going to make it *so* beautiful for you! You're going to be *so* proud!'

It was decided that she would do the house herself without telling me anything and then, one day, when it was all finished she would let me carry her through the door.

She had brought 'Pinkie' with her – a fresh-faced English girl who had spent the war in an anti-aircraft battery in London. 'Pinkie' adored the children and soon made the Spanish dungeon shine like a new pin.

Goldwyn loaned me to Universal to make an historical film with Ginger Rogers. Ginger was to play Dolly Madison and I was to portray Aaron Burr – the two most unlikely bits of casting of the century. The script was gibberish, but I was far too happy and the prospect of, at long last, settling down with my family in my own home was too good to be ruined by renewed quarrels with Goldwyn and by suspensions which I could ill afford.

Larry Olivier had left behind a large black Packard when he had last been in California. I bought it by cable, left Pinkie in charge of the children and with Clark Gable, Rex Harrison, Ida Lupino and Nigel Bruce, we set off in convoy for a week's gold at Pebble Beach. . . . They were golden days and Primmie showed me a letter she wrote to Bill Rollo saying that she never imagined she could be so happy. We came back on a Sunday because I had to do wardrobe tests the next morning.

'Ty' Power and Annabella gave a small party for Primmie that evening. John McClain had just arrived from New York and all my closest friends were there. As I looked around at them and at Primmie's radiant face, I wondered how it was possible for one man to have so much.

Nearly everyone was working the next day which meant being up by five or six o'clock so we had an early barbecue round the pool. 'Ty' cooked.

Afterwards, we went indoors and played some games. Someone suggested 'Sardines' – an old children's game, played in the dark. I was hiding under a bed upstairs when I heard 'Ty' calling me.

'Come down, quick, Primmie's had a fall!'

I rushed down.

In the dark she had opened a door thinking it was a coat closet – it was the door to the cellar and she had fallen down a dozen steps. She was lying unconscious on the floor.

We dabbed her head with water and she started moaning and moving a little.

Within twenty minutes the doctor arrived and within another half hour, she was tucked in bed in hospital.

'She's very concussed,' the doctor told me after his examination, 'but it's nothing to worry about. She'll have to stay absolutely quiet and in the dark for a few days – she'll be fine.'

I went back to Ty's house and told everyone the good news. Then I went to the Spanish house and Pinkie helped me pack up a few things Primmie might need, a couple of nighties, a toothbrush, some perfume.

Back at the hospital, they repeated that she was fine, said there was no good I could do by staying and to go on home: if I wanted to, to drop by before I went to work in the morning.

I was back about six the next day. They let me see her. She looked beautiful but very pale. Her eyes were still closed.

'She's had a good night,' said the nurse.

All during the day I called from the studio.

'Nothing to worry about – it's bad concussion – all she needs is complete rest and quiet.'

After work I went back to the hospital. They were most reassuring. I sat with her for a long time holding her hand. She was very still.

Suddenly, she opened her eyes, looked right at me, smiled a tiny smile and gave my hand a little reassuring squeeze. It was the first time she had recognized me. The matron said, 'Why don't you go on home and get some sleep yourself, there's nothing you can do. We'll call you at once, of course, if there is any change . . . go on home and don't worry.'

Bob Coote was in the house when I got back waiting for news. I told him everything was going along well, that no one was worried, and we raided the ice box for a snack.

About eleven o'clock, the phone rang. It was the doctor.

'I think you'd better come down,' he said . . . 'there are certain symptoms we don't like. I've alerted the best brain surgeon there is . . . we may have to operate.'

Bob came with me. An hour later, they started the operation. Two hours passed before the doctors came down.

I knew.

I knew as soon as I saw them come out of the elevator.

I knew by the way they walked.

I knew by the way they stood murmuring together without looking at me as I waited across the hall.

She was only twenty-five.

Somehow the dreadful days dragged by – somehow into weeks and months.

Friends tried valiantly to cushion the despair and I was infinitely lucky to have them.

Ronnie and Benita Colman took me into their home for I never again set foot in the Spanish monstrosity; then Douglas and Mary Lee Fairbanks gave me sanctuary. Joan Crawford took the children, with a stunned Pinkie, till they were settled on the Colmans' ranch at Montecito. Everyone tried to help, but there comes a time when friends must be allowed to get on with their own lives, so I went back to work at Universal and occupying myself with such a disaster was some sort of relief from the alternative. Even so, after work I walked for hours alone on the darkened beach, hoping, perhaps, that a merciful tidal wave might sweep out of the Pacific. Then I went to bed to toss in torment till dawn when exhaustion took over. A couple of hours of deep sleep would be brutally ended by an alarm clock and smashing down once more came the awful realization that it had not been a dream.

Work on the Pink House continued. Not because I wanted to transform it into a shrine: it held no memories: we had never lived in it . . . so work went on. After a while, with the rest of the house still gutted, one room, the cook's, and the kitchen, were finished.

With a few belongings, I moved in among the cement and sawdust, coils of wire, unattached radiators and toilets, buckets of paint . . . utter desolation that seemed somehow symbolic.

The so carefully collected furniture and china arrived from England but somewhere the container had been dropped and most of the contents were smashed beyond repair.

I had with me, for comfort, in the cook's room, a little case full of Primmie's most private things, childhood treasures, some photographs of our wedding and of the children's christenings, my letters written during the war and her tiny cache of inexpensive jewellery. While I was away at work one day, the case was stolen.

That night I nearly gave up.

The Pink House was finally finished and upstairs, a white carpet was laid.

That day, Rex and Lili Palmer gave me a Boxer puppy to keep me company. Within an hour, 'Phantom' had permanently changed the colour of the carpet.

On Sundays, the house was full of people from morning till night. Every week Gable arrived accompanied by some gorgeous creature while Lana Turner, Anita Colby, Rita Hayworth, Deborah Kerr, Ava Gardner, Ida Lupino and Patricia Medina set an unassailable standard of beauty and fun. Bob Laycock was stunned when he saw them. In his capacity as Chief of British Combined Operations, he came to California as the guest of the American Pacific Fleet at San Diego and stayed with me for several days. It cheered me a lot to think that he took back to Bill and Kathleen Rollo good reports of their grandchildren.

Like the understanding Gable who had been through a similar family tragedy himself, John McClain was a staunch and thoughtful friend. One day he said, ' "Betty" Bacall is giving Bogart a surprise party tonight – it's time you got out of your house.'

I didn't really want to go but the alternative was still something I flinched from. Pinkie would relentlessly keep the children up till I came home from work so they could have a half hour's 'play' with their father. It was torture for me and I dreaded seeing their gay, shining, trusting little faces.

After they had gone off to bed it was worse – a lonely meal and then pacing about the house like a caged lion till bedtime. By now, I was making an important picture for Goldwyn, playing the bishop in *The Bishop's Wife* with Loretta as the wife and Cary Grant as the Angel, so I was faced with getting up at six o'clock in house.

McClain, however, brushed aside all protests and I found myself with forty others hidden in different parts of Bogart's house as a surprise for his birthday.

'Betty' Bacall was the perfect mate for Bogie ... beautiful, fair, warm, talented and highly intelligent, she gave as good as she got in the strong personality department. Women and men love her with equal devotion.

Someone had been delegated by Betty to keep Bogie busy at the studio to give us all time to arrive and hide. When Bogie finally appeared, it was apparent how his busy time at the studio had been spent. He was loudly abusive and cries of 'who needs these bums!' and 'get the bastards outta here!' reverberated from the front door. For a few nervous minutes it was touch and go whether he would throw all forty of us out into the street, but Betty placated him, or rather, answered him loudly in the same vein and the party became a success after all.

Bogart was quite alarming to meet for the first time with his sardonic humour and his snarl that passed for a smile. It took a little while to realize that he had perfected an elaborate camouflage to cover up one of the kindest and most generous of hearts. Even so, he was no soft touch and before you were allowed to peek beneath the surface and catch a glimpse of the real man, you had to prove yourself. Above all, you had to demonstrate conclusively to his satisfaction that you were no phoney.

My test came soon. He asked me if I liked to sail.

'Done it all my life,' I said, blithely, 'in fact I once represented my country in eight metres.'

Bogie looked at me reflectively and sucked his teeth.

'Okay, come aboard *Santana* Sunday.'

Women were only infrequently made welcome aboard *Santana* so Betty was not there when I boarded the sixty-five-foot ketch at Balboa.

Tough and often argumentative ashore, I expected Bogie to be a veritable Captain Bligh afloat. Far from it, he was easy going, perfectly relaxed and highly efficient. I was lulled into a sense of false security and had no idea that this had been earmarked as the day of my entrance exam.

We were sailing along in a good stiff breeze; Bogie was at the helm, I was beside him, the solitary crew – a Dane he called Dum Bum – was forward keeping a sharp lookout because the stiff breeze was doing nothing to dispell a thick mist.

'Tuna boats ahead,' yelled Dum Bum suddenly.

Sure enough we were running fast towards a dozen big drifters, each with its net trailing out astern. It was a tricky situation that called for immediate action and because of the direction of the wind, there were only three solutions: one was correct, the second risky, and the third would have led to losing the mast.

Dum Bum was looking apprehensively at Bogie and I was just thinking to myself that he was leaving things dangerously late when he let go of the wheel, gave me a wolfish grin and said – 'Take over, Big Shot – I'm going to the can.'

He disappeared below.

Luckily, I knew what I was doing. I yelled a few orders which Dum Bum instantly obeyed, spun the wheel and the danger was past.

Christmas alone with the children was something I had dreaded.

Although they never ceased asking others when their mother was coming back, some extraordinary radar system prevented them from ever mentioning her to me. I knew one day they would ask me the direct question so until then I resolved not to broach the subject.

On Christmas Eve, with the lighted tree in the window behind me and a mountain of gaily wrapped presents from kind and even anxious friends beneath it, I was sitting on the patio steps swept suddenly by a wave of despair. A little arm went round my neck: they both stood there hand-in-hand.

'Are you very lonely?' asked the eldest and when I just nodded, he said, 'Mummy's never coming back, is she?'

'No, she's not,' I said.

'Has she gone up to Heaven?'

'Yes, that's right . . . she's gone to Heaven.'

The evening star was very bright over the distant ocean. He looked up.

'I can see Mummy's eye,' he said.

The Bishop's Wife turned out well. It, too, was chosen for the Royal Command Film in London and Goldwyn, loaning me out all over town, kept me blessedly busy. I made pictures with Barbara Stanwyck and Jane Wyman. I played all sorts of roles, including a world-famous pianist. During my big concert scene an expert played the piano with his arms through my tail coat while I rolled my eyes and looked soulful.

When a man is deeply unhappy, he brings out the very gentlest instincts in the very nicest women. They want to wrap him up, take him home and look after him. They give all of themselves but he, in turn, can give in only one direction and, inoculated by his unhappiness, rides roughshod far and wide.

This happened to me in full measure and I also believe at the same time I went a little mad. I began to resent and avoid the married friends who had showered me with kindness and protection when I had so badly needed it. Perhaps I was jealous of their happiness. Perhaps I was ashamed that they had seen me at my weakest and most vulnerable. This phase lasted several months, and, bewildered and hurt, some wonderful people must have found my coldness most difficult to understand.

The Pink House in the spring was a dream place for the children. They took swimming lessons in the pool. Peach trees, avocados, pomegranates, cherries, oranges, limes, lemons and guavas were in full blossom. Phantom dashed about the lawn chasing humming birds, the bantams crowed and the rabbits bred in great profusion. I planted a hundred rose bushes and at last, I, too, began to feel roots going down and some happiness seeping back up again. The boys were settling down marvellously, and some pattern for the future seemed to be emerging. I was, therefore, appalled when Goldwyn called me in and told me had had loaned me to Alexander Korda to make *Bonnie Prince Charlie* in England.

'You'll be away at least eight months,' he said.

I begged him not to send me and pointed out that not only would it disrupt the children's lives, it would also make new and hideous problems for me with the Inland Revenue.

He was adamant so I refused to go. Immediately, I was put on suspension.

Knowing that I was up to my ears in debt because of the Pink House, Goldwyn sat back and waited for me to crack. It didn't take long and, in the autumn, Pinkie and I packed up two resentful and mystified little boys and started the long trek back to England.

Korda, whose home was the Penthouse at Claridge's, was quite understandably surprised when I spurned the accommodation he had reserved for me in that excellent hostelry. I kept a room there for myself and moved the family into a country hotel near Shepperton Studios.

Bonnie Prince Charlie was one of those huge florid extravaganzas that reek of disaster from the start. There was never a completed screenplay and never at any time during the eight months we were shooting were the writers more than two days ahead of the actors.

We suffered three changes of director with Korda himself, for a time, desperately taking over and at one point I cabled Goldwyn as follows:

I HAVE NOW WORKED EVERY DAY FOR FIVE MONTHS ON THIS PICTURE AND NOBODY CAN TELL ME HOW THE STORY ENDS STOP ADVISE.

He didn't. He didn't even bother to answer.

I loved Alex Korda, a brilliant, generous dreamer, but with this film he was wallowing around in his own self-created confusion. I felt sorry for him but I felt much sorrier for myself as the Bonnie Prince who would assuredly bear the blame for the impending debacle and for Margaret Leighton and Jack Hawkins gallantly, against appalling odds, trying to infuse some semblance of reality into Flora MacDonald and Lord George Murray.

243

After nine frustrating months, the Bonnie Prince clanked towards its close. One more week, one more battle, one last mad charge and I would be rid of him. (Whenever we actors really started to breathe down the writers' necks, Korda ordered another battle to delay us for a few more days.)

The director at this point was a robust, hearty and immensely nice ex-naval commander – Anthony Kimmins. No fool, he knew only too well that he was captain of a movie ship heading like an arrow for the rocks, but bravely, he covered up and issued his orders to the several hundred extras as though he were Lord Louis Mountbatten addressing the crew of a badly listing destroyer.

'Now, Bonnie Prince Charlie has just won a great victory! You brave Highlanders have captured the English colours! When he comes out of his tent over there, I want all you Highlanders to give him a big cheer! Let him know you all love him!'

The wild Highlanders, in scruffy red wigs and uncertain kilts, were almost entirely recruited from London's East End. As I came out of the tent for the first 'take', there was scattered cheering. Then, crystal clear in the morning air came a fruity Cockney voice.

'Oi! David . . . we've got their — flag!!!'

The second 'happening' on that most important day came during the charge itself.

I was careering bravely along, skimming over the studio heather at the head of my Highlanders, pursuing the fleeing redcoats, when suddenly, claymore in hand, I found myself flying through the air. I still believe Jack Hawkins tripped me. In any event, my sword sank deep into the leg of the redcoat in front of me. It went in with an appalling 'thonk' just behind the knee and pinned him to the ground.

'Cut!' yelled the director (an unnecessary observation). Several women, hairdressers and other camp followers, screamed.

I pulled out the blade, trying not to throw up. The man got up and ran off with a pronounced limp. I chased after him.

'Are you all right? . . . I'm terribly sorry! . . . We'll get a doctor!'

'Wot's the matter, mate?' asked the man.

'Your leg,' I blabbered, 'my sword! . . . It went right in! We'll get a doctor!'

'Oh,' he said, 'thought I felt something . . . not to worry though, David.'

He rolled up the bottom of his trousers. His name was Bob Head. He had lost the original leg at El Alamein.

Happenings go in threes. I was dismissed early that evening and hurried off to get changed so I could go and play with the children. Because of the hours we had been working, I hadn't seen them for days. The gateman stopped me.

'Sorry, David – they just phoned up – they need you for one more shot.'

Furious, I stalked back into Make-up. Sullenly, I sat while the yellow wig was pinned on my resisting head and once more, like a spoilt child whose picnic has been cancelled by bad weather, I glowered my way on to the set, and snarled at the prop man.

'Where the hell's my chair?'

'Over there, David . . . there's a lady in it.'

'Then get her out of it!' I snapped.

'Take a look,' whispered Hawkins in my ear. 'Take a look.'

The French have the right word – *coup de foudre* . . . I had never seen anything so beautiful in my life – tall, slim, auburn hair, uptilted nose, lovely mouth and the most enormous grey eyes I had ever seen.

It really happened the way it does when written by the worst lady novelists . . . I goggled. I had difficulty swallowing and I had champagne in my knees.

Ten days later, we were married.

During the whirlwind courtship, there was a lot of activity. First of all, it turned out she was Swedish which posed all sorts of strange problems with the marriage authorities. Also, she didn't speak English too well which helped matters not at all when it came to explaining to them that she had landed in England en route from America to Sweden as the plane had been grounded because of sudden fog at London Airport and a friend on board had invited her to visit a film studio, etcetera, etcetera.

I had my problems too. I had to complete the *Bonnie Prince*, find gifts for all the crew, present Hjördis to Bill Rollo who adored her on sight and was gay and happy for me through his own sadness; I also had to submit to a series of loathsome meetings with the Inland Revenue because I had returned without being away for three years.

'But I was sent, dammit, by the American company that employs me . . . If I had refused, I would have broken my contract.'

'Well, we should read the small print before signing these foreign things, shouldn't we?'

Also, I had to find a ring, track down Trubshawe, who was to be best man again, and make all the arrangements to return quickly to California, where Goldwyn was holding up the start of my next picture.

Small wonder that I had a mini-collapse and when the official at the Chelsea Register office warned me pompously against the dangers of marrying a foreigner, I could barely croak at him to 'shut up and get on with it.' The number one model of Sweden found herself married to a man with red eyes, a running nose and a fever of 103°.

Audrey Pleydell-Bouverie gave us a wedding party in her little house strategically placed midway between the stables of Buckingham Palace and Watney's brewery, and next day we drove to Southampton to board the *Queen Elizabeth*.

Hjördis still swears that on the way there, I suddenly said, 'Oh! I nearly forgot, there are a couple of little things I have to pick up.'

According to her, I disappeared inside a country hotel and emerged later with two small boys.

On the trip to California, we got to know each other a little better and the little boys adored her.

She loved the Pink House and rose magnificently to the occasion of being pitchforked into the middle of all my old friends. McClain, Coote and Mike Romanoff gave her a 'welcome' party to make it easier and her gaiety and beauty captivated everyone.

Life Magazine had a 'spread' of the ten most beautiful women in Hollywood and Hjördis appeared on the cover. This generated a stampede of producers with offers of contracts but, mercifully, she just laughed and said she was too busy getting to know her husband.

The Pink House came alive under her hand and became everything I had dreamed about as a home. At night, the coyotes hunted in weirdly yelping packs in the canyon below: in the morning, the deer grazed on the hills opposite and the sunsets over the Pacific must have been ordered by the Chamber of Commerce.

Some highly decorative Scandinavian ladies now augmented the weekly gatherings ... Viveca Lindfors and Signe Hasso were often present; also the latest Miss Sweden – Anita Eckberg. The first naked female my sons ever saw was Greta Garbo, swimming happily in our pool.

'Goldwynisms' had been so widely quoted ... '... include me out,' 'a verbal contract is not worth the paper it is written on,' and of a 14th-century sundial, 'What will they think of next?' etc. that for a while I was suspicious that Goldwyn might foster the legend by dreaming up new ones for himself, but I don't believe this was the case. I heard him let loose many of them but I think his mind was so far ahead of what he was saying that he left it to his tongue to take care of thoughts he had left behind. In fact, he had great dignity but when thwarted, he tended to shout loudly.

After three months of my new found happiness, the pleasant routine was shattered. Goldwyn called me to his office and told me he had great news and that I was very lucky.

'I've just loaned you to Alex Korda to make *The Elusive Pimpernel* in England – you'll be away six months.'

Aghast, I told him that I didn't mind what he loaned me out for in Hollywood but that I had no intention of uprooting again so soon. Then the shouting began. He reminded me that he had picked me out of the gutter and given me my first break ... True.

I riposted by saying that with the enormous fees he was charging others for my services, I had already repaid him a thousand times over ... True.

Goldwyn pointed out that it would mean months of suspension if I refused ... True.

I said I looked forward to a good holiday anyway and I had plenty of money in the bank ... UNTRUE.

Goldwyn flicked a switch and said, 'Find out how much money Niven has in the bank.'

Within three minutes a disembodied voice came back, 'One hundred and eleven dollars ...' ... True, unfortunately.

Defeated, I prepared, once more, to make the necessary travel arrangements.

I lived in Hollywood for nearly twenty years without visiting a psychiatrist but my behaviour during the next few weeks was indicative of an unhinged mind and it was a pity I did not 'get help'.

I decided to make life unpleasant for Goldwyn which was tantamount to an eight-year-old with a pea-shooter assaulting Fort Knox. Everyone from Hjördis downwards warned me. My agent was horrified and pointed out that in mogul-controlled Hollywood, one word from Goldwyn could sink me. I knew better, of course, and proceeded very methodically to sink myself.

At the last minute, I refused to fly to London to keep the starting date of Korda's picture and insisted, instead, on being sent by train to New York and by boat – eleven days to Liverpool. Hjördis remained loyal but mystified throughout the trip. Once in London, I cabled Goldwyn reminding him that under the terms of my contract, I had six weeks' holiday each year and unless I was given my holiday at once before *Pimpernel* started, the contract would be broken as there would be no time left between the end of the picture and the end of the year.

'TAKE SIX WEEKS HOLIDAY IMMEDIATELY GOLDWYN' came the answer.

'THANKS VERY MUCH WILL TAKE HOLIDAY FROM TIME YOU RETURN ME TO MY HOME IN CALIFORNIA NIVEN.'

Poor, blameless Alex Korda, who wanted only to see his picture started, found himself in the middle of this lunacy. He offered me his yacht *Elsewhere* to go anywhere at his expense, but my mental imbalance was such that I forced Goldwyn to return me to the Pink House by boat and train: then, the next day, I flew with Hjördis to Bermuda for a delayed honeymoon.

Honeymoons are a great institution for getting to know one's spouse and the more I saw of Hjördis, the more amazed I was at my good fortune. The luck, the unbelievable luck that one man should meet, fall head-over-heels in love, marry within ten days and be blissfully happy – twice in a lifetime!

I revelled in Hjördis forthrightness, honesty and laughter and the holiday sped by. Towards the end, a full-scale hurricane hit the island – a nasty reminder of the impending storm with Goldwyn.

Six weeks to the day from the moment I had been brought back to California, I reported to the studio for work. Rather naturally, Goldwyn did not wish to see me and I detected a certain coldness towards me all over the Lot. Conduct such as mine, spoiled brat behaviour of the worst sort, was idiotic, conceited, indefensible and unforgiveable: the sort of thing that helped bring Hollywood to its knees.

Goldwyn, of course, had no further use for me and all the direst predictions came true. When we came back from England upon the completion of *The Pimpernel*. I was immediately loaned out to play the 'heavy' in a Shirley Temple picture, a disastrous teenage pot-boiler.

'Big shots' at other studios counselled me to break my contract with Goldwyn – 'just walk in there and tell him – the hell with it! . . . tell him you want OUT . . . then come and join us, we have a million properties for you!' I fell for that – it was not my finest hour. I asked to see Goldwyn and as he sat expressionless behind his desk, I said, 'Look, Sam, we don't see eye to eye any more. I have two years left of my contract – how about releasing me?'

He never took his eyes off me as he flicked his intercom lever.

'Give Niven his release as from today . . . he's through.'

Hjördis sounded doubtful when I told her the good news.

'Where will you work now?' she asked.

Where indeed? There is no question but that the Black List existed in Hollywood at that time but I have absolutely no proof that Goldwyn invoked its use in my case. On the other hand, the fact remains that the flattering studio 'big shots', who had painted such glowing pictures of my future with them once I was free of Goldwyn, were suddenly unobtainable. When I called their offices, the voices of their secretaries had changed subtly from fawning to evasive or even to faintly hostile.

Headlines put out by the Goldwyn Publicity Department were no great help –

GOLDWYN DROPS NIVEN

NIVEN FIRED

BRITISH ACTOR NO LONGER GOLDWYN'S CUP OF TEA.

Hjördis was nothing short of stoic because only too soon there was a shortage of cash. Nothing was coming in, everything was going out and the reserves were melting like butter on a hot stove. Friends such as the Astaires and the Fairbanks tried to cheer me by reporting that, at the latest Goldwyn dinner party, my photograph was still on the piano, but nobody suggested I should try a reconciliation.

Bogart, as usual, was down to earth.

'Let's fact it, kid – you've blown it! Keep going somehow, mortgage the house, sell the kids, dig a ditch, do anything but for Christ's sake, never let them think they've got you running scared because somewhere in somebody's desk is a script that's right for you and when they dig it out – it's you they'll want and nobody else and everything'll be forgotten.'

Bogie's life was either black or white – he had little patience with the greys, so he simply did not understand when I accepted the first offer that came along after months of near panic.

'You should've held out, kid – this is crap,' he said when I showed him the script.

The film, *The Toast of New Orleans* at MGM, was a success thanks only to the fact that it launched Mario Lanza's golden voice and with the proceeds, Hjördis happily paid the bills one short step ahead of the sheriff. The next picture was even worse – an appalling travesty of a costume thriller. The result was so bad that the audience thought it was a comedy and as such it became faintly successful.

'Get outta town, kid,' growled Bogart. 'They gotta have time to forget that one.'

I took his advice, let the Pink House for a year, took the whole family to England, and moved into a haunted manor house in Wiltshire on the edge of the Downs.

Hjördis somehow remained calm and outwardly unaffected by the rapid changes in our fortunes but my new role as a country squire was hard for her to digest. I had a 'gun' in the local syndicate dedicated to the slaughter of pheasants. I had a 'rod' on the River Kennet for the purpose of killing trout and I had a private pew in the village church (complete with hidden stove) for the good of my soul.

In the autumn, she came rushing to find me – 'Hurry! hurry! hurry! the garden is full of dogs and men blowing trumpets!'

Philip Hardwicke and Philip Dunne as joint Masters of the local foxhounds were merely following tradition. The opening meet was held each year at our Manor House. Hjördis, in tight, blue jeans and a white T-shirt with PALM SPRINGS RODEO written across her bosom, was a welcome if incongruous sight when I dispatched her outside with bottles of port and slices of fruit cake.

In England, we were able to catch up with Trubshawe, Coote, with Noël Coward and with the Oliviers who had moved into an Elizabethan abbey, near Thame. Arguments waxed and waned at Notley; causes were defended or attacked with vigour and professional reputations came under withering fire but there were few tears and gales of laughter, particularly when, accompanied on the piano by an hysterical Vivien, Larry, dead seriously, would sing *The Messiah*.

Friends were always championed to the death. One weekend, Larry, Vivien, Bobby Helpmann and Noël were trying to put Hollywood into its proper perspective for me.

'It's all very fine for you,' I argued, 'you are all theatre people who occasionally make a movie . . . I have nothing *but* the movies.'

If I had trodden on a wasps' nest . . . I couldn't have stirred up more action: everyone started shouting at once and when it died down, it was obvious that steps were about to be taken to get me started in the theatre.

Within a week, John C. Wilson, the Broadway producer and

longtime friend and associate of Noël's, offered me a play – *Nina*.

Gloria Swanson, who, the season before, in a spectacular comeback, had been the toast of Broadway in *Twentieth Century*, had already been signed and the cast of three was to be rounded off by that excellent English character actor, Alan Webb.

'I'm terrified,' I said to Noël. 'I've only been on the stage once over ten years ago and I was fired for being gassed.' The Coward finger wagged immediately.

'You will do it,' he ordered. 'You will do it well, and above all, you will do it sober.'

The boys stayed on in the haunted manor with Evelyn Walne, their new governess, poised to join us if the play looked like running and in October, Hjördis and I flew to the United States. First stop was to spend a weekend, pheasant shooting, with friends in New England.

I had by now seen Hjördis under a variety of conditions and had come to realize that one of the joys of being married to a 'foreigner' is being constantly surprised – nothing is automatically predictable.

I was not thrown off balance, therefore, when she came down to breakfast on the first morning, dressed not for the chase but for spending the day with an apple and a good book.

'I am not coming to watch you shoot,' she announced, 'because I don't want to be shot.'

The high-powered hunters and their wives tried to persuade her that it was perfectly safe, but she was adamant.

'I *know* I am going to be shot – so I stay home.'

Finally, after much badinage about Scandinavian sixth sense, trolls and spooks, she reluctantly consented to join us.

'But I will be shot,' she said sadly.

Less than an hour later, two guns turned to fire at a bird that was going back low and Hjördis fell to the ground, hit in the face, neck chest and arms.

I rushed over and as I cradled her, moaning, in my arms, a terrible thought went through my head – it's happened again.

Her beautiful face was a terribly swollen mask of blood; when she asked for a mirror, we pretended nobody had one. Within half an hour she was in the local hospital, where it was discovered that she had over thirty pieces of lead in her, including one which to this day remains embedded in the bone of her eye socket.

She was given an anaesthetic and they were preparing to remove the pellets when some strange force propelled me, uninvited, into the operating room.

'Stop, please!' I said to the astonished white-clad group. 'I'm sorry, before you cut her – I want another opinion.'

I don't know what made me do it – some half-forgotten wartime whisper about shrapnel wounds perhaps; anyway, white gauze masks were lowered and I was asked, icily, if I wanted to accept full responsibility. My host produced an ex-navy surgeon friend who was paged at the local fooball game. He came and examined her and gave it as his opinion that if the swollen tissues were operated on at that time, she would be scarred for life.

'Many will work their way out,' he said, 'the ones in deep we can get later. She should be X-rayed frequently to see if any move, especially the one near the jugular.'

Thank God for the US Navy. Hjördis is, today, unmarked but now when she hears those little northern voices, I listen with great attention.

A battered Hjördis and I moved to the Blackstone Hotel, New York. In a tiny room next to us was lodged a doe-eyed waif, a young actress, also making her debut on Broadway that season – Audrey Hepburn. Together, we shook with fear as our opening nights drew inexorably nearer.

Nina was a translation from a big French success by André Roussin. It was directed by a comic Russian, Gregory Ratoff. In English, it was pretty bad.

Gloria looked marvellous and took great pains to remain that way by eating the most loathsome concoctions of yoghurt, yeast, wheat germ and molasses. She also had a fixation that every actor should have another string to his bow – some other profession capable of padding out the lean times.

'I have a clothing business myself,' she said. 'The Pilgrim Company ... all my clothes for this show will be made by Pilgrim.'

We opened in Hartford, Connecticut, in front of a heavily partisan audience, most of whom had come up from New York to cheer us on, but among them was the usual sprinkling of carrion crows sniffing for the first scent of possible disaster and ready to fly back to Broadway, the bitchy bearers of grim tidings.

The show, at this point, went over quite well, and Otto Preminger, never a man to mince words, said he liked my efforts very much but by the time we arrived in Boston a week later, several scenes had been re-written and the show was half as good. Two weeks and many re-writes after that, we opened in Philadelphia. The carrion crows had every reason to be delighted – there was no question – we were headed for big trouble.

Rex Harrison and Lilli Palmer answered my SOS, and came down from New York to see the show and offer me some advice.

'Well, what do you suggest?' I asked over supper.

'Get out of it,' said Rex.

When we arrived in New York, Hjördis tried her best to appear optimistic and Garson Kanin suggested questionable aid for first night nerves.

'Go to the top of the Empire State Building ... don't throw yourself off – just look down at all those millions of lights and remember that only one of them is the Royale Theatre.'

When the big night came, neither the producer nor the director made it to the theatre and the last run through was conducted by Biff Liff, the stage manager, who read out the final instructions with all the enthusiasm of an undertaker.

All the professional first nighters were there and the dreaded critics. Also, Alfred Lunt and Lynn Fontanne, Tallulah Bankhead and Rex and Lilli – gluttons for punishment.

The house lights dimmed and an expectant buzz faded into a pregnant silence. I stood quaking beside the stage manager who made an abortive effort to bolster my sagging morale as he signalled for the curtain to rise –

'Get out there, Dave – there's nothing you can do about it now – the horse has left the barn.'

For a panic-stricken moment, I toyed with the idea of rushing madly out of the theatre and throwing myself beneath the hooves of the mounted police, then I tottered on stage.

Webb and I played the first explanatory scene together, then the doorbell rang signalling the entrance of Swanson. Webb, the husband, took refuge behind the curtain and I, the lover, moved across stage to admit my mistress. I was ill prepared for what I saw.

She had, I thought, worn some rather odd garments in Hartford, Boston and Philadelphia but now the Pilgrim Company had really excelled itself. Swanson stood there enveloped in a black taffeta tent. She stepped forward and a gasp of horror mingled with the applause.

She smiled seductively at her lover and I was supposed to smile back. I tried but I was so nervous and my mouth so dry that my upper lip became stuck above my teeth and I stood there leering at her like a mad rabbit.

The Bedouin tent with Swanson's head sticking out of the top of it rustled across the stage and flung itself into my arms. Swanson is not tall. She is, to put it mildly, petite, so when I clasped her to me, the top of her head nestled just to the right of my breast-bone.

Unfortunately, in my terror of the whole situation, I squeezed too hard in that initial clinch. There was a loud report. This was followed by a twanging noise and about eight inches of white whalebone shot out of Swanson's chest, and straight up my nose.

The audience was delighted – something new at last – they roared with laughter. Swanson half turned to see what was happening, thereby stirring the whalebone around in my sinus. Tears of pain streamed down my face but in my innocence of things theatrical, I thought maybe it didn't show and with the whalebone crunching about among the scroll bones, and with my gopher teeth gleaming in the limelight, I carried bravely on with the scene.

The audience hooted, and the 'flop sweat' broke out all over me like dew. Down in the area of my navel, Swanson hissed, 'What the hell's going on?'

In the morning, Walter Kerr, the critic for the *Herald Tribune*, wrote –

'We understood from the programme that Miss Swanson designed her own clothes . . . like the play, they fell apart in the first act.'

Nina trailed along for three months but by early spring we were all mercifully back in the Pink House. The movie business still wanted no part of me.

Hollywood is like a bird dog. When things are going badly, it tenses and sniffs at you. It scrapes away at the camouflage. It knows.

Hjördis told me not to worry because, she said, it made me put out an aroma of defeat. I must have been particularly smelly because she suggested a few days on a boat to take my mind off things. We chartered a small sloop and set off for Catalina Island with Garbo and a gentleman friend, an ex-navy man, completing the crew. Garbo was cook, Hjördis stewardess, and as befitted his background, the GF engineer and navigator. I was in charge of the sails.

When the wind fell away towards evening, I hauled them down and handed over to the GF.

For an hour he tinkered with the engine. I hovered nearby with useless advice while the Swedish members of the expedition drank schnapps, and made crude Nordic jokes at our expense.

'I wonder,' said Hjördis sweetly, 'if you should give us a bearing because if we miss Catalina, the next stop is Japan.'

Finally the engine spluttered into life and as we chugged hesitantly west in the gathering darkness, the man pored over charts and poked about with calipers. Then he announced heavily,

'Something's screwy here – according to my reckoning, we are eleven miles north of the Grand Canyon.'

The seafaring Swedes showed no sign of panic. One of them – both claimed the honour – saw a pinprick of light far away to port. We changed course and hours later with faltering engine, dropped anchor in a sandy cove.

Garbo during the weekend made up for some patchy and uninspired cooking by exuding sparkling fun and swimming, unselfconsciously, every day, Swedish style.

Television, in the early fifties, had begun to rear its ugly head. The major film studios, instead of grabbing it and making it their own, decided first to ignore it, then to fight it and wound up, a few years later, being swallowed by it.

I picked up some sparse but badly needed dollars by doing 'guest shots' on the Bob Hope and Jack Benny shows. Many people thought it was nothing short of suicide for a film star to fly in the face of the studio bosses and align himself with the enemy. I had no alternative. I was already dead. One well-known 'zany' red-head did a show with me and over a very inexpensive supper at the Brown Derby, confided that she was even more strapped for cash than I was. She turned out to be about as 'zany' as General Motors: within four years Lucille Ball had bought both the RKO studios.

In the spring, unable to raise another dollar in mortgage on the Pink House, I decided the sad moment had come – the Regency furniture had to go. I mailed carefully authenticated lists to Parke Bernet in New York and to the Shabbie Shoppe in Dallas, Texas, and enclosed a letter to each guaranteeing that their establishment was the only recipient of this golden opportunity. Their replies were sharp.

My own carelessness had saved me from losing my beloved collection. I had put the letters in the wrong envelopes.

In October, I was offered a live TV show of *Petrified Forest* in New York. Hjördis and I worked it out and after deducting air fares and three weeks' hotel expenses, we looked like clearing three hundred dollars so we took off in a hurry.

It was a good show and thirty million people saw it – a record at that time. Robert Sherwood sat in the control room watching us and professed himself delighted with our playing of his famous work.

Alex Segal directed it beautifully and Lloyd Gough, Kim Hunter and Art Carney rounded out the cast, but by the end of it I was so exhausted by the tension that we decided to blow the three hundred dollars on a trip to Barbados whence Ronnie and Marietta Tree had bidden us come and visit them for two weeks.

The day after we returned to the Pink House, Otto Preminger called up and offered me the best part in his forthcoming picture, *The Moon is Blue*. Something he had seen in my performance in *Nina* at Hartford had persuaded him that I was the actor he wanted. Hjördis and I were beside ourselves with excitement but Otto had a great deal of opposition from United Artists who were financing the picture.

'Niven is washed up!' they told him ... 'get somebody else.' But Otto is an immensely determined individual and what Otto wants, he usually gets ... he got me ... bless him!

Many actors don't like working with Otto because he shouts even louder than Goldwyn and can be very sarcastic. I love it. Actors have a certain amount of donkey blood in them and need a carrot dangled in front of them from time to time. The directors I dread are the ones who say, 'You've played this sort of thing before – do anything you want' ... Otto dangles carrots.

A highly organized man, he made a German version of his picture simultaneously with the American one. The German cast arrived, the two companies rehearsed for a month and the entire film was completed in two languages in eighteen days. It was also far ahead of its day in its attitude towards sex, was promptly banned by the Catholic Church in the United Stated and helped enormously by the ensuing publicity.

The Moon is Blue became a very big success all over the world and I, personally, was highly delighted to win the Golden Globe Award from the foreign press – for the best comedy performance of the year.

William Holden and Maggie MacNamara played the lovers in the film but before we started shooting, Otto asked me to play *The Moon is Blue* for three months on the stage in San Francisco with Scott Brady and Diana Lynn.

While we were doing so, Charles Boyer was performing in an adjacent San Francisco theatre. The two of us were having supper together one night when Boyer told me that he and Dick Powell were thinking of forming a company to make films for television.

In view of the film studios' attitude towards the upstart television, I was surprised that two such big names were prepared to risk so much, but I myself had little to lose and the net result of that after-theatre snack was the formation of Four-Star Television Inc., which to date has made between two and three thousand films for home consumption.

The idea of Four Star Playhouse was to have four well-known movie stars each appearing once a month in an anthology series. Since, however, we were unable to persuade a fourth star to join us, most people still being too frightened of the studio bosses who uttered the direst threats against 'black-legs', a few staunch friends helped us out during the first season by doing 'guest' shows – Ronald Colman, Joan Fontaine, Merle Oberon and Ida Lupino among them.

The three of us took nothing in salaries and with the proceeds at the end of the first year, we bought the rights to Somerset Maugham's short stories and started a second series with Henry Fonda as host: he even had the guts to blow froth in the beer commercials. The third year, we purchased the Zane Grey stories and launched a third series, 'Zane Grey Theatre'. This in turn spawned 'The Rifleman' which spun off another new series, 'Wanted Dead or Alive' into which we put an instantly successful unknown, Steve McQueen.

So it went on but it was not all smooth sailing by a long shot. Frequently, we overspent, or under-planned; often sponsors were weeks behind with their payments. Once on a Friday, I pulled all my savings out of the Bank of America to meet the studio payroll. The day before we were to start shooting a new series with Anita Eckberg as a female Tarzan, we received a very clear message from Howard Hughes's right-hand man informing us that the luscious Miss Eckberg had left town indefinitely for an undisclosed destination and would not be available in the foreseeable future. We took the high-powered hint and hastily re-cast another beautiful body in the leopard skin.

Several owners of today's biggest names started their careers with us as actors or directors and Jack Lemmon, Barbara Stanwyck, Steve McQueen, David Janssen, Chuck Connors, Robert Ryan, Robert Taylor, June Allyson, Gig Young, Ida Lupino and many, many others made series for us. One year we were turning out fourteen different series at the same time . . . as big an output of film as any of the major studios had made in their hey day. We had become big business; nerve-wracking big business.

My film career after *The Moon is Blue* also climbed back on to a most satisfactory plateau of important pictures.

The boys were growing fast and had settled down well in California though I always felt a tiny bit out of place with my polite hand-clapping Hollywood Cricket Club background when I found myself at Chavez Ravine, wedged between two cap-wearing, gum-chewing, mitt-thumping, raspberry-blowing little Dodger fans.

The days were full of promise and the friends with whom I could savour them were nearby.

Fred Astaire is a pixie – timid, always warm-hearted, a sentimentalist with a Lefty-Flynn-type penchant for schoolboy jokes. He is also a racehorse aficionado who owned a winner of the Hollywood Gold Cup.

Early one Sunday he called me.

'I've done a terrible thing – I don't know what possessed me, but at four o'clock this morning, I got out of bed and drove all over Beverly Hills, painting the city mail boxes with my racing colours.'

Freud might have had an explanation for Fred's behaviour – well-to-do ladies often abduct sausages from supermarkets – so when one day a voice on my telephone said,

'Good morning – I am the Bishop of Los Angeles.' I replied knowingly, 'And I am the Mother Superior – how's your cock?'

A quick intake of breath followed by a longish pause alerted me to the fact that it was not Fred. When the Bishop had recovered from the unaccustomed greeting, he told me what was on his mind.

'We have a Convention of several thousand Anglican clergy coming to Los Angeles from all over the world, we are holding a service in the Hollywood Bowl and we would be very happy if you would read the Second Lesson.'

He explained that it was several weeks away and when I enquired why he had selected me, he told me that as the Archbishop of York was coming from England, it had been decided to invite what he kindly described as a prominent British resident of Los Angeles.

The day approached and what had for some time seemed no more than a minor chore, now assumed the proportions of a major hazard. I had meetings with the Bishop and enquired about my wardrobe for the occasion ... dark suit.

We discussed the 'script' ... Galatians, Chapter IV.

I did not understand it ... 'What is *un*circumcision?' He explained patiently and told me with a smile not to worry about who was to read the First Lesson – 'You won't have to follow Bob Hope ... I will be reading that myself.'

On the night before my appearance at the giant Hollywood Bowl, I was so nervous I was unable to sleep. In the morning, I had a high fever and had completely lost my voice.

Hjördis telephoned the Bishop and explained while I listened on an extension . . . I could tell from the disappointment in his voice that he was having a hard time being a believer so I went down there anyway to let him hear me croak, I think. He said gently, 'You could try it, they will understand that you have something wrong with your voice and they will be terribly bored if I read them both lessons.'

When the moment came, with my knees clanking together like castanets, I walked out on to the desert-like stage while the thousands of clerics rustled themselves into seated comfort. A massed choir of hundreds stood in tiers behind me as I turned to face the vastness of the Bowl.

'Somebody' up there loved me that day. I opened my mouth to whisper the announcement of the Lesson and out of my hitherto totally constricted throat came the deepest and most resonant sounds I had ever heard.

On the Fourth of July in the United States American friends point out, with unholy glee, that the crack of each firework is symbolic of the breaking of a redcoat's neck. Bogart was always at his most sardonic on this occasion but once, in celebration, he broke all his rules and invited women aboard *Santana*.

'Betty', calling her husband 'Captain Queeg' after the half-mad sadist he had portrayed in *The Caine Mutiny* came along to keep Hjördis company. We dropped anchor in Cherry Grove and Frank Sinatra moored alongside us in a chartered motor cruiser with several beautiful girls and a small piano. After dinner, with Jimmy Van Heusen accompanying him, Sinatra began to sing.

He sang all night.

There were many yachts in Cherry Cove that weekend and by two in the morning, under a full moon, *Santana* was surrounded by an audience sitting in dozens of dinghies and rubber tenders of every shape and size. Frank sang as only he can, with his monumental talent and exquisite phrasing undimmed by a bottle of Jack Daniels on top of the piano.

He sang till the dew came down heavily and the boys in the listening fleet fetched blankets for their girls' shoulders.

He sang till the moon and the stars paled in the pre-dawn sky – only then did he stop and only then did the awed and grateful audience paddle silently away.

Noël Coward was about to appear in Las Vegas. He was sitting in a deep sofa at Bogie's one evening, discussing the problems of his show.

Bogie and I were facing him in two easy chairs. Suddenly, we realized that little Stevie, the five-year-old Bogart son and heir, was stalking Noël from behind, his target, obviously, the top of Noël's head. In his hands he bore a large brass tray.

The impending assault was so horrible that Bogie and I just sat there unable to move like two dogs watching a snake.

Little Stevie raised the tray high and brought it down with a crash on Noël's unprotected cranium. His head almost disappeared into his shirt.

Noël never looked round. His voice never changed nor did the rhythm of his speech alter.

'Bogart, dear,' he said, 'do you know what I am going to give darling little Stephen for Christmas? A chocolate covered hand-grenade.'

The famous 'Sinatra Rat Pack' should now be put in perspective. All sorts of people were for years stuck with this label, Dean Martin, Sammy Davis, Shirley MacLaine, Peter Lawford, Tony Curtis and Janet Leigh to name a few. They were guiltless.

During Noël's appearance at the Desert Inn, Sinatra invited a few friends to go with him to Las Vegas for the opening. When anything is organized by Sinatra, the arrangements are made with legendary efficiency and generosity. We boarded a bus outside Bogie's front door. Caviar and champagne sustained us during the drive downtown to the Union Station and there, with a cry from our leader of 'yellow armbands, follow me', we trooped aboard a private coach on the train for the overnight trip to Las Vegas. The group consisted of Betty and Bogie, Mike and Gloria Romanoff, Ernie Kovacs and his wife, 'Swifty' Lazar, Sid Luft and Judy Garland, Angie Dickinson, Hjördis and myself.

Sinatra provided individual apartments for everyone at the Sands Hotel and a large communal suite with hot and cold running food and drink twenty-four hours a day: a big bag of silver dollars was presented to each girl in the party to gamble with.

We saw Noël's triumphant first night and on subsequent evenings we visited all the other shows in Las Vegas. We gambled endlessly, only occasionally poking our noses outside to sniff the desert air and gauge the time of day. After three days, Judy Garland slipped me something that she promised would keep me going. It was the size of a horse-pill and inside were dozens of little multi-coloured 'energy' nuggets, timed to go of at intervals of forty minutes.

After four days and nights of concentrated self-indulgence, the only one of the party who seemed physically untouched was Sinatra himself. The rest were wrecks and it was then that Betty Bacall, surveying the bedraggled survivors, pronounced the fatal words – 'You look like a Goddam Rat Pack!'

A week after we returned to Los Angeles and forced ourselves back into some semblance of good health, the Rat Pack gave a testimonial dinner to Sinatra in the private room, upstairs, at Romanoff's. A surprise package, tied with pink ribbon and flown down by Jack Entratta, the entrepreneur of the Sands Hotel, awaited everyone of us. Inside each was a white rat. Several escaped during the unpacking and hot-footed it into the restaurant – sowing instant alarm among the chic clientele and eagle-eyed columnists belowstairs – thus heralding the end of the short, happy life of Sinatra's Rat Pack.

So much has been written about Sinatra, of his talent, his generosity, his ruthlessness, his kindness, his gregariousness, his loneliness and his rumoured links with the Mob that I can contribute nothing except to say that he is one of the few people in the world I would instinctively think of if I needed help of any sort. I thought of him once when I was in a very bad spot: help was provided instantly and in full measure without a question being asked. It was not, incidentally, money.

On New Year's Eve of 1956, Annie and Charlie Lederer stretched a striped awning across their back garden, boarded over their swimming pool and gave a very beautiful party for a couple of especially glamorous visitors, the Shah and the Empress of Iran. 'Le tout Hollywood' turned out in force.

Hjördis and I were dancing and beside us, 'Betty' Bacall, a particularly active and dedicated exponent of modern dancing, was gyrating, bumping and grinding round the guest of honour – a comparatively subdued performer.

In an effort to re-establish some sort of contact with his partner, the incumbent of the Peacock Throne said,

'You are a wonderful dancer, Miss Bacall . . . you must have been born to dance.'

'Betty' tossed back her mane of tawny hair, gave one more convulsive heave and answered loudly in her husky-sexy voice.

'You bet your ass, Shah.'

Betty Bacall was the perfect wife and companion for Bogie. I don't know how long she knew he was seriously ill but she was courageous and dedicated through the whole heartbreaking period. I had heard his nightly coughing bouts on my last trips with him in *Santana* but he said it was just his smoking, nothing more. Then, he began to lose weight but he never had been much interested in food.

Suddenly, there was an emergency seven-hour operation and the slow slide began.

'If I put on weight – I've got it licked,' he told me.

Hjördis and I went away to Rome for three months while I made *The Little Hut* with Ava Gardner and Stewart Granger and afterwards we spent a short time together in Sweden. From there, I brought back the radical plans and specifications of a new yacht that I thought might interest Bogie and took them to his house. I was shocked at the change.

We spent a day aboard *Santana*, but she remained tied up alongside her dock. She never put to sea again with Bogie.

He no longer referred to his illness and with Betty in permanent attendance, preserving somehow, God knows how, her marvellous gaiety and fun, he slowly wasted away. When he became too weak to make the trip downstairs for his ritual evening drink with his friends – now invited only one at a time and carefully selected by Betty – they converted the little service elevator, took out the shelves, and sharp at six o'clock, Bogie would have his terribly emaciated frame carefully dressed and be lowered below, sitting in his wheelchair.

One of us would always be waiting – Huston, Sinatra, Harry Kurnitz, Nunally Johnstone, Joe Hyams, 'Swifty' Lazar – a few others, and on special occasions, 'Dum Bum'.

At four o'clock one morning, Betty called us and said very quietly, 'My darling husband is gone.'

16

One Sunday afternoon, the phone rang in the Pink House.

'This is Mike Todd. I'm over at Joe Schenck's. I wanna see you. Get your ass over here.'

I was half way through a polite excuse before I realized that he had long since hung up. I had never met Todd but I had heard a hundred stories about the legendary master showman, gambler, promoter or con man – everyone saw him from a different angle.

We had a houseful of friends that afternoon and the consensus of opinion was that, whatever else, Todd was always interesting and I should indeed get my ass over to Joe Schenck's.

When I arrived, Todd was by the pool. Of medium height and perfect proportions, he was tanned dark mahogany. He wore the briefest of swimming slips. On his head was a white ten-gallon hat, in his mouth was a cigar of grotesque proportions.

He had no time for preliminaries.

'Ever heard of Jules Verne?'

'Yes, of course.'

'Ever read *Around the World in 80 Days*?'

'I was weaned on it.'

'I've never made a picture before but I'm gonna make this one. . . . How'd you like to play Phileas Fogg?'

My heart bounded. 'I'd do it for nothing.'

Todd tossed aside his hat and cigar.

'You gotta deal,' he said and disappeared beneath the surface of the pool.

From that moment till the time, six months later, that the picture was finished, I lived in an atmosphere of pure fantasy. Nobody knows where Todd raised the necessary seven million dollars and he certainly didn't raise it all at once because several times production ground to a halt while strange, swarthy gentlemen arrived from Chicago for urgent consultations. For weeks on end we went unpaid. Todd induced S.J. Perelman to write the screen play and employ John Farrow to direct it.

The Mexican bullfighter comedian, Cantinflas, arrived to play my valet, Passepartout, and Shirley MacLaine was signed to play Princess Aouda.

'But who the hell do we get to play Mr Fix the Detective?' said Todd, chomping on the inevitable cigar.

'How about Robert Newton?' I suggested.

Todd was enchanted with the idea and immediately put in a call.

'But I warn you, Mike,' I said, feeling every kind of heel, 'Bobbie is a great friend of mine but he does drink a lot these days and you must protect yourself. Lots of people are scared to employ him – he disappears.'

'I want to see Newton,' said Todd firmly, 'and when he comes in, I want you here in the office.'

'For Christ's sake, don't tell him I said anything,' I begged, 'he'll never forgive me.'

A little later, Bobbie Newton shuffled in. I hadn't seen him for some weeks and it was obvious that he had been on a bender of heroic proportions.

Todd went into his routine.

'Ever heard of Jules Verne?'

'Ah, dear fellow,' said Newton, 'what a scribe!'

'*80 Days Around the World*?'

'A glorious piece, old cock.'

'How'd you like to play Mr Fix?'

'A splendid role,' said Bobbie, rolling his eyes. 'Do I understand you are offering it to me, dear boy?'

'I might,' said Todd and I felt like the slimiest worm when he continued, 'but your pal, Niven here, says you're a lush.'

'Aah!' said Newton, 'my pal, Niven, is a master of the understatement.'

He was hired immediately and gave his word of honour to Todd that he would go on the wagon for the duration of the picture. He stuck manfully to his promise.

On location at Durango, Colorado, Bobbie and I went off every evening after shooting to catch big, fighting rainbow trout in the mountain lakes. One cold autumn sunset with streaks of blue woodsmoke clinging to the surface of the water and the last rays of the sun falling on the glorious colours of the aspens and beeches, Bobbie confessed to me that his promise to Todd had not really been all that difficult because that very morning his doctor had warned him that one more session with the bottle would almost certainly be fatal. Two weeks after we finished the picture, Todd called some of us back for an added scene on a ship. Bobbie Newton was only required for one day but when he arrived for work, a roaring delivery of 'Once more unto the breach...' announced alarming news. 'Oh, Bobbie,' I said, 'what have you done to yourself?'

He put his arm round my neck and tears rolled down his swollen cheeks.

'Don't chide me, dear fellow, please don't chide me,' he said.

Within a very few days, the doctors's warnings to that warm-hearted, talented and wonderful soul proved tragically correct.

If Todd had difficulty in raising money for his epic, he seemed to have none persuading the biggest names in show business to play small 'cameos' for fun. We started shooting in Spain with Louis Miguel Dominguin playing himself in the bullring, and there, after a falling out, Todd replaced the director, John Farrow, by the young Englishman, Michael Anderson.

In London, more cameo parts were played by Noël Coward, John Gielgud, Trevor Howard, Robert Morley, John Mills, Beatrice Lillie, Hermione Gingold, Hermione Baddeley and Glynis Johns, and back finally in California for the major portion of the work, I became inoculated against surprise when I found myself playing scenes almost daily with different distinguished visitors – among them Ronald Colman, Charles Boyer, Marlene Dietrich, Frank Sinatra, George Raft, Red Skelton, Victor McLaglen, Andy Devine, Joe E. Brown, Cedric Hardwicke and Buster Keaton.

Somehow Todd also found time to collect someone specially for himself and, radiant with happiness, Elizabeth Taylor became a permanent fixture.

Nothing 'phased' Todd . . . when a flock of several hundred sheep stopped our car on the way to location in Colorado, he bought the flock.

'Great idea!' he said. 'We put the sheep in front of the train to hold it up.'

The sheep had been on their way to market so now feed had to be provided at great expense to keep them alive till their big moment. When it came, far from stopping the train, they scattered before it like chaff.

'Sell the goddam sheep,' ordered Todd, 'we need a herd of buffalo.' He found them too, in Oklahoma, and the scene was reshot with several hundred gigantic beasts stampeding in every direction.

In Paris, shooting with Todd-luck on the only sunny day in five weeks of continual rain, we were joined by Fernandel and Martine Carol. Todd needed all the luck at his disposal when he took over the Place Vendôme and ordered cars towed away in the early morning which might interfere with his day's shooting.

One of the offending vehicles turned out to be the property of a Cabinet Minister who was spending the night away from home. Todd was ordered to stop shooting and the police moved in to enforce the order. Todd promptly paid two taxi drivers to stage a head-on collision in the rue de Rivoli and during the ensuing diversion, he completed his work.

In London, he 'stole' a shot of a company of Guardsmen marching out of Wellington Barracks and separating on either side of his camera by the simple device of camouflaging the machine on a vegetable barrow and pushing it directly in front of the oncoming soldiers at the last second . . . that, not surprisingly, proved to be our final day's shooting in the streets of London.

At Balboa, Todd converted an ancient sailing yacht into a paddle steamer of the period by building on deck a large superstructure which housed the ponderous engine of a San Francisco cable car to turn the paddle wheels. Not only was the yacht now dangerously top heavy, but, as we chugged out of the harbour, fully laden with actors, crew, lights and cameras, it was made clear to us that a nasty passage was ahead. I pointed to the storm warnings being raised by the coastguards at the end of the breakwater.

'I can't see a goddam thing,' said Todd, 'I'm Nelson.'

In the event the boat proved too dangerous to turn round in the heavy seas and we had to go all the way to Catalina before we dared try it.

With gorgeous Elizabeth by his side, Todd remained undefeated to the end even when the sheriff of Los Angeles locked up the finished footage of his picture, thereby immobilizing his only asset within the State of California till various local creditors had been mollified.

Todd was allowed to assemble and score the film during the day time under the watchful eye of a sheriff's deputy but at night, back it went into the vault.

Somehow, Todd staved off the enemy and, at last, the picture was ready for presentation. The sheriff was persuaded to allow the film to travel to New York for its big gala opening at the Rivoli Theatre.

'You gotta get your ass back East,' Todd told me. 'You gotta be there at the pay-out window.'

Todd sent air tickets and installed us in the most expensive apartment in the St Regis Hotel. There was a present for Hjördis when we arrived and the rooms were full of flowers; champagne and caviar were waiting for us.

The opening was a Todd bonanza; mounted police held back the screaming crowds as the audience of a thousand famous people in evening dress filed into the theatre. Every member of the audience received a beautifully bound and illustrated programme, embossed in gold on the cover with the name of each recipient. After the showing, Todd gave a champagne supper for fifteen hundred at the Astor Hotel.

Where did he get the money for all this? The answer, according to Bennett Cerf of Random House, who produced the programme, was that he didn't. The morning after the opening, his cheque made out to the publishers – bounced.

No matter, Gambler Todd had got right to the wire with his last penny and when the audience had finished cheering and the ecstatic reviews were being read, there he was standing happily at the pay out window.

The picture won the Academy Award as the Best Picture of the Year and became one of the biggest money spinners of all time.

Todd married Elizabeth and gave her a diamond the size of a skating rink. He bought himself a twin-engined plane.

Hjördis and I, with peculiar logic, decided that with a lot of good pictures now being offered to me, it was the ideal moment to go away from Hollywood for a few months so we flew off around the world.

Shirley MacLaine came with us to Tokyo and, with her husband, Steve Parker, as guide, we saw the best of Japan. The four of us went on to Hong Kong.

Shirely is a great traveller and a spectacular companion. She is also a lady of formidable crusading opinions and her anti-Establishment observations reverberated round the crown colony.

When she and Steve flew back to Japan, Hjördis and I continued on to Thailand, India and Turkey. In Greece we decided to spurge so we chartered a small ketch and the boys flew out to spend their holidays with us in the Islands of the Aegean and Ionian Seas. Hjördis caused a stir in every land we visited not only because of her spectacular beauty but because her idea of travelling light was to order a local costume in each country in turn. Somehow, her purchases always seemed to be delivered on the day of our departure, consequently, she contrived to be a country behind in her clothing. Her cheongsan from Hong Kong was, however, a huge success in Bangkok and her sari from Jaipur nearly caused a riot at a football match in Istanbul.

Back once more in the Pink House via Sweden and England, I

made *My Man Godfrey* at Universal before we decided to visit the scene of the Rat Pack inauguration.

The operator at the Sands Hotel located me at a blackjack table and told me Mike Todd was calling me from New York.

'Get your ass over to Palm Springs,' he said, 'Liz and I are flying out tomorrow. Come and spend the weekend.'

I explained that although Las Vegas is separated from Palm Springs by only a hundred miles as the crow flies, the bird would have to cross a hundred miles of mountains and desert to make the trip.

'Hold the 'phone,' said Todd.

After a while, he was back on the line.

'Okay, I'm sending the plane out there to pick you up – we'll come on out on a commercial – see you tomorrow night for dinner.'

He hung up.

The following day, Todd's twin-engined, twin-piloted pride and joy arrived from New York, picked us up and half an hour later, we were in Todd's Palm Springs pad.

Elizabeth Taylor has always fascinated me. I met her first when she was fifteen and got to know her well during her marriage to the gentle, self-effacing Michael Wilding. Her incredible beauty, her talent and her violet eyes have been the subject of endless paeans of praise; less well known are her courage, her down-to-earthness and her staunch defence of friends. That she is completely unspoiled and natural is a miracle when one remembers that with all the attendant sycophantic adulation, she has survived being a major world movie star since she made *National Velvet* at the age of ten.

She was gay and relaxed during the weekend but made no secret of her annoyance that she would have to stay behind and work in Hollywood when Todd flew back to New York in a few days' time to attend some testimonial dinner.

On the Sunday evening, we all returned to Los Angeles in Todd's plane. Hjördis and I needed little persuading when Todd suggested that we pick up our car and drive back to Palm Springs to relax in his beautiful house till the following weekend when he would be back again.

On the day we reinstalled ourselves in his desert home, Todd called us and said how he wished he could be with us and how little he relished the idea of going back to New York.

'Get out of the dinner,' I said, 'come on down.'

He said he couldn't as he had promised to attend. With typical thoughtfulness, he called again just before he took off to make sure we had everything and repeated once more, how much he wished he didn't have to go.

Four hours later, his plane crashed in New Mexico.

The word 'playwright' is spelled that way for a very good reason. Shipwrights build ships, wheelwrights fashion wheels, and playwrights construct plays. If they construct them badly, they quickly fly apart at the seams.

Terence Rattigan is an actor's playwright. To perform the characters he has invented is a joy because they are so well drawn and the plays that present them are so well constructed that so long as you can remember your 'lines' and don't bump into the furniture, you can't go wrong. *Separate Tables* is one of Rattigan's best plays and 'The Major' is one of his best written characters, so I was, naturally, overjoyed when I was offered the part in the film version. Burt Lancaster, Deborah Kerr, Rita Hayworth, Wendy Hiller, Gladys Cooper, Cathleen Nesbitt, Rod Taylor and myself rehearsed for two weeks under the expert eye of Delbert Mann – one of the best of the new brew of young directors who had been making names for themselves in 'live' television in New York.

It was a dream company to work with.

When the shooting was completed, Hjördis, who had just suffered through yet another miscarriage, was particularly delighted when we took off for a long-planned two weeks' holiday with Noël Coward at his home near Port Maria in Jamaica. On the first evening over rum drinks, having just heard sad news from England, I said to Noël,

'It's terrible – I've arrived at the age when all my friends are dying.'

'Personally,' said Coward, 'I'm delighted if mine last through luncheon. . . .'

'Incidentally', he added, 'you don't look too good yourself.'

I wasn't, it is true, feeling very well – feverish, and Hjördis had just discovered some spots on my back – they itched. By the next morning, more spots had appeared on my face and chest – and my fever had soared.

'I'm terribly sorry, Noël,' I said, 'but there seems to be a faint possibility that I may be coming down with chickenpox.'

Noël eyed my flushed face with mounting distaste then spoke very slowly and distinctly.

'I want to make one thing crystal clear – you cannot come down with it here.'

The next day when Hjördis counted my proliferating spots and reported to Noël that on my face and chest alone she had found over two thousand, Noël sighed resignedly.

'It's high time I wrote another play', he said, 'and painted some more of my excellent pictures, so we will now pull up the drawbridge, fly the Yellow Jack ... and the hell with it.'

He then fetched a bottle.

'The village postmistress,' he said, 'swears that pure rum will stop the itching and bring down the fever.'

While Hjördis watched apprehensively, he anointed my spots and gave me a hefty tot to drink for good measure.

The result of this piece of folklore was instant delirium and two attempts, bravely frustrated by Hjördis, to climb out of the window into the sea.

By the time, weeks later, that I was well enough to travel, Noël had indeed painted many excellent pictures. He had, also, written a very successful play – *Nude with Violin*. His real resilience, however, is demonstrated by the fact that he invited us to stay with him again.

Children's diseases are not to be recommended to adults. It was weeks before I could go back to work. When I did, I started *Ask any Girl* with Shirley MacLaine.

On the set one day, Shirley was called to take a phone call from New York; she let out one of her traffic-stopping shrieks.

'Hey, David! come here quick!' she yelled. 'You've just won the New York Critics' Award for *Separate Tables*.'

It was a tremendous surprise, I didn't even know I was a candidate. There were, I believe, fifteen voters and apparently after three ballots I had just scraped home over Spencer Tracy in *The Old Man and the Sea*. Bosley Crowther, the influential voice of the *New York Times*, had voted against me which, of course, he had every right to do, but finding himself in the minority, he behaved like a spoiled brat and devoted his Sunday article to saying what a disgrace it was that I had won.

Shirley got me all excited.

'If you win the New York Critics, you are almost bound to be nominated for the Academy Award! Hey! you may get the Oscar!!'

I tried to be cool and accepted congratulations all over town as unsmugly as I could but the weeks before the announcement of the five nominees for best performance by an actor were endless. When it finally came over the radio, I was on my way home from work and my receiver was on the blink. The attendant at a gas station gave me the good news when I stopped to fill up. When I arrived at the Pink House, Hjördis had the champagne out. The phone never stopped ringing. Basically, the awards system is a good one ... for the nomination, five in each category, one's peers vote. The actors nominate the actors, the directors nominate the directors, the writers the writers, the cameramen the cameramen – and so on. Then the whole lot, all three thousand members of the Academy, vote for the winners.

The other nominees in my category were Spencer Tracy, Paul Newman, Sidney Poitier and Tony Curtis.

I had ten weeks to wait before the final result and I started out by telling myself that at best, I was a four-to-one shot. I also felt a bit of a fake because playing the role of 'the Major' had, thanks to the way it was written and directed and the formidable help I had received from that high-powered cast, been far easier than I could have imagined.

As the ten weeks dragged by, the pressures built up. The winner of the Academy Award is supposed to add a million dollars to the potential of the picture he is in. His next film, too, is supposed to benefit largely. The advertising campaigns start in earnest one month before voting day. Film companies and some individuals spend thousands of dollars pushing their wares, everyone is speculating.

'Tracy will win because everyone loves him. . . . Newman will win because he is always so good – and it's time he did ... Poitier will win because he's black and Hollywood is colour-conscious ... Curtis will win because he's Jewish ... you can't win because you're British and they gave it to Alec Guinness last year' etc. etc. It was all very nerve-wracking but as the day came nearer, I found that I wanted that Oscar desperately.

My estimate of my chances was not very high at the best of times but it dropped to zero on the very day that the three thousand voters received their ballot sheets ... there in the *Hollywood Reporter*, the local Bible which would be read by all of them, was a reprint of a story by the eminent film critic and columnist of the Washington *Daily News*, Jim O'Neill. It stated that a well-known Hollywood producer had told that newspaper's columnist that the one person he would never vote for would be me, because I had copied Eric Portman's stage performance entirely, had seen the play forty times and had haunted Portman's dressing room till I had to be bodily thrown out of the theatre.

I was sunk. I cabled O'Neill in Washington and pointed out that not only was I not clever enough, or stupid enough, to copy anybody's performance – but it so happened that I had seen the play precisely once, four years before in London.

O'Neill checked with Portman who kindly corroborated this and wished me luck and O'Neill then, very graciously, apologized to me in print for 'irresponsible reporting'. He quoted Portman's cable and for good measure, told me, over the phone, the name of the Hollywood producer, 'as the very least I can do'.

It was far too late to hope to put the record straight, the votes would already have been cast and I had really given up any hope. However, I called the 'well-known producer' and thanked him for his help.

After a lot of spluttering, he said, 'Jesus; I'm trapped. I did it but I heard it from So-and-So. So-and-So told me it had come from "thingummibob"' – and so it went on.

Out of curiosity, I tracked it back through eight people and there I found who had originated the story – a publicist in the publicity department of a rival studio whose job it was to further his man's chances had decided that the best way was to chop down the opposition.

When there is a million dollars at stake, Hollywood has never believed in kid gloves. The actor, of course, had no idea it had happened, he would never in a million years have condoned it.

The night before the 'Awards', someone gave a large party for Ingrid Bergman, who, after years away from Hollywood and a romance on Stromboli which had shocked or titillated the world, had reappeared to make one of the presentations. Everyone at the party seemed to have voted for me; they didn't say so in so many words, they were content to signal the fact across the room by making a cross in the air and pointing to their own chests and winking knowingly.

I was greatly encouraged until I caught the eye of Rosalind Russell, a nominee for best actress for whom I had not voted – and found myself winking, pointing and drawing crosses in the empty air.

The night of the awards finally was upon us. I was slightly anaesthetized because for the hour-long show, Bob Hope, Jack Lemmon and I had been pressed into service as the three masters of ceremonies and this preoccupied me with a great deal of hard work. At Grauman's Chinese Theatre on Hollywood Boulevard, the scene was set.

The traditional searchlights weaved back and forth across the purple night sky and the bleachers were jammed with thousands of excited fans as the bearers of well-known faces arrived and popping flash-bulbs blinded their well-known eyes.

I had to be there early. Before I left home, our Celtic and Nordic blood sent us dashing superstitiously about the house gathering up good luck charms. Distributed about my person were several rabbits' feet, a silver pig that one of my sons had given to me, some heavy Swedish coins, a Hebrew inscription on beaten bronze which I hoped might have captured the Jewish vote, a Buddha with a tiny diamond in his navel which Hjördis had found in Thailand, and my other son's first fallen tooth.

Hjördis looked spectacular and, munching tranquillizers like popcorn, arrived later with Suzanne and Peter Ustinov.

My chores as a master of ceremonies over, I found my seat with them and sat knotted with indigestion as the show dragged on. I watched wretchedly as the happy recipients of Oscars made their carefully prepared acceptance speeches (more superstition had stopped me from preparing even one line – just in case). Ranged around the walls of the packed auditorium were five television cameras, each focused on a nominee and each ready to capture and flash to millions of viewers all over the world, looks of expectancy, disappointment, joy, studied indifference or tears.

Irene Dunne was finally introduced and I carefully composed my generous-hearted-loser-face for she it was who would open the big white envelope, sealed in guaranteed secrecy by Price Waterhouse and Company and containing the name of the winner of 'The Best Performance by an Actor'.

She opened the envelope and, after an interminable pause, read out my name. There was a roar. I didn't wait to diagnose whether it was a roar of approval or rage. I kissed Hjördis, leapt to my feet and with tail coat flapping, I cantered down the aisle – I thought 'I've got to get there quick before she changes her mind.'

Such was my haste to get on that stage that I tripped up the steps and sprawled headlong. Another roar rent the air. Irene helped me up, gave me the Oscar, kissed me on the cheek and left me alone with the microphone. I thought the least I could do was to explain my precipitous entrance, so I said. . . . 'The reason I just fell down was . . .'. I had intended to continue 'because I was so loaded with good luck charms that I was top heavy. . . .' Unfortunately, I made an idiot pause after the word 'loaded' and a third roar raised the roof.

I knew that I could never top that, so I said no more on the subject, thereby establishing myself as the first self-confessed drunk to win the Academy Award.

So many ingredients go into one individual's winning an Oscar – the material, the direction, the other actors, the photography, the editing, even the music, that in reality it's a team effort, but whatever the background and however sentimental the vote, it's a lovely feeling to accept first prize.

Cables and messages and scripts poured in from all over the world . . . King for a day? . . . Certainly! . . . after that, it's back to the old drawing-board.

The message I cherished the most was an invitation to go and see Samuel Goldwyn at his home. He opened the door himself and put his arm around my shoulders. It had been eight long years since we parted company.

In the drawing room, Frances caught me looking surreptitiously, at the piano: there in its silver frame stood my photograph in uniform sent from England during the war.

'Sam never took it down,' she smiled.

Live television, during its reign, proved one thing – that many actors are masochists. Without exception, the most ghastly torture ever invented for people in my profession, it incorporated all the worst features of films, radio and the legitimate theatre.

Before an unseen audience of millions, over-dressed and under-rehearsed actors struggled with badly written scripts in front of cameras which collided with sickening regularity and scenery that wobbled and often collapsed while the whole mess was directed by egomaniac directors, drunk with power in front of consoles studded with switches and buttons.

The actor's nightmare was ever present – the dread of forgetting the lines without any possible hope of being prompted back on to the track. My partner, Dick Powell, was the genius who overcame this on one occasion. When forgetfulness set in, he continued mouthing silently and all over the country hundreds of thousands of viewers frantically twiddled their dials and phoned their repair men.

Fortunately, film and tape gradually eliminated the live monster, leaving it to cope most efficiently with news, 'talk shows', and sports, but while it was in its final throes, masochist me could not resist one more exposure to its well-known dangers, so off I flew to New York.

It was an important show but the material was the usual gibberish: I was a spy or a doctor or a Congressman, I forget which – it would not have made the slightest difference. The strange thing was, I didn't really need the money that badly . . . it was an irresistible urge to be frightened . . . like skiing, but this time I was determined to be calm. After all, I was the star of the show and the major part of the burden was mine. My idea of being calm was this: I left my hat, coat and briefcase (my spy, doctor or Congressman equipment) in my little dressing room just off the sound stage and with only five minutes to 'air time', I wandered nonchalantly about in shirt sleeves.

An hysterical assistant rushed up, 'David! . . . for Christ's sake! . . .'

'Calm yourself, please,' I said, trying not to throw up, 'we have five, lovely, long cool minutes before we have to act this very bad play in front of several millions of people but, in the meanwhile, let us all relax. . . .'

'David! for Chrisss. . . .'

'Please,' I said, 'don't raise your voice, all I need is two minutes during which I will go to my room, put on my coat and hat and pick up my brief case.'

The man nearly disintegrated as I sauntered about, perhaps for the first time what Americans have always hoped a true Britisher might be – an ice-cold Gibraltar.

'David!' the assistant pleaded. '*Please* – you've just got two minutes!'

'Okay,' I said, 'no sweat', and followed by a forest of admiring eyes and with the slow measured tread of a London Bobby, I stalked to my little dressing room.

I had locked myself out.

Immediately, I was transformed into a shrieking, babbling, banshee.

'HELP! HELP!'

A quivering announcer started to extol the sponsor's wares against a background accompaniment of studio firemen hacking down my door and eventually, I made my entrance with my hat on back to front, my coat wrongly buttoned and covered in wood chips. I couldn't remember a word.

Orson Welles once said to me, 'We have now acted in theatres, on radio, in films and on live television – they *can't* think of anything else, can they?'

Oh! God! I hope not.

I stayed on in New York to make a film.

In this journal, I have, by now, firmly established myself as a name-dropper so I can, with equanimity, record that apart from re-establishing contact with McClain, the New York Giants and many other old friends, the only occurrence of note during the time I was filming in New York was my good fortune in getting to know Senator J.F.K. of Massachusetts and his beautiful wife, Jackie.

One night with a small party, we visited El Morocco and were seated at J.F.K.'s request in the Champagne Room at the back. I was dancing with Jackie in the main room and remarked on the fact that her husband remained out of sight all evening.

'Why's that? Doesn't he like to dance?'

'He wants to be President,' she replied.

The picture finished, I returned to the Pink House just in time for the boys' summer holidays. I had many offers. Four Star was mushrooming, the mortgage was paid off and the Oscar was gleaming on the mantelshelf. I should have known from experience that I was headed for trouble.

The astute reader will have noticed fewer references to Hjördis in the pages covering the last few months. Unfortunately and almost imperceptibly, this had become the pattern of our lives at that time.

I had fallen into the well-known trap of becoming so wrapped up in my career, myself and, lately, my success, that I had been taking the most important thing in my life for granted.

Hjördis told me that she was leaving me.

With complete honesty, Hjördis explained that she had to find out if she was still an individual, a human being in her own right, or just the trappings of someone else. It was very painful. Once Hjördis makes up her mind – that's it! She rented a small house nearby and moved into it to live alone and find out if she still 'existed'. The boys were nonplussed and refused to believe it had happened. Irreverently, they named her new residence. 'The Summer Pink House' and visited it daily on their bicycles.

Hollywood is an impossible place to work out family problems. There, several hundred resident correspondents peer through their microscopes at an ever-changing handful of goldfish who are news. Rumours flew; so we put out the traditional nauseating statement about 'a trial separation' and voiced our pious hope that 'friends would understand while we attempted to reconcile our differences'.

Looking sadly at an empty chair was no way of spending the summer holidays so I took the boys to Honolulu to try our luck on the surf boards. Forty-eight hours later, the Los Angeles papers were full of pictures of me being helped from the sea with blood streaming down my face – the result of a head-on collision with a rock.

Urgent enquiries from Hjördis – a good sign.

After six weeks, I returned to the Pink House, and diplomatic relations were re-opened between the two establishments, mostly in the form of SOS messages, relayed by the boys.

'The boiler's burst – she wants to know what to do.'

'Somebody's stolen the mowing machine and the landlord is suing her – who does she call?'

I went to work at MGM with Doris Day making *Please Don't Eat the Daisies* and, three months to the day from the start of our trial separation, I took my lunch box at midday and paid my first visit to the Summer Pink House. Hjördis was sunbathing in the garden when I walked in demanding beer to wash down my sandwiches. By the time I went back to the studio, the war was blessedly over.

It was a horrible experiment but by anyone as completely honest as Hjördis it could never have been undertaken except as a last resort. Most importantly, it worked and a whole new lease of life was given to our happiness entirely thanks to her having had the courage of her convictions.

As soon as I was through with the picture, we took off on a second honeymoon.

We had been invited to Brazil as guests of the Government. I was to be presented with the key of the city of Rio de Janeiro by President Kubitschek. We went via New York and while Hjördis busied herself finding clothes for the visit, I misguidedly enrolled myself at the Arthur Murray School of Dancing for a crash course in the tango.

For hours, closeted in a tiny cubicle, I nestled between the bosoms of a large, dark lady and swooped and dipped like a madman.

If anybody was still dancing the tango in Brazil they certainly were not doing so during our visit. I never had a chance to display my virtuosity.

North American hospitality is justly famous: the South American variety is exuberantly overpowering. It was a fascinating experience. Very few Hollywood faces had, thus far, been seen in that land of ardent moviegoers and we were fêted, cheered and mobbed wherever we went.

When the President, at the palace, presented me with a colossal key, Hjördis said, as a joke, 'What about me? Can't I have a little one too?'

With great gallantry, he ordered a small, golden replica to be made specially for her and delivered the same afternoon.

A fascinating man with a most attractive family, his pride and joy was the controversial city of Brasilia, which was then only half built. On the spur of the moment he said,

'We'll go up there together tomorrow.'

We flew up in the presidential plane accompanied by his wife, daughters and the architect of Brasilia – Oscar Neymeyer, who sat white-faced and miserable throughout the trip – he is frankly terrified of flying.

When we arrived in Brasilia, the President put us in his helicopter and pointed delightedly as we flew between the half-built skyscrapers of his new capital, landing finally on the lawn of the only finished structure in the city, his own 'Palace of the Dawn', there to spend the weekend. 'Tomorrow,' he said, 'you and I will officially declare the lake to be filled with water.'

In a dinghy with an outboard motor, dodging in and out of the half-submerged tree trunks, we made the grand opening tour of the huge half-filled man-made waterway.

After another week of being royally entertained in São Paulo, we spent a few days by ourselves in Bahia.

Soon after we got back to the Pink House, my birthday loomed up and Hjördis said, 'Let's go down to some little place on the beach and have lunch together.'

It was a Sunday and the weather was glorious, and dreading the bumper-to-bumper traffic, I advanced every excuse, but she was adamant. So I took my place resignedly behind the wheel and we headed out towards Malibu.

She pointed excitedly, 'Let's go in there . . . it looks sweet.'

'The Frigate Bird' was a well-known whore house with a very unsavoury reputation. I explained this to Hjördis.

'Oh, *please*,' she said. 'I've never been in one before. Please, do take me in there . . . and look . . . it says Dining Room!'

Still chastened by our short separation, I gave myself a good mark, for being attentive to my wife though luncheon in a brothel seemed a strange way to demonstrate it, and turned into the driveway.

As we entered, a parrot in a cage gave a wolf whistle and a sleazy madame greeted me with,

'Look who's here! Well, hullo there, Dave! . . . Long time no see' – a libellous and erroneous statement as it happened but I pretended not to hear and pressed grimly on towards the dining room. There I froze. In the gloom, I saw the well-known back of a close friend. His arm was around a blonde girl's waist . . . Lawrence Olivier.

'Quick!' I hissed to Hjördis. 'We've got to get out of here.' Then as my eyes became accustomed to the semi-darkness, I spotted another even more easily recognizable form . . . Peter Ustinov was pinning a dark girl to the wall. My head spun. My friends had gone mad – what a lunatic risk to take! I grabbed Hjördis by the arm and dragged her down the passage; the parrot whistled again, a peal of well-known laughter followed us – Patricia Medina!

Only then did I catch on. My surprise birthday party in surprise surroundings was a complete success.

In the spring of 1960, we had an overpowering urge to move. This urge became more and more pronounced and we knew with certainty that this was not something being signalled to our brains by our pathologically itchy feet. We knew that we wanted to make a big and permanent change. When I told my agent and my business manager that we were thinking of moving back to Europe to live, they were dumbfounded and lost no time pointing out that my career had never been in better shape, and asked what sort of pictures I thought I'd make over there.

'You'll be sitting on top of some goddamned mountain,' they said, 'praying for the phone to ring.'

They talked ominously about the boys' schooling, hinted darkly about my obligations to Four Star . . . they told me quite frankly that they reckoned I had gone mad, but the more they reasoned with me and the more valid their arguments sounded, the more certain I became that we would be going.

Hollywood had changed completely. The old camaraderie of pioneers in a one-generation business still controlled by the people who created it, was gone. The mystique had evaporated. Wrong it may have been, but when Joan Crawford, Norma Shearer and Marlene Dietrich had graciously consented to give interviews to the press, it was on the strict understanding that the copy would be submitted and could be altered to their taste before it was published. They created and perpetuated their images and – they became immortal.

Now, the inevitable reaction had set in and upon us was the era of the vicious, apparently law-suit-proof columnist, of *Confidential* magazine and the telephoto lens. The pipe dream was gone – the lovely joke was over. The asphalt jungle of highways was proliferating everywhere through the once lovely Californian countryside; the famous sunshine was dimmed by automobiles and industry and the scent of fear was attacking the smog-filled lungs of the professional film makers, already resigned to the fact that their audience was brainwashed by television. It was time to go, but even so and with our European roots tugging at us, it was a tough decision to make. Although we had lately received a nasty shock from the tax authorities who had taken all our savings to pay off a hefty reassessment of taxes from four years before, we still needed a clear sign that we should actually start making our reservations.

The message was delivered nearby in tragic and brutal fashion. . . .

On a bright Sunday during the Easter holiday, David and Jamie were on the patio helping me with the barbecue, Hjördis was indoors baking the potatoes. The garden was vivid with blossom and the yellow orioles had come back to nest once more. Around us the hills were misty and the blue jacaranda trees were in full bloom. In the distance Mount Baldy on one side reared its snow-topped head above the industrial haze of the Los Angeles basin, in the opposite direction, Catalina and the Santa Barbara Islands floated in ghostly isolation far out on the Pacific.

I don't think we even heard it ... if we did we would have dismissed it as the backfire of an automobile. It was a revolver shot. Four youths, 'junkies', had come up from Downtown in a taxi. After paying the fare, they had 'cased' our street for suitable victims and had settled on a neighbour's house a few yards away.

They rang the bell. The son of the house, a boy about the same age as mine, opened the door. They shot him.

While he was dying in agony on the threshold, they held up the distraught parents, took their available cash and then, inexplicably, allowed them to call a doctor.

They were all arrested within half an hour, and, receiving the sentences reserved for juveniles, have, presumably, long since been once more let loose on society.

Los Angeles is a violent city so I don't mean that we stampeded in panic as a result of this single tragedy, but it certainly tipped the scales, because we had lately decided to adopt and we wanted to bring up a new family somewhere in peace and quiet.

Finding a good home for the Pink House was our primary consideration. Many unknowns wanted it badly but we sold it much less advantageously to an old friend who loved it and who has lived there happily with his family ever since.

I resigned from the Board of Four Star, put the Regency furniture in storage and when the boys went back to boarding school, we flew off to find a new home and a new life in Europe.

First stop – Klosters in Switzerland – to catch the tail end of the skiing and to ask the advice of Deborah Kerr and her husband, Peter Viertel. They were adamant that we should follow their example and make Switzerland our base so when my agent finally trapped me after days of frantic search offering me several months in Greece and England making *The Guns of Navarone*, I left for the island of Rhodes and Hjördis stayed behind combing the Alps for a suitable chalet. She was brilliant and within a few weeks found exactly what we wanted, a comfortable cuckoo clock in a quiet farming village fifteen minutes from the ski resort of Gstaad.

The Guns of Navarone was a long and physically very arduous picture culminating with five weeks in England in November simulating a storm at sea by working nine freezing hours a day in a huge tank of filthy water.

After nine months, Gregory Peck and I were left alone with two weeks of exhausting night work still to do, shooting from dusk to dawn, filming the actual finale of the picture – blowing up the guns. As my character had been built up as 'a genius with explosives . . . the only man who can do it,' it will readily be appreciated that without my presence during those crucial last two weeks, the colossal seven-million-dollar epic could never be finished. With only three days to go, I picked up a fearsome infection via a split lip and at two o'clock one morning, was carted away with, what in the grim times before antibiotics, was known as general septicaemia. I lay dangerously ill for days while the experts from Guy's Hospital struggled to identify, isolate and eliminate the bug that had struck me down.

The picture ground to a halt amidst general consternation. The 'Big Brass' of the company arrived post-haste from America. They called a meeting with Carl Foreman, the producer, Lee Thompson, the director, the head of the finance department, representatives of the banks and insurance companies and various assistants.

One of these present reported the scene to me later.

Foreman read out the latest ominous bulletin from the doctors: murmurs of sympathy and alarm arose on all sides. After a suitable pause, the Biggest Brass spoke, 'We gotta problem here, fellers . . . so David is very, very sick . . . that's tough on him . . . and we all love him . . . but wadda *we* do if the sonofabitch dies?'

'The sonofabitch', pumped full of drugs, went back to work against the doctor's orders far sooner than was prudent, completed the crucial three days' work and suffered a relapse that lasted seven weeks.

The Big Brass never even sent me a grape.

While I was recuperating in the Chalet, Hjördis busied herself looking for the baby girl we had both set our hearts on. One day the miracle happened. A little round bundle, a few weeks old, was delivered into her arms. It promptly went purple with rage and tried to scream the house down, but one look at the madonna-like serenity of Hjördis face was all I needed. We were entering a period of pure joy.

Two years later, another little creature appeared and while Hjördis remained calmly confident, relentless competition for the affection of these two diminutive blonde bombshells set in between myself and my two sons. It continues, unabated, to this day; no holds barred.

After a while in Europe, the twin calls of sun and sea increased in volume. Hjördis, once again, was brilliant and this time, after combing the whole northern Mediterranean basin till she knew every rock by name, she found an old monstrosity, perched in an olive grove on a little promontory of its own on Cap Ferrat.

Any actor who voluntarily supports two residences should have a psychiatrist permanently installed in both of them.

However, the Regency furniture was sent for and the house was officially declared open by the more-beautiful-than-ever-Grace from next door in Monaco who sat on a packing case with her enchanting husband and ate sardines by candlelight.

During the next few years, we returned a few times to Hollywood including once to make a picture about two crooks with Marlon Brando and once to shoot the pilot of Four Star's most ambitious television series, *The Rogues*. The eye must really have been 'in' on the day when producer, Collier Young, and I did the casting because we chose as my leading lady, a complete unknown – Sally Kellerman.

Brando, contrary to what I had heard, was easy, sympathetic and generous to work with and a great help on a tricky political occasion.

Hjördis and I had received a message from the White House. Jackie was giving a very small surprise party for the President.

The producer of the picture, a staunch Republican, saw no particular reason to arrange the schedule to get me off a few hours early on Friday evening. Brando, a super Democrat, viewed it quite differently and the matter was quickly arranged. We flew to Washington; on arrival, we were smuggled by Fifi Fell into a small hotel where we changed and then boarded the Presidential yacht at a heavily guarded dock.

Apart from Fifi, ourselves and a senator from Florida, it was entirely a family affair – the R.F.K.s, the E.F.K.s, the Shrivers, the Smiths and so forth. Jackie had provided a small orchestra. When it struck up 'Happy Birthday to you' as the President boarded for what he thought was a quiet dinner alone with his wife, his face, luckily, lit up with pleasure.

We cruised up and down the river, followed by a secret service launch . . . a gay, happy family evening. We gave presents and in the early hours of the morning, played some fairly strenuous Kennedy games.

During one of these physical encounters, the entire left leg of Senator E.K.'s trousers was ripped off at the crotch. At four a.m. we came alongside for landing and it was evident that several marines, secret service men and others, were standing there to receive us.

'Please take my pants,' I said, 'it'll cause no stir if an actor comes ashore half-dressed, but it might look odd if you do.'

'The hell with it,' laughed Teddy Kennedy, 'it happened didn't it?' and with white underpants on the port side flashing bravely, he stepped jauntily ashore.

The next day, J.F.K. was in his office at eight sharp before attending a Decoration Day Service with his small son. At eleven, we had a rendezvous in his oval office.

'See how it feels,' he smiled and I sat for a moment at the Presidential desk.

With Jackie and the two children, we were whisked away in the Presidential helicopter to spend the rest of the weekend swimming, walking and skeet shooting at Camp David.

On the way up there, with a secret service helicopter in attendance, I noticed, at the President's elbow, a brightly coloured telephone. He saw me staring at it and started to laugh.

'Is that *the* one?' I asked. He nodded.

'The one you pick up if you want to blow up the world?'

'That's it', he said, then he looked down at the glorious, green countryside passing below us, glanced at the attendant chopper flying beside us and laughed again.

'You know,' he said, 'a guy could get to like this!'

Countless volumes have been written about this extraordinary human being and the earthshaking moments he lived through and often controlled. I shall never forget him for his simplicity, his humour, his kindness, his interest in other people and, above all, his love of life.

The end of the journal is now in sight so I will attempt to reward the reader's patience and loyalty by bringing it swiftly to a close without making it sound like my obituary.

Since the war, Trubshawe, long since married to the glamorous Mrs Tower, had tried his hand at many things, including becoming a publican. He had been the landlord of several hostelries including a small inn – The Lamb, at Hooe in Sussex. The honest burghers of Brighton, taking their Sunday drives over the Downs, were astonished to see a newly erected billboard that stated simply –

TRUBSHAWE HAS A LITTLE LAMB
– 12 miles.

Now he has given up that line of business and become an actor – a very good one too. He swiftly made a name for himself in television and one of his earliest screen appearances was in *The Guns of Navarone* – a lovely bonus for me.

Bill Rollo died. He died exactly as he would have planned it, except that he had every intention of living for ever. He worked hard all his life and put all he could afford into his delightful small farm in Rutland. Fox-hunting was his joy and his extravagance. He spent all the time he could spare with Dinie, his second wife, at Barleythorpe. At the age of seventy, mounted on his favourite hunter, on a glorious autumn morning, with the scent breast high and the Quorn hounds in full cry, he put his horse at a big thorn fence. It fell. Bill's neck was broken.

I was filming in Spain. Hjördis was visiting her family in Sweden, David was at the University of Florence and Jamie at school in Switzerland. We converged on London and the next day drove north for the funeral.

In London, it had been a happy family reunion, but as the miles sped by and Barleythorpe came nearer, the terrible sadness of the real reason for our coming together swept over us. We had all adored him. He had been indestructible. The little village church was packed with his old hunting and shooting friends sitting silently and stoically in their grief. In the family pew, the Niven contingent wept unashamedly. After the service, we walked miserably out into the pale sunshine. The Duke of Beaufort, a close friend of Bill's, approached.

'I take it you will be spending the night with Dinie?'

'I can't, I'm afraid,' I said. 'I have to go back to Spain – I'm shooting in the morning.'

'Ah,' he said, 'they've got a nice lot of birds down there this year, I hear.'

I didn't try to explain.

The boys completed their education in Switzerland, France, England and Italy. Jamie returned to the US and after leaving Harvard, married a very special girl from Philadelphia. He now works in New York, David in London.

Lately, Betty Bacall arrived to spend some time at Cap Ferrat with us. She brought with her the score of *Applause* and for ten days sat at the end of our promontory, belting out her numbers. The fishermen deserted the rocks below, the sea gulls departed and certain species of fish are no longer to be found in our waters, but when she opened on Broadway, she scored the greatest triumph that has come to any actress in the last ten years.

Well, that about rounds it off. . .

What else is there? Oh! yes! . . . the Movies! I almost forgot about them. Well . . . in the ten years since I left Hollywood, my itchy feet have spurred me, usually accompanied by Hjördis and the girls, to make films in Greece, Spain, England, France, Israel, Ireland, United States, Monaco, Switzerland, Austria, Mexico, Italy and the Lebanon – and more than one film in many of these countries.

During that time I have been directed by the highly intelligent such as John Huston, John Frankenheimer, J. Lee Thompson and Peter Ustinov and by other professionals, also by the heavy-handed, the hysterical and the half-wits. I have worked with drunkards and those who preferred 'pot', 'speed' or 'horse'.

As a result of these travels and all these exposures nothing really fatal happened but there was one extremely painful near miss.

We were shooting *The Pink Panther* in the Italian Alps; the following day I was required to do something very simple on skis and the producer, not knowing that I would rather ski than eat, told me to take the afternoon off and practise with a ski teacher. So anxious was I to profit from his rash instruction before he realized I might break a leg, that I bustled off up the mountain in my thin movie ski outfit, halfwittedly ignoring the fact that on the top it was 35° below zero . . . so cold in fact that no one else was skiing. Halfway down and travelling fast behind the instructor, I suddenly got a feeling of absolutely nothing in precisely the spot where I should have been the warmest . . . something was badly amiss amidships. A neon-sign flashed on in my brain FROSTBITE and cupping my hands over the danger area, I inadvertently put myself into the racing position and flashed past the astonished instructor. At the bottom three morose and mauve-coloured guides were warming themselves over a fire of fir branches.

'Catso gelato!' I yelled in my shaky Italian.

The men were galvanized into instant action. This was a fate worse then death.

'Put it in the snow,' they shouted, plucking feverishly at my zipper.

'You put yours in the snow,' I gibbered, 'mine's cold enough.'

My instructor arrived. 'Alcohol!' he commanded. 'We must put it in alcohol!'

We all clambered into his ancient car and I was driven through the main street of Cortina d'Ampezzo, one of the choicest resorts in the

Alps, lying in the back with four horny-handed mountaineers, trying to keep the circulation going in my stricken friend.

In the bar of the Hotel de la Poste, smartly dressed clients finishing a late lunch, gaped in amazement as we clumped to the bar and yelled at the barman to fill a balloon brandy glass to the brim with whisky 'prontissimo!'

In the lavatory, while the Italians formed a solicitous clucking semi-circle, I faced the agony of the thaw and prised out of my ski pants a pale blue acorn. Into the whisky it went and the pain was excruciating. This moment was chosen by a smart Milanese nobleman whom I happened to know to enter with a view to relieving himself. He took in the tableau at a glance.

'David,' he asked in a horrified voice, 'what *are* you doing?'

'I am pissing in a brandy glass,' I muttered between clenched teeth, 'I always do.'

Apart from that, nothing much happened on my wanderings.

I have been knifed (by mistake) in a Spanish production and nearly shot dead by a bedouin in Israel when the World War II rifle he was handling still had one up the spout. The bullet passed between our heads as I was talking to Duncan Macrae.

I have been knocked senseless by falling scenery in an English studio and overturned in a canoe in the loathsomely infested waters of a Mexican jungle ... all in all, about par for the course.

The results, too, have been average. Some pictures the critics loved and the audience hated; some despised by the experts were greatly appreciated by the paying customers. One effort became one of the great money-makers of all time; another broke the record at the Radio City Music Hall and a third was so bad that it never got shown anywhere – even on the airlines.

The whole movie industry, at the moment of writing, is in disarray – some say it will never recover.

When it was booming, nothing was put into research. With people, today, cavorting about on the moon, it is incredible to think that films are still made and distributed in much the same way as they were in the days of D.W. Griffith, Chaplin and Buster Keaton. If the film companies had been making motor cars or false teeth, they would have been bankrupt forty years ago. When the business men took over from the old-time movie makers and started chasing 'trends', disaster followed as the night the day and now there is little money left with which to make new pictures. Fingers of blame have been pointed freely in every direction including at the people who pulled in the customers.

Sitting in their yacht in Monte Carlo harbour, I was discussing the situation with the Burtons.

'What about the people who got a million dollars a picture?' I asked.

Elizabeth's reply was as down to earth as usual.

'If someone was stupid enough to offer me a million dollars to make a picture – I was certainly not dumb enough to turn it down.'

The movie business has often before proved its resilience and it will do so once more. In these days of super communications, it makes no sense to think that the greatest form of mass entertainment ever invented will just fade away.

Actors have a problem – often we don't know how to get 'off'.

'How do I finish this story?' I asked a writer friend.

'Quite simply,' he replied, 'just bring it up to date, then stop writing.'

After he had departed I was left in my London hotel staring at a blank sheet of paper digesting his brilliance and wondering how to avoid being sentimental while at the same time underlining my wonder at the ease with which two baby girls had altered my priorities and changed the whole process and meaning of my life when the phone rang.

'Uncle David!' said a sweet voice, 'this is your goddaughter!'

Noël Coward has twenty-seven godchildren – five more than I (eighteen of mine are girls).

Noël would never have floundered as I did ... his record for patience and helpfulness is legendary ... example –

'Uncle Noël! Look at those two little doggies! What *are* they doing?'

'The little doggie in front,' said Godfather Noël, 'has just gone blind, and his friend is pushing him all the way to St Dunstan's.'

'I have a friend with me,' said my unidentified goddaughter. 'He's dying to meet you ... can we come up?'

When she walked in and embraced me I remembered her. Eighteen years old, long, blonde hair, Indian head-band, willowy wasp-waist figure, suede jacket, fringed skirt, green eyes and a gorgeous smile.

Her companion was considerably less prepossessing.

'This is Big Top,' said my goddaughter offhandedly, as she indicated a morose, bearded creature lurking behind her. He sported an Afro hair-do, a grave error for a red-headed Caucasian. He, too, was festooned with love beads and his heliotrope bell-bottoms were kept up by a broad leather belt, the buckle of which was fashioned in the shape of a penis. Dirty, horned toenails jabbed out belligerently from between the thongs of his questionable sandals.

'You wanna blow some grass, man?' he demanded, his flat Lancashire voice winning easily over a phoney American accent. He ignited a joint and passed it to my goddaughter.

'You dig today's pictures?' he asked me. 'How come you only work for these creepy has-beens, man? I've got something that'll really blow your mind, very groovy.'

'What's it about, Big Top?' I asked, groaning inwardly.

'Just be cool,' he said. 'Be cool . . . if you wanna be in something really far out, really specific, something really against your bag . . . I have this story about this old guy, rich and weirdo: his daughter has freaked out, see, and shacked up with a spade who drops acid, who's a big wheel in some corny new African state. . . .' He droned out the rest of the well-known rubbish and then delivered a homily.

It was cats like me, it seemed, who had ruined the movie business with our bad taste and lack of imagination. The only way we could atone for our sins, was by coming up with some 'heavy bread' for his production company.

He finally withdrew, leaving my room smelling like a haystack I opened the windows.

'Isn't he awful?' giggled my goddaughter. 'I won't do that to you again . . . I got trapped.' She looked at me speculatively and took a long draught of champagne.

'Want to take me to a party? It's just around the corner.'

In the lobby many heads turned in her direction as she clung to my arm.

The party was located in a studio above an antique shop. A glassy-eyed transvestite admitted us and pointed limply into the gloom of a sickly-sweet haze . . . 'There's wine over there.'

The place was illuminated by carriage lamps; on the walls were garish posters, large, coloured numbers and blown-up photographs of Che and Mao. Through an open bedroom door to the right, I could see two young lesbians making slow, unhurried love. Our host offered us some pills from a Georgian snuff box.

'We have it all, man,' he said. '. . . California Sunshine even.'

Out of the gloom a tall girl rose, kissed me on the lips, said 'Peace', and sat down again.

Round the walls couples sat and smoked and stared at nothing in particular. From a record player, a female voice, Joan Baez, I think, was singing a sad ballad about children.

Not much happened for an hour, then a 16 mm. film was thrown on a portable screen. It was about homosexuality in Algerian prisons. The warders played prominent parts and the close-ups were quite repulsive. As the film unfolded, my blonde green-eyed Goddaughter became aware of my increasing restlessness.

'This isn't your scene is it?' she giggled. 'Do you want to split?'

She was giggling a lot by now and in the reflected light of the screen, I saw that her eyes were brightly out of focus.

Gratefully, I grabbed the offer and, ducking under the beam from the projector, I went quickly down the stairs. In the street, like a man who has just run a four-minute mile in thick mud, I leaned against the railings, gulping down great draughts of clean, windy Spring evening.

After a while, I looked up at the scudding clouds above and suddenly and unexpectedly, up there above the chimney pots, I beheld an old childhood friend, sailing calmly and confidently through a clear patch of sky . . .

> who knows if the moon's
> a balloon, coming out of a keen city
> in the sky – filled with pretty people?
> (and if you and i should
>
> get into it, if they
> should take me and take you into their balloon,
> why then
> we'd go up higher with all the pretty people
>
> than houses and steeples and clouds:
> go sailing
> away and away sailing into a keen
> city which nobody's ever visited, where
>
> always
>   it's
>   Spring) and everyone's
> in love and flowers pick themselves

David
Niven

Bring on the
Empty Horses

*With love to friends and acquaintances
who do not happen to be mentioned in these pages,
but who know, of course, that they, too,
are part of them*

Introduction

*I*F at this moment you are in a bookstore leafing through these early pages and wondering if the whole thing is worth a sizable expenditure, may I suggest that you keep your back toward the salesman and read on because, coming up, is a brief description of what this book is all about.

To be an actor, it is essential to be an egomaniac; otherwise it just doesn't work. The supreme act of egomania is to sit down and write 130,000 words about oneself. That I have already done in *The Moon's a Balloon*, so you will be relieved to learn that this is *not* a book about David Niven . . . at least, it is not *meant* to be. Unfortunately, the actor's urge to take up a firm position at center stage is a strong one, and if, despite valiant efforts to remain in the wings, I have, on occasion, eased myself forward, I apologize.

This book is about Hollywood; not the whole mishmash, because that has been done a hundred times, and anyway, the canvas is too huge and quite beyond my mini-brushwork, so I have attempted to splash a little color on just one corner—the twenty-five years between 1935 and 1960.

I was there from "extra" on down (or up—it's for you to decide), and I was part of it, but I have made little effort to keep things in chronological order; provided the people and events coincided with the allotted time span, I have just described them as I saw them.

The period covered in this book is often hailed as the Great Days of Hollywood. Perhaps they were, perhaps not, but, with those days gone forever, it is certainly not my intention to try to prove that they were superior to the Hollywood of today.

If now Hollywood is booming and full of talent, but controlled by conglomerates, lawyers, bankers, computers, and a handful of agents, then it was booming, filled with great personalities, but controlled by arrogant moguls, overcrowded and smelling of despotism, nepotism, and blacklists.

Hollywood was Lotus Land between 1935 and 1960 and bore little relationship to the rest of the world, but it was vastly exciting to be part of a thriving, thrusting "first growth" industry—the greatest form of mass entertainment so far invented—and if exaggeration became the norm, it was hard to recognize the fact, when a "great star" could confidently expect to receive 20,000 letters a week and newspapers all over the world daily set aside several pages for the news and gossip pumped out by the Hollywood self-adulation machines.

There was friendliness, generosity, excitement, sadness, success, despair, and no smog in that long-ago Hollywood, but, "high" on lotus, few of the inhabitants, when World War II shattered the calm, realized that all the old standards would be changed, including the public taste in canned entertainment, and like an out-of-condition heavyweight, Hollywood was ill prepared to cope with the second onslaught which followed quickly on the heels of the first—the sudden advent of television—and by burying its head in its arms and hoping that the enemy would go away, it very nearly went down for the count.

But before Hollywood was forced to shift gears, the moguls controlled the industry they had invented. They were master showmen; 200,000,000 people each week paid to see their product, and among the names in lights above their theaters were Garbo, Gable, Astaire, Cooper, Dietrich, Grant, Chaplin, Bogart, Garland, Hepburn, Flynn, and Davis. It was a fascinating canvas, there will never be another like it, and I hope, by trying to add a little firsthand light and shadow, that I have not spoiled it.

DAVID NIVEN

Kuala Lumpur, Malaysia

1

The Playpen

WHEN Gertrude Stein returned to New York after a short sojourn in Hollywood, somebody asked her, "What is it like—out there?"

To which, with little delay and the minimum of careful thought, the sage replied, "There *is* no 'there'—there."

To try to describe to the reader the self-styled "Glamor Capital of the World," it seems best to do so as it appeared just before the outbreak of World War II, because although this book describes some events between 1935 and 1960, that particular upheaval caused the number of inhabitants and automobiles in Los Angeles to double. Up until then there had been plenty of room and fresh air for everyone—one square mile for every four persons, to be precise—very little industry, the worst transportation system of any major U.S. city and clear blue skies without a hint of "smog"—not a word invented by a local wit, but borrowed from the city of Glasgow, where it had justifiably been in constant use since the turn of the century. The reader will find on page 13 a list of the actors and actresses who were that same year under contract to just one of the seven major studios, giving him an idea of the investment the moguls had in talent and the problems they must have had in keeping that talent gainfully employed.

There were four ways to approach Los Angeles from the East Coast: (1) by automobile, which took ten days of fast driving and entailed facing red dirt roads across large tracts of Arizona and

New Mexico with no prospect of a motel at the end of the day; (2) by train, leaving New York on the 20th Century Limited at 6 P.M. and standing respectfully aside while famous movie stars smiled for the New York papers as they were escorted by railroad officials along a red carpet to their sleeping compartments; on arrival at Chicago the following morning, the sleeping cars were shunted around the marshaling yards and by noon were tacked on to the rear of the Santa Fe Chief (steam locomotives until 1939), which two days later puffed to a stop at the Union Station, Los Angeles, where the famous movie stars perched on piles of matching baggage and smiled for the Los Angeles papers; (3) by plane, which was not for the fainthearted—a minimum of eighteen cramped and often nerve-racking hours flying in unpressurized and largely unheated twin-engined machines at low altitudes through sometimes appalling weather with the nasty possibility of thudding into either the Allegheny or Rocky mountains at one end of the trip—or (4), as I did it, by sea, an endless voyage of fluctuating comfort in a "dry" ship via Cuba and the Panama Canal.

The whole Los Angeles area was subject to frequent earth tremors, accounted for by an ill-advised proximity to the San Andreas Fault, and on the very day of my arrival in San Pedro I had noted from the deck of SS *President Pierce* that people at dockside beneath a swaying water tower were scurrying about looking nervously upward, wondering which way it would fall. It didn't, as it happened, and the next morning the Chamber of Commerce routinely reassured us that there had been no cause for alarm, but it was perhaps an early warning that I was heading for the breeding ground of stresses and strains.

The "film folk," I discovered, unwound at their favorite playgrounds, the beaches, the mountains at Arrowhead and Big Bear and the desert at Palm Springs—a tiny colony in the middle of Indian-owned land which boasted a main street and two hotels. Santa Anita Racecourse was also very popular with them, and there were various country clubs which dispensed golf, tennis, and an extraordinary degree of segregation. Not one had a black member, and several refused to have Jewish members, prompting the Jewish community to start their own country club and to take in no Gentiles. (They also found oil in satisfactory quantities beneath their fairways, which provided them with a splendid opportunity for nose thumbing.) But the topper was the prestigious Los Angeles Country Club which adamantly refused to have anything whatever to do with *anyone* in the motion-picture industry irrespective of race, creed, or color.

Greater Los Angeles, a city which grew more quickly than the city planners had planned, was not remarkable for its beauty, and it was necessary to disregard the largely temporary appearance of the buildings and the unsightly forests of poles and overhead wiring and concentrate on its truly remarkable setting, in the horseshoe of the San Gabriel Mountains, and on the sunsets.

In Hollywood itself, a place of dusty Baroque charm, one important thoroughfare, La Cienega Boulevard, with great subservience separated on either side of an oil derrick pumping slowly like a praying mantis, and in the scrub-covered hills above, underlining its claim to fame, was a forty-foot-high wooden sign: HOLLYWOOD-LAND.

Beverly Hills, another suburb, had gone against the haphazard planning of Greater Los Angeles, and when the Rodeo Land and Water Company decided to develop its gently sloping acreage, it had the great good taste and foresight to send for an expert from Kew Gardens, London, who planted a different species of tree for every street, and thereafter a fascinating variety of architecture proliferated beneath maples, magnolias, palms, corals, pines, sycamores, flowering eucalyptus, elms, olives, jacarandas, and oaks. A home in Beverly Hills was the status symbol of success in the prewar motion-picture industry, and the area boasted more private swimming pools and detectives to the square mile than anywhere else in the world.

Everything in Southern California seemed to me to be an enlargement—the bronzed and sun-bleached girls and boys of the beaches were representatives of a master race bred in freedom, sunshine, and clean air—but if the robins were the size of pigeons and the butterflies had the proportions of bombers, the diminutive honey-hunting hummingbirds brought things back into perspective as they whizzed merrily about with their tiny waistcoats of turquoise, vermilion, and gold flashing in the sunlight.

The relaxed villagelike atmosphere of Beverly Hills was very catching, and at the hub of the movie social wheel in the Brown Derby restaurant, the men wore loafers, open-neck shirts, and sports jackets, while the girls, lately liberated by Marlene Dietrich's earthshaking appearance in a man's suit, appeared enthusiastically in slacks, and the waitresses were pretty, would-be actresses in varying stages of disenchantment.

The two tennis clubs most highly regarded by the movie colony were the Beverly Hills and the Westside. The Beverly Hills was by far the better club, and the tennis there was of a much higher standard, with Fred Perry giving points and taking on all comers, but I myself joined the Westside because the committee had wisely decided that beautiful girls were a more digestible ingredient than perspiring professionals, and I will never forget a fancy dress party on the premises at which a young lawyer named Greg Bautzer arrived, on his face a grin so wide he looked like a Hammond organ and on his arm, aged seventeen, ridiculously beautiful, and dressed as Bopeep, Lana Turner.

The home of the phony phone call was the over-chlorinated pool of the Beverly Hills Hotel, around which little-known agents reclined, red-eyed and sweaty, waiting for the loudspeaker to relay messages which they themselves had carefully arranged to be broadcast: "Mr. Bleepburger, please be good enough to call Mr. Darryl Zanuck and Miss Claudette Colbert when you have a moment—urgent."

Written-out gag writers were also present, keeping their ears open for any anecdote that could be twisted to their advantage. "Fun-nee! . . . Fun-nee!" They would nod sagely without a glimmer of a smile, then hasten away to make notes, and all the time the long-legged, high-bosomed, tight-assed girls in swimsuits and high heels hopefully ebbed and flowed around the recumbent denizens of the water hole.

In the late thirties the twice-weekly program presented by most theaters consisted of a newsreel, a cartoon, a short, the second feature, and the first feature. The whole show lasted for a bum-numbing four hours, but as a result, Hollywood was booming, with Metro-Goldwyn-Mayer, one of the seven major studios, boasting that it alone turned out one feature film each week.

Edmund Lowe was famous for many films, but chiefly for the ones he made in partnership with Victor McLaglen, and he and his secretary befriended me soon after my arrival in Hollywood because she decided that I looked like her employer. She had noticed this resemblance because I had been standing outside the main gate of Paramount Studios watching for the stars in their fancy automobiles and had stood out, apparently, from the curious throng of sightseers and out-of-work extras, because in my mouth had been a large cork. This cork and the likeness to Edmund Lowe had so intrigued the lady that she had ordered the chauffeur to return and bring me before her master. Eddie Lowe was a friendly, smiling man; he explained that he was looking for a double and asked me if I would be interested in the job. I thanked him and told him that I was hoping to become an actor myself and did not mention that I thought he looked like my father.

"Why the cork?" he asked. I explained that E. E. Clive, an elderly character actor from the theater who had cornered the film market in butler and judge roles, had lately given me a valuable hint on how to increase the resonance of my voice which he had decided was neglible.

"Get a long cork, my boy," he had ordered, "out of a hock bottle preferably—though I doubt if many people drink hock in this backwater—shove it lengthwise between your teeth, and when you have nothing better to do, repeat the Lord's Prayer half a dozen times. It'll work wonders."

Eddie Lowe taught me much about Hollywood in the weeks to come, tried valiantly but unsuccessfully to arouse the interest of his producer friends in my stagnant career, and personally gave me a conducted tour of one Dream Factory in which he worked. He drove me around the cozily named back lot—a 200-acre spread upon which stood the permanent sets, including New York streets (some smart, some brownstone), New England, French, and Spanish villages, medieval castles, a railroad station complete with rolling stock, lakes with wave-making machines and rustic bridges, a university campus, an airliner, a section of jungle and another of pine forest, a Mississippi steamboat, a three-masted schooner, native canoes, a submarine, a stretch of desert with ruined fort and, in case anything was missing, several acres of carefully dismantled, docketed and stored streets, villages, cathedrals, mud huts, dance halls, skating rinks, ball parks, theaters, vineyards, slums, Southern plantations, and Oriental palaces.

Lowe also took me to the studio's Western ranch: several hundred acres of rolling hills in the San Fernando Valley upon which stood the permanent townships and Indian habitations. Huge tracts of make-believe were necessary to Hollywood because air travel was in its infancy, and if, for instance, a film were set in Venice, canals, churches, palazzi, gondolas, and bridges would soon be conjured up locally. Small wonder, then, that *Gone with the Wind* was filmed in Culver City, *Mutiny on the Bounty* just off Catalina Island, *The Charge of the Light Brigade* in the San Fernando Valley, *The Hunchback of Notre Dame* adjacent to Vine Street, *The Ten Commandments* behind the Western Costume Company, *The Adventures of Marco Polo* a hundred yards from the city gasometer, and Scrooge's breath in A *Christmas Carol* imaginatively photographed in a vast refrigerator near the Ambassador Hotel. Under Eddie Lowe's sponsorship I spent days wandering about the back lot and also the main studio at the heart of the Dream Factory, where for some reason the buildings, parking lot and streets were uniformly white or pale yellow, thus extracting the maximum amount of glare from the cloudless California sky, and where the whole place resembled a mixture of the business district of a thriving small town and the maintenance area of a busy airport. Twenty or thirty towering, hangarlike sound stages clustered together dominated the center, surrounded by the fire department, the generator turbines, the electrical grid, the transportation, construction, carpenter and plasterer departments, camera and electrical stores, wardrobe departments, legal departments, acres of dismantled sets and furniture repositories, tailoring and dressmaking shops, and ever-widening circles of photographic studios, painters' stores, cutting rooms, makeup, hairdressing, and sound departments, projection rooms and theaters, rehearsal halls, orchestra recording theaters, accommodation for set designers and set dressers, the story department, accounting offices, publicity offices, casting offices, fan mail departments, greenhouses, restaurants, a hospital, a gymnasium, and a shoeshine parlor.

An outer circle was rather stately by comparison, and green lawns softened the overpowering glare of the buildings, the barnlike dressing rooms allotted to the swarming extras and the double-decker rabbit warrens which housed the small-part actors. Shaded by trees, connected by paths, and surrounded by flowering shrubs, the bungalow dressing rooms of the stars gave an outward impression of an enclave of peace and tranquillity, but inside, as I was to learn, their walls bore the scars of countless exhibitions of temperament, noisy moments of triumph, and far too many lonely heartbreaks.

I was also to learn that writers got drunk, actors became paranoid, actresses pregnant, and directors uncontrollable. Crises were a way of life in the Dream Factories, but by some extraordinary mixture of efficiency, compromising, exuberance, gambling, shrewdness, experience, strong-arm tactics, psychology, blackmail, kindness, integrity, good luck, and a firm belief that "the show must go on," the pictures came rolling off the end of the production lines.

The star system was the logical answer to the first question asked by investors when it was hinted that they might put money into a film or by moviegoers when it was suggested that they should buy tickets to see the finished product.

"Who's in it?" they would cry.

The studios expended immense sums providing attractive answers to this question by signing established stars to long-term contracts and by discovering and developing young unknowns to take their places later. Once a studio was convinced that performers had "caught on" with the public, great care was taken to maintain their popularity by presenting them only in roles and vehicles in which their special talents and attractions would be displayed to the maximum advantage. On the other hand, when a studio became disenchanted and convinced that a star's popularity was waning, a wide variety of maneuvers were employed to bring their mutual contract to a speedy conclusion. The easiest way, of course, was to mobilize the forces of the actor's own congenital insecurity and give him an inferior part to play. The actor would fluff up his feathers of hurt pride and "refuse to be seen in such a crappy role." The studio then, piously referring to the wording of the long-term agreement between the actor and itself, would suspend the actor's contract for the duration of the picture and instruct its publicity department to leak the news to the world that their hero was a man who refused to honor his obligations. Certainly if an actor refused to perform, he could not expect to be paid, but the monstrous thing was that even if the studio handed an actor a bad part *truly* believing it to be a good one, and he turned it down, not only was he suspended for the duration of the filming of the picture (probably at least four months), but he was also suspended for an additional 50 percent of that time *as a punishment* . . . and the entire period of six months was added to the end of the contract.

Some of us gave twelve or fourteen sulfurous years of our short actors' lives working off a seven-year contract which had originally been conceived in mutual admiration and respect.

After one important actress had the guts to take her case against Warner Brothers all the way to the Supreme Court, a ruling was handed down that no contract with an employee could be extended without the employee's consent, and every contract actor in Hollywood blessed Olivia de Havilland . . . but after her courageous stand, she was seldom offered a role in a Hollywood picture. There were, of course, iniquities on both sides—the moguls were not the only villains and many stars behaved abominably to those who had discovered them and given them the keys to the local kingdom—but the classic use of a contract as a one-sided weapon has to be this:

An actor made a great hit in a Broadway play and celebrated the fact by having a not too well-camouflaged affair with the wife of a Hollywood producer. One day a representative of the producer's studio appeared in the actor's dressing room at the Shubert Theater and offered him a very lucrative seven-year Hollywood contract. The actor, overjoyed, packed up, kissed good-bye to New York audiences, and prepared to become the darling of the world. On arrival in Hollywood he was accorded the "A" treatment, press interviews, publicity layouts, et cetera; then the boom dropped. One day he was called to the makeup department at 6:30 A.M. to be prepared for "photographic tests" at 8 A.M. In a high state of excitement he arose at 4 A.M. and drove to the studio. For seven years, thereafter, he was called six days a week to the studio. If he did not show up, his contract was prolonged, if he did, he was paid handsomely, but he never appeared in front of a camera, and when he was last heard of, though he was a moderately successful and devoutly alcoholic real estate salesman in Canoga Park, his actor's heart had been broken.

Twenty-five years before Hollywood turned its first camera, the writer G. K. Chesterton wrote: "Journalism largely consists of saying, 'Lord Jones Dead!' to people who never knew that Lord Jones was alive." When a film was completed, the next trick was to sell it to the public, and studios allocated millions of dollars to their publicity departments to this end.

In the earliest days circus-type ballyhoo had been employed, and the first recorded press agent, Harry Reichenbach, was in fact lured away to the "moving pictures" from Barnum and Bailey's Circus. The first film he was hired to publicize was *The Return of Tarzan*. His method was effective. He booked into a smart New York hotel just across from the theater where the picture was opening, and a wooden crate was delivered to his room. He then called room service and ordered fifteen pounds of raw meat to be served for his luncheon. The waiter on arrival let out a piercing yell and dropped the meat—wearing a napkin, a large lion was sitting at the table. The waiter sued Reichenbach, and the headlines blossomed.

Francis X. Bushman was nervous about the possible non-renewal of his contract, so he hired Reichenbach to impress his studio by underlining his popularity.

Reichenbach made Bushman walk with him from Grand Central Station all across New York City to the studio office. By the time he arrived the easily identifiable figure of Bushman was being followed by enthusiastic thousands, traffic was jammed, and the studio heads witnessed a most impressive chaos from their windows. What they had not noticed was Reichenbach walking immediately behind Bushman and dribbling several hundred dollars' worth of nickels and dimes through a hole in his overcoat pocket.

As movies became more sophisticated, the efforts of the publicity departments did not always keep pace, and Gloria Swanson at Paramount was photographed being transported from her dressing room to the sound stage in a sedan chair, but finally highly intelligent men took charge, among them Howard Dietz and Howard Strickling at MGM, Charlie Einfeld at Warner's, Harry Brand at Twentieth Century-Fox, Russell Birdwell with David Selznick, and Jock Lawrence with Samuel Goldwyn.

Publicity departments went through their most difficult period when the studio heads decided that their stars should represent the sum total of all the virtues: They should not drink, swear, or, above all, copulate, and they must be presented to the public as the All-American Boy or the Girl Next Door. Self-inflicted dents in the facades of these paragons had, therefore, to be papered over without delay, so close contacts were forged with the police departments of Los Angeles, Beverly Hills, and the San Fernando Valley, and over the years only a thin trickle of the normal output of nightclub brawls, drunk drivings, scandals, accidents, assaults, attempted suicides, and rapes were reported in the press.

The policy of the studios was to sell their pictures on the names of their stars; they had a vested interest in their performers, and it was to their advantage to build them up. If they did so successfully, their investment was returned with interest, but the contracts of the actors were long, and the work of the publicity departments was painstaking; it was a case of piling up grains of publicity sand until they became mountains, and at the end of it the public might say, "Joe Doakes beats his wife," or "he drinks his bath water," but it did not ask, "Who is Joe Doakes?"

For each production a unit publicist was ordered to remain on the set from the first day of shooting in case anything newsworthy took place; in addition, in the main office, were specialists for the trade papers, general news specialists, magazine specialists, radio specialists, and legmen whose only job was to service the top columnists throughout the country, and all the while the still photographers dutifully pumped out reams of cheesecake, home layouts, and fashion layouts. Publicity campaigns for personalities and individual pictures were not always mounted with the meticulous planning of D day, and occasionally they misfired.

Mae West, at the height of her popularity, started a picture at Paramount titled *It Ain't No Sin*. One hundred and fifty parrots were bought and placed in intensive training to learn to imitate her sexy drawl and to repeat endlessly, "It ain't no sin," the objective being to park the unfortunate birds in theater lobbies and public places to coincide with the openings of the picture.

All went well, and at last the proud trainers reported that their troops were ready for action, but on the same day the Hays Office (charged with keeping clean Hollywood's public image) announced that the title of the picture must be changed because *It Ain't No Sin* was too "suggestive." The parrots were then given a crash course in saying, "I'm no angel." As a result, the theater lobbies and public places reverberated with frustrated whistles and rude noises, and the dejected birds were sent home in disgrace.

Warner's, with misguided zeal, tried to show its top "tough guy," Edward G. Robinson, out of character and persuaded the iron man to be photographed in a bubble bath, but it quickly had to mount a second campaign to nullify the first because whispers became widespread that Eddie Robinson was a "fairy."

Walt Disney's publicity department had its problems too. For the opening of *Pinocchio* in New York it was decided to hire eleven midgets, dress them in *Pinocchio* costumes, and have them gambol about on top of the theater marquee on opening day.

Food and light refreshments, in the shape of a couple of quarts of liquor, were passed up to the marquee top at lunchtime, and by three o'clock in the afternoon a happy crowd in Times Square was treated to the spectacle of eleven stark naked midgets belching loudly and enjoying a crap game on the marquee. Police with ladders removed the players in pillowcases.

Starting with Clara Bow as the "It Girl," individual girls were built up with catchy titles. Jean Harlow became the "Platinum Blonde" and Betty Grable the "Pinup Girl." Finally, lovely redheaded Ann Sheridan at a highly publicized dinner party paid for by the Warner Brothers publicity department was voted by the "Ten Most Eligible Bachelors in Hollywood" as the "Oomph Girl." (The "Most Eligible Bachelors," it is perhaps worth noting, were purely a Warner Brothers selection and included Edmund Goulding, Errol Flynn, myself, and seven others who just "happened" to be making pictures, of all places, at Warner Brothers—a good "double play.")

As press and public became less gullible and more cynical, the publicity gimmicks gave way to publicity junkets, although a few diehards still tried stunts. Jayne Mansfield got a certain amount of mileage out of wearing her pink nightie in her pink heart-shaped bed inside her pink house with her pink Cadillac standing outside, but nobody believed a word of her being shipwrecked on the pink sand of a tropical island in the Caribbean despite the fact that when she showed up, she was covered in pink sand fly bites.

Warner's splurged on a five-day junket to publicize *The Santa Fe Trail*, and reporters eagerly accepted invitations to congregate in Santa Fe, New Mexico. The studio, wary of Errol Flynn's capacity as a roisterer, assigned three men working twenty-four hours a day in shifts to keep him sober and in his own bed, but Errol outdrank and outmaneuvered the three men, and the junket lasted twice as long as planned.

One junket to Mexico City to publicize *Viva Villa* ended with strained relations between the two countries when one of the American stars of the film high up in his hotel room became tired of the noisy adulation of the vast crowd below and decided to dampen down their ardor by relieving himself upon them from the balcony.

A quite extraordinary rapport existed between many stars and the publicity chiefs of their studios—the sort of understanding that soldiers develop for one another when experiences have been shared—and many stars, who had been nursed through marriages, divorces, disasters, scandals, tremendous triumphs, and dreadful deflations, found themselves disproportionately dependent on the counsels of these men. A risky situation, when one considered the number of cupboards that were clanking with skeletons, and, with puritanism rampant across the country, how fatal to careers it could have been if there had been a misuse of the keys, but there was a flamboyant honor among the publicity men, and I never heard of one of them breaking his vows of silence.

Hollywood was a village, and the studios were the families. Everyone knew everyone else's business, weaknesses, kinky leanings, and good points. We were all in the same boat, involved in the early years of a terribly exciting experiment; it was an international community, and there was the maximum of camaraderie and the minimum of bitchiness. At all studios, employees from the most glamorous stars to the lowliest riveters on the heavy construction gangs felt that they were members of a team, gloried in the success of their "hit" pictures, and occasionally indulged in college humor at the expense of their rivals. "In case of an AIR RAID"—they chalked up on the main entrance at Paramount—"go directly to RKO . . . *they* haven't had a hit in years."

Hollywood was hardly a nursery for intellectuals, it was a hotbed of false values, it harbored an unattractive percentage of small-time crooks and con artists, and the chances of being successful there were minimal, but it was fascinating, and IF YOU WERE LUCKY, it was fun. And anyway, it was better than working.

Work consists of whatever a body is *obliged* to do . . .
Play consists of whatever a body is *not* obliged to do.
    --MARK TWAIN,
    The Adventures of Tom Sawyer

All the major studios kept stables of famous stars. The following is a partial list of those under contract to just one of them from 1939 to 1940:

Metro-Goldwyn-Mayer

June Allyson
Ethel Barrymore
John Barrymore
Lionel Barrymore
Wallace Beery
Ingrid Bergman
Louis Calhern
Joan Crawford
Melvyn Douglas
Marie Dressler
Nelson Eddy
W. C. Fields
Clark Gable
Greta Garbo
Ava Gardner
Judy Garland
Greer Garson
Van Johnson
Gene Kelly
Hedy Lamarr
Charles Laughton
Myrna Loy
Jeannette MacDonald

The Marx Brothers
Robert Montgomery
Frank Morgan
George Murphy
Walter Pidgeon
Eleanor Powell
William Powell
Luise Rainer
Debbie Reynolds
Mickey Rooney
Norma Shearer
James Stewart
Lewis Stone
Elizabeth Taylor
Robert Taylor
Franchot Tone
Spencer Tracy
Sophie Tucker
Lana Turner
Johnny Weissmuller
Esther Williams
Robert Young

2
The King

A blond sunburned fuzz covered his muscular forearms, and his potbelly hung over the top of his pants. Gross, pig-eyed and rude, Chet Liebert was a loathsome human being but he had one great asset—a 45-foot spear-fishing boat named *König*. He also had an undeniable talent in his chosen profession, and by the other charter boat skippers working out of Balboa, California, he was grudgingly acknowledged to be the most successful. They had no option but to bestow this accolade on him because every year he caught more broadbill and marlin swordfish than they did.

He kept his huge frame topped up with beer, swore endlessly in a heavy Dutch accent and never by any chance gave credit where credit was due. In an effort to keep deckhands, he paid generously, and this attracted me to him like a moth to a flame. As a $2.50 a day Hollywood extra, who worked only spasmodically, I was in no position to be choosy, so I swallowed the heavy insults and eagerly grabbed the $6 a day he gave me for ten hours of dangerous, dirty, and backbreaking work as a deckhand, spotter, spearman, hauler, gutter, and swabber.

When we were out spearing the giant broadbill swordfish for sale in the market, I took those six bucks, but I also gratefully pocketed the generous tips that were slipped into my hand when *König* was chartered by private individuals in the more exciting and less exacting pursuit with rod and reel of the blue and white marlin.

"Okay, so you're late," said Liebert when I showed up for work at five o'clock one morning. "Get her cleaned up from top to bottom, gut a dozen flying fish, and check two sets of gear and the teasers—make sure the head is spotless too, goddammit, because we've a charter today and the guy is bringing a broad with him. They'll be here at six thirty, and they'll need breakfast, so see that the coffee's ready, and stand by with ham and eggs and all the crap. They're picture people," he added, "so keep your goddamned trap shut about being a lousy phony actor, and get on with the job."

Liebert had a sneaking regard for me, I suspected, because on the very first day I had worked for him, he had slipped on the wet, pitching, gut-slick flooring and had misjudged the gaffing of a 200-pound marlin which an exhausted oil executive had finally brought alongside after a slashing, fighting, plunging three-hour battle. The giant fish with its last gasp had managed to spew out the hook and, with the gaff not planted, was free and sliding down tailfirst into the dark-blue water. In a moment of madness, I had grabbed the disappearing sword with my left hand, removing most of the skin off my palm, and with my right, I had punched the poor brute in its large saucer eyeball, thereby paralyzing it for the split second which Liebert needed to sink the gaff.

Not a word was said, but there had been a tiny flicker of recognition in the puffy red pig eyes of my employer.

By six o'clock on a still and cloudless morning *König*, as ordered, was swabbed down, mopped, dried, and polished, and by the time a large open Packard turned onto the quay, the aroma of good coffee was rising from the galley.

"Okay, now go over and fetch their gear, and don't get moviestruck," he added.

When I approached the Packard, I saw what he meant—the girl was blond and willowy with a fresh, open, fun-loving face. She wore a blue reefer jacket and red slacks, and her yachting cap was tilted at a rather exotic angle over her right eye. I don't think I noticed what the large, muscular man was wearing—he was opening the trunk of the car, and his back was toward me—but when he turned around, smiled, and said, "Hi, it looks like a good day," I nearly fell into the harbor. The man was Clark Gable.

I relieved him of rods, various professional-looking tackle boxes, a large ice bucket, a bottle of scotch, and watched him stride purposefully toward *König*; the blonde held onto his arm.

"Okay, Chet, bait 'em up and let's go," he yelled happily as he leaped aboard.

We had a lucky day. Gable landed two big blue marlin and was once broken after an hour's struggle with a gigantic, leaping mako shark. We also found a school of hungry yellow tail tuna which were striking at everything in sight, and even the blonde amid shrieks of excitement landed a couple of twenty-pounders. She also became rather maudlin toward late afternoon when she hooked a dolphin on a white feather lure and decided that it was the soul of a dead sailor . . . the whiskey bottle was almost empty by then. She pawed Gable a great deal.

The deckhand was working at full throttle throughout the day, and when not perched uncomfortably in the crosstrees of the mast looking for fins or telltale swirls, I was baiting hooks, gutting and cleaning the catch, making sandwiches, or mixing drinks.

When Gable heard my voice, he immediately pinpointed my accent and voiced a mild curiosity as to why I was there and doing what I was doing.

Liebert gave me a long, hard look as I prepared to answer, but suddenly, the first blue marlin hit, and forty-five minutes later, when he triumphantly unstrapped his shoulder harness, Gable's curiosity had vanished.

Six months later, in the spring of 1935, I landed something myself, a small contract with Samuel Goldwyn, the doors of Hollywood began to open, and I met Gable again. The iron man from Cadiz, Ohio, was looking rather trapped in white tie and tails, but the occasion demanded his discomfort. It was the Academy Awards presentation dinner—the annual handing out of the early Oscars.

The year before he had won one himself for his performance in *It Happened One Night*, and his acceptance speech was the shortest on record, two words—"Thank you!" That night Hollywood history had been made. Gable had been lent by MGM to the despised Harry Cohn and his struggling company, Columbia, as a punishment for intransigence in turning down too many mediocre scripts. Claudette Colbert was being similarly chastised for the same reason by her studio—Paramount—but between them they had outsmarted their bosses and persuaded the brilliant director Frank Capra to direct the picture for which Cohn had borrowed them. As a result, Claudette, Capra, and Gable all collected golden statuettes, the picture was voted Best Picture of the Year, and Columbia Pictures entered the big league.

Now, a year later, the Academy Awards had come around again, and Hollywood—still very much a village—was honoring its own with its strange tribal rites. Gable did not win this time, though his picture *Mutiny on the Bounty* came out on top. Excitement ran high among the 200 tribesmen and women who filled the private banqueting room downstairs at the Ambassador Hotel. A demure Bette Davis was proclaimed the winner for her performance in *Dangerous*, and Victor McLaglen (who, to everybody's delight, belched loudly when receiving his prize) was voted Best Actor for his portrayal in *The Informer*.

It was a vintage year, and the competition for votes must have been fierce because among other classic offerings that night were Gary Cooper in *The Bengal Lancers*, Fred Astaire in *Top Hat*, W. C. Fields in *David Copperfield*, and Garbo in *Anna Karenina*.

Less successful in all departments had been the Warner Brothers entry—*A Midsummer Night's Dream* with James Cagney as Bottom and Mickey Rooney as Puck. For the premiere in Beverly Hills, an elaborate program had been presented to each member of the audience, embossed on the cover of which were four golden plaques, each containing a well-known profile: the three Warner brothers and William Shakespeare.

Gable was seated at another table with a party from his studio—Irving Thalberg, the producer of *Mutiny on the Bounty*; Thalberg's wife, Norma Shearer; Jean Harlow; William Powell; Joan Crawford; and others. Ria, Gable's second wife, was also there, and I looked at her with interest. Several years older than her husband, she looked very calm and distinguished, and Gable was smiling across the table at her in the conspiratorial way happily married couples signal mutual boredom at dull parties. I was remembering with pleasure the unaffected charm and friendliness Gable had dispensed aboard *König* when, suddenly, he glanced directly at me. For a moment he looked puzzled; then my face must have clicked into place because he waved, smiled a friendly smile, and mimed the hooking of a big fish. I nodded and waved back, and after the presentations were over, he came to Goldwyn's table and shook my hand.

"Good to see you again," he said. "What are you doing here, try-ing to get Sam to go tuna fishing?"

I felt embarrassed at first telling it to the "King," as he was known throughout Hollywood, but bathed in the warmth of the great man's personality, I relaxed and explained that I had changed my job and had lately landed a contract with Goldwyn.

"Well, that's just *great*," he exploded. "Lots of luck, kid, and don't forget—the first thirty years are the hardest!" Then he added quite seriously, "And don't give up fishing—you'll find it's a great help sometimes."

When he had made the rounds of our table, followed every-where by looks of great affection, he spoke to me once more. "I'm moving over to the Goldwyn lot for the next one, so I'll hope to see you around. We can forget about making pictures for a while and yak about steelhead—is that a deal?"

"Fine," I said, delighted at the prospect of seeing him again and not unaware of the soaring of my personal stock among my high-powered dinner companions.

Several weeks later Goldwyn gave me my first speaking part: the role of a sailor in *Barbary Coast*—it consisted of one line. Thrown out of the window of a waterfront brothel in San Francisco and sailing past the madam, I was called upon to say, "Orl right—I'm goin'!" Then as I lay facedown in several inches of mud, the two stars of the picture, Miriam Hopkins and Joel McCrea, accom-panied by several donkeys and a posse of vigilantes, walked over the top of me.

Gable was by now working at the Goldwyn Studio making *The Call of the Wild*, and on the morning of my big moment he, the greatest star in the Hollywood firmament, took the time and the trouble to walk over to the back lot to wish good luck to an un-known beginner. He also insisted on stills being taken of the two of us, and the Goldwyn publicity department gleefully grabbed the golden opportunity to rub off a little of the "King's" glamor onto their nameless charge.

Several times I visited Gable while *The Call of the Wild* was being made, and I soon discovered that he had many other things to talk about besides fishing and hunting.

Certainly, more than anything, he enjoyed the great outdoors, and just as surely he felt uncomfortable at formal parties and despised the Hollywood hostesses and their "success lists."

"They only invite me because at the moment I'm on top of the heap," he said, "but when I fall on my ass, they'll just move someone else up a notch, and I'll go down to the bottom of the pile."

One January day we did more than talk about the big fighting seagoing rainbow trout of Oregon. His excited voice came over the telephone. "Hey! Let's go! . . . I've just been talking to some pals who have a fishing camp on the Rogue—the steelhead are running!"

"I don't have a rod," I said feebly.

"Forget it," said Clark. "I've got everything—I'll pick you up at midday, we'll spend the night in Frisco and be at Grants Pass by tomorrow afternoon."

He was a fast and dedicated driver, and he made it clear that he could do without the small talk because it ruined his concentration. This was perfectly all right with me, and I sat back and reveled in the glories of two-thirds of California.

At Grants Pass, where we stayed overnight at the fishing lodge, we were joined in the cold dark of the following morning by the guide, who came with his wife to fetch us. A squat, unsmiling, flaccid-faced Indian who smelled heavily of spirits, he was, according to Clark, the best man on the river. He was also the worst driver in the neighborhood and in the semigloom of that freezing winter dawn, his dilapidated Chevy, unbalanced by trailing a heavy fishing skiff behind it, swung terrifyingly around icy mountain bends. Clark watched me averting my eyes from the roaring river several hundred feet below, noted my tight smiles and high-pitched polite conversation, and correctly diagnosed my condition as one of abject terror.

"Don't worry," he said. "He'll make up for it when he gets on the river, and his wife, thank God, drives us back." He indicated the almost totally round and equally smelly lady who was huddled, unspeaking and blanketed, beside her erratic husband.

As the sky began to lighten, we slithered down a winding track and came to rest on a sandy beach between towering gray pine-topped cliffs. There we manhandled the skiff into the water, loaded it, and watched as the spherical wife took her husband's place behind the wheel and disappeared in a barrage of flying gravel up the almost perpendicular hillside, to meet us at dusk miles downriver.

Gable was wearing a heavy checkered mackinaw and his "lucky" long peaked cap. He had not bothered to shave, and a heavy black stubble was discernible in the growing light. It was bitterly cold.

"What are you giving us for breakfast, Chuck?" he asked the Indian.

"Small trout fried in butter," said the unsmiling one, "but you've got to catch 'em before I can cook 'em, don't you?"

"Sure thing, Happy." Gable grinned. "Let's get going."

The river was broad and sluggish where we put in, but the Indian knew the likely pools, and using a wet fly, we soon had half a dozen beautiful brook trout about eight inches long.

We pulled over to a sandbank, and while Gable and I collected dry driftwood, the guide, with a few quick flashes of his hunting knife, cleaned our catch.

On the east ridge high above us, the sun was backlighting the snow-covered firs. They looked as though they were on fire, but down on the sandbank it was still well below zero, and we huddled gratefully around the fire, sniffing the coffee and watching the deft movements of the Indian. A family of deer, seven of them, came down to drink at the riverbank opposite, a pastoral scene that was rudely shattered when an eagle flashed out of the sky and picked up a large rattlesnake from the rocks beside them. With his prey in his talons the great bird spiraled upward, gaining height till up near the ridge the sun caught them, and for a long time we could see the writhing silver underbelly of the reptile flashing out distress signals.

Clark was a true sport fisherman. He was uninterested in catching his limit of "meat," a comparatively easy achievement during the winter run when the silvery twenty-pound trout, slashed with vivid scarlet streaks at their sides after years away in the big ocean, were making their way in thousands far up the river to spawn in the selfsame gravel whence they had come. After a big January rain the barriers of flotsam had been washed from the river, the snow melt from the mountains had augmented the torrent, and the rapids between the pools were a roaring, rocketing menace.

The big pools were full of fish, and the air was so cold we had to dip our rods constantly in the water to free the guides of ice—it was very exciting. The fish were taking single salmon eggs washed free from the high spawning grounds, but Clark spurned the conventional use of these, and we cast with brightly colored salmon flies—a much trickier operation. Clark had two rods, a beautiful English Hardy, which he lent me, and a dream of a Cross, which he used with great effect himself.

You learn a lot about a man in four days of strenuous fishing and four nights of medium to heavy drinking. There was not a phony bone in Gable's body.

Around the log fire or drifting down calm broad reaches between the tumbling rock-strewn rapids of the aptly named Rogue, he would talk frankly and unemotionally about Hollywood and the people who controlled it.

The curvaceous blonde comedienne Thelma Todd had just been found dead in her garage near Santa Monica, found dead in the most mysterious circumstances, and for days the newspapers had hinted darkly at foul play and gangster connections.

"Thelma didn't read the small print," said Clark.

"The small print?" I queried.

"Yes. We all have a contract with the public—in us they see themselves or what they would like to be. On the screen and in our private lives, we are the standards by which they measure their own ideals of everything—sex, guts, humor, stupidity, cowardice, crumminess—you name it. They love to put us on a pedestal and worship us and form fan clubs and write thousands of letters telling us how great we are. But *they've* read the small print, and most of *us* haven't—they expect us to pay the price for it all . . . we have to get it in the end! So, when we get knocked off by gangsters, like Thelma did, or get hooked on booze or dope or get ourselves thrown out of the business because of scandals or because we just get old, that's the payoff and the public feels satisfied. Yeah, it's a good idea to read that small print."

Clark had a moderate opinion of studio heads.

"They're bastards," he said flatly. "They encourage people to be larger than life, they'll give 'em anything, take any crap from them provided they'll interest the public and the public pays to see them, but the moment they slip—oh, brother! Look at the kids on our lot at Metro now, Garland, Taylor, Gardner, Rooney, great kids, all of 'em, and loaded with talent, but they'll probably ruin 'em all.

Right now they can do anything they like, show up late, keep everyone waiting, go home when they want to, but God help them if the public stops coming—they'll pull the rug out from under 'em all over town."

I asked him how it felt to be in the number one spot in the whole industry.

"Well"—he laughed—"as sure as hell there's only one place I can go from where they've got me now! So I just go along with Tracy's formula and hope for the best."

"Tracy's formula?"

"Sure. Get there on time, know the jokes, say them the best way you can, take the money, and go home at six o'clock."

Gable talked about Hollywood and everything connected with it, but he remained completely unimpressed by it. He certainly never took his success for granted.

"Look," he said, "so they call me the goddamn 'King' at the moment, but there are dozens of people warming up in the wings, and anyway I'm just out in front of a team, that's all. Metro has half a dozen people, top writers, whose only job is to find the best possible properties for me, things that I fit into with the least risk of falling on my ass . . . that way I remain valuable to them, and everyone's happy—for the moment.

"Don't ever let them kick you around," he warned. "They squeeze people dry and then drop them. When you start to fade, they put you into skid pictures so you'll turn them down and they can put you on suspension and get you off the payroll. Be tough with them if you get up there, because it's the only language they understand, and that's the only place where you can use it. Remember you're dealing with people who believe that a two-thousand-dollar-a-week writer is guaranteed to turn out better stuff than a guy who is only asking seven fifty.

"Most executives at the big studios have no guts. They're so busy holding onto their jobs they never stick their necks out. Know how Lubitsch found out the other day that he was no longer head of Paramount? From his goddamn masseur, for chrissake! This guy had been rubbing down the studio brass, and they all told him what was happening, but nobody had the guts to tell Ernst to his face that he was through."

319

Next to fishing and hunting, Clark loved to play golf, and we played a great deal together. He was a splendid sight at Pebble Beach, his favorite course. He didn't walk between shots—he strode. He had a fearsome slice, which he never completely corrected, so we bent the rules slightly so that he could continue to play when his ball had drifted out of bounds onto the beach, and roars of laughter would rise from below as he hacked happily away among the seaweed, the crabs, and the small pools.

He was a doughty opponent, but he lacked concentration, and in an important foursome match I gleefully saw him falter because my partner was Group Captain Douglas Bader, the legless RAF fighter pilot.

Douglas visited me in California soon after World War II. He had come out to tour the hospitals and encourage hundreds of double amputees who were wondering what the future could possibly hold for them.

He did untold good recounting to them his own story of being shot down and bailing out over France, where he buckled one of his artificial limbs. The German commandant of the prison camp in which he soon found himself was so impressed by Bader that it was agreed at a prearranged time one Spitfire could fly over the camp and drop him a new leg. When the leg arrived, Bader thanked the commandant, put it on, and that night escaped.

At dawn he was recaptured, hobbling gamely along ten miles from the camp. Thereafter both his legs were taken away from him at night and locked up in the guardroom.

Playing golf against the legless Bader, as Gable soon discovered, was a hazardous undertaking, and knowing of Clark's feeble concentration, I was quietly confident of the outcome.

Bader's first ploy manifested itself on the second tee. Just as Clark was about to drive, Bader, with a noise like a machine gun, knocked the ashes out of his pipe against his artificial thigh. On the fifth green he winked at me and tightened a little wheel in his knee; then by moving very slightly just as Clark pulled back the head of his putter he produced a high, penetrating mouse squeak. Thereafter a jittery Gable and his unnerved partner never felt completely secure, and Bader and I coasted to an easy victory.

Gable never spoke much about his wives; he felt no urge to unburden his domestic problems on his friends, and he was strangely fatalistic when his marriages broke up, which they did with great regularity. In fact, he was strangely fatalistic about everything. He never went out of his way to make men friends. He reckoned that he was what he was, people could take him or leave him, and if they preferred to leave him, that was perfectly OK with him. Above all, unlike so many big stars, he felt absolutely no need to bolster his ego by surrounding himself with stooges and sycophants, so his circle of friends was small and independent.

It is difficult to paint a fascinating picture of a man whom nobody seemed to dislike. As David Selznick remarked during the filming of *Gone with the Wind*, "Oh, Gable has enemies all right —but they all like him!"

However, wherever there is competition there is jealousy, and where there is jealousy the knockers will knock. So in Hollywood people occasionally nudged each other and said, "Gable only likes older women."

It was the understatement of the century—Gable loved *all* women: older, younger, blondes, brunettes, and redheads . . . he loved the lot.

True, his first wife, Josephine Dillon, happened to be twelve years his senior, and his second wife, Ria, five years more than that, but Carole Lombard, Sylvia Fairbanks, and Kay Williams, when they became numbers three, four and five, were all in the junior league.

It was said by the knockers that Josephine, who was a well-educated drama teacher, had "invented" Gable, and the same source of bitchery passed around the happy word that Ria had paid for him to have his teeth capped. Clark just laughed when he heard this. "My mom and dad invented me," he said, "and L. B. Mayer paid for my teeth."

Clark was not really stingy with money; he was "careful." With the whiskey bottle, however, he was always lavish, and for years I was amazed at the amount he could consume with no apparent effect.

Gable said that acting did not come naturally to him—"I worked like a son of a bitch to learn a few tricks, and I fight like a steer to avoid getting stuck with parts I can't play."

As an unsuccessful Broadway actor he made three safaris into the Hollywood jungle. If the first trip in 1924 was a flop (he

321

worked only in small theatrical roles around Los Angeles or occasionally as an extra in the studios), the second was total disaster —he didn't work at all. Back again on Broadway, he finally smelled success when the egomaniacal George M. Cohan cast him as the lead in *Gambling*, but after the opening in Philadelphia, the sweet smell changed rapidly to something more unattractive. Cohan decided that he would like to play the part himself and fired Gable. Understandably short on self-confidence, Gable thereafter ricocheted off a succession of short-term flops till one day he was offered a part in a Los Angeles stage production of *The Last Mile*, and his third and final safari began. He never agreed that his subsequent breakthrough into the Hollywood big time was the glamorous rocket-propelled affair claimed by the MGM publicity department and always gave credit for it to two people: Lionel Barrymore and Joan Crawford.

Barrymore got him a test for the native boy in *Bird of Paradise*. Barrymore directed the test himself, and according to Gable, "They curled my hair; then they stripped me and gave me a G-string; a propman stuck a knife in my G-string, which scared hell out of me in case his hand slipped; then he stuck a goddamn hibiscus behind my ear and told me to creep through the bushes."

Irving Thalberg, the boy wonder of MGM, saw the result and told Barrymore, "You can't put this man in a picture. Look at his ears . . . like a bat!"

Nevertheless, he was finally hired by MGM to play a milkman in a Constance Bennett picture, and a small contract followed, which brought in its wake the all-important contribution by Joan Crawford. She bullied and cajoled the studio till Gable was given a major part in *Dance, Fools, Dance*—a tough hard-boiled character. His success was instantaneous. The critics raved, and the movie audience found a new hero, and for what it's worth, both Crawford and Gable always vehemently denied that their friendship was anything but platonic.

I have hinted that Clark was a little close with a buck, but this was only in connection with things his honest Dutch-German blood persuaded him were extravagant or unnecessary. For instance, none of the many women in his life were ever seen festooned with goodies.

Divorce, however, was something else again. Gable never

skimped on that, and to obtain his freedom from Josephine, Ria, and Sylvia, he, almost without arguing, was nearly wiped out financially three times in the process. Each time he was divorced, he issued the same hopeful statement: "I don't intend to marry again —ever" but each time he soon forgot what he had said.

One of the interim ladies to whom he was attached for a while observed, rather sourly, "Of course, Clark never really *married* anyone. A number of women married *him* . . . he just went along with the gag."

As I came to know him better, I became convinced that he would consider no marriage perfect without a son—he really longed to have a family.

In the mid-thirties there was a rather snooty success-conscious club in Hollywood named the Mayfair, whose members attended dinner dances in a small ballroom in the Beverly Wilshire Hotel. Norma Shearer, the reigning queen of MGM, and her brilliant, self-effacing husband, Irving Thalberg, arranged a foursome there one Saturday night and invited me to bring the delectable Merle Oberon.

Everyone at the club got dressed up to the nines; white tie and tails for the men, and the women were told most particularly to wear white. Everyone in the film business knew that a splash of red on the screen immediately drew all eyes, and the dress designers, in those early days of Technicolor, invariably swathed their leading ladies in crimson or vermilion. There was, therefore, a gasp of indignation when our party made its entrance and it was seen by the local vestal virgins that alone in the room, Norma Shearer was wearing a bright-red dress.

Gable that night was escorting the fascinating Carole Lombard, who was renowned for her uninhibited observations, but a second gasp went up when she asked in a loud voice, "Who the fuck does Norma think she is? The house madam?"

Carole and Clark made a highly attractive couple. Carole had everything that Clark wanted in a woman. Supreme blond good looks, a sense of humor, lovely wild bursts of laughter, his own brand of down-to-earthness and, most important, his love of wild country, hunting, fishing, and the same determination to separate her public life from her private one. They were soon openly living together, a situation made a little tricky by the fact that Clark was still married to Ria.

Hollywood was going through a housecleaning phase at that time, and people shacking up together came in for some tart observations from various organizations, church groups, legions of decency, and so forth.

The number one fan magazine, *Photoplay*, brought this simmering criticism to a boil with an article entitled "Hollywood's Unmarried Husbands and Wives."

It is difficult to imagine in these permissive days that such a dreary piece of journalism could so easily have put the cat among the local pigeons, but the cluck-clucking of disapproval first heard in the Bible Belt of mid-America became a rising crescendo of threats to box-office receipts by the time it reached California, and the big studio brass soon hauled their emancipated stars onto the mat and bludgeoned them into reorganizing their nesting habits.

Clark and Carole, Constance Bennett and Gilbert Roland, George Raft and Virginia Pine, Robert Taylor and Barbara Stanwyck, Paulette Goddard and Charlie Chaplin were all mentioned in the article, and most of them bustled briskly off to their nearest priest, minister, or rabbi and toed the party line.

Ria Gable played a cool hand with good cards, and Clark paid a stiff price to become respectable, so stiff in fact that whenever thereafter he criticized Carole, she was apt to crack, "Well, what did you expect for a lousy half million, for chrissake—perfection?"

In 1936, far away in Czechoslovakia, an unknown actress named Hedy Kiesler was chased naked through a wood in a film called *Ecstasy* and became an overnight sensation when the film was displayed in the United States. She was quickly signed up by L. B. Mayer, and her last name changed. Far more important for his studio than the discovery of Hedy Lamarr was that of Margaret Mitchell, a schoolmistress, in Atlanta, Georgia, who had given up teaching and been on the knife-edge of starvation for five years because she felt she had a great story to tell. Now she had finally and painfully arrived at the last chapter of her epic; *Gone with the Wind* was about to be published, and L. B. Mayer's son-in-law, the brilliant, independent producer David O. Selznick, from right under his father-in-law's nose had snapped up the film rights for a measly $50,000.

So great was the impact of the novel on the American public that the casting of the roles of Rhett Butler and Scarlett O'Hara took on the proportions of a national pastime. There was never any doubt in anybody's mind as to who was the perfect Rhett—Clark Gable—but Scarlett remained an international question mark, and Selznick greatly enjoyed the ensuing publicity. This enjoyment was tempered by the fact that Clark was under contract to Mayer and Selznick was determined to have Gable without his overpowering relative's hot, sticky breath on the back of his neck all during production. Finally, after two years of infighting, a deal was made between Selznick and MGM whereby Gable would be lent to Selznick to play Rhett Butler, but MGM would have the right to distribute the result. Gable, the pawn in the game, never forgave L. B. Mayer for refusing him even the minutest financial participation in the project which brought his company millions.

Selznick utilized the long months of negotiations with MGM by making scores of tests for the part of Scarlett. There was hardly an actress, great or small, in Hollywood who did not covet the role, and Selznick, as I can testify, put most of their aspirations on film.

I was making *The Prisoner of Zenda* for him at the time, so whenever I had a day off, Selznick would commandeer me, stuff me into a Confederate uniform to play Ashley Wilkes with my back to the camera, while the female elite of Hollywood hacked its way through dozens of versions of Scarlett O'Hara. Every evening I would report to Gable on the prospects—none seemed very promising, but all were different. One very perky little number by the name of Judy Turner was among those tested at that time. She had a perfectly packed little body and a behind that signaled a most beguiling message of welcome when she walked, which undoubtedly was the reason why Charlie Richards, Selznick's casting director, ordered her to wear a swimsuit instead of a crinoline for her test.

She did not land the part of Scarlett, but Mervyn LeRoy saw the test and signed her up for his next picture, *They Won't Forget* —a prophetic title as it turned out because Judy (renamed Lana for the occasion) made an instantaneous impact on the public.

After *The Prisoner of Zenda* I moved back to the Samuel Goldwyn lot to make *Wuthering Heights* with Laurence Olivier and Merle Oberon, and it was there that Scarlett was finally found.

The utterly delicious and kittenlike Vivien Leigh had come out to Hollywood to be with Laurence Olivier during the shooting of *Wuthering Heights*—they were deeply and touchingly in love.

Myron Selznick, the top Hollywood agent and David's brother, happened to visit the set one day when Vivien was there, and within minutes of meeting her, he put her firmly into a large black limousine and whisked her across town to be paraded before his brother. Her own personal magic struck twice that day, and by evening, much to the fury of countless local ladies, it was officially announced that the search for Scarlett O'Hara was over.

Mindful of *Photoplay*, David Selznick posted a heavy guard outside the modest little hideaway of Scarlett and Heathcliff.

Apart from a few almost clandestine games of golf, I saw little of Clark once Carole entered his life; they were completely happy in each other's company and needed no stimulation from outsiders. I tried to organize a couple of all-male fishing safaris, but Clark made no bones about the reason for sidestepping my invitations. "The trouble is," he said, "Carole thinks you're a pain in the ass." I must have looked a little crestfallen because he laughed and softened the blow by adding, "As a matter of fact, she thinks anyone is a pain in the ass who might be a better fisherman, a better shot, or a bigger boozer than she is. Don't forget this is my third time up at bat, and one lesson I have learned about wives is that the first thing they want to do is get rid of all their husband's friends. It'll soon pass, but I'm not going to fight it."

In September, 1939, they invited me out to the house for a farewell dinner. Clark and I sat in deep armchairs in the paneled den, and Carole sat on the floor at Clark's knee. We ate and drank, and the conversation was perhaps a trifle stilted because I was off to the war, and as none of us knew what the hell I was letting myself in for, we talked of other things. They were so happy and evidently had so much together that I wondered aloud if there could be anything else they had their eyes on. Carole looked up into Clark's face.

"I'll tell you what Pappy wants," she said quietly, "and I just hope to Christ I can give it to him. . . . He wants a kid."

"Yeah, that's right," said Clark, stroking her hair. "I'd give my right arm for a son."

There was a semi-embarrassed silence till Carole let out one of her famous yelps of laughter. "And he's sure as hell working on it!"

Shooting had just finished on *Gone with the Wind*, and Clark said he was delighted with the result. He had nothing but praise for Vivien—"She's going to be the biggest thing in this business when they see the picture."

David Selznick he admired enormously, but Selznick's penchant for bombarding him daily with memos about his performance left him unmoved—"I never read the goddamn things." He said, "All you can do is put your trust in the director and try to give him what he wants. If you start horsing around trying to please everyone, you wind up a nothing."

Gable insisted that his only contribution to the success of the picture had been arson.

Before shooting had started, it had been necessary to pull down a big cluster of old standing sets at the Selznick Studios in order to make room for the building of Tara and parts of Atlanta. "Why not," he suggested to Selznick, "put a match to the whole damn lot of 'em one night and photograph it? It'll look like Atlanta going up in smoke."

Selznick was delighted with the idea, and with some fire-proofed stunt men doubling for Rhett and Scarlett making their horse-drawn getaway from the burning town, that's exactly how flaming Atlanta came to the screen.

When I bade good-bye to them that night, Gable gave me a word of advice—"Stick to scotch if you want to be brave—gin only makes you piss"—and Carole gave me one of her silk stockings to remember her by and "to wrap round your neck if you get a sore throat."

Just before Christmas of that year, shivering and miserable with my regiment encamped on Salisbury Plain, I read of the highly publicized world premiere of *Gone with the Wind* in Atlanta. The picture was a smash and has rightly remained so to this day. Vivien Leigh and Victor Fleming, the director, won Academy Awards, and the film itself was voted Best Picture of the Year. Though an odds-on favorite, Clark did not win (the Oscar went instead to Robert Donat for *Goodbye, Mr. Chips*), and with a most uncharacteristic flurry of pique, Gable promptly gave his original Oscar to the small son of Carole's secretary, instructing him to prop open his bathroom door with it.

Margaret Mitchell, whose self-denial and near starvation had bought her the five years necessary to write her masterpiece, was shortly after the premiere knocked down by a car in Atlanta. She died of her injuries, and such was the ferocity of the income tax laws that having been relieved of an iniquitous percentage of her earnings from book and movie sales, most of which had accumulated during one year, she died penniless.

During our last evening together Carole had talked a little about Hitler. She really hated everything he stood for. Clark had been more phlegmatic—for him it all seemed like a famine in China, something one read about in the papers before one turned hurriedly to the sports page—but Carole was already arguing powerfully that the United States should get into the war. Later her sense of patriotism increased a thousandfold, and the day after Pearl Harbor she wired President Roosevelt offering both her own and Gable's services in any way they could be useful. This hardly earthshaking but nevertheless helpful offer to a harassed chief of state was duly filed in some government office, and later their help was invited to go on a bond selling tour. Clark was stuck finishing a picture, so Carole went alone.

The tour started in Salt Lake City and wound south through Texas. The last stop was Fort Wayne, Indiana.

Carole booked a sleeper on the train for Los Angeles, but at the last second, anxious to get home, she changed her mind and caught a milk-run plane instead. Gable was delighted when she phoned him and made plans for her early return. Carole loved gags, so Clark dreamed up a surefire one. He borrowed a wax nude dummy from the studio, fixed it up with a long blond wig, and carefully arranged it in a suggestive pose in Carole's bed. Then he spruced up to go to the airport. Carole's plane had already taken off from Las Vegas, the last stop, about an hour before, and Clark was just getting into his car when a call came from the studio police department. Something had gone wrong with Carole's flight, they said; they had no other details, but Eddie Mannix, one of the vice-presidents of MGM and a close friend of Clark's, was on his way out to the house; a plane had been chartered to fly to Las Vegas.

A terrible chill settled on Clark. He waited for Mannix. On the way to the chartered plane Mannix told him the latest news. Someone had seen an explosion in the sky thirty miles from Las Vegas, and another pilot had reported a fire burning fiercely on Table Rock Mountain. Carole's plane was still unreported two hours later, when Gable and Mannix reached Las Vegas and a search party with packhorses had been readied to make the ascent to the summit. Mannix talked Gable out of going with the searchers.

"It could be a false alarm, Clark," he said. "How will she feel if she arrives home and you're not there to meet her?"

Clark remained at the foot of the mountain, and Mannix went up with the climbers. After hours of toiling through deep snow the charred and smoking debris of the plane was found scattered over a large area. Mannix was able to identify Carole chiefly by a pair of earrings which he had helped Clark choose for her.

Clark did not delegate to anyone the making of the necessary heartbreaking arrangements. Ice-cold and monosyllabic, he supervised everything himself from the ordering of a hot meal for the exhausted search party on that dreadful night to the choosing of hymns for the funeral three days later. Then he went to the Rogue River, holed up at his favorite fishing camp, and for three weeks drank himself into a stupor.

MGM, with the soaring costs of an unfinished picture very much on their minds, dispatched mealymouthed emissaries to inquire as tactfully as possible when their star might be expected to report for work. Clark never saw them. He just roared through the locked door of his cabin, "I'll be back when I'm good and ready . . . now beat it."

Finally, he showed up unexpectedly at the Culver City lot. Outwardly he appeared unchanged. He kidded with old friends and dropped in to see acquaintances. Always on time, always knowing his lines and as always, the complete professional. Grief, like everything else, was very private to Clark.

The day his picture was finished he enlisted, asked to be trained as an air gunner and to be posted overseas.

329

By the summer of 1943 I had offset the misery of military life by the happiest of all acquisitions: a beautiful wife and a baby son. They lived in a thatched cottage two miles from Windsor Castle, and whenever I got leave, I rushed to join them. They had a few chickens and a vegetable garden to augment their joint rations of two eggs a month, two chops a week, and eight ounces of cooking fat every ten days. I was usually far away, leave was scarce, and communication with family almost nonexistent, but one summer evening I came home to find a large American Air Force officer sitting under *my* beech tree in *my* deck chair; on his knee was *my* little boy, and serving him from *my* last bottle of whiskey was *my* wife.

It was a great reunion. Clark was stationed in the Midlands, and from then on our cottage became his refuge from military life.

Gable had been dealt the cruelest of blows, but on the surface, at least, he was making the best of it. In his own deep misery he found it possible to rejoice over the great happiness that had come my way, and he became devoted to my little family, always showing up with unheard-of goodies such as concentrated orange juice and nylons from the bountiful American PX. He had had a difficult time, he told me, becoming an officer. Passing the written exam had been hell, but he had managed it, not by studying in the ordinary way . . . he had locked himself in the lavatory after lights out and, night after night, with his actor's mind, had memorized textbooks like scripts.

He found it rough being Clark Gable. He was caught between two extremes: those who fawned on him and those who automatically thought he ought to be chopped down. Whichever way it went, it was almost impossible for him to be just an ordinary guy— something he longed to be now more than ever.

For a year before I embarked, fumble-fingered with fear, for Normandy, we saw Clark frequently. The terrible wound of Carole's death seemed to be healing, but she was never far from him, and the very happiness of our little group would sometimes overwhelm him. Primmie found him one evening on an upturned wheelbarrow in the garden, his head in his hands, weeping uncontrollably. She held the huge bear of a man in her arms and comforted him.

Clark did several bombing missions over Germany as an air gunner, and one flak-shredded plane he was in nearly disintegrated over the Ruhr. No false hero, he said he was scared stiff the whole time, but the one thing that really put the fear of God into him was the thought of having to bail out. Not so much was it the prospect of the actual descent and landing that unnerved him; it was the thought of what Hitler might do to him on arrival: "That son of a bitch'll put me in a cage and charge ten marks a look all over Germany."

With the end of the war in Europe in sight Clark was released from the service.

GABLE'S BACK AND GARSON'S GOT HIM screamed the billboards all over the world. Clark was being relaunched by MGM in a dreary potboiler with, as costar, someone not among his most favorite leading ladies.

He lived at his Encino ranch, the thirty-acre spread in the San Fernando Valley where he had so far spent his happiest days. Carole's room was a shrine, and nothing was allowed to be touched —her clothes, photographs, perfume bottles, all remained exactly as she had left them—but the sprawling white brick-and-frame house did not become a mini-monastery. Far from it—its steps were polished by the expectant arrival and disappointed departure of a steady stream of carbon copies of Carole Lombard: beautiful blond ladies of the utmost attraction and sophistication whom he entertained, "used," perhaps, and in several cases, sent away brokenhearted, actresses, society ladies from New York, cover girls and secretaries.

They all did their best to fill Carole's shoes. They laughed with him, drank with him, and even apprehensively donned blue jeans and safari jackets and went duck hunting with him, but when each in turn failed to measure up, Martin, his faithful majordomo, would lower the electrically controlled boom at the end of the driveway and Clark would seek lonely comfort in his favorite whiskey.

When I returned to Hollywood after the war, Clark seemed to be withdrawing more and more into his shell. I think the arrival of Primmie and myself, by now with a second little boy, six months old, provided him with a tiny port in his personal storm. At any rate, hardly a day went by when he did not drop in at the appalling Moorish prison of a house which we had rented in Beverly Hills,

331

and as always, he arrived loaded with goodies for the children and played with them for hours, and as before, he found great peace and comfort in the calm serenity of Primmie.

We had been installed in the Moorish prison only six weeks when Clark called early one morning.

"Come on, kids," he said. "I've got it all fixed. We'll drive up to Pebble Beach and play golf for a few days. I've got a bungalow for you two at the country club, and I've got permission for us to fish in the reservoir up in the forest . . . that's elk country in there . . . maybe we'll show Primmie an old-fashioned California elk."

We took off, and Primmie's eyes were like saucers as we drove north through green rolling hills to Santa Barbara through the Alisal Ranch and San Luis Obispo, then along the coast road below W. R. Hearst's castle at San Simeon, through Big Sur, and along the high winding scenic route to Monterey with the tumultuous and incongruously named Pacific crashing against the rocks far below.

We played a lot of golf, stayed up much too late, caught very few fish, saw no elk, and laughed all the time. Clark was at his best, completely relaxed and reveling in showing Primmie such a spectacular section of his beloved California. During the weekend Primmie wrote to her father in England saying she had never been so happy in her life. Two days after we returned to Beverly Hills, as the result of an accident, she died.

I don't know how people can get through periods of great tragedy without friends to cushion and comfort them. To be alone in the world when disaster strikes must be an unbearable refinement of the torture, and I will forever bless those who helped me over the initial shock, but there comes a time when friends have to get on with their own lives and you have to face the problem alone— this is the worst part.

During that long period of utter despair Clark was endlessly thoughtful and helpful, and he checked up constantly to see if I was all right. Without my realizing it, he was drawing on his own awful experience to steer me through mine, and for the next eighteen months I saw a great deal of him, being one of the small handful whose voice on the intercom at the electrically controlled ranch gate was instantly greeted by Martin with "Why, drive right on up—Mr. Clark is right here."

Martin adored Clark and always had his best interests at heart, but sometimes his anxiety over his employer's well-being got the better of his judgment. Once I drove "right on up" with a particularly attractive companion who happened to be a happily married lady from San Francisco, and Martin decided that she was just his master's type, so he slipped an old-fashioned Mickey Finn into my drink and drove me home semiconscious.

Women adored Clark, but although he loved them and their beauty and gaiety, he was never a womanizer in the crude sense of the word.

"Hell," he said, "if I'd jumped on all the dames I'm supposed to have jumped on, I'd never have had time to go fishing."

If he ever discussed any of the aspiring beauties who visited the ranch, it was only in a generous, laughing, and flattering way—very unlike the broadsides he reserved for the new guard at MGM. L. B. Mayer, whom he had disliked but respected, had been replaced by others whom he disliked and despised. He also seemed to have lost interest in making pictures, a normal reaction among actors who had been away fighting a war; it seemed so childish for a fully grown man to put on makeup and spend the day playing charades.

He drank more than before and gained weight, which worried him. To counteract this tendency, he lapped down Dexedrine, which was supposed to make him lose his appetite. All it did, however, was make his head shake alarmingly.

I went away to Europe for six months to make a film, and when I returned, Clark seemed slightly perked up. He was even issuing occasionally from the ranch and being seen in public with a couple of his favorite dates, a sweet, gentle blond actress who lived near him in the Valley—Virginia Grey—and Anita Colby, a top cover girl from New York who was so beautiful she was known all over the United States as the Face.

He also seemed to take heart from the fact that, with great good luck, I myself, after two years, had again found great happiness and had remarried while in Europe. He approved mightily of Hjördis and was the first guest we invited to our house in Pacific Palisades. Hjördis decided to give a small dinner for half a dozen of my friends.

"We'll have a roast suckling pig," she announced as I was rushing out early in the morning in danger of being late for work.

This was a Scandinavian dish with which I was not too familiar, so when she inquired where she would be able to find such a thing, I mumbled through a mouthful of breakfast, "At the Mayfair market, I suppose," and headed for the car.

At that point Hjördis had a rather tentative grip on the English language, and nobody knows what she said that morning in the market. In any event, later in the day a van arrived at our house and deposited an entire hog of enormous proportions; dead, luckily. Our cook gaped at it apprehensively and suggested that instead of the traditional apple in its mouth, it would look better munching a melon; then she bravely set about cooking it in oven-sized sections, hoping, I suppose, to weld them together later like one of Henry Kaiser's Liberty ships.

"You all had better round up a few more friends," she advised Hjördis, "or this family'll be eatin' pig meat for five years."

Hjördis put out an SOS to her Swedish reserves. Viveca Lindfors, for one, leaped gallantly into the breach and rounded up a whole clutch of hungry Nordic pork lovers, plus her mother who had arrived that very morning for her first visit to the United States. "She doesn't speak a word of English," warned Viveca.

Gable showed up for the intimate dinner to find the house bursting at the seams with blue-eyed towheaded strangers, but he rose above it and did his best to make everyone happy.

"What do we do with the old broad?" he whispered to me, indicating Viveca's mother, who was sitting alone on a sofa.

"Slip her a belt of schnapps," I hissed, and hurried off to cope with some new arrivals.

It is possible that he gave the old lady a flower-vase full of the stuff because she became very uninhibited, suddenly burst loudly into song and, with skirts held high, went into a spirited dance.

Clark made no bones about it—he was longing to be married again—but when a man of fifty is looking around desperately hoping to fill a void, he is usually not seeing too clearly.

Sylvia Fairbanks, the widow of the inimitable Douglas, fascinated Clark from the moment he met her, and because of her ravishing blond beauty, her outspokenness, and her impeccable sense of humor, she seemed to him to be out of the same mold as Carole. There is no question—he rushed it. A few weeks after he had met Sylvia they called us from Santa Barbara in a haze of champagne (not his favorite drink incidentally).

"Guess what?" yelled Clark. "We've done it! We're married!"

As usual, Clark had kept his mouth shut about his love affairs, and it would have been grossly unfair, in the unlikely event that he had asked my advice, if I had by a single word tried to reverse the trend, but I had known both of them for many years, and I would certainly have marked them down as a high-risk combination.

Clark was a selfish man; Sylvia was a selfish woman . . . so far a standoff. Clark was a man's man, but Sylvia was a man's woman . . . a red light. Clark lived for the open air, blood sports, the big country, and large dogs. Sylvia was devoted to the great indoors, to her milky white skin, her flawless complexion, loathed the thought of animals being slaughtered, was happiest among the chattering chic of café society and owned a Chihuahua the size of a mouse named Minnie.

Possible friction points could perhaps have been welded into a great happiness by their mutual devotion to laughter had it not been for a further divergence: Clark was close with a buck, while Sylvia adored spending money.

Three weeks after they were married Clark was looking grim. Sylvia had blithely revamped Carole's room at the ranch and invited some smart friends from the East to come out and stay in it.

The King, with the expression of a man with a dead fish for a tiepin, was occasionally seen carrying Minnie, and when he returned from Long Island and Nassau, whither Sylvia had dragged him to meet some of the "beautiful people" of the day, it was obvious that a gross miscalculation had been made. After seventeen months of marriage Sylvia, claiming she had been locked out of the ranch upon returning from a second and this time solitary trip East, retained the great criminal lawyer Jerry Geisler to take care of her side of the divorce proceedings, only to discover that Clark had no intention of being wiped out for a third time by the California laws on community property and had taken certain evasive action. He had arranged for his contract to be suspended by MGM and had created a legal residence in Nevada, whence he moved everything he owned except the walls and roof of the ranch.

True to form, Gable kept his mouth shut about how much this latest and shortest idyll had cost him, but once the settlement had been made, his sense of humor returned, and he took a certain delight in displaying to his friends his Christmas card from Sylvia: "THANKS A MILLION." Then he issued his customary statement—"I don't intend to marry again *ever*"—and took off for Africa to make *Mogambo* with Ava Gardner and Grace Kelly.

When he returned from Africa, he spent a few months touring around Europe in a sports car; the passenger seat was seldom empty. I was filming in England and Italy, so Hjördis and I were treated to previews of the selected passengers, and inevitably the ones in whom he seemed most interested were all outwardly Lombardesque. Suzanne Dadolle was a very beautiful and intelligent French girl to whom Clark seemed genuinely attached. They came to visit us on location on Lake Como, and it seemed possible that the odds might be shortening when he hid her in a cupboard in his bedroom at the Villa D'Este and she stepped out suddenly to present us with a bottle of champagne.

Admirably but maddeningly close with information about all his liaisons, Clark was a difficult man on whom to place a bet, but with Suzanne beside him, the tour of Europe was prolonged again and again, and I had seldom seen him happier. But it ended suddenly—he never said why.

Mogambo was released and was a big hit, the most successful picture Clark had made since MGM wanted him to sign a new long-term contract, but the King was tiring. He was sick of the studio, the people who were running it, and the petty politics in which they indulged. So after fifty-four pictures and twenty-three years, he left MGM, never to return. He was oddly vitriolic about the company that had found him and built him up. Of course, he too had had a sizable hand in his own success, but surprisingly for such a down-to-earth man he fell into the actor's trap of thinking he had done it all by himself, and nothing would ever persuade him to make another picture at the studio. MGM, in turn, fell into the usual studio trap—they thought they could "buy" him back, and the more vehemently he refused to return, the higher went their offers. They finally gave up when they learned of his instructions to his agent: "See how high you can get those sons of bitches to go; then tell 'em to take their money and their studio and shove it up their ass."

His choice of pictures after leaving MGM was not inspired; in his mid-fifties even the King was finding it difficult to land good roles. A realist, he tried not to look over his shoulder, but he knew only too well that the Young Pretenders were breathing down his neck. A long love affair with scotch was also beginning to show. He was becoming heavy and bloated, but above all, he was lonely, and his dream of a happy marriage and perhaps a son was fading rapidly. There was a discernible air of quiet desperation about him, but he kept his own counsel, retained his humor, and soldiered on.

The sun when least expected came out for Clark at the age of fifty-five. One day he ran across someone he had seen only a couple of times in the past ten years, Kay Williams. Kay was his type in looks, blond, beautiful, and with periwinkle-blue eyes, but she also possessed something which attracted him even more, something which Carole had had in abundance. She was gutsy; she didn't kowtow to anyone; she was prepared to give as good as she got.

She had a couple of other things too that he liked the look of as soon as he saw them—a little boy of four and a girl of three.

"The kids'll screw it up for Kay," sniffed one of Clark's ex-girlfriends to me. "The son of a bitch might go for her if she had dogs instead of children."

Kay had been divorced three times, was now in her mid-thirties, and had decided that her acting career would never amount to much, so she was ready with a wealth of experience to settle down and make the right man happy. His friends knew it was serious when Clark disappeared from view, the boom was lowered at the ranch, and he no longer showed up at gun clubs and golf courses. A year later the two of them surfaced to get married in northern California.

Kay was perfect for Clark, and she set out intelligently to make him happy and content. Instead of sweeping the memories of Carole under the rug, she encouraged them. She became a good shot and an excellent fisherwoman, played golf with him and, if she didn't actually go drink for drink with him, usually contrived to have a glass in her hand at the same time he did.

Although she never asked for anything for herself, she gently indicated his purse till he loosened the strings. He bought a sports

Mercedes 300 XL and a piece of desert where he built a small house beside the sixth fairway of the Bermuda Dunes Golf Course, but even Kay was astonished when, on a Christmas shopping trip to New York, he suddenly steered her into Cartier's.

Jules Glaenzer, the ubiquitous head of the store, started washing his hands with invisible soap when he saw the prospective customers walk in through the Fifth Avenue entrance. He ushered them into a private room where the chairs had been polished by the bottoms of oil sheiks and maharajas and proceeded to display tray after fabulous tray. Gable began to sweat. Finally he got to his feet. "Er, I saw something down the street I like better," he said, and led a mystified Kay to Abercrombie and Fitch, where he bought her a shotgun. Soon after they were married, Kay became pregnant, and Clark was ecstatic with joy, but after eleven weeks, she lost the baby, and he doubted if his longing for a son could ever be fulfilled. Kay's two children adored Clark, and he was a redoubtable stepfather but—

Every picture was a job to Clark; the complete professional, he gave full value to the work at hand. He was always on time, always word-perfect, always prepared to do his utmost to give the director what he wanted. Engrossed as he was in his marriage, he did jobs as they came along, but his popularity remained enormous, and in spite of the rather mediocre material he selected, on the edge of sixty he seemed indestructible.

Early in 1960 he finished making *It Started in Naples*. The shooting of this nonsense had been mostly on the island of Capri, and bored by the smallness of the place and by the endless attentions of the paparazzi sent swarming over from the mainland by his leading lady's producer husband, he took heavily to the pasta and red vino. By the time he returned to the ranch he was thirty pounds overweight, but he couldn't have cared less and even talked blithely of retiring. Then one day a script arrived on his desk that really fascinated him. The screenplay of *The Misfits* had been written by America's number one playwright—Arthur Miller. John Huston was to direct, and for costars he would have the delectable and highly salable Marilyn Monroe and Montgomery Clift. The role was perfect for Gable, the best he had been offered in years, and in a high state of excitement he and Kay took off for the desert, where he promised himself he would get into top shape before shooting started. He played golf every day, watched his diet, and cut right down on the booze; the professional was getting down to his fighting weight for a special job. In July, 1960, he reported to the location near Reno, Nevada. He was the picture of health and vitality and looking forward eagerly to the start of the film. There was a delay. Monroe called from Los Angeles to say she was unwell and could not come up for several days. Shooting was postponed, but any annoyance or letdown that Clark might have felt was quickly eliminated when a radiant Kay arrived with the best possible news from her doctor: She was pregnant again. That was a lovely day for Clark. Everything at last seemed to be perfect, and it is unlikely that in his happiness he would have remembered the advice he had given to a young actor many years before: "Read the small print."

John Huston was not too happy with Arthur Miller's script—the first screenplay Miller had tackled incidentally—but the annoyances of rewrites and script conferences paled into insignificance with the arrival of Marilyn Monroe and Montgomery Clift. Marilyn had acquired a reputation for unprofessionalism and had a nasty habit of showing up late for work. She had become a mass of inhibitions, terrors, and indecisions, and the poor doomed girl was headed for a breakdown. Montgomery Clift a few months previously when leaving the hilltop home of Elizabeth Taylor and Michael Wilding had smashed through the guardrail on the twisting mountain road, and when he had been extricated from the wreck, many bones were broken and his face was terribly disfigured. Plastic surgery had done miracles, but the shock and the necessary pain-killing drugs had changed him terribly. Now he was subject to fits of the blackest depression, and he, too, frequently found it unbearable to show up on the set.

On the Reno location Miller kept rewriting the script and Huston kept rewriting the rewrites; then either Monroe or Clift would be hours late—sometimes they never turned up at all—and every day Clark was there on time ready to start work, and every day the sun climbed relentlessly in the cloudless sky. By eight o'clock it was 100 in the shade, by midday over 130, and every afternoon the hot desert wind covered everything and everybody with a thick alkali dust from the dried-up lake bed.

Out of pure boredom, Clark insisted on doing some stunts that would normally have been done by a double. Anything was better than sitting day after day in the baking desert just waiting, but roping a wild mustang in searing heat and being dragged along the desert floor at 30 mph behind a truck are not sensible pastimes for a man of sixty. Huston tried to dissuade him, and Kay was appalled when she nightly doctored his cuts and rope burns, but he persisted, and never once did he say a word against the others. He understood their problems and felt desperately sorry for Arthur Miller, who was married to Monroe and must have been bearing the brunt of all her difficulties behind the scenes.

At long last and weeks over schedule, the picture finished. Clark saw a rough cut, and although he hardly ever discussed his work, he told one and all that it was the best thing he had done since *Gone with the Wind*; then he forgot about the past miserable months and sat back and waited contentedly but impatiently for the birth of his child.

Early one morning Kay woke to find Clark standing by the bed half dressed, his face chalky white. "I've a terrible pain," he said simply.

The doctor was called and immediately sent for an ambulance. It was a massive heart attack. Kay moved into the hospital with him, and he improved steadily over the next nine days.

On the tenth day he looked like a new man, relaxed and happy. Kay says that he asked her to stand sideways against the light so that he could see her silhouette. Laughing happily, he used the doctor's stethoscope to hear the heartbeat of the little boy he longed for so much but would never see. During the night he was struck down a second time.

In Clark's copy of *The Misfits*, Arthur Miller had written: "To the man who did not know how to hate."

3
Our Little Girl
(Part I)

$\mathcal{M}$ ISSIE was described by the newspapers as a "sex symbol" or a "love goddess" and by us at the studio as "the Boys' Erector Set."

Her face, which was snub-nosed and pretty, was saved from being unremarkable by a pair of huge gray eyes. It was topped by a cloud of golden hair and had the great good fortune to be strategically placed above the most beautiful body in Hollywood.

Most of her adult life Missie had been part of the Hollywood scene. One year out of an Arizona high school and still thinking a chocolate marshmallow sundae was a "big deal," she had been spotted by a studio talent scout and offered a solo number in a Busby Berkeley musical. She had immediately kissed good-bye to her mother and headed for California. A long-term Hollywood contract had followed, and the paucity of her acting talent had been minimized by her pretty face, her gray eyes, and her quite extraordinary shape. The studio publicity department had encountered little difficulty in hoisting her to the top of "The Girl Most Wanted" list, and through the years she had accumulated a large and appreciative following in moneymaking pictures which had tested the guidelines of the Legion of Decency to the limits.

Missie was not the cleverest girl in the school, but she was smart enough to realize that her beautiful body and her enthusiastic use of it should not be distributed as largess to all and sundry, and as a general rule, she bestowed her favors where they would reap the most bountiful harvest—among the producers, directors, writers, and cameramen, in that strict order of "billing."

It was a "nervous" night. The hot desert wind—the Santa Ana—was blowing, skins felt dry and itchy, tempers were short, and problems were magnified. Missie, encased in the lightest of cotton sheets, was lying naked on her back—not her most unfavorite position, let us remind ourselves—but this time she was alone, naked because she liked the feel of the voile sheets around her curves and on her back because Cary Grant had told her that sleeping in that position was the only way to avoid getting wrinkles. The music was far away, and it entered her sleeping brain through a tiny attic window far up in her skull; slowly it filtered down, growing implacably louder until she could identify the song—"You smile . . . and the angels sing."

Missie stirred petulantly and made a brushing movement of her arm, but the music did not go away, and she realized it was the new alarm clock which "He" had given her, tuned in to the twenty-four-hour "music station." She knew that if she reached out a hand and switched it off, it would relentlessly come on again every thirty seconds until she climbed out of bed and yanked it out of the wall. She groaned and lay for a while listening to the song. When it ended and the all-night disc jockey started his hearty early-morning patter, she rolled out of bed and pulled the plug out of its socket—4 A.M.

Missie's head felt like lead, and her mouth like the bottom of a parrot's cage. Why, oh, why, she asked herself, had she been so stupid? "One of my sleeping pills a night, *only*," her doctor, "Needle Ned," had prescribed, but she had doubled the dose last night because "He" had invited a group over for supper and cards, and although she had tiptoed away at ten o'clock, making movie-camera, hand-turning signals, she had still found herself wide awake at midnight with only four hours to go before another exhausting day's work.

She tottered into her yellow tiled bathroom and switched on her mirror lights, but she was not happy with what she saw. Her famous creamy white skin was, despite Cary's advice, creased upon her face, her famous cat's eyes were half closed and puffy, and the stretch marks on her abdomen caused by little Sharon looked like streaky bacon held up to the light. She was thirty years old and felt fifty, but she doggedly set about making herself presentable for the gatemen, the studio police, and the departing shifts of maintenance men who might see her as she was driving through the studio gates.

At four-thirty she glanced out her bathroom window. Alvin was already there, and he knew his business, so he sat patiently in the driveway with his side lights on to show he had arrived on schedule.

"Thank God for Manny," she thought. "At least I don't have to drive myself to work at this hour of the night."

It was still pitch black when Missie let herself out of the house. She had peeked into "His" room on the way down and had blown a kiss to his sleeping form—a vague mound in the middle of the bed. Downstairs it had smelled of stale cigar smoke and booze, so she had opened the drapes and windows, then she had covered her cream-colored jacket and slacks with a mink coat, tied a silk scarf under her chin, and let herself quietly out of her house.

"Mornin', Missie," said Alvin, touching the peak of his soft black cap. "Sleep well?"

"Not enough, Alvin," she replied as she settled herself in the backseat, switched on a reading light, and during the half-hour drive studied the scenes scheduled for the day's shooting and cursed herself for not having been strong enough to say—"The hell with your party . . . *I'm* going to bed."

"Mornin', Missie," said "Red," the gateman. "Lovely mornin'."

Missie got out of the car outside her dressing-room bungalow and sniffed the cool fragrance of the California dawn; far away an orange glow was beginning to silhouette the semicircle of mountains that held Los Angeles imprisoned in a half-clenched fist.

"Coffee's all ready, Miss Missie." Vergis beamed. Missie kissed the shiny black cheek. "Who's looking after the kids today, Vergis?" she asked.

"Oh! I have good neighbors down there in Watts; they all take turns!" Vergis laughed a happy laugh as she poured the steaming Maxwell House.

At five thirty on the dot the makeup man appeared, lugging a huge leather-covered box containing all the bottles, brushes, pots, and pastes of his very considerable craft. He was as unemotional and methodical as a country policeman.

"Mornin', darling," he said, peering at her. "You look like hell—got your period?"

"No, thank God," said Missie. "Anyway, I get three days off when it comes—thanks to Manny . . . he got it added to the contract."

"Well, then get more sleep, for chrissakes," said Carl. "I don't want to lose *my* job! Like I said to Doris, the other morning, when she came in lookin' like that, 'Little Day—you've had a busy man!' . . . Eye drops first."

Missie lay back in her reclining chair and watched in the mirror while Carl transformed her from a pasty-faced dull-eyed woman of thirty into a vibrant, sparkling girl in her early twenties.

"Thank God the body's still good," muttered Carl, "but you'd better watch it, darling—those bastards in the front office have ice water for blood . . . they'll smile at you and tell you that you're 'their little girl,' but all you need is to get the blame for a couple of *their* big flops, and you'll be out on *your* cute little ass. . . . Hey! I nearly forgot. We have to put the scar on you today . . . just a tiny one on the right cheekbone." Carl applied fish skin, surgical spirit, liquid rubber, and Max Factor blood with great dexterity while Missie complained about her leading man's body odor.

"Honest, Carl . . . I can't stand it! It makes my eyes water! Can't you have a word with him?"

"Very difficult, darling," said Carl. "But I'll do my best. If we suggest he eat parsley all day long, he may get offended."

"I *dread* the love scenes." Missie sighed. "The poor boy's so nervous . . . that's probably the reason."

"Why don't you give him a piece?" said Carl. "He's obviously got the hots for you. That might do the trick . . . you know . . . relax the poor bastard?"

"Out! out! out!" came a high-pitched squeal from the dressing-room door, and clapping his hands, in swished Frankie, the head hairstylist. "Verg, darling, move your beautiful black ass and get Mother a cup of coffee."

"Yes, ma'am." Vergis, not to be outdone, giggled.

"Out, wrecking crew, I say, and leave this old bag to me."

"It's all yours, Buddy." Carl grinned good-naturedly. "Our girl needs help today, Frankie, so fluff her up and pray for backlighting. . . . See you on the set, darling." He withdrew.

Frankie soon had a mouthful of hairpins and was working with professional mastery at incredible speed. He never drew breath.

"Saturday night is bath night for me, sweetheart. . . . Only two more days, and I'll be in the full black nightie with one of Hedy's wigs on. . . ."

Missie had heard it all before, and she knew that two evenings hence middle-aged Frankie would be sitting hopefully on a tacky stool in Ricky's dingy bar on the Sunset Strip, checking on the "studs" and "scores" through a tangerine twilight of smoke, fluttering his eyelashes at the bikeless motorcyclists in their shiny outfits and the horseless cowboys in their unaccustomed buckles and boots. She only half listened to the depressing "drag" talk and the boasts of "juice" and "joints," "Bennies" and conquests.

She changed the subject. "I didn't think much of the dailies last night," she said.

"Nor did Mother, sweetheart," Frankie replied. "Between them, that camera queen and Mrs. Director really gave you a fucking . . . you looked *ninety!*"

"I don't want to rush you," said a calm Texas voice from the entrance hall of her bungalow, "but we'll be ready to turn over at nine o'clock sharp . . . it's not quite eight-thirty now . . . we'll go on where we left off last night."

"Okay, Chuck," she called. "I'll be there. Which gives you about five minutes more, Frankie," added Missie. "How're we doing?"

"The pink net's just going on, sweetheart," said the hairstylist with a last flourish of the curling iron. "Tell Vergis to wash you tonight—it's getting awful dry."

"It's those damn arcs," said Missie. "Nobody's ever used so many as this guy . . . he's baking my scalp."

"He's a lousy cameraman," said Frankie helpfully. "Why didn't you ask for Daniels or Stradling or Maté? You *know* what they do for girls."

"I did," said Missie, "and I also asked for Cukor or Franklin to direct because they're good for girls too . . . but they'd all been put on other pictures."

Missie's heart gave a little lurch as she said this. She knew she had made a big mistake, by evening it would be all over the lot that she was slipping.

Before she left her bungalow, Missie examined herself carefully in the long three-way mirror. Her morale rose, and she climbed into the backseat of Alvin's Cadillac. As the car wound through the studio streets to Stage 23, many workers waved a cheery greeting. Missie sighed and thought of those happy days when everyone at the studio had protected her and cosseted her and made it their business to approve or disapprove of her boyfriends and to watch with pride the development of her early-blooming figure.

Missie's portable dressing room, a large cubicle on wheels complete with dressing table, mirrors, a telephone and a comfortable couch, had, like her bungalow, been decorated to her taste. It had been towed to a quiet corner of the sound stage, conveniently close to the brightly lit activity where the day's shooting would soon take place.

Marie, from the wardrobe department, was waiting at the door. They kissed good morning.

"Afraid the costume weighs a ton, honey," she said, "and there's no way you can sit in it without creasing around the middle—I've asked Props for a slant board; he's gone to get one. Let's go, hon," she added. "The Creep's already looking at his watch."

The Creep was the nickname of the unpopular director. He was a brash but indecisive young man with a penchant for bullying those least able to defend themselves. The day before he had not endeared himself to the crew by standing two feet away from a quailing young actress and shouting, "No *good* . . . do it *again* . . . and this time, for chrissakes . . . *R E L A X!*"

"The Creep" had a couple of successful low-budget films to his credit and had been given the break of directing Missie's picture by its youthful producer, known behind *his* back as Coattails—a nephew of the studio head.

"Think positively," Missie told herself as she slipped out of her slacks and stood naked in the cubicle.

Marie ordered Missie to breathe in and hooked her into a Merry Widow which gave her a nineteen-inch waist, jutting bosoms, and acute discomfort. The basic hoop and petticoats came next, and at last the costume itself. Marie had been right—the weight was horrendous—but the result was spectacular, and Missie made a few pirouettes to watch the skirts swirl and fall.

346

"I hope my tits don't pop out," she said. "They're awful near the danger line."

"I'll keep an eye on them," said Marie.

"So will about fifty guys." Missie laughed.

A few last-minute dabs of powder by Carl, and sharp at nine o'clock, Missie walked out into the bright lights to start eight slogging, exhausting hours of nervous tension and high concentration.

Things went well for the first hour. "The Creep" was calmer and more inventive than usual, and the leading man appeared to have bathed in Knize 10, but the head of publicity cornered a resting Missie on her slant board.

"The front office has okayed some visitors today, darling," he said. "That dame from *Photoplay* wants to have lunch with you."

"No way," said Missie. "By the time I've gotten out of this dress I've less than half an hour before I have to get back into it again— all I do is grab a sandwich and call home—it's my only chance to talk to Sharon. She'll be asleep when I get back tonight."

The man sighed. He was used to rolling with the punches, and he got them from all sides, but he had a plan.

"Then there's the whole Ohio State football squad. They're playing at the Rose Bowl New Year's Day—they just want to come and look at you around three o'clock . . . they've elected you their mascot for the game . . . it'll mean a few pictures and autographs but tremendous coverage. How's about it?"

"Okay," she groaned, "but don't let me get trapped."

"A deal," he said. "I've turned down several others for today, the Boston *Globe*, the Des Moines *Register*, and the Washington *Star* —we can knock them off later. The president of the Foreign Press Association wants to come this morning—they're getting very important now, the foreign press. . . . He's a nice Swede and we might be able to swing an award from them later—that's getting more coverage every year. . . . Whaddya say, darling?"

"Not today, Eddie," begged Missie. "We've got a lot of awful tough scenes . . . maybe he could take me to lunch when the picture's over?"

"I'll tell you what I'll do, darling," said Eddie, looking away from her to lessen the impact. "I'll can the Swede . . . if you'll see Hedda."

"Hedda!" Missie almost screamed. "What the hell does *she*

want? . . . You mean she's coming out to the studio? She *never* does that!"

"She does when she's on to a story, darling," said Eddie smoothly, "and I'm afraid she's on to 'Him.' "

"Oh, Jesus!" said Missie. "What time is she coming?"

"She's here already," said Eddie, "over on Stage Nine at the moment. Just string her along. . . . She can be a good friend too, you know, and it's better to have her on your team than playing against you."

"On the set, please," said a calm Texas voice.

Missie worked on doggedly, but she kept looking into the darkness behind the camera, dreading the sight of the icy supercolumnist. At last, in an interval for relighting, Missie was confronted.

"We don't have much time, my dear," said the spare, overhatted Hedda, "so let's get down to business. . . . I hear that 'He' is living with you now. I know what he gets for breakfast, and I know he sometimes drives Sharon to school—a convent school, isn't it? . . . Do you think this is good for your image? . . . And what do you think will happen to your contract here if the Catholic Legion of Decency decides to ban your pictures?"

Missie's hand shook as she lit a cigarette.

"It's my private life, Hedda," she said defensively.

"Nonsense," said Hedda. "You *have* no private life—you sold that long ago for a contract, and you'll be getting twenty-five hundred a week if your option is taken up next month. You belong to the public, and a lot of people in the country still like people in the public eye to lead clean, decent lives and to rear their children in a clean decent home. They stomached your divorce because they'd loved you since you were a child, but they won't stand for 'Him' in your life . . . I'm warning you."

"Are you going to tell them, Hedda?" asked Missie in a quiet, little voice.

The columnist thought for a moment and gazed directly into the big gray eyes.

"No, my dear . . . not unless you force me to," she replied slowly, "but I'll tell you something that may make things easier for you: 'He's' a no-good son of a bitch . . . I've watched him for years

. . . he always was, he always will be . . . he's a crook in business, which we all know, but . . . he's cheating on you already."

"Waiting on the set, Missie," said a calm Texas voice. "Dialogue off camera, please."

In a daze and with legs turned to jelly, Missie walked toward the camera. She glanced back and saw Eddie deferentially shepherding Hedda's regal figure toward the door: then she faced her nervous young leading man, standing in his Gold Rush outfit under the full glare of the lights. It was his close-up in a difficult emotional scene, and he needed all the help she could give him. She put everything she could into it. The boy thawed out and responded, and when it was over, he bounded up to her like a big puppy. "Gee, thanks loads! . . . You sure did help me! . . . It's so lonely out there, I've been dreading that close-up ever since we started the picture!"

Impulsively, he hugged her. Missie burst into tears, ran to her trailer, slammed the door, and reached for the telephone. Stifling her sobs, she spoke to her secretary. "Morning, Pat. Did Sharon get to school okay?"

"Oh, yes," answered the girl. " 'He' took her—they only just made it—he had a tough time getting up, I guess!"

Missie took a calming breath.

"Is 'He' there now, Pat? I'd like a word with him."

"No, he just left for Lakeside . . . he has a golf game—said if you called to give you his love . . . he'll be back around six."

"OK, Pat, you come on out here then." She hung up.

A discreet knock, and the kindly face of Mac, the first assistant, peered around the door. Vergis was hovering behind.

"You okay, little girl? What's upset you? Anything I can do?" Missie dabbed her eyes and controlled herself.

"It was the scene, I guess . . . sorry, Mac . . . ask Carl to come and repair the damage, will you, please?"

"Sure, darling. Take your time; there's a lighting job coming up . . . call me if you need anything."

Carl went to work in silence—he knew better than to talk when temperament was on the boil whatever the cause—but the silence was broken by another knock on the door. Vergis opened it a few inches and relayed a whispered message.

"It's the man from the *Hollywood Reporter* . . . says to tell you they've reserved a full page for your Christmas ad again this year and to remind you the five hundred is deductible."

"Tell him to drop dead," said Missie, and she could feel hysteria rising within her.

The phone rang. It was her agent.

"I'll be out at the studio today, darling," said Manny. "I'll drop by and see you about five . . . okay?"

"It's a tough day, Manny," groaned Missie. "Can't it wait?"

"Won't take but a few minutes, darling . . . see you at five." He hung up.

"Ready on the set," came a calm Texas voice through the door.

Till noon the work was hard and mercifully needed the maximum of concentration, endless rehearsals that called for meticulous timing and the cooperation of two spaniels and three small children. The "child-actor mothers" were the usual mean-faced, grasping, jealous dragons, and the dog handler smelled of bourbon.

"Coattails," the producer, put in a brief appearance. He was full of concern.

"Missie, darling, I couldn't come before—I had a budget meeting—but they called to say you were not feeling well. Are you better now? . . . The studio doctor should see you during the lunch break—for the insurance, you know. . . ."

Missie reassured him he would not fall behind by a minute on his precious schedule because of her, but the thoroughness of the studio spy system irked her.

Just before the one o'clock lunch break, Coattails' uncle, the head of the studio, paid one of his infrequent visits to the set. At the very sight of him, surrounded by his henchmen, the whole tempo of work quickened.

The young director, who had been leaving the intricacies of coping with the dog and the children to the experienced Mac, immediately assumed full and ostentatious command, and everyone was scurrying about, reeking of efficiency. The grapevine had alerted Frankie, and he arrived in time to fiddle unnecessarily with Missie's curls.

"The Big Wheel" came over, tall and immaculate in a light-gray suit. His high-domed forehead was brown, blotched with bright pink patches where his beloved desert sun had peeled off one layer of skin and been too quickly allowed to burn its tender replacement—the pink patches were permanent. His wife, who baked herself for hours every day at Palm Springs, had achieved the complexion of a heavily worked Western saddle.

He smiled at Missie through rimless spectacles, but the smile only displayed his perfectly capped teeth—it did not extend to his eyes. He put his arm around her.

"And how's our little girl today?" he asked . . . not pausing for an answer. "Everyone tells me the picture looks real great . . . and you're giving a *great* performance . . . wish I had time to see all the dailies, but with fourteen pictures in production right now—you're the least of my worries—you got any problems, darling?"

Missie maneuvered him out of range of the flapping elephant ears of his entourage.

"Joe's a great cameraman, I know, but he uses so much *light* . . . I look like a death's head!"

"Damn right he's a great cameraman," said the studio head through a quickly diminished smile. "Tracy and Bogart fall over themselves to get him."

"But I don't want to look like Tracy or Bogart," wailed Missie. "I want to look like *me*. Couldn't he at least put a gauze over my key light?"

He patted her shoulder. "I'll have a word about it," he promised soothingly. "Leave it with me." He started away but turned back. "Oh, by the way, darling, I've sent for that agent of yours. He'll be in this afternoon . . . I want to have a little chat with him about our little girl's future . . . be good, darling, we all love you."

He shook a few hands on the set, listened to a few reports, checked the script girl's work sheet, and was gone.

Pat, the secretary, arrived just before the lunch break. She waited while Missie was released from the purgatory of her dress and then accompanied her in Alvin's limousine. Missie gazed absently out of the window as they threaded their way through the crowd headed for the commissaries, some seated in little gaily colored, awning-topped trolleys, but most on foot, and workmen carrying their lunch pails and radios headed for quiet corners behind buildings or for the vast acreage of the back lot. A multitude of extras in the varied costumes of fourteen different productions, the snooty dress extras in their white ties and tails with Kleenex stuffed inside their high collars for protection against makeup, and the girls with tissues in the tops of their dresses guarding the fabric from underarm stain. Glamor! thought Missie. The writers were headed for the writers' table in the private dining room, the directors would be huddled together at theirs, and the producers would be far removed in another enclave—all preferring the company of their peers in a rigidly class-conscious society. The stars in their allotted limousines were rolling toward their bungalows, and a few free souls were bustling off the lot for drinks and a snack across the street.

In her bungalow, while Vergis and Pat busied themselves in the kitchen, Missie spoke to Sharon, who had a free afternoon. The young clear voice cheered her.

"Mom, I'm going over to Virginia's for lunch and maybe stay till supper . . . a lot of the kids'll be there . . . we're going to play tennis and roller skate and stuff. . . . Work hard! Try and come home early so I can see you! . . . Bye now." She hung up with the single-mindedness of youth.

Missie dialed again and spoke to her cook.

"No, he's gone golfin'—went around eleven, I guess—Lakeside, I think he said."

She called the club, something she had never done before. Did she imagine an evasiveness about the secretary's voice at the other end?

"I got here late today, he's probably halfway around the course by now . . . I'll tell him you called when he gets in."

Missie picked dispiritedly at her low-calorie cottage cheese and pineapple while Pat sought to extract some decisions from her about Christmas.

"I reckon that including the staff at the house, the crew on the picture, and the usual studio list, you'll have to come up with around a hundred and thirty gifts," she said. "I'm mailing four hundred cards today and about a hundred telegrams on Christmas Eve. The stores stay open late starting next week. You'll want to pick up stuff yourself, won't you, for people like Manny and Louella and Hedda and, of course, family. . . . And don't forget Dan. . . ."

"No, don't forget *him* whatever happens," said a hearty voice from the doorway.

Missie jumped out of her chair and rushed to a large comfortable red-faced man in a loud sports jacket who was taking off a raincoat and removing from his head a homburg enveloped in a plastic covering.

"Radio said rain later on," he explained.

"Dan, darling," cried Missie, "do you want some food?"

"No, thanks, honey . . . I was on the lot, so I just dropped by to say hello. I'll take on a little scotch, though, if you have some."

"I'll fix it," said Pat. She liked Missie's business manager—he seemed honest and straightforward.

"Well, Dan, am I broke as usual?" Missie laughed. She was relieved to have something to wrench her mind away from Lakeside.

"Not quite, darling," said Dan. "But I'm afraid we've had a little setback: The government's come after you for sixty thousand bucks in back taxes from four years ago—they've turned down a claim for exemptions over the divorce settlement."

"Jesus," said Missie, "have we got it?"

"We can find it, honey," said Dan cautiously, "but we have to watch all the outlays next year . . . no big entertaining, no gambling on oil wells . . . no—"

"But all that's deductible, isn't it?" asked Missie. ". . . From taxes, I mean?"

"Honey," explained Dan gently, "lots of things are deductible— the ten percent of your earnings you pay to Manny, the five percent to me, Pat's salary, your lawyer's fees, your business gifts, clothes, publicity, entertaining—all sorts of things are deductible from tax, but you have to *pay* tax before you can deduct from it, and you don't pay tax unless you have an *income* . . . and actresses who don't work don't have incomes . . . and your contract comes up for renewal any day now . . . so, like I said, we have to watch it."

Missie spoke slowly. "They're . . . not going . . . to drop me, are they? . . . I mean, I've been here on this lot for more than twelve years."

"You've plenty more years ahead of you yet, darling," said Dan soothingly. "If not here, then someplace else, but the studios are all cutting their overheads, and your option calls for three years straight at a big raise. . . . Let's pray they pick it up." He drained his glass and made his good-byes. "Don't worry, honey," he said. "Just keep the positive thoughts."

The phone rang. Missie picked it up eagerly.

"Just checking," said a calm Texas voice. "We'll be ready to go right on the dot of two o'clock."

"Thanks, Chuck," she answered dully. "I'll be there."

As she got into Alvin's Cadillac, she said to her secretary, "Finish your lunch in peace, Pat, dear, and before you go, call the caddie shop at Lakeside and ask the pro what time he reckons 'He' will be finished . . . don't make a big thing of it."

The afternoon's work progressed normally, but it became increasingly oppressive on Stage 23 as the big sun arcs ate up the oxygen. Missie began to feel listless and edgy, and all the time, as though a door had been left open somewhere, there was a draft in her heart.

At last Pat reappeared, and Missie hurried across to her at the earliest moment.

"The pro says he hasn't been at the club all day," said the secretary.

"I see," said Missie in a small voice.

The head of publicity materialized in the offstage gloom. "The boys are all set, darling . . . over by the big doors . . . it won't take but a moment." She followed him and spent the next half hour surrounded by forty grinning behemoths, gracefully accepting heavy-handed compliments, signing autographs, filling in silences by asking, "And where are *you* from?" and praying that nobody would answer, "From Phoenix, Arizona, ma'am—*your* hometown."

"We're all ready for you," came a welcome Texas voice. "The director would like to rehearse the barn dance sequence . . . the dancers are all in position."

By late afternoon Missie was drained, mentally and physically, but there was still an hour and a half to go before the witching hour. "Thank God for Manny," she thought. "At least he got me the six o'clock clause . . . they can't ask me to work after that. *Manny!* Oh, my God! I'd forgotten all about *him*."

In a wave of near panic and with her mind feathering in different directions like a foxhound, she took a course of action she had never before taken—she called Frankie in the hairdressing department.

"I need your help, Frankie. I don't think I can get through the day I'm so exhausted. . . . Can you give me one of those little pills of yours to help me keep going?"

"Sure thing, darling," came the answer. "Mother will be right over, and I'll bring a spare for emergencies."

Whatever it was, the drug took almost instant effect. Missie soon felt clearheaded but slightly detached, and by five thirty when Manny arrived she was in a brightly gay mood.

Her agent was one of the most powerful in Hollywood, not physically—he was a little man despite his lifts, but he had muscle. He wore no spectacles, but there was a sheet of frosted glass between his eyeballs and his brain, and his face incompetently lifted, instead of youthfulness, gave an impression of drawn, lineless age. He invariably wore dark suits and tight white collars.

Manny had muscle in Hollywood because he handled some of the most illustrious names in the business, and he kept his stable valuable by poaching promising beginners from small agencies and pushing them into important pictures on the backs of his sought-after stars. As soon as he had concluded his business with Missie, he would be on his way to meet a young actor whose performance had caught his eye at a sneak preview in San Diego the night before.

Back in the bungalow, Manny waited while Missie made one more abortive call to her home; then he wasted no time.

"I've just come from talking to the Big Wheel," he said. "The studio is exercising its option—three years straight and the raise."

"Great! Wonderful! Yippee!" yelled Missie, jumping up and kissing him.

Manny held up a hand. "Not all *that* wonderful, darling," he said. "Your first picture under the new deal will be *The Green Shoot*."

Missie burst out laughing. "Is he out of his mind or something? I may get away with twenty-four or -five, but I'd still be ten years too old for *that* part . . . the kid's *fourteen*, for God's sake!"

"Twelve," corrected Manny. "But that's not the part. They want you for the mother."

Missie felt an icy hand clench itself around her intestines.

"I think I'm going to throw up," she said.

355

"She's a very young mother," said Manny, flicking a dead eye in her direction, "thirty-one, to be exact, so it wouldn't mean graying up or anything like that . . . and it's one hell of a script."

"Maybe," retorted Missie, "but it's not one hell of a *part* . . . everyone in town's turned it down . . . it's the kid's picture . . . it *has* to be."

"There's another thing. The Big Wheel thought," said Manny softly, "he thought it would be just great publicity-wise and in every other way if Sharon played the kid."

"I *am* going to throw up," said Missie. "Over my dead body will Sharon ever become a child actress—I know what it's like."

"The Big Wheel just put it out as an idea—that's all," said Manny. "He also said that he's worried because your fan mail has been falling off lately, and he mentioned that if it hadn't been for the pressure the studio was able to put on that Santa Monica judge, the more, er, spectacular parts of your divorce would have been on every front page."

"Oh God, Manny," Missie groaned. "What should I do? Help me . . . *please.*"

Manny had expected a longer struggle. He was relieved that it was over so quickly and that his 10 percent commission was safe for another three years.

"My advice, darling, is to grab it. That'll only be one picture . . . there'll be plenty more . . . this lot is where you belong . . . you're 'their little girl,' remember? . . . So *The Green Shoot* may turn out to be the kid's picture, but what the hell! You're still young and still beautiful . . . it's not over yet by a long shot. . . . I'll call 'em tomorrow and tell 'em they have a deal. . . . Be good now . . . stay happy." He left.

The phone rang, and Vergis answered.

"That was Chuck, Miss Missie, dailies in five minutes, projection room twenty-four . . . Alvin's outside."

"Give me a big drink," said Missie. "I'll take it with me. . . . Back in an hour. . . . Be an angel and wash my hair at home for me, so I can fall into bed . . . I'll get Alvin to take you downtown."

"Sure thing," said Vergis, "no trouble at all . . . be glad to."

The dailies were drawn out by the inevitable postmortem, and it was eight thirty before Missie and Vergis drove out of the studio gate.

The young Texan was on hand to say good-night and give the call for the morrow.

"Usual time," he said cheerfully, "five thirty makeup, and it's your big address to the miners."

Back at the house "He" was waiting. He looked very handsome with his curly black hair, white teeth, and blue eyes blazing out of a sunburned face. Her heart lifted when she saw him, but it immediately sank back again when she realized he was dressed for going out to dinner.

He hugged her and told her she looked great but that she ought to get the show on the road because they were late already.

Whether he had forgotten to tell her about the dinner or whether she had forgotten what he had said was of no importance. Hedda's words had been eating into her all day. "He's already cheating on you." She *had* to go with him.

"Give me half an hour," said Missie. "I must see Sharon and take a bath . . . call them up and explain . . . I'll be as quick as I can. . . . Vergis, you go on home with Alvin, honey. I'll come in half an hour early tomorrow, so we can wash my hair before makeup."

"OK . . . 'night, Miss Missie, see you tomorrow."

A few minutes with a sleepy Sharon, a quick bath and change of makeup and a hurried selection of clothes left Missie in a second trough of exhaustion.

In a reckless gambling mood, she swallowed the reserve pill which Frankie had given her for "emergencies" and ran downstairs. "He" was waiting impatiently at the wheel of her convertible.

As he drove, she once again began to feel lifted far above her petty problems. She gazed down from Olympian heights on the scene of her jealousy and listened in a floating, gliding way to her own voice as she calmly asked the opening question. "How was the golf?"

"Great." He laughed. "I was really hitting it good today . . . made a little dough!"

"Many people at Lakeside?"

He paused for a beat. "I guess so," he said.

"This is the moment of truth," thought Missie. "It doesn't hurt much after all." Very deliberately she said, "I called the club a couple of times, but they couldn't locate you."

357

"Perhaps time is elongated by drugs," she thought. She had heard it sometimes was, but it still seemed an eternity before he answered in an offhand way.

"Pity you didn't call Hillcrest. We decided to play there instead."

The party was a buffet-style affair for about forty people. Missie, the only well-known Hollywood face, was instantly the center of attraction. The rest were the Bel Air Bay Club group with a sprinkling of Easterners out for the winter—all ideal prospects for "His" real estate promotions—and Missie, sipping champagne, watched with a distant fascination as he moved effortlessly from one group to another. Hers were not the only female eyes that followed him, she noted with a mixture of pride and apprehension.

The pill and the champagne kept Missie "up" like a Ping-Pong ball on a water jet, but in the back of her mind the dictatorial voice of studio discipline was ordering her "Go to bed . . . go to bed."

Around eleven o'clock she whispered to him that she must leave. He reacted like a spoiled child interrupted in mid-angel-food cake.

"We've only been here an hour and a half, for God's sake! . . . There's a whole raft of people I want to talk to."

"*Please,*" she begged. "I've got to get some sleep. . . . I have a really tough day tomorrow."

"Oh, OK." He pouted. "Let's go then."

Missie said her good-byes and found her wrap. "He" kept her waiting in the doorway while he lingered. Particularly drawn out, she noticed with a little stab of worry, was his farewell performance for the benefit of a tall, sultry beauty from Philadelphia.

During the drive back to her house Missie snuggled against his shoulder, but there was no response, and she could feel his frustration.

"You go on back, darling, if you want to," she said.

"No . . . it's OK," he said shortly.

Missie longed to be enveloped in her soft sheets, to lie back and wallow in oblivion. She also longed to feel his warm body beside hers, but that stern studio voice was insistent: "Get some sleep! Get some sleep!"

There was an awkward and inconclusive embrace between them in the hallway, and Missie turned to go upstairs.

"I'll be up in a little while," he murmured, moving toward the drink tray.

In her room the sight of the turned-down double bed and shaded light overwhelmed her with fatigue. She glanced at the bedside clock—it was almost midnight. Automatically, she set the alarm for 4 A.M., then remembered about her hair and changed it to 3:30. She took off her clothes and climbed into bed, too tired to remove her makeup or to switch off the bedside light. For a while she lay there, waiting for the sounds of mounting footsteps; then in her mind she saw, like an illuminated scroll, the long, long speech she would have to deliver the next day before hundreds of "miners." She turned her head from side to side to try to erase the words; they would not go away. She tried to relax for sleep and at last reached out her hand for the pills which "Needle Ned" had prescribed.

"I'd better take two," she said to herself, "to knock down those damn things Frankie gave me," and as she swallowed them, she put a third—"in reserve"—beside the water glass. Then she switched off the light.

Dimly, she heard the handle of her bedroom door turn, but she was sinking down into a deep black pit. Faintly she heard the door click, and then an eternity afterward, far, far away, she heard the self-starter of a car and in the dim distance the sounds of its wheels crunching the gravel as it disappeared down her driveway.

Manny had been well pleased with the speedy conclusion of his business with Missie.

"Lucey's," he said to his chauffeur.

When he entered the small grottolike restaurant opposite Paramount Studios, it took a few seconds for his eyes to become accustomed to the gloom.

The dim lighting was not accidental. Lucey's was the favorite rendezvous of the starlets and young actors from the nearby studios, the Italian food was inexpensive, the steaks were good, and the kidneys grilled in their own natural cradle of fat were delicious.

While he waited for the young actor, he asked the waiter to bring him the daily trades. He sat back and perused the castings, assignments, the hirings and firings and the comings and goings announced in the *Hollywood Reporter* and *Daily Variety* and made a few entries in his notebook.

The young actor sent a message to say they were working a little late but that he would be over in fifteen minutes.

"He won't be that considerate once he hits the big time," thought Manny grimly.

The restaurant was filling up, and the discreet little alcoves around the main floor became nests of opportunity; at the exposed tables in the center, out-of-towners sat, taking their time over long drinks and trying to spot celebrities in the smoke-filled gloom. Manny glanced idly at them, and his attention was caught by a young girl sitting quietly with an older woman. As a flesh peddler he was normally as resistant to the lure of it as an attendant in the Louvre is to the "Mona Lisa," but there was something haunting about this girl's unaffected beauty and her almond-shaped gray eyes.

His perusal of the girl was ended by the young actor who arrived precipitately, very conscious of the fact that he was being seen in the company of such a powerful agent. With his customary dispatch, Manny got down to business. "Would you like me to handle your career?" he asked.

"*Would* I?" the young man yelled. "I can't *believe* it!"

When he had calmed down, he began to worry about his present agent. "He's been so good to me . . . lent me dough when I was broke . . . he's my friend."

Manny listened dispassionately; he'd heard it all before.

The boy's scruples quickly evaporated as he contemplated his good fortune. He sat in the alcove shiny-eyed with excitement.

Manny rose to leave. He could chalk up a successful day and he wanted his dinner, but his departure was delayed by the arrival of the middle-aged woman from the center of the room. She addressed the young man. Behind her stood the beautiful teenager who had momentarily aroused Manny's interest.

"We're from San Diego," said the woman, "my daughter and I, we came up for the day to do a bus tour of the studios . . . it's a big racket really, we never got to speak to any of the stars, they're always roped off . . . Caroline here was real disappointed . . . she's movie-struck, you see . . . well, now we've seen *you*, our day has been *made!*"

"Me?" said the young actor in surprise.

"Oh, yes," chimed in the girl, her face glowing. "Mom and me went to see a musical last night, and instead they showed a sneak preview of your picture—you know, to test the audience reaction and that—and after, they gave us cards to fill in saying what we thought about it, and we thought you were *wonderful*, didn't we, Mom?"

"Yes, just *wonderful*," said the mother, "and we loved the picture, too . . . we filled in the cards like that."

Manny stood quietly watching the young girl; he knew now why her looks had intrigued him. The young man was flushed with pleasure and preening himself before her excited eyes.

"Well . . . gee! Thanks!" he said, and stuck out his hand.

"Good-bye . . . congratulations, young fella," said Manny at the door of Lucey's. "We'll be seeing a lot of each other from here on."

He watched the young actor walking on air toward the parking lot; then, after a moment of decision, he turned back into the restaurant and invited himself to sit with the woman from San Diego and her daughter.

"Does Caroline want to become a film actress?" he asked.

"She dreams of nothing else, day and night," said the mother.

"Bring her to see me tomorrow at eleven o'clock," said Manny, handing her a business card. "You can check up on me any way you like before then . . . I can arrange for Caroline to make a test for *The Green Shoot* . . . it's the best part ever written for a young girl. If she does it, she'll steal the picture from the star."

4
Hedda and Louella

HOLLYWOOD invented a macabre party game called Airplane. This concerned a sizable transport which, owing to some mechanical defect, was destined to take off and never again to land, its crew and passengers doomed to fly around and around forever. The game consisted of providing tickets for those the players felt they could well do without. Hedda Hopper and Louella Parsons, unassailably the two most powerful gossip columnists in the world, had no difficulty whatever in finding space and, a refinement of torture, were usually allotted seats next to each other.

Compared to Lucretia Borgia, Lady Macbeth and others, Louella and Hedda played only among the reserves, but with their 75,000,000 readers all over the world, they wielded and frequently misused enormous power. Only Hollywood could have spawned such a couple, and only Hollywood, headline-hunting, self-inflating, riddled with fear and insecurity, could have allowed itself to be dominated by them for so long.

The reader must try to visualize that at every Hollywood breakfast table or office desk the day started with an avid perusal of the columns of Louella Parsons and Hedda Hopper. The fact that many had paid their press agents large sums of money to make up lies and exaggerations and then plant these items with Louella and Hedda detracted nothing from the pleasure they got from seeing this nonsense in the morning papers—they even believed it when they saw it.

A large part of their columns was pure fabrication, as I can witness. At one point Lord Beaverbrook asked me to cable a Hollywood page twice a month to the Sunday *Express*. My first article was on Clark Gable, and my second about Gary Cooper, but I soon realized that I could not wear two hats—I could not keep friends and at the same time disclose their innermost workings to several million readers—so I asked for and was given my release from the arrangement. However, before I could deliver the first article, I had perforce to become an accredited card-carrying member of the foreign press in Los Angeles.

At that time 500 journalists were encamped around Hollywood, covering the goings-on in the movie capital. My name was added to the mailing list, and every day thereafter bundles of gibberish arrived at my home, churned out by the public relations officers of studios, including, to my great delight, pages of complete fantasy about myself which had been dispatched by the Samuel Goldwyn Studios, to which I was under contract.

It took guts and ability for Hedda and Louella to rise to the top of this inkstained pile of professional reporters, and it took tremendous stamina and craftiness on their part to remain there for a quarter of a century.

Louella, short, dumpy, and dowdy, with large brown eyes and a carefully cultivated vagueness of smile and manner, was a Catholic, married three times, first to a real estate man, secondly to a river boat captain, and thirdly to a doctor who specialized in venereal diseases. From the earliest days she had been a newspaperwoman and during her Hollywood reign was one of the star reporters of the W. R. Hearst publishing empire. Her flagship was the Los Angeles *Examiner*.

Hedda, who came on the scene later, was tall, thin, and elegant, with large blue eyes and a brisk, staccato way of demanding replies rather than asking questions. Of Quaker stock, she had been married only once to a four-times-divorced stage actor twenty-seven years her senior, whom she herself had divorced when she caught him cheating on her at the age of sixty-three. An ex-chorus girl, she graduated to small parts on Broadway and in films and was a washed-up middle-aged Hollywood character actress when she took to journalism as a last resort. Her flagship was the other local morning paper, the Los Angeles *Times*.

They were an unlikely couple, but they had one thing in common—they loathed each other.

Hollywood folklore insisted that Louella held her job with W. R. Hearst because she knew literally where the body was buried. In 1924 Hearst had organized a trip aboard his yacht *Oneida*. Among others on board were Louella and the producer Thomas Ince. Far out in the Pacific, so the story went, Hearst entered the cabin of his mistress, Marion Davies, and found her thrashing around naked beneath a similarly unclothed Ince. An altercation followed, during which Hearst shot Ince. He then carried the body on deck and dumped it over the side. Louella, who was dozing unseen in a deck chair, was supposed to have heard the splash and reached the rail just in time to see the dead producer bobbing past, and Hearst was supposed to have told Louella to keep her mouth shut, in exchange for which she was promised a job for life.

The two major flaws in that story were, first, that Ince left the yacht in San Diego suffering from indigestion and took the train to Los Angeles, where he died two days later of a heart attack, and secondly, that Louella Parsons was never a member of the yachting party. The truth of her beginnings with Hearst was that she was a very good reporter who appreciated the excitement that was being generated by the infant film industry and Hearst knew a good reporter when he saw one.

Hedda's emergence as a newspaperwoman came some ten years after the beginning of Louella's reign as the undisputed queen of the Hollywood scene. In 1935 Hedda was in trouble. She was fifty years old and a very bad actress. She was a striking-looking woman, however, who spent every cent on her clothes, sparkling company too, always equipped with the latest juicy pieces of information, but she was hardly ever offered a part in films. She somehow kept going, doing anything that came along, including modeling middle-aged fashions and a stint with Elizabeth Arden, and on the proceeds she managed to give her son a good education and to run an attractive little house near the Farmer's Market. She had some staunch friends, among them the beautiful and talented writer Frances Marion, who took her along with her on trips to Europe. On one of these she picked up a bogus English accent, complete with the broadest A in the business. On her return she informed me that London was "ARBSOLUTELY FARNTARSTIC."

Another champion of hers at that time was Louella Parsons, who frequently mentioned her activities in her column and introduced her to W. R. Hearst and Marion Davies. It was at the Hearst ranch at San Simeon that a fellow guest, Mrs. Eleanor Paterson, the publisher of the Washington *Times-Herald*, became so captivated by Hedda's brittle and spicy observations about Hollywood that she invited her to write a weekly newsletter, and Hedda's first step toward becoming Louella's archrival was taken.

Once it was available for syndication, the number of newspapers subscribing to Hedda's column was far from spectacular until lightning struck in 1937—she was bought by the Los Angeles *Times*. Now she was read by everybody in the motion-picture industry, and overnight sources of information were opened to her that had remained firmly closed when her output was only being glanced at in remote corners of the country. As news and gossip flooded in on Hedda from hundreds of press agents and private individuals, her column received a blood transfusion and improved immeasurably. Within a very short time it was syndicated in as many newspapers all over the world as that of an increasingly resentful Louella Parsons.

The arrival on the Hollywood scene of a second queen who had to be pandered to, pacified, or prodded posed some very tricky questions for the publicity-hungry citizens. How to plant a story with one while still keeping the amiability of the other? How to arrange a private showing of a new film for one without offending the other? And above all, how to give the story of an impending marriage or divorce to one without incurring the implacable wrath of the other? It seems incredible, but in a town with a herd instinct and a concentration of insecurity, it needed only one of these ladies to hint that an actor or actress was "box-office poison" for contracts to be terminated and studio doors to be slammed. Discretion was, indeed, the better part of valor, and the great majority of us played a humiliating game of subterfuge and flattery, having long since decided that it was far less troublesome to have them with us than against us. If they were susceptible to flattery, they were also very astute, and it was fatal to try to get by with an untruth—for that there was no forgiveness.

They could help careers, and they could hinder careers, and they could make private lives hell, but if there was talent, they could not stop people from getting to the top, and, as Hedda knew from experience, if there was no talent, they could not manufacture it.

Hedda should have been the easier to deal with. Having been so long a frustrated actress herself, she understood, but she was unpredictable and ruthless in her championship of causes and in her attacks. With her private list of "pinkos," she made Senator McCarthy sound like a choirboy.

Louella was a much softer touch, easily humored by a bunch of roses, but also erratic because she was apt to listen to the last voice before her deadline, and many of her scoops were a long way off target as a result. On one occasion she announced that Sigmund Freud, "one of the greatest psychoanalysts alive," was being brought over from Europe by director Edmund Goulding as the technical adviser on Bette Davis' picture *Dark Victory*. This posed a difficult logistical problem because Freud had been dead for several months.

When conducting interviews for her big Sunday full-page story, Louella, in her comfortable house on Maple Drive, invariably set the oldest of tongue-loosening traps—she plied her subject with glasses the size of umbrella stands, filled to the brim with whiskey or gin—but often she trapped herself by keeping the subject company and her notes became illegible.

Hedda used the same technique and plied her subjects with booze, but she shrewdly sipped tonic water herself. She always swore that her short marriage was the only sexual foray of her life; she certainly had a long procession of admirers, but she stoutly maintained that she had preserved her near virginity against overwhelming odds, and probably because of this puritan outlook, she attacked ferociously those she suspected of any extracurricular activities. She infuriated Joseph Cotten and greatly disturbed his wife, Lenore, when she printed heavy hints that Joe had been caught by the Malibu Beach patrol in the back seat of his car bestride the teenage Deanna Durbin. Joe Cotten, the epitome of the Southern gentleman from Virginia, warned Hedda that if she added one more line on the subject, he would "kick her up the ass"! Sure enough Hedda went into action again a few days later, and the next time Cotten saw Hedda's behind entering a smart Hollywood party, he lined up on the target and let her have it.

In spite of this lesson, she became a little power-mad and soon after the war laid herself wide open to lawsuits when she wrote a book, *The Whole Truth and Nothing But*. In it she wrote that she had summoned Elizabeth Taylor to her house and tried to dissuade her from marrying Michael Wilding because not only was he too old for her but he had also long indulged in homosexual relations with Stewart Granger. She had some qualms about printing this passage, however, and one Sunday afternoon she called me and asked me to come see her urgently.

Her address had changed with her fortunes. She had left the Farmer's Market neighborhood and was now settled in a charming white house on Tropical Avenue in Beverly Hills—"The House that Fear Built" she called it. As usual, I was given a hefty gin while Hedda toyed with tonic. Then she came to the point.

"Isn't it true," she asked, "that Michael Wilding was kicked out of the British navy during the war because he was a homosexual?"

When I had recovered from the shock of this nonsense, I told her of Michael's gallant record and explained the true meaning of being "invalided" out of the service.

"Well"—she sniffed—"I know that he and Granger once had a yacht together in the south of France, and I know what went on aboard that yacht."

"So do I," I answered, "and it's a miracle that the population of France didn't double."

She let out her great hoot of laughter and then read me the passage she had written.

I told her I thought she was mad to print it and was bound to get sued if she did, but she said that the publishers wanted her to spice up the book and be more controversial. "They won't sue me," she said airily, "it would only make it worse for them to drag it into court—they'll be sore for a while; then they'll forget it."

In any event, Hedda and her publisher were sued for $3,000,000 and had to cough up a hefty settlement and an abject apology.

The two ladies were made of very durable material. Producing an interesting column every day and a feature story on Sunday entailed an immense amount of hard work and very long hours. True they employed legmen and legwomen, who scurried about on their behalf digging for gossip, but all the openings and major social events they attended themselves. They also manned the telephones for hours each day, sifting pieces of information and tracking down stories. Each nurtured an army of part-time informants who worked in restaurants, agents' offices, beauty parlors, brothels, studios, and hospitals, and no picture started shooting without its complement of potential spies eager to remain in the good books of Hedda and Louella.

Neither of them was above a little gentle blackmail through the suppression technique. People dreaded an imperious telephone message—"Call Miss Parsons/Hopper—urgent"—but it was better to comply because at least there was a chance to stop something untrue or damaging from being printed; if the call went unanswered, the story was printed without further ado.

COLUMNIST: Who was that girl you were nuzzling in that little bar in the San Fernando Valley at three o'clock this morning?

ACTOR: I was with my mother.

COLUMNIST: You were *not* with your mother, you were with Gertie Garterbelt. I suppose she told her husband you were both working late?

ACTOR: Well, we were—we just dropped in for a nightcap on the way home.

COLUMNIST: According to my information, you had one of her bosoms in your hand.

ACTOR: It fell out of her dress. . . . I was just helping her put it back in.

COLUMNIST: Rubbish! . . . But I won't print because I don't want to make trouble for you.

ACTOR: Bless you—you're a doll.

COLUMNIST: Got any news for me?

ACTOR: Afraid I haven't right now.

COLUMNIST: Call me when you hear anything, dear.

ACTOR: (wiping brow): You bet I will.

And he would, too.

Both had their favorites, and these were the happy recipients of glowing praise for their good looks, talent, kindness, and cooking, but when they fell from grace, retribution was horrible—and millions were informed that they could do nothing right. Sometimes, however, because of the good ladies' antipathy one toward the other, pedestals broken by one would be pieced together by the other, and life for the fallen idol would go on much as it had before.

Jealousy might have been the reason Hedda failed to appreciate great creative talent, but Louella had no excuse for joining her in scoffing openly at such giants as Garbo, Hepburn, Olivier, and Brando, and out of the ranks of the supertalented, each chose a target for real venom. For Louella it was Orson Welles; for Hedda— Charlie Chaplin.

When she discovered that *Citizen Kane* was modeled on her boss, W. R. Hearst, and Marion Davies, Louella screamed in print like a wounded peahen and flailed away at Welles on every occasion, accusing him of avoiding war service, stealing Rita Hayworth away from brave Victor Mature (who was in the Coast Guard), and dodging taxes by moving to Europe. She pilloried RKO Pictures, which had financed the film, and, backed by the power of the Hearst press, campaigned so effectively to have the picture destroyed before it was shown to the public that the heads of the industry got together and offered RKO $3,000,000 for the negative. Fortunately, the offer was spurned, and a movie milestone was preserved, but Welles was only infrequently invited to display his talent in Hollywood thereafter.

Hedda's stream of bile played for years upon Chaplin. She hounded him in print because of his avowedly liberal politics and for the fact that after making a fortune in the United States, he was still, forty years later, a British subject, and, having been herself married to a man twenty-seven years her senior, for some reason she nearly went up in flames when she heard that Eugene O'Neill's eighteen-year-old daughter, Oona, was planning to marry Chaplin, who was thirty-six years off the pace. When she published a string of stern warnings and dire prognostications, harping always on Chaplin's suspected preference for young girls, Chaplin ignored Hedda completely and went ahead with his wedding plans.

One day a weeping pregnant girl appeared on Hedda's doorstep and announced that she was the bearer of startling news— Chaplin's child.

According to Joan Barry, she had been engaged by Chaplin to play in a film with him. She had been seduced by him, and when she became pregnant, Chaplin canceled the film and had her arrested on a vagrancy charge, for which she had received a suspended sentence.

Hedda reacted like a firehorse. She took the girl to a hospital and had her examined. She was indeed pregnant. Then she dispatched her posthaste to Chaplin's home on Summit Drive to tell him that "Hedda Hopper knows everything." Chaplin's answer to that was to call the Beverly Hills police, who arrested Joan Barry and put her in jail for three weeks.

Thanks to the publicity, however, Chaplin was now involved in a paternity suit, and Hedda crowed when his marriage was postponed. She may have stopped crowing when blood tests proved that Chaplin could not have been the baby's father, but she bypassed this in her writings and concentrated instead on the fact that Joan Barry had been awarded child support. Chaplin rose above the whole episode, however, gave no indication that he even knew of Hedda's existence, and made the announcement of the new date of his marriage—in Louella's column.

If our heroines were long on self-importance, they were also the possessors of very short fuses when it came to having their legs pulled. Thanks to the aforementioned carefully cultivated informers, stars heading for an illicit love affair ran the risk of reading about it before they had undone the first button, and happily married couples having a difference of opinion about the number of shots taken on the eleventh green at the country club could read the next morning about their impending divorce.

Ida Lupino and Howard Duff had been happily married for several years; so had Hjördis and I, but for some reason both couples had lately been subjected to a spate of printed rumors, so we decided to have a little fun with Hedda and Louella. We chose as the battleground Ciro's, the "hot" restaurant of the moment and one of the most spy-infiltrated, and after dinner at Ida's home, I called the headwaiter.

D.N.:   Could you keep a table for me around midnight?

HW: Oh, yes, indeed, Mr. Niven—it'll be a pleasure— on the dance floor . . . and for how many?

D.N.:   (in conspiratorial tones): No . . . not on the dance floor . . . in a dark corner . . . just for two—*you* understand.

HW: Oh! Yes, indeed, sir, just you and madam . . . leave everything to me.

Around midnight I arrived with Ida Lupino on my arm, and the headwaiter's eyebrows shot up into his hairline. Vibrating with suppressed excitement, he led us to a dark corner at the far end of the room and stood with eyes glistening as Ida started nibbling my ear.

Somebody wasted no time in getting to the phone because by the time Ida and I had finished our second drink a battery of photographers was massing in the bar.

Howard and Hjördis timed their arrival perfectly, and the entire restaurant watched spellbound as a jittery headwaiter led them to a table as far away as possible from Ida and myself.

They made a lovely couple, and out of the corner of my eye, I could see Howard draping himself over Hjördis like a tent.

Howard had quite a reputation as a brawler, and as I was pretending to be quite high, there was an expectant hush when Howard, judging his moment with great expertise, suddenly pushed his table over with a crash and rose to his feet, pointing at me across the room with a dramatically accusing finger.

Hjördis tried to restrain her partner, as did Ida when I staggered to my feet, though I thought Ida overacted a bit by screaming, "No, no! Darling! You must flee! . . . He'll kill you!"

Shrugging off the ineffectual clutching hands of women and waiters, Howard and I advanced upon each other from opposite sides of the restaurant. The place was deathly quiet, and the photographers, headed by the veteran Hymie Fink, moved expectantly into position for the scoop when like two cowboys in the classic ending of Westerns, stalking each other down the empty street at sunset, we moved inexorably forward through the crowded and silent tables. At the edge of the now-deserted dance floor, with eyes immovably locked, we removed our jackets and rolled up our sleeves. Then we advanced again and circled each other a couple of times. You could have heard a pin drop; people at the back were standing on chairs. Suddenly, we sprang, grabbed each other around the waist, kissed on the lips, and waltzed slowly around the floor. A disappointed headwaiter set up a new table for four, and the ensuing revelry was recorded by the more sporting among the photographers, but the two queens of the columns were not amused. . . . I got calls from both the next day telling me that they would not tolerate being woken up in the middle of the night over a false alarm.

Louella and Hedda were not averse to a little "payola." Louella had earlier conned important stars into appearing on her radio show, *Hollywood Hotel*. Hedda had been less successful with her program, *Hedda Hopper's Hollywood*, but later made a successful transition with it to television, where she "persuaded" the biggest names in movieland to appear with her. This program stole a lot of viewers away from the Great Stoneface (Ed Sullivan), appearing at the same time on a rival network, and Sullivan complained bitterly that he was paying full salary to the performers on his show whereas Hedda was paying nothing to the lineup she had announced for hers—Gary Cooper, Judy Garland, Joan Crawford, Bette Davis, Lucille Ball, and Charlton Heston.

Some of Louella's payoffs were subtle: She persuaded Twentieth Century-Fox to buy the film rights to her unfilmable autobiography and made it quite clear to producers that whenever her husband, Dr. Harry Martin, was hired as "technical adviser" on their films, they would not lack for publicity.

Being a "clap" doctor, "Dockie" Martin was a very useful member of the community. Venereal disease increases in direct proportion to promiscuous fornication, so with Hollywood not being famous for the chastity of its citizens, it was inevitable that through the good doctor's waiting room passed some of the most famous private parts in the world. Many sufferers who had survived Dockie's extremely painful pre-penicillin treatments were understandably worried, in view of his marital setup, that news of their misfortunes might leak to the press, but the doctor in his bedchamber or in his cups stoutly stood by his Hippocratic oath.

Dockie, who resembled a gone-to-seed middleweight, was a heavy drinker, and people with uncomfortable appointments ahead of them on the morrow watched apprehensively as he consumed huge quantities of alcohol on the eve of the encounter.

It was on just such an occasion, during a dinner party, that he slid quietly under the table. Two men moved to pick him up but were stopped by Louella, who said, "Oh, let poor Dockie get a little sleep—he's operating in the morning."

Irving Thalberg and Norma Shearer chartered a yacht and took a party of us one weekend to Catalina. The doctor was determined to catch a fish during the four-hour crossing to the island and sat in a wicker chair, trolling a big white bone lure astern. A steward kept him topped up during the voyage with a steady stream of his favorite beverage—gin fizz. After a couple of hours he turned to me.

"Hold the rod for me, willya, Dave? . . . I've gotta take a leak."

No sooner had the doctor's head disappeared belowdecks than with a bang! and a screech! a twenty-pound tuna hit his lure. By the time a relieved doctor reappeared his fish had been brought to gaff, and the yacht was once more gathering speed.

Almost exactly two hours later a now well-oiled physician asked me once more to hold his rod. Bang! Screech! It happened again, but this time he heard it and came weaving back on deck with his dress not adjusted, causing Eddie Goulding to say in a pained voice, "Dockie, please do up your fly; we've all *seen* Louella's column."

Later that day, when we dropped anchor in Avalon Bay, Dockie rowed Louella ashore in the dinghy "to have a couple of snorts at the hotel." When they returned, not only was his oarsmanship most peculiar, but on arrival he ungallantly stepped onto the gangway ahead of his wife, at the same time pushing off from the dinghy. Louella, dutifully and equally unsteadily following her husband, stepped into forty fathoms of water, which was embarrassing for her because she couldn't swim. Goulding and I fished her out.

Louella and Dockie were a devoted couple, and evenings at their home were relaxed and unpretentious. The conversation was strictly movie shop. At Hedda's, evenings were gayer, brighter and, because of Hedda's friends and interests outside Hollywood, more cosmopolitan and much more stimulating.

She was a sparkling hostess, chic, gay, witty, and acid. She used a great variety of four-letter words and enjoyed hearing her two poodles sing to her piano playing. Hedda always stated that she would make up for her late arrival in competition with Louella "by outlasting the old bag." By the mid-forties both ladies were nearing seventy, and some heavy bets were laid in movieland as to which one would run out of steam first, but seemingly indestructible, they continued to work punishing hours, and their columns were still widely read despite a certain erosion of readers. The old stars who had played the publicity game with Louella and Hedda were fading fast, and the new ones—Brando, Holden, Newman, and Dean —and the young producers and directors found it old-fashioned and unnecessary to bother about Hedda and Louella. The war was over; tastes were changing; like most royalty, they were an anachronism; and anyway, newspaper circulations were dropping all over the country. But if Hedda and Louella recognized all this, they gave no sign of it except, sensing perhaps that they were entering the last few furlongs, each redoubled her efforts to outdo the other, and oneupwomanship became the order of their day.

The super love goddess Rita Hayworth decided to take her first trip abroad and asked my advice on a trip around Europe. Knowing how genuinely shy and gentle she was and respecting her longing to avoid the goldfish bowl of publicity, I worked out a complicated itinerary for her, starting with a small Swedish liner to Gothenburg, quiet country hotels and mountain villages all the way south, and ending up in an oasis of Mediterranean calm, the Hotel La Reserve in Beaulieu-sur-Mer.

Rita departed with a girlfriend and the works of Jean-Paul Sartre. Everything went beautifully according to plan, and after three leisurely and peaceful weeks, she arrived radiantly relaxed at La Reserve. The champion charmer of Europe, Prince Ali Khan, saw her walk in, and a new chapter was added to Hollywood history.

It was indeed a romantic match, and Hedda and Louella spent frustrating weeks angling for invitations to the wedding. The ceremony was to be held at L'Horizon, the Ali's pink villa near Cannes —an enchanting place to look at from the sea with its feet in the blue water, but a difficult place in which to carry on a conversation when the express trains to Italy thundered past the kitchen door.

The Ali had no intention whatever of having a Hollywood-style wedding, and all newspaper reporters received a blank refusal to their requests for inclusion on the guest list.

Hedda and Louella could not believe that this treatment of the press included them, and they were particularly irked that with their immense power, their supplications received the same cold shoulder as that turned toward the local reporter from Nice *Matin.* Poor gentle Rita with her inbred Hollywood fear of Hedda and Louella needed all the Ali's Olympian calm when threatening and ominous calls came from Beverly Hills, but she held her ground, and neither was invited to the wedding. Both ladies, however, goaded by their powerful employers, headed for the south of France, hoping for a last-minute breakthrough.

Louella, much to Hedda's chagrin, persuaded Elsa Maxwell, the famous party giver and sometime columnist, to take her along with her to a large buffet luncheon at L'Horizon a week before the wedding. Once she had her foot in the door, Louella pulled out all the stops, and appreciating the pressure that was piling up on Rita, the Ali finally agreed that Louella's name could be added to the wedding list.

If Louella was in a position to crow, Hedda was more than ever determined to square the account. She harangued the frustrated French reporters milling around Cannes, Antibes, and Juan-les-Pins. "How disgraceful," she told them, "that such favoritism is being shown to an American journalist."

At last, an embittered Parisian newshawk broke the deadlock. He unearthed a Provençal law from Napoleonic times which stated that no wedding could be held in private if one citizen objected. Dozens of citizens—reporters from all over France—signed the objection, and the local mayor announced that the wedding must be held in public at the *mairie*. Hedda had squared the account, but both she and Louella, after all their efforts, had to swallow their pride and join a cast of thousands hoping to catch a glimpse of the bride and groom.

When Louella reached the age of eighty-one, she was still writing her column, but the flagship of her syndication fleet was foundering, and one day it sank without trace. The Los Angeles *Examiner* ceased publication, leaving the Los Angeles *Times* as the sole morning newspaper in the city. Louella retired, and the stripling seventy-six-year-old Hedda had realized her wish—"to outlast the old bag."

She continued writing her column till the age of eighty-one, when illness incapacitated her, but she went down firing broadsides from her deathbed.

"I hear that son of a bitch Chaplin is trying to get back into the country," she told all and sundry. "We've *got* to stop him!"

Neither of them would have won a scholarship at MIT, or even obtained good marks for grammar, and most of their crusades turned out to be a waste of ink. Chaplin returned in triumph to receive a special Oscar in Hollywood; Orson Welles was forgiven; *Gone with the Wind* rose above the fact that David O. Selznick had "insulted Hollywood by employing an English actress to play Scarlett O'Hara"; Ingrid Bergman overcame the screams of outrage caused by her romance on Stromboli; Senator McCarthy inevitably became a nasty word; and Brando continued to be Brando.

Hedda and Louella had power out of all proportion to their ability and a readership out of all proportion to their literacy. They had delusions of grandeur and skins like brontosaurs, but they were gallant, persevering, and often softhearted. They interfered in casting and were partisan in politics; they helped some beginners and hindered some established filmmakers, but they could not be faulted when it came to their devotion to Hollywood, and they tried daily to preserve it as it stood—a wondrous structure of corruption, fear, talent, and triumphs, a consortium of Dream Factories pumping out entertainments for millions.

Perhaps they did not do much good, but on the other hand, they didn't do much harm either, and it's a good thing they were both spared the spectacle of the once-mighty Metro-Goldwyn-Mayer in its death throes auctioning off Fred Astaire's dancing shoes, Elizabeth Taylor's bra, and Judy Garland's rainbow.

5
Degrees of Friendliness

REPUTATIONS and fortunes were made out of movies by producers, directors, and actors, but if they had not had good screenplays to work with, they would have sat around picking their noses. For some incredible reason, however, the writers were treated by the studios as second-class citizens, grossly underpaid, housed in rabbit-warren offices, ordered to punch a time clock, and instantly blamed if a director or a star could not cope with the matter in hand. "Get the goddamned writer on the set" would be the cry. As a result of this folly a permanent state of war existed between some of the best brains in the world and the movie moguls.

Counterattacks were launched. Charles MacArthur introduced an illiterate London-born garage mechanic to L. B. Mayer as "the hottest playwright in England since George Bernard Shaw," and the young man was promptly given an office and $1,000 a week.

Wilson Mizner announced that working for Warner Brothers was like fucking a porcupine—"it's a hundred pricks against one"—and William Faulkner, rebelling against the Metro-Goldwyn-Mayer edict that writers must be in their miserable little broom-closet offices, pounding their typewriters from nine till six, demanded that he be allowed to work at home. Two months later, after frantic nonproductive phone calls and a spate of telegrams to his Hollywood apartment, someone remembered that he lived in Mississippi.

Samuel Goldwyn early on appreciated and paid for the writers' true worth and, as a result, attracted the best, among them Somerset Maugham, Maurice Maeterlinck, Robert Sherwood, Sinclair Lewis, and Lillian Hellman.

Writers, being human and usually broke, scenting the easy money to be picked up in Hollywood, had packed up their typewriters and headed west. Once there, they separated into two main groups, those who blessed Hollywood for paying them money and those who cursed it for the same reason. There was also a third group, headed by the hornet Evelyn Waugh (who insulted my nice black housekeeper by referring to her as "your native bearer"), which grabbed the Hollywood gold and departed at high speed to rail against the place and to denigrate its inhabitants.

Of the various writer cliques, the Garden of Allah set was the most flamboyant—living in small, badly furnished stucco cottages, clustered around a central kidney-shaped pool, a well-frequented bar, and a suspect dining room which dispensed instant ptomaine poisoning.

Lodged there myself for a while, I became a sleepless wreck from the nights made hideous by the laughter, battles, and mating cries of Robert Benchley, Dorothy Parker, Charlie MacArthur, Donald Ogden Stewart, and others, all alumni of the Algonquin Group from New York and a fascinating mixture of talent, booze, eccentricity, and liberal ideas. They were regarded with some alarm by Hollywood.

"Mr. Stewart, I feel so silly with you dancing in that long black overcoat. *Please* take it off."

He did—and was stark naked.

Charlie MacArthur found a way to travel back cheaply to New York. He contacted the local undertakers and asked them to let him know if any Eastern families required an escort for their loved ones who had died in California.

On one trip, according to the Garden of Allah barman, with the casket in the goods van, Charlie got waylaid by friends during the Chicago stopover and decided to take in the Kentucky Derby. The corpse went with him on the side trip to Louisville.

Dorothy Parker specialized in making "immortal" quotes.

Rollicking, pear-shaped Robert Benchley hated birds. "They're not too bad in profile, but have you ever seen the sons of bitches head on?"

He called me early one morning when I was away in San Francisco. "Is it raining up there?" he asked.

"No, it's lovely," I assured him.

"Raining like hell down here," he said and started to laugh. "You know that little pathway outside my bungalow? Well, it's got a lot of water on it right now." Another paroxysm of mirth. "A bird, a big black bastard with a yellow beak, just came in for a landing, and it skidded and sat right on its ass!"

And one writer wandered about the garden bemoaning the fact that he owed his teenaged son $40,000.

"I wanted him to get off his ass during the summer vacation," he said, "so I told him I'd double anything he earned. Well, the little son of a bitch wrote a pornographic book, and it's a best-seller."

The thing that worried the man most was the research that must have gone into his son's literary effort.

In the summer of 1939 Samuel Goldwyn called me to his office. I was about to make *Raffles—The Amateur Cracksman* for him.

"I'm not happy with the script," said Goldwyn, "so I'm going to put back the start for a few days and get a new writer on it—Scott Fitzgerald. He starts tomorrow."

That same day I ran into a producer, Walter Wanger. I had lately finished a picture for him.

"How's *Raffles* coming?" he asked.

I told him the latest news, and he was horrified.

"Fitzgerald! Forget it! He's nothing but trouble. I just had him with me on location in New England, and it was hopeless. Drunk as a skunk the entire time, missing trains, getting lost, insulting people. He never wrote a line I could use. Finally, I kicked him off the picture."

Merritt Hulbert, the head of Goldwyn's story department, was an ex-editor of the *Saturday Evening Post*.

"Fitzgerald is a lush," he said when I questioned him, "and he's never made it as a screenwriter, but he's written some beautiful stuff in the past. We bought a lot of his short stories for the *Post*."

I had never read it, so he handed me a copy of *Tender Is the Night*.

"Mr. Goldwyn has given him the job because he feels sorry for him, but I don't think he'll come up with very much for this picture. Your agent talked Mr. Goldwyn into it," Hulbert added.

"Scott's a drunk, but he's still a brilliant man. Also, he's sick, so be nice to him," said my agent, Leland Hayward.

Fitzgerald is impossible for me to describe because he gave the impression of being absent, and he looked so frail that he seemed to be floating: mid-forties, Valentino profile, rather weak mouth, and haunted eyes. He carried a large writing pad and a cardboard container of Coca-Cola bottles when I first saw him and made a little nest for himself in a corner of the sound stage.

After a few days' delay, the picture had finally started shooting with, as far as I could judge, only minimal changes to the original script. I introduced myself, and Fitzgerald rose from his chair, which, as he was over twenty years my senior, surprised me; then he passed me a bottle of Coca-Cola—a strange gesture at eight thirty in the morning.

"I drink dozens a day," he explained, and added, with a flash of fun in the vacant eyes, "it's all I *can* drink these days."

I offered him the use of the icebox in my comfortable dressing-room suite, a short distance away. He gratefully availed himself of this and, as the picture progressed, of the divan bed that stood near it. He rested a lot.

Scott Fitzgerald did not contribute very much in the way of sparkling dialogue in the weeks to come, and if ever the director asked him for a quick change of a line or a piece of business, he looked scared and dithered, but he never took a drink. He just melted into the background, scribbling away on his big writing pads and, to the annoyance of the sound man, coughing continually.

At lunchtime he liked to come across the street with me to the Mimosa Café, a crummy Chinese restaurant, frequented by bookies and minor crooks; while I ate, he gulped down more Coca-Colas.

"I'm on the wagon for good," he said.

Actually, I found him rather heavy going, with his long silences and tales of bad luck at the hands of the movie moguls, but his was a genuine frustration because he had really studied filmmaking, was fascinated by the medium and, unlike many of his contemporaries, did not feel that all producers were illiterate half-wits.

I mentioned, one day, how much I had enjoyed *Tender Is the Night*, and he was galvanized. He suddenly came alive; he could not believe that a spoiled young actor had ever heard of it, let alone wished to discuss it. Little did he know that I had read it the night before, simply and solely to give myself some conversational ammunition.

He told me how pleased he was to have the job on the picture because he could now afford to put his automobile back on the road. When I looked disbelieving, he said that no writer worth a damn misses a chance to utilize his own experiences however dire: "that is why I have made Raffles explain to his friend that he has to do something desperate because he's just hocked his convertible."

In the middle of the filming Hitler attacked peaceful Poland and unleashed the horror of World War II. I told Fitzgerald that as soon as the picture was finished, I would go back to Europe and volunteer for the British army.

He was fascinated by this quixotic decision and became very maudlin about it, declaring his intention of coming with me.

"I missed out last time," he said wistfully. "I left it too late. I didn't join up until 1917—I never got to go overseas." He became quite dreamy-eyed about the impending heroics with his mind firmly focused on Agincourt and white chargers.

Just when I was beginning to like a lot, and perhaps understand a little, this strange, haunted, withdrawn, and massively insecure man, Goldwyn fired him.

Goldwyn had told him that he was contributing little to the picture and, in particular, had taken exception to a love scene Fitzgerald had written for Olivia de Havilland and myself:

RAFFLES:	Smile!
DE HAVILLAND:	(pressing closer . . . smiles)
RAFFLES:	Wider! I'm going to ask you a *very* important question.
DE HAVILLAND:	(expectantly) Oh! Darling!
RAFFLES:	Tell me. . . who is your dentist?

Fitzgerald took his dismissal calmly. "It always happens," he said and buoyed himself up with the thought that, thanks to Goldwyn, he could now afford to work full time on a novel which he had started and upon which he had presumably been using up his yellow pads at a great rate.

I thought no more about him till one day, at the tail end of the production, we were doing a cricketing sequence—supposedly at some English county house which I was about to rob, and the game, in 110-degree heat, was being photographed on a polo field in Pasadena.

The director, Sam Wood, had been taken ill, and the great William Wyler had taken over. He knew nothing about cricket and had set things up like a baseball game, leaving me to unravel the shambles.

Just as we got things straightened out, a cry rose from the outfield, and the actors froze in their unaccustomed white flannels. "Hey, hey, my buddy! . . . I've been looking all over for you, buddy! Where the helluvya been, buddy?"

Scott Fitzgerald came tottering across the green turf like a stage drunk, weaving in great arcs.

Wyler, a meticulous professional, not renowned for his patience, was compassion itself, while I, profoundly embarrassed, like a little boy attempting to get rid of a piece of sticky paper in a breeze, tried to disentangle myself from my clinging visitor.

At last, I persuaded him to go and rest in my caravan till we had finished the day's work. He was escorted there, cosseted and given refreshment by Irving Sindler, the propman, but this retreat was only agreed to after much loud bartering, on condition that I would accompany him later to Don the Beachcombers to "drink all the rum in California."

Don, a thin, good-looking, philosophical, raffish character, was just that—a genuine beachcomber.

He owned a minute bar on McCadden Place just off Hollywood Boulevard which could accommodate, at most, twenty people. There he mixed his own inventions, delicious and exotic drinks composed of various rums, fruit juices, and flower petals. He served these wearing white dungarees and a dirty white undershirt. Frequently, he was fined for causing a nuisance; he had installed a powerful watering system above his establishment and delighted in requests for tropical rain, turning it on and deluging the passersby.

When Don had made enough dollars from dispensing his marvelous concoctions, he hung a sign outside the door of his bar—

GONE TO THE ISLANDS—and off he went: to remote parts of Hawaii, there to sit on white sand beneath the palm trees and drink rum from coconuts. When he was broke, he returned to McCadden Place and removed the sign.

I spent the greater part of that night with Scott Fitzgerald listening to an outpouring of woe, charm, lost-youth sadness, boasts, family disasters, nostalgia, fears, hopes, pure babbling, and a lot of coughing. I suppose to me, numbed by Don's endless ministrations, it was, by turns, flattering to be the confidant of a man twice my age and a crashing bore to be pinned against the end of the bar, the recipient of so much self-pity and so many intellectual rationalizations. I longed to go to bed.

I never saw him again.

A little over a year later, at the height of the London blitz, I read that back in Hollywood, "the unemployed writer" Scott Fitzgerald had died of tuberculosis and that he had left behind him a brilliant, unfinished novel, *The Last Tycoon*. Later I learned that Dorothy Parker had looked at his coffin and quoted from *The Great Gatsby:* "Poor son of a bitch."

An endless stream of writers washed up on the Hollywood shores. Some were unappreciated, most were underpaid, and a few could hardly be trusted to address an envelope.

The refugees from Hitler arrived in droves and headed for the Hollywood Hills: Thomas and Heinrich Mann, Leon Feuchtwanger, Franz Werfel, Bruno Frank, Emil Ludwig, and Bertolt Brecht. When Erich Maria Remarque was not wrapped around Marlene Dietrich or other local beauties, he acted as a sort of liaison officer between the German-speaking foreigners, the Garden of Allah set, and Musso and Frank's Restaurant on Hollywood Boulevard, where the brilliant William Saroyan and Budd Schulberg made their headquarters. Sooner or later they all showed up, a tidal wave of talent.

Besides Fitzgerald, the American writers who came and went while I was there included Hemingway, Thornton Wilder, Zane Grey, Robert Sherwood, John Steinbeck, Irving Stone, Raymond Chandler, George Kaufman, Moss Hart, Lillian Hellman, John O'Hara, Irwin Shaw, S. N. Behrman, Elmer Rice, Paul Gallico, and a thousand others; and the British contingent alone contained, among others, Maugham, H. G. Wells, P. G. Wodehouse, Hugh

Walpole, J. B. Priestley, Graham Greene, Arnold Bennett, R. C. Sherriff, Christopher Isherwood, Eric Ambler, and Frederick Lonsdale. It was the greatest convention of brilliance ever assembled, but so much was watered down, wasted, or filtered out by megalomaniac producers that tragically little of the output of these famous authors ever reached the screen.

The writers, for the most part, swallowed their pride and rolled with the punches.

Clifford Odets gracefully admitted that he appreciated the money because "of thirteen plays I have written, I have made a living out of only two."

Nathanael West agreed: "Before I came here I tried to work seriously at my craft but was unable to make a living."

James Hilton murmured, "A movie writer must make his own reckoning as to whether he would rather say, a little less exactly what he wants, to millions or, a little more exactly, to thousands."

George Bernard Shaw was more cynical and, after listening to Samuel Goldwyn expatiating on the art of making pictures, closed the conversation by saying, "That's the difference between us. . . . You talk of art, Mr. Goldwyn, I think of money."

It was left to the rebel William Faulkner to lay it on the line: "I get sick of those people who say if they were free of Hollywood what they'd do. They wouldn't do anything. It's not the pictures that are at fault. The writer is not accustomed to money. It goes to his head and destroys him—not pictures. Pictures are trying to pay for what they get. Frequently they overpay, but does that debase the writer? Nothing can injure a man's writing if he's a first-class writer. If he's not a first-class writer, there's not anything can help it much."

The writers of Hollywood, however opulent they became, clung tenaciously to their prerogative to be inquisitive crusaders and could not keep their pens shut when they sniffed the whiff of suppression.

Less than two years after the end of World War II the first microbes of a foul disease that was to spread across the fair face of the United States surfaced in Hollywood. Senator Joseph McCarthy and his two loathsome lieutenants, Cohn and Schine, had not yet succeeded in infecting the land with McCarthyism, but a cry of "There are Reds under Hollywood's beds" was raised in Washington, and the House Committee on Un-American Affairs opened an investigation on Communist infiltration of the motion picture industry. Immense publicity was generated by the ensuing circuslike proceedings under the chairmanship of a highly biased gentleman named Parnell Thomas. Richard Nixon was a member of the investigation team.

Some full-blooded support for the theory that Hollywood was in grave danger of becoming a tool of the Communist Party was given by a long list of "friendly" witnesses, including L. B. Mayer, the head of MGM; Jack Warner of Warner Brothers; Walt Disney; Gary Cooper; Robert Montgomery; Adolphe Menjou; George Murphy, later U. S. Senator from California; Ronald Reagan, who became governor of the same state; and Ginger Rogers' mother, who remained Ginger Rogers' mother. Between them these "friendly witnesses" named a few of their fellow workers as Communists and pointed to a larger group as "acting like Communists." Before long, all these people were paraded before Parnell Thomas and Co.; many became known as the "unfriendly witnesses."

Hollywood, by instinct and common sense, was a town largely disinterested in politics; it was a community dedicated to the manufacture of mass entertainment for people all over the world, regardless of how they voted, but it was also traditionally relaxed about those who took their politics seriously. Of course, we know that a few among us were Communists, but we also knew that others were Holy Rollers and that quite a number practiced black magic, but so long as the Communist Party was officially recognized by the government and not outlawed in the United States, Hollywood did not feel that people who felt strongly enough to join it should be treated like criminals.

So the great majority watched sadly while a small minority tore itself to pieces. It all seemed so unnecessary, because it was quite impossible for a tiny group of writers, directors, and actors to subvert for Communist propaganda the motion-picture industry when the whole business was in the hands of a dozen men.

The writers and directors could possibly inject small doses of Communist ideology into innocent-looking scripts, and perhaps the actors might be capable of giving an innocuous line a sinister twist, but the producers controlled the finished pictures, and there was just no way that the Seven Dwarfs could be Reds under Snow White's bed unless Walt Disney wanted them there.

The macabre farce unfolded, and Parnell Thomas allowed the friendly witnesses to make opening statements but denied the same opportunity to the unfriendly witnesses.

The crunch question which the unfriendly witnesses all faced was this: "Are you now, or have you ever been, a member of the Communist Party?"

If a witness stated that he was a Communist, he was then required by Parnell Thomas to inform on his fellow party members. If he declined to do so, he went to jail for contempt. If he denied that he was a Communist and was then proved to be a party member, he went to jail for perjury, and if he refused to answer the question at all, he could go to jail for contempt of Congress.

In the end ten witnesses went to jail, the best known of whom were the writer John Howard Lawson, whom Parnell Thomas ordered to be forcibly removed from the witness stand by armed guards when he insisted loudly that his rights as an American citizen were being invaded; Dalton Trumbo, the writer, who was refused an opportunity to cross-question witnesses when they stated that he had Communist Party affiliations; the writer Sam Ornitz, who was also forcibly removed after an altercation with Parnell Thomas; the well-known director Eddie Dmytryk, who, because he claimed constitutional immunity, was refused a chance to cross-question witnesses; and the writer Ring Lardner, Jr., who was denied the opportunity to read a closing statement in his own defense.

Two breaths of fresh air blew through the committee room when Eric Johnston, the president of the Motion Picture Association, and Dore Schary were called as witnesses. Somehow they managed to be neither "friendly" nor "unfriendly" and to get in some fairly sharp criticism of Parnell Thomas' handling of the investigation. "Don't put any American who is not a Communist in a concentration camp of suspicion," warned Johnston, and Schary, who was the head of production at RKO Studios, made it quite clear that he would not hesitate to hire a Communist unless it was proved that he was a foreign agent and pointed out that the Supreme Court had ruled that an employer could not refuse a man work because of his political convictions. Schary's attitude so infuriated the columnist Hedda Hopper that from then on she waged a campaign against him, accusing him of everything "pinko" and only stopping short of announcing that he himself was a paid-up member of the party.

As Hollywood had predicted, the top brass of the industry stoutly denied that any Communist propaganda could possibly get by them, and Hollywood was indignant when Parnell Thomas handed down his report on the investigation: "The outlines and pattern of Communist activity in the industry was clearly disclosed." When the unfriendly witnesses returned from jail, they were promptly blacklisted by the studios and were only able to work abroad or by using false names. One writer won an Oscar with a pen name which caused an embarrassed lull in the proceedings on Academy Award night, when the winner's name was announced.

Apart from that, the only fun Hollywood extracted from the whole unfortunate episode was when it learned that at the very moment the Unfriendly Ten were being released from prison, Parnell Thomas was himself being locked up for padding a government payroll with fictitious names and keeping the salaries for himself.

So much for the curtain raiser. Three and a half years later there was a much bigger investigation, covering not only Hollywood, but the whole spectrum of the entertainment industry; it lasted from March, 1951, to November, 1952. Almost a hundred witnesses appeared before the chairman, John S. Wood, and his committee: they were roughly divided between "friendlies" and "unfriendlies." The names of the witnesses were more illustrious, the committee members more reasonable, and most of the acrimony and ill temper displayed before by both sides were avoided.

This time nobody went to jail.

In three and a half years, times had changed. Not, let it be said, thanks to Senator McCarthy's myopic misrepresentations, but by the actions of the Russians themselves, who by focusing the attention of the free world on their own brutal purges and the Berlin Wall among other things, had made it painfully obvious to Americans that their brave allies of World War II still had a highly unattractive side to them.

It had become increasingly difficult to justify the U.S. Communist Party, and many of its Hollywood members, including a large percentage of the original Unfriendly Ten, this time around not only told the committee how disenchanted they had become with it, but were happy to help along its demise by volunteering a list of erstwhile friends who were still members.

Directors Eddie Dmytryk, Elia Kazan, and Frank Tuttle and actor Sterling Hayden were not thought of highly in Hollywood for "shopping" their friends, but their motives, as they described them, seemed perfectly sincere. Sterling Hayden had doubts about his behavior, however, and later described his effort as a "one-shot stoolie show," but those who knew him for an extremely honest human being and a courageous fighting man who had spent many months in Yugoslavia during World War II with the partisans behind the German lines realized that he was once more putting country before self and self at great risk—this time from the blacklist.

The Hollywood blacklist swelled considerably during these second hearings. Those who were exposed as present or past members of the Communist Party or who refused to answer the crunch question as to whether they were or not risked the total eclipse of their careers, and those who "squealed" risked, in addition, the hatred of their fellows and the cold shoulders of the pious noninvolved, and by the time the John S. Wood investigation had finished, McCarthyism was in full spate and the Hollywood blacklist was bursting at the seams. All unfriendly witnesses were automatically blacklisted but a sort of gray list was reserved for some friendly witnesses as well. The smell of fear was everywhere.

The actors suffered most. They could not change their names or their faces, and for several years they endured terrible hardships; many saw their careers collapse completely.

The writers suffered less financially because they could always go on writing under assumed names. Many did so abroad, but it was humiliating and soul-destroying work, and no one will ever know how much inventive and progressive talent during that period was stifled and stultified.

The tiny Communist group in Hollywood was certainly crushed like a beetle as a result of the two investigations, but it was never proved that it was even remotely possible that it could have "infiltrated" the motion-picture industry.

390

Hollywood was deeply wounded, however, and for years friendships, careers, marriages, and reputations lay in tatters as the arguments waxed and waned about who had behaved well, who had behaved badly, and who had saved their skins at the expense of others. "It is not enough to have informed. . . . You must also have talent!" became a favorite slogan on the walls of Warner Brothers.

Since I had worked with dozens of friendlies and unfriendlies, it was horrifying to see what happened to some of them as a result of the investigations and the spreading disease of McCarthyism. The bigger they were, the more likely they were to survive. The small ones mostly went under, and some, completely unconnected with the whole operation, suddenly found themselves under suspicion. No explanations were given; no responsibility was accepted; no one felt safe.

F. Hugh Herbert was the highly respected president of the Screen Writers Guild. I had done a play and a movie of his and was a great admirer of him and of his work.

As vice-president of Four Star Television, I was always on the lookout for good short stories for the many series our company was producing.

"Help yourself," said Hugh, when I was discussing this with him. "I have a whole trunkful of them. Take any you like."

I spent some time at his house reading through his output and soon found one that was perfect.

Nat Woolf was our contact man at the advertising agency which had provided the sponsor for the series in question.

When I told him I had obtained a story by F. Hugh Herbert, he was elated, and when he read the story, he agreed with me that it was exactly right for the show.

A few days later Nat came to see me at my house and was evidently embarrassed.

"That story of Hugh Herbert's, it's not going to work, I'm afraid," he said.

"Why not?" I asked. "You said you loved it, and you're the one I have to clear it with."

"It's not the story," said Nat. "It's Hugh."

Then I dragged out of him the fact that "someone," and Nat refused to say if it was someone at his agency or with the sponsoring company, had said, "We don't want anything from F. Hugh Herbert because he's a Commie."

I roared with laughter. "There's no way Hugh could be a Communist!" I said. "I've known him personally for years, he's president of the Screen Writers Guild, and his name never even came up in connection with the committees."

Nat was very uncomfortable. "Well," he said, "I'm not happy about it either, believe me. I think it's a load of crap, but you'll have to look for another story."

Hugh Herbert was incredulous when I told him; then he laughed; then he became very angry indeed.

"This is the sort of thing I hate with every bone in my body," he said. "Will you tell them you insist on doing my story and then ask for their reasons in writing if they refuse? I've got over two million dollars in the bank, and I'll happily spend the lot to find the son of a bitch who started this campaign against me."

In any event, Hugh Herbert never did find out. In due course I received a letter from the agency regretting that the first appraisal of F. Hugh Herbert's short story had been a trifle hasty and that they had decided that they would like me to present an alternative property for consideration. I did, I sent three more of Hugh Herbert's excellent stories and received three more refusals.

The fourth Hugh Herbert story I presented was accepted with alacrity. It did not make Hugh or Nat or myself feel any better when I confessed that I had changed the name of the author.

6
Errol

IT was a typical warm, scented south of France evening. It was, also, an ostentatious, scented south of France party, taking place in the beautiful gardens of a monstrosity of a house constructed at the turn of the century, with the maximum of financial outlay and the minimum of taste, by a Belgian textile millionaire. Now the place had been rented by a socially ambitious American couple—he the head of a proliferating conglomerate, she, on a voluntary basis, writing for a New York fashion magazine.

Not knowing any of the local residents or the so-called beautiful people from Paris and Rome, the American couple had cut the corners by hiring an international pederast, who had at his fingertips a list of the sort of people they believed would be good for their image.

The house and garden had been facelifted and lit by a decorator brought from California. Maxim's in Paris had provisioned the extravaganza, and a hot "group" from London had been flown down to ensure, with the aid of electronic equipment, that conversation would be cut to a minimum. The wine flowed, and the beautiful people, miming that they were having a marvelous time, pointedly ignored their host and hostess and paraded around, smiling vacuously at each other.

The evening brightened for me in the early hours when a young couple approached. She was a very beautiful Italian actress with whom I had made a film not too long before; he was tall, extremely good-looking and had something about him that seemed vaguely familiar.

The girl smiled her beautiful smile, all lovely white teeth and glowing brown satin skin, and embraced me warmly as she breathed in my ear an introduction to the young man behind her. I put out my hand, which he seemed not to see.

"I know you were a friend of my father," he said in a loud voice. "Please don't mention his name to *me*." I replied, perhaps a trifle tartly, "That would be difficult because I haven't yet heard *yours!*"

The Italian girl made a quick up-rolling-of-the-eyes "sorry" and steered the young man away. Intrigued, I cornered the pederast and requested information.

"Why, that's Sean Flynn," he said. "Isn't he *beautiful?*"

Yes, undoubtedly he was, and it is sickening to think that as of this writing he is still "missing believed dead" as a particularly gallant news photographer in Vietnam.

Errol Flynn had indeed been a friend of mine; for a while a very close friend. We started together in Hollywood at exactly the same time.

The great thing about Errol was you always knew exactly where you stood with him because he *always* let you down. He let himself down, too, from time to time, but that was his prerogative and he thoroughly enjoyed causing turmoil for himself and his friends.

When we started off in the Hollywood studios, the flacks went to work on us. I was publicized as the "son of a famous Scottish general" (in actual fact, my father had been killed in 1915 with the rank of second lieutenant), and Flynn was widely reported to be "as Irish as the potato and coming straight from a successful career with the Abbey Players." By some inscrutable logic, Warner Brothers decided that Errol would be more palatable to the American public as an Irish potato than as himself—an Australian whose upbringing had been in Tasmania and New Guinea.

I first met Errol in Lili Damita's bungalow at the Garden of Allah in the summer of 1935.

Lili was a beautiful hourglass-shaped creature who epitomized the sexy French cover girls of *La Vie Parisienne*, but she was also one of those insecure ladies who feel the necessity to be surrounded by devout homosexuals, and as her usual little coterie was around her that night, for a while both Flynn and I thought the other was a fag.

After sniffing suspiciously, we got this sorted out, and a tour of the dives off Hollywood Boulevard became the logical outcome of the evening. Flynn had that day completed his first part under his contract with Warner Brothers, playing a corpse on a marble slab in *The Case of the Curious Bride,* so we had much to celebrate, and during our foray he unburdened himself of his obsession with Lili. Their love affair blossomed quickly thereafter, and they were soon permanently bedded down in a house in the Hollywood Hills —an adventurous move at the time because Hollywood was still reeling from the highly publicized excesses of the "Silent Days," and the spectacle of two people openly living together was both abhorrent to the hypocritical big studio brass and a salacious bonanza for the gossip columnists.

"Tiger Lil," as Errol called her, taught him a great deal about living and living it up, but a quick marriage in Arizona did nothing to dispel her pathological possessiveness, and in the next few months, during a spate of Herculean battles, Flynn drifted away from her. The truces between the battles became shorter and shorter, and one day Flynn called me and asked if I would like to set up a bachelor establishment with him. "Let's move in together, sport," he said. "I can't take that dame's self-centered stupidity for another day."

We rented 601 North Linden Drive, Beverly Hills, from Rosalind Russell, chartered a nice understanding black housekeeper, and pooled the expense.

Flynn was collecting rather more from his contract with Warner Brothers than I was receiving from Samuel Goldwyn, so he forked out more in rent and insisted that he had prior claim to the largest bedroom, the one which housed the double bed. Flynn was fairly tight about money matters, so although on state occasions I was allowed to borrow his room, it was only in consideration of a small readjustment to our financial arrangement.

One winter's evening I came back from work, and as I turned my car into the driveway, I perceived a sinister figure, his hat pulled down over his eyes and with the collar of his camel's-hair overcoat turned up; he was lurking in the bushes by the kitchen door. Never the bravest of men, I let myself in hurriedly by the front door and went looking for reinforcements in the formidable shape of Flynn. I discovered that he was not yet back from his studio, so I took a hefty nip from the whiskey bottle ever present on our hall table and went out to deal with the intruder. I stalked him successfully and grabbed him from behind. He turned out to be the highly erudite and popular producer Walter Wanger. He was in a very nervous condition. Wanger was very much in love with the gorgeous Joan Bennett, and in matters pertaining to her, he suffered from a very low threshold of jealousy. As I released him, he blurted out that he knew that his loved one was upstairs in the big double bed with Flynn. I was able with truth to tell him that Flynn was not in the house, but I withheld the information that downstairs in the living room awaiting Flynn's arrival was Joan.

Wanger, mollified, left, and Joan, rather precipitately, left soon after.

Flynn was lucky that day because a short time later Jennings Lang, an agent, also raised Wanger's possessive instincts to a high level and one evening in the parking lot in front of the offices of the Music Corporation of America, Walter produced a revolver from the pocket of his camel's-hair overcoat, took careful aim, and shot Jennings Lang in the testicles.

Ten or fifteen years before Robert Mitchum was unlucky enough to be arrested for puffing on a joint in a house in Laurel Canyon, Errol had introduced the stuff into the life of 601 North Linden. Under the name of kif he brought it back from a trip to North Africa and was apt to offer it around, saying rather grandly that the painter Diego Rivera had introduced him to it in Mexico. Smoking it or chewing it, however, was a nonrisk pastime in those days, war on pot having not yet been declared.

I gave it up early on, chiefly I think because I was already hooked on something probably far more lethal—scotch—but Flynn pressed on, and twenty years later, at the last meeting I was to have with him, he told me that apart from mainlining heroin he had by then used everything, including, as an aphrodisiac, just a pinch of cocaine on the end of his penis.

In those prewar days, Errol was a strange mixture. A great athlete of immense charm and evident physical beauty, he stood, legs apart, arms folded defiantly and crowing lustily atop the Hollywood dung heap, but he suffered, I think, from a deep inferiority complex—he also bit his nails. Women loved him passionately, but he treated them like toys to be discarded without warning for new models, and for his men friends he really preferred those who would give him the least competition in any department.

He was not a kind man, but in those careless days he was fun to be with, and those days were the best of Flynn.

Humility was a word unknown to Errol. He became a big star overnight with his first Hollywood superproduction, *Captain Blood*, but it never crossed his mind that others—the producer, the director, the writers, the technicians, and above all, the publicity department—might have had a hand in his success. It all went straight to his head, and by the time I joined him in his second superproduction, *The Charge of the Light Brigade*, he was cordially disliked by most of his fellow workers—particularly by the extras.

Guts he always had. We were seated on our chargers in front of 600 of the toughest "Western" riders and stunt men in the business when Errol let his reins go slack and busied himself with mirror and comb before a close-up.

The "soldiers" had been equipped with rubber-tipped lances to cut down accidents in the impending "charge." One of them leaned forward and waggled the rubber tip of his lance in Errol's horse's behind.

The animal reared up, and the star of our film looped the loop, landing flat on his back to the accompaniment of roars of laughter.

Errol got up slowly and dusted himself off.

"Which of you sons of bitches did that?" he asked quietly.

"I did, sonny," said a large broken-nosed character. "Want to make something of it?"

"Yes," said Flynn. "Get off your horse."

The man did with winks at his cronies. . . . He was taken to the infirmary ten minutes later, and Errol's stock rose dramatically.

Errol always said that physically the toughest picture he ever made was *The Charge of the Light Brigade*, and he had a point. We spent several months at Bishop, California, in the dusty, windy foothills of Mount Whitney.

The location started easily with decent late autumn weather and with the only hotel in town taken over for the exclusive use of the company, but after a week shouts and profanities at two o'clock in the morning alerted us to the fact that someone had put a match to the place. It burned to the ground very quickly, providing us with the last warm evening we would spend for the rest of the engagement, and thereafter in tents and other miserable makeshift accommodations far out in the desert in sandstorms or high up in the freezing winds blowing off the mountain snows, we shivered and grumbled in our thin tropical uniforms. Flynn's big love at this point, apart from an unrequited obsession with the leading lady, Olivia de Havilland, was Arno. Arno was a schnauzer, and Flynn adored the dog, so much so that he fought a duel over him.

The owner of the local bar in Lone Pine, a large oxlike moron of permanent belligerence, objected to all dogs, particularly those lifting their legs on the corner of his building. "To teach the sons of bitches to find someplace else to piss," he installed a steel plate on the sidewalk and another on his doorpost, both wired to a battery inside the establishment. Poor Arno came bouncing along as we were about to enter the bar and lifted his leg in the danger area. The amber arc completed the circuit, and the luckless animal, collecting a high voltage shock in his offending organ, was hurled into the air and went careering off down the street, howling with pain and terror. Flynn strode into the bar, and the place fell quiet. The customers were evenly matched, local cowhands and ranchers and a sprinkling of tough stunt doubles from our picture. All prudently remained on their stools while Flynn took the barman apart. It was a bloody battle, Flynn reveled in it, and Arno was the last dog in Lone Pine to get shock treatment in his private parts.

Flynn loved fighting. He took it seriously and kept himself in a permanent state of readiness at 601 North Linden by sparring twice a week in the garden with Mushy Callahan and other professionals. John Huston also liked a good punch-up now and then.

On one famous occasion he and Flynn decided that they were bored at a Hollywood soiree. "Tell you what, kid," said Huston. "Let's get the hell outta here and go down to the bottom of the garden and just mix it a little. Whaddya say?"

"You're on!" said Flynn, and while the rest of the guests tried to concentrate on their dinner, the sound of strife filtered through the open windows as Flynn and Huston whaled away endlessly at each other. They both ended up in the Cedars of Lebanon Hospital for emergency repairs.

Barroom brawls were a specialty with Flynn. Sooner or later every well-known actor, particularly those specializing in tough roles, received a drunken shove in the back and heard the inevitable challenge: "Okay, sonny boy, let's see how tough you are." Gable, Cagney, and Bogart perfected sensible and peaceful ways of ridding themselves of these nuisances, but Flynn would gleefully wade in to the attack.

He met his match once. His beloved Arno fell overboard and drowned, and a particularly nauseating gossip columnist named Jimmy Fidler wrote a snide piece about Flynn's failing to rescue his dog. We spent a whole evening looking for Fidler, and when we found him sitting with his wife in a nightclub on the Strip, Flynn flattened him with a single punch. Mrs. Fidler, however, stuck a fork in Flynn's ear, and they both took him to court for assault.

Mike Curtiz was the director of *The Charge* and his Hungarian-oriented English was a source of joy to us all.

High on a rostrum he decided that the right moment had come to order the arrival on the scene of a hundred head of riderless chargers. "Okay," he yelled into a megaphone. "Bring on the empty horses!"

Flynn and I doubled up with laughter. "You lousy bums," Curtiz shouted, "you and your stinking language . . . you think I know fuck nothing . . . well, let me tell you—I know FUCK ALL!"

Toward the end of the picture Errol and I were placed in a large basket atop an elephant; for some obscure reason Warner Brothers had decided to twist history and to let the Light Brigade charge across the North-West Frontier of India instead of the Russian Crimea. The scriptwriters had been ordered to insert a tiger hunt into the proceedings to warm things up, and we were shooting this sequence at the studio instead of in open country. This proved just as well because the elephant, driven mad by the arc lights, and by Mike Curtiz's megaphone, went berserk and dashed madly all over the back lot trying to scrape off the basket with us inside it against trees, archways, and the side of the fire station.

Studio workers scattered like chaff as we trampled and trumpeted our way toward the main entrance, and only the astute closing of the gates by the studio police stopped us from careering out into the traffic of Pico Boulevard and heading for the Punjab. It was a most unattractive interlude.

When the charge itself was shot, one man was killed and many more were hurt, but the wretched horses suffered most. Curtiz ordered the use of the "running W," a tripping wire attached to a foreleg. This the stunt riders would pull when they arrived at full gallop at the spot he had indicated and a ghastly fall would ensue. Many horses broke legs or backs and had to be destroyed. Flynn led a campaign to have this cruelty stopped, but the studio circumvented his efforts and completed the carnage by sending a second unit down to Mexico, where the laws against maltreating animals were minimal, to say the most.

Perhaps it was the proximity to so many horses that caused it, but by the end of *The Charge* Flynn was really beginning to feel his oats. He sensed that Jack Warner was building him up to be the top box-office star of the studio, and he reckoned he could begin to throw his weight about. It started in the usual way with demands for a more lucrative contract, for a larger dressing room and all the trimmings, but as the years went by, Jack Warner found he was reaping the whirlwind he had sown. Flynn's pictures brought in millions, but he made a habit of breaking down the door of Warner's office when he was kept waiting for an appointment. Their contractual battles became legendary. It was a love-hate relationship, and there was admiration on both sides, but in the end King Jack ridded his court of his "turbulent priest."

After *The Charge* with the proceeds of a greatly increased contract, Flynn had bought himself a 65-foot ketch, which, after some hulk he had once owned in New Guinea, he named *Sirocco*. I was presented with a white T-shirt with her name proudly embossed across my chest, and we put to sea every weekend accompanied by helpful female "crew members." As I have already indicated, Flynn was never happier than when witnessing the discomfiture of his friends. One of my chores aboard *Sirocco* was the mixing of the drinks—a full-time job. As there was only a primitive refrigerator aboard, a large block of ice was purchased at the beginning of each voyage. In a rough sea, I was steadying the weekend block with my left hand while hacking off suitable chunks with an ice pick held in my right. *Sirocco* gave a violent lurch, and I found that I was unable to remove my left hand from the ice. Looking down, I noticed with a sort of semidetached interest that I had plunged the ice pick right through my middle finger.

I yelled to Errol to come and to get ready with the first-aid kit. He was delighted at what he saw.

"Hey, that's *great*, sport," he said. "Don't pull it out yet, we must show this to the girls!"

Impaled on the ice block, I waited below while Flynn rounded up the "crew." Much to his delight, one of them fainted when she saw what had happened.

Flynn read somewhere that a man named D'Arcy Rutherford had invented a new sport in the south of France—water skiing— and he showed me pictures of Rutherford skimming along behind a speedboat off Eden Roc.

"Look, sport," said Flynn, "we've *got* to try that," and he designed a pair of very painful, heavy wooden skis which the studio carpenters knocked together for us. The following weekend we tried them out off Catalina Island—they worked. There is no record to prove it, but I am pretty sure that on that day in the mid-thirties, Flynn and I introduced water skiing to California and maybe even to the United States.

Be that as it may, on that memorable weekend, Ronald Colman aboard his *Dragoon* was anchored in a nearby cove a couple of miles away from *Sirocco* in Avalon Bay, and we decided to give Colman and his guests an exhibition of our newfound sport. Flynn was driving the speedboat when we arrived, and my girlfriend for the weekend was sitting beside him. I was slapping merrily along on the heavy boards astern. After we had suitably impressed the customers aboard *Dragoon*, Flynn pulled a typical "friend-discomfiter," and instead of stopping or turning back toward Avalon, he headed out into the open sea. By now I was getting very tired indeed. I signaled to him to stop, and about half a mile from *Dragoon* he obligingly did so. I sank gratefully into the blue water and waited to be picked up. As the boat came near me, Flynn pulled in the towrope. "So long, sport," he called. "Why don't you drop in on Colman for a nice cup of tea? Betty and I are going back to *Sirocco* to take a nap." Betty, I noticed with some annoyance, seemed to be putting up only token resistance to this infamous suggestion, and with a roar of laughter, Flynn swept away, leaving me to face a long swim in mid-Pacific. However, it was a lovely afternoon, there was no adverse current, the sea was warm and oily calm, and when I wanted to rest, I had only to use the skis to support me. So I took my time, paddling gently along, rather enjoying my languorous journey.

About half the distance to *Dragoon* was covered when I got a nasty feeling that I was no longer alone. About ten yards on my right was a very large shark, its greasy black dorsal fin undulating above the surface as it moved effortlessly through the water.

Panic gripped me. I stopped swimming and tried to push the skis beneath my body for protection. With the uncoordination of fear I let go of one of them, which drifted toward the shark. The brute immediately flicked its giant tail and changed course to investigate. Some half-wit once said that you can frighten sharks away by splashing violently and making a noise . . . it's nonsense. . . . I splashed and shouted like a maniac, but my shark just came closer to find out what all the fuss was about. With one ski now beneath me, I hoped protecting my underbelly et cetera from being ripped away, I paddled slowly, gibbering with terror, toward Colman's yacht.

The shark in increasingly close attendance accompanied me the whole way. I prayed that he would remain on the surface, and I never took my eyes off his fin. Periodically, I yelled "Shark!" and "Help!" at the top of my lungs.

At long last I saw field glasses pointing in my direction and stopped paddling when Colman and a sailor jumped into the tender and started up the motor. Only when they were right on top of him did the shark lose interest in me. Then, with a mighty swirling convulsion, he slid into the depths below.

Aboard *Dragoon* a much-needed tumbler of brandy was pressed into my hand while I borrowed somebody's hand mirror to see if my hair had turned white, and when Flynn came over later to pick me up, I had a few words with him. He hooted with laughter. "Jesus!" he roared. "I wish I'd seen *that!*"

I planned my revenge carefully. First I enlisted the help of a writer friend, that redoubtable Teddy bear John McClain, who came up with a short script in which the leading part would be played by the unsuspecting Flynn.

McCLAIN: Oh, Errol, on Friday, my aunt from Marion, Ohio, is coming out with her daughter Eunice,

402

	and they'd just love to meet you—especially Eunice. You remember Eunice, don't you, Dave?
NIVEN:	I certainly do! . . . Really gorgeous! . . . But don't let Errol get near her—she's just the age he likes.
MCCLAIN:	Now, Errol, goddammit, you keep your cotton-pickin' hands off my niece!
FLYNN:	(with famous smirk): I'll do my best, fellers, but don't bank on it.
NIVEN:	Why don't you bring them both over to North Linden for drinks on Saturday, John? You'll be there, won't you, Errol?
FLYNN:	You're damn right!

After that it was just a case of subtle reminders and praise for Eunice and her measurements.

McClain and I enlisted a high-class whore of about thirty-five for the part of the aunt, and she in turn undertook to appear with a real stunner of seventeen in the role of her daughter. I was to be the director.

On "F Day" I left the Westside Tennis Club first and drove to North Linden at high speed, to rehearse and position my waiting actors. McClain and "Eunice," a sexy-looking blonde with the most awful hog-calling voice I had ever heard, I stationed at the bar. Then I moved the sofa so that it would be in full view through the curtains of the garden window and ordered the "aunt" to join me outside.

When Flynn came into the room, the "aunt" breathed in my ear, "Wow! He's really something!" I shushed her, but I had to agree. Errol was a magnificent specimen of the rampant male.

McClain as an actor was nervous, I noticed, but that is often the way with writers. Luckily, his poor performance went unnoticed by Flynn, who had eyes only for "Eunice." Nor did he seem to hear her blaring voice and preened himself outrageously in front of her. "Eunice" almost stole the show. She gave a stupendous performance, undulating with suppressed desire, making rapturous quick intakes of breath every time Flynn came close to her and darting the pink tip of her tongue between sensuous lips.

We had two phones in the house, so when I was satisfied that all was going according to plan, I nipped around to the kitchen and dialed the number which rang in the bar. McClain picked up the phone, and I listened carefully to hear him get off his most difficult speech.

McCLAIN: Hello! . . . Oh, Auntie, it's you. . . . Where are you? Oh, at the hotel. . . . Okay. . . . I'll come right over . . . no problem. . . . I'll be there in fifteen minutes. (Turning to Eunice) Eunice, I'm just going to pick up your mother at the Bel Air . . . back in half an hour.

EUNICE: (ogling Flynn): Take your time, Uncle John. I'm sure Mr. Flynn will take good care of me.

McClain made his exit and joined the "aunt" and myself outside.

McClain had given Eunice some carefully worked-out speeches here to make her seductive and to lure Flynn delicately across to the sofa—they were wasted. Before she could get the first line out, she found herself on that sofa and her skirt over her head.

This was a tricky time for the poor girl because if she gave in too quickly, the whole structure of the piece would be suspect. Flynn took her desperate time-consuming moves, the maidenly hauling down of her skirts, her frantic hitching up of panties, and her wild hand slapping as the real thing and pressed home his attack with admirable expertise. The watchers at the window were in agonies of suppressed laughter and when Flynn leched into her blond curls, "Oh, Eunice, we only have about twenty minutes," I stuffed a handkerchief somewhere down around my tonsils. I pulled myself together, and once Flynn was well and truly in the saddle, I sent in my reserves.

McClain and the "aunt" made a dramatic entrance just at the high point of the performance.

AUNT: Eunice! What *are* you doing?

EUNICE: (peering out from beneath Errol): I don't know, Mom, ask Mr. Flynn.

AUNT: Mr. Flynn! Get off my daughter *Immediately* and explain yourself.

FLYNN: (buttoning up desperately):
          Oh! . . . Oh! . . . I lost my head . . . I lost
          my head.
AUNT: Eunice! You're a mess! Go to the car and wait
          while I have a word with Mr. Flynn.
McCLAIN: Come, niece (then, turning ponderously toward
          Errol) Flynn! . . . You swine! (Exeunt)
AUNT: Now, Mr. Flynn, I'd just like you to explain
          yourself.
FLYNN: (shaking head and muttering) I lost my head, I
          lost my head!
AUNT: (slowly) I sent Eunice out because (grabbing at
          his fly) I want a bit of that myself!

CURTAIN

During the years McClain and I occasionally dusted off the
script and recast the principals with great effect.

Christmas in Hollywood was like something from another
planet. Festoons of reindeer and giant bells were first stretched
across Hollywood Boulevard in late November, and thereafter
lighted trees proliferated in the snowless gardens of Beverly Hills.
All work stopped or rather staggered to a halt during the late morning of Christmas Eve, and the rest of the day was dedicated to parties—parties on the set, parties in the producers' offices, the directors' offices, the stars' dressing rooms, the cutting rooms, and the
casting office. Everyone at the studio expected presents, from the
night watchman to the chief of police, and from the head of
the studio to the lowliest secretary, but the biggest outlay was in
the realm of personal gifts to friends and business acquaintances.
One was constantly getting caught short. I once gave Miriam
Hopkins half a dozen handkerchiefs, and she gave me a Stude-
baker. All in all, it was a difficult and expensive time.
Errol and I decided that the whole Peace and Goodwill Department was getting completely out of hand. So we decided to buy no
personal or business gifts at all. Instead, we invested in some fancy
wrapping paper, yards of multicolored ribbons, and several dozen
greeting cards. We then sat back at North Linden Drive and

waited for the deluge. As the presents poured in, it was a simple matter to rewrap them, add something personal on a card, and dispatch them elsewhere.

Trade was brisk for several days before Christmas, and all went well till someone sent us a case of champagne, which we gratefully opened instead of sending on its way. After that we became careless. Our rhythm faltered, and the operation lacked synchronization with the embarrassing result that Walter Wanger received a beautiful black silk evening wallet on which, in gold lettering, was inscribed "To D.N. from W.W."

I never quite understood Errol's hero worship of John Barrymore. Still of blazing talent and unquestioned, if somewhat blurred, profile, Barrymore seemed to go out of his way to shock and be coarse. He was also conspicuously unclean and smelled highly on many occasions.

He had an abiding love of the theater and treated filmmaking as a financially necessary evil. Watching him work, I was amazed at the carefully arranged phalanx of boards, some stationary, some held aloft by moving stagehands, and all bearing the lines John Barrymore was required to speak during the scene at hand.

Painstaking rehearsals went into the placing and progress of these boards to enable the great man to move freely about during the playing of a scene without giving a hint that he was reading the whole thing.

Like boys who go to complicated lengths to cheat in exams, it would probably have been less time-consuming and nerve-racking to have learned the lesson in the first place, but Barrymore was adamant and had a stock answer when anyone dared to make such an observation.

"My memory is full of beauty—Hamlet's soliloquy, the Queen Mab speech, the fifteen-minute monologue by King Magnus in *The Apple Cart,* and most of the Sonnets . . . do you expect me to clutter all that up with *this* horseshit?"

Barrymore had a tempestuous marriage with a lady named Elaine Barrie, and their partings and reconciliations were joyfully reported by the nation's press.

After a spat in New York, he boarded the train for Los Angeles. Elaine Barrie by leapfrogging over him in a series of plane trips tried to head him off and, surrounded by a snowballing number of reporters, made dramatic appeals from wayside railway platforms across the country while her husband gazed down dispassionately upon her from the safety of his locked stateroom aboard the Santa Fe Chief.

The Barrymores' progress west was followed avidly in the daily papers, and "The Caliban-Ariel Chase," as it was labeled, came to an end at San Bernardino, the last stop before Los Angeles, when at last Barrymore unlocked his door and allowed his wife to ride the remaining sixty miles in his company.

Shortly after this interlude Flynn took me to lunch with Barrymore at the Brown Derby in Beverly Hills. This restaurant was designed so that everyone could see everyone else; the tables were set at a series of semicircular brown leather banquettes, the backs of which fitted uncomfortably into one's lumbar region. The waitresses, all would-be actresses, wore very short bell-shaped and highly starched skirts and spent much time dropping and provocatively retrieving forks and spoons before the tables of producers and directors. Barrymore caused a stir as we entered, and he boomingly table-hopped his way to our corner.

He was a fascinating ham, and everything he did or said was accompanied by rolling eyes and extravagant gestures. His beautiful voice was pitched for the most effect, and he was far from reticent about its reaching the farthest corners of the room, particularly when Flynn asked him a loaded question: "But tell us, Jack, what do you *see* in Elaine?"

Barrymore banged the table, and the glasses jumped. Heads turned, and conversation stilled.

"You want to know what I see in my wife?" he roared. "Well, I'll tell you! You put it *in*, and it goes right through the main saloon and into the *galley*; then the cabin boy comes down a ladder and rings a bell. . . . In other words, you stupid bastard, *IT FITS.*"

Errol had sporadic reconciliations with "Tiger Lil" during his tenancy of 601 North Linden, but they amounted to little and did not seem to interfere with the main trend of his activities—a big turnover was the thing, with the accent on youth. One afternoon he said, "Come on, sport, I'm going to show you the best-looking girls in LA." We headed down Sunset Boulevard, and I thought he was taking me to the theater of *Earl Carroll's Vanities* which boasted an illuminated sign over the stage door: THROUGH THESE PORTALS PASS THE MOST BEAUTIFUL GIRLS IN THE WORLD.

He glanced at his watch.

"They should be coming out any minute now," he said, and stopped the car.

We were directly opposite the Hollywood High School.

Out came the girls, and they were indeed an eye-catching lot with their golden California suntans, long coltlike legs, and high, provocative breasts. All were made up, and many clutching their schoolbooks to their curves looked eighteen or nineteen. Flynn sighed and shook his head.

"Jail bait," he said. "San Quentin Quail. What a waste!"

A patrol car pulled up behind us, and a cop got out. "You fellows waitin' for someone?" he asked.

"No, Officer," said Flynn, "we are just admiring the scenery."

"Beat it," said the cop.

Early in 1939 Errol surprised me by informing me that his marriage was patched up "for keeps." "There's a whole new deal coming up with Lil," he said. "I'm going home."

601 North Linden was disbanded, and we went our separate ways.

During the inevitable wrangle over the "damages" we had done to Rosalind Russell's house during our long tenancy, tightfisted Flynn, who had been stupid enough to sign the lease, met his match. Our landlady had counted every piece in the woodshed when we moved in, and although we had constantly replenished her fuel supplies, in addition to other damage, we were asked to pay for thirty-seven small logs.

The following year we made *Dawn Patrol* together at Warner Brothers. Edmund Goulding directed, and it was a most happy assignment except that I could not help noticing that Flynn had really got the "star" bit between his teeth and was beginning to behave outrageously to the people who employed him and even toward some of those who worked with him.

In September, 1939, Hitler invaded Poland, and before World War II ended six years later 55,000,000 lay dead. How to behave as a young man when your country is invaded or in danger is a very personal decision, and anyone who rushes off brandishing a sword should never point a finger of scorn in the direction of those who decide not to do so.

I decided to go, and Flynn decided to stay—it was as simple as that.

During my absence a lot of things happened to Errol. Britain and Australia were at war with Germany and Italy, but he had no intention of being called to the colors. He felt no loyalty to Britain, and little to Australia; the United States had given him his big chance, so he took out American citizenship. Then the Japanese bombed Pearl Harbor, and young Americans started flocking to the recruiting offices. Errol hesitated, but he was confronted by "Tiger Lil" with a baby boy, Sean, in one hand and, in the other, one of the most punitive settlements ever handed down by the notoriously tough California divorce courts. But working on in Hollywood, Errol misguidedly accepted a series of war films in which he appeared playing highly heroic roles: *Dive Bomber, Edge of Darkness,* and *Objective Burma* to name a few. The press reacted angrily to his efforts, particularly in beleaguered England, where Zec, in the 4,000,000-circulation *Daily Mirror,* depicted Flynn in a half page cartoon, dressed in battle dress, seated in a studio chair with his name stenciled on the back and in his hands the script of *Objective Burma.* On the studio grass beneath his chair was a multitude of tiny crosses and, beneath the jungle trees, stood the ghostly form of a soldier. The caption read: "Excuse me, Mr. Flynn, but you're sitting on some graves."

Errol retreated to a mountaintop. High up on Mulholland Drive he built a luxurious one-floor bachelor pad. It had a Finnish sauna bath and a battlefield for a bed with a mirror on the ceiling. It had glorious views of the San Fernando Valley below and some stables in which highly illegal cockfights were staged on Sunday evenings, but apart from the inevitable girls, it became, according to Flynn, "the mecca of pimps, bums, gamblers, process servers, and phonies." It also became a refuge for the great John Barrymore, whose end was visibly drawing near. For a while he lived up there with Errol, but there was general relief in the household when he left and the frame of the living-room window could be revarnished because during his visit Barrymore had made it a nightly habit to urinate out of it in the hopes, he said, of spraying Warner Brothers Studios in the Valley below.

Errol liked to tell of arriving home drunk after drowning his sorrow at Barrymore's demise. According to him, he let himself into the house and in the dark living room with the picture windows presenting a panoramic view of the whole glittering San Fernando Valley, he beheld John Barrymore sitting in his usual chair with a drink in his hand. He thought it was a ghost, but on closer inspection Errol claimed it turned out to be Barrymore's corpse, which his cronies had persuaded the undertaker to lend them for a few hours.

Errol never explained satisfactorily why any undertaker would jeopardize his livelihood by breaking the law and handing over a body to anyone other than the next of kin, nor could he convince me that it had been medically and physically possible to overcome rigor mortis so conveniently.

Late in 1942 high jinks aboard *Sirocco* boomeranged on Errol, and he was arrested on four charges of statutory rape.

In the state of California statutory rape meant that a male had fornicated with a female below the age of eighteen. The fact that the lady in question had long since been deflowered and, far from withholding her consent, had entered enthusiastically into the proceedings made no difference, and conviction carried a sentence of five years. Looking back on many weekends aboard *Sirocco*, I could not remember any "crew members" flashing their birth certificates as they trooped expectantly up the gangplank.

It seemed obvious that Flynn was being framed, and young America was aroused. William F. Buckley, Jr., then at prep school, told me later that he had joined A.B.C.D.E.F., American Boys Club for the Defense of Errol Flynn. The accusing girls, Betty Hansen and Peggy Satterlee, had always looked like sophisticated well-upholstered twenty-two-year-olds, but for the trial the prosecution ordered them to take off their makeup, do their hair in pigtails, wear bobby socks, and carry schoolbooks.

It didn't work. The jury, confronted by the masterful tactics of Jerry Geisler, saw through the camouflage and pegged the girls for what they really were. Errol was acquitted, but the stigma of rape was attached to him. He never shook it off, and for years he gritted his teeth when hailed with cries of "In like Flynn!"

The long trial over, Errol married again—a quiet, pretty girl, with an uptilted nose, Norah Eddington—but by now he was so dependent on his bachelor life on Mulholland Drive that his new wife lived in a little house in Hollywood and never became the chatelaine of his mansion on the mountain. In 1945 Norah gave birth to a baby girl, but she and Flynn continued to live apart.

Errol was stuck with making a lot of Westerns, which he hated doing, but they made money for the studio and amid renewed sounds of strife he bowed to Jack Warner's directive and walked through his roles with haughty disdain. He also discovered vodka in a big way and proceeded to drink it as though it were going out of style. At seven o'clock in the morning he was gulping it down in the makeup chair—mixed fifty-fifty with 7-Up.

It was not a happy man I found upon my return to Hollywood at the beginning of 1946.

Miraculously, Errol still looked in good physical shape and gave the outward impression of being the same, insulated with charmingly cynical self-sufficiency, but there was something infinitely sad about him, something missing, and behind his eyes there was a shield—I could no longer see into his face.

With pride he showed me the spread on Mulholland Drive and, having discarded *Sirocco* as a bad dream, with loving care introduced me to every inch of his new "wife," *Zaca*—a 120-foot schooner which he had found in San Francisco. She was a dream, and he had spent a small fortune refitting her.

"And let me show you the house flag," he said as he unfurled a symbolic crowing rooster. "A rampant cock, sport, get it? That's what I am to the world today—goddammit—a phallic symbol."

He didn't smile as he said it.

Perhaps I had become smug, self-satisfied, and "square" in the years I had been away. I had come back with a beautiful young wife and two tiny children, and I found I had little in common with the group which now surrounded Errol—hangers-on almost to a man.

The worst, I thought, was Bruce Cabot, an actor who specialized in playing villains, who drank hard, played golf beautifully, and gambled prodigiously, but who had a nasty habit of being absent when the debts were being settled. Flynn was always good to Cabot and never failed to keep him afloat or to see that he was lucratively employed in Flynn pictures, but it was Cabot in the end who delivered the unkindest cut of all—"Et tu, Bruce?"

Because of the implications, Errol tried hard to get away from making sex-symbol pictures, but they made money, and the studios kept him churning them out till the pointed fingers and the snide "rapist" cracks so depressed him that he drank more and more and even contemplated suicide, on one occasion sitting up all night with a bottle of vodka in one hand and a loaded revolver in the other.

Occasionally and unexpectedly during this low period Errol came down from his mountaintop to see us, and I would arrive home from work to find him playing with my little boys or helping my wife get supper. His tremendous charm enveloped us all like a tent, and he in his turn seemed to extract a certain peace from the closeness of our family. "This is the life, sport," he would say. "You've really got it made."

Norah had a second baby, and Flynn made a stab at family life for himself. He suggested that she move into Mulholland with their children, but the invitation came too late, and they were divorced. Errol, more restless than ever, then took *Zaca* through the Panama Canal and headed for the Caribbean where he fell in love with Jamaica and looked for a while like settling down, but he pulled up the anchor, set sail for the Mediterranean, and tried his hand at a new role—as international playboy in competition with Rubirosa and Freddie McEvoy.

He gambled, drank, fought, and became the target for every freeloader and trollop between Malaga and Taranto. He seemed to have lost all interest in making films, and although he still had a contract to make several more with Warner's, he never ran out of excuses for not returning to do so, but *Zaca*, with her large crew and complement of guests, was costing him a fortune, and it finally dawned on him that if he didn't make films, he didn't get paid.

Good luck, which Errol was beginning to believe had deserted him forever, appeared out of the blue in the shape of a lovely and calm young actress from New York—Patrice Wymore. She became an island of peace and common sense in the middle of his sea of false values, and eighteen months after his divorce from Norah,

Errol and Patrice were married. On the day of his wedding in Nice with his adoring new wife holding his arm and looking trustingly up into his face, he was handed a document that turned him to stone—a seventeen-year-old French girl named Denise Duvivier was accusing him of something she said had occurred aboard *Zaca* one year before: RAPE!

All over the world headlines once more attacked, ridiculed, and pilloried Errol, but Patrice behaved immaculately, and sat beside him during the preliminary inquiry holding his hand. After visiting *Zaca* and asking Denise Duvivier a few searching questions about the small shower cubicle in which she insisted the action had taken place, the judge ruled that the girl had never even set foot aboard.

Patrice persuaded Errol to return to Hollywood and work out his contract, but when they arrived there, she was appalled by the inroads that had been made into his capital by lawyers, courts, wives, mistresses, alimonies, and, of course, the hangers-on, so when Errol went back on the payroll, she persuaded him to grab the weekly checks and buy land on Jamaica—the island of his dreams.

This advice Errol took, and by the time his contract was finally terminated (in the course of one last convulsion with Jack Warner) he was the owner of more than 5,000 acres, but he still had not cleared up his astronomical debts. Convinced that his career and earning power were over, he had no intention of doing so, and as Patrice had produced a baby, the three of them took off in a hurry for Europe to live on *Zaca*. "Let Tiger Lil and the whole god-damned lot of them come after me and try to collect," said Errol. "I'm sick of being taken."

First stop was Rome, where Errol put up half a million dollars—all the cash he could raise—as a half share in the costs of a picture, *William Tell*, but his Italian partners walked out, the picture collapsed halfway through, and Flynn found himself more in debt than ever. He cabled an SOS to his business manager in Hollywood, Al Blum, and discovered that his trusted adviser had just died—a blow not softened when he learned that in his last few weeks Blum had used the power of attorney Flynn had conferred on him to make some very peculiar financial arrangements which had effectively scraped the bottom of Errol's barrel. He also

413

learned that "Tiger Lil" had taken possession of Mulholland Drive.

This was Flynn's lowest ebb, and it was then that his great friend Bruce Cabot showed his hand.

Flynn had brought Cabot over from America to play an important part in *William Tell*. When the picture collapsed, Flynn flew to the Geneva banks to try to salvage it. He returned, empty-handed, to find that in his absence the man he had befriended for years had sent around a process server for unpaid salary and had removed his car and his wife's and his baby's clothes.

Flynn never went to look for Cabot—he was afraid he might kill him.

For four years after the demise of *William Tell*, Flynn was a floating, boozing bum. He made some trips to Jamaica to try to keep hold of his land and was able to convince the banks there that its value had increased. He also made a couple of disastrous films in England for which he was happy to be paid a fraction of his former salary.

Most of the time *Zaca* remained tied up in the minor ports of the Mediterranean while her owner caroused and brawled, intent, apparently, on his own self-destruction. Vodka and other stimulants made terrible inroads into his health, his looks were fading fast, and with one exception, Hollywood washed its hands of Errol Flynn. Sitting in his beautiful house above Beverly Hills, surrounded by a most enviable collection of paintings, was a quiet, almost professorial man named Sam Jaffe—a highly successful agent. He had not forgotten Errol Flynn, and he had a hunch. He packed, left for Europe, and tracked Flynn down in Palma de Majorca.

He cajoled Flynn, and he appealed to his pride, and the loyal Patrice helped him. Flynn pulled himself together and before long was back in Hollywood, making a picture, *Istanbul*. He was not playing a beautiful young sex symbol anymore. He was playing himself, a middle-aged rake with the remains of elegance stamped on a face that had been lived in, and he loved doing it. After *Istanbul*, his old antagonist Jack Warner offered him the part of John Barrymore in *Too Much Too Soon*. Drawing heavily on his personal experience of the man, he turned in a performance that delighted critics and public alike. Next came *The Roots of Heaven*

—another role from the same mold to be shot in Africa with John Huston directing and $4,000,000 being spent on the production.

In 1958 I met Errol by chance in London. Ten years had passed since I had last seen him, and it was a joyful reunion. We lunched, largely on Pouilly Fumé, at a little place in Soho, and I cannot pretend that I was not shocked by the physical change; he had been doing himself grave damage, the face was puffy and blotchy, and the hand that had once held the bow of Robin Hood could not have put the arrow through the Taj Mahal at ten paces, but there was an internal calm and a genuineness about him that I had never seen before.

He brought me up to date about all his wives—he had just separated from Patrice, and he talked wistfully of how hard she had tried to help him and how impossible he must have been to live with. He told me with pride of his children, especially of Sean, and when he spoke of Jamaica, he positively glowed.

Then he said something very unexpected: "You know, sport, I've felt a heel about you for ten years. When your wife died in that accident when she'd just come out to California, I never did a goddamned thing to help, did I? Never came to see you or anything. Well, I wanted to, and I thought about it all the time, but I couldn't bring myself to do it—I don't know why. . . . Anyway, I always wished I had."

We filled our glasses and sat in that wonderful silence that old friends can afford.

After a while I said, "I see you've still got a couple of lawsuits going and all the usual tax problems. You seem very relaxed about everything—how do you do it?"

"I've discovered a great book, and I read it all the time—it's full of good stuff," said Errol.

I looked at him inquiringly.

"If I tell you what it is, sport, I'll knock your goddamned teeth down your throat if you laugh."

"I promise," I said.

"It's the Bible," said Flynn.

On the evening I finished writing down these inadequate words about Errol Flynn, I left my house on Cap Ferrat and took the footpath around the end of the point, the one used by the *douaniers* in their search for smugglers. When I came to the Baie de Villefranche, I had a glass of wine with my friend Bidou in his little quayside bistro, before walking on past the old fishing village with its sun-washed houses and festoons of multicolored laundry, past the fourteenth-century fort to the Vieux Port. Very much the second-class citizen in these days of smart marinas is the old port of Villefranche. It gives refuge to elderly fishing boats and to a few seedy private yachts. In its little boatyard, a big Piggiotti 35-knot cruiser was being repainted by some shifty-eyed Algerians. Moored near her were two or three impounded motor cruisers which had been caught smuggling dope from North Africa. I wandered along the old seawall, looking down at the sad and rejected little fleet sheltered below: many were for sale. Rigging and mooring ropes slapped and creaked in the rising mistral. The place was full of ghosts.

Suddenly, I felt goose pimples rise up all over me. A large dismasted hulk lay before me. Her teak decks gaped to the sky, the planks of her sides were thinly covered with a cracked and flaking grayish paint, but despite the old bus tires that did duty as fenders swinging on frayed ropes along her sides, she still had a defiant elegance enhanced by her bowsprit still rigged and thrusting out belligerently before her.

My eyes followed along her beautiful, if aging, lines. I knew now what I was going to see, and there it was, proudly emblazoned on her great arclike transom:

7
"Mr. Goldwyn"

WHEN a history of Hollywood is written, the name of Samuel Goldwyn is bound to get top billing.

For half a century he towered like a colossus above his contemporaries, and the results of his taste and his single-minded determination to settle for nothing short of his own ideas of perfection are preserved for all to see.

It was long a habit among the jealous and the snide in the Hollywood jungle to ridicule Goldwyn and try by the all too easy manufacture of Goldwynisms to diminish his stature. "Include me out," "I'll tell you in two words—im-possible," "A verbal contract is not worth the paper it's written on," "We can always get more Indians off the reservation," and "We've all passed a lot of water since those days" have become part of the Goldwyn legend, but who can claim to have been present when these pearls of wisdom were dropped? Another Goldwynism faithfully repeated to me during the shooting of *The Real Glory*—"Elevate those guns a little lower"—was actually an Andrew Jacksonism which erupted from the lips of the future seventh President of the United States at the Battle of New Orleans in 1815. I was under contract to Goldwyn for fifteen years, and I only heard him produce one malapropism, and as it could not by any stretch of the imagination chip a piece off the colossus and as it occurred in the presence of thirty witnesses, I will quickly get it out of the way.

In 1946 for some reason to do with a visit to the American Pacific Fleet in San Diego, Field Marshal Montgomery appeared in California, and Goldwyn gave a dinner for him.

Because of Montgomery's foolish military whim about being punctual, the guests were selected from among the more reliable of the local citizenry. The field marshal arrived on time, wearing his blue patrol uniform, and on his left breast were several layers of medal ribbons. The guests were smartly seated at rows of small tables for four and six. Frances Goldwyn placed the field marshal on her right, opposite her she positioned Gary Cooper's wife, Rocky, and on the fourth chair, because he had served under Montgomery, sat the author. Small talk and Hollywood gossip washed over Montgomery's head; he only came to occasionally when the word "shooting" was used, so Frances became increasingly nervous and signaled to Sam to cause a diversion.

Goldwyn, at the other end of the room, obediently rose from his table and beat a knife against a wineglass. The clatter was cut to a minimum, and we braced ourselves to hear the inevitable words of welcome to the distinguished guest.

Goldwyn cleared his throat.

"It gives me great pleasure tonight to welcome to Hollywood a very distinguished soldier . . . ladies and gentlemen, I propose a toast to Marshall Field Montgomery."

A stunned silence, during which Frances Goldwyn sat very still, looking as though she had been hit with a halibut, was finally broken by Jack Warner, who cracked, "Montgomery Ward, you mean."

Like many others, Goldwyn did have a problem remembering names. Joel McCrea, who was under contract to him at the same time as myself, was invariably referred to as Joe McCreal, and his European public relations chief, the impeccable and immaculate Welshman Euan Lloyd, became resigned to being addressed as Urine. Goldwyn was no mean wit. When I was leaving Hollywood to go off to Montgomery's war in September, 1939, I went to Sam's office to say good-bye. He was very put out that I was leaving voluntarily and not waiting until I was called up, so he put me on suspension till the end of the war or of my life, whichever came sooner, and said, "I'll cable Hitler and ask him to shoot around you."

Goldwyn was a zealous preserver of a buck. In July, 1939, I paid the first down payment on a New York Life insurance policy. Exactly a year later and shortly after Dunkirk, I received a reminder from New York Life warning me that my second installment was now due and that if it was not paid very quickly, I would lose the coverage and the first installment. As Russia was still an ally of Germany and Hitler was opposed only by Great Britain, I did not rate my chances of survival as a soldier too highly and sought to do my dependents a good turn.

I cabled Leland Hayward, my agent, asking him to see if Goldwyn would advance the money against my suspended contract.

Goldwyn had been reading the daily papers and apparently had also evaluated my chances. He refused, and unable out of my soldier's pay to preserve the policy myself, I lost it.

Six and a half years later, when I returned to the Goldwyn fold, a forgotten, broke, and valueless commodity, Goldwyn somberly pointed out that during my absence there had been a change in the law as a result of which my suspended contract had lapsed. Then, unpredictable as always, he laughed at my stricken face, gave me a new five-year contract at a greatly increased salary, and lent me enough money to make the down payment on a house.

I purposely placed the start of these notes on Goldwyn at one of his dinner parties because a special determination of his was to be a great gentleman, and in his own home he was. An impeccable host, even if an hour before he had been banging his office desk and hurling imprecations at you across it, once at his house on Laurel Way, he would meet you smiling at the door, look after your every need during the evening, and personally escort you to your car when it was time to depart. People found this Jekyll and Hyde quality disconcerting because the reverse could happen, and despite their being lulled into a sense of false security during a cozy dinner, accusations and abuse could be awaiting them at the Samuel Goldwyn Studios first thing the following morning.

The key to understanding Goldwyn was to know that his total obsession was making pictures of which he could be proud, and apart from his private moments with his family, every waking minute of his day was dedicated to that end alone.

Above average height, deep of chest and high of voice, he was always dressed in suits, shirts, and shoes of perfect fit, clothes being one of his few personal extravagances. He also took great trouble to see that he remained trim. His light, almost spartan luncheons at the studio were served in his private dining room, invariably with his wife in attendance, and every evening on his way home, he ordered his car to stop as soon as he reached the city limits of Beverly Hills so that he might walk briskly the remaining mile and a half to his house.

Head high and eyes glazed in thought as he strode along, he had a habit of talking to himself and frequently became so engrossed in his own conversations that he ignored the salutations and greetings of aggrieved neighbors.

I never dared play gin rummy or backgammon with Goldwyn because I had heard tell of some nasty feuds and vendettas that had come the way of some who did, but then in everything, competition was his lifeblood, and to win was essential. Playing croquet with Sam could be a real "hazard."

He had a beautifully manicured lawn, and the best players in Hollywood gathered there on Sundays, but it was necessary to have an extra man stashed away in the trees because after disagreements Sam frequently stalked into the house and locked the front door. On particularly fraught occasions he dispatched a butler to fetch the drinks into the house after him. Nobody would have accused him of actually cheating at games—he just *had* to come out on top. I was playing a single at tennis with Goldwyn one day, and Fred Astaire (in reserve in case of emergencies) was watching. It was the first serve of the match, and I delivered a perfect ace into the corner. A puff of white dust arose to acclaim my feat.

"Doubles," said Goldwyn, and marched purposefully across to the other court.

Fred witnessed another bit of Goldwyn gamesmanship on a golf course. Sam sliced his ball into some trees, and it ended up in a virtually unplayable position. Fred grabbed my arm, shaking with laughter. "Look at him," he said. Goldwyn very methodically was moving stones and fallen branches and placing the ball in a position from which he had an uninterrupted view of the green. Then he produced a wooden tee from his pocket and put the ball upon it.

"Sam!" I yelled. "You can't *do* that!"

"I know," he shouted back. "My caddie *told* me I shouldn't."

If he was competitive at games, he displayed the toughness of stainless steel in business, and the fields were littered with the vanquished. Ronald Colman, after years under contract to him, refused even to speak to him again, and Eddie Cantor swore that working for Goldwyn put him in the hospital. In Goldwyn's office the rows with his top director, William Wyler, were so noisy that Merritt Hulbert, a distinguished editor of the *Saturday Evening Post*, who had become the head of Goldwyn's story department, asked to have his office moved to another floor. "Quiet story conferences make quiet pictures," retorted Goldwyn firmly, but eventually he and Wyler arranged a truce.

"Look, Willie," he said, "from now on when we meet, we each put a hundred-dollar bill on my desk, and the first one to shout loses his money."

"OK," said Wyler.

As a result, Hulbert stayed on in his office while, next door, appalling insults were traded in whispers.

I don't believe that Sam was rude on purpose. I think his thoughts flashed through his head with lightning speed, and sometimes he just didn't give his tongue enough time to check its possible effect on people. Once he shook the normally imperturbable Laurence Olivier by being too quick on the verbal draw. Goldwyn came on the set on the second day of shooting, having just seen the rushes of the first day's work on *Wuthering Heights*. We all stood nervously around waiting for the great man's comments.

He put his arm around Olivier's shoulders, and Larry prepared himself for the compliments which he thought must surely be coming his way.

"Willie," said Goldwyn to Wyler, who was hovering nearby, "would you look at that actor's *ugly* face?"

(Olivier told me that he objected chiefly to being called "that actor.")

Goldwyn had immense presence and a great dignity. His walk was athletic and always brisk. He lifted his heel at each stride. His head was almost completely bald from an early age, and his eyes were dark, small and deepset. His jaw was pronounced and very determined indeed. Employees from top to bottom at his studio were in awe of him for a very good reason—there was not a technical job on the lot that he could not fill perfectly himself. He was well aware of his awesome presence and seldom visited the sound stages because he knew that his appearance there sowed instant alarm and a feeling of impending doom in the breasts of one and all.

Directors, actors, cameramen, and sound technicians who had not reached the high standards he demanded of them were "sent for"; invariably they returned looking as though they had witnessed a terrible accident on Santa Monica Boulevard.

He never asked the banks to put up the money for his productions; however expensive, the sole financier of a Samuel Goldwyn film was Samuel Goldwyn himself. "The banks can't afford me," he said.

He had a deep and abiding interest in seeing that he got full value for his every dollar. It was not only we in his immediate vicinity who came under the microscope; exhibitors all over the world who showed Goldwyn's pictures received personal calls at all hours, demanding explanations of the finer points of their bookkeeping.

Little Samuel was born in 1882 in the Warsaw ghetto. At the age of eleven he ran away from home and found sanctuary with relatives in England, who quickly "placed" him as a blacksmith's assistant. He saved enough in the smithy for a steerage passage to New York, where an Irish immigration official, unable to cope with his unpronounceable Polish name, told him that from then on he would be known as Samuel Goldfish.

Young Sam migrated to Gloversville, New York, and became a glove salesman; a very good salesman, he sold enough gloves to be able at the age of twenty-eight to marry his first wife, Blanche Lasky.

In 1912 Samuel Goldfish decided that he could not look another glove in the face and that his future lay with the infant motion-picture business. His brother-in-law, Jesse Lasky, was a vaudeville producer, doing quite well, so he was not overly tempted when Sam proposed that they should join forces and take a gamble. Lasky, however, conjured up a possible partner in the shape of an actor and a writer of vaudeville acts—one Cecil B. DeMille.

DeMille fell for Sam's idea, and a year later the two of them prevailed on Lasky to put up $25,000. DeMille was dispatched to Flagstaff, Arizona, to direct their first picture—a Western with William S. Hart, *The Squaw Man*. Flagstaff was chosen because with the exception of Death Valley, it was reputed to have the lowest rainfall in the United States.

In any event, it poured with rain there for five consecutive weeks and a dispirited DeMille moved on to the more salubrious climate of California, whence he wired his partner that he had "rented a barn for $75 a month in the middle of an orange grove in a place called Hollywood." Hollywood was born.

The Squaw Man was a success, and with Samuel Goldfish handling distribution and exploitation, the company made twenty-one films that first year, but success bred mergers, and mergers bred palace revolutions, and Samuel Goldfish became allied with a theatrical producer from New York, the quiet, self-effacing Edgar Selwyn.

Using half their respective names, in a moment of mental aberration, they registered their combine as "The Selfish Company," but wiser counsel prevailed, and the halves were reversed. The Goldwyn Company flourished and its name became a household word, whereupon Samuel Goldfish, with what quiet, self-effacing Edgar Selwyn described as a piece of monumental commercial treachery, nipped down to City Hall with his lawyer and legally took the name of Goldwyn for himself.

The Goldwyn Company boomed, and more palace revolutions followed. Goldwyn discarded his wounded partner, Selwyn, but was himself bought out by new associates who merged the Goldwyn Company with Metro and L. B. Mayer.

Goldwyn agreed to this merger but cagily insisted that his name should remain in eye-catching sloping letters between the stereotyped ones of Metro and Mayer. Then he left METRO *Goldwyn* MAYER with their snarling lion trademark and became in 1924 what he was to remain until his retirement in 1965: the greatest independent producer the world has ever seen.

After Goldwyn became an independent producer, he joined forces for a while with other independent producers—Douglas Fairbanks, Charlie Chaplin, and Mary Pickford. Together they formed the United Artists Company to distribute their products, and among them they bought studios on Santa Monica Boulevard. Before long Goldwyn realized that he was the major contributor to the company's output and in a final major convulsion, unloaded his partners, plus the United Artists Company, and wound up owning the studios.

The aforementioned palace revolutions assuredly occurred because if Goldwyn found it difficult to work with partners, the partners found it just too nerve-racking working with him.

Around this time, having for several years been divorced from Blanche, Sam married a calm and beautiful young actress—Frances Howard, who presented him with an enchanting heir and provided him with a quiet, uncomplicated home and an enduring Hollywood marvel, a happy married life.

The house in the hills they built together on Laurel Way was a charmingly unpretentious white structure surrounded by an attractive garden, a pool, and a tennis court—the croquet lawn came later. Decorated by Frances with a light and happy touch, it had, apart from a few good Impressionist paintings and a comfortable projection room, none of the traditional trappings of the vintage movie mogul.

Goldwyn loved this sanctuary and guarded it jealously against all intrusion. One evening sitting on the veranda with him, inhaling the smell of magnolia blossom in the clean champagne air and enveloped by my boss's very considerable charm, I pointed out to him the splendid spectacle of a family of quail parading across his lawn. Father was in front, proudly bearing his antennae headdress, mother fussily at the back, and in between, in strict line-ahead formation, were eight scuttling little babies.

"They don't belong here," said Goldwyn coldly.

The Goldwyns entertained quietly: no big ostentatious parties, no monstrous striped tents covering a boarded-over swimming pool —just a few friends on a Saturday evening invited to enjoy dinner and afterward a movie or cards.

All the top producers and stars had movie theaters either inside their houses or as outcrops of their playrooms and pool houses; this was known as the Bel Air Circuit, and a menace it was, too. The competition to display the latest film to weekend guests was intense, and to obtain them, a great deal of rank pulling and subtle blackmail was employed.

Producers, directors, and actors quailed when they learned that their lifeblood was about to be poured out at one of these private showings where months of effort could easily be ruined if their film was heckled, mocked, and torn to shreds by loudmouthed and overlubricated know-alls talking back to the screen. The reputation of a picture was frequently blackened before the paying customers had a chance to judge for themselves, and it was not uncommon for a studio head, hearing of the hostile reception thus accorded one of his productions, chickenheartedly to downgrade the exploitation budget he had already apportioned to it.

This never happened in Goldwyn's house. Once the guests were comfortably seated, Sam manned the sound controls himself, Frances settled herself, full length and rug-covered on a sofa, and the film, good or bad, was unfolded with honor and dignity. Afterward Goldwyn might invite discussion of its merits or demerits, but always his was the most generous and constructive of criticism. Secure in his own integrity as a filmmaker, he felt no need to chop down the opposition.

"The play's the thing"—Goldwyn early believed that Shakespeare had a point there. Although he produced only two or three pictures a year, he entered into long contracts with big established stars such as Ronald Colman and Gary Cooper and signed with a view to building them up to follow in the footsteps of their betters, a small band of unknowns, but his major outlay was always in the direction of the authors, and frequently, he would have several screenplays prepared by different writers from the same material; then he would choose the best and make his picture.

Employed by Goldwyn, but never incarcerated in the chicken-coop writers' buildings, the iniquitous "script batteries" of the major studios were, among others, F. Scott Fitzgerald, Robert Sherwood, John Huston, Maurice Maeterlinck, Lillian Hellman, Ben Hecht, and Thornton Wilder.

Could such a man *really* have held the following conversation with Edward G. Robinson?

ROBINSON: Sam, my studio is going to make *The Merchant of Venice*. They want me to play Shylock. Should I accept?

GOLDWYN: Screw 'em. . . . Tell 'em you'll only play the Merchant.

Robinson swore it happened.
I doubt it.

Goldwyn had an instinct, an instinct about everything to do with filmmaking. As far as music went, for example, he was incapable of differentiating between *Firebird* and "The Flight of the Bumblebee," and Al Newman, the musical director on many of his pictures, told us that Sam had congratulated him on his "wonderful new sounds" when by mistake he had played a new composition backwards on the sound track, but Sam in his own inscrutable way was right—the sounds fitted the scene, so Newman just accepted the praise and kept his mouth shut.

If Goldwyn surrounded himself with the best creative talent that his own money could buy, his formula for making a successful movie was deceptively simple:

1. Forget what other people are making.

2. Never worry about trends.

3. Buy a property that *you* think will make a good picture.

4. Hire the best writer or writers to give you a screenplay.

5. Employ the best director to translate that screenplay onto celluloid.

6. Give him the cast he wants and the cameraman he believes in.

7. Control the whole thing yourself, and *above all, take the blame if it goes wrong.*

"Goldwyn is not an easy man to work for. . . ." For half a century that remained the understatement of the year. Many people suffered under his arrogance and bullheadedness; tact was a word unknown to him, and his feuds were deep, bitter, and sometimes endless, but he, too, was fallible, and in spite of a spectacular string of successes, he inevitably suffered a few disappointments. In 1934 he signed the Russian actress Anna Sten, who had appeared in a silent version of *The Brothers Karamazov*. She duly arrived in America long on avoirdupois and short on English. Goldwyn uncorked a costly campaign of publicity and to no avail employed a regiment of physical culturists and several Professor Higginses. He then threw the result into the hesitant arms of Gary Cooper. "Coop" reeled under the impact of his leading lady, who remained resolutely incomprehensible for several films. The whole operation cost Goldwyn a small fortune. Gable he once turned down because "his ears are too big," and after buying the *Wonderful Wizard of*

Oz, he decided that it would never make a picture and sold it, a cut-rate bargain, to MGM.

One setback he sustained particularly irked him. He was trying to coax the elusive Garbo into working for him. He managed to lure her up to his house for dinner—a most carefully prepared meal catering especially to her Nordic taste—intending once she had thus been softened up on smorgasbord and "Jonson's Temptation" to persuade her to sign a contract. After dinner, however, Garbo spent two hours talking to his Swedish cook, then slipped out through the kitchen door and went home.

Goldwyn could extricate himself from apparently impossible situations with the dexterity of Houdini. At great expense he bought the hit Broadway play *Children's Hour.* As it was about lesbian schoolmistresses in a girls' school, it was not surprising, in those days, that the Hays Office flatly refused to let him make it into a film.

Undaunted, he changed the title to *These Three* and had the plot altered to focus on the problems of two sex-starved schoolmistresses competing for the affections of a rampant schoolmaster. With Miriam Hopkins, Merle Oberon, and Joel McCrea in the leading roles, the picture was a huge success.

Sam early learned to make the newspaper correspondents his friends and never repeated an early error when he "gave away" Vilma Banky, one of his first stars, at her marriage to her leading man, Rod La Rocque. The ceremony took place at Goldwyn's studio, and the suspect molars of several reporters flew apart when they bit into cakes and fruit provided by Sam's plasterers and painters. Thereafter Goldwyn's publicity department was geared to promoting Goldwyn the producer. The stars, directors, and authors he employed became of secondary importance, and the result of this, coupled with the almost unbelievably high standard of his product, was that all over the world distributors fought to obtain the next Samuel Goldwyn Production before he announced what it was about or who would appear in it.

"The Goldwyn Touch" was legendary, and he spared no expense to perpetuate it. "Good taste" were his watchwords on the screen.

We were rehearsing that subtle fantasy *The Bishop's Wife* (all Goldwyn pictures were carefully rehearsed in their entirety before shooting started). I was playing the Bishop, Loretta Young, the wife, and Cary Grant, the Angel. Bill Seiter, normally a director of broad comedy, was at the helm.

The day before shooting was to start, Goldwyn decided that the interiors of the Bishop's house were not ecclesiastical enough and ordered several sets to be torn down, redesigned, and rebuilt. For three weeks, while this was going on, production was halted; then, two days after the cameras finally had a chance to turn, Goldwyn decided that Seiter's hand was a little too heavy on the tiller; he was removed, paid his full salary, and after a week Goldwyn hired Henry Koster to start again from scratch—with another two weeks of rehearsal. All this must have cost Goldwyn several hundred thousand dollars, but in the end, he got what he wanted.

Always a perfectionist, when we were preparing a picture in which I had to age from twenty-five to seventy, Goldwyn talked me into having my hair bleached white for the last scene instead of wearing a wig. He examined the result of several trips to a women's beauty parlor, ignored the fact that my own dog had attacked me on sight the night before, and said, "It looks good. Now we have to slow down your movements as the old man."

So saying, he ordained that sixty pounds of lead should be distributed in the soles of my shoes and about my clothing. When he called me again to his office to inspect the result of his brainstorm, I arrived like a heavily handicapped racehorse.

An argument developed over the physical fatigue that I stoutly held would prostrate me during the long, hot hours of shooting. During this altercation I sprang from my chair to make my point and strode briskly about his office, but Goldwyn was right: My spring had become a rheumaticky rise, and my stride a stately totter. As a result of carting that lead around for weeks, I was a gibbering wreck by the end of the picture, but on the last day of shooting Goldwyn came on the set and gave me a complimentary lecture about how I had proved the necessity of always having a completely natural makeup.

"Well," I said, "I'm glad you're happy. Now what are you going to do about my hair?"

"What's the matter with it?" asked Goldwyn.

"I want it put back the way it was," I said.

"What was it before?"

"I can't remember—a sort of rich mouse color, I think."

Bob Stephanoff, the makeup man, was instructed to dye me back to normal, but it came out jet black and shiny, like that of a Japanese general, and during two weeks' holiday in Bermuda, the salt water and sun turned it into a metallic magenta. I was stuck with it for about a year, and the review of our joint efforts which I liked least came from the Los Angeles *Examiner*: "a pity Goldwyn allowed Niven to ruin his performance by wearing an appalling wig."

This, of course, is not intended to be a portrait of Samuel Goldwyn. At most, it is a few hesitant lines of a preliminary drawing, because in spite of many years of close association with him, I was never able to see him clearly. By an accident of birth, I was not born Frances Howard or Samuel Goldwyn, Jr., and I suspect that only they could do so.

To me he was like crème brulée—rock hard on the outside and surprisingly soft underneath. When he first pulled me out of the extra ranks and offered me a contract for seven years starting at $100 a week, I was in such a hurry to sign it, before he changed his mind, that I failed to notice that he had reserved the right to drop me at the end of every three months during the first two years and that I would have to face twelve weeks of layoff without pay each year. I just grabbed the contract gratefully and signed it with a heart pumping at the realization of the unbelievable good fortune that had befallen me. Then I walked to Hollywood Boulevard and did something I had always wanted to do: I went to the Ford dealer and flashing my golden credit card—my contract with the great Samuel Goldwyn—pointed to a two-seater convertible and said, "I'll take *that* one." Then I drove slowly back to the studio to display my shiny beauty before the admiring employees in the casting office.

Bob McIntyre, the kindly head of that department, looked embarrassed.

"Take it back again, son," he advised. "Mr. Goldwyn has just called down. You're on layoff for six weeks."

So much for the hard outside, but the gooey inside was often revealed by massive and unpublicized blood transfusions to charities and by unexpected generosity to the people who worked for him as lesser employees at his studio. To them he was a father figure who demanded and got an awesome standard. They gave him their best, and he looked after them. They loved him and would not hear a word against him, especially from the smart manufacturers of Goldwynisms. For a beginner it was incredible luck to be picked off the floor by Goldwyn. From 1935 to 1950 I had happy times with Goldwyn and sad times, some dizzy heights and some heartbreaking lows: arguments, battles, silences, suspensions, handshakes, meanness, sudden generosity, rages, and sunny smiles. In the end I repaid the man to whom I owed so much by getting too big for my boots and was, with great justification, fired. Only then did I really find a friend.

It is just possible, in spite of what I have intimated, that Sam perpetrated more Goldwynisms than I thought. If so, then I was the recipient of one sent by cable. It was delivered to me in London during World War II at a time when selected actors were released from military service to make films considered to be of importance to the national war effort.

PARAMOUNT INQUIRING IF YOU COULD OBTAIN RELEASE FROM ARMY TO PLAY J.M.BARRIE'S HERO QUOTE THE ADMIRAL CRICHTON UNQUOTE. GOLDWYN.

I still prefer to think the slipup was at Western Union.

8
"The Emperor"

IN the summer of 1947 I was settling myself luxuriously into a booth in the bar of Romanoff's Restaurant in Beverly Hills. It was lunchtime, and the smartest, the chicest, and the owners of the best-known faces in Movie Town were arriving in droves, pausing to make their "entrances" into the main dining room. It was nice to be in the dark air-conditioned cool of the bar, nice to be out of the glare of the midday sun, above all, nice to be in the company of the diminutive proprietor of the joint—His Imperial Highness, Prince Michael Alexandrovich Dmitri Obolensky Romanoff.

"Old boy," my diminutive host intoned in his deep, slightly "off" Oxford voice, "your Emperor has ordered an ice-cold bottle of Dom Pérignon and some grouse which were flown in specially this morning from your native Scotland."

He extracted a monogrammed cigarette from a heavily embossed golden case (monogrammed with the imperial R of course), and I noticed once more that his thumbs arched back when he was gesticulating, almost to his wrist—a sign of great generosity, it is claimed, and with Mike Romanoff it was often proved.

The headwaiter approached with a deferential inclination of the head.

"We must find room for this party, Mr. Romanoff. They're very important . . . eight of them."

"Who are they?" demanded Mike.

"Oilmen from Texas and society people from Pasadena—very rich."

"Peasants," said His Imperial Highness. "Fuck 'em."

Ten minutes later the scene was repeated. "Very important, Mr. Romanoff—Main Line society people from Philadelphia."

"*Canaille!*" said Mike from the imperial tumbrel.

"And there's a general waiting in line too, Mr. Romanoff . . . from St. Louis. . . ."

"Cannon fodder," commented the prince, "from the Interior, too," he added with disgust.

Harry F. Gerguson of Chicago, as Mike was known in the records of the New York police department, had also been described officially by Scotland Yard as "a rogue of uncertain nationality." He had been jailed countless times in the United States and in France and had received two suspended sentences in England. He had been deported regularly from all three countries and twice on transatlantic liners had been caught, a first-class stowaway using empty cabins. In December, 1922, unable to prove his American citizenship, he was held on Ellis Island. He escaped, by swimming he claimed, to the Battery. It is a matter of record that he disappeared from Ellis Island at that time, but it is equally true that without water wings, he could never swim a stroke. All his crimes had been what he termed "moves of self-preservation"— failing to return things he had borrowed without asking, selling *objets d'art* which did not belong to him, and passing enough dud checks on both sides of the Atlantic to provide his own ticker-tape parade. All these misdemeanors had been perpetrated in what he considered the best possible cause—to help Harry F. Gerguson live in the style to which Prince Michael Alexandrovich Dmitri Obolensky Romanoff would have been accustomed.

There was absolutely no malice in the man, and even when he had been at his most reprehensible, he had behaved like a latter-day Robin Hood, extracting cash from the wealthy and joyfully sharing the benefits accruing therefrom with his friends.

Many people who had been "taken" by Mike became his most ardent supports, and slowly he had evolved from being a full-time impostor and international con man into the honest burgher of Beverly Hills who was pouring ice-cold Dom Pérignon on that warm July day.

The headwaiter approached again and whispered in his ear, jerking his head disapprovingly toward the bar.

"Give them my Imperial greetings," said Mike, without hesitation, "take them to the best table you have, and serve them anything they want; then send the account to the Winter Palace."

I watched the headwaiter approach two men at the bar and recognized them as a well-known actor and an excellent writer; both had served with gallantry with the Marines on Okinawa, and Mike was one of the few who cared that since their return to Hollywood they had found themselves largely forgotten and the going very rough.

I first met Mike in New York at the tail end of Prohibition; we frequented the same speakeasy, Jack and Charlie's at 21 West Fifty-second Street, where I had just been taken on as their first salesman of legitimate booze. I was not selling very much, so after his initial effort Mike realized that putting the bite on me for ten bucks was living in Mother Hubbard Land, and we became good friends in need. He never seemed to lack for invitations to meals, but he was very reticent about where he lived, and depending on whom he was talking to and his estimate of their gullibility, he operated a sliding scale of claims of kinship to the murdered czar. It fluctuated wildly. Sometimes he was the czar's nephew, occasionally his half brother, often he was the son of Prince Yusupov, who had pumped booze and bullets into Rasputin, and on particularly low-risk occasions, he became Yusupov himself. When he operated in the "Interior," he occasionally dropped his Russian connections, and in Chicago he took on a British aura, sticking closely to the Duke of Wellington, wearing a monocle and calling himself Sir Arthur Wellesley, Count Mornington, or plain William Wellington, Esquire, but he sometimes got his priorities a little mixed and referred to the Prince of Wales as "my cousin David."

In spite of his acquired accent, Mike's heart was never English, and as the years passed, it seemed as though he increasingly came to believe a large part of his Romanoff fantasy.

With New York harboring countless Russians of noble birth, Mike was again and again denounced as an impostor, but on such occasions he conducted himself with such immense dignity that he added to his growing coterie of admirers, who remember with awe his occasional courageous defenses of his indefensible situation and his battles against appalling physical odds in a number of barroom brawls. A particularly unattractive verbal confrontation occurred when somebody invited the Grand Duke Dmitri of Russia to meet his kinsman. The grand duke peered suspiciously at the top of Mike's hairbrush crew cut and spoke to him rapidly in Russian. Mike made for the door, raising a languid hand to silence him.

"I don't think," he said, "that we should insult our hosts by talking in any language but theirs."

Afterward he confided that he had never much cared for that branch of the family.

For anyone with Mike's flair and humor it was inevitable that sooner or later he would feel the call of the Hollywood wild, and in 1927 His Imperial Highness arrived aboard the Santa Fe Chief, took a large suite in the Ambassador Hotel, and started dispensing princely amounts of champagne and caviar to all and sundry. Vowing haughtily that the Romanoffs never dirtied their fingers with common currency, he tipped headwaiters and bellhops with great abandon by check and, at the end of his visit, signed his bill with a flourish and departed for pastures new.

The prince was lavishly entertained by Hollywood hostesses, and Warner Brothers begged him to be their technical adviser on *The Desired Woman*, a picture with a Sudanese background and a British army foreground. Mike admitted modestly that he had indeed served with the British army in the Great War and that it just so happened that he knew the Sudan like the back of his hand. He pulled down a royal salary for many weeks and became much sought after by the studios as technical adviser on all pictures with Russian or British overtones. These for a while he haughtily turned down and undertook instead a lecture tour of Pasadena, Whittier, Santa Barbara, and Pismo Beach—his subject "Russia Past and Present." When the proceeds from the tour dried up, Mike took a calculated risk and accepted one of the studios' offers. It proved his undoing. An old friend of the late czar—an ex-general, named Theodor Lodijensky—was working as an extra on the film, and he promptly alerted the Los Angeles *Examiner*. The next day a frontpage story exposed Mike as an impostor, and he was publicly defrocked.

Finding Southern California suddenly uncomfortably warm, Mike decided to disappear for a cooling-off period, and the "Interior" was soon papering itself with his dud checks. He kept on the move, however, and, apart from the odd night in jail, largely stayed ahead of the sheriff, and from his uncomfortable perch on various flatcars, he enjoyed uninterrupted views of a large portion of the United States. But if the authorities found it hard to catch up with him, that ghastly creature bearing scythe and hourglass was breathing down his neck. Well into his forties by now, Mike was longing to settle in one place, and soon he was back in Los Angeles, broke as usual but with a new light in his eye—he had determined to stop moving and to go straight.

Mike's true genius was his ability to make admiring and staunch friends out of the very people who had the best reasons for disliking or distrusting him. His turn into the straight was a gradual one. Instead of borrowing money, he now preferred winning it at backgammon or chess, at which he was an expert, playing several games at once all over the country by telegram. Throughout his metamorphosis, he clung tenaciously to his Romanoff fantasy, but however much he believed it himself, he now traded on it openly and encouraged people to pay false court to him and became more widely admired, feted, and entertained as a famous impostor than he ever had been in the days when he was accepted as the real thing.

He foreswore his time-honored role of freeloader and now, if he joined a friend's table for luncheon, he would meticulously pay his share if he was in funds; if not, he would sit nibbling a roll and sipping a glass of water. We knew better than to press him.

Twentieth Century-Fox employed him occasionally as a reader of possible film material or as a synopsis writer, and he acquitted himself well there and at other studios, but on Friday nights we made a point of avoiding him because payday to Mike was merely an excuse to entertain his friends at the Trocadero, snapping his fingers and ordering large quantities of the best wines to wash down out-of-season delicacies.

By 1939 I was living in comfort in a small house on the beach at Santa Monica. Mike was a frequent and most welcome visitor; he never borrowed money but occasionally asked if he might have the loan of a bed "on which to lay the Imperial head." He made the trips to Santa Monica by bumming lifts. One day he drove up to the door in an immense drophead Duesenberg.

"Greetings, old boy," he said smugly.

"Who did you borrow it from?" I asked.

"It's mine," said the prince, "I bought it last week."

"I don't believe you," I said ungraciously.

Mike frowned his displeasure at my bad taste. "Allow me to show you the pink slip."

He then displayed the coveted document proving that he had indeed made the purchase.

I goggled.

"Where are you sleeping?" I asked.

"Why, in the Duesenberg, of course," said the Imperial motorist.

Even though by now he was playing his impostor role for a different effect, he still used the trappings of his calling, wearing an Old Etonian tie one day and a Brigade of Guards scarf the next. His conversations still pulsated with "when I was up at Oxford," "during my time at Sandhurst," or "he was a classmate of mine at Harvard."

It was no easy job to catch him out; many tried and failed. There were dozens of witnesses to prove that in 1923, for a few months at least, he had indeed studied at the Graduate School of Arts and Sciences at Harvard, and I heard an old Etonian question him about Eton.

"Who was your housemaster?" he asked.

"You mean who was 'me tutor,'" countered Mike swiftly, and followed up his advantage by saying, "I suppose you'll be asking me next if I went to Thomas' in the High Street to get my hair cut."

As an ex-Sandhurst man myself I found his knowledge of the goings-on, the military procedure, and the habits and hideaways of the cadets at the Royal Military College to be just as extensive as my own, and I did not doubt that when he poured out the names of officers, cadets, and staff of his supposed period there, he would have been correct down to the last hyphen and decoration.

"How many schools and colleges *have* you attended?" I asked him once.

"Let me see," said Mike. "St. Paul's, Andover, Choate, and Harvard in the United States. Eton, Harrow, Winchester, Oxford,

Cambridge, and Sandhurst in England and, of course, the Sorbonne and Heidelberg. Believe me, old boy"—he chortled—"this business of being an impostor is a full-time job!"

It was Mike's British accent that always fascinated me. I could never put my finger on it. It was the sort of camouflage that English curates perfect to cover up honest Cockney voices. This "plummy" delivery never left Mike, and even on the very few occasions, those testing times when he took a glass or two too many, it remained as much a part of him as his bristly crew-cut pate and his military mustache.

I could never discover whence this strange sound originated. The secret of its source was locked away in the same little mental strongbox in which he kept the key to his whereabouts during the blood-drenched years between 1914 and 1918. The twin mysteries have never been solved, but during his many unveilings as an impostor, Mike stated under questioning that he had passed World War I as an officer with a British regiment in France or with Allenby in Palestine; he also claimed that the eastern front had enjoyed the benefit of his presence and expertise as a Cossack reconnaissance captain (though his horsemanship was later proved to be on a par with his prowess at swimming). He hinted at driving a taxi for the French army during the epic defense of Paris and vigorously defended his right to wear in his buttonhole the red ribbon of the Légion d'honneur, but whether or not he gathered any decorations during that period it was certainly then that he acquired his British accent and his military mementos.

In 1937 Mike struck gold. He obtained an option on the lease of a defunct restaurant on the Sunset Strip. His friends became stockholders in the shoestring enterprise, and the place reopened in a blaze of black ties, mink, well-known faces, and publicity.

The invitation was a classic:

I AM COMMANDED BY HIS IMPERIAL HIGHNESS PRINCE MICHAEL ALEXANDROVICH DMITRI OBOLENSKY ROMANOFF TO REQUEST YOUR PRESENCE AT A SOIREE HE IS GIVING IN HIS OWN HONOR . . . COUVERT FIFTY DOLLARS
BRING YOUR OWN WINE AND KINDLY FEE THE WAITERS

HARRY GERGUSON
COMPTROLLER TO THE IMPERIAL HOUSEHOLD

Le tout Hollywood turned out in force, and so many people brought wine that few realized the place had no arrangements whatever for cooking. A sparse menu was serviced by a nearby hash joint on a strictly cash basis (the money collected for the first two couverts started the ball rolling), a riotous evening was had by all, and enough money raised to install a kitchen and launch Mike on a fabulously successful career as a restaurateur.

In 1939, when I was headed for Europe and the British army, Mike came to say good-bye and gave me some advice: "If you become an officer, invent a pair of trousers that immediately drop around your knees when you are ordered to charge. Then you just say 'On! On! Men! Don't wait for me. I'll catch you up.'"

He also gave me a hand-knitted balaclava helmet ("saved me near St. Petersburg, old boy") and a large blue and white spotted scarf with a burn in the center ("mustard gas . . . Cambrai . . . silk is the only thing against it"). I lost the hand-knitted balaclava helmet, but I still have the blue and white spotted scarf; a laundress told me that careless ironing was responsible for the burn.

Restaurateur Mike prospered during World War II, and by 1945 he was firmly established as the owner-manager of the highly lucrative Romanoff's in Beverly Hills. The imperial R was emblazoned on the front door. When he branched out into an even larger and more elaborate establishment, his loyal staff and clients and the imperial R made the move with him. Around that time he also started a subsidiary on an escarpment near Palm Springs called Romanoff on the Rocks, accumulated a bulldog named Confucius, and an extremely attractive young wife, Gloria. His Imperial Highness had made the big switch from con man to capitalist and, in a strange reversal of form, had not lost a friend in the process.

Mike loved children, and one of my reasons for visiting him on that hot summer's day was to thank him for yet another kindness toward mine. As a widower I had been finding it a difficult job to bring up two small boys and at the same time earn my living. Friends had come to my aid, and Mike, with a constant flow of ideas, had been in the van of the rescue operation.

The evening before, I had arrived home from work to find the children waiting at the garden gate, shiny-eyed with excitement.

"Mr. Romanoff took us on a treasure hunt! Look what we

found!" and they proudly displayed ropes of pearls, huge rubies, and handfuls of "doubloons."

Mike had staged it all meticulously, arriving unexpectedly with a picnic basket and a carefully drawn pirate's map of a lonely part of the beach ten miles away near Trancas. There had been clues and red herrings and arrows made of pieces of driftwood, and finally, after a long search, the corner of a treasure chest had been spied just showing above the sand in a pirate's cave. Mike must have spent hours arranging it all, but he brushed aside my thanks. "The pleasure was all mine, old boy . . . children are nature's gentlemen . . . I far prefer their company to that of grownups."

Over luncheon I sought to enlist Mike's help for a project of my own. Robert Laycock was coming to visit me, and I wanted Romanoff's to cater a party I was planning for him.

"Ah, and how is young Bob?" asked Mike the minute he heard the name. "I haven't seen him since he was at Eton."

"Now, Mike," I said patiently, "Bob Laycock is twenty years younger than you. You were never at Eton with him or anybody else for that matter."

Mike looked pained.

"I did not suggest that young Bob was a schoolmate of mine—I merely mentioned the fact that I had not seen him since he was at Eton."

It was always fun to play along with Mike, so I gave him a cue. "And where did you meet him while he was a schoolboy?"

"At Wiseton, of course, he was home after the summer half and Sir Joseph had invited me for the weekend for a spot of country house cricket."

Wiseton was indeed the Laycock home in Lincolnshire, and Sir Joseph was certainly Bob's father, so I could not suppress a start of surprise. Mike noticed this and pressed home the advantage.

"Yes, old Joe and I were very close and Kitty, too, of course . . . too bad she lost a leg on their honeymoon."

Mike had obviously had reason somewhere along the line to research the Laycock family very carefully, but the mental picture of him in blazer and white flannels, sitting in a deck chair, sipping tea and eating cucumber sandwiches while waiting his turn to bat, was too much even for me.

"Mike, please," I said, "please don't get into a thing with Bob

439

Laycock about his mother having only one leg because he may not appreciate it, and he's a very rough character indeed—he was the chief of all the Commandos, you know."

"And the youngest general in the British army," said Mike, unmoved. "I'm very proud of him."

I shook my head. "Mike, please, on this one occasion, *please* don't press your luck." There was a pause.

"A'ter luncheon," said my host, "we will go to my house—I have something to show you which may put your mind at rest."

Back at Mike's white stucco residence on Chevy Chase Drive, he took me up to his bedroom; there he nonchalantly displayed a pair of ivory hairbrushes. The ivory was a little yellow with age, but what brought me up all standing was the insignia in worked silver on their backs. It was something I knew very well—the crest of the Laycock family.

"A present from old Joe," said Mike smugly.

Bob Laycock duly arrived on his visit, and the party as catered by Romanoff's was a great success. I had warned Bob about Mike and hoped against hope that Mike would stay off the subject of Wiseton. Far from it. For a large part of the evening, Mike cornered Bob, who seemed to be enjoying thoroughly the company of the mini-monarch from whose expressive gestures I could see from across the room that both cricket and hairbrushes were being discussed at length. Nothing awful happened, however, and the happy guests finally departed. After they had gone, Bob and I had a nightcap and held the usual postmortem on the evening.

"What did you think of Mike?" I asked.

"Fascinating," said Bob. "He had me stumped completely. There is no question but that he has been to Wiseton and no question at all that he has played cricket there. There is also no question that long ago a team of Durham miners came over to play. I well remember it because Father was so furious. When they left, it was discovered that someone had swiped his favorite hairbrushes." Prince Michael Alexandrovich Dmitri Obolensky Romanoff remained enigmatic when I tried to pump him.

"Golden days, old boy," was all he would say dreamily. "Golden days."

He steadfastly refused to answer my question: "What was Harry F. Gerguson of Chicago doing down a Durham coal mine?"

9
Two Queens

CONNIE

*A*T five o'clock on Sunday afternoons in the late thirties, tennis courts would empty and streets would become thinly populated. America liked to be by a radio set at that hour so it could listen to Edgar Bergen and his wooden top-hatted and monocled ventriloquist dummy, Charlie McCarthy.

The audiences for the big radio shows were enormous with 40,000,000 or 50,000,000 addicted to the like of Cecil B. DeMille's *Lux Radio Theater* and the *Lucky Strike Hit Parade*, but just as the advent of sound had a winnowing effect on the popularity of the silent film stars, so was the arrival of television destined to put an end to the careers of many radio personalities. Bob Hope, Jack Benny, George Burns, Gracie Allen, Jimmy Durante, and a few others made the transition with flying colors, but Edgar Bergen went under because people thought they could see his lips move when Charlie McCarthy was talking, and they were distracted by his strained smile and bobbing Adam's apple. Gravelly-voiced Fred Allen, who headed a wonderfully well-written weekly show which included Allen's Alley, a street peopled by hilariously contemporary characters, faded away because he was unveiled as a crotchety, sour-faced man with a bad complexion, and the longest-

running show of all, heard nightly for twelve years—*Amos 'n'*
Andy, the comic antics of two blacks in the Deep South—disintegrated when the cameras disclosed the fact that the well-known
voices had been issuing from two whites.

After the big radio shows had departed, the performers were long
remembered with affection complete with their signature tunes
and sayings:

> "Thanks for the Memory"—Bob Hope
> "When the Blue of the Night Meets the Gold of the Day"—
> Bing Crosby
> "Inka-Dinka-Doo"—Jimmy Durante
> "Wanna buy a duck?"—Joe Penner
> "Vas you d'ere, Sharley?"—Jack Pearl
> and the squeals of Baby Snooks—Fanny Brice

Even the Morse sender which the gossip columnist Walter
Winchell used to attract attention to his scurrilous gibberish was
mourned in some quarters:

> Tap. Tap. Tap. "Good evening, Mr. and Mrs. North
> America, and all the ships at sea. Let's go to press!"

During World War II radio's foreign correspondents became
household pets, William Shirer, Charles Collingwood, Cecil
Brown, and Quentin Reynolds to name some of the most beloved,
and the defiant growl of Churchill became as much a part of
America as President Roosevelt's Fireside Chats beginning "My
friends," but it was the deep clear voice of Edward R. Murrow
broadcasting from London during the 190 days of the blitz which
brought tears to American eyes. "This is London. . . . I am speaking to you from a city in flames."

Radio acting was not easy, the trick being to sound as though
you were not reading, even though many rehearsals had bred over-
familiarity and suddenly a simple word could stare up at you from
the page—an unrecognizable jumble of letters. Radio actors were a
fascinating breed—performers who lived by their voices alone,
never seen by their admirers and often preferring it that way. There

was, for instance, one middle-aged lady whose minimal physical attractions were compensated for by the fact that she could produce the most seductive tones ever to come out of a twenty-year-old. Several times I was called on to play ardent love scenes with her, and for a young film actor, it required the marshaling of every reserve of imagination to be able to speak adoringly to her over the top of a microphone while averting my eyes from the gray roots of her hair and the heavy deposit of dandruff on her shoulders.

Some radio actors could produce twenty or thirty accents and dialects, while comedy voices were the forte of others, among whom the most sought after was Mel Blanc, famous for supplying the endearing quack words of Donald Duck and the strange mechanical sounds of Jack Benny's Maxwell automobile. But the backbone of the dramatic shows was the sound-effects men. These individuals were highly regarded by the studio audiences who watched their every move as from a forest of gadgets they coaxed the sounds of popping corks, electrical storms, galloping horses, crying babies, crashing aircraft, escaping steam, and burning buildings, but sometimes they elicited a response from their admirers which puzzled the unwary performer. Struggling through the thornbushes of the North-West Frontier with Victor McLaglen in *Gunga Din*, I was panting as ordered by the script and whispering "audience orientation" dialogue. "Phew, this undergrowth is heavy." To which McLaglen replied, "So's this dynamite I'm carrying, but we'll teach 'em a lesson with it when we get to the fort up ahead there in the clearing . . . don't make a sound." It was supposedly a tense and exciting moment, but the studio audience was tittering loudly, and we did not have far to look for the reason. The sound-effects man was simulating the heavy crackling of the bushes by wrapping toilet paper around his microphone.

The studio audience became specialists in their field. They lined up from early morning outside the enclaves of the Columbia Broadcasting System and the National Broadcasting Company on Sunset Boulevard, waiting patiently for free passes to see their favorite shows and to watch their favorite performers. Radio producers were pleased to see these "professional" audiences because they paid for their free passes by enthusiastically obeying the instructions waved aloft on boards emblazoned with LAUGH! or APPLAUSE! A select few could be relied on to sniffle.

The big radio shows carried tremendous publicity value, and the movie producers were delighted when their stars were offered the exposure. Some shows were popular with the top film performers, others, if possible, they avoided like the plague, but Louella Parsons had a blackmailing show called *Hollywood Hotel*, and a few years later Hedda Hopper, the other all-powerful columnist, came up with her own con game—*Hedda Hopper's Hollywood*. The big stars, goaded by their studios, performed on these programs at great inconvenience and for no salary because the chickenhearted producers believed that refusal to "lend" their stars would bring swift retribution in the shape of bad publicity and poor reviews.

The revulsion of the big film stars against the Parsons and Hopper shows was widespread, but they lined up happily to be heard on the big dramatic offerings or even as guest stars on comedy programs with Bergen, Crosby, Benny, or Hope, being well aware that exposure to the listening millions in well-written and well-produced material could do their film careers nothing but good. Some, like Constance Bennett, were a trifle condescending in their attitude toward what they considered the poor relation of the entertainment world, and this was a hazard for which I had been ill prepared when my first boss, Samuel Goldwyn, gave the electrifying news that he had lent me to the *Shell Hour* to play opposite the most highly paid film star in the world in selected love scenes from Pirandello.

Constance Bennett I had long worshiped from afar. She seemed to me the quintessence of a movie queen. She radiated glamor from her exalted position in the Hollywood firmament, and everything about her shone! Her burnished head, her iridescent skin, her jewels, her famous smile, her lovely long legs, and the highly publicized fact that she pulled down thirty thousand bucks a week. If Marlene Dietrich possessed a Cadillac the length of a subway train, driven by a chauffeur named Briggs who had a mink collar on his uniform in winter and a brace of revolvers on his hips, and Jeanette MacDonald was ferried about in her conveyance by a smart gentleman who shared the front seat with a large gray and white sheepdog, then Constance Bennett was out of place in anything but her Rolls-Royce, a shiny black beauty of a phaeton, with *her* chauffeur sitting outside in all weathers while she sat behind in a velvet-lined compartment decorated on the outside with yellow wickerwork. I was excited at the thought of what the next few days had in store for me, but the Shell people were overwhelmed to have such a glamor queen on their program, and their awe of her seemed to inhibit them from giving her precise calls to rehearsal.

"Here's her home number, Dave," said the director ten days before the fatal Saturday. "Why don't you give her a call, then go over to her place and kinda kick it around together before we start full rehearsals Tuesday?"

Over the first weekend I familiarized myself with the scenes, and on Monday, about midday, I dutifully called Constance Bennett's house.

"Miss Bennett does not awaken before three o'clock," said a butler. "Kindly leave a message and your phone number with her secretary." He switched me over. I explained to the secretary the reason for my call. She was sympathetic but unimpressed.

"Well, there's plenty of time, isn't there? . . . The show's not till Saturday, and it's only radio! . . . We'll call you later."

I hung around my boxlike apartment for the rest of Monday, but nothing happened. On Tuesday morning early the director called me.

"How's it been goin', kid?" he asked, and from the anxiety in his voice, I knew that he too had enjoyed little contact with his star.

"Jesus!" he shrieked when I told him. "The first rehearsal's at two o'clock."

Later he called back and said that it had been canceled for that day but that he had arranged an appointment for me at Constance Bennett's house on the morrow.

"And you'd better be there," he snarled as though I were responsible for the nonevent so far.

As ordered, I reported at a most attractive house in Carolwood Drive at eleven o'clock on Wednesday morning. The butler showed me into a library, where I read magazines till two o'clock. At three I heard a car leave, and the butler brought me a tuna fish sandwich and a glass of beer.

"Miss Bennett has fittings at the studio," he said. "She said she was sorry to miss you and to come back tomorrow at the same time."

"I'd like to speak to the secretary," I said.

"She's gone, too," said the butler. "Coffee?"

On Thursday morning about ten o'clock the secretary called. "Sorry to disappoint you," she said. "Miss Bennett can't make it today, after all, but you have an invitation to lunch tomorrow, two thirty and bring a tennis racket." She hung up.

Nobody called from the *Shell Hour*, so I decided they must have been keeping themselves abreast of events.

I awoke on Friday morning in a highly nervous condition. One did not fool around with Pirandello, even if one was reading it, and certainly not in front of 20,000,000 people. The dress rehearsal with full orchestra and effects was scheduled to begin the following morning at ten o'clock, and the show itself would be broadcast at five that evening. Much depended on my forthcoming luncheon date with the star.

I arrived on the dot of two thirty to find a couple of dozen people already sampling various beverages on the patio. The secretary introduced herself and presented me to the others. It was a friendly and extroverted group, and I was able to relax. The talk was mostly about a poker game the night before at which, I gathered, my hostess had been the big winner. Good-humored threats of revenge were being issued, but La Bennett did not hear them—she was sleeping peacefully upstairs. After luncheon her resident and permanent "beau," the romantic-looking Mexican actor Gilbert Roland, took me by the arm. "Let's get some exercise, amigo," he said, and led me down to the tennis court.

We played singles and doubles till the light began to go. As it faded, I remembered Pirandello, and my nerves started twanging anew. I enlisted Gilbert Roland's sympathetic help. "I'll talk to her," he promised.

Up at the house people were arriving for cocktails, and a poker game was already under way. At the table I noticed Myron Selznick, the top agent in Hollywood, Joseph Schenck, the head of Twentieth Century-Fox, and Irving Berlin. Constance Bennett was also there. I had seldom seen a more beautiful human being: straight, shiny, very blond hair, pencil-thin brows over big, blue, intelligent eyes, a finely chiseled face with high cheekbones, and a rather determined jaw. Her skin was creamy white, and her beautifully slim body was encased and encrusted in and by the latest in fashion and the most expensive in jewelry.

Gilbert chose a lull in the action and bent over her. She let out a peal of delicious laughter, waved gaily at me, and turned her concentration once more to the business in hand.

"She says," said Gilbert, "why don't you go home and change. It's buffet supper, and she's running *The Good Earth* afterward. She'd be delighted to have you join us."

"My God," I croaked, "what about tomorrow? . . . We've got to do that show!"

"You only have to *read* it, amigo," said Gilbert, "but I'm sure she'll find time to run it through with you during the evening."

By the time I returned an hour later forty or fifty people had converged on Carolwood Drive and presupper conviviality was in full swing. The poker game was still in progress in the cardroom, and from the totally engrossed expressions of the players I judged it unlikely that much rehearsing of tomorrow's radio show would be taking place. The buffet supper came and went. *The Good Earth* with two good Jewish actors, Paul Muni and Luise Rainer, looking determinedly Chinese while swatting away at swarms of MGM's homemade locusts, was dutifully applauded, and around two o'clock in the morning the party began to thin out. I checked on the situation in the cardroom—it was unchanged, and the sight of discarded ties and jackets, plus the presence of plates of sandwiches and the monumental size of the pots, made it obvious that it would remain that way for some time to come.

At four o'clock I went home, none too relieved by Gilbert's latest piece of information: "She can't quit now because she was such a big winner last night. . . . She says she'll be ready at nine o'clock in the morning, so you be here then. . . . You can drive down with her and run it through a couple of times down at the studio before the rehearsal. . . . Don't worry, amigo, it's only radio!"

I couldn't sleep and had visions of a promising career going up in smoke, so I worked till dawn on the scenes determined by now to embark upon a policy of *sauve-qui-peut*.

Sharp at nine, eyes blinking in the blinding California sun and shaking with black coffee and Benzedrine, I rang the doorbell at Carolwood Drive. A housemaid looked surprised. "I've an appointment with Miss Bennett," I said.

The girl motioned me toward the still heavily curtained library redolent with the smell of after-party staleness. I couldn't believe my eyes. In the cardroom beyond, I beheld the poker game still going full blast; the players, with the exception of Constance Bennett, looked haggard and blue of jowl.

The hostess saw me and announced, "Last hand, fellows. I have to go to work."

Soon it was over, and an hour later I found myself seated in the Rolls-Royce phaeton beside an incredibly beautiful and apparently well-rested Constance Bennett. She must have been made of different stuff because with her unlined face and clear blue eyes she looked as though she had awakened from a dreamless sleep of at least ten hours.

During the twenty-minute drive to Vine Street, she filled me in on the outcome of the marathon game. "Poor Myron," she said, "I think he really will quit now. . . . He lost almost a hundred thousand bucks, but you can't mix martinis and cold hands . . . not with that group, you can't. . . . He was that much ahead at one time, but at the end he blew it."

At the radio studio everyone was determinedly trying to look as though he was not at panic station. We were at least two hours late for dress rehearsal, but such was the awe in which my glamorous partner was held by the executives of the *Shell Hour* that they welcomed her as though she had come to inaugurate a new wing of the building. Waiting, too, were several hundred of her fans, screaming her name and begging her to spare them a smile, pleading for autographs and apparently undismayed by the fact that they were kept at a respectful distance from their idol, having been herded since early morning into a prisoner of war cage of high wire netting.

The director fawned on her and immediately acceded to her request that for the next half hour she and I should be left undisturbed in her dressing room so that she could "check a few things in the script."

Constance Bennett was completely composed as she took her first look at Pirandello's lines which she would be delivering later in the day to the expectant millions. Totally absorbed, she read for a few minutes then stopped and frowned. In silence she leafed ahead through the rustle-proof pages; then she threw them in the wastebasket.

"I'm not going to do this shit," she announced.

The producer and director were summoned; so too was the advertising agency man. She would not tackle Pirandello, she said, under any circumstances. A dew of sweat stood out on the assembled group. "But, Miss Bennett, it's almost one o'clock, and we go on the air at five," pleaded the director.

"Too bad," she answered.

"The orchestra has been rehearsing since eight this morning," murmured the producer.

"They get paid," said the star.

"Shell will cancel the account," groaned the man from the advertising agency.

"Screw Shell," said Miss Bennett.

For half an hour the men pleaded and cajoled but at one o'clock with air time a scant four hours away, the men agreed that she could instead play a couple of scenes from the picture she had just finished at Twentieth Century-Fox. Quite apart from the hideous spot into which this last-minute switch now put me (a situation which nobody even mentioned), there was the question of obtaining the permission of Twentieth Century-Fox.

"You go ahead with that," said C. Bennett loftily. "Just call Darryl Zanuck; we'll go on back to the house and grab a bite to eat while we read through the scenes together. I have some scripts up there. You'd better send someone to pick one up so you can find out what it's all about. . . . Let's go," she said to me over her shoulder and headed for the door. As we departed, I saw the director conversing with the orchestra leader; their faces were a very odd color.

Constance B. smiled charmingly at her caged fans on her way to the Rolls-Royce, and on the long drive back to Carolwood Drive she remained cool and confident. She patted my wet hand. "Don't be nervous," she said. "These are great scenes, you'll love them."

Around two o'clock I was given a hamburger which turned into a bicycle in my stomach, and between bites I read the scenes. They were light and airy and, compared to Pirandello, much easier to play. I felt a little less apprehensive of my impending ordeal, but my optimism was short-lived when the *Shell Hour* spoke to Constance Bennett. They were desperate: Nobody at Twentieth Century-Fox except Joseph Schenck or Darryl Zanuck could give the necessary permission; Zanuck was on his way to Santa Anita Racecourse, and even if they could locate him there, it would be too late. Schenck was at his home, and no one would give out his private number.

"Leave it to me," said the star. She glanced at the clock; it was almost three o'clock. Already the lines would have formed outside the radio station. She couldn't find her phone book, and the secretary was off for the day. Several calls later the secretary was tracked down, loudly relaxed at a liquid brunch in Santa Monica, but the whereabouts of the book were wrung out of her. It made no difference. Schenck, according to someone at his house, had given strict instructions not to be awakened till four o'clock. "He got home real late," said a soft black voice. "I know that, goddammit," said La Bennett loudly. "C'mon. Let's go."

"Where?" I asked, panic rising.

"To Joe's place," said La Bennett. "I'll wake the son of a bitch up."

The chauffeur of the Rolls, spurred on now by a far less relaxed employer, catapulted the phaeton with smoking tires through Holmby Hills, but to no avail. We arrived to a head-on confrontation between a big film star and the stone-faced entourage of a big producer. His butler, the gardener, and a private detective lurking in the bushes all made it crystal clear that they had not the slightest intention of waking their boss before the appointed hour.

The big star wheedled, threatened and ranted. "But he was still in my house at nine o'clock this morning," she yelled, stamping a pretty foot.

They were unmoved. "Sorry, Miss Bennett . . . orders is orders!"

Finally, she gave up. "Let's go," she growled. "Back to the studio."

The Saturday afternoon traffic by now was bumper to bumper, and every light seemed to be red. Down in Hollywood an expectant audience of hundreds was settling itself, twittering with excitement at the prospect of seeing its own Constance Bennett, and millions all over the country were gathering around their radio sets to hear her voice. "We'll stop at Schwab's Drugstore," she said. "You go call those creeps at Shell and tell 'em it's Parendillo or whatever the hell his name is."

From a pay booth I called the *Shell Hour,* and a noise like boiling water issued from our producer, but I promised that I would indeed "get that bitch down here in fifteen minutes."

By the time we had run the gauntlet of the swollen number of her fans behind the wire netting (and I had to admire her—she smilingly took her time and even signed a few grubby slips of paper poked at her through the holes) it was less than half an hour before air time, and she was swept off to her flower-filled dressing room, where she nonchalantly changed her makeup and put on a stunning silver lamé dress. I sat bolt upright on a wooden chair, alone in a corner of the stage, avoiding the hostile glances of the orchestra, and with trembling fingers and unseeing eyes pretended to be working on my script.

At a quarter to five the curtain rose, and the announcer warmed up the studio audience with a few nervous jokes, explained to them how much their applause would contribute to the listeners' pleasure, extolled the beauty, brilliance, and dedication of our hardworking star and introduced the orchestra leader and the director. This individual found time to hiss at me, "You both work on the same mike . . . take stage right so she can show her best profile . . . when there's a music bridge, sound effects, or pause, watch me for your cue before you start speaking and . . . God help us all!"

Five minutes before air time the announcer remembered me and told the studio audience that the young man playing opposite Miss Bennett came from the Abbey Players in Dublin—a black lie which aroused little response.

Thunderous applause and gasps of admiration then greeted the appearance of the star. She smiled beautifully and calmly settled herself on a chair next to mine and crossed her impeccable silken legs. After what seemed an eternity, the red sign ON THE AIR flashed; a fanfare, and the announcer began extolling the smiling efficiency of the Shell station attendants, the unequaled excellence of their product, and the cleanliness of their lavatories. Another fanfare, followed by a moving introduction of the main event, and Constance Bennett and I were alone in the center of the stage, facing each other and twenty million Americans over the top of the microphone.

I didn't feel anything very much: I was numb with terror. I had to speak first; the director signaled frantically to me to begin. I stared back at him like a dog watching a snake; then I looked across at my partner, hoping that miraculously some of her superhuman

451

calm might rub off on me. What I saw made me relax completely. She was human, after all—she was pale green and shaking like an aspen.

GARBO

In our itchy fustian trousers and jackets of the same material stained at the armpits with salty sweat rings and redolent of a hundred earlier occupants, we extras working on a Marie Dressler potboiler were making the most of our short lunch break on the MGM back lot, stretched out on the grass and foraging dispiritedly among the unappetizing contents of small cardboard boxes provided for our refreshment.

A dusty road separated the well-tended campus lawns on which we sprawled from the fronts of a row of prim New England clapboard houses. They had no interiors and no backs.

"Here she comes!" somebody announced in an excited whisper, and the message spread with the rapidity of a forest fire among the half hundred depressed citizenry.

"Who?" I asked my neighbor, a large Mexican lady of uncertain cleanliness who, I had noticed, earlier in the day, when pinned against her in a doorway, had a cluster of blackheads between her bosoms.

"Garbo!" she replied, rising to her feet. "Every day at lunch time she takes her exercises."

The road at its nearest point to us was fifty yards away, and the extras, with one exception, making no move to close the gap, stood respectfully and watched in fascinated silence as a slim figure wearing dark glasses, a baggy sort of track suit, and a large floppy hat strode purposefully past. Upon the hardened, cynical faces of those long exposed to every great star in the business were looks of wonderment and awe. Suddenly the spell was broken. A young boy broke from the ranks, and brandishing a pencil and a grubby piece of paper, he ran across the grass toward the dusty road. "Miss Garbo!" he called.

The trim figure missed a beat and stiffened perceptibly; then she accelerated by lengthening her stride; as the cantering youth closed the gap, she broke first into a trot, and finally, as he gained upon her, she opened the throttle and, leaving him pounding along in her wake, disappeared at a graceful gallop toward the sanctuary of the main studio and her dressing room. She had never looked around, but she had the radar system of a bat when it came to avoiding contact with a stranger.

When the panting and crestfallen boy returned, the Mexican lady cuffed him hard and shook him. "Why you not leave her alone?" she demanded loudly. "She likes be *private!*"

She did indeed, and the studio was filled with stories of her determination to preserve her privacy. She liked to work always with the same crew and demanded that the redoubtable Bill Daniels photograph all her pictures. A great professional, she seemed perfectly at ease among others working on the same film, but as Bill said, "She could sniff an outsider a mile away, and if anyone, no matter who, came on the set to get a peek at her, she'd sense it even with a coupla hundred extras around and she'd just go and sit in her dressing room till they'd been put out."

Stories of her elusiveness were legion, and much enjoyment was extracted from the names, "Gussie Berger" and "Harriet Brown," under which she booked hotels and travel arrangements. The great Garbo quote "I want to be alone" was probably never uttered by her, but there was no question that she was a loner—painfully shy with people she did not know and preferring her own company to that of most people. "Making a film with Garbo," said Robert Montgomery, another star at MGM, "does not constitute an introduction." Garbo had an icy look in her eyes when anyone sought to impose upon her, as, according to studio gossip, Groucho Marx discovered one day. He saw a well-known figure approaching in slacks and floppy hat, waylaid her, bent down in his famous crouch, and peeked up under the brim. Two prisms of pure Baltic blue stared down at him, and he backed away, muttering, "Pardon me, ma'am. I thought you were a guy I knew in Pittsburgh."

When the talkies came in, there were many casualties among the great silent stars, but none suffered a more dramatic and humiliating decline than John Gilbert. The established number one male box-office attraction of the MGM Studios was wrecked upon the rocks of his first talking film, mistakenly titled *His Glorious Night*. Gilbert did not have a voice of great resonance, he had a light, pleasant voice, but somehow it did not suit the dark, flashing eyes and gleaming white teeth of the great screen lover, in addition to which sound in its infancy was unreliable in the lower registers and poor John Gilbert's first squeaky declarations of passionate love brought down the house. He was allotted no more roles by the studio where he had reigned supreme for so long, and stories abounded that the studio heads were trying to break his very expensive contract by trapping him with whores or getting him drunk in public and then invoking the morals clause whereby an actor undertook not to bring himself into disrepute with the public. In fact, the poor man was so desperately humiliated and unhappy that he refused to be seen in public, but his drinking bouts in private became legendary.

Garbo and Gilbert, some years before the debacle of *His Glorious Night*, had embarked on a highly publicized love affair. Too highly publicized perhaps for Garbo's taste because at the very moment when Gilbert thought that all was set for a wedding and a honeymoon in the South Pacific aboard a yacht specially and romantically outfitted for the occasion, Garbo had taken to her heels. Gilbert, thereafter, married twice elsewhere, but both marriages fell apart, and with his career in tatters he was badly in need of a friend.

Garbo at the height of her popularity was preparing to make *Queen Christina*, and Laurence Olivier with great fanfare was brought over from England to play opposite her, but for some never fully explained reason, the studio decided at the last minute that he was wrong for the part and sent him home again. To see such a glorious opportunity blown away before his eyes and before the eyes of the world must have been a body blow to a young actor as yet unknown outside his own country, but Olivier, blessed with a massive talent and a highly justified faith in himself, returned later to Hollywood to take his pick of the best roles at all the studios. MGM, in the meanwhile, received a body blow of its own when Garbo informed it that she would make *Queen Christina* only with . . . John Gilbert.

The picture was a triumph for Garbo, but Gilbert's performance failed to rekindle the flame with his fans, and he sank back once more into despondency. Around this time (1935) Ronald Colman, who had befriended me, took me frequently to Gilbert's house to play tennis. The house, which was later purchased by David Selznick when he married Jennifer Jones and completely modernized and rejuvenated, was in Gilbert's day a somber place, a rambling Spanish-style structure at the end of a long winding and highly dangerous mountain road with only the flimsiest of barriers at hairpin bends to save one from terrifying drops.

From the property the view was spectacular; below as though photographed from an airplane lay the whole of the Los Angeles Basin, ringed on the left by the high snow-topped mountains and to the right clamped against the great horseshoe of the Pacific Ocean with Catalina Island like a giant humpbacked whale anchored fifty miles offshore. The decor in Gilbert's time was heavy and the gloom of the place was intensified by curtains permanently drawn against the light. When he showed up to play, the tennis was desultory, but the conversation, bonhomie, and refreshment were abundant. In his mid-thirties he was a man of sparkling good looks, but his good humor and laughter seemed dredged up with great effort. Often he did not appear at all, and Colman and I would take a swim in his sad leaf-filled pool. Once or twice I caught a glimpse of a beautiful face watching us from a window, and on one occasion, as we were climbing into Colman's car, a figure in a man's shirt, slacks and a big floppy hat approached from the scrub-covered hills and, with head down, hurried past us into the house.

"When Jack's drinking, she goes walking," said Colman phlegmatically. John Gilbert made only one more film before his heart gave out—*The Captain Hates the Sea*. Columbia Studios chartered a liner and dispatched an entire film unit and a troupe of hard-drinking actors to complete the picture at sea. It proved an expensive experiment, the filming became ever extended, and finally, as the budget was revamped with sickening regularity, a desperate head of production cabled the director far out on the Pacific: RETURN IMMEDIATELY. THE COST IS STAGGERING. He received a laconic reply: SO IS THE CAST.

I was afforded one more mini-glimpse of the famous recluse when Edmund Goulding, the director, invited me for a weekend at his desert retreat above Palm Springs. I arrived hot and dusty after a long drive, and Goulding pointed the way to his swimming pool in the palm trees below. "Go and cool off," he ordered.

As I neared the pool, it became apparent that standing in the shallow end was a naked female figure. As this incident took place in the mid-thirties, the reader will understand that I retreated to the house and asked my host for a clarification of the situation.

"Oh," he said, "it's only Garbo. She's staying somewhere down there and uses the pool when she feels like it."

I hastened once more down the garden path, but I was too late. All that remained was the disturbed surface of the water.

Garbo was finally dethroned as a working actress but remained inviolate as the most mysterious personality in Hollywood's history.

Her dethronement was sudden and remarkable because she apparently went down without a struggle. It could have happened to anyone—and frequently did. She chose the wrong film. Certainly in her position she could have refused it, but because it was wartime, she had agreed to do the sort of picture that was cheering people up—a farce.

Nothing in show business is more horrendous than a farce when it is not funny, and *Two-Faced Woman* was a four-star, fur-lined, oceangoing disaster. It also contained a surprising quota of "dirty" dialogue, was banned by the Legion of Decency, and roasted by the press with one eminent reviewer referring to Garbo's appearance as "embarrassing—like seeing Sarah Bernhardt swatted with a bladder."

The actors have always been the principal targets when shows flop, and they accept this as an occupational hazard—the producers rarely get blamed—but Garbo, instead of sweeping *Two-Faced Woman* under the rug of her memory, drawing comfort from an unassailable record of success, and being more selective in future, just stopped making films.

Certainly she was intensely shy and as sensitive as a seismograph, but it was an extraordinary abdication and rocked Hollywood to its foundations. Possibly she reasoned that she had always longed for privacy, she could certainly afford it, and to quit at the very pinnacle may have seemed to her the ideal time to go—no one could find out. She did not go far—just to New York—and she came back occasionally to haunt Hollywood like a lovely ghost and nonchalantly pushed aside a hundred offers to return to the screen. Only once was she tempted, by the producer Walter Wanger, who had a moment of glory when he was able to display a contract on which she had affixed her name, but she never went before the cameras. Hollywood could not believe that she would not make a well-timed comeback, not to do so was contrary to all Hollywood thinking, so the longer she stayed away, the stronger and stranger with every passing day grew the Garbo myth.

About five years after Garbo's retirement I purchased an old house in Pacific Palisades with "all mod cons, views, ocean and mts." It had been built by Vicki Baum, the author of the best-seller *Grand Hotel*, which had been made into a hit film starring Garbo. A neighbor of ours there was a rarity—a Hollywood hermit.

Richard Haydn first made his name imitating fish. "I was standing on a street corner as happy as could be, minding my p's and q's, when a large man tied a horse and cart to me. I uttered a cry. A passing fishmonger said 'Why! that is the mating call of the Goo Boo or Blushing Fish!' I was *amazed*."

Richard's act as "Mr. Carp—the only living Fish Mimic" went down to history, and Hollywood commandeered him. He became a much sought-after director, as well as character actor, but his joy in life was to be completely alone, tending the most beautiful concentration of flowers and plants in any garden in California. I suspected that he went near the studios only in order to earn money to buy seeds and fertilizer, and it took weeks of patient prodding and the absorption of countless rebuffs on our part before this enchantingly fey creature could be persuaded to visit our house. When he finally became tame enough to do so, he appeared unexpectedly, saying, "Come quickly. I *must* show you my phlox and scabiosa." I had an urge to call the doctor.

One evening Hjördis and I were sitting on our terrace, watching the ostentatious setting of the sun upon the distant Pacific and listening to the weird yelping of coyotes in the hills around us, when Richard Haydn materialized. His eyeglasses glinted mischievously.

"I've brought someone who says she spent some of her happiest days in this house," he announced. "She would like to see it again if it's not inconvenient."

Birds of a feather had evidently flocked together because behind Richard stood Garbo.

I don't remember what she wore on that occasion because I was so stunned by the beauty of her face. She was utterly unaffected and completely easy and relaxed with a spontaneous and highly infectious laugh. My wife, being Swedish, took over the tour of the house, and by the time they came back the two of them were jabbering away like two Scandinavian conspirators. Garbo told us about our house during the Vicki Baum days—it must have been a fascinating place, a rendezvous for Leopold Stokowski and a host of European writers and artists.

During the years to come Garbo often came to see us. Always the same, of undiluted beauty and spontaneity, but always something was held back in reserve. She reminded me of a child living in her own secret world, and with childish directness she came and went as she wished, swam when she felt like it or when she missed the rains of her native land, walked about under the lawn sprinklers, but no amount of pleading on behalf of our Swedish cook could coax an autograph out of her. "I never give autographs or answer letters," she said firmly.

Normally an infallible way of getting to know someone and of ferreting out their good and bad points is to be cooped up with them for several days aboard a small and unreliable sailing boat. I forget who organized the trip, but Hjördis and I, Garbo and a friend of hers, who claimed he could navigate, set off for a few days in a small sloop I chartered in San Pedro. It was a miracle we survived the experience because on the first evening out the wind dropped at dusk, the engine failed, and Garbo's navigator friend got loose among the schnapps bottles. Trying to find Catalina Island with ourselves a forlorn little speck on the ocean, we were not reassured when he informed us that we were several miles north of the Grand Canyon.

Eventually we found the island, which was lucky because the next stop would have been Japan, and there spent a most enjoyable few days. Garbo was going through a health food period and tried to interest us in the contents of a brown paper bag she had smuggled aboard—foul-looking walnut burgers fried in sunflower oil. Her swimming outfit was far more intriguing—a white bathing cap and a pair of boy's swimming trunks. Throughout the cramped trip she had been a model crew member, the fountainhead of gaiety and fun, uncomplaining and always courageously volunteering to help in our many emergencies, but when we docked once more at San Pedro, I realized that I knew her no better than when she had first bobbed out from behind Richard Haydn, and the only thing I had discovered about her was that she did *not* have big feet.

The jealous always try to detract from beautiful women, but Garbo's beauty was so unassailable that the jealous, in desperation, pointed at her feet. "They're *big!*" they exulted.

Actually Garbo's feet were beautifully shaped and long, in correct proportion to her height, but she had an unfortunate habit of encasing them in huge brown loafers which gave the impression that she wore landing craft.

Robert Taylor, who played opposite Garbo in *Camille*, told me it was a fascinating and totally satisfying experience except for her fixation about having comfortable footwear.

"There she was," he said, "playing love scenes and death scenes with me and wearing these gorgeous crinolines, but all the time I *knew* that underneath she had on a crummy old pair of bedroom slippers."

Garbo was in our house one summer evening when the time came for Hjördis and me to leave for a large cocktail party which we had promised to attend. We explained the situation to our visitor, who asked who was giving it, how many would be there, and so on.

As it was to be at the home of a close friend who was celebrating the end of a long suspension by his studio, we were able to supply the answers and to hazard a guess that about a hundred people would be on hand.

"May I come too?" Garbo asked suddenly.

We were stunned and wondered what had brought about such a phenomenal "turn up for the books."

The party, when we arrived, was in full and boisterous swing, and when Garbo walked into the garden chockablock with young filmmakers, the effect was magical. They just could not believe their eyes. For a while she was left in a clear space, chatting happily with people she had worked with, but gradually as the throng pressed ever closer in its enthusiasm, her eyes took on the look of a hunted fawn, and suddenly she was gone.

Garbo's visits to California became rarer, but the myth remained as deeply entrenched as ever. The newspapers showed pictures of her fleeing from their photographers in European cities and printed reports of her aimlessly and alone walking the New York streets or haggling over the price of carrots and small antiques, and her apartment was reputed to contain a priceless collection of Impressionists stacked on the floor and all facing the wall. At the end of the period covered in this book we found ourselves in a house in the south of France. To our joy we discovered that Garbo was installed in a house on a neighboring promontory, the guest of a Russian-born New Yorker—George Schlee. The property was ideal for her, isolated and perched high upon jagged rocks far from prying eyes. In calm weather she could descend some steps into the blue Mediterranean, and when it was rough, she could take her beloved exercises in the pool. Schlee was the ideal companion for Garbo, a cosmopolitan of immense knowledge, charm, kindness, and understanding. She seemed completely happy in his company and, after the passing of several years, more beautiful than ever. One day, when they were at our place, we laid out food and wine in the garden on an old table among the olive trees, but an unseasonable rainstorm arrived just as we were about to sit down to luncheon. "Help me carry everything into the house!" I ordered, grabbing something light.

"Nonsense," said Garbo firmly. "We put it all under the table and eat it there."

People who have climbed a cliff and are resting peacefully on the summit have been known to glance casually down into the void below and for the first time realize to their horror that they suffer from vertigo. With knees of jelly, pounding hearts, and spinning heads, they then inch their way down and never climb again.

I often wondered if something of the sort had overtaken Garbo at the pinnacle of her career, so seeing her before me, carefree and happy, munching away contentedly with the rain cascading off the table, I decided it might be a propitious moment to try to find out.

"Why *did* you give up the movies?" I asked.

She considered her answer so carefully that I wondered if she had decided to ignore my personal question. At last, almost to herself, she said, "I had made enough faces."

"A riddle wrapped in a mystery inside an enigma" was how Winston Churchill described 170,000,000 Russians. And one lovely, lonely Swede, too, perhaps?

10
Summit Drive

RONALD COLMAN

$\mathcal{I}$N Beverly Hills, Summit Drive was well named but not for topographical reasons. It was a short street winding up a valley from Benedict Canyon. There were only six estates on the ridges on either side of this valley, but in prewar days in these six houses, hidden by magnificent specimens of sycamore, pine, eucalyptus, jacaranda, chestnut, and oak, reposed some of the crown jewels of Hollywood.

Up Summit Drive, the largest estate of all was at the bottom on the right, a rather untidy, comfortable, secluded, rambling hideaway belonging to one of the Hollywood pioneers—Harold Lloyd.

On the ridge opposite his estate was a more imposing structure— a large "stockbroker Tudor" edifice complete with beams, eaves, sloping roofs, ivy, and mullioned windows. From the stately wrought-iron gates at the entrance, a winding driveway led to the house past beautifully manicured lawns flanked, not by orange trees, brightly colored hibiscus, oleanders, or trumpet flowers, but by dark foreign-looking yew hedges. Waiting, somberly dressed, at the top of the drive would be a diminutive general factotum named Tommy. "Mr. Colman," he would intone reverently, "is in the library. Pray follow me."

Ronald Colman, if not a recluse, had a mania for preserving his privacy—understandable really when one remembers that on any given day, hundreds of fans would be cruising, goggle-eyed, around Beverly Hills in limousines, jalopies, or buses equipped with loudspeakers, clutching in their hands the maps they had purchased for $1 from beery ladies parked beneath beach umbrellas at the city limits: "Maps of the Movie Stars' Homes." Many of these documents were wildly inaccurate, and the guides of conducted tours were also badly informed. Important putts on the greens of the Bel Air Country Club were frequently muffed by prominent local citizens, thanks to a blaring voice from the nearby road describing their distant clubhouse as "the palatial home of the beautiful platinum bombshell—Jean Harlow . . . where champagne flows and anything goes."

Colman, a quiet man, was English. He had been recruited from an obscure position on Broadway when, panicking at the sudden event of talking pictures, Hollywood had convinced itself that none of the "silent" stars could talk. The choice of Colman as a standard-bearer was fortunate because he was indeed the possessor of a matchless speaking voice, plus darkly handsome good looks, massive charm, and great acting ability. He was also the lucky owner of a pair of dark-brown eyes, dark eyes being much the most photogenic and expressive on black-and-white film—the worst were the pale-blue ones which looked washed out and somehow dishonest. The owners of dark eyes also suffered much less from the sun arc lights which were capable of burning the skin of the eyeballs. "Klieg eye" was a painful and unattractive occupational disease.

Ronnie Colman lived alone in the large, rambling pseudo-Tudor house, surrounded by a beautiful collection of Chippendale and Sheraton furniture; only English painters of the eighteenth and nineteenth centuries graced the walls, and the rooms were comfortable in a leathery sort of way. The place was masculine to a fault and screamed out for a lady of the house. Ronnie, under heavy camouflage in the late thirties, was laying the foundations of just that. Having lately tottered away, mentally bruised, from a most unhappy marriage, followed by an extremely painful divorce, he was highly nervous of any further entanglements, but egged on by his close circle of men friends, he was hesitantly chipping away at his mental barriers. The chipping soon passed the stage of wishful thinking, and working at night, he knocked a large hole in the wall bounding the back garden of his estate. Tommy produced some hinges, cement, and a heavy oak door, and the beautiful actress Benita Hume, who lived in a small Spanish-style house immediately behind Colman's kitchen garden, was able to come and go in the greatest secrecy.

This delightful intrigue by Hollywood's most eligible bachelor ended, as his friends always hoped it would, with the gate being removed, the wall being bricked up again, and Benita moving into the manor house as the second Mrs. Ronald Colman.

The misogynist Colman slowly thawed out under the warmth, gaiety, and humor of Benita. The small coterie of his old-time friends was enlarged, a daughter, Juliet, was born, and the house was filled with flowers and laughter, but if the flowers were usually stocks, roses or chrysanthemums, the mirth too remained predominantly British.

Colman was never part of the "British Colony" as personified by the Hollywood Cricket Club, Ernest Torrance's Sunday afternoon tea parties, and the tournaments on C. Aubrey Smith's croquet lawn, but his old American friends, William Powell, Richard Barthelmess, and the cowboy star Tim McCoy, found themselves outnumbered by the Nigel Bruces, the Basil Rathbones, and Herbert Marshall with a bewildering succession of wives and mistresses.

Christmas dinner at the Colmans' was a permanent fixture. On went the dinner jackets, down went the turkey, plum pudding, and champagne, and out poured the speeches.

After dinner the women withdrew, and over port and brandy, the older men reminisced while the younger ones, Brian Aherne, George Sanders, Douglas Fairbanks, Jr., and myself, remained respectfully silent because mostly they talked about the Great War: Colman had been gassed in it, Rathbone had won the Military Cross, Nigel Bruce had absorbed eleven machine-gun bullets in his behind, and Herbert Marshall had lost a leg.

Before his second marriage Ronnie had invested large sums to protect his beloved privacy. First, he bought the San Ysidro Ranch in the hills above Montecito 100 miles north of Los Angeles. This was no cattle-raising spread; it consisted of several hundred acres of gently sloping land. Immensely tall eucalyptus trees framed the property, on which were groves of oranges, avocados, and lemons, and hidden among these were twenty or thirty white-painted frame bungalows with private gardens and verandas. There was a main dining room and bar, tennis courts, stables, a swimming pool, and a stunning view of the mountains and ocean. It was a Mecca of calm to which the same clientele returned faithfully each year at the same time like the swallows to Capistrano. A hundred years before, Robert Louis Stevenson had loved the place, and the little cottage in which he wrote many of his works was preserved with pride. Later Galsworthy wrote much of *The Forsyte Saga* in the same cottage, and J. F. Kennedy spent some of his honeymoon there.

Ronnie's second investment in peace and quiet was a box of oil paints and an easel, a less costly extravagance than his third—an 85-foot copper-bottomed ketch, *Dragoon*. No sailor himself but cosseted by Tommy and an excellent crew, he liked at sundown to sit at the wheel with his yachting cap at a rakish angle, a large whiskey and soda in his hand, and fulminate against Samuel Goldwyn, for whom he had worked for many years and at whose hands he vowed he had suffered unimaginable injustices. Apart from Goldwyn, I never heard Ronnie say an unkind word about anyone.

Bill Powell loved the sea as much as I did, and we were frequently invited aboard *Dragoon* for weekend trips to Catalina or the Santa Barbara islands.

One cold October evening *Dragoon* dropped a lonely anchor in a little bay off the sheltered eastern coast of Santa Cruz Island. We had enjoyed a couple of days' fishing en route, but the heavy autumn swells had made most anchorages among the islands uncomfortable sleeping places, and we looked forward to a good night's rest ashore at Eaton's Fishing Camp.

Expectantly, therefore, Ronnie, Bill Powell, and I climbed the hundred rickety wooden steps from the landing stage to the small cluster of cottages roosting on the rock face above, owned and operated for many years by Mrs. Eaton.

Santa Cruz Island was large and was a privately owned cattle and sheep ranch. The Eaton family had long held the only concession of any sort allowed on it.

The widow Eaton was a wild-eyed, harridan-type woman with straggly gray hair, dirty fingernails, and a gray woolen sweater which made one's eyes water, but the beds she assigned to us looked clean, the water was hot, and in the dining hut the menu promised a welcome change from the baked beans and corned beef dispensed by Tommy.

Nobody was there but us.

After taking showers, we repaired to the dining hut, and while Mrs. Eaton and a gap-toothed Mexican were preparing our meal, we relaxed around a roaring fire. The conversation, as usual, was about movies, which was unfortunate because having plonked down our plates, Mrs. Eaton suddenly fixed us with her mad eyes.

"You guys movie folk?" she demanded belligerently.

Feeling uninvolved, as I had as yet hardly appeared on the screen, I looked at my companions, two of the biggest stars in the business, and waited for their modest acceptances of the fulsome compliments that would soon rain down upon them.

"Yes," said Powell, "we are—er, in a small way."

Mrs. Eaton was instantly transformed. She grabbed up our sizzling steaks and headed for the kitchen.

"Clear that goddamn table, Ramon," she shrieked at the Mexican. "No film people set foot in my camp . . . fuck off, the lot of you!" She started pulling us out of our chairs. "Get off this island—I hate you all, you're a bunch of no-good chiselers . . . the dog gets your steaks."

A mangy, twitching mongrel lying in front of the fire opened one unenthusiastic eye.

"Here," she babbled, ripping our wind jackets off hooks. "Take your goddamn coats and get the hell outta here."

She started raining blows on our retreating backs.

"Why, madam. . . . Why?" asked Colman, trying to lend some dignity to our retreat. "What have we done to you?"

"Barrymore!" she yelled. "Ever heard of a creep called John Barrymore? . . . Well, ten years ago the bastard dropped anchor down there in a big white schooner . . . he came up to the camp for supper, he and his lousy friends . . . my little girl was here on vacation; she was gorgeous and only seventeen. She waited on table at the Happy Halibut Seafood and Steak House at Pismo Beach. This drunken shitheel, Barrymore, was old enough to be her granddad, but he kept making passes at her. Finally, she says, 'Mom, I've been invited off to the yacht for a beer,' and off she goes. . . . I never seed hide nor hair of her since. . . . That goddamned Barrymore sailed away that night with my little girl, and I never seed her no more."

Tears were pouring down the woman's dirty cheeks, and she kept shoving us through the door.

"She married some fella . . . a cameraman or some such, they told me . . . she never wrote to me, and she never come back . . . I hate all of you . . . get off my camp, you lousy bums, and stay off of it."

As our crestfallen and stomach-cheated trio clambered down the dark rotting steps, we were bombarded with half grapefruits, empty beer bottles, and cries of "Lousy actors—who needs you?"

Harry Cohn, the foulmouthed and dynamic head of Columbia Pictures, once enlisted Colman's help in another situation that called for quiet charm. Cohn had fallen in love with "The White Cliffs of Dover," a piece by Alice Duer Miller, but was meeting resistance from her because she feared that he might not have the taste and finesse to translate it to the screen. Colman was shooting a picture at Columbia, so Cohn begged him to invite Alice Duer Miller to the studio, give her luncheon, show her around, and generally soften her up. "Tell the old bag how goddamned tasteful I am," said Cohn. "Shit! I'm making the *Lost Fucking Horizon*, ain't I?"

Colman dutifully did his best, and Alice Duer Miller was visibly weakening during luncheon in his dressing room. Afterward he took her on a tour of the rabbit warren of a studio, avoiding its seamier parts.

He thought she might be impressed by a walk through the writers' building because on the doors were the titles of forthcoming productions and the well-known names of those slaving over the screenplays within. The place, smelling of coffee, was impressive with its air of quiet concentration, and the steady clacking of typewriters underlined the industry of Harry Cohn's employees.

"This picture will be going into production soon," said Colman, pointing to a door on which was written:

TOM BROWN'S SCHOOLDAYS
Writers—TOWNE AND BAKER

Alice Duer Miller was genuinely delighted. "Why, that's just wonderful! They are going to make a film of that . . . what a charming idea!"

At that moment the door flew open, and out rushed the diminutive Gene Towne. He grabbed Colman by the lapels of his jacket. He was glassy-eyed with excitement.

"Hey, I've got it! Goddammit, I've got it! It wasn't the boys who did it—the sons of bitches—it was the masters, the bastards!"

"The White Cliffs of Dover" was, not surprisingly, made by Metro-Goldwyn-Mayer.

I had first met Colman in the pre-stockbroker-Tudor period, when he lived a hermitlike existence in a cul-de-sac above Hollywood Boulevard, Mound Street. I was still an extra.

I was taken there by Alvin Weingand to make up a four at tennis. After that I was invited back often, but *only* for tennis. Tommy each time would meet me at the gate, escort me through the back garden to the court, and escort me out again at the end of the game.

The players were always the same—Weingand, Colman's agent Bill Hawkes, Clive Brook, Warner Baxter, Colman, and myself. I was much the youngest, so usually I was teamed with Colman, who had, I noticed, rather flat feet; he left most of the running to me. When he finally became convinced that his inner self would not be imposed on by me, I was no longer escorted by Tommy to the gate at the end of a game—I was invited inside for a drink, and a lasting friendship slowly developed.

In all the years I knew him he was only interested in one woman —Benita. His favorite film leading lady had been lovely Alice Terry, a blithe and free spirit whose weakness was eating cream cakes.

Her studio remonstrated with her about this. "You can't do that and remain a star," they told her.

"All right," she replied. "I shall make a million dollars as fast as I can; then I'll retire and eat cream cakes."

According to Ronnie, she did just that. She no longer read the scripts the studio sent her.

"Just tell me two things," she said. "Do I have to get wet or ride a horse?"

If they said no, she would agree to make the film.

The last Ronnie heard of her, she had made her $1,000,000, had retired to the San Fernando Valley, and was up to her armpits in cream cakes, as happy as a clam.

Ronnie tried hard to further my fledgling career and when he was about to make *Lost Horizon* with Frank Capra, he did all he could to persuade Capra to cast me in the role of his younger brother. Capra reacted kindly to the suggestion but, after meeting me, was only moderately impressed. He did, however, say that he might give me a test the following week.

For six days I never moved more than a few feet from the phone, but it never rang. On the seventh day I concluded sadly that my chances were slim and decided to go fishing. Before I left, I took a small precaution in case by some miracle Frank Capra still might call and asked a girlfriend to stay in the house for me. If Capra rang, she promised to drive north of Malibu and to wave a sheet from the cliffs of Point Dume (pronounced DOOM—and for me it very nearly was).

The all-day boat from Malibu Pier pulled out on the dot of seven o'clock. It was a beautiful still morning with the sun just rising above the sea mist, not a ripple on the surface, just a long, lazy swell.

The fishermen were a jolly cross section of locals from Las Tunas, Santa Monica, and Venice, retired businessmen, carpenters, garage mechanics, house painters, and the like on their day off, with a sprinkling of college kids stealing a day away from their classrooms. We started fishing about three miles offshore, and while the live bait was being chummed overboard to attract the big fish, several fishermen, with a conspicuous lack of husbandry, started munching the contents of their lunch boxes, and beer cans were being opened freely even at that early hour. All in all, it promised to be a good day.

Suddenly, the water all around the boat erupted as a school of yellowtail tuna found the sardines and anchovies. The fishermen, with eager cries, flung aside their sandwiches and started overhead casting, with gleaming silver spoons—a dangerous time, that early first excitement, when the inexperienced caster frequently hooked somebody's ear with his backswing, but that morning no ears and a lot of fish were caught, and everyone was happy.

By noon the schools of big fish had completed their feeding, and we moved in toward the kelp beds off Point Dume, to tackle the bass and halibut. The sun was beating down, and the swells were heavier. A few fishermen changed color and became strangely silent. Such had been my total absorption that I was halfway through my lunch before I remembered my arrangement with the girlfriend and the sheet signal.

I alerted the captain, and he made a comic announcement over the loud-hailer, asking everyone to keep an eye open for a flapping sheet.

"How the hell are you going to get ashore, Dave?" he asked.

"I'll swim," I said blithely. "It's only a couple of hundred yards."

"More like five," said Jack doubtfully, "and don't forget that kelp . . . it can really hold you . . . that swell's real heavy."

Half an hour later a cry went up: "The sheet, Dave! . . . the sheet!"

My heart nearly stopped beating. There, far away on a bluff, stood a leggy blonde waving frantically.

A test with Frank Capra! For an important role in one of the biggest pictures to be made that year! Hurriedly, I stripped down to my underpants, and to the encouraging yells of "Attaboy, Dave!" and "Good luck, kid," I dived over the side and headed for stardom.

The kelp beds which form an unbroken chain along hundreds of miles of California coastline are about 200 yards in diameter; the great golden-brown slimy weed branches out to cover the surface, and the thick, weaving roots go down to the ocean floor a hundred feet or more below. Kelp feels very unpleasant to the naked body and has to be navigated carefully from open patch to open patch. It is not advisable to fight it or panic, or one becomes entangled.

In the middle of a clearing, I was resting, floating on my back before tackling the next slippery barriers, when I thought of the sharks. Suddenly, about six feet away from me there was a swirling commotion, and a black shiny head with two huge eyes and a bristling mustache shot out of the water. When my heart restarted, I saw it was a baby seal, and it wanted to play. It swam all around me and under me and stayed with me all the way to the clear water on the beach side of the kelp beds. In fact, its presence gave me courage because by now I had heard the ominous sound of heavy surf—big oily swells rising and falling several feet in water a hundred feet deep are transformed into a series of giant foaming rollers when they arrive at a sloping shore.

From the tops of swells I obtained momentary glimpses of the girl and two men scrambling down a cliff path. I paddled on, but I still had quite a way to go. I was tired after my long struggle through the kelp. I was growing cold, too, and my fingers were curling up toward my palms. I began to wonder if I had made a horrible mistake.

Looking landward from the top of one swell, I could see a dozen more, and the farthest ones were curving out of sight away from me. Plumes of spray from their crests were flung back by an offshore breeze. For a few minutes, listening to the alarming pounding of the surf, I rested beyond the broken water, conserving my strength. I had decided to ease my way in, then swim fast with the last unbroken swell. This would carry me ten or twenty yards shoreward. The next one would break, and I would body-surf with it in the approved style, sliding, head down, from the crest. This, I guessed, would take me safely to the beach.

I guessed wrong.

Suddenly a mountainous surge gathered beneath me, and I found myself propelled forward in a crest of foam. I struggled, head high, for a lungful of air and somehow got into my surfing position. I was whizzing beachward at an alarming rate. Feeling myself sliding down the far side, I raised my head again for another much needed gulp of oxygen and beheld a horrifying sight: Beneath me, about fifteen feet below, was nothing but sand liberally sprinkled with stones and small rocks. I had picked up the surfer's nightmare—a big shore breaker. The giant wave flung me onto the hard, unyielding foreshore. Tons of water crashed down on top of me, turned me over and over, and ripped me out again along the ocean floor. My mouth and nose were full of sand and water. The breath had been knocked out of my body. I was inside a giant washing machine. I tried to swim to the surface, but everything was dark brown. I didn't know which way up I was. Somehow, with bursting lungs, I found myself on the surface. I was picked up by another roller and flung once more shoreward. Providentially, this wave broke behind me and bore me along, rolling me over and over like a log almost to the high-water mark.

The girl and the men dragged me up among the stinking decayed seaweed, where someone turned me face down and pressed the water out of my lungs. Then I was sick. My chest had been almost stripped of skin.

The girl drove me home, anointed me with iodine, and bandaged me. Then I called Frank Capra's office at Columbia Studios.

Capra had gone for the day, but his secretary was still there.

"Oh, you shouldn't have bothered to rush back from your fishing," she said. "Mr. Capra just wanted to tell you that he will not be making your test because he has cast John Howard in the part."

DAVID SELZNICK
AND *The Prisoner of Zenda*

Colman was not put off by Capra's indifference, though he was full of misgivings when I landed a small contract with Samuel Goldwyn, and when he was preparing for his next picture, *The Prisoner of Zenda*, he walked across Summit Drive and talked about me to the producer, David O. Selznick.

Selznick lived fifty yards away in a white, brightly decorated, rambling one-story house; a belt of towering trees marked the boundary between his property and that of Harold Lloyd. The gardens were full of color, and the place was equipped with the inevitable pool and tennis court. There was no front gate; one turned off Summit Drive into a semicircular driveway.

Selznick was a huge giant panda of a man, standing about six feet two and permanently struggling with a weight problem. He wore thick glasses and had thick, curly hair. He chain-smoked incessantly, had a broken nose, a wild sense of humor, a great deal of kindness, a weakness for dry martinis and terry-cloth bathrobes, and a completely nonexistent sense of punctuality.

Not even his friends, and he had hundreds of them, could have called him handsome, but such was his charm that it never crossed one's mind that he was anything else. Selznick was married to dark, flashing-eyed Irene, the daughter of the all-powerful chief of

Metro-Goldwyn-Mayer, the foxy, mercurial and frequently vindictive Louis B. Mayer.

Selznick's courting of Irene must have been a nail-biting period. When it came to the affairs of his daughters Irene and Edith, Mayer made Papa Barrett look like Winnie-the-Pooh. His ambitions for Edith were shaken to the core when she announced her intention of marrying quiet, witty Billy Goetz, who had just lost his job as an assistant studio supervisor, and when the young couple asked for an unobtrusive wedding, Mayer nearly blew a gasket.

After endless arguing, they reluctantly agreed to what he thought was more fitting to *his* station, an overproduced publicity-oriented bash at the Biltmore Hotel, but as a reward he presented them with a hefty chunk of stock in a new film company which he was largely financing—Twentieth Century-Fox.

If he swallowed with difficulty the marriage of Edith to Bill Goetz, he found the possibility of a match between Irene and David Selznick totally indigestible. "That schnook, that bum" he called David, "that son of a Selznick." David's father, Louis, had been a partner of Mayer's in earlier days, a partner, according to Hollywood legend, who had been unloaded and destroyed by massive jiggery pokery. This belief was certainly held by David and his brother, Myron, a powerful agent, both of whom had sworn to get even on their father's behalf.

Myron was often successful at this and, by manipulating his stable of sought-after stars, was able, from time to time, to give his father's old enemy a right royal financial screwing. David, of course, did not fall in love with Irene in order to do his bit in the Selznick-Mayer war, but he did cause the enemy great anguish. Mayer did all he could to dissuade Irene from the enterprise, and his house shook with emotional scenes, but Irene was unmoved, and finally he gave his consent.

Mayer genuinely admired David's success as head of production at RKO Studios, and once he realized he had lost the battle for Irene, his search for good potential manpower overcame his personal distaste, and he offered David a comparable job at MGM plus, as an inducement, the same amount of stock in Twentieth Century-Fox that he had lately given to the other newlyweds. Selznick spurned the stock offer, took the job, quickly turned out a string of great successes, and then announced that he was leaving MGM to form his own production company.

L. B. Mayer did everything in his considerable power to hold Selznick, but David was wary of him. Above all, he was wary of the aforementioned vindictiveness, of which a classic example surfaced when Mayer fell in love with a beautiful young actress, Jean Howard. Mayer put a detective on her trail to report on any extracurricular activities on her part. Not only were the reports "positive," but Jean fell in love and married Charlie Feldman, a handsome, moderately successful young agent, so Mayer promptly barred Feldman and all his clients from MGM Studios and tried to persuade the other company heads to do likewise.

Charlie Feldman refused to panic and kept his ears open. When he heard that Garbo, the brightest jewel in L. B. Mayer's crown, was scheduled to make *Conquest* and would do so only if a newcomer from France, Charles Boyer, played opposite her in the role of Napoleon, he talked Boyer into letting him handle his affairs. Garbo would work only with Boyer, but Boyer would speak to Mayer only if his agent was present, so Feldman was back in MGM Studios; he took great joy in putting the boot in, and Boyer wound up being paid almost twenty times his former salary.

Selznick stuck to his guns, left MGM, and even won the final jackpot. In a bewildering series of plots and counterplots, he maneuvered Mayer into lending him Clark Gable, the biggest box-office star at MGM, for his picture *Gone with the Wind*.

Colman's good words on my behalf fell on receptive ears, and one Sunday I received an invitation from Irene Selznick to come play tennis. I arrived at two thirty to find David Selznick in the hall, wrapped in a terry-cloth robe, consuming a plate of smoked salmon, cottage cheese, and pumpernickel.

"Like some breakfast?" he asked cheerfully.

I had just finished lunch, but I thought it might be diplomatic, so I accepted.

"Ronnie Colman talked to me about you," he went on between mouthfuls. "He thought you could play Fritz von Tarlenheim . . . I'll kick it around with John Cromwell tomorrow—he's going to direct—but don't raise your hopes too high because I'm aiming for an all-star cast. I've signed Madeleine Carroll to play Princess

Flavia opposite Ronnie, Mary Astor will play Madame de Mauban, Raymond Massey I'm negotiating with for Black Michael, and I may bring Doug Fairbanks, Junior, over from Europe, if he can tear himself away from Gertie Lawrence, to do Rupert of Hentzau. Dear old C. Aubrey Smith wants to play Colonel Zapt, which will be great, so that leaves Fritz."

He stared at me for a long time over the top of a cup of coffee, and I sat there thinking about the last two times I had seen him—lying flat on his back, having been knocked cold at Hollywood parties. Both David and his brother, Myron, compounded their weakness for dry martinis by having very short fuses when arguments started, and they were continually getting into fights which they lost. Chronically bad performers in the noble art, they were further handicapped by very short sight, so the locals when challenged by one of them had a way of bringing matters to a speedy conclusion by first flicking off their eyeglasses and then delivering a quick one-two punch.

The crash of falling Selznicks was frequently heard around midnight in Hollywood high society.

"It might work out," said Selznick suddenly.

He lit a cigarette and rose, his bathrobe fell open. "Oops, sorry," he said. "Let's go down to the court and see who's there."

I followed him past rows of bookcases and out into the garden.

Some good tennis was being played by a men's four and some spectacular ladies were watching, including Marlene Dietrich, Paulette Goddard, and Claudette Colbert.

David and Irene Selznick introduced me around and made me feel completely at home. Never for one moment during that long day was I allowed to feel out of it in the presence of an endless procession of the mighty and the talented of Hollywood. I was pressed to stay for drinks and then for a buffet supper and a movie and, like many before me, fell completely under the spell of David Oliver Selznick.

When he bade me good-night, my heart jumped. "Good night, Fritz," he said. "I'll talk to Cromwell tomorrow. Maybe we'll make a test."

All went well. A test was made, and during a game of gin rummy, probably as part of the stakes, Selznick acquired my services from my boss, Samuel Goldwyn.

The Prisoner of Zenda, the classic story of intrigue and high adventure in Ruritania, was an ideal film subject. Donald Ogden Stewart and John Balderston turned out a masterful screenplay full of duels, chases, coronations, and ballroom spectacles.

Selznick assembled the cast he had hoped for, and for four months a great time was had by all. Usually when one makes a film, it is a little like being too long on an ocean voyage. At the end of the trip, total strangers who have been thrown together for several weeks part, swearing eternal allegiance to each other, but never doing much about it. *Zenda* was different. Everyone became friends and remained so.

Colman was the leader and very much the star—a most serious and dedicated performer who was never his easygoing self until the end of the day when Tommy would come and lead me to the star bungalow to join him in his ritual six o'clock "beaker."

Madeleine Carroll was a porcelain beauty of great sweetness and fun, and Mary Astor, who looked like a beautiful and highly shockable nun, had a sweet expression and a tiny turned-up nose and made everyone feel she was in desperate need of protection. In point of fact, she was by her own admission happiest and at her best in bed. She was also, it turned out, highly indiscreet and confided all in her private journal, starting each revealing daily entry "Dear Diary. . . ."

"Dear Diary" right in the middle of the picture caused a major reshuffling of the shooting schedule because it was stolen and turned up as prime evidence in a highly publicized divorce case, and Mary had to give evidence.

If "Dear Diary" caused a stir among the *Zenda* company, it was nothing to the upheavals and near heart attacks it perpetrated throughout the upper echelons of the film colony. Mary, it appeared, had been a very busy girl indeed, and her partners had gleefully been awarded marks in "Dear Diary" for performance, stamina, et cetera.

After being absent for days in a blaze of scandal and being laid bare (to coin a phrase) for all to see, Mary returned to the set of *Zenda,* looking just as sweet and demure as ever, and everyone, as usual, desperately wanted to protect her.

C. Aubrey Smith was over seventy when *Zenda* was made, six feet four, ramrod straight, alert and vigorous. Never did he forget

a line or misunderstand a piece of direction. Unfailingly courteous, kind and helpful, he was beloved by all.

Every Sunday he ordered me to turn out for the Hollywood
Cricket Club, I always called him "sir," and though dreading long
hot afternoons in the field, I obeyed.

His great, craggy face was frequently creased by worry because he
loved England very deeply, and as it was early in 1937, he had little
faith in the way Neville Chamberlain was coping with the Rome-
Berlin Axis and Germany's anti-Comintern Pact with Japan.
Refusing to read the "local rags," the Los Angeles *Times* or the *Examiner*, trusting only the London *Times* to keep him up to date,
and with airmail across the Atlantic almost nonexistent, Aubrey
was usually eight to ten days behind a crisis. Nobody spoiled his
fun by telling him the news, so it was almost two weeks after it had
happened that the old man flung down his morning paper and
boomed across the set, "The bloody feller's done it!"

"Who, sir? What, sir?" we chorused.

"That whippersnapper Hitler! He's marched into Austria!"

John Cromwell, the director, was highly respected and highly
efficient, but he was a little low on humor, which created certain
hazards for Raymond Massey and Doug, Jr., two of the most inveterate gigglers in the business.

The scene at the state ball was most important. Colman,
masquerading as the king, was proposing to Princess Flavia in a
small anteroom. Outside, a courtier was eavesdropping. At the end
of the long intimate love scene this courtier, a large fat man with a
mauve face, had to hurry to Fairbanks, Massey, and myself, waiting
in our resplendent uniforms at the bottom of a long flight of steps
at the entrance to the castle. On arrival he had to say two words:
"Good news!"

It was what is known as a production shot, designed to give
richness, size, and color to the film by showing the maximum
number of people in their magnificent costumes and the most ad-
vantageous views of the extravagant sets.

The famous Chinese cameraman James Wong Howe had excelled himself, and by a "marshaling yard's" arrangement of tracks
and overhead trolleys, his cameras were able, all in one flowing
movement, to witness the love scene, then follow the mauve-faced

courtier through several anterooms filled with beautifully gowned ladies and bemedaled gentlemen across a giant white marble multipillared patio, around a lily pond on which cruised haughty black swans, thence up a flight of ornate stairs into the candlelit main ballroom, where 300 couples of the handsomest and most glamorous extras were executing a carefully rehearsed waltz.

Past the minstrel's gallery the mauve courtier hurried, on through the kitchens and vestibules, followed everywhere by a battery of wondering eyes—what would his message be?

Finally, the big moment came. Satin-breeched flunkies flung open the huge main doors, and as the tension mounted, he ponderously descended 120 steps to our little group waiting at the bottom.

"Good news!" he said loudly, and we reeled back. It was bad news for us—he had a breath like a buzzard.

When the courtier tramped back to his starting position for the next run-through, we dared not look at one another. Fairbanks, I sensed, was beginning to vibrate, and out of the corner of my eye, I could see that Ray Massey was making a great production of polishing his monocle.

We suffered through half a dozen more rehearsals and six more broadsides from "Halitosis Harry." By the time John Cromwell was satisfied and ordered the first take we realized we were doomed. A sort of schoolboy hysteria had gripped us, and although we still avoided one another's eyes, we knew we could never get through the scene.

"Let's pretend it's drains," I whispered.

We could hear the love scene being played in the distance, and with dread we followed the sounds of the courtier's slow progress toward us. The orchestra in the ballroom fell silent as he approached the end of his journey so that his two golden words could be recorded for posterity.

The doors above us were flung open, and our tormentor, relieved to be at the end of his complicated trip, descended smugly toward us.

"Good news!" he said.

We greeted his announcement with gales of pent-up laughter.

"Cut! What the hell's going on?" demanded a furious Crom-

479

well, rushing up, but the more angry he became, the more uncontrollable became our mirth.

Fairbanks behaved in a most craven manner. "Ask Mr. Massey what's wrong," he blurted out with tears streaming down his face. "He's the oldest."

Ray's suggestion didn't help at all. "Gee, Mr. Cromwell, perhaps it would give us a kind of springboard if the gentleman *whispered* the line."

The whisper brought us a whiff of pure phosgene.

In the end Cromwell rearranged his shooting schedule so that our reactions to the fateful "news" could be photographed the following day when, as he succinctly put it, "You bastards will have had a whole night to calm down."

Hollywood always felt that the leading characters of costume pictures should be seen riding prancing, frothing, and often unmanageable steeds, so when we came to the shooting of the coronation procession, I had a few words with the head wrangler, some currency changed hands, and I was mounted on a nice quiet old mare. Unfortunately, she was in heat. Trotting through the cheering citizens beside the golden coach bearing Ronnie and Madeleine, resplendent in cuirass and silver helmet topped by a golden eagle, I was blissfully unaware of danger gathering like a storm astern of me. Ray was riding a large black stallion.

A high-pitched whinnying rose above the screams of hurriedly departing townsfolk, and about six feet of easily identifiable stallion equipment passed me like a torpedo. I turned in my saddle to find thrashing hooves and gnashing teeth all around me. Far above, I saw Ray's horrified face. Not wanting to go down with the ship, I hurriedly disembarked by flinging myself to the ground, leaving my mare to her happy fate and Ray to a ringside seat. For a while it looked as though he were riding a rocking horse.

David Selznick's *Prisoner of Zenda* was a triumphant success, critically and financially, and a testament to what happens when a producer infuses all those around him with loyalty, enthusiasm, and a real joy in their work.

Fifteen years later L. B. Mayer decided to make some easy money and ordered a remake of *The Prisoner of Zenda*. Feeling that he could not improve on the way his son-in-law had captured the Anthony Hope classic, he insisted that the new version be made with identical sets, word for word, shot for shot, and close-up for close-up; it had to be exactly the same as the old one, but with new faces. He cast Stewart Granger in the Colman role, and James Mason misguidedly attempted to follow Doug, Jr. To David Oliver Selznick's great amusement the result was a critical and financial disaster.

DOUGLAS FAIRBANKS

At the top of Summit Drive stood Pickfair, a walled estate that had long been the focal point of all that meant Hollywood.

The home of the two biggest stars of silent pictures, Douglas Fairbanks and Mary Pickford, Pickfair had hosted the most ostentatious parties and royal entertainments of the great dawning of Hollywood.

The "King of the Silent Films," the most popular male star in the world, hero of such muscular, exciting, and intentionally amusing spectacles as *The Three Musketeers*, *Robin Hood*, *The Mark of Zorro*, *The Black Pirate*, and *The Thief of Baghdad*, had married "America's Sweetheart"—a Hollywood bonanza!

Fairbanks had a hold on the filmgoers of the world, young and old, that has never to this day been equaled. Mary Pickford, too, "Little Mary of the Golden Curls," had her own immense and devoted following. The marriage had ended in divorce the year before I arrived in Hollywood, and the Pickfair I saw was a sad, overfurnished, and melancholy place of memories and closed doors. Mary was a wan and gallant little hostess, relying more and more on the companionship of a serious curly-haired young actor-singer whom she subsequently married—Buddy Rogers. Fairbanks was far from wan and sad. He was being comforted in England by the glorious, willowy, lemon-meringue blond Lady Ashley.

Sylvia Hawkes had been a chorus girl and small-part actress till she met dull, good-looking Lord Ashley. Before long, she met the far from dull, but equally good-looking, Sir Tim Birkin, a rich racing motorist, but a year after her divorce from Lord Ashley she upset the books by marrying Fairbanks.

Doug, an ex-Harvard graduate, was a chronic Anglophile. He openly and unashamedly loved the country, the people, the customs, and the climate. He rented a large country house in Hertfordshire, had his suits made by Anderson and Shepperd, his evening clothes by Hawes and Curtis, his shirts by Beale and Inman, his monogrammed velvet slippers by Peel, and he drove a Rolls-Royce. Although a self-confessed snob enjoying the company of the more flamboyant British aristocracy ("Burke's steerage," he called them), he never lost the common touch. He was worshiped wherever he went.

When he departed from Pickfair, Fairbanks moved down to a Santa Monica beach house with Sylvia and a huge oversexed mastiff called Marco Polo.

This dog was a bisexual menace: nobody was spared its attentions. It weighed about 200 pounds and pumped up and down indiscriminately on anything that moved.

Doug in his mid-fifties still had the figure of a young athlete, and he paid constant attention to keeping it that way. He took a sunbath daily in a small green canvas compartment in the garden, burning himself the color of chewing tobacco. He was curiously coy in the presence of the friends he invited to join him there, always covering his private parts with his two cupped hands.

Chuck Lewis, his personal trainer, was always in attendance, giving massages and organizing workouts, steam baths, tennis, golf, or long-distance swims. Doug enjoyed hugely displaying his acrobatic talents and watching those half his age trying to catch up with him. I nearly killed myself jumping off his high diving board onto the low springboard alongside, which he had assured me would give me a "real tremendous bounce." It did. I missed the water altogether and landed in some petunias below the drawing-room window. While we disported ourselves in the business end of the pool, Sylvia, ever careful of her famous creamy white skin, paddled about in the shallow end beneath a huge floppy hat. Douglas was an overgrown schoolboy reveling in practical jokes, simple and elaborate.

The simple ones ranged from giving people exploding cigars, lighting orange flash papers, playing ostentatiously with a twenty-pound cannonball, exchanging it unseen for a rubber replica, yelling "catch," and tossing it to some poor unsuspecting wretch, to disappearing beneath the dinner table on serious evenings, crawling on hands and knees, and gently opening the fly of a pompous man sitting between two equally haughty ladies at the far end.

The elaborate ones turned sometimes into expensive productions. He announced in the trade papers that Dr. Hans Strassmann, the head of the German film company UFA, was coming out to visit him. Then he arranged for a "professional insulter"—a small bald actor named Vince Barnett—to board the Santa Fe Chief at San Bernardino, the last stop before Los Angeles.

Barnett, in Tyrolean hat and green cloak, made a triumphant entry into the film capital, and Fairbanks welcomed him at Union Station with red carpet, photographers, and a large crowd. The next night Fairbanks gave a white-tie dinner, and everyone was in the know except Samuel Goldwyn. At the end of the meal, cigars were lit and speeches of welcome were made. The last guest called on was the unfortunate Goldwyn. When Barnett rose to reply, with a heavy German accent, he thanked all the speakers but said that he was a little surprised that Goldwyn had been invited to meet him because he considered him to be the least talented filmmaker in the United States. He went on to say that Goldwyn was famous for stealing actors like Gary Cooper away from other studios, that everyone in Berlin knew that the only reason he had brought the Russian actress Anna Sten out to Hollywood was "because he wanted to get into her bloomers."

Poor Goldwyn was slow to catch on, and it took Fairbanks a long, long time to put matters right.

Fairbanks was a low handicap golfer, an excellent tennis player, and a top-class performer with saber, épée, or foil. His film duels were high spots in all his productions, and his daring stunts, as a matter of pride, he did himself, scorning the use of doubles.

One was really spectacular: Escaping from the heavies from a high balcony in *Robin Hood*, with both hands he plunged his sword into an eighty-foot-high velvet curtain and whizzed down to safety. He repeated this stunt in *The Black Pirate*: trapped in the highest crosstrees, he slid down a billowing mainsail and arrived safely on deck, leaving his adversaries in the rigging.

Plagued by questions on how his hands and wrists could possibly have been strong enough to keep the sword at exactly the right angle, he one day divulged to us that on the other side of the curtain and sail the swords had been bolted into a large board—but it was still a very dangerous descent.

Doug's prowess and ability aboard movie ships did not extend to his seamanship in real life. One Fourth of July he and Sylvia chartered a motor cruiser and invited a small group to sail with them to Catalina. The idea was to anchor on arrival alongside Cecil B. DeMille's sleek white three-masted schooner. Our captain had an ominous name—Jack Puke.

Except for the deckhand who really had been prostrated by seasickness, the four-hour trip to the island had been uneventful, and without difficulty, we located DeMille's schooner. Nearby was a large circular mooring buoy, and Captain Puke decided to attach his boat to the ring on top of it. With DeMille's smartly dressed guests applauding our arrival, we rammed this buoy at considerable speed because when Captain Puke rang down to the engine room for "full astern," the engineer was on deck picking his teeth and contemplating DeMille's yacht.

Finally, we maneuvered into position for someone to jump down onto the buoy and secure us. "Now," yelled Captain Puke.

"I'll go," said Fairbanks bravely. "Quick, David, up to the sharp end!"

I followed him to the bow, where he grabbed a rope I was holding and, with his famous grace and feline agility, leaped down onto the pitching buoy. Further applause greeted this effort, but it was premature because the rope turned out to be attached to nothing on our boat, and when the engineer at last obeyed Captain Puke's unnautical command to "BACK UP . . . YOU SON OF A BITCH!" we pulled away, leaving our host stranded.

I fetched him later in the dinghy.

Fairbanks owned a large country property near San Diego—the Rancho Santa Fe—and there he delighted, for short periods only, in the simplicity of ranch life, keeping us up all night coyote hunting, lying, heavily armed, in wet grass, waiting for the ghostly slinking packs to devour the dead chickens he had impaled on stakes.

His duck hunts were more civilized and of minimal danger to the timid mallard, teal, and widgeon which swarmed around the reservoir. He would wake us stealthily before dawn, in whispers distribute guns and ammunition, and then drive us three miles to the waterside in his Rolls-Royce with headlights blazing and radio blaring. No humans were shot either. Such heady stuff was it for an unknown young actor to be accepted by one of the Hollywood giants that it was some time before I realized that beneath all his gaiety, flamboyance, and love of youth, Fairbanks lived with a great sadness. He fought off the advancing years valiantly and perhaps a little desperately, but the afternoon light was already softening the contours of a career that had long been illuminated more brightly than any other in the history of the movies, and it was with a rather sad smile he bade me one day bend down and look at myself in the mirror top of a coffee table. The blood ran into my cheeks and under my eyes, and I found myself staring at a warthog.

"That's what you'll look like when you're fifty!" He laughed.

Still acclaimed, applauded, and stopping traffic wherever he went, even in the remotest parts of the world, he accepted the adulation with a flashing smile, but it must have been a knife in his guts to know that, at an age when his contemporaries in other walks of life were just reaching their zenith, he had already been turned out to grass.

CHARLES CHAPLIN

On the same side of Summit Drive as Pickfair and Ronald Colman's house sprawled an estate of about the same acreage as that of Harold Lloyd. . . . It also was owned by a founding father of Hollywood—Charles Spencer Chaplin.

It boasted stands of beautiful trees, green lawns sloping down to a swimming pool and, of course, a tennis court. The house was large, cluttered, of yellow-ocher color and Victorian design: high french windows giving on to the gardens retrieved it from being supersuburbia. Few people were invited there, not because Charlie

Chaplin shunned all contact with the Hollywood he had done more than any other to change from a citrus-growing community into one of the biggest industries in the United States, but for two very basic reasons: The greatest public entertainer in the world had only a sketchy idea of how to entertain in private, and he was also allergic to laying out large sums of money for food and drink to be guzzled by those he reckoned to be passengers and noncontributors. He enjoyed going out, however, to selected houses, and nothing made him happier than playing the elder statesman, sitting in a chair after dinner, with the faithful at his feet, while he held forth with gestures and sublime caricature.

Not the greatest listener in private life, Chaplin was a great advocate of it as an essential part of the actor's equipment. One night Doug Fairbanks ran a film after dinner at the beach house, and in it was one of my earliest efforts. When it was over, the others made the insincere but flattering noises so dear to an actor's heart, but Chaplin sat still, saying nothing.

Finally, I plucked up courage to ask him what he thought.

"Don't just stand around like most actors waiting for your turn to speak," he said flatly. "Learn to listen."

The uncompromising directness of this excellent advice was typical of Chaplin. The folk hero of millions in every land, the tattered courageous little tramp who loved flowers and children and raised two rude fingers at the Establishment, he was in himself an extremely opinionated man with a highly developed sense of his own place in history. He loved being asked for advice and gave it freely.

Beside Fairbanks' pool one day, the playwright Charles MacArthur, who had lately been lured from Broadway to write a screenplay, was bemoaning the fact that he was finding it difficult to write visual jokes.

"What's the problem?" asked Chaplin.

"How, for example, could I make a fat lady, walking down Fifth Avenue, slip on a banana peel and still get a laugh? It's been done a million times," said MacArthur. "What's the best way to *get* the laugh? Do I show first the banana peel, then the fat lady approaching; then she slips? Or do I show the fat lady first, then the banana peel, and *then* she slips?"

"Neither," said Chaplin without a moment's hesitation. "You show the fat lady approaching; then you show the banana peel;

then you show the fat lady and the banana peel together; then she steps *over* the banana peel and disappears down a manhole."

Chaplin was devoted to Douglas Fairbanks and never wearied of telling that it was Fairbanks' business antennae which had sensed the fact that with Mary Pickford the three biggest stars in the business were overpricing themselves so heavily that producers, seeing little profit from their pictures, would soon be unwilling to employ any of them.

"It's simple," Fairbanks had said. "We cut out the producers; then we make our own pictures and employ ourselves."

The result had been the highly profitable United Artists Company.

When Fairbanks was around, Chaplin delighted in telling stories against himself because Doug, with his schoolboy humor and infectious laugh, was the world's best audience.

Egged on by Doug, Chaplin reenacted, one evening, an embarrassing arrival in the little French port of Cagnes-sur-Mer.

Aimee Semple McPherson was a beautiful blonde with a fascinating superstructure. She was also an evangelist with a faithful following of thousands who called her Sister, subscribed $1,000,000 to build her Angelus Temple in downtown Los Angeles, and watched breathlessly as she publicly baptized immense truck drivers swathed in see-through sheets.

"Come to Jesus!" she would cry.

The faithful also purchased a license for her Angelus Temple Radio Station and financed her personal travels "to the Holy Land."

One day Aimee Semple McPherson disappeared, and headlines screamed that she had been kidnapped on her way to Mecca. These were later reoriented toward suicide, murder, or simple drowning beneath the Santa Monica Pier, but in point of fact she had run away with the burly operator of her radio station.

During one of her aforementioned travels to the "Holy Land," "Sister" Aimee had joined Douglas Fairbanks on a yacht he had chartered for a Mediterranean cruise. Another guest had been Chaplin.

Wherever the yacht anchored, thousands had lined the shoreline, hoping for a glimpse of their heroes, and landing for a stroll or a little shopping had produced mob scenes reminiscent of a DeMille epic, so they worked out a careful plan to enjoy a quiet picnic in the hills behind Grasse. The yacht anchored a mile offshore. The crew reconnoitered the little port and reported nobody about except a few fishermen. A car was ordered to wait at a certain flight of steps with engine running, and the party, complete with rugs and picnic baskets, descended into the motorboat for the trip ashore.

For dinner, the night before, however, they had eaten a mound of mussels and, just as they rounded the breakwater and slid into the calm water of the little harbor, one of these shellfish struck.

Chaplin felt two fists clenching and unclenching around his intestines. He broke out in a sweat and knew that he must immediately get to a toilet. He was in agony.

The launch came alongside the landing, and Fairbanks stood up to help Aimee Semple McPherson ashore—he was instantly recognized.

"Dooglas! Dooglas!" yelled a fisherman, dropping his rod and disappearing at high speed into the nearest bistro. Out poured the inmates; children were dispatched to spread the glad tidings to the village.

"Dooglas! Dooglas!" chanted the swelling throng. Bathers and tourists, attracted by the cries, circled excitedly at the perimeter of the crowd like sea gulls around refuse.

"*Regardez!*" yelled someone, excitedly pointing at a bent-over figure clasping his abdomen in the stern of the boat.

"*C'est lui! C'est Charlot!*"

Chaplin was undergoing paroxysms of pain.

"*Où est le lavabo?*" he croaked in faltering French. Fairbanks, already ashore, turned and was so unnerved by the sight of his friend's ashen face that he released his grip on the evangelist, who slipped and baptized herself between boat and landing.

The populace applauded: "*Formidable! Bravo! Bravo!*" They were convinced that high comedy was a way of life with the world's two greatest entertainers.

Fairbanks tried his hand at enlisting the help of the crowd.

"*Le can pour Charlot!*" he shouted. "*Où est le can?*"

Chaplin tried sign language to help things along and, clasping one hand to his stomach, pantomimed the pulling of a chain with the other. This really brought down the house.

"Bravo, Charlot! Bravo, Charlot!" the crowd shrieked, delighted at the prospect of a free show beyond their wildest expectations, and convinced that they were about to witness some marvelously inventive comic ending; so they helped him from the boat and carried him shoulder high to an evil-smelling cell at the far end of the port.

Inside, in the most appallingly insanitary surroundings, nature took its long and horrendous course to the accompaniment of at first encouraging, then impatient, and finally disgruntled shouts, clapping hands and time beaten upon the door and walls: "CHAR-LOT! . . . CHAR-LOT! . . . CHAR-LOT!"

When Chaplin finally emerged from his noisome sanctuary, the shadows were lengthening on the little port. As he boarded the waiting launch, the fallen idol was treated to turned backs, shrugs of Gallic dismissal, and mutterings of *"Ce Chaplin . . . il est rien."*

I recounted to Chaplin some of the experiences I had endured in the "meat market," the loathsome practice of some directors when casting the smaller parts of their films, calling twenty or thirty "possibilities" to the sound stage and making each in turn play a key scene *in front* of the remainder, finally dismissing all except one.

Chaplin told me that this embarrassing and unfair system was a legacy from Broadway and that it had not changed since he had come to New York in 1913 with Fred Karno's *A Night in an English Music Hall* (another member of that small troupe had been Stan Laurel, later of Laurel and Hardy). Chaplin was interviewed by William Gillette, a great actor-manager of that time, who was casting for *King Henry V*, and twelve nervous young actors were lined up on the stage, hoping for the microscopic part of Williams, one of the English soldiers.

Gillette, an intimidating figure draped in a long black coat with a fur collar, addressed the group.

"Gentlemen," he intoned, giving full range to his famous voice, "I shall approach each of you in turn and say, 'The dauphin is dead!' Your reply will be one word: 'Dead!' He who makes the most of that one word will play the part of Williams."

The group of young hopefuls shuffled nervously about. At the

489

farthest end of the line in a black suit with a high white stiff collar stood Chaplin—by several inches the shortest.

"The dauphin is dead!" boomed Gillette at the first actor, but the young man was so terrified he just managed to roll his eyes and emit a pitiful squeak: "Dead?"

He was dismissed. "The dauphin is dead!" roared Gillette, but the next actor decided that an English soldier would be delighted at the news. "Dead?" he asked, smiling happily as though his stock in the Union Pacific Railroad had risen twenty points. He too was dismissed.

As the line was thinned out and an impatient Gillette drew inexorably nearer, Chaplin became increasingly nervous. Eight actors had been dismissed with ignominy, taking with them every inflection and every nuance with which he had hoped to embellish the word "Dead." Three more dismissals followed in quick succession, and the diminutive Chaplin found himself alone on the stage confronted by the towering figure of the now-exasperated actor-manager.

Gillette looked down with distaste upon the sole survivor. "The dauphin is dead!" he yelled.

Chaplin's mind went blank.

He shook his head mournfully from side to side, then clicked his tongue loudly on the roof of his mouth. "*Tch! tch! tch! tch!*" he went.

Gillette slowly raised his arm, pointed scornfully to the exit, and Chaplin, not for the last time, disappeared alone and with dignity into the sunset.

Feeling himself pilloried too long in the American press for not taking out his U.S. citizenship, for his leftist political views, for his former love affairs with young actresses, and finally for his marriage to the teenaged daughter of Eugene O'Neill, Chaplin folded his tents and one night silently stole away to live peacefully in Vevey, a small, sleepy town on the shores of Lake Geneva.

Reclining in a hospital bed into which Chaplin had inadvertently put me, I read of his sudden departure and was amazed because a few hours before I had been playing tennis with him on Summit Drive.

A highly organized man, as his military-style withdrawal demonstrated, he liked his tennis games neatly arranged. With a clearly defined preference for winning, he had given me as a partner for the afternoon's sport Tim Durant, a slow-moving elderly man, later famous as the galloping grandfather courageously flogging also-rans around the Grand National Steeplechase. As his own partner Chaplin had invited none other than Big Bill Tilden, questionably the greatest tennis player the world had ever seen.

Tilden served first to me, and because of his great height, the ball came out of the sun. I never saw it—but I *heard* it as it went by and became embedded in the wire netting behind me.

Durant fared no better, and Chaplin looked smug.

"Thirty-love," he crowed.

For the next serve to me, Tilden decided to be kinder and instead of acing me with another bullet, he uncorked a delivery that had so much spin on it that the ball was egg-shaped as it floated over the net. When it hit the ground, it shot straight up in the air above my head. With visions of smashing the Great Tilden's top-secret delivery, I leaped in the air and flailed at it.

I thought I had received a blow with an ax behind my leg, and I fell to the ground writhing in excruciating agony. I had not pulled a tendon; I had snapped my entire calf muscle clean in half.

Tilden was galvanized into action. He leaped the net. "I know what it is," he said. "Quick, somebody, get adhesive tape!"

Chaplin disappeared toward the house, and with hindsight, I suppose he must have done some unpacking. At any rate, the most appalling pain I have ever experienced was relieved when he reappeared.

"I'm going to tape your heel up as high as it will go," said Tilden. "That'll point the toes down and make the muscle go slack. It'll help the pain; then we'll put you in the hospital."

He did as he promised; then he and Durant carried me to his car and drove me away. My final view of Chaplin, with his last day's tennis in California ruined, was of a small, white-flanneled figure disconsolately hitting balls against the green canvas of the backing.

Within a few hours, Hollywood's one true genius was gone forever to the land of peace, understanding, milk chocolate, and all those lovely snowcapped tax benefits.

11
Mary Lou

*I*N the earliest days of Hollywood the professional extra did not exist. If a director needed bodies to fill out the screen, he dispatched his assistant to find them. For a while onlookers and others in the vicinity, with nothing better to do, enjoyed the experience of appearing in front of the camera—for fun. Later they demanded to be paid, and the going rate became 50 cents a day. This munificent offering attracted every drunken bum and panhandler in the area, and the streets around the studios became clogged with flushed citizenry with outstretched hands. The producers then invented the bullpen, a sort of central corral into which, early each morning, hundreds of eager bodies were herded, and from which, as the day progressed, assistant directors siphoned off the types they needed.

As the original Hollywood studios became bigger and new ones sprang up all over the sprawling Los Angeles area, each studio built its own bullpen and used, in addition, the services of independent hiring halls in downtown Los Angeles.

By the mid-twenties Hollywood was attracting a tremendous monthly influx of young hopefuls, from trained or semitrained actors and actresses to what seemed like every beauty contest winner in the world—and all with a one-way ticket.

By 1926 the studios realized that their prehistoric methods of hiring extras must be revised; potential talent was being trampled underfoot by the bums and panhandlers in the bullpens and hiring halls, and no coherent records were being kept.

The time had come to move from utter chaos to simple confusion, so the Central Casting Corporation was born.

A filing system was at last instituted, but an "open door" policy still persisted, and by 1930 an unwieldy 18,000 names were on the books and Hollywood film actors found themselves members of the most overcrowded profession in the world. A few, very few, percolated upward from the crowded extra ranks, among them Carole Lombard, Joel McCrea, Paulette Goddard, and Lucille Ball, but the chances of such success were microscopic, and the luck had to be colossal. Much talent withered and died from frustration.

Central Casting made ineffectual efforts to stem the surging tide of the star-struck and, in the early thirties, hung over the front door a large banner upon which was emblazoned a piece of advice which I noticed with some alarm when I joined a long rain-soaked line awaiting registration: DON'T TRY TO BECOME AN ACTOR. FOR EVERY ONE WE EMPLOY WE TURN AWAY A THOUSAND.

We newcomers had been warned, but worse was to come; within a few weeks the pay of the extras was arbitrarily cut by 20 percent.

It was grim. The wage for a crowd extra fell below $3 a day, and Central Casting reported that, including the highest paid of their 18,000, fewer than 60 extras were earning more than $2,000 a year; the rest were averaging less than $500.

Most of us were forced to take part-time jobs, and we became carhops, manual laborers, shop assistants, janitors, or waitresses; I worked on a fishing boat. Many went on relief.

The lucky ones among us who received studio calls were expected to report for work at 6 A.M., to accept inedible meals when it suited the producers, to continue working, or rather to continue being herded about like cattle, till all hours of the night with no additional pay and to report again at 6 the following morning. For the same pittance we had to work right through the night on Saturdays, and we had to face the fact that on days when shooting was canceled at the last minute because of bad weather, a drunken leading man, or "acts of God" (a favorite studio ploy), we would be sent home without touching a cent. There was no compensation for the hours of travel spent on the erratic transportation system of the metropolis, and if we got hurt during filming, there was no redress except by suing the studio heads, which was tantamount to asking them if they would kindly find room for more names on their blacklists.

The powerless and leaderless extras became desperate. They were saved by their more opulent fellow actors who conceived the idea of a Screen Actors Guild to give protection to all film performers in Hollywood. Leading man Leon Ames, comedian James Gleason, and the glowering figure of Frankenstein's Monster Boris Karloff were the founding fathers of the movement, and the first to join them "to help the less fortunate than ourselves" was that splendid old gentleman C. Aubrey Smith.

His example lit the torch, and Gary Cooper, Clark Gable, Spencer Tracy, Paul Muni, James Cagney, Robert Montgomery, Fredric March, Groucho Marx, and many other great stars quickly affixed their names to the crusade which resulted by 1935 in the producers' being forced to recognize the guild and to treat their highly profitable cattle more like human beings.

The ambitious mass of extras registered at Central Casting were divided into four classes:

1. *Dress extras.* These owned garments for every occasion: ball gowns, white tie and tails, riding habits, clothing for business, weddings, graduations, beaches, racetracks, et cetera. The more outfits they owned, the more often they worked. They numbered only 200 or 300 and were a very upper-class closely knit group in extra land. They were led by a dignified dowager named Mrs. Wickes, a tall, professional-looking gentleman named Larry Dodds, and an elderly white-mustachioed ex-Indian army man known as Major. They were paid $10 per day, lived in a country-house atmosphere, and played bridge endlessly among themselves, gossiping and chattering together, spurning the common box lunches and munching goodies from their picnic baskets. Mostly, they were devoid of all acting ambition and, like all extras, had only a sketchy idea of what masterpiece they were currently engaged upon.

2. *General extras.* These could look presentable and move well in street clothes or uniforms.

3. *Atmosphere or crowd extras.* And comprising nine-tenths of the main herd of cattle. We were rounded up and mercilessly harried from morning to night by brash young assistant directors. In

this group we were classified ethnically—Latin, Middle Eastern, Far Eastern, Asian, Indigenous U.S. (white, black, or red). My card was stamped "ANGLO SAXON TYPE 2008."

4. *The "shit kickers" or cowboy extras.* These habitually hung out in "Gower Gulch," on the corner of Gower Street and Sunset Boulevard, strategically placed between several bars and the small independent studios which churned out cheap Western quickies.

In addition, the studio gates were daily besieged by crowds of freakish opportunists hoping to catch the eye of directors being signaled through in their limousines: giants, dwarfs, midgets, the grotesquely ugly, the fat, the emaciated, the maimed, and those waggling newly arrived bosoms and bottoms.

All registered extras followed the same routine: Between five and eight o'clock every evening we would call Central Casting and state our names and classifications.

At the other end the operators—and there were dozens of them working frantically at a huge board—would check the latest requirements:

Paramount	180 Indians
Universal	25 Greeks
RKO	150 Asians
MGM	200 Nondescripts
Fox	230 U.S. (white)
	25 " (black)

Then, till the quotas were filled, the first to call who fitted the required groups would be hired and told where to report on the morrow.

With up to 18,000 inquiries coming in for an average of 800 jobs, the evening hum of disappointment rising from the switchboard was numbing.

"Nothing, call later. . . . Nothing, call later. . . . Nothing, call later"—but most people continued calling till at long last the switchboard went dead.

After years of exploitation, it is not hard to imagine how much the extras relished getting a little back from the producers; even the snooty dress extras indulged in this game. They were periodically called to "dress parades," where before an audience of casting directors and assistant directors from all the studios they displayed their entire wardrobes and, according to the number of changes they could muster, were marked down for future calls. By deft maneuvering in the changing rooms, it was possible for them to arrange for one cutaway or white fur stole to appear on a dozen different backs with most beneficial results.

We of the lower classes found more plebeian ways of revenge.

It was a simple matter to show up early, for example, at Paramount for a big crowd call to collect our voucher (which had to be dropped into a box at the end of the day's work for later payment), to entrust this document to a chum to drop with his, and then hotfoot it over to another studio, draw another voucher there, and collect a second day's pay for one day's work.

The obvious refinement of this was to do no work at all at any studio and still get paid for a full day's labor. A group of us perfected this, and when employed on the back lot at Metro-Goldwyn-Mayer, we were able to put it into practice. We had loosened some boards and rearranged some wiring in the high surrounding fence. At 6 A.M. we drew our costumes and our pay vouchers and showed up with hundreds of other Friends, Romans, Countrymen, or whatever. Later we drifted lavatoryward and kept going to the escape hatch in the fence, where we stripped off the studio clothing, and in our bathing costumes (thoughtfully worn underneath) joined a friend in his convertible for a lovely day at the beach. Toward evening the reverse procedure was employed, and we arrived back in ample time to drop the vouchers and hand in our costumes.

If we worked later than expected, damp salty swimsuits beneath breastplates or doublets and hose became itchy reminders of a golden day of hot dogs and surf enjoyed at L. B. Mayer's expense.

One athletic girl, Mary Lou, was an avid beach lover and an eager recruit on these expeditions. Like thousands of others among the extras, she had come to Hollywood with stars in her eyes, but a veteran of three years in Hollywood, she had still not spoken a line, and she was becoming disillusioned.

"I've tried it all," she told me. "I've worked at night in acting classes and theater groups, and I've paid those phony makeup schools that guaranteed employment, but no talent scouts ever came near me. I've been on parties with producers and gone to Vegas with casting directors, and I've held my nose and laid some of the creepiest agents in the business, but no dice, nothing ever happened."

She was a beautiful, open-faced girl, tall, creamy-skinned with wide, almost golden eyes and rather broad shoulders. We called her Miss Corn on the Cob because she had once won a high school beauty contest in her small farming community in Iowa. She was a quiet, private person, mysterious and aloof, and no matter how well one knew her, a part of her was always held in reserve. Going through a bad financial patch, she was evicted by her landlady and showed up at my little Hollywood pad till things got better. To start with, this unexpected bonanza went the traditional route, and she shared my bed, but even there she held back, and I had an uncomfortable feeling that she was merely paying rent. After a few days we made other sleeping arrangements, which included a mattress for me on the floor.

We remained good friends but it was infinitely frustrating to see such a gorgeous creature wandering about in all sorts of provocative stages of undress, cooking things and tidying up, and to have to face the fact that my romantic or sexual fulfillments were subject to the most stringent rationing, and I was quite relieved when she got a job on a long location picture and left.

By a series of highly unlikely gyrations, the wheel of fate had picked me up, shaken me, rattled me, and finally spewed me upward from the extra ranks into the coveted strata of contract players, so at the end of 1935 I left my sordid little South Hollywood pad and rented a slightly larger and marginally less sordid one in a once-smart residential area on a North Hollywood hillside.

It comprised a bedroom below and a large living room above, complete with kitchenette and a permanently sealed picture window, through which, when I cleaned it, I could see at night the electrical rash of the Los Angeles Basin and by day in the far distance, the water tower of Metro-Goldwyn-Mayer Studio and the oil derricks beyond Culver City. I also had a small terrace.

Directly below me, in a beautifully manicured garden, stood a large cream-colored Colonial-style mansion with a pillared front entrance which I could not see and a private parking lot at the back which I could not only see but hear. Expensive cars backed and filled from early afternoon to dawn on its gravel surface; laughter and sometimes altercations disturbed my slumber.

Eddie, the mailman, brought me up to date when I asked him about my neighbors.

"Hey! Whaddya know!" He chortled. "You been livin' here a month and you don't catch on you're lookin' inta the back windows of a whorehouse! You want a piece of tail—you better get yer ass down there and talk to the Baroness—she's got the best-lookin' bunch of hookers in LA."

Thereafter I borrowed a pair of binoculars from the studio property department, hoping to catch a glimpse of some friend in action, or at least at pre- or postcoital parking, but the windows were heavily curtained, and as the days passed, I became disenchanted with the attractive girls and the well-heeled gentlemen who ebbed and flowed on the parking lot below me. I had not seen one familiar face.

One evening I received a shock: Mary Lou was locking the door of a green two-seater Pontiac convertible. I watched the familiar figure pass around to the front entrance; she did not reappear.

Thereafter I kept an eye open for that car, and when I realized that it was a semipermanent visitor to the parking lot, my curiosity was understandably aroused.

I made some inquiries and learned from Central Casting that Mary Lou had withdrawn her name from their books. The next time I saw the green car, I left a note under the windshield wiper, indicating my whereabouts and suggesting that it was time we resumed contact.

One calm evening I was sitting content on my little terrace, sniffing a sunset scented by the orange blossoms of an adjacent grove, when there came a knocking at my door. Mary Lou walked in, looking ravishing. She settled herself down with a drink, crossed long silken legs, shook her sun-kissed hair and, without any prompting from me, brought me up to date.

She was an extremely forthright girl and explained her new life clinically and concisely. There were no excuses, and there was, apparently, no remorse.

"I'm a whore now," she announced cheerfully, "but I am also going steady with Bobbie."

"Who's Bobbie?" I asked.

"You'll see for yourself in a little while," she answered. "I gave up sleeping around when I met Bobbie because for the first time I had found someone who suited me in every way. With Bobbie it really *works*."

"Are you in love?" I asked.

"I dunno . . . I guess so . . . Anyway, for the moment I've never been so happy. . . . I was really getting desperate in Hollywood. I was going noplace fast and not earning enough to pay my laundry. I didn't want to go back to Iowa." She paused, spread her hands, and smiled down at her white pleated skirt and expensive shoes. "Now look at me—I'm *loaded!*"

I looked at her, and she really was a dish.

"How does Bobbie feel about you being a whore?" I asked. "That's sleeping around, isn't it?"

"Just *great!*" She laughed and did not elaborate.

"Who is the Baroness?"

"Oh! You'll *love* her, she's a great old broad . . . she really is a baroness, too . . . German . . . she's like a mother to me." She giggled.

"I'll bet," I said sourly. "Is she the madam?"

"Yes, but she doesn't run it like a cathouse. She has a great bunch of girls working there, and it's mostly done on a 'date' basis. The guys call up for a date with one of us, and we have lovely apartments to entertain them in, and there's a butler and two maids and drinks and snacks. We get a lot of dough, and the fellows are nice too, mostly important businessmen from back East or society people from Pasadena, or Palos Verdes, and the LA Country Club. In fact, the Baroness won't accept anyone from the movie business; she says they're 'common' and talk too much, and she doesn't need them anyway."

A car stopped outside, and a horn honked.

Mary Lou's face lit up. She rushed to the door. A beautiful tall girl of about twenty-eight with close-cropped dark hair and wearing white slacks strode into the room.

"Hi!" she said. "I'm Bobbie."

When I saw Mary Lou's glowing face, I knew how a Brooklyn Dodger fan must have felt on hearing that his favorite pitcher had defected to the New York Giants.

The girls shared an attractive ground-floor apartment near the Garden of Allah, and there I was frequently invited for Sunday brunch. They were very happy together, and it was obvious that they treated their time spent under the roof of the Baroness strictly as office hours. They had no intention of breaking the old lady's number one rule: "Private telephone numbers are never under any circumstances to be given to clients."

The Baroness, they told me, sometimes sent her girls out on dates to private addresses but never to hotels, and she carefully vetted, personally, all prospective clients, inviting them around for afternoon tea to see if she "approved"; she had no intention of paying protection money to Mickey Cohen.

Bobbie was great fun and painted enthusiastically in oils. She explained that she ran the "correction unit" for the Baroness, and billed as "Deborah de Sade—strict disciplinarian," she climbed into her leather bra, open-sided leather shorts, high-heeled thigh boots, gauntlet, and black mask and meted out lusty punishment with belt and whip to those who came to pay for humiliation and pain.

"It doesn't mean a goddamn thing to me," she said. "It's a pleasure to be able to help out the poor bastards. The funny thing is most of them are big guys in business, running corporations and that, and the moment I get through with them or they've had enough of being kicked around the floor, they're on the phone to their offices, cussing hell out of their secretaries and issuing orders all over the joint."

Mary Lou was happy in her work, too. "The dates I have really pay good money, and most of them are real nice. I guess they're not getting it at home. Some of them just like to sit around and talk— they must have lousy wives. Of course, we have a few specialists— like Brenda, who was trained for opera; she does specialties and hums 'The William Tell Overture' at the same time—but most of us are straight. The humping doesn't mean anything to me, of course, but I've finally become one hell of an actress! I give the best service I can and help them out with their little problems.

"Quite a few like to dress up, and the Baroness always sends those to me. She's given me a whole load of wigs and a makeup table for them, and they'll take forever choosing black underwear or a dress or a French maid outfit. I help them with their eyelashes and suspender belts and tell them how beautiful they look while they mince about in front of the three-way mirror. . . . It's a lot easier, I can tell you, than standing around on some goddamn hot movie set for twelve hours a day to earn what I now give the maid for tidying up the room. . . . Those guys don't do anyone any harm anyway."

One day I asked her how it could be arranged because I had generated an overpowering curiosity about the Baroness. "How can I meet her?"

Mary Lou and Bobbie decided that the best plan would be for them to tell her they had met a lonely young foreign visitor on the beach and ask the old lady if she would like to interview him as a potential client.

So it was put in train, and a few days later I was bidden to take tea with the Baroness.

I walked down from my aerie above and rang her front doorbell. A butler dressed in white coat and striped trousers opened the door.

"I have an appointment with the Baroness," I said, and told him my name.

"Yes, indeed, sir," he said in a sibilant German accent. "Follow me please."

We passed through a large beautifully furnished hall and knocked upon a door.

"Mr. Niven," he announced, and bowed.

I entered a small, cool, tastefully decorated green-tinted sitting room, cluttered with pieces of Meissen china, silver, bric-a-brac, and a profusion of oval-shaped photographs of square-headed gentlemen with spiky mustaches and ironclad military expressions. Above the mantelshelf was an oil painting of a girl; her dark hair was swept up at the back, and the fact that it sat upon her head like an inverted falcon's nest did nothing to detract from the serene alabaster beauty of the aristocratic face beneath.

"Good evening, young man," said the Baroness, extending her hand. "Come and sit down."

She indicated an armchair facing hers.

"Mary Lou tells me you are English, so we are having my favorite tea—Lapsang Souchong. I am sure you will appreciate it."

502

The white-haired old lady smiled, and I saw how beautifully the young girl above the mantelshelf had aged.

She asked what part of the British Isles I was from and launched into rhapsodies over the good times she had enjoyed as a young girl when she had been presented at court.

"Ah, those beautiful houses! And those gay weekends! Chatsworth! Drumlanrig! Eaton! Belvoir! Badminton! It was all so elegant and carefree, and we loved each other so much—till that stupid Kaiser ruined everything."

I was fascinated by my chic, carefully coiffed hostess, and as I looked across the three-tiered silver cake dish, happily munching mille-feuilles I wondered if the other girls in her establishment would measure up to the beauty standards set by Mary Lou and Bobbie.

I asked how long she had lived in California, whereupon she treated me to a harrowing description of the Baron's financial difficulties under the Weimar Republic when runaway inflation had cut the value of his Deutschmarks in half every hour.

"In 1923 he sold his estates near Münster for what he could get, and we moved here. He became interested in growing oranges and walnuts in the San Fernando Valley, but he passed away before he could get started." She sighed. "It was difficult for me at first being alone in a foreign country, but I made friends quickly, and now I run classes in deportment and social graces for young girls. The house is always full of young people, and I am content. All work and no play is not good for the girls, so I allow them to entertain their friends here between classes, and they organize swimming parties and so on."

I was just about to ask her if I could meet some of her pupils when she forestalled me by pulling a bell cord. The butler appeared and bowed.

"Wolfgang, I believe Miss Tessa, Miss Judy, and Miss Mary Lou are having a rest period at the moment. Tell them I would like them to join me for tea." The butler bowed again and withdrew.

"Dear Wolfgang," said the Baroness, "so loyal, he insisted on coming with us when we left the Schloss. I would be lost without him." She poured me another cup of tea.

"Mary Lou tells me that you are lately arrived and don't know many people out here. That is why I have asked two of her friends to join us—they are charming girls, rather shy, but if you feel you would like to have a private word with either of them and perhaps make a date with them?" She wagged a finger. "I know what young people are!"

I went along with the game.

"I can't thank you enough, Baroness, it's most kind of you, and I do appreciate it—but how can I, er, speak to one of the girls and not hurt the feelings of the others?"

She smiled a sweet smile and waved a hand. "The girls will be seated in those three chairs. If you feel you would like to have a private word with one of them before you go, signal the fact to me by turning the handle of your teacup in her direction and I will see that she stays after the others leave—no feelings will be hurt."

The girls came in together, Mary Lou leading and obviously going to have a hard time not bursting out laughing. The other two followed, and a most spectacular couple they were, too. The Baroness had thoughtfully provided a choice of coloring so, as they seated themselves, Mary Lou's blond fresh good looks were flanked by a sultry red-lipped, olive-skinned brunette and a green-eyed redhead whom I remembered seeing on several movie sets.

Both had spectacular figures, and their bosoms longed to burst out of their flimsy dresses. All had nice "toothpaste ad" smiles, they were carefully made up, and there was no hint anywhere of a hard-boiled trollop.

Tea and cakes were dispensed, and Mary Lou opened the ball game with a fast delivery. "Have you visited any of the studios since you've been out here?" she asked innocently.

I ducked that one with a clever shake of the head, and the conversation became more general.

The Baroness was kind and thoughtful with the girls, and they obviously enjoyed her company. It was a well-mannered and successful tea party, and only the muffled sounds of footsteps above and the distant flushing of toilets reminded me of my true whereabouts.

Discreetly raised eyebrows on the part of the Baroness signaled that she would like to conclude the business in hand, so I turned the handle of my teacup firmly toward Mary Lou. The Baroness rose, and we all stood. She glanced at a china clock. "Tessa and

Judy, darlings, I promised your mothers you could be home early today, so you had better run along, both of you."

The girls smiled good-bye and said it had been nice meeting me.

"Mary Lou, darling, I have so much to do. Why don't you show your friend the house? He tells me he is very interested in furniture. . . . Come and see me often, young man; you'll always be welcome."

The Baroness elegantly lifted to me the back of her hand, and I found myself bowing and kissing it. She swept regally from the room.

Mary Lou collapsed into a chair with laughter.

"Jesus, isn't that some act? But you should see her when she wants to get rid of someone—she's like a bouncer in the Bowery! Come on, let's go. You can see my workbench, and if Bobbie is not beating the bejesus out of some poor bastard, you can case her torture chamber."

Mary Lou's room was comfortable and functional. There was a large double bed and a thick rug on the floor for the "rough trade." The aforementioned well-stocked dressing table, wardrobe, and three-way mirror for the fetishists were in evidence, as was an imposing selection of spiky high-heeled shoes and "kinky" underwear for Mary Lou's own use if such aids were requested by the customers. A bathroom was adjacent, the lighting was discreet, and the radio was tuned to the music station.

We sat on the bed, and a strangely silent Mary Lou held my hand. Then she started crying, quite suddenly, gently at first, then with deep, heaving shudders. In great embarrassment I tried to console her, but she turned her head into the pillow. "Go away," she sobbed. "For chrissake, go *away*."

At the bottom of the stairs, Wolfgang materialized. He glanced at a pocket watch which he withdrew from his waistcoat. "The Baroness says you have most generously donated a hundred dollars toward the new pool house for the students," he said.

I handed over what amounted to my weekly salary, walked out into the poolless garden, and inhaled the warm Californian evening, thoroughly depressed.

I was sent away on a location picture in northern California for six weeks. When I returned, it was two days before I noticed an unnatural calm below me. The Colonial mansion was quiet; there were no curtains at the windows and no cars in the parking lot; pieces of newspaper were blowing about in the garden, which looked unhappy and deserted.

My little shack was the highest point, physically, of Eddie the mailman's morning round, and he made it a point to refresh himself there before proceeding downhill.

I heard him upstairs opening my icebox and joined him. He poured out a bottle of beer and brought me up to date.

"There's a carload of great-lookin' hookers loose around here someplace," he said. "They cleaned out the old lady below."

"Who? The cops?"

"Nah. The Mob . . . Bugsie Siegal, Mickey Cohen, and that bunch of hoods. Seems they wanted a big piece of the action down there, but the old dame just told them to go fuck themselves and closed up the joint in twenty-four hours. I seen a coupla big Bekins interstate vans loadin' on all her junk, and the girls were standin' around cryin'. Some people think she's moved to Vegas, but I don't think that's refined enough for her—my guess is Frisco. I feel sorry for them hookers, though." He shook his head sadly.

"Information" informed me that the phone had been disconnected, so I went round to Mary Lou and Bobbie's flat near the Garden of Allah. A suspicious Grant Wood-type lady wearing curlers and a flowered dressing gown opened the door a few inches.

"Yes?"

"I'm looking for the girls who live here—are they around?"

"No—they left town almost a month ago, and from what I understand from the folks around here, no one's going to miss them. . . . Whores!"

She slammed the door.

12
Bogie

HUMPHREY Bogart was born in December, 1899, which, up to a point, was perfectly all right with him. The thing he deeply resented about it was that it happened on Christmas Day. "Got gypped out of a proper birthday, goddammit."

Bogie's father, a well-to-do New York physician, was incessantly nagged by his wife. Bogie too enjoyed needling people, and he practiced it from an early age.

"Guess I inherited it from my folks—they were always griping at each other."

His famous lisp was caused by a badly performed operation on his lower lip in which a splinter of wood had become embedded.

"Goddamn doctor—instead of stitching it up, he screwed it up."

I asked him how the piece of wood had got into his lip in the first place. "Accident as a kid." He shrugged.

The Warner Brothers publicity department improved upon this and announced that it was a "shrapnel wound suffered in combat during World War I."

Bogie endured a well-to-do eastern seaboard upbringing, attended Andover, and headed for Yale. He didn't make it there, much to his mother's annoyance. She told him he was a failure and ordered him to go get himself a job. He complied, the next day enlisted in the U.S. Navy, and at seventeen and a half aboard the troop carrier *Leviathan* did indeed see service in the closing months of World War I.

After two years he was honorably discharged from the Navy and for the next eighteen months was employed as a runner for a Wall Street brokerage house. He didn't run fast enough apparently and resented openly the financial Establishment which employed him, so to the accompaniment of catcalls from his mother and with very little encouragement from his father, he drifted little by little into the theater.

First, he became stage manager to William Brady, the father of a school friend, who was producing plays in Brooklyn, and later he played his first part for the same suburban impresario in a play called *Swifty*. Opposite him was a young actress, Frances Howard, who left the production to become the wife of my own future boss —Samuel Goldwyn.

Bogie caught on in a small way and, by the age of twenty-six, was regularly employed in New York and the suburbs as a sleek juvenile lead complete with white tie, tails, and occasionally a tennis racket. These being the Roaring Twenties, he also set about making a name for himself in the speakeasies of Prohibition, where he took happily to the use of scotch. Although never at any time was he near alcoholism, Bogie maintained from then on an awe-inspiring level of consumption—he enjoyed it; he liked the taste of it; he approved mightily of its effect upon him—but he never allowed it to interfere with his work.

Bogie married a successful young actress named Helen Menken. The marriage fell apart after eighteen months, with Bogie blaming himself for putting his career before the possibilities of a happy home life—a lesson which remained unlearned because one year later he married another successful young actress, Mary Phillips, and promptly departed for Hollywood, where he had been offered a small contract.

The fulfilling of this long engagement 3,000 miles away from his new wife did nothing to help his new marriage or to further the career which he still found all-important, and on his return to New York he was only routinely surprised when Mary Phillips informed him that she had fallen in love with a New York-based actor, Roland Young.

The depths of the Depression coincided with Bogie's return to Broadway, and work for actors was scarce to nonexistent, but against this somber background Bogie and Mary made a brave stab at putting together the Humpty-Dumpty of their partnership. They moved into peeling, crumbling lodgings on the East Side and for a while were supported solely by Bogie's prowess at chess; he played for 50 cents a game in sleazy Sixth Avenue dives.

To be thirty-four years old, an unemployed married actor, small in stature, short on presence, with a pronounced lisp and little professional experience, must have been daunting even for Bogie, but he gamely plodded off on his rounds of agencies and producers' offices, and in 1934, a few weeks after the death of his bankrupt father, Bogie struck theatrical oil. Arthur Hopkins was casting *The Petrified Forest* by Robert Sherwood, and Bogie was given a chance to read the part of the sentimental killer, Duke Mantee. He shaved off most of his thick thatch of hair and delivered his lines with a snarl made even more menacing by his lisp.

Neither Hopkins nor Sherwood was impressed, and from the darkness of the stalls Bogie heard the dreaded "Thank you very much, don't call us, we'll call you." As Bogie slunk from the stage, renewed whispering broke out. Leslie Howard, the star of the play, had been sitting quietly in the back row. Now he moved forward and urgently begged the others to reconsider. He was convinced that Bogie was ideal for the part. Bogie read again, Sherwood agreed with Howard, and finally, Hopkins nodded his assent.

The play was a huge success, and Bogie made a personal success of enormous proportions. He was signed with Leslie Howard to make the picture for Warner Brothers at the end of the Broadway run, but when he and Mary in high excitement arrived in Hollywood, all set to knock the film world for a loop, he learned to his stunned dismay that the studio had decided to pay him off and put one of their biggest contract stars into the role of Duke Mantee—Edward G. Robinson.

Bogie had no intention of meekly swallowing this, his first taste of big studio duplicity, so he fired off an SOS to Leslie Howard in England. Howard reacted immediately and unleashed a return salvo at Warner Brothers: "It's either with Bogart or without me."

Bogart it was, and film history continued smoothly on its way.

He never forgot, never ceased to acknowledge the helping hand he had received when he had most needed it and, as a gesture of his gratitude, named his second child, a girl, Leslie.

The brothers Warner, never renowned for the delicacy and

foresight with which they handled their contract players, decided that they had hatched a golden egg, so Bogie was treated like a battery hen and in the next four years was forced to pump out no less than twenty-nine gangster films, in each of which he played a carbon copy of Duke Mantee; this nearly finished his career and completely ruined his marriage. Seeing nothing of her husband except glimpses of a zombie who worked punishing hours on Warner's production line, Mary took off for New York to do a play. Bogie was sad to see her go but consoled himself with an undulating blonde of conspicuous cleavage named Mayo Methot. Mayo was a hard case, a drinker who went refill by refill with Bogie, but unlike him, she was unable to handle it, and by the time Mary divorced Bogie Mayo was well on her way to alcoholism. In 1938 Mayo and Bogie married, and at a famously liquid reception the Russian actor Mischa Auer appeared from behind the giant wedding cake and danced before the befuddled guests stark naked.

Bogie settled down for the third time to married life, but his latest partnership soon developed into the toughest situation he had ever had to handle.

I witnessed some of it. I had met Bogie the year when he had been lent by Warner Brothers to Samuel Goldwyn to make *Dead End,* and one day we drank lunch together at the Formosa Café across the street, but we did not like each other very much. I found his aggressively tough and needling manner rather tiresome, and he obviously marked me down as a prissy Englishman. We parted with expressions of mutual respect and a determination from then on to avoid each other like the plague.

The next time I came face to face with Bogie he was underneath a table in the Restaurant La Maze on the Sunset Strip. This was a favorite hangout of the younger Hollywood group because it boasted the best music in town and the manager made a welcome specialty of keeping it off limits to the prying eyes of the columnists, possibly because the place also catered to the Mickey Cohen gangster element of Los Angeles, and indeed there had lately been a full-scale killing on the premises.

Bogie, like all movie mobsters since the beginning of films, was plagued by drunks who would lurch up to him in public, trying to pick a fight in order to impress others with how they had "taken care of the tough guy." Bogie was an adept at avoiding all forms of physical combat. It was not that he was cowardly; it was just that he was quite small—a bantamweight—who had not the faintest intention of being knocked around by people twice his size. His love of the needle, however, sometimes ended in dangerous brinkmanship.

That night at La Maze Bogie was confronted by a large man with a flushed face wearing an open-neck shirt turned down outside his jacket.

I was sitting in a corner with the "Oomph Girl," Ann Sheridan. Bogie with Mayo was a few tables away. We couldn't hear the confrontation, but we could see that the scene was developing along traditional lines. The large man was bending over their table and poking Bogie in the chest with a forefinger, Bogie was smiling insults, Mayo was rising like a ruffled hen turkey from her seat, and waiters were circling warily around, taking up action stations to isolate or eliminate the impending conflict.

Suddenly all hell broke loose. Bogie threw a full glass of scotch into his aggressor's eyes, and at the same moment Mayo hit the man on the head with a shoe. I caught a momentary glimpse of flinty-eyed characters rising purposefully from the table whence the large man had come and of a solid phalanx of waiters converging on the battle area. Cries of rage and alarm rose on all sides, and the air became thick with flying bottles, plates, glasses, left hooks, and food.

"Quick," screamed the Oomph Girl. "Under the table."

This was a suggestion with which I was only too happy to comply, but for some technical reason, it was impossible to get beneath our own table, so we threw ourselves to the floor and crawled on hands and knees to a larger sanctuary a few yards away.

We had not been installed there for more than a few seconds before Bogie came padding in on all fours; he was laughing like hell.

"What's going on up there?" I asked.

"Everything's OK," he chortled. "Mayo's handling it. . . . I wish I'd brought a fork, though—I might be able to jab the bastard in the leg."

Mayo did indeed handle it. The attacker and his party were ousted, and the evening dusted itself off and returned to normal.

After that night Bogie nicknamed Mayo Sluggy, and she lived up to it. The skirmishes between the "Battling Bogarts," as the Hollywood press corps christened them, were noisy in the extreme, and complaining neighbors insisted that they were nonstop. Jealousy on the part of Mayo seemed to be the spark that ignited the flames —jealousy mixed with booze, a lethal cocktail, with Bogie playing his role of "stirrer." He and Mayo would drink: then her jealousy, generally of his current leading lady, would come to the boil, and Bogie would gleefully go into action, goading her till the bottles started whizzing past his head. It must have been a most exhausting period for him, and it was certainly dangerous, because on one occasion Mayo slashed her wrists, on another she set fire to their house, and on a third she stabbed him in the back with a carving knife. "Only went in a little way," he said as he was being stitched up.

The "Battling Bogarts" were still at it hammer and tongs in September, 1939, when, in a moment of military lunacy, I departed for Europe. I did not see Bogie again till I returned in 1946, but a great mutual friend, the writer John McClain, serving with the American navy, had kept me up to date.

Bogie, he told me, had widened the area of conflict and had decided to take on Jack Warner at the same time as he was conducting his running battles with Mayo. He had realized that he must get away from his gangster screen image because he saw clearly that with the wartime carnage being fully reported, the "Mob" in action had become tame stuff indeed, so he refused to work at all and was suspended. After much resistance from Warner, John Huston was allowed to put Bogie into *The Maltese Falcon*, a picture regarded at the studio with undisguised apprehension. With the success of this picture a new career opened up for Bogie, and in *Casablanca* he played a romantic soldier of fortune opposite Ingrid Bergman. He became the pet of the Warner Brothers' lot, and a beaming Jack Warner told him he could have the pick of all the scripts.

As Bogie's film popularity soared, so his home life deteriorated. Mayo became a confirmed alcoholic; her looks and figure collapsed, and she made an increasing number of hideous scenes in public, but Bogie, trying nobly to keep the ship afloat, would never hear a word against her.

"She's an actress," he would say with menacing quiet, "a god-damn good one, but she's not working much at the moment, which is tough on her . . . understand?"

When Mayo heard this, she was apt to scream out that Bogie was "a Four-F coward and a phony," but somehow he got through the battle-scarred nights and still arrived on time for work early the next morning.

It couldn't last at that pace, of course, and when in 1944 Bogie made *To Have and Have Not*, he fell head over heels in love with his nineteen-year-old leading lady, an ex-theater usherette and cover girl, Lauren Bacall. Mayo's antennae picked up the message early, she scented battle and sailed into the studio, and Bogie's next love scene was interrupted by the strident voice of his wife inquiring how he was getting along with "that poor child half your age."

Betty Bacall was equally in love with Bogie, but all she could do was suffer and pray that Bogie could work things out so that he would be free to marry her. Bogie gave his marriage to Mayo another try to see if he could forget Betty, but it didn't work. Poor Mayo—her jealousy made her ugly, and her ugliness made her drink, and a guilt-ridden Bogie ducked her flying bottles and pretended not to hear her abuse, but even he was not made of steel, and his nerves finally cracked under the strain.

One morning in the studio makeup department, a girl was washing Bogie's hair. His chin was cupped sleepily in the aluminum bowl, and the hairdresser was proudly giving him the benefit of her best friction rub. Suddenly the poor creature stared aghast into the basin; then she let out a piercing shriek and fainted dead away. The entire growth of hair on the head of the most valuable star in her studio had come away in her hands. It grew back in time as his nerves recovered, but Bogie never again had the same luxurious thatch. From then on it always looked to me as though the cat had been at it.

Divorce became inevitable, and Mayo, a classic Hollywood casualty, departed for her Oregon birthplace, and there six years later, as the tragic decline accelerated, she died all alone in a motel.

When Betty and Bogie married in the Ohio home of Louis Bromfield, there was exactly twenty-five years' difference in their ages. This sparked off some spicy observations about "old folks' homes" on the part of Betty's father, and the Hollywood smart money went on an early breakup. The locals, over the years, had been afforded ample opportunity to study Bogie's form, but they underestimated Betty, who was an unknown starter. In spite of her extreme youth, she had a mountain of common sense and the guts to put it to work. She never kowtowed to Bogie, she never nagged him, and above all, she truly admired him as a man and as an actor. For his part he adored her and was proud of her looks, her honesty, and her spirit. He cut back conspicuously on his whiskey consumption because "Betty doesn't go for it too much, and it's no fun drinking alone." Her explanation was probably nearer the mark: "Bogie drank a lot because he was unhappy. Now he's happy."

This then was the couple that John McClain took me to visit when we both returned to Hollywood in 1946. Nobody likes being dropped in on, especially when tired after a long day's work, but Betty had arranged a surprise party for Bogie on his forty-seventh birthday—a potentially dangerous tactic.

When Bogie walked in and discovered thirty people hiding in cupboards, seated on toilets or under beds, he became loudly abusive, and it seemed that no amount of singing "Happy Birthday" could soften his attitude. Betty finally won the day by playing it his way. "All right then, you son of a bitch," she yelled. "You stay here alone, and we'll all go out for dinner."

He bared his teeth in the famous wolf grin and snarled, "Okay, you bastards—you're welcome." The party went on till dawn.

Bogie bought a sailing boat from Dick Powell, the 65-foot ketch *Santana*, and next to Betty, she became the most important thing in his life.

He was a first-class sailor, an ocean racer of repute, and his love of the sea was deep, almost mystical. Betty was smart enough not to be jealous of this other love and realized that he derived much peace and strength from his weekend voyages. Occasionally she went along, but mostly she encouraged him to go alone with Pete, his Danish crewman, and a couple of pals.

During his forty-seventh birthday party, Bogie learned that I, too, had sailed all my life, and his face softened.

"There's hope for you yet," he growled. "Come to the island next weekend."

I enjoyed the trip immensely, but I subsequently discovered

that while I had been reveling in being told to take the helm or put up a spinnaker, I had, in fact, been under Bogie's microscope. His theory was simple—if a man could handle a boat in rough weather or be a good shipmate in days of calm, he should be awarded one star like a reliable restaurant in the *Guide Michelin*. If in addition, he proved to have interests, experience, and curiosity outside the small world of filmmaking and enjoyed a game of chess, he might receive a higher rating. I never learned my own classification, but imperceptibly almost, our understanding prospered from then on, and one day I looked up to find Bogie and Betty among my closest friends.

This was flattering because Bogie did not really like actors as a breed, and apart from Tracy, Sinatra, and Peter Lorre, he usually kept his distance, much preferring the company of writers such as Huston, Bromfield, Nunnally Johnson, Mark Hellinger, Alistair Cooke, and Harry Kurnitz.

On the many, many subsequent trips I had aboard *Santana*, I grew to realize what a very special man Betty had married. Things to Bogie were either black or white; he had little patience with the grays. To sort people out quickly, he used the shock technique. Early on in an acquaintanceship he would say or do something completely outrageous, and the reaction of the other person told Bogie most of what he wanted to know. People in movie theaters saw him as the personification of the tough and the sardonic, and up to a point they were not far wrong. He gamely presented the same facade in real life, but my own theory was that he worked to maintain it and had a difficult time covering up the fact that he was really kind, generous, highly intelligent, and deeply senti-mental. Animals loved him, too—the best sign of all.

I think he had a horror of being unmasked, and being very publicity-conscious, he gradually eliminated nearly all contact with the press, preferring, if he had anything to say, to give it to one man who wrote a column in the New York *Herald Tribune*—Joe Hyams. Other people would then pick it up.

Joe was an intelligent and respected newspaperman, and he kept Bogie's image alive in exactly the colors Bogie wanted. Whether he was taken in by Bogie or whether his personal friendship impeded him in his reporting of some of the subtler shadings of his subject, it was hard to decide, but he certainly played the game according to Bogie's rules.

Bogie set himself up as a nonconformist, and this was no act. He really intended to do his own thing and despised those who pandered to the Hollywood code of good behavior.

"I'm not one of the boys next door. I leave that to all those good-looking bastards with their button-down shirts."

And he would go on his merry way, tilting at the windmills of convention, arriving at nightclubs with giant panda dolls, arguing with all and sundry, championing left-wing causes, and making heavily quoted statements about the unreliability of people who never drank.

Once, sitting on the deck of *Santana* in a quiet cove off Catalina Island, eating delicious lobsters caught in his illicit trap (his publicity incidentally stated that he never fished because he loved animals too much), I heckled him about his obvious determination to bend the rules.

"You're very clean about your own house," I said. "Why do you make such a point of going out to dinner unshaven and wearing a stinking old tweed jacket when you've been asked to arrive in a tuxedo?"

"The point I'm making," he said, "is that if I choose to show up unshaven and stinking, it's nobody's goddamned business but mine, and nobody gets hurt but me."

"Working on the Bogart image?" I asked.

"How far can you swim, you jerk," he countered, "because it's sixty miles from here to Santa Monica!"

Bogie one day was reminiscing on how great a part luck had played in his early days at Warner Brothers; he reminded me yet again that he had played *The Petrified Forest* only because of Leslie Howard's determination and added that he had got *The Maltese Falcon* only because George Raft had turned it down and *High Sierra* had come his way because Paul Muni had huffily refused it on the grounds that it had first been offered to George Raft. "But that's the way the piss pot cracks," he said.

I couldn't resist it, as I had been husbanding the dangerous morsel for years. "Now I'll tell you how you got an Oscar for *The African Queen* in 1951," I said.

"Please do," said Bogie with chilling calm.

"Because Bette Davis turned it down!" I announced smugly.

When the explosion died away, I told him more.

C. S. Forester wrote the story in 1935, and Warner Brothers bought it for Bette Davis. In 1938 their producer, Henry Blanke, borrowed me from Samuel Goldwyn to play the Cockney "river rat" opposite her. The deal was signed, and bemused by my glorious opportunity, I had spent four weeks polishing up a Cockney accent. I even grew a beard which made me look like a diseased yak, but at the last minute, Bette Davis fell out with Blanke and told him she refused to be photographed out of doors (a likely story), so the picture was canceled and the property sold to Twentieth Century-Fox, where twelve years later John Huston unearthed it.

When I finished, I waited for the Bogie bombshell. It never came. He put a consoling arm around my shoulders and said very thoughtfully, "Kid . . . I think you would have stunk up the screen in that part." It was a hundred to one that he was correct in his assessment, but he was sensitive enough to know that when it had happened, it must have been a crumpling disappointment not to get the chance to find out.

Bogie, above all, loathed the phonies and the pretentious. At one evening party I settled down happily when I discovered that he was sitting opposite me and beside him was an overdressed lady from Cincinnati whose money had restored the façades of both her husband, a bisexual Roman count, and his crumbling palazzo.

"Do you have servant problems in Hollywood, Mr. Bogart?" she asked.

Bogie helped himself to some bread and made a large gray ball of it; then he shrugged.

"It's *quite* impossible in Italy now," continued the lady from Cincinnati, missing these first ominous signs. "We used to have only English, then they became impossible, so we took on Germans, but they became difficult, too, so we had to fall back on Italians—nothing but trouble."

"Too bad," said Bogie, fixing her with the needling eye I knew so well. "Whaddya got now?"

"Greeks," she said. "Of course, they're peasants and have to be taught everything from the start. I never let them near the nursery."

Bogie flicked the gray bread ball with his thumb and watched it perform a graceful parabola in the direction of John Huston at another table.

"Who looks after the kids?" he asked.

"Oh, I have a wonderful Dutch girl, and the children just *adore* her. She never complains and doesn't mind at all eating her meals off a tray. Of course, I overpay her, but it's worth it because I feel secure when I go to Paris. . . ."

I waited expectantly. The pause was long.

"Does she fuck?" Bogie asked.

Bogie had a slight predilection for that particular Elizabethan word and enjoyed the shock waves it could produce when used to the greatest effect. He once spent an afternoon in 21 in New York, flanked by John McClain, Quentin Reynolds, and myself drinking stingers and poring over various telephone directories. We worked out that by forging the signature of the Con Edison Company and sending 438 telegrams to selected officeholders in Radio City requesting them, for testing purposes, to leave their lights blazing at the end of the day, we could emblazon the word in letters sixteen floors high.

Sitting long evenings below decks in *Santana*, I was constantly amazed at the simplicity of Bogie's character; he just could not be bothered to camouflage his weaknesses. Although right at the top of his profession, he also possessed the actor's Achilles' heel—he was jealous and showed it.

The actor he admired most was Spencer Tracy. They were highly professional performers, and both despised the "stars" who were not. Bogie wanted to make a picture, *The Desperate Hours*, and the "dream casting" was to play Spencer and Bogie in the two tailor-made roles. Both were longing to do it, and both wanted badly to play with the other. Again and again, they met and got all steamed up about the prospect, but each time it mysteriously collapsed, the reason being that the moment they parted they quickly contacted their respective managers—neither of them would take second billing. They never worked together.

If he was childish about billing, which is something the public is blissfully unconscious of, he was also overly quick to react to the threat of "new faces."

"Why the hell don't they lift some of the old ones? All those bastards at the studios are trying to do is find fifty-dollar-a-week Gables, Coopers, and Bogarts." And he was positively vituperative about the Method acting of the New York Group Theatre and the Actors Studio—the "scratch-your-ass-and-belch school" he called them and had the lowest opinion of Lee Strasberg, the group's founder. Actually Bogie and Tracy, the down-to-earth-no-frills actors par excellence, had been performing naturally for years in just the way the pupils of these schools were now learning to do. Bogie had no time for people who took their talent for granted or for actors who denigrated or downgraded their own profession; he admired the ones who worked hard to improve what they had been given.

Bogie took me, when I was in a nasty financial bind, to see his business manager, Morgan Maree. From then on, Maree picked up my earnings, paid my bills, and worked out my taxes, but like Bogie, I was put on a tiny weekly allowance and only permitted to sign for necessities—no bar bills or things of that ilk. Bogie and I spent hours trying to work out ways to cheat Morgan, but over the years he was too smart for us and saved our collective bacon.

I don't for a moment believe that Bogie had any premonition, but he became increasingly exercised over the fact that a successful actor's life is a series of short bursts of high taxation with no chance to spread the earnings over the lean years. "I've got to get some decent dough put away for Betty and the kid." He worked continuously toward that end, making pictures through his own company and finally selling the company with the rights to all his pictures for a very large sum.

When the sale was consummated, Morgan Maree called to say that the check had arrived. Bogie rushed over. "Can I borrow it for an hour or two?" he asked like a child. Then he took Betty to lunch at Romanoff's and made a grand tour going from table to table, waving the check like a banner.

Being married to Bogie even for someone with the understanding and intelligence of Betty could have been no smooth ride. For a start he was as set in his ways as a streetcar and had an utter disregard for personal comfort. Betty was soon champing at the bit to break out of his small gloomy canyon house with its disturbing memories. For a long time her pleas for more elbowroom fell on deaf ears—"you were raised in one room in the Bronx, for chris-sake, and there's nothing wrong with *you.*"

Finally, with the help of the trusty Morgan Maree, who touched a nerve by persuading him that it would be an excellent investment —"something to leave to Betty and the offspring"—he forked out a down payment on a beautiful tennis-courted and pooled house in the high-tax-bracket area of Holmby Hills. Bogie felt he was being conned into joining the Establishment, which he wholeheartedly despised, and *Santana* for a while rocked with resentment, but Betty smiled like a big cat and smoothed him down and became pregnant a second time, and he grew to be obsessively proud of his new acquisition. He never dressed the part of a Holmby Hills squire and forever slopped about the place attired in a grisly selection of antiquated moccasins, sweaters, windbreakers, and dun-garees—usually with a battered yachting cap on his head; dogs and cats were everywhere.

Betty was the perfect mate for Bogie, and as they were both com-pletely honest with each other and utterly straightforward in their approach to life, the friction points were few and far between. Oc-casionally there would be an almighty explosion, but it never lasted long, and with the air cleared, life went on more smoothly than ever. Betty gave as good as she got, but she also understood his love of his men friends, his need for male companionship, and she appreciated his longing for arguments, though she was never too happy when his extreme needling tactics were used to provoke them. She never was just a decoration in her husband's home, though Bogie loved her to be beautiful and admired her looks, her taste, and her talent. He was, above all, proud of the fact that he had a partner with whom he could share everything good or bad. He never looked at another woman.

He was a good father, I'm sure, though his idea of entertaining his children on a free day was odd—to take them to lunch at Romanoff's. The lack of discipline was something he felt could be put right later by Betty. The longest wince I ever witnessed was the one which contorted the face of the elegant Noel Coward when lit-tle Stevie was introduced to him and piped up, "Hi there, Mr. Dog-do-in-his-pants."

Bogie, like Flynn, was always greatly amused by the discomfiture of his friends, and on one Fourth of July trip aboard *Santana* was at his sardonic best. We sailed over to Catalina Island and dropped anchor in Cherry Cove. As a special concession on the big national holiday Betty and Hjördis were grudgingly invited, too. This cramped the sleeping quarters considerably and, for me at least, turned the occupancy of the single confined toilet, with its unreliable hand pump, into a hazard of insurmountable proportions. To circumnavigate this embarrassment, in the early morning, I told Pete that I was taking the dinghy as I wished to take a little stroll. Silhouetted on the top of the barren hills of the Wrigley Ranch which surrounded the bay, I had spied the top of a large clump of bushes; donning a pair of red sailcloth slacks and a white cotton shirt, I rowed ashore and toiled up a precipitous goat track toward my objective. It was a long, hard, hot climb, and even at that hour I soon took off my shirt and rested awhile enjoying the sight below of fifty or sixty yachts floating lazily on the glassy slate-blue early-morning calm of the bay. On some of them people were already stirring, stretching and yawning and swabbing vaguely at decks; the boat noises took a long beat to reach up to me.

On arrival at the summit and just out of sight of the fleet below, I entered the clump of bushes.

I was making some preliminary adjustment to my red slacks when I had a nasty feeling that I was not alone. Five yards from me and regarding me with undisguised hostility was a monolithic Brahma bull—the sort of animal that drives rodeo riders into early retirement. Red slacks at half-mast, I hobbled a hasty retreat from the clump.

The bull followed. On the crest of the hill I stood facing it; it faced me. We both stood perfectly still. Then it lowered its head and pawed the ground, but I was so frightened that quite apart from the sack race impediment of my lower garments, I was unable to move. This then was the tableau, in perfect silhouette on the skyline, which the owner of *Santana* perceived when he rolled back the hatch and took his first tentative breath of fresh air.

Bogie took in the juicy situation at a glance and alerted Betty and Hjördis. Then he reached for his loud-hailer and addressed the awakening fleet.

"Now hear this . . . hear this . . . *Santana* calling all yachts. . . . Happy Fourth of July, folks! . . . This is the day we celebrate ridding ourselves of the British. . . . Just take a look up the hill, ladies and gentlemen . . . This production comes to you by courtesy of your friendly neighborhood Yankee."

Then the noise started—a cacophony of sound as loud-hailers opened up from all over the fleet, "Olé! Olé!" and many crude suggestions to do with my red slacks. By a miracle the bull instead of being maddened by the bedlam below became momentarily distracted; it stopped pawing the ground and looked uneasily toward the source of the interruption. When it turned its head once more toward me, the contact was broken. The bull made a noise, a snort of pure disgust, the sort of sound that daily help make when they give notice; then very slowly it turned away and lumbered off along the skyline. This elicited a veritable thunderclap of enthusiasm from below, cheers and bravos for me, catcalls and whistles for the bull. I hauled up and secured my red slacks (more applause and more tasteless instructions); then, idiotically, I decided to make a gesture of defiance toward the tail end of my departing antagonist. I flapped life into the white shirt which had remained clasped in my trembling hands and, for the benefit of my noisy aficionados, executed a few passes.

The crowd was delighted by my farols and largas and roared its approval of my series of veronicas.

Success went to my head. I turned my back on the bull to demonstrate the insulting pase de pecho. A roar of warning from the loud-hailers told me that the bull had got the message. He turned in a flash, and the earth shook under his charge. There was nothing for it—I flung away the offending shirt and went down that hillside the shortest way . . . straight—jumping, bumping, cartwheeling, and ricocheting. I don't know why I didn't kill myself, and Bogie spent most of his Independence Day happily pulling cactus spines out of the behind of a redcoat.

John Huston was always a joy to Bogart, probably his favorite companion and certainly his favorite director. Bogie could never measure up intellectually, but Huston stretched him to the utmost, and some classic discussions developed.

Director Huston got the most out of Bogie as an actor, and if they worked perfectly as a team and together turned out some classics—*The Maltese Falcon, The Treasure of Sierra Madre, The African Queen,* and *Beat the Devil* among others—the leg pulling was also mutually satisfactory. Huston was waiting to hear news about his induction into Special Services with the Army during World War II. The word came by phone when he was in the middle of directing Bogie in a small building. His escape had been carefully rehearsed—whom he shot, whom he knifed, and through which window he would jump, et cetera.

Huston never said a word about the receipt of his call-up, he just tripled the number of Japanese around the building, boarded it up with the hero inside, and left for Europe. A hastily summoned takeover director found a note on the door: "I'm in the Army—Bogie will know how to get out."

Occasionally, when in England, I had been invited by His Grace, the Duke of Marlborough to shoot birds at Blenheim Palace in Oxfordshire. I was not a very good shot; the duke was one of the best in the country. It was, therefore, with some surprise when walking up partridge across frosty stubble fields that I noticed the duke preparing to dispatch a high-flying pigeon which was heading for the line of guns. I was surprised because to everyone present, it was perfectly obvious that our host was taking aim not at a wood pigeon, but mistakenly at a carrier pigeon, hot winging it to its waiting owner somewhere in the industrial north. To general embarrassment the bird thumped to earth at the duke's feet. In the ensuing silence, I could not resist shouting down the line a vintage pigeon joke: "Are there any letters for me?"

I was not asked to shoot at Blenheim again, and indeed, two or three years passed before I set eyes on the Duke of Marlborough.

In London, Hjördis and I were having a midsummer dinner at Les Ambassadeurs with Betty and Bogie and John Huston. In midfun, I perceived that the immensely tall pink-faced duke had materialized beside me. Always fascinated by films and film people, he now made it obvious that he wished to meet my famous companions.

Hjördis he already knew, so I introduced him to the others. That done and a few pleasantries exchanged, he sought for a gracious exit line and said, "Well, David, when are you coming to shoot a pheasant with me?"

"Any time," I said blithely, "just give me a date and I'll be there."

"Ah, well . . . How about the, er, last week in January?"

"Splendid," I said, "thank you so much."

The duke rejoined his female companion at a nearby table; Bogie followed him with his eyes and then leaned toward me, the big needle poised.

"Hey, get a load of you! . . . Hobnobbing with the aristocracy! . . . Shooting goddamn pheasant with a Dook for chrissake . . . a lousy ham actor wearing a deerstalker!"

Huston was at that time enjoying full country squire status in the Irish bogs, so he put things in their correct perspective.

"It's not really much of a compliment, Bogie, being asked to shoot during the last week in January. The season is over by then, and a few bad shots are invited, the local butcher and people like that. They go round the outlying hedgerows and kill off the old birds—cocks only."

Bogie mulled this over and glanced somberly across at the duke's table. "Cocks only, eh?" he muttered.

The evening at our table resumed the course on which it had been set, and wine, arguments, and mock abuse flowed in an endless stream.

Finally, the duke and his guest rose to leave. His departure happened to coincide with some remark of Bogie's which amused Huston greatly. He threw his head back and roared with laughter. Unfortunately, he threw his head so far back that his chair overbalanced and he landed with a crash at His Grace's feet.

Huston caught sight of the ducal disapproval etched on the pink face far above him, and his laughter redoubled.

Marlborough stepped haughtily over the helpless body and said, loudly, to me, "I don't think much of your Hollywood friends. . . ."

People nearby heard his calculated rudeness, and there was a hush. Bogie was out of his chair like a terrier. He only came up to the duke's navel, so instead of grabbing him by the lapels and lifting him off his feet in approved movie tough-guy style, he grabbed the slack of his trousers somewhere around the top fly button; then he lifted, hard. The duke found himself teetering on tiptoes, his face congested with acute discomfort, and he started to splutter.

"Now get this, Dook," snarled Bogie in his most menacing style, "get this and get it straight! You quit insulting my pal with your goddam . . . COCKS ONLY!"

When Bogie released his hold, John Albert Edward William

Spencer-Churchill, tenth Duke of Marlborough, Baron Spencer, Earl of Sunderland, Baron Churchill, Earl of Marlborough, Marquess of Blandford, Prince of the Holy Roman Empire, Prince of Mindelheim in Swabia, returned to terra firma and shook his ruffled feathers.

His companion plucked at his sleeve. "Come along, Bert," she said.

I don't remember when I first noticed Bogie's cough, probably sharing sleeping quarters with him aboard *Santana*. I expect I thought it was just a smoker's cough because he used up a great number of cigarettes—"coffin nails" he called them. But the cough slowly got worse, and Betty prevailed on him to see a doctor. The doctor made some tests and then called Bogie in to tell him the news—it was as bad as a man could hear.

There followed an eight-hour operation, and the slow slide began. "I've got it licked if I can put on some weight," he said. But as the weeks went by, he lost weight steadily. His eyes became enormous in his pitifully gaunt face, but his courage shone out of them.

At the funeral service on January 17, 1957, his friends were determined that his departure should be dignified and purged of all Hollywood gloss and bad taste, and we unceremoniously bundled outside into the sunshine several newsmen who had attempted to enter the church with concealed cameras.

John Huston was always the closest to Bogie, so it was right and fitting that he should write and speak a few words of farewell at the service. No one could have done it better, and he has most graciously given me permission to remember some of them here.

"Bogie's hospitality went far beyond food and drink. He fed a guest's spirit as well as his body, plied him with goodwill until he became drunk in the heart as well as in the legs.

"This tradition of wonderful hospitality continued on to the last hour he was able to sit upright. Let me tell you at what effort it was extended through the last days. He would lie on his couch upstairs at five o'clock, when he would be shaved and groomed in gray flannels and scarlet smoking jacket. Then, as he was no longer able to walk, his emaciated body would be lifted into a wheelchair and pushed to a dumbwaiter on the second-floor landing. The top of the dumbwaiter had been removed to give him headroom. His nurses would help him in, and sitting on a little stool, he would be lowered down to the kitchen, where another transfer would be made, and again by wheelchair he'd be transported through the house into the library and his chair. And there he would be, sherry glass in one hand and cigarette in the other at five thirty when the guests would start to arrive. They were limited now to those who had known him best and longest, and they stayed, two and three at a time, for a half hour or so until about eight o'clock, which was the time for him to go back upstairs by the same route he had descended.

"No one who sat in his presence during the final weeks would ever forget. It was a unique display of sheer animal courage. After the first visit—it took that to get over the initial shock of his appearance—one quickened to the grandeur of it, expanded, and felt strangely elated, proud to be there, proud to be his friend, the friend of such a brave man. . . ."

13
The Pleasure
of Your Company

*C*HRISTMAS parties! New Year's parties! Birthday parties! Parties to celebrate the end of a picture or a marriage, the signing of a contract, or the birth of a baby! There was always an excuse for a party in Hollywood. And at the end of a strenuous six-day week Saturday night was dedicated to letting off steam. The needle measuring Hollywood parties swung between orderliness and orgies.

Income tax was low, salaries were high, and if a few of those entertained could be deemed helpful to the career, the cost of the binge could be deducted from taxes, provided the presence of the helpful guests could be proved.

A good plan was to have the arriving guests sign the Visitors Book (it was risky to leave it till they departed at 4 A.M.), and an essential was to invite a few press photographers to record on film the presence of the "useful" ones. Hollywood, conscious always of its public image, indulged in a token purity at the beginning of most parties, and while the photographers were snapping away, glasses and bottles were kept out of sight and husbands, wives, and established "couples" sat close and smiled fondly at each other. Once the press had departed freedom of movement, speech, and behavior was restored, and the opportunity for all hell to break loose was welcomed with open arms and lifted elbows.

Parties, of course, varied enormously in size and content, from a super bash for 2,000 in costume at Marion Davies' beach house to half a dozen eating Mexican food prepared by Aldous Huxley in his tiny stucco pad on the wrong side of the Beverly Hills tracks.

Some of the biggest party givers held annual events: Marion Davies to celebrate the birthday of her boyfriend W. R. Hearst, Sonja Henie to celebrate her departure on her spring trip to Norway, Joseph Cotten, who gave an all-day party each Fourth of July, and wealthy oilman Tex Feldman, who loved to illustrate the fact that every year Hollywood was full of sensationally beautiful girls.

The big black-tie parties for 200 or 300 usually followed the same pattern: Men in white coats parked the cars, the food and drink was catered by Romanoff's or Dave Chasen, the swimming pools were boarded over to make dance floors, and green and white striped marquees were erected in the gardens. In the early mornings, fights and scandals were frequent.

Basil Rathbone and his Russian wife, Ouida, were inveterate middle-sized party givers, and several times a year this kindly man, the highest-paid free-lance actor in the world, who specialized in playing mean, hiss-provoking villains, provided extravaganzas into which went a great deal of inventive thought.

He badly misjudged the climate one Christmastide, however, when he covered his lawn and driveway with 300 tons of snow trucked down at high speed and great expense from Big Bear, and we splashed and skidded through brown slush when torrential warm Southern California rain took care of the arrangements. The city of Beverly Hills sent Basil a ferocious bill for cleaning up the mess.

Many parties were given with full press coverage to publicize the emergence of a finished film, the theme of the production being worked into the decor.

The first night Deborah Kerr spent in Hollywood, I took her to one such affair being given by producer Nunnally Johnson. We arrived early and found lying outside his front door half a dozen sour-faced topless blondes with everything below their hipbones squeezed into shiny green fishtails.

"We're waiting to be carried in and propped up at the bar," they told us. Nunnally was launching his picture *Mr. Peabody and the Mermaid*.

Small parties, as usual, were the most satisfying, and many people were experts at giving them. They ranged from beach parties and full-moon searches for the mad grunion fish, which came in on one big wave, laid its eggs hurriedly in the sand, and departed on the next, to ranch parties in the San Fernando Valley—Western style. These were very popular, and Darryl Zanuck allowed us to ride his polo ponies through the darkened countryside after dinner.

Mike Todd, always flamboyant, had steaks flown out from Kansas City on his private plane for a party of six and proudly displayed them to Elizabeth Taylor, Eddie Fisher, Debbie Reynolds, Hjördis, and myself. He was going to cook them a new way, he announced, and at his barbecue pit on a hillside he left them surrounded by sauces, oil, and brushes; then he took us into the house to wait till his charcoal fire was perfect. A fox ate the steaks and Todd sent out for Chinese food.

Many, many houses had projection rooms, and a normal evening was twenty or thirty people for dinner and a preview of one of the latest films, but the wiser producers refused to expose their pictures on the highly critical and often destructive "Bel Air Circuit." David Selznick, when he married Jennifer Jones, moved into John Gilbert's old mountainside mansion and transformed it. The parties there were my favorite in the fifties—very relaxed and always an intriguing mixture of Hollywood and the big world outside. Bill and Edie Goetz too provided much fun for their friends among their staggering collection of Impressionists, and it was intriguing to see the works of Renoir, Picasso, and Toulouse-Lautrec wafted upward at the touch of a button to make way for the unrolling screen and the twin projectors moving into firing position through the gaps left on the wall.

The Goetz family lived in a splendid residence on the same street as Sonja Henie. It was a short walk to Sonja's annual party, but Bill wanted to drive his new Rolls-Royce. He drank too much, which was very unusual for him, and Edie issued the driving instructions for getting home.

"Just stick right on the curb," she ordered, "keep in low gear, and don't go more than five miles an hour."

Bill followed her suggestions to the letter, glued himself to the curb, and motored slowly into the back of a parked police car.

Speech-making was a grisly Hollywood habit, and in some houses one risked being called upon to say a few words after dinner.

Jack Warner was a popular, if high-risk, speaker, and at a dinner for Madame Chiang Kai-shek brought on a deathly hush by concluding, "So, folks, if you have any laundry, you know where to take it!"

Some comedians never let up even at parties. Sitting at a table with Red Skelton, I alerted him to the fact that a caterpillar was roaming around in his salad.

"HMMM . . . NICE," said Red, and ate it.

Streaking is an old sport. Carole Landis did it to great effect in the early evenings, but people swimming naked in a floodlit pool toward dawn merely drew attention to the lateness of the hour.

Smoking plants, other than tobacco, was not widely practiced, but parties were conducted in a sweet sickly haze in remote glens off Laurel Canyon, and in dim nightclubs, where jam sessions went on all night, joints glowed brightly in every corner. Cole Porter gave intimate dinners of great taste with masterpieces presented by his French chef washed down by wines to match, and after dinner, when he and George Gershwin and Irving Berlin tried out on each other their latest compositions for the great new musicals, we lucky guests were at jam sessions of the gods.

At one party champagne flowed out of a statue's nipples, and when a nude party was being held in a beach house, two guests slipped out and came back dressed as cops. A well-known character actor broke a leg when he jumped out a window.

Charlie and Ann Lederer gave a party for the Shah of Iran. When the incumbent of the Peacock Throne complimented Lauren Bacall by saying, "You were born to dance, Miss Bacall," she replied with gusto, "You bet your ass, Shah."

A white horse was the guest of honor at an indoor party with disagreeable results for the carpets, and when Premier Nikita Khrushchev of the USSR was guest of honor at luncheon in the commissary at Twentieth Century-Fox, this event, too, left a bad odor.

With the exception of Madame Khrushchev and her daughter, it was strictly a "men only" affair. About 300 of us were bidden to attend, and Frank Sinatra and I were detailed to sit with the two ladies and jolly them along with the help of an interpreter. This proved to be no chore. Madame Khrushchev was a sweet-faced motherly lady with an almost totally square frame encased in a black tent. Her grayish hair was pulled straight back into a bun; she smiled benignly at one and all and, within a minute of being seated, delved into a voluminous black handbag and passed to me across the table photographs of her grandchildren.

Her daughter was a quiet, thirtyish, large-nosed blonde, and both she and her fleshy husband, the editor of *Izvestia,* were equally affable. I asked Madame Khrushchev what they were planning to do after luncheon, and she looked very crestfallen.

"We were so much looking forward to visiting Disneyland," she said, "but the police have told us they cannot be responsible for our safety."

I passed this information on to Frank, who reacted in typical fashion. "Screw the cops," he said. "Tell the old broad you and I'll take 'em down there, this afternoon—we'll look after 'em."

I tactfully rephrased and then, via the interpreter, relayed this suggestion to Madame Khrushchev, whose face lit up at the idea.

She delved into her huge bag and scribbled a note to her husband, which was dispatched to the speakers' table. Khrushchev reacted angrily and signaled *nyet* to her with much wagging of a forefinger. When Spyros Skouras, the president of Twentieth Century-Fox, rose to make his address of greeting, he chose, with elephantine bad taste, to describe how he, too, had risen from being a workingman to become the head of a great enterprise and sought to draw a parallel between his rise and that of the guest of honor, who had gone from coal miner to become the most important man in the USSR.

When Khrushchev's turn came, he stood, obviously flushed with anger, and proceeded to rend the wretched Skouras. He also poured scorn on the perfunctory airport welcome he had received that morning from Mayor Norris Paulson of Los Angeles and ended by acidly observing that it must be a sad state of affairs if living in Mayor Paulson's city was so dangerous that Madame Khrushchev and his daughter would not be safe in a children's playground.

After this ill-fated and well-televised meal, a further risk was taken by Twentieth Century-Fox. The publicity department, scenting a big break for their forthcoming picture *Can-Can,* herded the visitors across to a sound stage where Shirley MacLaine and a large troupe of carefully rehearsed dancers were "just by chance" about to shoot a take of the famous dance by the same name.

The Khrushchev party were seated in a specially built box and looked down with undisguised horror as Shirley and Company, complete with garter belts and black fishnet stockings, kicked their legs, swirled their petticoats, waggled their knees, and ended up with their skirts over their heads and their bottoms pointing directly at the guest of honor and his family.

As the publicity department gathered around for Khrushchev's eagerly awaited quote, he gave it to them in one word: "DISGUSTING!"

There was a band of butlers headed by Marcel and Theodore who catered and served small parties. With their wives or other female helpers they arrived during the afternoon and took over, bringing with them hors d'oeuvres, bottles, and food. They commandeered the kitchen and the bar. The only information they required was the number of guests, what liquor to serve, and whether to push it early on to get the party going or to hold back and let nature take its course.

They knew all the guests, their preferences and dislikes, and a great deal too much about their private lives, but they were impeccable servitors and for a large sum relieved hosts and hostesses of all worry. Nothing ruffled their calm.

Theodore, at the home of Frank Ross and Joan Caulfield, demonstrated this when he was offering me a platter of goodies during the cocktail hour around their pool. He bowed and stepped back into eight feet of water. Somehow he managed to keep his hold on the tray and, ignoring the encouraging cries of the common herd, swam with it before him to the shallow end, climbed the steps, and without any change of expression stalked majestically toward the kitchen. Later that night from inside a dinner jacket belonging to our host, he watched enigmatically while guests, in various stages of undress, ate little sausages, deviled eggs, and small squares of cheese off the bottom of the deep end.

Several rich neighbors from Santa Barbara and Pasadena gave parties because they enjoyed rubbing shoulders with "movie folk," and the "movie folk" went along because they enjoyed parties.

Dorothy Earel, a dark-eyed socialite beauty, invited us to come to the downstairs room of the Vendome Restaurant dressed as children. On arrival we were announced and discovered that we had to make our entrance down a canvas fire chute, but altercations broke out when it became apparent that at the bottom of the chute the Pasadena Polo fraternity was making book on which girls would not be wearing panties.

Errol Flynn once utilized a favorite Hollywood ploy on a pompous Washington diplomat who was pestering him for an invitation to a "real" Hollywood party. The man arrived at the appointed hour and was delighted when a gorgeous maid wearing nothing but shoes, stockings, and a little white cap opened the door.

"The undressing room is here, sir," she said, indicating a room full of discarded clothing.

"When you are ready, sir, I'll take you in to the party." She smiled seductively.

The man soon appeared naked, his eyes shining with excitement.

"I hope you'll have some fun, sir," said the maid. "Follow me, please."

He did, appreciating the sway of her hips and her twinkling behind.

She stopped at a door. The sound of revelry came from within. She asked his name, opened the door, and announced it. The diplomat charged in like a bull at a corrida.

Thirty people in full evening dress looked at him disapprovingly.

When Jimmy Stewart was getting married, about twenty of us gave him a bachelor party in a private room at Chasen's. It followed predictable Hollywood lines with the usual jokes, speeches, and gags, including a huge covered dish which was put before the bridegroom-to-be; inside was a midget dressed as a baby.

I sat next to Spencer Tracy that night, and he gave me a jarring insight into his great personal problem.

"What is this?" he asked me, pointing to the dessert.

"It looks like a trifle," I answered.

He sniffed at a spoonful like a bird dog. "There's something in it," he said. "What is it?"

I, too, sniffed. "A touch of rum—I think," I said.

Spence pushed his plate away. "Jesus!" he said. "That's all I need—one mouthful of that, and I'd be gone for a week."

When I looked disbelieving, he elaborated. "I'm not kidding. I have to fight it all the time, I'm a real alcoholic, and just that little bit would start me off."

If parties were given to launch new films, they were also occasionally given to launch new faces.

When Sophia Loren first thrust herself, chest first, into the limelight, *le tout* Hollywood was invited to meet her by the producer of her first Hollywood picture, and an elaborate dinner was given. The photographers outnumbered the guests, but Sophia was delighted and, in a very low dress, gave them everything she had. Convinced that she was the possessor of a bad profile, Sophia, when making a film, liked to choose a spot about three inches to the right of the camera and play all her scenes to that spot, irrespective of where the other actors were standing, so facing a battery of still cameras on her introduction night, Sophia's highly professional eyes soon found a suitable spot which would ensure her best angle, and she directed her smiles accordingly. The popping bulbs reached a sudden crescendo, but Sophia did not realize till too late that she was being "outboobed." Bending low over her right shoulder, with the most famous orbs in the world gleaming in all their creamy glory, was Miss United Dairies herself—Jayne Mansfield.

An eccentric and lonely little old millionaire named Atwater Kent gave sumptuous parties at his statue-encrusted estate above Beverly Hills, Capo di Monte. No expense was spared, and a good time was had by all, but many people never set eyes on their host because he usually took refuge in a huge leather wing chair in a remote library and stayed there all night.

A majority of the guests never discovered why they had been invited, but they swallowed their curiosity and the Moët et Chandon and attacked the beluga with reckless abandon.

If occasionally the better-mannered would go to the remote library to seek out Atwater Kent and thank him, he was almost pathetically touched, smiled a wispy little smile, and marked them down in his heart as "friends." When he departed this earth, he left bequests to seventy-three "friends" and enjoined them to use the money "for happiness," something, perhaps, he had always been short of.

Two mature ladies from New York became the superhostesses of Hollywood: Lady Mendl and the Contessa di Frasso. They had nothing in common except New York beginnings, an urge to live in California, and a love of the questionable excitement generated by people in the film world.

Lady Mendl was born Elsie De Wolf, and after blossoming into a near nonentity on the New York stage, she became internationally renowned as an interior decorator, salvaging Louis XV's tumbledown Villa Trianon in Versailles from complete disintegration and making it a gem of beauty and converting two rat-infested East River slums into New York's most desirable quartiers—Sutton Place and Beekman Place.

At the age of seventy she descended full of vim and vigor upon Hollywood. With her nice elderly ex-diplomat husband, Sir Charles, she bought a really horrible little Spanish-style monstrosity in Beverly Hills and transformed it, by using a lot of trelliswork, mirrors, eighteenth-century French furniture, and clever lighting, into a mini-monument to good taste in the middle of the surrounding "Cape Cod style," "adobe style," "ranch style," and "Ye Olde Englishe style."

Her tight white curls she colored according to her moods, pale green, pink, or mauve; she wore gloves a lot and stood on her head in a corner after dinner. Her little house was Mecca for the young and unsophisticated, and she seemed, while fostering our romances and ambitions, to draw a curious strength from us. In spite of the daunting sight of the good furniture, we were encouraged to lounge around on comfortable chintzy sofas upon which were mounds of silk cushions with embroidered advice: "Never complain. Never explain."

Elsie Mendl's parties were small, the food was simple and beautifully cooked, and she loved to produce on each occasion somebody "new," a "new" face, a "new" talent, or a couple in the throes of a "new" romance.

She one day invited a group to meet the artist Ludwig Bemelmans, lately arrived from Paris. For the occasion she decided to offer a buffet-style dinner, and the young and unsophisticated duly faced a long white-clothed table upon which reposed a great array of chafing dishes filled with chicken à la king, goulash, vegetables, and fruit salad, surrounded by bottles of wine.

The buffet opened for business at nine o'clock, but there was as yet no sign of the guest of honor. By ten Elsie Mendl was visibly disappointed, and coffee was being taken in a general mood of anticlimax.

At last Bemelmans walked in, looking very small and round and bright pink. He was obviously splendidly drunk. "This," he said, pointing to a large, equally well-oiled individual behind him, "is Hank."

Hank was wearing a raincoat and a black hat. He lifted this hat to the astonished company.

"I have only one *great* parlor trick," he announced, "and that is my ability to remove a tablecloth from a table *without* disturbing the crockery."

With that, Hank took hold of a corner of the cloth and very slowly, like a fisherman on the Volga pulling in a net, and humming the while "Yo-ho heave-ho!" he yanked it toward him. Crashing down inexorably went the chafing dishes, the bottles, and the coffee cups; the amazed guests, ankle-deep in chicken à la king and fruit salad, watched fascinated as Hank lifted his black hat once more, put a fatherly arm around Bemelmans' shoulder, and departed saying, "Come, Bemie, we must away to pastures new."

Dorothy di Frasso was born in New York, and Hollywood legend had it that her father, Bertrand Taylor, onetime president of the New York Stock Exchange, had left her $12,000,000; in any event Dorothy was one of the early swingers. She first married Claude Graham White, the British adventurer who owned the first gasoline-driven motorcar in England and possessed the first British pilot's license; then she married good-looking, impecunious Count Carlo di Frasso, brought back to life his crumbling Villa Modama in Rome, and became an intimate of both Mussolini and Count Ciano.

When Dorothy descended on Hollywood, she did so without her husband and moved into a large Beverly Hills estate off Coldwater Canyon, filled it with Italian servants, and entertained nonstop. Luncheon parties melded into tennis and swimming parties, and the afternoon parties went on till the early hours of the morning.

Dorothy resented with a passion the passing of the years and, like Elsie Mendl, down the road, felt that the presence of the young and beautiful around her might help to keep at bay that threatening old gentleman with his hourglass and scythe.

She was a truly generous person and loved nothing more than to give pleasure and provide fun for those less well fixed financially than she. Cary Grant became a great friend, and she and Marlene Dietrich were inseparable. When Marlene in the mid-thirties made her historic appearance in a man's suit, thus liberating women and giving them the necessary lead to take to slacks, Dorothy egged her on to make her "outrageous" move.

Dorothy loved gossip and sometimes went to odd lengths to obtain it: At one of her parties she placed chairs and mattresses in pairs in secluded spots all over the garden and had them bugged—the result was scheduled to be played back at luncheon the next day to, she hoped, our great embarrassment. Luckily, Ann Sheridan found a bug in her mattress and rushed all over the garden alerting recumbent shapes. When Dorothy played the results the next morning, she heard nothing but salacious gossip about herself.

Gossip about Dorothy was never difficult to come by because she was nothing if not direct in her approach when she saw something she fancied.

On Friday nights she went regularly to the Hollywood Legion Arena to occupy her ringside seat at the fights. Lupe Velez, another extrovert, sat nearby, and the two ladies enjoyed competing for the limelight. Lupe, being Mexican, made all Mexican fighters her protégés, and if one lost, she would storm into the ring, flashing tantalizing expanses of thigh and buttock as she climbed the ropes and physically attacked the referee.

One night Dorothy noticed a handsome young Italian prizefighter named Enzo Fiermonte and decided that she too could be a racist. Throughout the bout she screamed advice and encouragement at the young man in his mother tongue while Lupe was shrieking at his opponent in Spanish. The Italian won, and Dorothy was out of her seat and into the ring before Lupe could move. A commanding figure with her blue eyes and sapphires to match, brilliant under the arc lights, she stood congratulating both Fiermonte and the referee.

Dorothy's relationship with the fighter was not a long one. She announced first that she was going to adopt him and later that she was about to marry him, but strangely weakened at his next appearance in the ring, he was knocked cold in the first round, and she never saw him again.

Early in her Hollywood days she met a gangling young actor from Montana and decided, though he was several years her junior, that she would dedicate a great deal of her time to polishing this rough diamond and turning him into a sophisticated man of the world. Gary Cooper resisted the polishing and remained his own man, but he enjoyed greatly his long liaison with the effervescent Dorothy, particularly African safaris and trips to the capitals of Europe. Well-publicized voyages these were, because Dorothy was not renowned for avoiding the attentions of the press, and they prompted Bill Goetz to remark, "The best way to cross the Atlantic is on the *Countess di Frasso*."

One of Dorothy's maritime adventures made headlines. She had accumulated a young male companion from a most unexpected quarter. He was extremely good-looking in a dark, swarthy way and a very natty dresser. His name was Charles Siegal.

"Bugsie" Siegal was a gangster fairly high up in the California underground hierarchy, who had hitherto indulged his appetite for young blond actresses. This sudden switch to the titled hostess was an electrifying titillation for Hollywood, and much to Dorothy's delight it received generous coverage in the newspapers.

She stoked up the fires of local imagination by setting off on a four-month sea voyage with Bugsie, Jean Harlow's stepfather, Marino Bello, and his girlfriend.

The trip ended in charges of piracy and mutiny and suits for assault. There were whispers of the discovery of buried treasure in the Cocos Islands and the delivery of an illicit cargo to Louis "Lepke" Buchalter, another gangster currently on the lam, who was later strapped to the electric chair in Sing Sing.

Dorothy appeared before a federal grand jury and fended off all questions with wide-eyed innocence. Asked if she did not find it peculiar that she had been in the company of a well-known gangster, she said stoutly, "On the contrary, I was in the company of a *good friend*, and anyway, Mrs. Bello was there to chaperon me."

(What Dorothy did not mention was that Mr. Bello had married his girlfriend on the last day of the trip.)

Bugsie did not get off lightly. Not long afterward a man with a tommy gun walked up to a house in Beverly Hills, drew a bead on him through the window as he sat on a sofa in his living room, and squeezed off a long burst.

There was no malice in Dorothy. She was generous to a fault, and she was one of the first to "do her own thing." She died wrapped in a mink coat aboard a train between Las Vegas and New York. She left her entire fortune to her housekeeper and afforded Hollywood one last titillation and speculation—the fortune amounted to less than $40,000.

There was a very unattractive kind of snobbery about Hollywood's social life—the snobbery of success.

The guest lists to the highly publicized big parties reeked of it. The successful and the established were invited; the struggling and the passé were not. I was never invited when I was an extra, and later when I was invited, I don't remember seeing any extras as fellow guests.

This nasty differentiation percolated down to those invited to most of the children's parties, unhealthy competitions to see who could provide the most exotic and novel entertainment for the pampered little creatures.

The kids were showered with expensive gifts and the latest in miniature fairgrounds and sideshows, ponies and motorbikes to ride, clowns to laugh at, orchestras to dance to, and a proliferation of conjurers, magicians, and illusionists to watch. Without doubt, the children would have been far happier turned loose in blue jeans and inventing their own games, but some were sent off to their parents' studios to be waved, ringleted, and made up, and all arrived impeccably dressed and surly, ready to face the inevitable photographers. Professional parents, who used their children for their own publicity, were among the sadder sights in Hollywood, because the kids sensed it and did not always forgive, and the list of bad parent-child relationships in Hollywood was long.

One Christmas I gave a party for my two small sons, and Tyrone Power offered to play Santa Claus. Ty was everybody's favorite person, and all agreed that he was that great rarity—a man who was just as nice as he seemed to be. With his flashing good looks, graceful carriage, and easy laughter, it was no surprise that he was a

Pied Piper to women—they followed him in droves wherever he went—but Ty was a simple person, with a great down-to-earthness and modesty about himself. He lived a few blocks from me, and I went over to help him dress and brief him on the impending operation.

He was extremely nervous.

"This is worse than a first night on Broadway," he said, helping himself liberally to the scotch bottle. "I've never performed for a bunch of kids before."

I pushed and pulled him into the padded stomach, bulky red outfit, and high black boots rented from Western Costume Company and helped him fasten on a black belt, a huge white beard, and little red cap.

"Don't worry about it," I said. "It's all fixed. I've left the gate open at the bottom of the garden. I've rigged up some sleigh bells down there and stashed away the presents, and at exactly six o'clock we'll give 'em the bells; then you pick up the sack and make it up the lawn to the house—they're all expecting you."

"Oh, God!" Ty groaned. "Why the hell did I suggest this? Hand me that bottle."

Another hefty swig passed through the cotton wool beard.

"Whose kids are they, anyway?" he asked.

"Two of mine, Maria Cooper, Roz Russell's kid, the Fairbanks' and Deborah's, Loretta's and Jerry Lewis', Michael Boyer, and Edgar Bergen's little girl Candy, about fifty all together. You'll know a lot of them; the rest are neighbors."

"Fifty!" yelled Ty. "Hand me that bottle."

"Don't worry," I said. "I've written all the names clearly on each present. Just read 'em out, ad-lib a little, and don't forget to go HO! HO! HO!"

"Jesus!" said Ty. "Let's go. . . . I can't stand all this waiting around."

One last nip, and we were off: we took the bottle along.

During the five-minute drive to my house Ty begged me to let him off the hook. "Why don't *you* do it?" he asked. "It's your party."

"You suggested it," I said firmly.

By six o'clock Santa Claus was loaded in every sense of the word and, sack on shoulder, was hidden in some bushes at the bottom of my garden.

I tugged the string and pealed the sleigh bells.

Immediately excited cries broke out from the house, and little heads appeared at every window.

"Off you go," I said to my quivering companion. "Lots of luck!"

"Son of a *bitch!*" hissed Father Christmas, and he lurched off up the lawn.

When his shadowy form was spotted by the excited children, shrill shrieks and applause broke out. At that point I had intended to turn on the garden lights to illuminate the scene, but for some reason I missed the switch and turned on the sprinklers. With a crack like a pistol shot, geysers of spray shot out of the grass all around him, and Ty fell down. I readjusted the situation; Ty picked himself up, gave me a marked look, and squelched on toward the shining, expectant faces in the windows.

Like all actors, once the curtain was up and the adrenaline had started pumping, Ty was relaxed and happy in his work. "HO! HO! HO!" he boomed. "And *who* is this lovely woolly lamb for, eh?"—fumbling at the card—"Aha! I remember now. Candice Bergen. . . . Come here, little girl . . . HO! HO! HO!"

He was doing beautifully by the time I had sneaked in by the back door, seated in a big chair in the hall with excited children climbing all over him.

"And who is *this* gentleman?" he asked my eldest son, indicating me.

"That's my daddy," the little boy piped up.

"Well, now, I wonder if your daddy could spare old Santa a glass of lemonade. I've come a *long* way tonight."

A sizable bolt of scotch disappeared into the white foliage, and Ty became too sure of himself.

"Maria Cooper! *My*, what a pretty girl! HO! HO! HO! You tell your daddy that old Santa thought he was just dandy in *High Noon* . . . and ask him for Grace Kelly's phone number while you're about it. . . . HO! HO! HO!"

Maria Cooper was a little more sophisticated than the other children. "Where did you see the picture, Santa?" she asked sweetly.

"Oh," said Ty, pointing vaguely above him, "up there!"

After a while Santa made his good-byes and staggered off down the lawn. Some of the children cried when he left; one complained about his breath.

Back at the bottom of the garden, I helped him out of his outfit. He was as excited as if he had just given a triumphant Broadway performance of King Lear. "I really enjoyed that!" he said. "Weren't the kids a *great* audience!"

Up at the house he mingled unnoticed with arriving parents and was beside me when my youngest son emerged from a bedroom flushed with embarrassment.

"Daddy, Daddy! Guess *what*? That Candy Bergen has been trying to *kiss* me."

Some Hollywood children *never* knew when they were well off.

14
The Ace

*E*UROPEANS, particularly the British, have a loathsome habit of arriving on American doorsteps bearing "letters of introduction," and upon receipt of these missives, Americans have an endearing habit of asking no questions and opening wide the doors of their boundless hospitality.

I had such a letter to Fred Astaire, from a slight acquaintance in England—Lord Graves (the only titled bookmaker to be found taking bets on the rails)—and I decided to present it one evening in 1935 after a hot game of tennis. I wandered over to the Astaire house, but I forgot to put my shirt on.

I rang the bell.

After a while the door opened and a doll-like, ravishingly beautiful redhead stared at me coolly. She looked about fifteen.

"Is Mr. Astaire at home?" I inquired.

"Who wants him?" she asked, raising eyebrows at my attire and sniffing slightly.

"Well, he won't know who I am, but I have a letter here."

"Who's it from?"

"Er, a bookmaker . . . Tommy Graves is the name."

"Your name?"

"No, the bookmaker's name."

The redhead looked at me with distaste, held out a slim hand for the letter, and started to close the door.

"I've met Mr. Astaire's sister," I added hastily, but as the words came out, I knew they were rash because under cross-examination I was bound to be exposed as having once been taken backstage for two minutes to her London dressing room when Adele Astaire was the toast of the town in *Stop Flirting*.

"Stay here," commanded the redhead icily.

From inside I heard her calling, "Fwed, Fwed, come quickly! . . . There's a perfectly *dwedful* man at the door without a shirt . . . he says he knows your sister and has a letter from a bookie called Gwaves."

From these unpromising beginnings, a friendship grew which perhaps meant more to me than any other in Hollywood.

The combination of Fred and Phyllis was a joy to behold. They blended together with an almost uncanny smoothness, though the mixture had been potentially an unreliable one: the highly bred New York society girl with no interest whatever in the theater or theater people and the dedicated professional entertainer born in Omaha, Nebraska, the son of a small-time brewer, an Austrian immigrant. Fred had been a vaudeville performer at the age of five, doing a touring act with his sister. They had worked hard, and their talents had not gone unappreciated for long. Soon Fred and Adele had taken both Broadway and London by storm, and when Fred met Phyllis at a Long Island luncheon given by Mrs. Vanderbilt, the Astaires' musical *The Bandwagon* was the hottest ticket on Broadway.

Fred immediately fell in love with the slim, steady-eyed girl who could not pronounce her *r*'s, but it took him two agonizing years to persuade her that marriage to an actor would not necessarily mean entering a den of iniquity.

RKO Studios offered Fred a contract, his first picture to be *Flying Down to Rio*, and he decided to take a flyer in the movies.

Would Phyllis give up her Long Island summers and winters in North Carolina and take a flyer, too?

"Yes, I will," said Phyllis to Fred's unbounded joy, and after a one-day honeymoon, the newlyweds flew to Hollywood.

Before Fred started work on *Flying Down to Rio*, in typical Hollywood style, his studio bosses decided first to lay off the bet they had made by lending him out at an exorbitant fee elsewhere, thereby securing his services free for themselves. Fred found himself reporting to MGM and ordered to do a couple of dances with Joan Crawford in her movie *Dancing Lady.*

In Fred's own words, "I didn't have much to do so I just did as I was told, but when I saw myself on the screen . . . gosh! I looked like a *knife.*"

Fred was just about to start filming *Flying Down to Rio* when that "perfectly dwedful man without a shirt" came banging on his door. He had actually started the rehearsals of his one number with the star, Dolores Del Rio, but he had already spotted that his best opportunity in the picture would be in the "Carioca," a subsidiary dance number which he considered the best thing Vincent Youmans had ever written.

A full-time worrier, Fred was very concerned about who would be his partner for this big opportunity. When he heard the name, he was overjoyed. It was to be an old friend and an excellent dancer whom Fred, a year before, had been called in to help when she was having choreographic troubles in her own Broadway show—Ginger Rogers.

As partners they caught fire in "The Carioca," and the rest is movie history, but Fred always swore that he "never realized we were starting something."

As their smash hits piled up—*Gay Divorcee, Roberta, Top Hat, Swing Time, Shall We Dance,* and many, many others—Fred and Ginger together became the top box-office attraction in the world, but Fred remained mystified by his success. "I'm just a hoofer," he said. Phyllis stayed outwardly aloof but inwardly glorying in his success.

"You go ahead, Fwed, and make the money . . . I'll look after it for you." She did too, quite brilliantly, spurning the local business managers with their get-rich-quick schemes of golf courses in Mexico, oil drilling in Mozambique and Black Angus herds on windswept Colorado escarpments. She talked quietly to friends in New York, made minute entries in ledgers the size of Ping-Pong tables, and enabled the family to live in comfort for the rest of their days.

Self-effacing Phyllis only infrequently visited the studio to watch Fred working, and there was a widely believed rumor that she forbade him to kiss Ginger. This was, of course, complete fabrication. Ginger and Fred had a mutual distaste for slowing things up with what Fred described as "long, mushy love scenes," but the rumors provoked a counterattack, and in *The Barkleys of Broadway*, they took a deep breath and were glued together in the longest and most unrelenting kiss so far recorded on film.

Fred invited me to RKO Studios to watch the filming of his "Cheek to Cheek" number in *Top Hat*, and Phyllis came with me. Fred spent a minimum of two months meticulously preparing his dance routines for each picture; then, on shooting days, he would run the pertinent number through for the camera, lighting, and sound experts, put on his costume, turn up the playback of the music, and usually have it "in the can" at the first take—the supreme professional. People begged for a chance to be present on those historic shooting days.

Phyllis settled herself down unobtrusively to watch Ginger and Fred do their run-through on the vast sound stage.

Ginger rehearsed in slacks, and when she appeared for the first take, she looked ravishing in a dress composed almost entirely of red feathers.

"She looks like a wooster," Phyllis giggled.

It transpired that the dress was only just ready in time owing to some sartorial hitch in the wardrobe department. The playback blared forth, and the dance started. Slowly, one at a time at first, the feathers parted company with the parent garment. Then, as Fred whirled Ginger faster and faster about the gleaming set, more and more flew off. It became reminiscent of a pillow fight at school, but they pressed bravely on with the number, and by the end Ginger looked ready for the spit.

Altercations broke out between the director, the cameraman, and the wardrobe mistress. Phyllis pulled my sleeve.

"Let's get out of here," she said. "Fwed will be so embawassed."

The Astaires took me down to Dolores Del Rio's house in a quiet street in Santa Monica. Dolores, a spectacular black-haired, dark-eyed Mexican beauty with skin whiter than a hen's egg, was married to good-looking military-mustached Cedric Gibbons, the head set designer at MGM Studios. Their house was covered with climbing plants of various kinds, the choice of which perhaps contained a clue to the odd relationship of the two householders. Dolores had a large sunny room on the first floor containing a huge and inviting bed. Gibbie lived in comparative squalor in a small room immediately below. The only connection between these two rooms was by way of a stepladder which could be lowered only when a trapdoor in the floor of Dolores' room had been raised. There was a long stick in Gibbie's room with which, we conjectured, he signaled his intentions or hopes by rapping out signals on the floor of his wife's bedchamber.

Phyllis and Fred delegated me to find out more, but despite many happy hours spent in the company of Gibbie and Dolores, they declined to unravel the mystery.

Serious music has an unfortunate effect on me unless I am prepared for it. With Fred and Phyllis I went to Joan Crawford's house one night for dinner, a rather formal affair, served to the four of us by white-coated menservants. Crawford, one of the reigning movie queens and a lady of extraordinary beauty and drive, had decided to branch out and become an opera singer in her spare time. She had taken a few lessons locally and had made some ill-advised recordings of the result with the MGM Studio Orchestra. After dinner she put record after record on her solid mahogany radiogram, and for what seemed a very long time, we were treated to her interpretation of famous arias from *Tosca, Aïda,* and *La Bohème.* As her courageous but fluctuating notes rose and fell, Joan watched us keenly, and we, not daring to look at each other, nodded appreciatively back. I was highly relieved that Raymond Massey and Douglas Fairbanks, Jr., had not received invitations to attend.

Summit Drive appealed to Fred and Phyllis, not because of its glittering inhabitants, but because of Phyllis' bird-dog nose for good business. They occupied two houses on that illustrious street in fairly quick succession. Phyllis invested in some choice acreage just below Pickfair, on the Colman ridge. She divided this land in two and on one half built a nice, comfortable, easy-to-run family house complete with swimming pool and tennis court.

Fred remonstrated about the court. "I don't like tennis; everybody beats me," he complained.

"David and I will play on it," said Phyllis smugly, "and anyway, this house is not for us . . . it's for sale."

She then put the house on the market, sold it at a succulent profit to William Wyler, the director of *Wuthering Heights, The Best Years of Our Lives, Ben Hur,* and many other movie milestones, and built a second and bigger one on the other half of the land.

Peter Potter, the child of a brief former marriage of Phyllis', was a three-year-old when Fred and Phyllis married, a serious-minded citizen even then, destined later to serve many remarkably useful years as a law enforcement officer in Los Angeles and Santa Barbara counties. He was early fascinated by explosives. Fred misguidedly gave him a chemistry set on his tenth birthday, and quiet dinners at the Astaires' were thereafter punctuated by appalling explosions upstairs.

Once upon arrival at the house, I found the whole family in the living room, cowering behind sofas while outside a huge projectile lay hissing and smoking ominously on the lawn.

"Peter's wocket wefuses to take off," said Phyllis nervously. "It's been making that tewibble noise for ten minutes and it's pointing this way—can you do something bwave about it?"

Prudently, I waited till the noises ceased altogether; then I went out and stalked it. When I was about six feet away, the monster suddenly came to life with a burst of orange flame and an appalling *woosh*. It missed my head by inches, arched up high over the house, disappeared in the general direction of Pickfair, and Peter's arsenal was ordered to be dismantled.

Peter had been joined, very early on, by two enchanting Astaire children, Fred, Jr., and Ava, and it was impossible to find a more devoted family. Fred and Phyllis had everything in common, love of their three children, a longing for a peaceful life, a loathing of Hollywood parties and "chichi," and a fascination with horses and horseracing. This last resulted in the purchase of a ranch at Chatsworth in the San Fernando Valley and the accumulation, by judicious buying and breeding, of a very handy string of racehorses.

One, Triplicate, bought as a three-year-old for $6,000, a beautiful animal with a coat of beaten bronze, went on to earn well over $250,000 in prize money, capturing, en route, the Hollywood Gold Cup and the San Juan Capistrano Stakes. Other horses they owned did well too, including one oddly named The Fag.

The ranch became the center of their lives. It was always spick-and-span, as I can witness, having been frequently bullied into painting and repainting what seemed like miles of white paddock fencing. Fred, one of the few people in the world about whom it could be claimed that he would never hurt a fly, in point of fact loathed the insects because they annoyed his beloved horses. He invested in electric "fly crematoriums" for the stables; any flies landing on their seductive surfaces were instantly incinerated. Another gadget was less successful. Fred loved the family maid, and he bought an electric carpet sweeper to ease her burden. Something went wrong, and the machine left tracks like a mowing machine on the rugs. The maid was in tears, so Fred trimmed the bristles of the revolving brushes down to nothing with his nail scissors. Little was swept thereafter, but the family maid was wreathed in smiles. Fred loved gadgets. He began losing his hair early, and although philosophical about it, referring to "my high intellectual forehead," he fought a permanent battle to try to maintain the status quo: hence the purchase of an electric hair restorer, a strange, throbbing rubber cap containing elaborate coils and impulses. He must have misread the directions and assembled it incorrectly because on opening night it went into reverse and yanked out a large proportion of what he had left. Fred dreaded "social" dancing, and Ava swore that the most embarrassing night of her life was at a debutantes' ball. There was a father-daughter dance, and according to his daughter, Fred, the focal point of all eyes, "tripped all over me." Above all, he dreaded lugging around a dance floor some eager matron or starry-eyed teenager who would breathe, "Gee, I just can't believe I'm dancing with the *great* Fred Astaire!" But an inhibited and self-conscious social dancer, he would occasionally "take off" in private. Coming home one night in 1950 and hearing loud canned music booming out of my house, I found Fred leaping from staircase to bookcase, to sofa, to floor, using my golf clubs as swords for a sword dance and Hjördis for a partner and, all the time, beating an incredible tattoo with his winged feet.

Since Fred was established as a dedicated worrier, it was inevitable, after a string of ten consecutive box-office smashes, that he would become convinced that he was due for a slump. The interest of audiences toward all musicals had indeed started, slowly, to erode all over the world, and as his last two pictures with Ginger had been merely "great successes" instead of "sensational hits," he talked so persuasively to his costar that she too decided that they

549

might indeed have done enough together and agreed to a "trial separation."

Ginger chose to do a straight comedy, *Bachelor Mother*, with a new, young leading man—David Niven—and Fred took a whole year off to enjoy himself.

Ginger bloomed in her success as a straight actress, but poor Phyllis, instead of spending twelve months of hard-earned relaxation with her husband, found herself cooped up with a hand-wringing wreck who was convinced that he was permanently unemployed, could no longer hit a golf ball, spot a winner, or get a job, but the scene changed unexpectedly. Musicals became the perfect antidote to the grimness of the latest intercontinental lunacy— World War II. Suddenly they were back with a rush, and Fred, with a variety of sparkling partners (of whom Rita Hayworth was his favorite), found himself back on top of the tree.

With the war over, Fred was immediately consumed with renewed doubts about continuing dancing and even went so far as officially to announce his retirement. Photographs were flashed to a horrified public of Fred performing his "last dance," but "Somebody Up There" had no intention of letting Fred off the hook that easily and allowing him to spend the rest of his life with racehorses and mashie niblicks, so he sneakily arranged for poor Gene Kelly in the middle of rehearsals of *Easter Parade* to break a leg.

An SOS went out to Fred, and much to everyone's delight, including Gene's, Fred Astaire's "retirement" ended overnight.

Fred was such an honest person that he just could not believe it was fair that he should be getting such real pleasure out of working. More than 90 percent of the people of the world, he reckoned, were slaving away at jobs they hated in order to support themselves and their families. The most balanced of men in every sense of the word, he only once to my knowledge went mad. At dawn one day Fred called me and announced his mental aberration.

"I'll never know what made me do it," he moaned, "but I had this overpowering urge . . . so I got up in the middle of the night and drove all over Beverly Hills painting the mailboxes with my racing colors."

Fred never ceased to say that he was "the luckiest hoofer and luckiest guy in the world," and it seemed to his friends that he had indeed been dealt an unbeatable hand.

Apart from his soaring talent, this kind, generous, and gentle man had three children who adored him and whose adoration he had earned by being unfailingly understanding and helpful during their growing-up problems, their early careers and marriages. He had a home where he felt safe and at peace; he had his racehorses and had earned and kept money enough to minimize all the everyday problems. Above all, he had Phyllis, the vibrant, vital little auburn beauty he worshiped with all his heart. Theirs was the prototype of a gloriously happy marriage, but Fred, the worrier, deep down felt that his luck was too great, and that it was all too perfect, that something was *bound* to ruin it all, and, one day at Belmont Park Races, Phyllis, who had never known a day's illness, asked to be taken home. "I feel dizzy," she said.

The next day she felt fine, and Fred thought no more about it till a few weeks later, this time at Santa Anita Races, she said in a quiet voice, "I feel faint—please take me home." Fred went cold, and at his insistence Phyllis visited a doctor who ordered a series of X rays, the result of which was an emergency operation.

On a hot afternoon I sat with Fred in a small waiting room at St. John's Hospital, Santa Monica, during her five hours of surgery. Finally, relieved doctors came in and told him the good news. "Looks like we've got it all." They beamed, but their optimism was short-lived: Complications set in, and at 4 A.M. back she went into the operating room, and there was little hope of survival. Fred was numb, but friends can do nothing to help on these occasions—all they can do is stick around in case they are needed and try somehow to share the awesome helplessness.

As the cool, flower-scented California dawn broke, Fred was told that a miracle had happened. Phyllis had come through once more. Frail, waiflike Phyllis was made of stainless steel. Alone in a lead-lined room, she endured weeks of X-ray treatments, put on weight, and even joked about her past ordeal.

"The only time I thought I was in twubble was just before I went in for the second time . . . a lot of nuns came into my woom, knelt down, and started pwaying."

Two months of euphoric remission ended abruptly with further emergency surgery, and Fred's own words will postscript his lost happiness:

"She lapsed into a coma for several weeks. I *knew* she would snap out of it. She didn't. She looked like a beautiful child. She never lost her sweet facial expression. Phyllis . . . slipped away from us."

15

The Enchanted Hill

EVEN by the standards of Hollywood in the mid-thirties it had been a very heavy night.

It was after five o'clock, and already the sky was becoming lighter behind me as I sped, none too safely, westward down Sunset Boulevard. High in the hills to my right, the giant sign looked luminous in the ghostly predawn glow: HOLLYWOODLAND.

I was in a great hurry. I had to drop a Wampas Baby Star back at her mother's apartment in Beverly Hills, watch her sneak in, slippers in hand, then return to my own nest in Hollywood, shave, shower, and check in at the studios by seven o'clock.

I pushed the accelerator right down to the floor, and the passenger stirred uneasily as we whizzed through a red light. Suddenly she screamed, but I had seen it too. Slowly crossing the boulevard fifty yards ahead of us was a sizable building.

My unreliable brakes came through nobly, and we stopped with the radiator a yard away from a white front door. Angry men with lanterns surrounded us, including two in the uniform of the Los Angeles police department. When I was allowed to get a word in, I inquired why a large building was crossing a main thoroughfare.

"It's Marion Davies' dressing room," they said.

"Where's it going?" I asked.

"To Warner Brothers," came the reply.

It was too. After ten years as a top star at Metro-Goldwyn-Mayer, Marion Davies was literally moving house, and her fourteen-room bungalow was being towed in sections ten miles from Culver City to the San Fernando Valley.

Louis B. Mayer had stood blubbering at the main gate when this strange cortege had moved out of his studio. "The queen is leaving us," he wailed.

When she was eighteen and one of the most beautiful girls in New York, Marion Davies had a walk-on in a revue, *Stop! Look! Listen!*

William Randolph Hearst, the multimillionaire head of a vast publishing empire, saw her and promptly fell in love with her. She became his mistress, but there were snags to the smooth running of this arrangement because Hearst was thirty-four years older than Marion, he was also married, and the United States was still rigidly puritanical with regard to people "living in sin."

Hearst, however, decided that there was one code of behavior for himself and another for the rest, so he openly flaunted their relationship, and his presses pumped out praise of the talent of his beautiful girlfriend. Aided by that and a genuine flair as a comedienne, Marion quickly passed through the showgirl school of Florenz Ziegfeld, graduated to small parts in musicals, and arrived in the upstart film business. Hearst formed Cosmopolitan Pictures and, after a beginning on the East Coast, moved his production company to Hollywood. He longed to make Marion a big star adored by the public, and he very nearly succeded, but the very intensity of his efforts upset the apple cart. Marion was perfect material for Lombard-type comedies, and the audiences warmed to her beauty, her charming little stammer, her naturalness, and her obvious sense of fun, but they became suspicious of the constant blast of publicity that issued from the Hearst press and sniggered openly at the sycophantic drooling of Hearst's super columnist, Louella Parsons, whose every description of a Hollywood gathering inevitably concluded with "and Marion has never looked lovelier."

Marion, an utterly genuine person, had no illusions about her talents and must have fulminated endlessly against Hearst's efforts to promote her as a great dramatic actress. If his well-meaning interference in the choice of roles made things difficult for her, it was nothing compared to the way in which his meddling during production upset her directors. He rewrote scenes, ordered retakes, fired hairdressers, demanded that certain favorite pieces of his own furniture be used to dress the sets, and insisted, however out of place, that somewhere in the picture Marion should sing a song.

He loved her deeply and truly, and she repaid his devotion in kind. Above all, she loved him for himself, not for what he could do for her. She was not at all ambitious, and although she enjoyed the fun and camaraderie of making pictures, she did so to please him, not to polish her own ego, and large chunks of the money she earned she gave away to charity or to less fortunate friends. The one thing she wanted desperately for herself was his name, but although Hearst was reputed to have made a few halfhearted attempts to arrange this, it was denied her and she tried reluctantly to reconcile herself to the status quo.

It was important to Hearst that his mistress was not looked on by the world as just another ex-Follies showgirl, so he pressed on relentlessly to try to propel her right up to the number one spot in the Hollywood galaxy. MGM had been chosen by Hearst as the instrument for the push.

The presence of Marion Davies among L. B. Mayer's stars had guaranteed an incalculable amount of benevolent publicity in the Hearst publications, but matters had come to a head when Hearst insisted that Marion should play Elizabeth in *The Barretts of Wimpole Street* and the title role in *Marie Antoinette*. Both had already been earmarked for the reigning queen of MGM—Norma Shearer, who happened to be the wife of Irving Thalberg, who happened to be the producer designate of these productions.

The negotiations, which had been long and acrimonious, had ended up with Hearst ordering Marion's bungalow to be towed across town to Warner Brothers and Norma Shearer's name to be banished from his newspapers and left L. B. Mayer using his main gate for a wailing wall.

Hearst's roughneck gold-mining prospector father many years before had finally struck it rich. He didn't strike gold, but he hit on the next best thing, in enormous quantities—silver.

George Hearst, a firm believer in the future of the West, with the proceeds bought up large hunks of California, including, for 60 cents a time, 40,000 acres in San Luis Obispo County, stretching from San Simeon Bay to the Santa Lucia Mountains; there he developed a famous stock farm and constructed, on a grassy slope not far back from the ocean, a modest ranch house called the Hacienda.

Son William Randolph, at the age of twenty-four, refused to follow in his father's footsteps as a mineowner or a rancher and, already fascinated by the world of journalism, talked his parent into making him a present of a failing little publication, the San Francisco *Examiner*. His huge, sprawling, octopuslike publishing empire was born that day and was destined to become the largest consumer of newsprint in the world, but he never lost sight of that acreage in San Luis Obispo County. There he decided he would one day build his castle, and as his fortunes prospered, he assiduously bought up more and more land in the area till his holdings at San Simeon totaled almost 250,000 acres.

A man of incredible energy, he found time to weld his colossal empire, to rule it with a rod of iron, to revolutionize and 'sensationalize the whole spectrum of journalism, to oppose U.S. entry into World War I, to fight the League of Nations, to wage a private vendetta against both the British and the French, to warn the United States that the Brooklyn Bridge was about to fall down, and to run twice for mayor and once for governor of New York. At the same time he became the biggest collector of antiques and *objets d'art* in the world, ending up with a many-floored warehouse covering a whole city block in the Bronx and serviced by a permanent staff of thirty. It was stuffed to the roof with treasure, most of it still unpacked, including entire rooms, staircases, and ceilings, ripped from within the walls of disintegrating British, French, and Italian stately homes, plus one complete Spanish monastery with its stones still individually wrapped and numbered. He also collected real estate with the same abandon, garnering, among other choice plots, 1,000,000 acres in Mexico, a hotel in New York and St. Donat's Castle, an eleventh-century pile in Wales, but in the middle of all these and a thousand other activities the apple of his eye remained San Simeon, and there as he had long promised himself, he constructed with loving care a castle of his own design.

On a craggy, treeless spur, high above the original Hacienda, he blasted rock, dragged thirty-foot trees over ranges of mountains, and slowly, securing for itself a spectacular 360-degree panoramic view of unmatched beauty, the incredible edifice arose.

The housekeeper of what Hearst liked to call La Cuesta Encantada—The Enchanted Hill—proudly boasted that the place cost $7,000 a day to run, not counting the mounds of fish and meat consumed by the packs of wild animals in the open range zoo which surrounded it.

At weekends it was full of guests, but for Marion, the chatelaine, it must have been a lonely mist-shrouded domain during midweek when the ocean fog crept clammily up the Enchanted Hill and she found herself alone, surrounded by forty pairs of see-all-miss-nothing eyes belonging to Hearst's hand-picked Filipino servants.

About a year after my early-morning near collision with her dressing room, I received a phone message: "Call Hacienda one immediately."

I enlisted the studio operator's help, and she informed me that it was the Hearst estate at San Simeon. "Miss Marion Davies is trying to contact you."

Marion sounded enchanting on the phone, and I greatly enjoyed my first exposure to her most attractive stammer. She invited me up for the following weekend and explained that Bill Hearst had suggested that I be part of the house party which she was organizing. "The boys will all be here," she said.

W. R. Hearst had five sons: George, the eldest, rather portly and distrait, Bill, Jack, and the twins, Randy and David. Their mother, Millicent, lived on a large estate at Sands Point, Long Island, and the fun-loving boys moved between these two poles of interest, intrigue, and luxury without, at least on the surface, the slightest dent in the armor of their common sense or their attitude toward their parents.

They were completely relaxed about the Hearst-Marion relationship, though it could not have been easy to assimilate it under the prevalent conditions. They were very fond of Marion, loved their mother, and adored and admired their father. San Simeon was their dream place, too, and there they were happiest.

They were contemporaries of mine, and Bill and his wife, Lorelle, I had come to know very well, so I was relieved that they too would be at the Ranch, as the castle was cozily referred to by the family, when I arrived for the weekend. I was fascinated and a little scared at the thought of meeting W. R. Hearst.

As a beginner in the film industry, I had necessarily become aware of the power of the press. In those days the Hearst press columnist, Louella Parsons, wielded undisputed and immense power mixed with a limited sense of right and wrong, so I thought it might do no harm to let drop in her ear that I would be spending a few days with her boss. I passed the happy word along to one of her spies at my studio and packed my bag.

The route north in early April was beautiful. For several hours I drove through hills still green from the rainy season; wild flowers grew in great profusion. At San Luis Obispo, I turned left to the coast road and drove for another hour through Morro Bay, Harmony, and Cambria till I reached the boundary of the Hearst ranch and found an unobtrusive sign: HEARST HACIENDA.

I turned right into the hills; far above me I beheld, in the glow of the sunset, the castle. I had heard many descriptions of it, some flattering, some derisory, but I personally found it breathtaking. It looked from the coast like a green oasis enclosing a white Spanish village, dominated by twin cathedral towers, and I pressed eagerly up the winding road. Signs were everywhere—"Animals have right of way"—and every mile or so it was necessary to open a heavy gate, and while one did so, it was advisable to keep a wary eye on the zebras, bison, ostriches, and water buffalo which stood around glaring balefully. I was passing through the largest private zoo in the world.

When I arrived at the castle, the boys met me and escorted me through beautifully manicured flower gardens to the guest "cottage" which had been allotted to me—it seemed to my eye, as yet unaccustomed to the Hearst scale of things, to have the proportions of a mansion. They told me that the huge carved bed in which I was to sleep had belonged to Cardinal Richelieu. I have since read that Hearst always slept in Richelieu's bed. If he did, I certainly did not notice him that night, but then the thing was the size of a battlefield.

The sun was over the yardarm, and the boys watched expectantly as I unpacked. Sighs of relief went up when I produced the bottles of scotch and gin they had instructed me to bring.

We settled back with our drinks, and they explained the reason for their predinner thirst. Marion for years, it seemed, had been drinking too much, and W.R. had instituted a campaign to remove the temptation. He himself would mix an innocuous cocktail for the guests, wine would flow like glue during the meal, and afterward it might just be possible to extract an occasional glass of California champagne from the butler, but the "old man's" eye would be on everyone's intake, particularly that of Marion.

We had several more drinks; then I cleaned up for dinner, and munching handfuls of peppermints, we strolled past a treasure trove of garden statuary to La Casa Grande. The entrance was most impressive—a huge door topped by ornate balconies and a portico, flanked by the twin cathedral towers I had seen from the coast road. On top of each tower was a set of church bells encased in a circular colonnade capped by a beautifully proportioned dome and a crucifix. The overall effect was Spanish, and the detailed work in wood and stone was magnificent.

Inside the castle I was led into a cavernous reception hall which must have been thirty yards long and twenty across. The fireplace, in which enormous logs were blazing, was framed by a mantelshelf of gargantuan proportions; the ceiling was almost out of sight. On an immense Spanish table in the middle of this room stood a very large silver bowl full of fruit juice, and into this bowl, W. R. Hearst was pouring a thimbleful of gin. He, too, was huge; almost six feet six inches tall and shaped like an avocado, with sloping shoulders and sizable paunch. His straight grayish hair behind a high-domed forehead was plentiful, parted in the middle and falling forward in two unruly locks. He wore coat, trousers, and waistcoat of thick tweed of overcheck design.

When Bill introduced me, his father turned and treated me to a charming, if rather vague, smile, but his eyes beneath brows that sloped down in harmony with his shoulders were the bluest and the coldest I had ever seen. I had a nasty feeling that he knew about the empty bottles of gin and whiskey now reposing under Richelieu's bed.

He had a curiously high voice. A dachshund sniffed at his shoes. Marion bustled up, and I was captivated by her. She was all bubbling fun and laughter, and despite her fortyish figure, her long blond hair, huge baby-blue eyes, and sexy mouth and teeth made her seem fifteen years younger.

Introductions happened piecemeal, and of the thirty or forty present, I remember two or three mature ladies who were friends of Marion from her days in the *Follies*, one with a permanent leer caused by an erratic operation to remove the bags from under her eyes, Frances Marion, a talented screenwriter who had written many of Marion's movies, Gutzon Borglum, the Danish sculptor who was currently hacking the likenesses of four American Presidents out of the side of Mount Rushmore in South Dakota, and several gray, noncommittal gentlemen from the hierarchy of the Hearst empire, including Richard Berlin and his top columnist, Arthur Brisbane. Among this older group, I was excited to see Charlie Chaplin, though my excitement faded after dinner when he held court, telling long and surprisingly dull stories.

Guests at dinner were seated by Marion at the "longest refectory table in the world" in the longest dining room I had ever seen. The chairs were extremely uncomfortable, having been designed for knights who ate in their armor. Behind us, against the entire length of the walls, were monks' stalls of solid oak removed from some medieval house of worship, and high in the gloom above us, on long poles arching over our heads like swords at a military wedding, were several dozen beautifully embroidered banners from the leading families of Siena and Florence. Arranged at intervals of a yard or so down the center of the vast table were three-foot-high heavily worked silver candlesticks, and between these were surprising but somehow reassuring little outcrops of paper napkins, Worcestershire sauce and ketchup. W.R. liked to keep things simple at the Ranch.

Hearst sat at the middle of the table. Marion sat directly opposite him, and I noticed that his cold blue eyes, which had alarmed me earlier on, were looking warmly at her throughout the meal. In the middle section of the table, flanking W.R. and herself, Marion had parked the elder statesmen and stateswomen of the group, while the boys, their wives, and their friends, jogging the arms of the wine-serving Filipino servants in vain attempts to encourage respectable rations, were phased out into the half-light at either end.

There was no general conversation. The dinner itself was buffet-style and hearty—man-eating steaks, baked potatoes, salads, and desserts. Self-service from another large and well-laden table at the end of the room was the order at all meals, and throughout these repasts one became accustomed to yards of ticker tape and other pieces of hot news being slipped beneath one's host's nose by a male secretary.

After dinner we filed into the private movie theater and from deeply comfortable seats watched one of the latest as yet unreleased films, which were sent up every week to San Simeon by the major studios, hoping to garner some favorable publicity by this genuflection in the direction of the all-important Hearst press.

To an unknown young actor it was a revelation and a mixed joy to listen to the acid comments and catcalls that greeted some of the efforts that were selected nightly for dissection. It was a rough audience for a bad film, but the best audience in the world for a good one.

Well past midnight the film ended. W.R. and Marion disappeared inside a claustrophobic little elevator which held only two people and were borne jerkily aloft to his Gothic library, and there, before retiring four or five hours later to their "Celestial Suite," the charming, relaxed host of San Simeon surrounded by telephones became the dynamo, and some said the demon, who put the fear of God into editors, bankers, captains of industry, and statesmen all over the world.

When the cat was away, the mice began to play, and the young indulged in all sorts of harmless pursuits, moonlight swims in the giant marble and colonnaded outdoor pool or the gold-leafed indoor one, card games, music, and always dormitory-type raids, booby traps and water fights. W.R. knew everything that went on, and sometimes damage was extensive, but nothing was said, provided none of the three cardinal rules was broken: No drunkenness, no bad language or off-color jokes, and above all, no sexual intercourse between unmarried couples. This last was a strange piece of puritanism from a man living openly with his mistress, but it was rigorously enforced and any misdemeanor immediately punished by banishment, the offenders receiving a note with their breakfast saying that it would be advisable to make an early start. Nobody lingered, though all marveled at the efficiency of the local intelligence service.

Dorothy Parker was said to have received her marching orders—being sent down the hill, it was called—and bridled at the indignity that she felt had come her way for making love in the middle of so much beauty and treasure.

561

San Simeon lore had it that before her early-morning departure she opened the visitors' book and in it wrote:

Upon my honor I saw the Madonna
Standing in a niche
Above the door
Of a well-known whore
And a first class son of a bitch.

On a subsequent visit to the Ranch I myself fell foul of the local Gestapo.

I had been encouraged to drive up from Los Angeles with a very beautiful girl. The first evening of the weekend had developed along normal lines, and when the movie and other jollities were over and I judged that everyone was sound asleep I set out from my guest cottage in the gardens intent on finding my friend somewhere high up in the main house.

During the evening this project had become a joint planning operation, and my partner in crime had given me minute instructions on the exact location of her bedchamber.

Undeterred by the fact that we had been allotted rooms at the farthest extremities of San Simeon, I tiptoed quietly along garden paths, inhaling the overpowering sweetness of night-scented jasmine, and gained the impressive front door of La Casa Grande. Inside, the great hall was warm and smelled of lingering cigar smoke; the embers of the dying logs still gave out a faint glow which helped because all the lights had been switched off. I groped my way around looking for some stone stairs and found instead the door to the two-seater elevator. This I entered and pressed the button that would propel me past the danger area of the Gothic library and the Celestial Suite. In the stillness of the night the elevator sounded like the elevated railway on New York's Third Avenue, and when it finally clanked to a stop, I stayed in it for an eternity, not daring to come out, and toyed with the idea of giving up the whole project, but as the girl had hinted that she didn't think I had the guts to try the assault on the stronghold, I decided to press on.

In the darkened elevator I had misjudged the number of buttons, so when I did emerge, I found myself on a veranda which had no place at all in our meticulous planning. I began to long for the safety of Richelieu's bed, but there was nothing for it. I had to go back into the elevator.

The noise going down was deafening, and I couldn't wait to get out of the damn thing, but I had once more miscounted and this time I emerged into a dank passage full of pieces of sharp masonry upon which I left the leading edges of my shinbones.

After two more clattering trips in the elevator I finally surfaced among acres of pitch-black and recognizable reception rooms where I blundered about until miraculously I bumped into the "longest refectory table in the world." I don't know how I did it, but I had found the dining room.

Almost prostrate with nervous exhaustion, I sank gratefully into one of the monks' stalls. From there I could work my way to the front door. I was saved!

Suddenly all the lights in the place went on.

I hastily prepared a thin excuse about foraging for a snack, but nobody appeared. In the full glare of the lights and in the certain knowledge that my entire promenade had been monitored, I summoned what dignity I could for the benefit of the watching eyes and sauntered from the room, humming a brave little tune. In case I was still under any misapprehension, the moment I swung the front door open an unseen hand once more plunged La Casa Grande into darkness.

I went unpunished for my nocturnal ramble and had the great good fortune to be invited frequently to the Ranch during the next few years.

Marion was always warm and gay. Even in repose she seemed about to burst out laughing. She was a sort of den mother to the young and was never happier than when she was fostering romances.

W. R. Hearst remained courteous, thoughtful, and charming, but I cannot claim that I ever came close to him. I was always in awe of him, despite the fact that he sought out the company of the young and encouraged us to talk to him.

Although at the time in his mid-seventies he was full of amazing physical energy. Picnics were organized which W.R. would lead in full Western costume, riding for hours to some remote ranch on the estate, where, as if by magic, everything had been prepared for the arrival of his troupe.

Playing tennis singles with him was something of a hazard because he plainly liked to come out on top, and as he had no intention whatever of running for the ball, he took up a strong position in the center of the court and waited for it to be hit within his reach. When this was achieved, he struck it very hard indeed and unerringly returned it out of one's reach. It was incredible to think that when this man was sitting on his father's knee, Abraham Lincoln was balancing a piece of paper on his own and drafting the Gettysburg Address.

I had heard much about Hearst's chronic anti-British feelings, and indeed a glance at any of his publications in those pre-World War II days showed how stubbornly he still held to them. Often I wondered why anybody with my blood was tolerated near him, but he never said a word of criticism to me and only once put my American loyalty in question.

In order to get rid of an extra who was pestering me on the set, I gave him $10 toward some fund for which he was collecting. He had mumbled something about the starving Mexican lettuce pickers of Salinas.

It turned out that along with dozens of other unsuspecting people I had subscribed to a Communist front organization.

Hearst's Los Angeles *Examiner* picked up the story, and along with such well-known "Communists" as C. Aubrey Smith, Ronald Colman, Basil Rathbone, and Cedric Hardwicke, I was pilloried in its columns for days.

"Who needs these British bums?" was the theme, if not the actual wording, of the attacks, and we were publicly hauled over the coals for taking jobs from clean-cut American actors and undermining the fabric of the country that had befriended us. It was, therefore, with some trepidation that I accepted my next invitation to the Ranch, but Hearst was his usual charming self and even singled me out for a personal tour of the cages of his favorite dangerous animals behind La Casa Grande.

W.R. loved animals great and small with a most endearing passion, but he could not bear their injuries or deaths. When the dining hall of La Casa Grande became infested with mice, far from destroying them, he left out tasty tidbits for them before retiring at night. When they multiplied alarmingly, he reluctantly agreed to have them trapped, provided they were not hurt. Special cages were constructed to capture them alive, and each morning resentful Filipinos emptied the catch into the front garden. The little captives, hardly believing their good fortune, then hotfooted it happily back in the direction of the kitchen entrance.

At the end of our walk he smiled his vague smile and said, "And when are you going to become an American citizen?"

I had been lulled into a feeling of false security by his charm, and while I fumbled around for an answer he continued. "After all, you *do* owe a great deal to this country, don't you?"

"I certainly do, sir," I said sincerely, "but I am proud of my own country, too . . . and after all, thousands of Americans work happily all over the world, but they don't feel they have to become British or Arabs or Chinese."

Hearst did what I least expected: He let out a high cackle of laughter and patted me on the shoulder. "Good boy!" he said. "Good boy!"

If I had hoped that the "Limeys, go home!" trend in the Hearst press might abate as a result of my brilliant riposte, I could not have been more mistaken, and two years later, after Hitler marched into Poland, the crescendo was reached when President Roosevelt lent Britain fifty old destroyers and several thousand rifles, hoping to stave off the inevitable involvement of the United States. "Pulling the British chestnuts out of the fire!" proclaimed Hearst, and he stuck to his guns right up to the moment when the Japanese bombed Pearl Harbor. Then he put all his resources unreservedly behind an all-out war effort.

It seemed strange that a man of pure Anglo-Saxon heritage should conduct such a virulent crusade against the land of his forebears. Perhaps the fact that his wet nurse had come from Southern Ireland had something to do with it. Personally, I don't believe he was anti-British. I think he was just 100 percent pro-American.

When he sent his son Bill to England for the first time, he told him he liked the English very much but warned him to be careful. "They are charming," he said. "Don't let them charm you off your American perch."

565

W. R. Hearst's love for Marion was plain for all to see, and in spite of the difference in age, it remained so to the end. Marion's love was equally strong, but there was an appalling gap in her contentment. She longed to be Mrs. Hearst and knew it could never be. Probably therein lay the cause of her increasing reliance on the bottle to help her maintain her gaiety, and Hearst was permanently on tenterhooks because of her drinking. By all accounts he was far more concerned about that than any thought of losing her to a younger man. It seemed that she did occasionally have flirtations with actors in her films, but she must have known that information of such goings-on was bound to be relayed to W.R. even before the bed had been turned down; perhaps she hoped that she might spur him on to make the one move she longed for.

If one became a frequent visitor at the Ranch, one also became involved in Marion's near alcoholism. There was one heart-stopping occasion when she opened her handbag upside down during dinner, and after a loud crash of broken glass, the unmistakable smell of Booth's Gin rose from the stone floor. "My new perfume." She giggled nervously at W.R. He smiled indulgently across the table, but the hurt and the fear were in his blue eyes.

I, for one, cursed myself when I grew older and wiser because after dinner when the champagne went around, Marion would wink at one of her "trusties" and whisper, "Isn't it about time you went to the can?" This was the signal for a full glass to be left in there for her.

It seemed fun at the time to stoke up her fires of outrageous fun and laughter, and I got a kick, I suppose, out of feeling that I had outwitted one of the most powerful and best informed men on earth, but what a disloyal and crummy betrayal of someone who had shown me nothing but kindness and hospitality and what a nasty potential nail to put in her coffin.

On my visits to San Simeon the balance of the invited was always much the same: top-ranking employees from his empire mixed with authors, politicians, statesmen, explorers, and other figures of world renown, never anyone from the rich froth of international café society—they bored him to distraction—and old friends of Marion's from the theater and movies.

The boys invited their friends, and from their vantage point, it was fascinating to observe the imperfections and pretensions of the great and near great. Though I was not fortunate enough to be present when Albert Einstein, George Bernard Shaw, or Winston Churchill was a guest at the Ranch, it was tempting to speculate if it had ever been hinted to them that a good place to leave a glass of champagne was in the bathroom.

Hearst's preoccupation with furthering Marion's career had led him to surround her with the trappings he thought befitted a great film star.

In 1926, realizing that many of the Hollywood greats, including Douglas Fairbanks, Joseph Schenck, Will Rogers, L. B. Mayer, and Marion's great rival, Norma Shearer, owned beach houses at Santa Monica, Hearst set out to give her the most luxurious beach house of all. Marion went along with the idea, not that she particularly wanted it, but she knew that showering her with gifts gave Hearst great pleasure and also helped him paper over his conscience.

Hearst bought up the necessary beach frontage, including a small adjacent lot belonging to Will Rogers upon which he intended building a tennis court. The lot was worth a few thousand dollars, but Rogers had decided that Hearst should be taught that money could not buy everything, so each time Hearst made an offer, Rogers had put up the price. Finally, he accepted a round sum of $100,000, thereby learning what money *could* do.

Reminiscent, with its pillars, porticoes, and symmetrical wings, of Buckingham Palace, the white frame structure, named Ocean House, rose slowly on the Santa Monica beach, and Hearst filled it with treasure, sometimes driving the architect to distraction by mentioning that the shape of a particular room was dictated by the fact that he had already bought it intact in Europe, and now it was up to the architect to fit it into the house.

There was a ballroom, a gigantic staircase, fifty-five bathrooms, and lockers for more than 2,000 guest swimmers—it was not very cozy. The parties at Ocean House were on a different scale from those at San Simeon—they were strictly Marion, and there with gaiety, generosity, and bubbling fun she entertained her multitude of friends. Each year she gave a costume ball on W.R.'s birthday. There was a Forty-Niner Party; a Kid Party, when Gable came as a Boy Scout and Joan Crawford as Shirley Temple; an Early American Party, when Hearst dressed as James Madison; and a Your Favorite Movie Star Party, which saw Gary Cooper as Dr. Fu

Manchu and Groucho Marx as Rex, the Wonder Horse. But the most lavish of all was the Circus Party.

Two thousand guests assembled. Cary Grant and Paulette Goddard arrived with a party of friends dressed as tumblers and, after days of practice, were able to make a most impressive entrance cartwheeling across the dance floor. Henry Fonda came with a group of clowns; Bette Davis was a bearded lady, Dolores Del Rio a bareback rider, and Claudette Colbert showed up as Pocahontas.

I forget what Marion wore, but I do remember thinking, in spite of his noble profile, how forlorn and self-conscious W.R. looked as the ringmaster.

There was a carousel and sideshows and prizes for the most original costumes. Among the less popular contestants for these were Errol Flynn and myself, who arrived dressed in baggy white suits and white peaked caps, inquiring where the elephants were. We carried shovels and buckets on which was painted "IT."

It was estimated that Ocean House cost more than $7,000,000 by the time it was completed and furnished. Gratuitous additions for me were a couple of white frame guest cottages. Bill Hearst talked to Marion, and for a while I rented one of these from her for a minimal sum. I shared it with two bachelor friends, and our parties, if not on the scale of the big house, were such that Carole Lombard nicknamed the place Cirrhosis-by-the-Sea.

We had this painted on a board above the front door, where it remained till Harry Crocker, a great friend of Hearst's, dropped by and suggested that I take it down.

"Imagine," he said, "how W.R. would react if he ever thought it was a crack at Marion."

Some days Marion walked down the beach and dropped in to see if her tenants were behaving themselves. Our free and easy lifestyle fascinated her and made her a little wistful, I think. She adored and revered W.R.—"Hearst come, Hearst served" was her favorite parting line when she terminated her visits. Occasionally, one heard rumors that she had cuckolded him, but in so doing, she somehow would have remained true to him. It would have meant nothing to her; she was just being generous and making someone happy. There was no bitchiness or underhandedness in Marion's makeup.

Undoubtedly, by the end of 1937 if I had had my eyes and ears open, I would have detected certain undercurrents at San Simeon. I would have realized that the gray, uncommunicative top brass of the empire was now outnumbering the friends of Marion and the boys, and I would assuredly have noticed that these men were looking drawn and worried.

I might also have spotted that Marion was antagonistic to these same high executives, and I would certainly have sensed that this antipathy was heartily reciprocated, but never by word or deed would my shy, generous, courtly, and thoughtful host have alerted me to the fact that he was under an almost intolerable strain.

The Hearst empire was cracking up. The debts amounted to a monumental $126,000,000, and Hearst at the age of seventy-five was facing personal bankruptcy and the total dissolution of everything he had single-handedly built up.

I don't know if the boys realized how close above their heads Damocles' sword was dangling. If they did, they kept their own counsel, and the fun at San Simeon seemed to the self-indulgent guests to be as constant and unforced as usual, but behind the scenes W.R. was taking what must, for him, have been heartbreaking decisions. He formed a committee of his top advisers to take over his financial affairs with orders to cut away the deadwood and liquidate everything that was not making a profit, so during the next few months dozens of his favorite newspapers and radio stations were sold, much of his real estate went, and finally, his beloved collection was put on the market. No single antique dealer in the United States was able to cope with the thousands of items, so the accumulated treasure of the most prolific collector in the world ignominiously went under the hammer at Gimbel's and other department stores throughout the country. The castle in Wales did not find a bidder, nor did the 164,000 outlying acres of San Simeon itself, but one can imagine the wrench Hearst must have felt when his "committee" ordered him to divest himself of the very heartland of his empire. The animals went off to zoos in 1938, and a year later Hearst asked the bank for a mortgage on the Enchanted Hill itself.

The strain on Hearst and on Marion must have been crippling when stockholders, rivals, and even some of his own committee openly and most unfairly blamed her for his almost lunatic outpourings, but the unkindest cut of all came when he discovered that the mortgage he had finally obtained on the Enchanted Hill was held by his archrival, Harry Chandler, publisher of the Los Angeles *Times*.

If W. R. Hearst was made of very special stuff, so was his mistress. At the most critical point, when his aged head was only just above water, he needed just one more million dollars to keep afloat. Marion, without a moment's hesitation, pooled her film savings, jewelry and real estate investments and presented W.R. with a check which, over his vehement protestations, she insisted he cash immediately and for which she refused all security.

The empire shrank, but Hearst's remaining newspapers and radio stations were run with all his old vigor, and his feelings toward Great Britain remained unchanged.

In 1939, just before Hitler finally went berserk, W.R. addressed a stern radio warning to the American people: "It is no part of our duty to support the British Empire in her ambitious schemes to dominate Europe, absorb Africa, and control the Orient. England has never in our whole history extended any aid, comfort, or consideration to these United States of ours!"

When he made that statement, what was left of his empire was at the edge of the precipice, but a few weeks later mankind embarked on its bloodiest self-inflicted wound, and the Hearst empire was saved. With the outbreak of hostilities, profits from newspapers and radio stations soared, the 164,000 unsold acres of San Simeon were snapped up by the U.S. army, and a sizable and timely slab of hard cash came from, of all people, the despised British government, which took St. Donat's Castle in Wales and turned it into a training school for officers.

If 1939 was a turning point in Hearst's business career, it was also the harbinger of a particularly difficult time in his private life. The "boy genius," Orson Welles, descended on the film capital, and *Citizen Kane* was prepared in great secrecy at RKO Studios.

The screenplay was not written by Welles, as most people believe; it was the work of the hard-drinking, brilliant and erratic Herman Mankiewicz. It was directed and acted by Welles, and it was photographed by the young Sam Goldwyn protégé Greg Toland, whose deep-focus photography gave a three-dimensional illusion which brought paeans of praise from the industry.

The story, of an egomaniacal, power-mad, acquisitive publisher and his drunken blond ex-actress mistress living in a hilltop castle, left no one who saw it in much doubt as to who were the prototypes.

Hearst, when shown the picture, was furious; not for himself, because, as he had lately demonstrated during the near eclipse of his publishing world, if he could dish it out, he was perfectly prepared to take it, but the pointing up of the failure of comedienne Marion's career as a dramatic actress and the underlining of what was now becoming her near-chronic alcoholism were more than he could bear. He fought back savagely. The Hearst press was still a power to be reckoned with by the film industry, and a great deal of pressure was brought to bear on RKO. L. B. Mayer offered to pay the entire cost of the film if they would destroy the negative. They refused, and the film won international acclaim, not so much for its content, which was a very local affair, but for its brilliant revolutionary, youthful, and long-overdue approach to picture-making.

The name of Orson Welles was banned from all Hearst publications, and for a considerable time RKO Studios received no reviews whatsoever for their pictures, but *Citizen Kane* survived the onslaught and won the Academy Award for Best Picture.

When World War II ended, Marion was forty-eight years old, Hearst was eighty-two, and Ocean House was a beached white elephant. Marion sold it for a song to a developer, who turned it into a beach club which failed, and before long it was pulled down and made into a public parking lot, giving a local wag a chance to write, "Marion Davies' Beach House—no more—thousands homeless."

More and more, W.R. and Marion retreated to San Simeon, but the parties were fewer, and the tempo of the place was slowed to walking pace.

The remaining 75,000 acres still enabled Hearst to look to the horizon in any direction, and everything he saw except the ocean was his, and if the beloved animals were no longer surrounding him in various stages of freedom, in the evening light he could still look down from the Enchanted Hill and rejoice in the sight of herds of elk grazing peacefully on his golden slopes below.

Returned from the war which Hearst had so much hoped his country could avoid, I did not see San Simeon again with W.R. in residence. Bill Hearst I had met up with many times in Europe where he had served as war correspondent, and back in California, he became a great favorite with my wife, Hjördis, and my two small sons at our house in Pacific Palisades. "Mr. Useless" they named him because he consistently failed to demonstrate the tiniest glimmer of know-how or invention when called on to assist in small household chores such as changing a light bulb, controlling a runaway toilet, changing a fuse or boiling an egg, but fun-loving, intelligent and generous Bill, with big blue eyes as warm as W.R.'s were cold, became "Mr. Useful" as far as reporting went and created a record in the·chilliest weeks of the cold war, when he interviewed Khrushchev, Bulganin, Molotov, Zhukhov, Churchill, and Eisenhower.

There were those who said that W. R. Hearst had an overdeveloped dread of death, and they argued in a rather convoluted way that it was this fear of the inevitable which drove him to surround himself with the young and hinted that he felt he could postpone the end so long as he continued making additions and alterations at San Simeon. Certainly I had never seen the place without scaffolding enveloping some corner of it, but if he harbored greater than normal apprehensions about the end, by all accounts, he covered them up most gallantly when he realized that his time was approaching.

For most of his life he had suffered from a suspect heart and in 1947 was struck down by a heavy attack. He was ordered to live the rest of his life near a specialist and realized that his days at San Simeon were over.

Marion found a rambling Spanish house in Beverly Hills, the gardens were touched up with a few pieces of his favorite statuary, and a dozen of his faithful San Simeon retainers were dispatched to prepare the place for their master.

How all-enveloping must his sadness have been when he went down for the last time from his Enchanted Hill. For four years in Beverly Hills he clung to life and with occasional spurts of superhuman energy still ripped off spiky directives to his editors and perpetuated one last, gloriously defiant act of horrendous extravagance when he bought fifty thoroughbred Arab horses and ordered them to be sent to San Simeon, but in August, 1951, at the age of eighty-eight he finally gave up the struggle. Nobody knows what conversations took place during the last months between the frail and weakening W.R. and Marion, who had at last lost her long battle against alcoholism.

Probably she reiterated her dislike and suspicion of the committee; certainly the dying man saw only too clearly how desperately unprotected her life was soon to become. In any event, there was mystery and high drama from the instant of his passing.

A few months ago I was trapped halfway up a Swiss mountain in a two-seater chair lift. A sudden blizzard had so violently rotated the wind gauges on the pylons that the lift motor had automatically cut, and with my companion I was left swinging, perilously, seventy feet from the ground.

Stanley Flink, because he was an ex-paratrooper, was less terrified than I.

"I think we can jump from here," he calculated. "The snow looks deep enough, so we'll only break our legs . . . but if this goddamn chair comes off the wire, we'll go down in it and break our backs."

I had long since resolved to stay in the chair come what may, so I set about ensuring that Flink would not leave me in the lurch by hurtling to his own doom.

I started a jerky and strained line of conversation that encompassed the days we had spent together in Hollywood when Flink had been the resident correspondent for *Life*. Suspended from a wire that seemed in imminent danger of snapping and swinging wildly about with the horizontally blown snow blinding us and trying to rip the skin off our faces, Stanley Flink told me what had transpired in Marion Davies' house in Beverly Hills.

Marion had been at Hearst's bedside most of that last night. By dawn the old man was sleeping, and she was exhausted. The doctor gave her a sedative and told her to rest for a few hours. When she awoke, she found not only that W.R. had died but that the undertakers had obeyed prior instructions from the committee to remove the body—she was alone. As she recounted it, "The nurse said he was dead. His body was gone whoosh! . . . like that. Old W.R. was gone. . . . Do you realize what they did? They stole a possession of mine. He belonged to me. I loved him for thirty-two years, and now he was gone. I couldn't even say good-bye."

Flink found that the guards from around the house had been

removed, and a *Life* photographer took a picture of the large four-poster in which W.R. had died. Sitting on it, whining piteously, was a little dachshund—Hearst's favorite animal and his only companion when the end had come.

The funeral, attended by the family and more than a thousand friends, rival press lords, and dignitaries, took place in San Francisco.

Marion was not invited.

W.R. had loved and admired his sons, and in his last days he must have been inordinately proud of them.

George with the San Francisco *Examiner* and Jack, aide to the Hearst newspapers' general manager, perhaps showed less flair as newspapermen than the twins, Randy, publisher of the San Francisco *Call-Bulletin*, and David, publisher of the Los Angeles *Herald-Express*.

Bill (Mr. Useless) was the star performer, publisher of the New York *Journal-American*, and being groomed to step full time into his father's shoes.

Much as the boys and their families loved the Enchanted Hill, not one of them fancied the idea of maintaining the castle and its remaining 75,000 acres.

In 1957 the state of California accepted the boys' gift of San Simeon, with 123 acres surrounding it, as a state park to be opened to the public.

At the end of that year Bill Hearst and his gorgeous second wife, "Bootsie," invited Hjördis and me to San Simeon for the last private weekend before it became public property.

Except for the giant great hall with mammoth logs blazing for the last time, La Casa Grande was dark and cold, so the four of us were housed in the largest guest "cottage," La Casa del Mar, a Spanish-style structure adjacent to the 100-foot marble outdoor Neptune pool.

For a few days we explored and played tennis and remembered the tournament organized with such helpful partners as Helen Wills, Bill Tilden, Fred Perry, and Alice Marble. We hiked and pretended we enjoyed ourselves, but Bill was obviously weighed down with a deep sadness which affected us all. In the evenings before simple meals in the "cottage," we mixed cocktails in the vast ghost-filled hall; the logs did their best, but there was a bone-chilling unhappiness about the place which Bill tried valiantly to exorcise by taking me down to the cellar on a foray for wine for dinner.

Below was a colossal underground depository, and I was amazed that W.R., with his well-known feelings about alcohol, would have laid down such a mammoth supply. We found there thousands upon thousands of dust-covered bottles. Nothing had been cared for, and the contents of bottle after bottle were quite undrinkable, including several cases of 1890 Tokay which looked and tasted like the bottom of San Pedro Harbor.

On New Year's Eve we drank beer and ate hamburgers in the "cottage," and at 10:30 P.M., too depressed to see in the New Year, we went to bed. The next morning the sightseers from their trailers and motels below arrived in buses and started filing through the gardens and reception rooms of La Casa Grande, gaping at the banners and the monks' stalls, nudging each other in their flowered shirts, giggling in the Gothic library, and posing in their ten-gallon hats beside the Neptune pool.

The state park guides seemed to be doing a well-informed job on the history of the place, but not one of them mentioned Marion Davies.

The sea fog slowly seeped up toward the castle. First the flower beds and "cottages" were covered; then the palm trees were no more. For a while the soaring twin towers made ghostly appearances as the cold mist swirled about them. Finally, they, too, were obliterated.

In silence, William Randolph Hearst, Jr., drove us down the road from the Enchanted Hill.

16
Our Little Girl
(Part II)

*L*ET'S pull 'em up and head back," said my companion, a general practitioner from Santa Monica. "It's gettin' late, and nothin' goin' to hit now."

We reeled in our lines, and he gunned the motor; it was four o'clock in the afternoon, and we'd been trolling for marlin since six o'clock in the morning. "Just one of those days, I guess." He sighed. "We might just as well break out the scotch!" We had an hour's run back to Balboa, so we settled ourselves comfortably, glasses in hand. Silence is not an embarrassment between friends, and we sat back contentedly watching the horizon astern thicken to purple as it prepared to receive the great red ball of the sinking sun.

"That's one hell of a profession you've gotten yourself into," said the doctor later with a smile. "D'you think you'll come out OK at the end of it?"

I asked him what he meant. "I have very little contact with people in the film business myself," he said, "but d'you have any idea how many wind up in our hospital as alcoholics, addicts, suicides, attempted suicides, or with breakdowns?"

"Just what I see in the papers," I replied.

"That's only the tip of the iceberg," said the doctor. "It's frightening! A guy at the hospital has written a paper on stress, there's a chapter on what it does to actors; I'll send it along to you."

I told him I hoped that I personally would survive; he laughed and said, "Yes, you probably will, because you're perfectly happy sitting on your ass for ten hours holdin' a rod and not catchin' a fish."

Some weeks passed before I got around to reading about the dire effects of stress in the motion-picture industry. High-powered executives, it appeared, were prone to everything from heart attacks, to hemorrhoids and premature ejaculation. Agents and publicists cornered the market in ulcers, while writers and actors frequently became alcoholics or drug addicts. An alarming number of actresses, the article stated, either killed themselves, attempted to do so, or suffered nervous breakdowns. I was still not reading seriously until the writer provided an up-to-date casualty list starting back in the silent days with Clara Bow, Barbara La Marr and Jeanne Eagels—it was a profoundly disturbing catalogue of collapse, which included the names of many people I knew or had known.

The main point the writer made was that the players most likely to suffer were not the talented "personalities" such as Garbo, Joan Crawford, Bette Davis, Katharine Hepburn, Dietrich, Mae West, or Claudette Colbert, because they would always be able to adjust to the fact that each day everyone becomes twenty-four hours older; the targets for attack were the young, of minimal talent, who had been plucked from obscurity, spoon-fed on publicity, taught how to walk, to talk, to dress; and then how to undress and expose themselves to the world as sex symbols or love goddesses.

The article printed a lurid picture of what could happen to the mind of a female in her late twenties or early thirties who was beginning to realize, after years of adulation and secure in the knowledge that half the male population of the world wanted to sleep with her, that in fact her famous face and curves were showing signs of losing the battle against gravity, and to be told by her studio that her public was tired of her.

That, the writer concluded, would be a traumatic enough experience for anyone, but to have to cope with it in the full glare of publicity in front of millions of people could prove too much. She would have to fall back on her "real" self; if she discovered that her "real" self was absent because it had never existed, then collapse in some form would follow as the night the day. The article on stress went the same way as other sad-ending scenarios because I mentally pushed it aside. Famines in India seemed far away, too.

Three years had passed since I had first met Missie. "He," the boyfriend, had gone to jail for defrauding gullible ladies (including Missie). A third mate had given up the unequal struggle of being married to a sex symbol, and now she was married to a close friend of mine, a cameraman, one of the best in Hollywood, a master of diffused lighting, and in great demand by the female stars. Missie, by now twenty-eight years old Hollywood time (thirty-three Eastern Standard Time), was still a gay, sparkling creature, but according to local gossip, her thickening body was making her exceedingly jealous of her husband's proximity to the most glamorous ladies in the world, and lately, whispers had been filtering back from the South Pacific, where he was photographing an extremely predatory lady. Rumor also had it that the film Missie was currently shooting was a skid picture designed to be the last one at the studio where she had worked for fifteen years but which was now preparing to dump her. She seemed in good spirits when she called to invite me to a small party at her house a few days hence. "Just friends," she said, and she talked rapidly and at great length about its chances of success.

Missie was a meticulous and house-proud hostess, who took endless pains to ensure that her guests were happy and that everything —company, food, drink, and lighting—was as near as possible perfect. True, she was shooting a picture so as a mid-week party we did not expect a late or elaborate affair, but the twenty or thirty guests were a trifle surprised to find on arrival that Missie had ordered no food or made any apparent efforts to accommodate them. She was overly bright and gay and said she was delighted that we had all dropped by, but she still wore the sweater and slacks in which she had returned from work and had not removed her heavy studio makeup. It didn't matter. People disappeared to their houses and came back with ham and eggs, cheese, bread, candles, and a couple of cases of wine; the girls invaded the kitchen and calmed down Mae, the longtime "help"; and with Missie behaving like the most animated of guests, we ended up having a very good time.

As I drove home, I thought back over the evening and decided that Missie must have been high on something. I was perhaps a little surprised, because she habitually drank very little and I had never seen any signs of her taking drugs, but I dismissed it from my mind and went to sleep.

At six o'clock in the morning Mae called me on the telephone.

"Mista David, you git over here *real* quick! . . . Somethin' terrible's happenin' to Missie."

"What?" I asked sleepily.

"She's *possessed*—that's what! . . . You git over here real *quick* now!"

Within twenty minutes I drove up to the little white garden gate and jumped out of the car. Mae was waiting for me. She was shaking. She clutched my arm and repeated over and over, "She's possessed! She's possessed! She's throwed me out! . . . I'm quittin'. . . . I'm quittin'!"

I tried to reassure her, but nothing would persuade her to come back into the house with me, so I took her key and watched her head quickly down the treelined street in the direction of Sunset Boulevard—she never looked back.

It was still dark, and no lights showed in the small house as I quietly let myself in the back door. I didn't know what to expect, so I stood inside the kitchen and called out softly a few times, "Missie, it's David!" There was no answer, then the sound of footsteps above. I pushed the swing door into the hall. Suddenly all the lights went on, and there stood Missie at the top of the stairs. Her hair was hanging down in straggly clumps; the mascara and makeup made a ghastly streaked mask down to her chin; one false eyelash was missing; her eyes were staring and wild. She was naked and looked quite, quite mad.

I had never seen real hysteria before and didn't know how to cope with it. I tried walking up the stairs toward her, but she backed away, screaming, "Go away! Go away! I hate you! . . . Don't touch me!"

When I tried to reason with her, she sat on the landing, alternately sobbing like a child and snarling down at me through the bannisters like a caged animal.

I knew I must get her a doctor, but the very mention of the word brought on the most terrifying reaction. I knew also that she must be overdue at the studio makeup department, and any minute the assistant director would be calling up to find out if she had overslept; above all, I knew that if Missie had cracked up, no word of it must leak out to the press or she'd be finished in Hollywood.

In desperation I tried an offhand approach.

"Look, darling," I said, "you can sit up there on the floor as long as you like, but I'm bored, and I want to watch television."

At that hour of the morning in the early days of TV, there were no programs on the air, but I had a feeling that I must coax her downstairs and try to keep her busy. I switched on the set, which cracked and hummed and displayed nothing but horizontal lines, and settled myself on the sofa to watch them. After a few minutes the stairs behind me creaked, but I did not look around. I could sense that Missie was standing watching me. Then she came shyly into the room, like a child, and curled up on the sofa next to me to watch the blank screen with a funny private smile. We sat there together for a long while. Occasionally she would let out a peal of laughter and point at the set; sometimes she would shrink back in horror; once she screamed with fear and moved up close beside me.

Goosebumps rose on my back.

I put my arm around her naked body to protect her from whatever it was she saw in her poor faraway mind—she was icy cold.

The phone rang in the kitchen. I glanced at my watch. It was only eight o'clock, but I already felt I had been in that house for a lifetime.

Having succeeded, so far, in calming her by playing a game of lies, I continued by saying, "Oh, that's for me. . . . I'll be back in a second."

It was indeed Mac, the assistant director. He was in a highly choleric condition.

"Where the hell is Missie?" he demanded. "She's over two hours late!"

By a great stroke of good luck I had worked with Mac and knew him for one of that priceless breed of true professionals who can guide unsure directors, make life pleasant for actors, and save money for producers. Once he had identified himself, I whispered down the phone.

"Missie is sick, Mac, and it's real trouble, so for her sake don't say a word to anyone except the producer. . . . Who is he?"

Mac mentioned a fairly obscure name and added, "And he's a jerk."

"Tell him to come over right away," I said. "Not to come up to the house, just blow the horn in the street, and I'll come out to him."

I fetched Missie's husband's overcoat from the hall closet and joined her once more before the television set. She snuggled under the coat and clasped my hand. "Isn't she lovely?" she said, pointing at the empty screen. Around nine o'clock I heard the front doorbell ring. Missie was transformed.

"Don't let them in!" she pleaded. "They'll take me away!" I promised that I wouldn't let anyone in if she would be a good little girl and go up to her room and shut the door. I watched her still-gorgeous back view ascend the stairs.

On the doorstep I found a highly strung, fat, youngish man dressed in white slacks and a puce open-neck shirt. His black hair was slicked down, and his eyes were obscured by dark glasses.

"What gives, for chrissakes?" he asked, and before I had time to phrase an answer, he added belligerently, "And how did *you* get into the act?"

I brought Missie's producer up to date and told him that in my opinion she would be unable to report for work for some time.

"Are you screwing her?" he asked. "What the hell do you know about it? . . . You're not her goddamn physician. . . . Where is she? . . . I want to talk with her."

He was prevented from doing this and finally left, having jabbed a finger in my chest and promised to sue me, to call the police, to get me barred from all the studios and to "take care of Missie for fucking up *my* picture."

When he had gone, I found Missie cringing among the shoes at the bottom of her wardrobe.

After another hour of empty television I claimed an urge for a cup of coffee and left Missie reacting to the horizontal flashes while I headed for the kitchen and another whispered phone call, this time to the new head of her studio—a quiet, dignified man I had met only once.

He was light-years ahead of his image-conscious producer.

"The only thing that matters is that girl's health," he said at once. "We'll keep the picture going and wait for her as long as we can; if necessary, we'll recast and reshoot Missie's part, but what about *her?*"

I underlined the urgent need for a doctor, and he instantly agreed to alert my old friend from Santa Monica, whose office, far from Beverly Hills, was unlikely to be infiltrated by gossip columnists' spies, eager for the hot news of an impending abortion, a drying out, or a breakdown. He also promised to locate Missie's husband and get him an immediate message, telling him, from me, in the most urgent but least frightening terms, what had happened to his wife and to urge him to return posthaste. We both agreed it would take him at least three days to make the trip.

Probably from her hours of naked exposure in a drafty house, Missie was coughing intermittently, so I told her that my doctor would be passing by to give me "an injection" and that I'd ask him to check her over at the same time and perhaps recommend something for her cold. To my surprise she agreed without much ado, but when I suggested that she clean up her face for the impending visit, it provoked another screaming spate of abuse: If I didn't think she was beautiful the way she was, why didn't I get the hell out? . . . Who'd invited me anyway? et cetera. After she calmed down, we returned to the television set, and Missie ate some cottage cheese.

The doctor arrived punctually, and I went down to the gate to brief him. He followed me into the house, and when Missie saw him administering my bogus jab, she held my hand during the proceedings. When he turned his attention to her, she babbled incoherently but allowed him to listen to her heart and lungs. He produced a bottle of pills and said to me, "She should take two of these every two hours. . . . She has the beginnings of a nasty infection there. . . . I'll drop by again around six."

Missie had been unnaturally calm during his visit but the storm broke when he asked if she had a girlfriend who could come and sit with her "because you might feel drowsy and you don't want to take a fall."

She suddenly turned on the poor man and started belaboring him and pushing him toward the front door. She yelled and screamed and poured out torrents of abuse on him and on all her girlfriends, naming them one by one, reviling them and accusing them of plotting against her.

When she collapsed with the inevitable tear storm, she sobbed, "David's the only one I trust . . . and he's looking after me."

583

At the doctor's car he said, "There's no question . . . the girl's in big trouble and must go in for psychiatric treatment at once."

The responsibility was being lifted from my shoulders. I was relieved and said so, but he shook his head. "You told me it would be three days before the husband gets here, and by California law the next of kin is the only one who can sign her in. . . . Even I can't do it. Till he gets here, she *must not be left alone* whatever happens. And lock up all the kitchen hardware because she might do anything."

He paused and said kindly, "It's going to be tough on you, but you're the friend of the family, and it looks as though you're stuck. . . . How's the sex thing between you?"

"There isn't any," I said. "There never has been."

He opened the door of his convertible. "She's going to offer it to you," he said. "That's part of the pattern. If you accept, you'll make matters worse, and if you refuse, you'll still make matters worse because she'll feel rejected by the only person she trusts. . . . I don't envy you the next three days."

"What the hell do I do?" I asked. "I've only been here four hours, and I'm already exhausted. . . . I have my own life to lead, too."

"Give her those pills," he said, "and keep in touch with me. Remember, when they're like this, they're very, very cunning. Good luck."

He drove away.

Back in the house the nightmare took its course. First the phone rang, and a voice said, "Hold the line for Miss Louella Parsons, please."

It hadn't taken long; probably a secretary in the fat producer's office had heard him pressing the panic button. Louella's well-known drawl came over the phone. She demanded to speak to Missie.

"She sick," I said, putting on what I hoped was a Filipino houseman's voice. "She sleeping . . . she no come to phone . . . you leave message."

"Tell her to call Louella Parsons as soon as she wakes."

"Yes, ma'am," I said.

"Who was that?" asked Missie when I went back into the television room.

584

"Oh, just Louella," I said offhandedly.

Missie was instantly transformed. "Why don't you want me to speak to Louella?" she yelled. "She probably wants to do a Sunday story on me. . . . You *know* I love Louella." She ran into the kitchen and started looking up the columnist's number. I grabbed the phone from Missie's hands, and a battle royal took place for its possession. She went for my eyes and testicles with fingers like hooked claws, so during the sobbing period that followed the encounter I took the doctor's advice and locked up all the sharp kitchen implements I could find.

The dreadful day dragged on. During the afternoon I finally persuaded her to take two of the doctor's pills, which she had hitherto regarded with the deepest suspicion, but first she wanted to take a walk around the small swimming pool. Stark naked as usual, she paraded about the garden, and I prayed that prying journalistic eyes could not see through the hedge. When the moment to take the pills came, she grabbed the bottle out of my hand and ran off like a naughty child, hid it behind her back, and demanded a kiss in exchange for it. This payment having been extracted, she deliberately emptied the contents of the bottle into the deep end of the pool.

The doctor paid his second visit, and Missie refused to let him inside the house, saying he was one of "Them." I managed to have a few words with him in the garden.

"I'll get you some more pills," he said, and showed me where he would leave them by the gate. "They're strong sedatives; it'll make your life much easier if she'll take them. . . . Is she eating anything?"

"Only cottage cheese," I told him.

"Try pounding them up and mixing them in there," he suggested. "Is she drinking?"

"She asks for a glass of wine now and then . . . is that bad?"

"Any stimulant is bad, of course, but don't refuse it—water it down."

He gave me news from the head of Missie's studio. "I'm in contact with him; he sounds like a good guy. He said to tell you that the husband is on his way. He's due in eight o'clock Sunday morning."

My heart sank—it was only Thursday evening.

585

"He said to tell you that he's put out a press release that she's in bed with a virus infection under doctor's care . . . good luck, Doctor!" He added with a smile, "Try to get a couple of those pills into her stomach, and take the phone off the hook."

Missie made the offer the doctor had predicted during our first night together.

"I've something for you," she said seductively, and ran upstairs, giggling.

Half an hour later she called down. Her face was cleaned at last, her makeup redone, her hair brushed and falling in a golden cloud over her shoulders, and she was wearing a short black see-through nightie. She looked lovely.

"Come and get it," she whispered from the top of the stairs, turning her back in a parody of sexiness and lifting the hem of the nightie. It was not an easy evening for me, to put it mildly, and it ended in a glass- and bottle-throwing scene with Missie ordering me out of the house, an instruction I longed to, but dared not, obey.

The pills did not seem to have much effect on Missie. Around midnight she ate some cottage cheese which contained a couple and drank some wine into which I had stirred a third, but they slowed her down for only an hour or two; then she was as bright and demanding and as terrifyingly unpredictable as before. I dared not go to sleep for five minutes, and as the long days and interminable nights melded into each other, a dreadful thought began to assail me—that it was not Missie whose mind had become deranged . . . it was mine. I became a hollow-eyed zombie, sleepless and utterly exhausted, but Missie never showed any signs of tiredness and harried me endlessly to play hide-and-seek with her, to flatter her, to comfort her, to fight with her, or to go to bed with her.

I found I had come to hate her.

Twice a day the doctor met me in the garden to give me news of the husband's progress and to inject me with floods of B_{12} to keep me going. By Saturday evening I could go no further.

"I can't make it through tonight," I told him. "The plane's on time . . . he arrives tomorrow morning. For God's sake give her a jab and put her out so that I can *sleep*. . . . *I can't go on*."

He looked at me carefully for a long time. "It's completely illegal," he said, "but OK, I'll do it."

He outlined the plan. I was to leave the front door open, and at nine o'clock exactly he would slip in with a trained nurse, who, he said, would act as a witness, help with the injection, and also stay the night to take care of Missie when she came around. The two of them would hide in the downstairs bathroom; then, on some pretext, I would coax her into the hall, grab her, throw her on the ground, and hold her down while the deed was done.

"It's going to be very rough," he said, "and God knows I hate to do it—but it's the only way."

Missie seemed to sense that something was going to happen. For the first time her eyes lost their wild look; she seemed calm, almost normal and very vulnerable. She followed me wherever I went. Also, for the first time, she talked about her husband. She had not mentioned him once during the whole time I had been with her. "I hope he comes to see me," she said sadly.

It was eerie.

A few minutes before nine o'clock I told her I was hungry and asked her to come help me fix a sandwich. She left her favorite place in front of the television set and put her hand trustingly and childlike in mine. As we passed through the hall into the kitchen, I caught a glimpse through the curtains of the doctor's darkened car at the gate.

We puttered about in the kitchen, and I received another reminder of the premonition that had awakened within my charge. Suddenly Missie said, "You won't let them take me away, will you?"

For a moment I thought she too might have seen the car.

"Who?" I asked.

"Oh!" she said mysteriously. "*They* will be coming for me one day. . . . They want to take me away, but you won't let them, will you?"

"Of course not," I said, loathing every second of the dreadful charade that was unfolding. Slowly I ate my sandwich.

When I judged that sufficient time had elapsed for my co-conspirators to be in position and ready, I took Missie's trusting hand in mine and led her into the hall; a chink of light showed from beneath the bathroom door. Clumsily I spun the poor naked girl around, hooked one leg behind her knees, and flung her to the ground.

After a first startled gasp she fought with incredible ferocity and strength. She didn't scream; she was spitting like a panther, biting, clawing, and kicking. I finally managed to spread-eagle her on the floor and to pinion her arms by kneeling on the elbow joints. I yelled for the doctor.

When she saw two strange forms approaching, one in white uniform and the other bearing a hypodermic syringe, Missie screamed at last, long, piercing notes of pure animal terror.

"They've *come!* They've *come!*"

The nurse held Missie's feet, and between us we controlled her convulsive struggles while the doctor did his work.

It was soon over, and as she began to calm down I avoided her eyes, filled as they were with such blazing hatred at my base betrayal.

Later, when we carried her to bed, her face was as innocent and as peaceful as a baby's.

The nurse cleaned up my many bites and scratches, and the doctor gave me something that would enable me to go to sleep at last. None of us spoke.

At six o'clock the next day, refreshed, but with a leaden conscience and a three-day growth of beard, I drove, on my way to the airport, through the peaceful emptiness of the early-morning streets.

A few kids were already abroad, experimenting with brightly colored bikes, and some early risers in curlers and bedroom slippers were retrieving carelessly delivered Sunday papers from beneath bushes in their front gardens.

I felt as though I had returned from far, far away.

> To gild refined gold, to paint the lily,
> To throw a perfume on the violet,
> To smooth the ice, or add another hue
> Unto the rainbow, or with taper-light
> To seek the beauteous eye of heaven to garnish,
> Is wasteful and ridiculous excess.
>
> —WILLIAM SHAKESPEARE

17
Long Shots and Close-Ups

CARY

*I*T is very easy to write about Cary Grant's pedigree as an actor, to enthuse over the way he comported himself as a great star, and to be amazed at the extraordinary composure he displayed on the screen—appearing utterly relaxed and therefore, like a magnet, drawing the eye of the beholder—but it is another thing altogether to try to describe Cary, the private individual, because he was a will-o'-the-wisp.

Enthusiasm was a most important ingredient in Cary's makeup, and it shone out of that side of his character which he presented to his friends; the other side was as mysterious as the dark side of the moon. Cary's enthusiasm made him search for perfection in all things, particularly in the three that meant most to him: filmmaking; physical fitness; and women.

He found it without too much difficulty in the first two categories, becoming a perfectionist in his work and a living monument to bodily health, but in the third group he struck a few snags. He passed rapidly through his marriages to Virginia Cherrill, Barbara Hutton, and Betsy Drake and filled in the lonely gaps between them by falling in and out of love with most of his leading ladies, which, as his output of films was prodigious, underlined the excellence of his physical condition.

"The trick," he said, "is to be relaxed. If you can attain true relaxation, you can make love forever." This was heady advice, but it seemed odd coming from the mouth of one who freely admitted that from the age of twelve when he had run away from school to join an acrobatic troupe, he had been searching for peace within himself. When I say Cary attacked his amours with enthusiasm, I don't mean to conjure up a picture of him in an executioner's outfit, advancing purposefully with a rawhide whip; he was gentle and thoughtful, and they all loved him dearly, but he went headfirst into the affrays, throwing caution to the winds and quite convinced, in his boundless enthusiasm, that each romance was the one for which he had been put into the world. If his disillusionments were many, his defeats were few, and he always, with great gallantry, took the blame when things went wrong, saying that he had been too egocentric to give the union a proper chance.

He showed great resilience when things didn't work out, his recipe being "to stay within the pattern" and to try again with another lady of much the same physical appearance as the last. When he met the earthy Sophia Loren during the shooting of her first Hollywood picture, Cary took unto himself the role of "patron" and taught her carefully how to pick the most rewarding path through the Hollywood jungle. He often proclaimed that while doing this, he had fallen in love with her, but if so, he got over it with typical alacrity when Sophia, not the least ambitious of actresses, suddenly announced that she was marrying her portly producer, Carlo Ponti. Upon receipt of this news Cary allowed no grass to grow under his feet. He "followed the pattern" and was off like a flash in a gypsy caravan with a younger and more voluptuous edition of Sophia—a bouncing lady called Luba, a Yugoslav basketball player.

The first day that Cary, the perfectionist, walked into my house, he went immediately into high gear. He pursed his lips, made clucking noises, and set about straightening the pictures. Through the years to come he made generous efforts to straighten out my private life by warning me of the quirks and peculiarities of various ladies, by giving me complicated advice on how to play a part in a film I was making with him, by telling me which stocks to buy when I could not afford a phone call to a broker, and by promising that he could cure my liking for scotch by hypnotizing me. These offers of help were spontaneous and genuine, and if they did not noticeably improve my shortcomings, they did at least help me perceive that if Cary spent a great deal of his time worrying about himself, he spent much more worrying about others.

His was a restless soul. He changed houses the way most of us changed agents—without a backward glance—and long before computers went into general release, Cary had one in his own brain. A brilliant businessman himself, he was fascinated by the very rich and the ultrasuccessful and was in his element in the company of Howard Hughes, Onassis, Kirkorian, Hearst, and assorted tycoons.

His perfectionist urge with regard to his own body was nothing short of mystical. He invariably looked, moved, and behaved like a man fifteen or twenty years his junior. "I just *think* myself thin—and it happens," he was fond of saying, but he conveniently forgot his frugal eating, his daily workouts, and his appointments with the masseur.

Early one morning at his Palm Springs hideaway (he was passing through his Desert Period at the time), I heard loud commands followed by hideous grunts and splashing. Cary was taking lessons in how to swim the crawl. "Why lessons?" I asked sleepily from my bedroom window. "You swim the crawl beautifully—I've seen you do it for years."

"I want to do it *perfectly*," he gurgled, and plowed on.

During the same period Cary, who had seldom thrown a leg over a horse, invested in a white stallion and a beautifully cut riding outfit of black Levi's, discreetly decorated with small silver stars, and within an incredibly short space of time he was a Valkyrie, galloping about the dunes with great panache and perfect control.

Anyone as silhouette-conscious as Cary was bound, sooner or later, to go through a health food period, and some of us suffered stoically through his Days of the Carrot. A vast clanking machine was installed in his kitchen, shaped like the mouth of a great white shark.

"Today we'll have nothing but carrot juice," Cary announced, and emptied a couple of sacks of roots into its gaping maw. Fearful throbbings and crunchings followed us into the garden, where we were given a preluncheon cocktail of buttermilk, wheat germ, and molasses. When the sinister sounds died down, we reentered the house to find that the machine had gone berserk and had redecorated the kitchen from top to bottom; walls, windows, ceiling, and linoleum flooring were covered with a fibrous yellow paste.

Cary's exercises in hypnotism were less messy, and he certainly cured himself of smoking by saying over and over for weeks, "Your fingers are yellow, your breath smells, and you only smoke because you are insecure." He also claimed that he had cured a nasty slash on his back collected in a film duel by applying oxygen to the affected area and commanding his lungs to dissolve the useless tissues. This so impressed us that before long we were lying like stranded tuna on his drawing-room carpet, waiting for him to bring us around.

Betsy, Cary's third wife, had a very unattractive experience after visiting him on location in Spain. She booked on a luxury liner to return to America, and when she landed in New York, she was badly in need of therapy to help her forget her trip. The name of her ship had been *Andrea Doria*.

Betsy spent a great deal of time with a Dr. Mortimer Hartman, who gave her a series of treatments which included doses of LSD. Betsy then reported that she was completely released from her haunting memories of the liner settling beneath her feet but said she now had the feeling that it was time she scuttled Cary—which she did. Cary, to whom the unknown was an irresistible challenge, promptly registered himself with Dr. Hartman and spent many weeks contentedly munching LSD, listening to music, and baring his soul. Apparently, it was a most salutary experience, sometimes joyful, sometimes shattering, but he persevered until he could announce to his spellbound friends, who were half envious and half horrified by what he had willingly subjected himself to, that he was a totally new man, cleansed and purged of all inhibitions, with a subconscious which could no longer cause him any problems.

"All actors long to be loved," he said. "That's why we become actors . . . but I don't give a damn anymore. . . . I'm self-sufficient *at last!*"

It seemed to the rest of us a most hazardous trip for Cary to have taken to find out what we could have told him anyway: that he had always been self-sufficient, that he had always been loved, and that he would continue to give a damn about himself—and particularly about others.

GEORGE

If Cary Grant was an optimist then George Sanders was the opposite, and he genuinely harbored all the cynicism he so joyfully displayed.

Russian-born George, a giant grizzly of a man, had a face, even in his twenties, which looked as though he had rented it on a long lease and had lived in it so long he didn't want to move out. He was a highly undervalued actor probably because he didn't give a damn whether or not his efforts were appreciated. "I don't ask questions," he said. "I just take their money and use it for things that *really* interest me."

As early as 1937, when we were working on a John Ford picture together, he said, "I will have had enough of this earth by the time I am sixty-five. After that I shall be having my bottom wiped by nurses and being pushed around in a wheelchair. I won't be able to enjoy a woman anymore, so I shall commit suicide."

I don't remember George's ever taking any exercise. He would show up immaculately dressed and watch the rest of us playing tennis or would sit comfortably near the eighteenth green till we finished playing golf and would throw up his hands in horror at any suggestion that he might like to take a walk along the beach.

His reaction to war service was one of instant repulsion, and he never modified it. "The stupidest thing young men can do is to throw away their youth, as Thomas Carlyle said, 'With clenched teeth and hell fire eyes hacking one another's flesh.' They'll never get me to do it." And they never did. "I shall keep ahead of the sheriff," he announced. "Luckily I hold three passports—Russian, American, and British. I shall play one off against the other till they either give up or order me to do something. Then I shall immediately become a Quaker, and if they tell me to drive an ambulance, I shall crash so many learning how to drive that they'll send me home."

George did, however, try to make a tongue-in-cheek contribution to World War II. In 1943 he forwarded to Washington a detailed suggestion for the organization and administration of an infantry battalion equipped with roller skates. He enclosed a graph of gradients and the estimated attack speeds of troops along main roads. To me, in England, around the same time, he sent an envelope "To be forwarded instantly to Winston Churchill." It contained the specification of an attachment to be clamped to the nose cone of RAF bombs. On their way earthward, he claimed, they would sound the German all-clear and the ensuing disaster among those issuing from their shelters would add "a gratifying bonus in casualties."

George suffered bouts of black oppression which his friends dismissed as "another of his Russian moods," but when they were on him, he was inconsolable. He was a loner and would often disappear for days on end into his beautifully equipped workshop; several strange but very clever inventions awaited patents as a result.

Women were fascinated by George, and before Zsa Zsa Gabor decided to become a caricature of her real self, the two of them made a fascinating couple. She enjoyed and encouraged his peculiar outlook on life and his sometimes outrageous utterances; he was fascinated by her very great beauty and her vivacity. No mean hand with an acid quip herself, Zsa Zsa once told me that she and Conrad Hilton, her millionaire ex-husband, "only had one thing in common . . . *his* money."

When Zsa Zsa "left" George, she somehow contrived to stay on in their Bel Air home facing the fifteenth fairway of the Country Club and took in as a houseguest "the great Parisian lover" himself —Porfirio Rubirosa. If this infuriated George, he gave little sign of it, but it certainly awakened him to the very grave financial dangers of the California divorce laws.

"This is no time to behave like a gentleman," said George. "I am a cad and shall react like one."

On a misty evening in late December with the surrounding hills twinkling with half a hundred illuminated Christmas trees, George left his car near the fifteenth green and set off up the fairway. He was accompanied by his lawyer and a man with a big black camera.

The lawyer and the photographer carried a ladder. George carried a brick.

The plan was simple. The french windows of the master bedroom, in which George was convinced action sooner or later would be taking place, overlooked the golf course. The french windows opened onto a veranda. Bedroom and veranda were on the first floor—hence the ladder.

Once inside the room, George had every reason to believe he would find his wife in bed with Rubirosa—hence the camera.

But, George reasoned, the french windows might well be locked —hence the brick.

The lawyer, with the caution of his ilk, was worried that police might intercept their cortege and ask embarrassing questions. "Certainly," he said, "there's not a reason on earth why a householder shouldn't enter his house by ladder if he so desires, but a brick could be construed as an offensive weapon. . . . I'm worried about that brick."

George had a brainwave. "I'm bringing my wife a present on Christmas Eve," he said. "So we gift-wrap the brick."

The operation, according to George, went without a hitch. When the signs were that the big double bed above was working overtime, the ladder was placed in position and the assault was mounted, but Zsa Zsa, an unwitting fifth columnist, had forgotten to lock the window, and the brick became redundant.

Zsa Zsa and Rubirosa, their eyes wide with apprehension and dazzled by flashbulbs, were photographed clutching the sheets to their chins; then, like two plump partridges, they broke from the undergrowth and scuttled for the bathroom.

George and his henchmen waited, but the culprits, in a sudden burst of modesty, refused to come out again because there was only one towel. At last matters were arranged, dressing gowns were permitted, and the whole party descended the stairs in an embarrassed silence. Hesitant farewells were being made when Zsa Zsa, with a flash of great style, said, "Oh, George darling. . . . I almost forgot, I have a gift for you under the tree!"

To which George could not resist replying, "And I have a gift for *you*," and he handed her the brick.

The calmest time of George Sanders' life was during his marriage to Benita, Ronald Colman's beautiful widow.

The most understanding and generous-hearted of women, Benita encouraged George's inventions and eccentric ways, applauded his excellent screen performances, survived the soaring arias and Wagnerian bellowings that blared permanently from his homemade hi-fi, and even invested heavily in his manufacturing company, named Cad Co. The company went down to defeat quixotically trying to make English sausages in Scotland filled with Italian meat.

George was not a man endowed with optimism and hope, so when Benita died, he became daily more cynical and disillusioned, and at the age of sixty-five, he did what he had always promised he would do: He took his own life.

Ernst Lubitsch

Ernst Lubitsch was a pixie. There were three or four master directors in Hollywood in the thirties and forties, men for whom the biggest stars in the world tripped over each other in their anxiety to be invited to work. Ernst Lubitsch was the master's master. For a big established star to perform for Lubitsch was the sign that a career had reached its zenith, and for a beginner to be cast in a Lubitsch picture was notification that a new career was off to the most promising of starts.

One day in 1936 the "producers' producer" called me in to his office. I had lately been signed by him to a long-term beginners' contract, and I held him in such awe that if he had said, "I have cast you as a performing dog," I would have rushed out and taken barking and hoop-jumping lessons. The great Samuel Goldwyn looked at me unsmilingly out of his small, deepset eyes. "You are a very lucky young man," he said.

I nodded in agreement.

"But you don't know it," he added.

I nodded again.

"I have just loaned you to Ernst Lubitsch for *Bluebeard's Eighth Wife*. Report to Paramount Studios tomorrow. Keep your ears open and your mouth shut, and put yourself in Ernst's hands—they're the best in Hollywood."

Tottering on legs made rubbery by my unbelievable good fortune, I made my way to the office of Reeves Espy, the calm and considerate right hand of the volcanic Mr. Goldwyn.

"This is a real break for you," said Espy. "I've read the script—it's written by Billy Wilder and Charlie Brackett—it's marvelous, and your part is *great!*"

"What is it?" I asked breathlessly.

"Secretary to Mr. Brandon," said Espy.

"Who's Mr. Brandon?"

"Gary Cooper," said Espy, "and you're also in love with his girl."

"Who's his girl?"

"Claudette Colbert—and they both get to beat you up. . . . It's a very sympathetic role."

What a bonanza! An unknown beginner to be directed by Lubitsch, in a script by Wilder and Brackett, and to play with Paramount's two superstars, Gary Cooper and Claudette Colbert, and to be beaten up by both of them!

The next morning, shining like a new pin, I checked in at the Paramount lot, was handed the key to a dressing room and given a script.

"Read it right away, David," advised the casting director, "then about eleven go over to Ernst's office—he wants to meet you and talk to you about wardrobe et cetera."

By eleven o'clock I was in poor shape. The part was indeed beautifully written, but I was quite convinced that I could never play it.

Lubitsch was a tiny man, with a heavy German accent, straight black hair slicked down, twinkling black eyes, and a cigar out of all proportion to the ensemble. When I walked into his office, he was in shirtsleeves with heavy suspenders supporting his pants. He rose from behind his desk and greeted me with both hands outstretched and a slice of blatantly overdone flattery.

"This is indeed a pleasure." He beamed. "We are so lucky to get you for this part! Now before we sit down," he said, "would you mind dropping your trousers?"

"I beg your pardon?" I said nervously.

Gales of laughter swept over the little man. "Don't worry." He chortled. "I have a very beautiful wife! But I have to see your legs, because your opening scene is on the beach with Claudette. If you have strong legs, there will be no problem, but if you have twigs like mine, we'll have to rework the scene so you can wear slacks."

I dropped my pants, and he pronounced himself satisfied. "Good"—he nodded—"like a Bavarian bullock."

Then he sat me down on a sofa and proceeded to act out all my scenes, giggling and hugging himself as he explained the visual business he was intending to incorporate into them, and the more he gesticulated and pranced about, the more convinced did I become that I did not have the equipment or the training to deliver to him that which he obviously thought was his for the asking.

Finally, sensing that I was holding something back, Lubitsch asked me what was the matter.

"I don't think I can do it, Mr. Lubitsch," I mumbled.

He looked at me, and his eyes shone with merriment. "Do I frighten you?" he asked.

"No, sir," I said, "but I'm terrified of Gary Cooper and Claudette Colbert. . . ."

He jumped up and hooted with laughter.

"Do you know something?" He chortled. "Claudette is frightened of Coop because of his natural acting, and Coop is frightened of Claudette because she's so expert and this is his first comedy, and both of them are scared out of their wits by the small-part players Edward Everett Horton, Franklin Pangborn and Herman Bing, because they are supposed to be scene stealers . . . but d'you know who is the most frightened of all? . . . Me!"

He put his arm around my waist (because he could not reach my shoulders) and led me to the door.

"Everyone will be nervous on the first day," he said, "even the electricians in case they set fire to the studio, but we're all going to be together for many weeks, and I promise you it'll be fun. Now run along to wardrobe and makeup, they have some fittings and tests set up for you. . . . Drop in to see me anytime. . . . We don't start for two weeks—you're a member of the family now!"

I couldn't wait to start.

When Ernst Lubitsch described us as his family, it was no understatement, and we all had complete respect for the father figure. I never once heard him raise his voice, and he loved to be given suggestions, listened patiently to them, and then just as patiently explained why they wouldn't work.

Billy Wilder, the future master director, was constantly on the set, and there was obviously a great rapport between him and Lubitsch: he may even then have set his sights on directing, because he was unfailingly understanding and appreciative with the actors, a nice change from many writers who winced painfully as their golden words fell from the performers' mouths.

Lubitsch took infinite pains with everyone, especially with me, the novice, and for several days before I started work, he ordered me to be on the set so that I could get to know everyone and feel at home.

"I don't know what I'm going to do about Gary." He chuckled. "He's just *too* relaxed!"

Cooper had ambled onto the set in a crumpled flannel suit.

"Just look at him!" said Lubitsch. "It's the first time he's played a comedy, and we had that business-tycoon suit made by Eddie Schmidt, but he still thinks he's a cowhand. Where've you been, Gary?" he asked conversationally.

"I just grabbed me a little shut-eye on that pile of straw back there on Stage Six," drawled the tall man from Montana.

Lubitsch sent for Slim, Cooper's gangling stand-in, and Cracker, his small devoted dresser from Georgia.

"Now you two!" He giggled. "Coop is playing a business tycoon on holiday in Cannes, France, his wardrobe is very elegant, and he has to be stopped going to sleep in it every time he finishes a scene, so get him out of that suit and into pajamas, then have it pressed *again!*"

Gary Cooper was no poseur—he was exactly what he seemed, a charming, slow-talking, gentle country boy who loved animals and open air and avoided problems—but he was also a phenomenal natural actor with spectacular good looks and a great sense of timing. I was fascinated by the way he "thought" on the screen, and during a lull when we were shooting a scene together, I asked him about this.

"You have such great concentration," I said. "How do you do it?"

Coop looked genuinely startled. "Concentration?" he said

slowly. "Bullshit! I'm just tryin' to remember what the hell I have to say next!"

My first big scene was indeed on the beach with Claudette Colbert—outside the Carlton Hotel, Cannes (where Brigitte Bardot was later discovered by a photographer, and a naked starlet by Robert Mitchum). It was simulated by dumping a few truckloads of sand inside Stage 4, and gaudy umbrellas above bronzed extras completed the illusion. The scene was a long one, and the comedy content was delicate. Claudette and "Bullock Legs" were in swimsuits, and the sun arcs blazed down from on high. Claudette, the soul of enchanting fun and a most generous performer, did all she could to calm my twittering nerves, but she made things a little difficult for the cameraman because, convinced that it was her best side, she insisted that she be photographed only on the left side of her face. Many stars harbored the same beliefs and specified in their contracts which one could be presented to the camera.

Lubitsch perched himself atop a small stepladder at the side of the camera, the inevitable howitzer-type cigar in his mouth. He rehearsed us carefully and finally said, "Let's shoot it!" Very conscious of the fifty or so bronzed extras (all would-be stars), I was about as relaxed as a bulldozer, but Claudette patted my knee and whispered, "It's going to be great." We started the comedy scene, and I noticed that Lubitsch was crying.

"Cut!" he sobbed helplessly at the end. "That was *wonderful!* You made me laugh so much I nearly choked! . . . Now, just a couple of little suggestions. . . ."

We absorbed them eagerly, and he clambered back up his stepladder. "Action!" he commanded. Again we played the scene, and again Lubitsch wept.

"Wonderful! Wonderful! *How* you made me laugh! . . . Now just a couple of little suggestions. . . ."

We probably played the scene a dozen times, each time our efforts were saluted by paroxysms of mirth from the master director, and each time he managed to blurt out "a couple of little suggestions" before climbing back onto his perch. By the time we had performed the scene to his complete satisfaction we had, of course, like many before us, given performances of "pure Lubitsch," and as Claudette pointed out, "And why not? . . . He's better than any of us!"

John Huston

All the directors had their little idiosyncrasies. Lubitsch had his cigar and his stepladder. John Ford sat beneath the camera chewing the corner of a grubby white handkerchief. Michael Curtiz strode about wearing breeches and riding boots and brandishing a fly whisk. William Wyler liked to make anything up to forty takes and then print the first. Otto Preminger seemed to enjoy working in an atmosphere of tension, and generated it by screaming loudly at people. Henry Hathaway objected to chairs on the set for actors—"I'm on *my* feet all day . . . they should be on theirs." W. S. Van Dyke chain-sipped gin out of paper cups, and Bill Seiter, who specialized in comedies, employed a goosing stick on the touchy bottoms of the unsuspecting—a long cane on the end of which was clenched a plaster fist with the second finger rudely extended.

Of the master directors (Ford and Wyler were also on everybody's list) the most relaxed, with his poet's heart and misleading broken boxer's face, was John Huston. "Let's just kick it around, kids," he would say to his actors, and from their first natural and tentative playing and thereafter through many rehearsals, he would build up a scene piece by piece till he was satisfied; then he would invite the cameraman to watch a run-through. "That's it," Huston would say. "Now go ahead and light it." While that was being done, he would wash all problems from his mind by settling down with a box of panatelas and a good book.

I first met John in 1935 when he was a scriptwriter at the Samuel Goldwyn Studios; his father, Walter, a monumental actor, was playing the name part in the film of *Dodsworth*, directed by William Wyler. I was playing a small part in the picture, and John was constantly on the set. In spite of his many great directorial successes there, John never fully settled for the Hollywood way of life and found his ultimate happiness with a home in Southern Ireland, leaping fearlessly over jagged stone walls as Master of the Galway Blazers Fox Hounds. He once made a tentative stab at living in Hollywood and moved into a house near Clark Gable's in the San Fernando Valley. It was a revolutionary structure consisting almost entirely of glass with some necessary beams and supports of redwood. John lived inside this bizarre cage with an extremely beautiful wife and a very ugly monkey. History does not relate where the monkey came from, but John persuaded delicious Evelyn Keyes to join him during a long dinner at Romanoff's Restaurant. They flew that night to Las Vegas to get married after Mike Romanoff had first bustled off to his house and retrieved a wedding ring which had fallen off somebody's finger into his swimming pool. Evelyn was a highly intelligent girl, and for a while great happiness reigned, interrupted admittedly by the gibberings and shrieks of the monkey.

Only those involved can ever know what tensions have pulled apart a marriage, and John maintained a gentlemanly silence when he and Evelyn finally called it quits. Evelyn, too, had nothing but the deepest affection and respect for John, and they remained firm friends. Evelyn enjoyed relating the final scene before they went their separate ways:

EVELYN: John, darling, I'm sorry. One of us has to go. . . . It's the monkey or me.
JOHN: (after long pause) Honey . . . it's you!

During World War II John Huston headed a particularly gallant photographic unit and became a familiar figure among front-line troops at Monte Cassino and other Italian battlefields, puffing away at his panatelas and calmly photographing the moments of maximum danger.

The war over, John returned to the United States and was there when I arrived aboard the *Queen Mary* with 15,000 joyful fighting men, mostly of the 101st Airborne Division. We were welcomed by several bands and a posse of beautiful Powers models, whose cover-girl smiles froze on their faces when the returning warriors released several hundred fully inflated condoms from the boat deck far above their heads. During drinks that evening at Jack and Charlie's, I reconstructed for John's benefit the spectacle of coveys of flying French letters eddying about the clifflike sides of the giant Cunarder, and he was moved to quote the observation of a Parisienne countess of the eighteenth century upon her first view of one of those well-intentioned envelopes: "A battlement against enjoyment, and a fishnet against infection." The conversation having taken such a soldierly turn, I was not surprised to hear John say, "While we've been away, they've opened the greatest whorehouse right here in New York, better than anything in Rome or Paris—what d'you say we go take a look at it?"

I shook my head like a bishop finding a fly button in the collection. "No, thanks—I'm a happily married man these days."

"Oh, come on!" said Huston. "You don't have to *do* anything. . . . Just come and case the joint, then we'll take the madam out for dinner—she's a lot of laughs."

I was hungry, so after John had made a phone call, we set off. The house on Park Avenue had a most imposing façade. John pressed the bell, and a saucy-looking maid opened the door and took our coats. "Good evening, Mr. Huston." She smiled. "May I get you a drink while you're waiting?" Huston ordered a scotch, and I did the same. The maid served us the drinks in an attractively decorated drawing room, and John pointed casually to a Monet on the wall.

"Of course this is a clip joint on a big scale," he explained. "The madam has the greatest girls in New York, all shapes and colors, and anything goes, but boy, does she charge for it!"

"I'll bet," I said, "but even so—a Monet!"

"Well," said Huston, lighting up one of his smokes, "she has some old guy for herself who collects paintings, and she screws an occasional Impressionist out of the poor bastard—she has a dandy Braque right over her bed . . . it leaves marks on the wall as it swings!"

After a while the madam, very petite, beautifully dressed, and bejeweled, descended the stairs and walked into the room. John rose, kissed her hand, and introduced me.

"I'm so glad you could join us," she said in a charming voice. "John is an old friend, and he's told me so much about you."

"Well," I said, "I don't really want any action tonight, I just came to take a look at the place. . . . Where are the girls . . . all upstairs banging their brains out?"

The madam looked mystified, and Huston, like a canary-swallowing cat, smugly broke the news to me that she was in fact Nin Ryan, the most elegant society hostess in New York City.

John, the director, was famous for being easy and thoughtful with his actors; as a writer he was famous for being easy and thoughtful with his directors, and as an actor (he was an excellent performer when the spirit moved him) he was the soul of discretion in his relationships with one and all. A paragon of all virtues, so it seemed, but when the smoke of his panatelas cleared away, it was invariably found that John had quietly achieved whatever he had been striving for, no matter which hat he had been wearing. He even ended up with Jack Warner of Warner Brothers eating out of his hand.

JACK WARNER

Loud, gregarious, flashy, wisecracking Jack Warner, with· his slicked-down hair and carefully plucked pencil-thin mustache, was the prototype of the Hollywood mogul. The son of a cobbler in Lynchburg, Virginia, he and his brothers were delighted when their father diversified by becoming a butcher, and they hacked happily away at the remains of dead animals, "counting," as Jack liked to say, "their thumbs along with the purchases." He freely admitted that he was a frustrated actor, and his after-dinner speeches were so long and so corny that Jack Benny was moved to remark, "Jack would rather tell a bad joke than make a good movie." Jack Warner had early worked off some of his actor urge by using the stage name of Leon Zuardo and singing in vaudeville as a boy soprano, but he listened to the advice of one of his older brothers, who said, "Don't *be* an actor. . . . *Pay* actors—the money is where the customers are."

Later, as head of production, Jack amassed a reputation as the most unbending employer of talent in Hollywood. "I pay 'em— they do what I tell 'em," he said, and conducted through the years epic running battles with most of his stars, including Flynn, Bogart, Bette Davis, and Paul Muni. When Lauren Bacall questioned his ability to handle her career, she was led to the window of his office and invited to contemplate the sprawling, humming, thriving acreage of the studio below. "Would all *that* be there," Warner inquired, "if I didn't know what the fuck I was doing?"

The Warner Brothers Studio buzzed with frustrations, which tended to be ventilated late in the day, and long after shooting had finished, cries of rage, threats of vengeance, and the sounds of rebellion issued from offices, bungalows, and dressing rooms.

Afternoon tea on the set became a popular feature while I was making a picture there with Jane Wyman. Toward the end of the day we made it a point to invite friends from nearby sound stages to drop over and join us at the charming ritual. I handed around little cakes while Jane from a large Rockingham teapot dispensed lethal dry martinis, and our Warner-contracted guests obtained an extra charge from these clandestine sips, from the knowledge that they were enjoyed on Jack Warner's time.

Jack Warner lived the way a movie mogul was supposed to live: He was a generous host, a big gambler at work and at play, and with supreme confidence he put his money where his mouth was. In his spare time he became a well-known figure in the casinos, harbors, and other playgrounds of the Mediterranean, and entertained at his sumptuous estate in Beverly Hills with splendid abandon, but at his studio, efficiency and closely watched budgets were the watchwords. His writers were encouraged to get up early, read the papers, and then produce screenplays based on what they had read, and his actors were advised to accept the roles they were assigned without argument, to take the money and be grateful.

Many felt that his highly publicized wars with his stars were the outward signs of Jack Warner's unfulfilled inner longings to be a star himself, but one thing was sure: He never practiced discrimination, and he fought with equal gusto against producers, directors, writers, and agents.

Cecil B. DeMille

If Jack Warner was the militant mogul, Cecil B. DeMille, the man who "discovered" Hollywood, was the prototype producer-director. Also a onetime actor, he was the possessor of a beautifully modulated speaking voice and a very definite set of principles.

Long after he had become world-famous with his superspectaculars, such as *The Sign of the Cross, Cleopatra, The Crusades,*

The King of Kings, Samson and Delilah, The Greatest Show on Earth, and *The Ten Commandments,* he voluntarily gave up, for a principle, a yearly salary of more than $100,000 which he could have continued to collect by paying just $1.

DeMille's epic career at Paramount had started when he persuaded the heads of the studio that they could no longer afford to pay the mountainous salary demanded by the queen of the box office—Mary Pickford (known to an adoring public as America's Sweetheart and to the heads of the studio as the Bank of America's Sweetheart).

"Let her go," DeMille had counseled, "and give the money to me. I'll make big pictures for you with small names, and when the small names get too big, I'll let *them* go."

It worked, and then, in 1936, as a sideline, DeMille, fascinated with radio, became producer of the *Lux Radio Theater.* Every Sunday evening thereafter for the next nine years his pear-shaped tones announced, "Greetings from Hollywood," and 40,000,000 listeners settled back and prepared to enjoy one of the most popular shows on the air.

In order to perform on radio, DeMille had long since joined the American Federation of Radio Artists, but in late 1944, around the time that American soldiers were producing their own superspectacular at the Battle of the Bulge, DeMille was informed by the AFRA that all members of the union were being assessed $1 for a fund to fight an amendment to a California law. DeMille saw the law in question as one which preserved the freedom of workers to decide whether or not they wished to join a union, he refused on principle to be ordered to subscribe toward altering it, and his "nuts" to AFRA shared the headlines with General McAuliffe's famous reply to the German High Command when he was invited to surrender Bastogne.

General McAuliffe won the Battle of Bastogne, but DeMille lost his with AFRA, and the most prestigious producer in radio was prevented from working by his union.

Watching DeMille direct a film crowd was a spectacular in itself. I was one of a thousand extras naked except for a loincloth, and as I was being constantly belabored with special "hurt-proof" whips, I gathered that I was a slave and the film was probably *Cleopatra.* (Extras focusing on the $2.50 they would be paid for their efforts seldom bothered about the titles of the pictures they worked on.) For two days I saw DeMille in the far distance high up on a platform dressed in riding boots, breeches, and an open-neck shirt and watched him issuing his instructions for the shoallike eddying of our vast throng around some pillars. Occasionally, DeMille would seize the loud-hailer and chastise some unfortunate individual among us for some minor lapse. DeMille, with his aristocratic face and fringe of hair at the base of a shining skull, looked like a benevolent bishop, but he did not sound like one. Once he had singled out his whipping boy he would berate him publicly: "Thanks to the inattention of Mr. Kowalski, I must ask you all to do this long and arduous scene once again."

The set was volcanic with discontent during my days under the lash, as we were endlessly harried by the patrician figure on high. We were cheered, however, by a story that passed among us like wildfire. DeMille on a previous production had selected his daily "Mr. Kowalski" from among the thousands and had chased him relentlessly throughout a hot, dusty day; rehearsal after rehearsal had been endured, always "Mr. Kowalski" had been blamed for everything that went wrong. Finally all was prepared. "We will now shoot the scene," came DeMille's voice, "provided Mr. Kowalski is ready."

"Mr. Kowalski," at the end of his tether, threw his $2.50 to the winds, cupped his hands, and bellowed back, "I'm ready when you are, Mr. DeMille."

He was removed.

Later I worked many times for DeMille on the *Lux Radio Theater*, but on those occasions he was always the soul of courtesy, appearing only for the dress rehearsal and the shows themselves, attired invariably in a dark suit and white shirt. After several performances on the show he presented me with a coffee mug with my name on it and singled me out for long lectures about Hollywood's moral and intellectual obligations to the public.

In 1959 DeMille called me and bade me come to his house that afternoon "for tea." I drove downtown intrigued by the invitation, because I had never set eyes on DeMille at a Hollywood function, nor had I ever seen it reported that he had attended one. I was delighted to be afforded this opportunity to glimpse the hideaway of the great man. As I passed through Beverly Hills and Hollywood, my curiosity increased in direct proportion to the smog. From my sun-drenched home on a hillside near the ocean I had looked down with dread upon a yellow-brown stagnant haze hanging over the distant restless city, and by the time I had reached Western Avenue the sun above me was diffused to a brassy glare, my chest felt encased in a lead vest, my eyes were prickling, my nose was dribbling, and even the wheezing birds were walking. I arrived at last at the bottom of a tree-covered hill surrounded on all sides by the sprawling mass of Los Angeles. I passed through a gate, drove up a winding private road, and at the summit came at last upon DeMille's abode. He had lived there all his Hollywood life, and the low, rambling structure set in its considerable acreage seemed peaceful and contented and far removed from the Hollywood he had created.

DeMille's wife, a charming gray-haired lady, met me at the door and led me through a maze of wonderfully cluttered passages and rooms to a final chintzy resting place where DeMille was reading and where she later dispensed tea and cakes. At last, with the tea things and Mrs. DeMille gone, he told me the reason for my visit, but not before he had launched into another of his dissertations on "Hollywood's obligations to the public."

"I have made seventy films," he said suddenly. "I will make only one more; and you will be in it."

Having just completed six exhausting months making a picture for Mike Todd and knowing of DeMille's predilection for Biblically oriented ventures, I was less than fascinated by the prospect of spending the next year beneath forty pounds of false hair and being yelled at from the middle of a burning bush. He noted my hesitation.

"I am appalled by the violence in the world today," he said, "and I am going to do something about it. I am going to show that there is something else for youth besides street gangs and switch blades."

DeMille rose from his chair and paced the floor with the purposeful resolve of a planner of the Mayflower Caper; then he stopped in front of me.

"I'm going to tell the story of Baden-Powell and the Boy Scouts," he said, "and you will be Baden-Powell."

I think I voiced some mild surprise that such a gentle-sounding subject could have the ingredients for a massive DeMille epic because he spent the rest of the afternoon outlining the action-filled life of the man who had longed to be a poet, who had fought with the British cavalry in India, had developed Scouting as a martial art during service in Matabeleland, had conducted the heroic defense of Mafeking during the South African War, and had then thrown up his medal-encrusted military career to campaign against violence and to dedicate the rest of his life to helping youth. He formed the Boy Scouts and Girl Guides and saw those movements flourish in two-thirds of the countries of the world.

"Imagine!" said DeMille. "The final Jamboree, when the old man is almost eighty, with a hundred thousand youngsters of every race and color from all over the world gathered around him in peace and happiness . . . it will be my last film," he said again, "and my greatest."

It was a tragic loss when DeMille died before he could turn the cameras on his "last and greatest film."

BOBBIE

It will never be known if Utrillo or Van Gogh would have painted better pictures if they had drunk less or if Picasso would have excelled even himself if he had drunk more. Many modern musicians are convinced that they play finer music when high, but when Arthur Rubinstein or Yehudi Menuhin performs, he is stone cold sober. Certainly surgeons, airline pilots, and racing drivers avoid the stuff, but for writers and actors it presents a rather special problem.

How much of Scott Fitzgerald's brilliance and perception was aided by the bottle? How much of John Barrymore's or Spencer Tracy's was dimmed? Certainly, if the actor is not at ease, the audience is restless, so the temptation to relax oneself artificially before or during a performance is very real, and on average, I suppose, actors and writers do expose themselves to the hazards of drink more than most.

During World War I a great entertainer of legendary conviviality named Herbert Mundin volunteered for the Royal Navy and served as a stoker in a minesweeper.

For four years he obeyed regulations, so he ate, slept, and presumably stoked encased in a hideously bulky and uncomfortable cork life jacket, the theory being that there was always a possibility that the ship could hit a mine instead of sweeping it.

Herbert Mundin grew to loathe that life jacket with a passion, but this hatred notwithstanding, for four years, day and night, he was trapped inside it.

On November 11, 1918, in the middle of the North Sea he was called on deck with the rest of the crew, and after triple rum rations had been issued, the Captain announced that the war was over. In the midst of the general excitement, the cheering, the backslapping, and the sobbing, Herbert Mundin quietly looked down at his detested life jacket, his prison for four years; then he left the group and very deliberately undid its canvas straps one by one. Next he slid the loathsome garment over his head and approached the rail, smiling secretly to himself and savoring the delicious moment. Holding it in both hands, with the grip and narrowed eyes of a strangler, he looked it right in the eye. "Fuck *you!*" he said quietly, and flung it into the cold gray northern waters.

The life jacket sank like a rock.

When, a brief twenty-one years later, the Germans came on for their encore and launched World War II on a trembling and ill-prepared world, Robert Newton was near the peak of his career as a London stage actor and was already receiving the most flattering offers from Hollywood. Himself a carouser of some repute, it seemed natural that he would follow in Herbert Mundin's footsteps. He promptly joined the Royal Navy and served as a stoker in a minesweeper. His ship was very possibly the same, the equipment probably was identical, and the regulations certainly were unaltered, so, with the exception of one short respite, Robert Newton for four years wore a life jacket in which he ate, slept, and presumably stoked.

The short respite came in 1942. Submarines and bombers had taken heavy toll of His Majesty's ships and the loss of life had been appalling. Short of good officer material as a result of this tragic attrition, the Admiralty brass was poking around in the most unlikely nooks and crannies, looking for suitable candidates for commission.

Deep in the bowels of his minesweeper, they found Able-bodied Seaman Newton. His nose by now was a threat to the memory of W. C. Fields, and the legend of his intake of bottled goods was firmly established, but these were not the factors that made the brass dispatch him, posthaste, to the King Alfred Training School for Officers at Devonport; the big attraction to them was that he held an excellent degree from Oxford University.

Degree notwithstanding, the mysteries of navigation eluded Bobbie Newton, and he viewed with apprehension his final examination after four months of intensive coaching.

He saw to it that he was suitably relaxed when a stern-faced master-at-arms called out his name, "Able-bodied Seaman Newton!" Bobbie shuffled forward and found himself on a mock-up ship's bridge. Awaiting him was the selection board, two admirals and a captain. The imitation bridge was fully equipped with a wheel, engine room telegraph, compasses, calipers, binnacles, radars, depth sounders, log-books, and gadgets for shooting the sun and, when in great difficulty, oneself.

The captain blew down a tube and issued brisk orders to a nonexistent engine room staff, rattled off a lot of information about rhumb lines, GMT nulls, fixes, lorans, and sonars; then he spun the wheel.

"Newton," he said, with something of a flourish, "that is the situation—what is your course?"

Bobbie peered dazedly at the maze of sophisticated hardware, the helpful possibilities of which had largely escaped him during his tuition. The admirals consulted their notes and leaned expectantly forward.

"Well," said Bobbie, trying an engaging smile, "I should hazard a guess . . . that . . . we . . . are . . . heading . . . roughly, er, west?"

"Thank you," said the senior officer present. "Report back to your ship."

Bobbie Newton was a brilliant actor, but in his case the bottle, little by little, took charge. With just the right amount on board he could be fascinating, for he was a highly intelligent, erudite, kindly, and knowledgeable man, but once he had taken the extra one and his Plimsoll line had disappeared below the surface he changed gear and became anything from unpredictable to a downright menace.

Demobilized from the Royal Navy in 1945 and before taking off from a sparkling career as a character actor in Hollywood, he made a film of Noel Coward's *This Happy Breed* and at the same time performed at night in a play in London's West End.

It could have been brought on by overwork or a longing for the play to close so that he could indeed "head west," but one Saturday night at the St. James's Theatre the curtain did not rise. The audience became first restless, then impatient, and finally, from the gallery, the slow handclapping started and spread to the dress circle and the stalls.

At last the middle of the curtain wobbled uncertainly and a pair of shoes appeared beneath it. Sensing an announcement, the audience hushed itself into silence. Unsteady hands pulled the curtain apart just enough to frame the purple countenance of the star.

"Ladies and gentlemen," roared Bobbie Newton, rolling his eyes at every corner of the house, "the reason this curtain has so far not risen is because the stage manager . . . has the fucking impertinence to suggest that I am *pissed.*"

Very shortly after that episode Bobbie was on his way to Hollywood.

He did well, and his work there was greatly admired, but as word of his barhopping and extravagant behavior got around, the bush telegraph between studios signaled a preliminary warning and producers began to ask embarrassing questions about his reliability.

With millions of dollars being spent on production the last thing anyone wanted was to have precious shooting time wasted because of an actor's self-indulgence.

It was dreadfully sad to see such a flowing talent being destroyed, and Bobbie's friends tried hard to stop the rot. He would listen to us with great solemnity and agree with everything we said, and for weeks on end he would keep his promises, but some little bell inside would sooner or later summon him to the bar, and off he'd go again.

The astonishing thing was that though drunk, he could still give great performances, so long as his memory remained unimpaired,

612

but gradually that vital part of the actor's equipment showed signs of stress, and the bush telegraph beat out another set of warnings.

As he became more and more eccentric, assistant directors watched the clock apprehensively every morning to see if he would throw the cameraman into utter disarray by arriving too late to put into the makeup department for urgently needed repairs. During the filming of the Kipling story *Soldiers Three* at MGM he arrived on several occasions just in time for the first shot but still in pajamas.

Throughout the long weeks of shooting on that picture, I dreaded the magic hour of six o'clock because at the close of work Bobbie had accumulated a man-eating thirst, but he hated to drink alone.

"Dear fellow," he would wheedle, "a little light refreshment this evening? . . . A tiny tipple on your way home to the old ball and chain?" I made up a variety of excuses; they were coldly received.

"Getting a little settled in our ways, are we? A little sedentary perhaps? No sense of adventure anymore?"

On the last day of the shooting, Bobbie made it crystal clear that he had no intention of letting me slip away without a "farewell posset."

"I know a little bistro, dear fellow; it's just around the corner—come, let us away."

He shoveled me, protesting, into his car, both of us still wearing the bemedaled khaki drill uniforms, pith helmets, and drooping mustaches of Queen Victoria's army in India.

The car was a 1921 Rolls which he had found in a Burbank junkyard and had renovated at huge expense. The chauffeur in full regalia with the Rolls-Royce cockade on his cap was an ex-stuntman whom Bobbie had befriended when he found him working as a bouncer in a Gardena gambling hall. The "bistro" turned out to be thirty-three miles away in Long Beach. The Rolls had a top speed of about twenty-five miles per hour, and the honest citizens of Southern California blinked in amazement as we rolled sedately through their communities perched up like two visiting generals with the phony chauffeur pinching a big black rubber bulb at the end of a long curling brass horn and coaxing therefrom a mournful upper-class baying.

On arrival at Long Beach, I warned Bobbie for the umpteenth time that I had no money on me.

"My treat, old cock . . . and I'm loaded with the good stuff . . . we'll only stay a few minutes."

We entered Bobbie's "little bistro," and I shuddered. It was a long, dimly lit, evil-smelling bar. There were many customers, some on stools, others playing cards at tables. All were fishermen from the big tuna boats: Russians, Yugoslavs, and Japanese. They looked a little perplexed when they noticed the entrance of two soldiers of the Queen but soon returned to their drinking and playing.

"I knew you'd love it, dear fellow," said my host. "Full of color, don't you think?"

We gave our order to the barman, who prepared it in sulky silence. He was blue-black and would have made Sonny Liston look like a choirboy. The "chauffeur" remained with the car. "Can't have people removing souvenirs from Old Mary, can we?" said Bobbie.

He called for constant refills, and for the first half hour the time passed pleasantly enough, but quite suddenly he interrupted a quiet, sentimental description to me of a hill farm on the Welsh borders to roar at some Yugoslavs the first lines of a lengthy poem by Thomas Lodge:

> Love in my bosome like a bee
> Doth sucke his sweete:
> Now with his wings he playes with me,
> Now with his feete. . . !

The Yugoslavs backed away in some alarm, and the barman muttered, "Hey, you—cut that out, willya?"

Bobbie fixed him with a stony eye; then in a conspiratorial aside to me, he delivered a few lines from the Clown in *Antony and Cleopatra*:

Look, you, the worm, is not to be trusted but in the keeping of wise people; for, indeed, there is no goodness in the worm.

"Wazzat you say, man?" demanded the barman belligerently.

"If you don't like Shakespeare, dear fellow," said Bobbie, "then I shall give you a taste of Andrew Marvell," and off he launched into the whole lengthy "Nymph Complaining for the Death of her Faun":

> The wanton troopers riding by
> Have shot my faun and it will die. . . .

By the time he had finished there was no doubt that Bobbie had lost his audience; he was the recipient of several complicated pieces of advice from the barman and quite a number of Bronx cheers from the tuna boat men. I had a nasty feeling that things were getting out of hand and said so to Bobbie. "Let's pay and get the hell out of here."

"On the contrary," said Bobbie firmly, "the greatest joy an actor can have is to tame a hostile audience and make them his own. . . . I now propose to do what Laughton has lately done in a film . . . I shall deliver to this scum the Gettysburg Address."

"Let's deliver everyone a drink first," I pleaded, hoping thereby to soften the impending blows.

"Good thinking," said Bobbie with enthusiasm, and ordered drinks all around. Then, an incongruous figure in his creased uniform, he began pacing up and down the bar, roaring and declaiming, whispering or giving it the full bellows. He went, without a hitch, the whole route from "fourscore and seven years ago" to "that government of the people, by the people, for the people, shall not perish from the earth."

He did not finish to a standing ovation, it's true, but at least he came to the end in a respectful hush, a slightly embarrassed hush, perhaps, because by the time he was reveling in the last rolling sentence, the Russians, the Japanese, and the Yugoslavs, whether they understood what he was saying or not, had caught on to the fact that tears were streaming down his face.

"Let's go, Bobbie," I begged.

"Of course, dear fellow . . . do you have any money, dear boy?"

"No," I hissed. "I told you forty times that I haven't."

"Ah!" he said, pressing a forefinger against the side of his nose and rolling his eyes. "We have a tricky situation here."

It was indeed tricky, and the big blue-black barman, with the antennae of his ilk working at full volume, was sidling up the bar in our direction flicking overnonchalantly at the top of it with a dirty napkin.

"Dear boy," said Newton in a ventriloquial whisper between unmoving lips, "nip outside and prepare the getaway car; then call me from the door."

I wandered away, looking vaguely at my watch, and caught a last glimpse of that huge man, arms akimbo, staring straight into Bobbie's face from across the bar. Bobbie was smiling back uneasily.

Outside, the ex-stuntman caught the urgency of the situation and cranked the starting handle. The Rolls stood throbbing like an elderly "wolfhound in the slips," and leaving both doors on the curbside open, I hurried back to the entrance. The tableau had not changed during my absence.

"Bobbie!" I yelled, and keeping a foot in the door, I made ready to flee.

Newton started to back toward me, and I heard him get off his exit line.

"Barman, dear, just put it on my mother's charge account at Sears, Roebuck."

The barman's roars, like those of a wounded stag, we heard for quite a while as we motored peacefully away.

As Bobbie's unreliability increased, so the number of scripts sent to him decreased. This depressed him, and he sought more solace—it was a vicious circle. Living now in Bogart's old house far up on Benedict Canyon, his wife tried loyally and desperately to help him. His friends tried too, but his charm was so great and, when he took only a couple of drinks, his entertainment value was so spectacular that there was always some idiot who would press him to take the fatal third and fourth.

In 1956 before New York's supershowman Mike Todd died when his plane crashed in New Mexico, he realized a long-cherished ambition—he brought to the screen Jules Verne's classic *Around the World in 80 Days*. It was his first and sadly, because Hollywood needed him so badly, his only film. It won the Oscar and became one of the top grossers of all time. A key role was that of Mr. Fix, the detective, and Todd cast Bobbie Newton. Not before some soul-searching, however, because the red-flag warning of Newton's unreliability had been waved, and with Todd's shoe-string financial structure, he could ill afford delays in his shooting schedule. He called Newton in and said, "I hear you're a lush."

"An understatement, dear fellow," said Bobbie blithely, and was hired on the spot.

Todd extracted a promise from Newton that he would go on the wagon for the entire four months of his engagement, and Bobbie stuck manfully to his word.

In early autumn on location at Durango, Colorado, Bobbie was in his element. He was a superb fisherman, who "tied" his own flies, and we went fishing every evening after work. With the golden colors of the fall reflected on the mirror surface of the lakes, I saw him bring to gaff countless huge fighting rainbows.

It was becoming cold on those high lakes, so one evening I thoughtlessly put a half bottle of bourbon with my gear. Thoughtlessly, because I had not appreciated how great was Bobbie's struggle to keep away from the stuff.

As I opened it, I caught his eye and quickly slid the bottle back into my tackle bag.

"Dear fellow," said Newton, "that was very kind of you, but please don't worry. First of all, I daren't ask for a little nip because quite apart from having no intention of breaking my word to Todd, my doctor has told me that if I really get at it again, I shall very likely leave the building for good. So please don't feel that I am tempted by the sight of it"—he paused and chuckled—"however, kindly pass me the cork from time to time so I may sniff it. . . . I really do *love* the stuff, dear boy."

Bobbie completed his role in the picture and left the company, looking fitter than I had seen him for a long time. Two weeks later he was called unexpectedly for an added scene. At seven thirty in the morning I was sitting in the makeup room when the passage outside was shaken by a roaring delivery from *King Henry* V, Act IV:

> We few, we happy few, we band of brothers;
> For he to-day that sheds his blood with me
> Shall be my brother. . . .

I was horrified at Bobbie's blotched and puffy face when he lurched into the room.

"Don't chide me, dear fellow," he said. "Please don't chide me." Tears coursed down his cheeks.

Within a very short time Bobbie Newton's doctor's diagnosis was proved tragically correct.

EDDIE

Edmund Goulding was eccentric, but he was also a first-class director. Performers, male and female, loved to work with him because, an actor once himself and unlike Jack Warner, he understood their problems, tiptoed over their egos and, above all, never made light of their built-in insecurities. A highly sensitive man, he was especially sought after by the important actresses and became famous as a "woman's director." He was, however, allergic to this label, and to prove that he was bisexual in his work, at the height of his fame, he took on *Dawn Patrol*, an extremely tough picture with an all-male cast, including Errol Flynn, Basil Rathbone, myself, and other unreliables.

His greatest triumph in the realm of personality handling was *Grand Hotel*, which boasted a potentially explosive cast: first—introverted Garbo, who was genuinely timid with strangers and suffered from acute claustrophobia in public; next—extroverted John Barrymore, who enjoyed nothing so much as blowing apart myths with a whiskey breath and treading heavily on sensibilities; then—Joan Crawford, very entrenched at the studio, very cognizant of her own box-office appeal, and determined to play second fiddle to nobody; and, finally—the ex-female impersonator Wallace Beery whose lovable "aw shucks, ma'am" onscreen personality was in direct contrast with his belligerent, rude, egotistical side which made him easily the most unpopular actor at Metro-Goldwyn-Mayer.

Goulding flattered, badgered, bullied, or cajoled this spiky troupe until it was individually and collectively eating out of his hand, and the picture—the biggest of its year—won the Academy Award.

Goulding's wife—the dancer Marjorie Moss—died, and thereafter he lived a rather sad bachelor existence, but he was never without friends, except at the studio, where he had somehow run afoul of studio politics, and for reasons he could never discover, his intangible enemies destroyed him. Irving Thalberg, the head of production, had been his greatest admirer, and Goulding was probably the only person on the lot, L. B. Mayer included, who could walk, unannounced, into the great man's office.

Once he barged in and said, "Irving, I've a brilliant idea for Harlow and Gable!"

"Tell it to me, Eddie," said Thalberg.

When Goulding had finished telling his story and even acting out some of the roles, Thalberg was ecstatic.

"We'll buy it!" he announced, and they settled the terms there and then.

"Let me have a few pages of outline by the end of the week, and we'll decide who to put on the screenplay."

When the end of the week came, Thalberg called and asked for the outline, but Goulding had completely forgotten what his brilliant idea had been. Within a week, however, he retrieved the situation by coming up with another which Thalberg bought.

After Thalberg died, so tragically young, the knives were honed for the outspoken and eccentric Goulding, and he was slowly maneuvered out of his contract and off the lot. He directed spasmodically at other studios, but his heart was at MGM. The pictures he was given were not up to his old standard, and the trickle of offers finally dried up altogether.

Goulding became deeply depressed, and when he found the depression unbearable, he would seek refuge in the bottle but in a very methodical way. Before he took the first swig, he would call an ex-boxer-chauffeur he knew and tell him for how many days he thought his bender would be therapeutically good for him. Then, secure in the knowledge that he would come to no harm nor, above all, bring harm to others, he would take off.

Goulding died, and his friends were stricken. He was much loved and had passed through the Hollywood jungle dispensing nothing but kindness, thoughtfulness, generosity, and talent with both hands. He had a wild and woolly sense of the ridiculous, and I am convinced that from some private Valhalla he directed his own funeral.

Goulding's sister Ivis called me and said that her brother had left a note saying that he would like me to be one of his pallbearers.

As instructed, I dusted off my dark suit and black tie and drove sorrowfully to a grotesque little slate-roofed church in the middle of several hundred acres of rolling hills which make up Hollywood's much-publicized burial complex, Forest Lawn.

At the door of this gray-stone monstrosity a professionally mournful undertaker's assistant gave me a white carnation, my badge of office, and instructed me to join the other pallbearers already seated in the front pew. The church inside was every bit as grisly and depressing as its name: the Wee Kirk o' the Heather. Seated in it were friends of Goulding, and at the back I noticed several pious-faced members of the very studio hierarchy which had left no stone unturned to ensure that his last years had been so unproductive and frustrating.

As I sat down, I was alarmed at the sight of Goulding's casting of the other pallbearers—alarmed because he had put on quite a lot of weight in his last years, and the people I was now teamed up with were quite evidently not up to the job. My disquiet mounted when I noticed that the open coffin directly in front of us was of the heaviest and thickest black mahogany and its fittings of solid brass. Herbert Marshall was next to me. He had one leg, the other having been blown off during World War I. Next to him was Reginald Gardiner, who had only one serviceable arm; the other had been badly mangled in an appalling headfirst fall down the iron steps of the fire escape outside his apartment down which for some reason best known to himself he had been chasing Hedy Lamarr.

Beyond Gardiner, I spotted the diminutive Al Hall, Mae West's director, who was hardly far enough out of the ground to be sanitary, and the heaviest thing he could lift with any cohesion was a scotch and soda.

Craning forward, I saw beyond Hall a business manager, a man of immense girth with a purple complexion and a concertina of double chins. At the moment in the humidity of that Los Angeles August, he was overflowing out of a tight blue suit, sweating profusely and wheezing loudly.

Just as I registered that we were a potentially unbalanced five in number—four and a half if one remembered Al Hall's specifications—our full complement was made up by the welcome arrival of a gigantic young man of Tarzanesque proportions wearing a light-gray suit and a pink shirt. The raised eyebrows and shaken heads of the original incumbents of the pallbearers' pew betokened the fact that none of us had the faintest idea who he was. Indeed, he seemed to be only a distant friend of the deceased because he leaned forward, peered directly inside the coffin, and said with a loud lisp, "Oh, my *God!* Is that *him* in there? . . . In a goddamn *tux!* How did they put his socks on, for heaven's sake?"

This query caused a certain restlessness among the congregation, but it was instantly stilled by the appearance of the priest, minister, moderator, or high lama of the strange Hollywood cult which professed atheist Goulding had, unbeknownst to his friends, embraced during his last days. This individual appeared before us wearing a sensible business suit beneath a seedy greenish-black gown reminiscent of graduation day. True, the mortarboard was missing, but in its place he sported a wig of flaming red hair. He had eyebrows and a drooping mustache to match.

He stared at us menacingly for a long time. We stared mournfully back. Suddenly, he clapped his hands together. "This is ridiculous," he said sharply. "Come along now. . . . *Perk up!* . . . Why are you all sitting there looking so miserable? . . . Let's see a little smile. . . . Edmund is perfectly happy. . . . What right have you to be so downbeat? . . . Just look at yourselves with all your gloomy faces! Edmund *hates* it!"

We looked at each other uncertainly. He clapped his hands together more loudly. "Perk up," he ordered us. "Everybody *smile!* . . . Let's see those teeth!"

I glanced at the back of the church. The studio brass were sitting there, staring straight ahead with flat, expressionless eyes, but dutifully exposing their expensive, perfectly graded dentures—it looked like a piano shop.

"This guy is *fantastic!*" breathed the young man from Muscle Beach, nudging Al Hall and nearly knocking him off his perch. After a twenty-minute pep talk we dutifully filed with averted eyes past the open coffin and waited outside for matters to be arranged so that we might bear it to the waiting hearse.

In the hot sun, standing before one of the many flaming hibiscus bushes which relieved the gloom of the Wee Kirk o' the Heather, I found myself bathing in the cheerful incandescence of Ginger's red-fringed smile.

"Nice to have you here, Dave," he said. "Hope to see you again, real soon." (An unnerving wish, I thought.)

"I so much enjoyed your talk just now," I said truthfully. "It really did cheer me up. . . . I suppose we all wonder about what happens next, and it's hard to believe that great brains like those of Einstein or Marconi or Sophocles just faded away when their bodies gave up."

"You said it," said Ginger heartily. "It would be such lousy economy, wouldn't it?"

He looked at the back door where a church attendant was nodding conspiratorially.

"It's OK. You boys can fetch Edmund down to the collection bay now."

The motley troop of "boys" returned to the church, and three on each side, we managed to lift our incredibly heavy cargo and struggle with it down the path to the waiting Cadillac hearse. The church attendant followed us and instructed us minutely how to deposit it near the curb at a special angle.

"So's there'll be no slipups this time," he said ominously.

The chauffeur of the hearse pressed a switch on his dashboard, and the glass side rolled back. Then two obscene chromium pincer arms unfolded themselves from the interior and fastened themselves avidly onto each end of the coffin.

The church attendant signaled his satisfaction, another button was pressed, and the coffin in one smooth, silent convulsion was lifted from the ground and rotated slightly so that it fitted perfectly onto a velvet-covered tray which had slithered out from the inside; then, with just a hint of a hydraulic hiss, the whole thing disappeared, and the glass side of the hearse slid back into place.

"Plot seventeen ninety," said the church attendant, briskly nodding down the white road shimmering in the heat, "about three hundred yards. . . . The grave is just over the brow of the hill shaded by those pines and blessed with a beautiful panoramic view of all Hollywood."

The hearse pulled slowly away from the curb, and we stared after it, saying nothing. Bart Marshall broke the silence. "That is one hell of a walk for me," he observed. "Let's get the cars."

622

"We'll never get Goulding up that hill," said Al Hall. "The thing weighs a ton."

We sorted out our transport problems and arrived at the foot of the pine-covered knoll to find that the coffin had already been electrically ejected from the hearse.

"It's all yours, fellows," said the driver of the hearse, nodding toward the crest and removing his cap and jacket. "This is as far as I go." He winked and waited expectantly for a tip, then drove off rapidly.

"We have to have a little discipline here," said the large unknown in the shocking-pink shirt. "Fall in now, you guys, three on each side—it's gonna be a long haul up there."

Grateful to find we had a leader, we waited a couple of minutes while Bart Marshall made some mysterious adjustments behind the knee of his artificial leg. "Just shifting into 'climb,'" he explained. Then obediently we lined up as directed. The giant young man placed himself in front, followed by Al Hall and Reggie Gardiner on one side, Bart Marshall, the purple business manager, and myself on the other. We grunted and groaned, but finally we hoisted our cargo onto our shoulders and started up the steep incline toward the silhouetted pines. Zigzagging carefully between headstones, we toiled manfully uphill.

The business manager was the first to go. He started quite early on, making the most extraordinary noises—trumpetings and belches in about equal proportions.

"Sorry, fellows, can't make it," he finally spluttered, and producing a large red handkerchief, he staggered out from in front of me and settled himself, fanning and mopping on a grave; his color had changed from purple to sap green.

Although Al Hall, on the other side, with upstretched arms, had so far been making but a token contribution to the fair distribution of the load, trotting beneath the coffin and occasionally making contact with it with his fingertips, he was the next to decide to take time out.

With his black silk suit clinging stickily to his birdlike frame, he treacherously deserted us. "See you on top," he muttered like a mutinous Sherpa, "if I can make it up there." He fell behind.

"Get with it, fellows, *please*," commanded Tarzan. "It's only another twenty yards—we can't let him down now." A strange choice of phrase, I thought as, blinded with sweat, I plodded grimly upward, wondering which would be the next to go: me, with a hangover, Marshall with his leg, or Gardiner with his arm. In any event, about ten yards from the summit, they both went together. Bart's performance had been truly heroic, but he had come to the end of the line. "Sorry, boys, can't go another yard. In fact, I don't think I can even make it down again."

"I'll help you," panted Gardiner, basely grabbing his chance.

"Okay, fellows, let's put it down for a moment," grunted our leader.

Bart and Gardiner collapsed together against a nearby headstone and took off their jackets. Twenty yards away Al Hall was lying facedown in the grass, and far below him, we could see the red dot of the business manager's handkerchief as he rhythmically stirred some movement into the blast furnace air.

"Dave," ordered our leader, "go on up to the top and see what gives."

As I toiled on by myself, I noticed with mounting apprehension that the wind had detached a fair proportion of pine needles from the trees. Brown and dried out, these had formed a carpet which decreased my traction with every step I took toward their parent clump.

Puffing and slipping, I reached the shade of the trees. Twenty yards down the reverse slope below me, I saw the freshly dug grave banked with flowers on the far side and seated on wooden chairs, with their backs luckily toward me, was a small group of relatives. Glancing impatiently at his watch was Ginger. Beside him stood a church attendant, and far below, in the golden heat haze, the whole panoramic view of Hollywood as advertised. The hum of traffic rose.

I returned, skidding on the icelike surface, to find that Marshall and Gardiner had already started down to base camp, but their place had been taken by a refreshed and invigorated Al Hall. I also noticed a smell of spirits when he beat his hands together like a quarterback and said, "OK, you guys, let's go."

I gave Hall a dirty look and made my situation report to Tarzan. He issued commands with commendable clarity.

"We can't get it on our shoulders, so I'll take the top end and

624

you two push at the back. When we get to the top, we'll get those guys from the church to give us a hand."

"It's slippery as hell near the top," I warned.

We struggled upward, and my warning became painfully true: painful for Hall, whose feet suddenly shot away from under him. As he pitched forward, he was all but knocked unconscious when his jaw connected with the top of the coffin.

Gravely unbalanced as a result of this, I pleaded with the leader to rest for a minute and reconsider our strategy.

He was adamant. "We *have* to make it to the top . . . the family's waiting."

"But it's like going up a glacier," I argued. "We should be roped."

"Why don't you two take off your shoes and socks?" mumbled Hall. "You'll be able to grip with your toes."

"That's a disgusting idea," Tarzan said sternly. "Let's go, Dave!"

Sourly I spurned Hall's proffered flask and God alone knew (I choose those words advisedly) how much actual poundage Tarzan and I, with minimal help from Hall, manhandled up those remaining yards, but by the time we reached the top my heart was pounding in my ears, and I was on the point of blacking out.

"We made it!" whispered Tarzan ecstatically. "Try to act unconcerned. Al, you go on down there and speak to the preacher." Hall slithered off on this mission, but luckily he did not get far.

The little group below were unaware of our arrival on the summit above them which was just as well because almost imperceptibly at first the coffin began to slide forward. Transfixed with horror, I had a vision of Goulding in his heavy container happily tobogganing past his own grave, pursued by the remnants of his friends, and with increasing momentum charging down the hill, crossing Hollywood Boulevard and winding up in the bar of the Roosevelt Hotel.

In front the Man from Muscle Beach grabbed wildly at the passing coffin, was caught off-balance, and fell down. Al Hall it was who made up for his past incompetence and unreliability with a heroic save. He just lay on his back in the path of the oncoming Goulding with his knees bent and the soles of his shoes positioned like buffers at a railway terminal. The impact shunted him several feet and forced a hissed oath from between his clenched teeth, but apart from that, the day was saved in silence and no head was turned in our direction.

A few minutes later, suitably reinforced, we completed a dignified delivery of our much-loved cargo, but I will always remain suspicious of Goulding's casting of his pallbearers.

WINIFRED

Despite the fact that she was permanently teetering on the verge of bankruptcy, Clemence Dane, known to her friends as Winifred, was the richest human being I have ever known.

The normal dread that we mortals harbored—that we would not be able to earn enough to fill our stomachs, to care for our dependents, or to pay for any prescribed drugs we might need—never entered into Winifred's head. If her bills remained unopened, so did the check she earned remain uncashed; she did not regard money as filthy lucre—she just did not have the faintest idea what it was.

I was in a temporary state of financial shock when I met Winifred. I had decided one December evening in the late fifties to take a long walk in the hills behind my heavily mortgaged house, hoping, if not to find a seam of gold where the fire roads had been ruthlessly gouged out of the beautiful lonely landscape, at least to arrive at a possible solution to my problem.

It was bitterly cold, and there was an unheard-of sprinkling of snow on the tips of the surrounding Santa Monica Mountains.

"Sssh!" whispered a voice.

So engrossed had I been in my thoughts that I had failed to notice in the gathering dusk a very large lady in a bush by the roadside, with a finger to her lips.

"Come and help me," she ordered in a calm but authoritative voice. "The poor little darling is so cold it can't fly, and I can't quite reach it."

The large lady was spread-eagled in the branches of a scrub oak, in imminent danger of snapping the branches of that notoriously treacherous growth and cartwheeling to her death several hundred feet below on the canyon floor.

Whatever "it" was became of secondary importance to extricating the large lady from her position of heart-stopping danger. It was a difficult operation because she weighed in the neighborhood of 220 pounds and, despite the extreme cold, was firmly impaled upon the thorny branches in a voluminous garment of black chiffon. She had a lineless face of great beauty and infinite sweetness and was at least seventy years old.

"It's a hummingbird," she explained.

At grave personal risk I managed to extricate the large lady, and then, because she was watching me with eyes filled to the brim with trust and confidence, with lunatic bravery I rescued the semicongealed hummingbird from its perch above the horrifying drop.

"How kind of you," said Winifred. "The little darling has a tummy of cadmium yellow."

We wandered back down the fire road together, she with the tiny honey-eating creature fluttering in her cupped hands as it thawed out and I, like Hernando Cortez when he first set worshipful eyes on Doña Marina, forgetting all my petty problems and impending disasters.

Winifred, a top-class sculptor and painter, was also the author of half a hundred plays, novels, and books of short stories. Hollywood had wooed her, and she had lately arrived with considerable fanfare to work on a screenplay.

Her studio, once the red carpet had been rolled back into mothballs, had allocated her to a small cell in the writers' building, and the producer designate had tried to make her feel at home with an antique Hollywood joke. "Miss Dane," he said, "we need this script in a hurry, so those pencils on your desk I expect to see half as long by tonight. HA! HA! HA!"

If Winifred had been amused, she had given no sign, but she had immediately relinquished her apartment in the Beverly Hills Hotel and moved into a two-room cottage in the trees on the canyonside below my house which had no telephone. The cottage, the property of my neighbor Douglas Fairbanks, Jr., was accessible only by a flight of sixty almost perpendicular wooden steps, hazardous for a mountaineer, but no problem apparently for an old lady with arthritis of the hip, and further protection against interference by her producer designate. Its small front porch was the rallying point for the local rattlesnakes . . . Winifred slept on the porch.

My family adored Winifred, and the children became the recipients of a constant stream of handmade presents. Hjördis and I were introduced to painting by Winifred, and after turning out a steady flow of canvases that looked like the bottom of Lake Erie, we were persuaded by her to convert our living room into a studio.

My wife, a lady of spectacular beauty, became Winifred's favorite model. She also became resigned to the gradual change that overtook her carefully chosen color scheme in the living room thanks to Winifred's habit of catching the sleeves of her flowing garments on the corners of still-wet canvases, sweeping bottles of linseed oil onto the sofa, and sitting heavily on capless tubes of Yellow Ocher and Venetian Red; gray modeling clay was also trodden into the carpet.

One morning I was awakened by a jangling telephone.

"I *have* to paint the sunrise over the mountains," announced Winifred. "Will you be a darling and pick me up at the top of the steps in five minutes and take me up into the hills?"

I did as I was asked because, for some strange reason, however eccentric, one always acceded to Winifred's requests. She was waiting for me at the top of the steps wearing a nightgown overlaid by a Japanese kimono; her still-brown hair, usually worn in a bun, reached to her waist. In one hand was a large wicker basket full of paints and bottles, and in the other, a collapsible easel.

We drove up a winding road in the virgin hills, and as the first silver streaks were appearing in the sky, Winifred indicated her spot. On foot we toiled up a deer track, and at long last she pointed imperiously to a flat, relatively scrubfree space on top of a knoll.

"That will do nicely," she said.

I fixed up her easel and prepared to take my leave.

"What time would you like the car, madame?" I asked facetiously.

"About eleven," she replied, squeezing enormous dollops of paint onto her palette, "and would you be a darling—I badly need a roll of lavatory paper . . . for the brushes," she added, banishing a bizarre spectacle from my imagination.

I was back in about half an hour with her request and found her utterly engrossed, standing like the figurehead of an ancient sailing ship and attacking her canvas with bold slashes of color. Winifred's pictures were as magnificent as herself and as full of vitality, but her friends had learned forcibly to take her canvases away from her after her first instinctive onslaught because she invariably ruined them later by fiddling.

"Be a darling," she said through a mouthful of brushes, "pop up here a little later on with a thermos of tea and a packet of biscuits."

"Watch out for the rattlers," I said as I turned to go. "The hills are full of them."

"Oh, the little dears," she said, "they won't hurt me—they're my friends."

I made several trips during the morning, keeping Winifred topped up with tea, biscuits, turpentine, and Titanium White, and by midday her large canvas was finished—a glorious impression of the first rays had been preserved with the distant snows of Mount Baldy touched with pure gold and the awakening foreground kept in perfect balance. The colors on the canvas were subtler than those on Winifred herself. As the sun had risen, she had realized the need to protect her head. Making a nest of lavatory paper on the ground, she had tipped into it the paints from her large wicker basket and placed the basket on her head. The hot rays of the sun had melted the residue of paint at the bottom of it, and Winifred looked, when I came to take her home, like an Apache brave. Hair, face, kimono, and nightdress were caked and streaked with Vermilion, Cobalt Blue, Rose Madder, Ivory Black.

"Be a darling," she said, completely unconscious of this blaze of color, "take me home now—I really *must* wash my hands and do some work on that script. They *keep* sending messengers for it."

During her months as our neighbor, Winifred ruined our living room for genealogical time, but she also painted some beautiful pictures and completed some remarkable sculptures. She found time to write many children's stories for my offspring and gave endless pleasure to the rest of us with her outpourings of wit and wisdom, but there is no record with the Screen Writers Guild of her having completed a screenplay.

She left quite suddenly because she missed an immensely crusty mongrel named Ben and a cluttered flat in the middle of London's Covent Garden vegetable market. Soon after she returned there, the market was largely destroyed by fire. The residents evacuated in a hurry, all except Winifred, who stayed to paint the conflagration from her bedroom window. When firemen finally came to force her to leave, they found her rummaging around, looking for a two-gallon can of highly inflammable turpentine.

Her next residence was in a field in the midst of beautiful Sussex woodland. As a grudging concession to her arthritic hip she had allowed the locals to replace its steps with a wooden ramp, and there, writing, sculpting, and painting, surrounded by the birds and little animals from the woods, by her priceless collection of Meissen, Dresden, and Nymphenburg porcelain, and, above all, by her friends, she spent her days—in a gaily painted gypsy caravan. Winifred was not a Hollywood type.

The Eleventh Commandment (Thou Shalt Not Be Found Out)

Some people liked L. B. Mayer, many were fond of Samuel Goldwyn, everyone loved Fred Astaire, Tyrone Power, and Clark Gable, but hardly any were devoted to their agents. Actors, writers, and directors all had contracts with them, and all, with varying degrees of resentment, paid them 10 percent of everything they earned.

At the beginning of a career it was virtually impossible to get started—to graduate from the extra ranks, for example—without an agent, because he knew about the pictures that were being planned, and if he was a high-class agent, he had contacts among those who were doing the planning. The giant step was, of course, the first good job, but if that job led to a coveted seven-year contract, the agent who had found it became a financial albatross around the neck and was entitled to 10 percent of the client's earnings for the next seven years without the obligation even to send him a card at Christmastime. The spectrum of agents went from the cheap little flesh peddlers, confident that they had a proprietary right to play grab-ass with their clients among the bit players and dancers, to the big wheels in their receptionist-controlled and beautifully furnished offices, who could walk unannounced into the sanctums of the moguls and there play power politics because of the demand they had generated for their high-priced stable of stars. In between these two extremes was a variety of agents, most of whom worked hard to find and develop talent, but who became resigned to seeing ambitious clients drifting away from them to join the stables of the big wheels with the possibility of a power-assisted boost up the ladder.

Big wheels such as Myron Selznick, Leland Hayward, Harry Eddington, Charlie Feldman, Lew Wasserman, and Bert Allenberg represented the Holy Grail for actors whose principles were apt to melt like butter on a hot stove when the chance of being represented by one of these men presented itself. A particularly unattractive example of this was the behavior of an actor I knew very well. This man was under contract to an excellent, hardworking, clear-thinking, honest, middle-of-the-spectrum agent named Phil Gersh. Gersh had been very successful with this actor, and under his guiding hand his client's career had prospered exceedingly. They had been together for some years, and although their contract had only a few more weeks to run, it would be renewed: Neither had any intention of dissolving the association; also, the men had become good friends. The actor, however, like most of his profession, was susceptible to flattery and made uneasy by suggestions that his progress up the ladder could be accelerated by a new approach.

One night, in a house on the crest of Mulholland Drive, with the whole of Los Angeles twinkling like a million stars on one side and with the San Fernando Valley glowing like the Milky Way on the other, the actor was listening with rapt attention to the siren words of one of the big wheels—Bert Allenberg.

Tall, good-looking, charming Bert Allenberg personally guided the fortunes of half a dozen of the biggest stars in Hollywood, and to be one of his handpicked clients was the dream of every actor, the underwriting of a career.

"I'd like to handle you," Allenberg was saying. "I've a whole lot of ideas for you. . . . What d'you say?" The actor took a deep breath; he had visions of being catapulted over the heads of his contemporaries and into the very forefront of the Hollywood galaxy. He thought about the offer all evening and carefully weighed his ambition and greed against his integrity.

"I'll talk to Phil Gersh tomorrow and tell him I'm leaving him," he said to Allenberg as he was saying good-night, and was surprised at how easy it must have been for Judas Iscariot.

The actor liked Phil Gersh very much and wished him no harm, but he was dazzled by the golden gates swinging on their hinges before him. The confrontation between the actor and Phil Gersh was unpleasant for both. The agent listened in amazement as the actor explained that he would not be renewing his contract.

"But why?" asked Gersh.

"Of course, it's nothing personal," said the actor. "It's just that . . . I feel like, er, changing my butcher," he finished lamely. The agent rose to leave.

"You were the first actor I had ever *really* liked . . . ever *really* trusted," he said quietly. "Now I know you are just the same as all the rest. . . . I'll stick with writers and directors from here on in. . . . I'll never handle another."

In his comfortable leather-bound office, Bert Allenberg lolled back in an armchair and listened as the actor recounted the scene. "Gersh'll get over it," he said flatly. Then he broke out the champagne and outlined his plans for the future. "I'm meeting with Darryl and L.B. tomorrow," he said. "I'll have big news for you by Wednesday. Call me first thing in the morning."

The actor slept little on Tuesday, and on Wednesday morning, in a high state of expectancy, he called his new agent's office. The secretary's voice was muffled. "Mr. Allenberg died last night," she sobbed.

The name of the actor can be found on the next page.

David Niven